Inflammatory Bowel Disease: Role of Nutrition

Handbook of Research on Training Teachers for Bilingual Education in Primary Schools

José Luis Estrada Chichón
University of Cádiz, Spain

Francisco Zayas Martínez
University of Cádiz, Spain

A volume in the Advances in Early Childhood and K–12 Education (AECKE) Book Series

Published in the United States of America by
    IGI Global
    Information Science Reference (an imprint of IGI Global)
    701 E. Chocolate Avenue
    Hershey PA, USA 17033
    Tel: 717-533-8845
    Fax: 717-533-8661
    E-mail: cust@igi-global.com
    Web site: http://www.igi-global.com

Copyright © 2023 by IGI Global. All rights reserved. No part of this publication may be reproduced, stored or distributed in any form or by any means, electronic or mechanical, including photocopying, without written permission from the publisher. Product or company names used in this set are for identification purposes only. Inclusion of the names of the products or companies does not indicate a claim of ownership by IGI Global of the trademark or registered trademark.

Library of Congress Cataloging-in-Publication Data

Names: Chichon, José Estrada, 1980- editor. | Zayas Martínez, Francisco, editor.

Title: Handbook of research on training teachers for bilingual education in primary schools / José Estrada Chichón, and Francisco Zayas Martínez Editor.

Description: Hershey, PA : Information Science Reference, [2023] | Includes bibliographical references and index. | Summary: "Primary teacher training has always been a relatively uncontroversial discipline for researchers as it has traditionally focused on different professional expectations, depending on the specific social and cultural perceptions of the primary teacher in each country. However, as a result of globalization in recent decades, societies have driven and demanded educational modalities in which foreign languages are used for communication from very early educational stages. As a result, educational authorities administer how bilingual education should work in the different geographical areas or countries. This book focuses on a review of the theoretical foundations and practical approaches to didactic processes undertaken by many tertiary education institutions around the world to train future teachers of bilingual education in primary schools. Today, most teacher trainers at the university level are experts in foreign language teaching who are looking for ways to train their students to integrate the content and communicative use of the target language. This work includes chapters referring to this panorama in different countries, with the corresponding descriptions of the language policies that contextualize them. In this sense, the central chapters present good training practices to reflect on experiential formulae or more theoretical approaches that could also guide the process"-- Provided by publisher.

Identifiers: LCCN 2022039918 (print) | LCCN 2022039919 (ebook) | ISBN 9781668461792 (hardcover) | ISBN 9781668461808 (ebook)

Subjects: LCSH: Education, Bilingual--Study and teaching (Primary) | Teachers--Training of. | Primary school teaching. | Language and languages--Study and teaching (Primary)--Bilingual method. | Bilingualism in children.

Classification: LCC LC3723 .H36 2023 (print) | LCC LC3723 (ebook) | DDC 370.117/5--dc23/eng/20220909

LC record available at https://lccn.loc.gov/2022039918

LC ebook record available at https://lccn.loc.gov/2022039919

This book is published in the IGI Global book series Advances in Early Childhood and K-12 Education (AECKE) (ISSN: 2329-5929; eISSN: 2329-5937)

British Cataloguing in Publication Data
A Cataloguing in Publication record for this book is available from the British Library.

All work contributed to this book is new, previously-unpublished material. The views expressed in this book are those of the authors, but not necessarily of the publisher.

For electronic access to this publication, please contact: eresources@igi-global.com.

Advances in Early Childhood and K-12 Education (AECKE) Book Series

Jared Keengwe
University of North Dakota, USA

ISSN:2329-5929
EISSN:2329-5937

Mission

Early childhood and K-12 education is always evolving as new methods and tools are developed through which to shape the minds of today's youth. Globally, educational approaches vary allowing for new discussions on the best methods to not only educate, but also measure and analyze the learning process as well as an individual's intellectual development. New research in these fields is necessary to improve the current state of education and ensure that future generations are presented with quality learning opportunities.

The **Advances in Early Childhood and K-12 Education (AECKE)** series aims to present the latest research on trends, pedagogies, tools, and methodologies regarding all facets of early childhood and K-12 education.

Coverage

- Performance Assessment
- STEM Education
- Literacy Development
- Head Start and Pre-K Programs
- Poverty and Education
- Bullying in the Classroom
- Pedagogy
- Learning Outcomes
- Common Core State Standards
- Diverse Learners

IGI Global is currently accepting manuscripts for publication within this series. To submit a proposal for a volume in this series, please contact our Acquisition Editors at Acquisitions@igi-global.com or visit: http://www.igi-global.com/publish/.

The Advances in Early Childhood and K-12 Education (AECKE) Book Series (ISSN 2329-5929) is published by IGI Global, 701 E. Chocolate Avenue, Hershey, PA 17033-1240, USA, www.igi-global.com. This series is composed of titles available for purchase individually; each title is edited to be contextually exclusive from any other title within the series. For pricing and ordering information please visit http://www.igi-global.com/book-series/advances-early-childhood-education/76699. Postmaster: Send all address changes to above address. © © 2023 IGI Global. All rights, including translation in other languages reserved by the publisher. No part of this series may be reproduced or used in any form or by any means – graphics, electronic, or mechanical, including photocopying, recording, taping, or information and retrieval systems – without written permission from the publisher, except for non commercial, educational use, including classroom teaching purposes. The views expressed in this series are those of the authors, but not necessarily of IGI Global.

Titles in this Series

For a list of additional titles in this series, please visit: http://www.igi-global.com/book-series/advances-early-childhood-education/76699

Theoretical and Practical Teaching Strategies for K-12 Science Education in the Digital Age
Jason Trumble (University of Central Arkansas, USA) Sumreen Asim (Indiana University Southeast, USA) Joshua Ellis (Florida International University, USA) and David Slykhuis (Valdosta State University, USA)
Information Science Reference • © 2023 • 298pp • H/C (ISBN: 9781668455852) • US $215.00

Practical Strategies to Reduce Childhood Trauma and Mitigate Exposure to the School-to-Prison Pipeline
Belinda M. Alexander-Ashley (Independent Researcher, USA)
Information Science Reference • © 2023 • 350pp • H/C (ISBN: 9781668457139) • US $215.00

Preparing Pre-Service Teachers to Integrate Technology in K-12 Classrooms Standards and Best Practices
C. Lorraine Webb (Texas A&M University, San Antonio, USA) and Amanda L. Lindner (Texas A&M University, San Antonio, USA)
Information Science Reference • © 2022 • 340pp • H/C (ISBN: 9781668454787) • US $215.00

Cutting-Edge Language and Literacy Tools for Students on the Autism Spectrum
Katharine P. Beals (Drexel University, USA)
Information Science Reference • © 2022 • 298pp • H/C (ISBN: 9781799894421) • US $215.00

Handbook of Research on Family Literacy Practices and Home-School Connections
Kathy R. Fox (University of North Carolina Wilmington, USA) and Laura E. Szech (University of North Carolina Wilmington, USA)
Information Science Reference • © 2022 • 353pp • H/C (ISBN: 9781668445693) • US $270.00

Rethinking Inclusion and Transformation in Special Education
Maria Efstratopoulou (United Arab Emirates University, UAE)
Information Science Reference • © 2022 • 348pp • H/C (ISBN: 9781668446805) • US $215.00

Best Practices for Trauma-Informed School Counseling
Angela M. Powell (Lone Star College, USA)
Information Science Reference • © 2022 • 331pp • H/C (ISBN: 9781799897859) • US $215.00

Disciplinary Literacy as a Support for Culturally and Linguistically Responsive Teaching and Learning
Leslie Haas (Xavier University of Louisiana, USA) and Jill T. Tussey (Buena Vista University, USA)
Information Science Reference • © 2022 • 391pp • H/C (ISBN: 9781668442159) • US $215.00

701 East Chocolate Avenue, Hershey, PA 17033, USA
Tel: 717-533-8845 x100 • Fax: 717-533-8661
E-Mail: cust@igi-global.com • www.igi-global.com

List of Contributors

Alonso-Díaz, Laura / *University of Extremadura, Spain* 90
Böttger, Heiner / *Catholic University of Eichstätt-Ingolstadt, Germany* 208
Conesa, Isabel Maria García / *University Defense Center in San Javier, Spain* 292
Costa, Francesca / *Università Cattolica del Sacro Cuore, Italy* 379
Delicado-Puerto, Gemma / *University of Extremadura, Spain* 90
Durán-Martínez, Ramiro / *University of Salamanca, Spain* 155
Espinar, Magdalena Custodio / *Comillas Pontifical University, Spain* 109
Ferrero, Valerio / *University of Torino, Italy* 41
Gkaintartzi, Anastasia / *University of Thessaly, Greece* 67
González-García, Francisco / *University of Granada, Spain* 351
Jovanović, Ana / *University of Belgrade, Serbia* 186
Kostoulas, Achilleas / *University of Thessaly, Greece* 67
Manchado-Nieto, Cristina / *University of Extremadura, Spain* 90
Mañoso-Pacheco, Lidia / *Autonomous University of Madrid, Spain* 22
Martínez, Amaia Aguirregoitia / *University of the Basque Country (UPV/EHU), Spain* 129
Martín-Pastor, Elena / *University of Salamanca, Spain* 155
Milla, Ruth / *University of the Basque Country (UPV/EHU), Spain* 129
Müller, Tanja / *Catholic University of Eichstätt-Ingolstadt, Germany* 208
Pla-Pueyo, Sila / *University of Granada, Spain* 351
Ramos-García, Ana María / *University of Granada, Spain* 351
Rubio, Antonio Daniel Juan / *University of Granada, Spain* 292
Ruiz, Gerardo Reyes / *Center for Higher Naval Studies (CESNAV), Mexico* 321
Ruiz-Madrid, María Noelia / *Jaume I University, Castellón, Spain* 237
Salvador-García, Celina / *Jaume I University, Spain* 1, 237
Ting, Y. L. Teresa / *The University of Calabria, Italy* 259
Torres-Zúñiga, Laura / *Autonomous University of Madrid, Spain* 351
Valverde-Esteve, Teresa / *University of Valencia, Spain* 237
Vitsou, Magda / *University of Thessaly, Greece* 67

Table of Contents

Foreword xvi

Preface xviii

Acknowledgment xxiii

Section 1
Theoretical Approaches and Pedagogical Reflections on Bilingual Primary Teacher Education

Chapter 1
A Journey Into CLIL-Friendly Pedagogies to Inform Teacher Professional Development 1
Celina Salvador-García, Jaume I University, Spain

Chapter 2
Teachers' Code-Switching in Bilingual Primary Education: A Literary Review of its Pedagogical Functions 22
Lidia Mañoso-Pacheco, Autonomous University of Madrid, Spain

Chapter 3
Let's CLIL! Pedagogical-Linguistic Reflections Between Teacher Education and Classroom Teaching – A Focus on the Italian Context 41
Valerio Ferrero, University of Torino, Italy

Section 2
Case Studies and Proposals for Teacher Training in Primary Bilingual Education Contexts

Chapter 4
"English in the Kindergarten: Towards Multilingual Education": Good Practices From a Teacher Training Program in Greece 67
Anastasia Gkaintartzi, University of Thessaly, Greece
Achilleas Kostoulas, University of Thessaly, Greece
Magda Vitsou, University of Thessaly, Greece

Chapter 5

University and Primary Schools Co-Teaching Together: Challenges Towards a CLIL Training Program.. 90

Cristina Manchado-Nieto, University of Extremadura, Spain
Gemma Delicado-Puerto, University of Extremadura, Spain
Laura Alonso-Díaz, University of Extremadura, Spain

Chapter 6

Collaborative Lesson Planning for CLIL Student Teachers of Primary Education............................ 109

Magdalena Custodio Espinar, Comillas Pontifical University, Spain

Chapter 7

CLIL Teachers' Beliefs and Practices: How Can Teacher Training Help?...................................... 129

Ruth Milla, University of the Basque Country (UPV/EHU), Spain
Amaia Aguirregoitia Martínez, University of the Basque Country (UPV/EHU), Spain

Chapter 8

Bilingual Education and Attention to Diversity: Key Issues in Primary Education Teacher Training in Spain... 155

Ramiro Durán-Martínez, University of Salamanca, Spain
Elena Martín-Pastor, University of Salamanca, Spain

Chapter 9

A Service-Learning Program for Multilingual Education at an Early Age: Tandem Teaching Experiences... 186

Ana Jovanović, University of Belgrade, Serbia

Chapter 10

Learning in Two Languages: A Long-Term Study at Bavarian Bilingual Elementary Schools......... 208

Heiner Böttger, Catholic University of Eichstätt-Ingolstadt, Germany
Tanja Müller, Catholic University of Eichstätt-Ingolstadt, Germany

Chapter 11

Teaching Physical Education Through English: Promoting Pre-Service Teachers Effective Personality Through a Learning-Practice Approach.. 237

Teresa Valverde-Esteve, University of Valencia, Spain
Celina Salvador-García, Jaume I University, Castellón, Spain
María Noelia Ruiz-Madrid, Jaume I University, Castellón, Spain

Section 3
Innovative Techniques, Resources, and Materials for Bilingual Teaching in Primary School Contexts

Chapter 12

CLIL: Towards a Transdisciplinary and Literacy-Focused Approach to Language-Learning........... 259

Y. L. Teresa Ting, The University of Calabria, Italy

Chapter 13
Benefits of the Application of Task-Based Learning Within the Bilingual Field in Primary
Education 292
 Antonio Daniel Juan Rubio, University of Granada, Spain
 Isabel Maria García Conesa, University Defense Center in San Javier, Spain

Chapter 14
Augmented Reality as an Innovative Tool for the Training of Bilingual Education Teachers in
Primary Schools... 321
 Gerardo Reyes Ruiz, Center for Higher Naval Studies (CESNAV), Mexico

Chapter 15
Example of a CLIL Teaching-Learning Sequence About Geology and Evolution for Pre-Service
Teachers 351
 Sila Pla-Pueyo, University of Granada, Spain
 Francisco González-García, University of Granada, Spain
 Ana María Ramos-García, University of Granada, Spain
 Laura Torres-Zúñiga, Autonomous University of Madrid, Spain

Chapter 16
Training the BE Trainee Teacher in Drama: A Focus on English and Science 379
 Francesca Costa, Università Cattolica del Sacro Cuore, Italy

Compilation of References 393

About the Contributors 444

Index 450

Detailed Table of Contents

Foreword xvi

Preface xviii

Acknowledgment xxiii

Section 1
Theoretical Approaches and Pedagogical Reflections on Bilingual Primary Teacher Education

Chapter 1
A Journey Into CLIL-Friendly Pedagogies to Inform Teacher Professional Development 1
    Celina Salvador-García, Jaume I University, Spain

CLIL effective pedagogy has been uncovered during the last two decades, and literature points to a number of considerations that CLIL teachers should take into account if they aspire to ensure optimal teaching and learning practices. Among other aspects, CLIL effective pedagogy may bear in mind a range of issues such as multimodal communication, oral communication, pedagogical translanguaging, collaborative teaching, critical thinking, and cooperative learning. In the present chapter, these will be described and justified from a theoretical perspective as relevant pedagogical ideas that CLIL professional development should consider. In addition, each of these CLIL-friendly pedagogical practices will be accompanied by an illustrative exemplification settled in a primary education context to facilitate their understanding and let readers clearly perceive how they may be operationalized at the classroom level.

Chapter 2
Teachers' Code-Switching in Bilingual Primary Education: A Literary Review of its Pedagogical Functions 22
    Lidia Mañoso-Pacheco, Autonomous University of Madrid, Spain

Code-switching is a linguistic phenomenon that is widespread among the bilingual communities of primary school learners. Despite the school administrators' disapproval, teachers commonly resort to this practice as a pedagogical tool to facilitate the dual-focused aim pursued through the content and language integrated learning (CLIL) approach. The present chapter aims to explore the most significant theoretical contributions concerning code-switching in bilingual settings, with an emphasis on its pedagogical functionality in primary education. Data on code-switching were mainly gathered through the bibliographic databases Web of Science (WoS) and Scopus. This literary review categorizes the functions reported by scholars into two broad categories: code-switching as a conceptual-understanding facilitator, focused on mathematics attainment, and code-switching as an interpersonal facilitator, divided into classroom management and affective development. The results point to the need to regulate its use and acknowledge the practicality of code-switching among bilingual school populations.

Chapter 3
Let's CLIL! Pedagogical-Linguistic Reflections Between Teacher Education and Classroom Teaching – A Focus on the Italian Context...41
 Valerio Ferrero, University of Torino, Italy

This chapter articulates its reflection on content and language integrated learning (CLIL) methodology in Italian primary schools from a pedagogical-linguistic perspective, emphasising its educational potential for the personal growth of children. Moving between teacher training and didactic action in the classroom, it will highlight how CLIL is useful in making students citizens capable of acting in the globalal world as people in possession of linguistic, cognitive, metacognitive, and emotional tools for analysing reality. An example of a teaching project using CLIL methodology will be proposed to anchor theoretical reflection to educational practice.

Section 2
Case Studies and Proposals for Teacher Training in Primary Bilingual Education Contexts

Chapter 4
"English in the Kindergarten: Towards Multilingual Education": Good Practices From a Teacher Training Program in Greece...67
 Anastasia Gkaintartzi, University of Thessaly, Greece
 Achilleas Kostoulas, University of Thessaly, Greece
 Magda Vitsou, University of Thessaly, Greece

This chapter presents a teacher education program that aimed to prepare early childhood educators and English language teachers to collaboratively introduce multilingual learning opportunities in preschool education in Greece using English as a bridge-language among students' languages and cultures. The program, which was designed to support education policy that introduced the English language into the curriculum of Greek state preschools, had four goals. Firstly, it aimed to approach English as a bridge-language that can help promote multilingual meaning-making. Secondly, it encouraged the use of pedagogical translanguaging in order to support teachers to challenge prevalent monolingual instruction patterns and build upon the children's entire linguistic repertoires. Teachers were also trained in experimenting with and employing arts-based learning and creativity. These learning outcomes are illustrated in the chapter by drawing on teacher training materials and participant output, which provide useful data on the implementation and overall impact of the program.

Chapter 5
University and Primary Schools Co-Teaching Together: Challenges Towards a CLIL Training
Program.. 90
Cristina Manchado-Nieto, University of Extremadura, Spain
Gemma Delicado-Puerto, University of Extremadura, Spain
Laura Alonso-Díaz, University of Extremadura, Spain

Bilingual education is getting great achievements because of the performance of bilingual programs. In Spain, these programs have been developed at the university thanks to the efforts made during the previous decades of their implementation. The autonomous region of Extremadura has been working cooperatively with other institutions since then, and now it is time to look back to recapitulate what has been done and what needs to be done from now on. This chapter aims to gather the main milestones of this process in order to review its internal and external aspects, as well as to reconsider the ways of improving bilingual programs. Final remarks show that bilingual programs have brought benefits, but there are still some aspects that require attention, such as a homogeneous national regulation or minding the methodological qualification of bilingual teachers. These issues need to be addressed in future research for the welfare of bilingual education.

Chapter 6
Collaborative Lesson Planning for CLIL Student Teachers of Primary Education........................... 109
Magdalena Custodio Espinar, Comillas Pontifical University, Spain

The introduction of content and language integrated learning (CLIL) in mainstream education in Spain demands specific teaching competencies. For this, Spanish universities have adapted the design of their degrees in education to meet the challenges of this demanding scenario. However, there is still a heterogeneous scenario among Spanish universities for preparing prospective teachers for CLIL. This chapter aims at exploring the profile of the primary education teacher specialized in CLIL teaching and proposing a collaborative lesson planning task likely to develop some key competencies of this profile in a group of student teachers. The collaborative lesson plannings designed by students are described and discussed in relation to recent literature. Moreover, the answers of 17 of these students to a questionnaire are analyzed to unveil the potential of this type of training for actually developing the collaborative competence of prospective CLIL primary teachers. A final reflection on the need to provide more homogeneous preparation connected to the CLIL classroom is also provided.

Chapter 7
CLIL Teachers' Beliefs and Practices: How Can Teacher Training Help?.. 129
Ruth Milla, University of the Basque Country (UPV/EHU), Spain
Amaia Aguirregoitia Martínez, University of the Basque Country (UPV/EHU), Spain

This chapter presents the main aspects of a study conducted to explore existing beliefs and perspectives on CLIL-teaching specific practices and methodological aspects. The study aimed at identifying the educational practices accepted by CLIL experienced teachers and comparing them with prospective primary education teachers' underlying assumptions both before and after explicit instruction on CLIL based on experts' advice. The analysis of the results seems to indicate that instruction has modified students' beliefs and that specific training may contribute to the alignment of in-service teachers' praxis with the suggestions by experts in the field, in areas such as identifying problems in advance, using the learners' mother tongue, correcting language errors, using authentic materials, or presenting content. Interestingly, the answers of both teachers and students acknowledge the effectiveness of CLIL, although they reveal that appropriate qualification and training are a matter of concern that could benefit teachers greatly.

Chapter 8
Bilingual Education and Attention to Diversity: Key Issues in Primary Education Teacher
Training in Spain... 155
    Ramiro Durán-Martínez, University of Salamanca, Spain
    Elena Martín-Pastor, University of Salamanca, Spain

Inclusive and bilingual education programs are two facets that can define quality education today. This chapter begins by focusing on the convergence between inclusion and bilingual education through a brief analysis of the impact of both in the field of education, and then addresses the principles that define content and language integrated learning (CLIL) and universal design for learning (UDL) approaches. Starting from the aspects shared by CLIL and UDL, five strategies and an example of an educational resource are presented that respond to the needs and characteristics of all students in primary education classrooms. This proposal can serve, in turn, as an element of reflection and analysis for future primary school teachers involved in bilingual programs.

Chapter 9
A Service-Learning Program for Multilingual Education at an Early Age: Tandem Teaching
Experiences 186
    Ana Jovanović, University of Belgrade, Serbia

This chapter explores the effects of a service-learning program on the development of competences for teaching Spanish to young learners during initial teacher education. The framework of action science provides guidelines for the design of participative inquiry in which the student-teachers evaluate their theories of language teaching and embrace opportunities for developing a more efficient, flexible, but also a more critical approach to early language education. By implementing interpretative phenomenology as a research tool, a particular attention is dedicated to the participants' understanding and interpretation of specific pedagogical events of tandem teaching, which marked their positive and negative didactic experiences and influenced reconsideration of their theories of teaching.

Chapter 10
Learning in Two Languages: A Long-Term Study at Bavarian Bilingual Elementary Schools 208
    Heiner Böttger, Catholic University of Eichstätt-Ingolstadt, Germany
    Tanja Müller, Catholic University of Eichstätt-Ingolstadt, Germany

In the school years 2015/2016 and 2018/2019, the authors accompanied and evaluated 21 public elementary schools in Bavaria, Germany, in a research collaboration with the Bildungspakt Bayern Foundation about bilingual (German/English) instruction in German elementary schools. The goal was to investigate how high the potential of implicit teaching and learning in a bilingual primary context is. Altogether, over 900 students, parents, and 42 teachers participated in the empirical long-term study (over 5 years) Learning in Two Languages –Bilingual Elementary School English. The findings not only show that students taught in the bilingual classes have a foreign language advantage and perform at least as well in mathematics and German as students in regular classes do, but also that they have a very positive attitude towards learning English in elementary school. These findings, the study, and its theoretical background are aimed to be portrayed in short in this chapter.

Chapter 11
Teaching Physical Education Through English: Promoting Pre-Service Teachers Effective
Personality Through a Learning-Practice Approach...237
    Teresa Valverde-Esteve, University of Valencia, Spain
    Celina Salvador-García, Jaume I University, Castellón, Spain
    María Noelia Ruiz-Madrid, Jaume I University, Castellón, Spain

Applying a learning-practice approach to CLIL in teacher education may be instrumental not only to promote the development of CLIL professional skills, but also to improve pre-service teachers' 'effective personality.' This chapter provides, first, a detailed description of a specific course of physical education teacher education that has been successfully applied for three years, in which pre-service teachers are required to implement CLIL through a learning-practice approach. Subsequently, it presents an explanatory mixed-methods study to examine how pre-service teachers' effective personality was influenced by the learning-practice approach to CLIL used. Informed by the results obtained, the chapter finishes by sharing some clues on how to foster effective personality through CLIL teacher training to help lecturers design and develop proper CLIL teacher development activities.

Section 3
Innovative Techniques, Resources, and Materials for Bilingual Teaching in Primary School Contexts

Chapter 12
CLIL: Towards a Transdisciplinary and Literacy-Focused Approach to Language-Learning........... 259
    Y. L. Teresa Ting, The University of Calabria, Italy

By integrating content and language learning-objectives, one gains a transdisciplinary literacy-focused perspective that brings into focus the thinking skills, literacies, and soft skills that all children need to succeed. This proposition is grounded in two sets of CLIL-materials. For preschoolers, this transdisciplinary literacy-focused perspective transformed must-learn vocabulary and grammar into tasks for cultivating early numeracy, logical thinking, and self-regulatory behaviours. For primary-level learners, this approach recognized the cognitive maturity and reasoning abilities of 8-year-olds: age-appropriate disciplinary concepts regarding natural history were presented through materials using age-matched academic language, thus providing children whole complex discourses for thinking whole complex thoughts. To help readers incorporate such a perspective into their own practice, a workshop format presents some cognitive-neuroscience principles guiding the development of these materials alongside specific design considerations, implementation processes, and classroom observations.

Chapter 13
Benefits of the Application of Task-Based Learning Within the Bilingual Field in Primary
Education 292
    Antonio Daniel Juan Rubio, University of Granada, Spain
    Isabel Maria García Conesa, University Defense Center in San Javier, Spain

Over the last two decades, the second language acquisition field has been influenced by new pedagogical approaches and innovative trends, which have reframed the principles of how foreign languages should be taught. The emergence of the task-based language teaching (TBLT) since the late nineties, and its increasing implementation, transformed it into one of the trendiest pedagogical approaches. Later, the dual-focused vision of the content and language integrated learning (CLIL) approach gained momentum in European countries, and it was included as an essential part of schools' curricula. Nowadays, although CLIL and task-based instruction are well established in educational contexts, the combined use of the two still produces doubts among teachers. In this chapter, a thorough exploration of the main pedagogical constituents of CLIL and TBLT is carried out to analyse their commonalities and set relationships between them. To sum up, this paper will convince bilingual teachers about implementing authentic and meaningful task-based experiences within their CLIL curricula.

Chapter 14
Augmented Reality as an Innovative Tool for the Training of Bilingual Education Teachers in
Primary Schools 321
    Gerardo Reyes Ruiz, Center for Higher Naval Studies (CESNAV), Mexico

Children know a language when they associate words with images and sounds—this facilitates the assimilation of knowledge. This research uses applications based on augmented reality, which are designed to help teachers who want to teach another language, particularly English. The set of useful terms for the student to learn is defined in various categories such as animals, colors, and things. These terms are stored in a database with different formats such as text, 3D image, audio, and video which are associated with items that contain, in turn, a vocabulary which represents abstract entities, which are necessary to complement the learning of a language. The words are associated with the images and with the corresponding audio so that the students learn to read, write, listen, and, consequently, pronounce the words correctly. This research is projected as an innovative technological support that helps primary school teachers in the process of teaching the English language, and it is expected that in the short term it will become an indispensable basis for this educational dynamic.

Chapter 15
Example of a CLIL Teaching-Learning Sequence About Geology and Evolution for Pre-Service
Teachers 351
Sila Pla-Pueyo, University of Granada, Spain
Francisco González-García, University of Granada, Spain
Ana María Ramos-García, University of Granada, Spain
Laura Torres-Zúñiga, Autonomous University of Madrid, Spain

The present chapter describes in detail a teaching-learning sequence using the CLIL approach to teach contents related to sedimentary rocks, fossils, and evolution to pre-service primary education teachers. The sequence was designed and implemented during two consecutive semesters of the academic year 2021-2022. The target students belong to the bilingual strand of the courses 'Didactics of Experimental Sciences' I and II, dealing with physics, chemistry, geology, and astronomy contents (course I) and life sciences contents (course II). The courses are taught mainly in Spanish, but this particular sequence was delivered, produced, and assessed in English. Students' performance was assessed by means of self-evaluation, peer-evaluation, as well as immediate or delayed feedback from the lecturer.

Chapter 16
Training the BE Trainee Teacher in Drama: A Focus on English and Science 379
Francesca Costa, Università Cattolica del Sacro Cuore, Italy

This paper presents a teacher training experience for bilingual education (BE) using drama activities and techniques within a university degree in primary education. Many studies have underlined the similarities between teachers and actors, seeing teachers as performers, especially in regard to the correct and effective use of the voice, body language, and involvement of the audience. The type of training described here has a twofold objective: to make trainee-teachers participate as learners of drama techniques, and to help them use these techniques with their pupils. This paper will investigate studies on teacher training and BE and on BE and drama, describe the Italian context, and show the activities carried out in the teacher training. It will also analyze the script of a science play in English from a lexical point of view and show one of the lesson plans produced by the trainees. This study is theoretical-descriptive and has no research-based aims.

Compilation of References 393

About the Contributors 444

Index 450

Foreword

In recent decades the seeming historical certainties of Europe's largely monolingual national education systems have come under siege from various directions: long-standing linguistic minorities have gained more self-determination and stronger language rights, mass immigration has led to the influx of new language groups, the linguistic capital represented by the global lingua franca English has created demand for using it in classroom teaching beyond traditional language lessons. Interestingly, all these trends fit under the umbrella of the European Union's language policies which aim at creating plurilingual citizens that know two languages on top of their first. And so it is under this umbrella that CLIL (Content-and-Language Integrated Learning – the teaching and learning of non-language curricular content through an additional language) started to take hold in many European countries, with the EU policy rhetoric ensuring the benevolence of national educational administrations. The strongest impetus however – let there be no mistake – came from the grassroots level: parents and teachers saw leverage in CLIL for increasing the foreign language attainment of their children and students because such competences would be an asset in an increasingly interconnected world. CLIL with its focus on meaning promises to take foreign language learning beyond what is usually achieved through foreign language lessons alone – a perspective that seems particularly attractive in contexts where foreign language learning outcomes are traditionally considered inadequate.

The intense research and development work that has taken place over the last 20 years has shown that CLIL programmes are quite diverse and deeply context-dependent rather than representing a unified approach or a "teaching method". Nevertheless, the cumulative work of numerous CLIL researchers and practitioners has begun to crystallize around a number of key ideas that are considered either foundational for our understanding of CLIL or as enhancers of good CLIL practice. Without claim for completeness, these are:

- the multimodal nature of communication
- the key role of language in all types and all subjects of formal education
- the importance of subject-specific as well as transdisciplinary literacy for educational success
- the fact that the bilingual nature of CLIL classrooms represents an asset that ought to be actively exploited
- the importance of student engagement and task- or project-based learning
- attentiveness to the diversity of learners, and
- cross-curricular teacher collaboration

Foreword

So what does all this mean for the professionals who are supposed to deliver this type of bilingual education? Obviously, they need to be prepared for it beyond enhancing their proficiency in the target language. The fundamentally monolingual traditions of most of Europe's education systems are quite naturally reflected in the teacher education embedded in them, a circumstance which is likely to create tensions and complications in preparing teachers for bilingual education. But teacher education institutions are beginning to face their responsibility, and to the extent that CLIL has become part of the mainstream (more in some education systems than others) they have started to include learning opportunities for their pre- and in-service students to prepare them for being CLIL teachers. This always needs to happen on top of everything else that requires coverage in teacher education programmes, which are highly complex undertakings at the best of times.

In tackling such a challenging and delicate task it is natural to turn to the experiences of fellow professionals. The present book provides teacher educators with just such a platform for sharing pedagogical designs, lessons learned, research findings, and good practice, linking expertise across geographical and institutional contexts. CLIL teacher educators will find inspiration as well as confirmation on at least two accounts. Firstly, with regard to what should be the most important learning goals of CLIL teacher education modules (see the bullet points above), and secondly, with regard to the pedagogical designs used by proven CLIL teacher education modules. Such designs range from experiential learning (i.e. students experiencing CLIL as part of their own general teacher training), practice-learning (i.e. students implementing CLIL lessons while also building conceptual knowledge about them), using Universal Design for Learning as a dual tool for pedagogical planning as well as self-reflection, and using drama pedagogy. One further concept for CLIL teacher education namely that of service learning deserves special attention. In this model, future CLIL teachers learn to focus on the role of language for curricular learning through teaching the main language of education to children with migration backgrounds in a service learning situation. In this way, the deep connection between different situations of bilingual education becomes obvious despite differences with regard to social status, academic preparedness and language prestige. Because at the core, there always lies the task to make knowledge accessible to the learners who are studying through a second or foreign language. The fact that CLIL is strongly associated with high-prestige target languages and is commonly taught by teachers who share their non-native speaker status with their pupils seems to create a higher degree of openness and tolerance towards questions of language and accessibility of knowledge. Giving future teachers a firm grounding in good CLIL practices might – just might – also benefit their dealing with the multilingual learner groups they teach in every lesson, as long as the teacher development creates awareness regarding the transferability of good pedagogical practice.

Christiane Dalton-Puffer
University of Vienna, Austria

Preface

Quality education is one of the 17 Sustainable Development Goals (SDGs) included by the United Nations General Assembly in the 2030 Agenda. It would seem less urgent than other goals, such as zero hunger or climate action, for example. However, quality education is closely related to both, as well as to most of the remaining goals (non-poverty, well-being, gender equality...). In this sense, quality education is the gateway to social sensitivity and empathy for future societies, on which most possible sustainability strategies depend. In this context, bilingual education emerges as a firm commitment to the future, that is, the first step towards cultural diversity. It is an opportunity to fight against the deceptive simplicity of monolingual and monocultural education, where learning risks becoming a pinchbeck of a unique and hegemonic discourse.

From a pedagogical point of view, bilingual education refers to the teaching-learning process in which the agents involved work with two languages –thus also with two cultural backgrounds–, most of the time one of them being the language of learning. In the growing didactic phenomenon known as CLIL (Content and Language Integrated Learning), the target language is used partially or wholly for teaching, most of the time for content that has little or nothing to do with the target language itself. Bilingual teachers use specific strategies to enable their students to develop a wide range of competencies employing a vehicular language that they do not yet know. This particular use of the target language, whatever it may be, is the most authentic and therefore the most valuable opportunity for language acquisition.

Bilingual education was until a few decades ago a possibility only accessible to a few elite minorities who could afford it. It was almost exclusively devoted to the pragmatic training of privileged students to become economic or political leaders. However, the rapid development of technical globalization, together with the increase in the mobility of learners around the world, has brought about a drastic educational change in the field of foreign language teaching. So, Content-Based Teaching (CBT) teaching models, including CLIL, as well as EMI (English Medium of Instruction), in which English is used as the only language of instruction, and some other methodological approaches to applied foreign language learning, have become widespread. The actual use of more than one language for educational purposes is a reality for millions of learners today, so a central question arises: Are teachers ready for this new challenge?

The level of proficiency in a foreign language may not be questionable at the university level, where researchers are supposed to work with more than one language for scientific and academic purposes. Yet, with the only exception of foreign language teachers, most of them are likely to lack a clear conceptual understanding of 'educational bilingualism' as well as specific techniques for using foreign languages in teaching. This pedagogical shortcoming becomes more and more controversial as we move away from university teaching, with primary education being the stage where teachers' linguistic and methodological skills are most sharply questioned. Regardless of whether this is fair or not, the fact that bilingual

Preface

teaching can fail at the basic educational stages is a real threat to modern societies, including the goal of quality education, and therefore, to some extent, other SDGs as well.

Most primary school teachers involved in bilingual programs do not know how their colleagues are dealing with this same situation in other areas of the world, often not even within the same country. In addition to this global lack of knowledge, the content subjects affected by one type of CLIL teaching may vary from one school to another. Even CLIL changes according to the teachers who lead the processes within the same school. Methodological diversity is therefore extreme, and it is difficult for experts to evaluate whether a teaching technique is more or less appropriate for specific content, or whether it depends on the circumstantial variables of a particular application. The importance of sharing theoretical foundations, pedagogical perspectives, and good practices lie in the possibility of minimizing this threat.

Those of us who are committed to the effectiveness of our daily teacher training work cannot ignore that, along with basic conceptual knowledge –both epistemic and didactic–, attitudes and intuition will play a decisive role in the success of our student teachers. These intangible virtues will be essential where communication constitutes a high danger zone, so bilingual teachers often rely on their deepest convictions about what they do, how they do it, and why they do it. To enhance this less easily observable part of the training, many of us do our best to leave student teachers with an indelible imprint of our passion for teaching: We promote mobility to countries where foreign languages and cultures are daily accessible; we make them visit bilingual schools and develop formulas for academic cooperation with teachers; we supervise school internships; etc. The results can be poor if we do not concern ourselves with what other bilingual teachers are doing in other places, with other languages, with other content subjects, with different group compositions, etc., if we do not have the opportunity to reflect on the various circumstances.

Taking all this into consideration, this book is devoted to the review and analysis of the theory and practice of bilingual primary teacher training in a broad sense. On the one hand, it may be useful for trainers' reflection upon case studies and concrete proposals for primary teacher training in bilingual contexts. On the other hand, it is also an invitation to primary bilingual pre-service and in-service teachers who would like to update their knowledge of theoretical perspectives and practical approaches, among others. In this respect, some chapters also refer to innovative techniques, resources, and materials successfully used in bilingual primary education contexts.

The first section of the book, titled "Theoretical Approaches and Pedagogical Reflections on Bilingual Primary Teacher Education," includes three chapters. The first chapter by Salvador-García is rooted in the CLIL approach as a basis for ensuring optimal teaching-learning practices in bilingual education contexts. From a theoretical perspective, the author addresses concepts such as multimodal communication, oral communication, or pedagogical translanguaging, as significant elements to be taken into account in in-service teacher training. For a better understanding of the readers, the author incorporates examples that illustrate each element, contextualizing them in the primary education classroom. The second chapter by Mañoso-Pacheco presents, based on a review of the current literature, the potential benefits in the primary education classroom of one of the pedagogical techniques most widely used by CLIL teachers: Code-switching. To this end, the author classifies the functions into two broad categories: code-switching as a conceptual-understanding facilitator and as an interpersonal facilitator. The findings include the need to regulate the use of code-switching, but also the need to recognize the convenience of code-switching among the bilingual education community. The third and final chapter of this section by Ferrero focuses on the Italian context to highlight the value of the CLIL approach in bilingual teaching for the personal growth of learners. In other words, he aims to enable learners to act

xix

Preface

in a globalized world as individuals in possession of linguistic, cognitive, metacognitive, and emotional tools to analyze reality. All of this is based on an approach centred on teacher training and didactic elements in the classroom in the form of illustrative examples.

The second section of the book, called "Case Studies and Proposals for Teacher Training in Primary Bilingual Education Contexts," includes eight chapters. The first chapter by Gkaintartzi, Kostoulas, and Vitsou is contextualized in early childhood education, as it is the stage that precedes primary education and often serves as a pioneer for the implementation of educational programs that are subsequently applied in successive stages. The importance of the chapter lies in the presentation of a teacher training program to create multilingual learning opportunities, using English as a bridge between the different languages and cultures of the pupils. The learning outcomes of the program are illustrated in the chapter based on the teacher training and on data provided by the participants, which provide useful information on the implementation and overall impact of the program in Greece. The second chapter by Manchado-Nieto, Delicado-Puerto, and Alonso-Díaz provides information on the co-teaching process between the University of Extremadura (Spain) and primary schools in order to review internal and external elements and to reconsider ways of improving bilingual programs. They conclude that bilingual education programs have brought important benefits, but there are also important elements for improvement. Among others, they propose a homogeneous national regulation of bilingual education and the consideration of methodological qualification of bilingual teachers.

The third chapter by Custodio-Espinar explores the profile of the primary education teacher specializing in CLIL teaching. The author presents a collaborative lesson planning task to develop some key competencies of the CLIL teacher. This is supported by the student teachers' views on the proposal. She offers a final reflection on the need to provide more homogeneous training related to CLIL teacher training. The fourth chapter by Milla-Melero and Aguirregoitia-Martínez involves a study carried out to explore beliefs and perspectives on teaching practices and methodological aspects of teaching CLIL subjects. One of the novelties of the study is the inclusion of the views of in-service CLIL teachers and pre-service primary education teachers before and after receiving specific methodological training. They conclude that training has been effective in changing the beliefs of student teachers and that it may contribute to improving the teaching practices of in-service teachers. The fifth chapter by Durán-Martínez and Martín-Pastor introduces one of the most significant issues in bilingual education today: Attention to diversity. Here, the authors focus on the convergence between inclusion and bilingual education through a brief analysis of the impact of both elements in the field of education. They then discuss the principles that define CLIL and *Diseño Universal para el Aprendizaje* (DUA) or Universal Design for Learning. Finally, they propose five strategies and an example of an educational resource that respond to the needs and characteristics of primary school pupils.

In the sixth chapter, Jovanović presents the results of a service-learning program aimed at the development of competences in Spanish as a foreign language during initial teacher training. The importance of the paper lies in the focus on the participants' understanding and interpretation of tandem teaching. This determines both their positive and negative teaching experiences, which, moreover, served to directly influence the reconsideration of their ideas about teaching foreign languages (i.e., Spanish). The seventh chapter by Böttger and Müller presents a five-year research study carried out together with the Bildungspakt Bayern Foundation to investigate the potential of implicit teaching and learning in a bilingual primary education context in schools in Bavaria (Germany). The typologies and the high number of informants (pupils, teachers, and parents) involved in the research are remarkable. The results show that pupils who attend bilingual schools have an advantage in language proficiency and perform at least

Preface

as well in content subjects such as mathematics as pupils who do not attend bilingual schools, together with developing a more positive attitude towards foreign languages. The final chapter in this section by Valverde-Esteve and Salvador-García describes a specific CLIL physical education teacher training course that has been running for three years. This training course provides CLIL teachers with specific instruction through a learning-practice approach, shaping their teaching personality as teachers of a very specific CLIL subject. The chapter concludes by providing guidelines for effective teacher training for CLIL teaching based on practical activities.

The third section of the book, that is, "Innovative Techniques, Resources, and Materials for Bilingual Teaching in Primary School Contexts," includes five chapters. The first chapter by Ting explores, through the integration of content and foreign language, a transdisciplinary perspective on literacy development. The author develops her proposal based on two typologies of sets of CLIL materials aimed at pre-school and primary school pupils, respectively, in order to develop linguistic-cognitive competencies. In addition, she facilitates the reader's understanding by means of a workshop-like chapter, in which, among other considerations, the theories and principles of learning that shaped the development of the materials are presented. The second chapter by Juan-Rubio and García-Conesa focuses on the benefits of applying project-based learning to bilingual teaching in primary school contexts. In doing so, the authors aim to address concerns about the joint application of project-based learning and the CLIL approach. The objective is to establish patterns of teaching practice around the meaningful application of project-based learning in CLIL classes. The third chapter by Reyes-Ruiz invites the reader to learn about the application of augmented reality to the training of teachers of bilingual education in primary education. Through the use of different applications, the author presents innovative technological support that helps primary school teachers in the process of teaching English as a foreign language.

The fourth chapter by Pla-Pueyo, González-García, Ramos-García, and Torres-Zúñiga describes an example of a CLIL teaching sequence on geology and its influence on the training development of pre-service teachers. The sequence was designed and implemented in English as a foreign language in 2021-22 at the University of Granada (Spain) with students of the courses Didactics of Experimental Sciences I and Didactics of Experimental Sciences II. Working with the didactic sequence brought important benefits for the students' training, especially considering that for many of them it was their first contact with the CLIL approach. The fifth and final chapter by Costa presents an experience of training bilingual education teachers using drama activities and techniques with pre-service primary school teachers. The novelty of the work lies in the author's twofold goals: to involve pre-service teachers as learners of drama techniques; and to help them use these techniques with their pupils.

So, this book includes different examples of activities carried out to illustrate the contents, as well as the work done by pre-service teachers in the form of lesson plans. In a nutshell, bilingual education is not a didactic trend. It is here to stay so that in the coming decades, primary schools will move towards this new pedagogy. Primary school teachers will have to be proficient in a foreign language in a practical sense; to be able to use it spontaneously in their classes; and to organize and check out every single linguistic use necessary for any specific issue related to the content subject they deal with. Trainers must therefore be capable of carrying out linguistic and technical training by adopting a CLIL approach to their courses themselves. We are more than aware that bilingual teaching can be affected by very diverse and various circumstances in different regions of the world. In response to this variety, the corresponding training itineraries for bilingual primary school teachers are also diverse, depending most of the time on the educational and social reality of a particular area. In this sense, the analyses and

xxi

evaluations of bilingual primary education made by the several contributors to this book should always be taken with reserve.

José Luis Estrada Chichón
University of Cádiz, Spain

Francisco Zayas Martínez
University of Cádiz, Spain

Acknowledgment

We would like to thank all the contributors to this book, the reviewers, the development editors of IGI Global, as well as Dr. Christiane Dalton-Puffer (University of Vienna) for their work and collaboration. In addition, we would like to acknowledge and give our warmest thanks to all those who are passionately committed to teacher training for bilingual education on a daily basis. In our case, this role is assumed by Ms. Elena Romero-Alfaro (University of Cádiz).

Section 1

Theoretical Approaches and Pedagogical Reflections on Bilingual Primary Teacher Education

Chapter 1

A Journey Into CLIL-Friendly Pedagogies to Inform Teacher Professional Development

Celina Salvador-García

https://orcid.org/0000-0003-0776-8760

Jaume I University, Spain

ABSTRACT

CLIL effective pedagogy has been uncovered during the last two decades, and literature points to a number of considerations that CLIL teachers should take into account if they aspire to ensure optimal teaching and learning practices. Among other aspects, CLIL effective pedagogy may bear in mind a range of issues such as multimodal communication, oral communication, pedagogical translanguaging, collaborative teaching, critical thinking, and cooperative learning. In the present chapter, these will be described and justified from a theoretical perspective as relevant pedagogical ideas that CLIL professional development should consider. In addition, each of these CLIL-friendly pedagogical practices will be accompanied by an illustrative exemplification settled in a primary education context to facilitate their understanding and let readers clearly perceive how they may be operationalized at the classroom level.

INTRODUCTION

From a general perspective, CLIL (Content and Language Integrated Learning) may be seen as a pedagogical approach focused specifically on content and language learning. Nevertheless, this might be a quite short-sighted understanding of the concept. CLIL holds a pivotal position for reframing its potential as a pedagogic, rather than a linguistic, phenomenon. Currently, CLIL aspires to be more than a mere language teaching methodology, since it may foster more than the simple learning of content and language. In fact, it emerges as a possibility of leaving behind traditional approaches of learning and moving forward towards an updated approach of educational practices (Coyle, 2018). Well-prepared CLIL practices respond to the necessities of the 21st Century's world. Therefore, this pedagogical approach might be considered as an innovative practice aimed at promoting quality education. In spite of this, for

DOI: 10.4018/978-1-6684-6179-2.ch001

Copyright © 2023, IGI Global. Copying or distributing in print or electronic forms without written permission of IGI Global is prohibited.

proper quality education to be promoted, teacher professional development is of utmost importance, since it should ensure that educational programs are not only well articulated, but also effectively implemented at the classroom level (Martínez-Agudo & Fielden-Burns, 2021).

Even though a sharp increase and an enormous uptake of CLIL have been taking place in numerous countries all over the world (Lasagabaster & Doiz, 2016; Siqueira et al., 2018),

Its rapid spread has been considered to outpace teacher education provision. Teachers, undoubtedly the actors who have been more deeply impacted by CLIL, have often been thrown out to teach according to this approach without sufficient or adequate training, because the demands placed on them by the implementation of this new approach have been largely overlooked. This situation needs to be countered and teacher training should figure prominently on the present and future CLIL agenda, as the success, sustainability, and continuity of CLIL schemes are considered to hinge largely on teacher education and preparation (Pérez-Cañado, 2018, p. 1).

This is concerning because CLIL teachers should possess scientific knowledge, which is connected not only to their expertise regarding the specific contents of the subject they teach, but also to the pedagogical practicalities of CLIL, with which they need to be well-versed too (Mehisto et al., 2008). According to previous literature, some CLIL teachers lack the necessary awareness of pedagogical essentials that are key for adequate CLIL implementation (Hu & Gao, 2021). In addition, some CLIL teachers have reported that they feel underprepared to properly apply this pedagogical approach (Contero, et al., 2018; Salvador-Garcia & Chiva-Bartoll, 2017). Consequently, if CLIL attains to stay deservedly within the educational scenario without hindering quality education, the challenges it poses linked to teacher professional development must be faced.

Against this backdrop, Pérez-Cañado (2018, p. 3) proposes several lines of action aimed to guarantee enduring bilingual education. Particularly, two of these lines of action are precisely focused on teacher professional development. One of them refers to 'modifying existing undergraduate degrees to guarantee that preservice teachers receive sufficient methodological and theoretical grounding on CLIL'. The other raises that 'preservice teachers can also be more adequately prepared to step up to the bilingual challenge by reinforcing CLIL preparation in university teacher trainers'. All in all, to ensure quality of bilingual education, proper and specific teacher training for CLIL is critical. Taking into account the aforementioned ideas, the aim of this chapter is to describe several CLIL-friendly pedagogical options on which CLIL teacher professional development may be focused to guarantee a success-prone implementation of this approach and foster quality education.

CLIL: YOU WILL NEVER WALK ALONE

CLIL effective pedagogy has been uncovered during the last two decades in an attempt to better understand how this pedagogical approach functions and optimize its implementation, since 'adopting a CLIL approach does not automatically lead to effective learning and increased subject-specific performance' (Meyer & Coyle, 2017, p. 200). In fact, there is a growing awareness of the need to better understand the nature of CLIL leading to the question of 'how' to put it into practice properly (Coyle, 2015). In this sense, for example, the pluriliteracies framework (Coyle & Meyer, 2021) or the Cognitive Discourse

A Journey Into CLIL-Friendly Pedagogies to Inform Teacher Professional Development

Functions construct (Dalton-Puffer, 2016) have been specifically developed for CLIL to show teachers how they can guide students through their learning path.

Nevertheless, in addition to these CLIL specificities and according to the large body of research revolving around this pedagogical approach, CLIL is not an isolated phenomenon, and besides of its own pedagogical tenets, additional pedagogies may offer valuable support to enhance CLIL practice. This vast sum of literature points to a number of considerations that CLIL teachers should take into account if they aspire to ensure optimal teaching and learning practices. Among other aspects, according to research in this field, CLIL effective pedagogy may be underpinned by a range of issues such as multimodal communication (i.e., Evnitskaya & Jakonen, 2017), oral communication (i.e., Estrada & Otto, 2019), pedagogical translanguaging (i.e., Liu, 2020), collaborative teaching (i.e., Pappa et al., 2019), critical thinking (i.e., Romeu et al., 2020) and cooperative learning (i.e., Casal, 2016). Although there might be additional options that could have been included in this list, the length restrictions to which this chapter is subjected made it impossible to add more. Therefore, the author considered that this compendium of pedagogies was sufficiently theoretically sound and supported by empirical research to be chosen for this text.

The aim of the present chapter is to describe and justify this set of six CLIL-friendly pedagogies from a theoretical perspective as relevant pedagogical ideas that professional development focused on the use of CLIL could bear in mind. As it will be seen, all of them may help CLIL teachers to optimize educational practices, promoting the development of a number of competencies among students while learning a content and a language. In addition, each of these CLIL-friendly pedagogical practices will be accompanied by an illustrative exemplification settled in a primary education context to facilitate their understanding and let readers clearly perceive how they may be operationalized at the classroom level. These ideas are not expected to provide 'recipes' of how CLIL lessons should be taught, since neither of these pedagogies is indispensable nor exclusive; but rather to show how CLIL practice might be enhanced by paying careful attention to a set of practicalities. Finally, it is worth mentioning that each of the pedagogical considerations presented should be adjusted to the specific settings where it is to be applied.

CLIL-FRIENDLY PEDAGOGIES

Multimodal Pedagogical Affordances

Multimodality refers to conveying meanings thanks to the integration of elements such as language, images, resources, interactions or events. In this sense, Archer (2014, p. 189) asserts that the teaching and learning act "is multimodal as it happens through speech, writing, gesture, image and space". Most of the times, CLIL learners are not proficient in the vehicular language, therefore fostering meaning-making and understanding becomes critical in settings where CLIL is applied. Consequently, multimodal communication emerges as a valuable means for mediating and optimizing the teaching and learning process (Fernández-Fontecha et al., 2020).

The communication process might be hindered in CLIL lessons due to the language limitations to which students may be subject. However, regardless of these difficulties, teachers still need to ensure that the subject content is understood. This is worrisome since the cognitive load theory establishes that exposure to new content in a language that is not mastered and without any appropriated instructional support will probably pose an additional challenge to students, resulting in ineffective learning (Roussel et al., 2017). As a consequence, if CLIL is not properly articulated, language and/or content learning may be negatively affected. In fact, this is one of the most frequently repeated reproaches against CLIL and bilingual education.

In order to overcome such a challenge, CLIL teachers are not expected to rely solely on language to convey meaning. In fact, they may use a range of multimodal elements to deal with subject specific content. These pedagogical affordances (Airey, 2016) or scaffolding strategies (Bruner, 1984) bridge discourse with reality to enhance learners' comprehension of the specialized content. These strategies may be perceived by different senses, thus, adding extra information to the teacher's discourse and helping to convey its meaning (Airey, 2016).

There is ample research on the use of multimodality in learning scenarios (Magnusson & Godhe, 2019), and its analysis in CLIL contexts is also increasing notably because of the benefits it may entail (Evnitskaya, & Jakonen, 2017; Fernández-Fontecha et al., 2020; Forey & Polias, 2017). Multimodal pedagogical affordances may take the form of gestures, pointing, visual aids (i.e., posters, videos, objects), visual organizers (i.e., timelines, infographics, schemes), language adaptations (i.e., synonyms, periphrasis, reiterations, «echoing», questioning, rephrasing), or paralinguistic features (i.e., intonation, voice tone, stress systems), among other aspects. If CLIL teachers are able to bear in mind and properly use multimodal pedagogical affordances in their lessons, they will probably enhance their teaching practices and aid students better understand and engage in the teaching and learning process.

An Exemplification in the Physical Education Subject

Table 1.

Level: 6th level (11-12 years old)	**Topic**: Australian Rules Football

Description:
This exemplification is developed within a proposal focused on Australian Rules Football, a team sport. 6th grade students are learning its rules and how to play this sport. In order to show how multimodal pedagogical affordances may play a meaningful role, subsequently, a couple of ideas are going to be described.

Example 1 – Introductory video
When a new sport (content) is presented to the students, it is interesting giving them some initial information for them to get the gist of it. A number of options are possible. Among them, one that CLIL teachers might choose are videos. In this sense, an introductory video showing several images about Australian Rules Football could be watched in the first session of a unit. Videos are a multimodal visual input that contains words, pictures, and gestures that will help CLIL learners discover what the sport they are going to start working is. To enable this, while watching the video, the teacher could ask a few questions to make sure the students are following it (i.e., In which country is this sport played? Is this an indoors or an outdoors sport? How many players are there?). In addition, after watching the video, students, in pairs, could do an activity to identify similarities and differences with a sport they already know.

Example 2 – Multimodal speech
Physical Education CLIL teachers may rely on a range of multimodal pedagogical affordances to present activities, tasks or games. All these strategies may be instrumental to help students better understand what the task consists of, how it is developed and what they are expected to do. In the following example, a teacher is explaining a game, and she supports her explanations with different multimodal pedagogical affordances. The next excerpt displays her speech, but subsequently additional strategies accompanying her words are going to be explained.

> *T: If you have the ball at this moment [Seq. 1], you have to go and touch your classmate with the ball [Seq. 2], you have to try to touch with the ball. Ok? To touch [Seq. 3], ok?*

In this case (Figure 1), the teacher is holding a ball, since this artifact is basic to play the game. Anytime she utters the word "ball", she is stressing it by increasing her tone of voice while holding harder the ball [Seq. 1]. In addition, when she is explaining that players have to touch each other with the ball, she exemplifies the action by doing it herself [Seq. 2 and 3]. These gestures act as visual aids for those students who might struggle to understand the language or imagine what she means with her words. Likewise, she uses reiterations and repetitions, since she repeats three times the verb "touch" and slightly rephrases the way she explains the same idea.

Seq. 2 | Seq. 3

Continued on following page

Table 1. Continued

Seq. 1			

Figure 1. Example of multimodal sequence.

Key issues:
-Multimodal affordances may be jointly applied and each of them may support the others. Therefore, teachers should be aware of how they may orchestrate all the options they have to help foster understanding.
-It is also interesting making students aware of their own possibilities to use multimodal strategies when speaking. If they know that interacting is much more than the mere speech, they may feel more comfortable and be more prone to engage in the communication process.

Fostering Meaningful Oral Communication

Oral communication skills are critical in any CLIL context. In fact, one of the main goals of this pedagogical approach is to develop this type of skills. These may be attained as a result of using the target language with communicative purposes when listening to and speaking with the teacher and/or other classmates. In this sense, thanks to the nature of CLIL, educational settings using this approach let students use the language meaningfully as well as be conscious of how it works. Likewise, CLIL lessons provide learners with more input and exposure to the target language, and they should be able to engage in oral communicative practice in a number of occasions during the sessions. In fact, Martínez-Agudo and Fielden-Burns (2019) assert that the increased and continued exposure to the target language emerges as one of the key aspects for CLIL programs to succeed in terms of language benefits.

Although learners' oral skills may be substantially benefited and improved when CLIL is applied (Martínez-Agudo & Fielden-Burns, 2019; Pérez-Cañado, 2018), these outcomes are not expected to be achieved by simply translating the lessons to the target language (Meyer & Coyle, 2017). In fact, if CLIL aspires to promote oral language use and learning, students should be provided with opportunities to effectively interact in class. To do so, Mehisto et al. (2008) suggest that building a psychological and physical safe environment, letting students experiment with the language, using an appropriate language level or generating a myriad of opportunities for students to use the language are some of the key issues that every CLIL teacher should consider.

Oral interaction in class may be established between teachers and students or solely among students. Regarding the former, teacher's strategic use of questions has great potential (Tagnin & Ríordáin, 2021). While closed questions are commonly limited to one-word answers, thus entailing limited communication and interaction; open questions leave more space to the students to express themselves and engage cognitively. Moving now to the latter, pair work and group work seem to be essential strategies to get students speaking to each other (Attard-Montalto et al., 2015).

Regardless of the participants engaged in the oral communication process, one thing seems clear, careful planning is of utmost importance to avoid difficulties and promote it in class. In this sense, CLIL teacher training may focus on how different methods, strategies and techniques could be more or less adequate to raise proper questions and/or develop pair and group activities with the aim of enhancing meaningful oral communication.

A Journey Into CLIL-Friendly Pedagogies to Inform Teacher Professional Development

An Exemplification in the Music Subject

Table 2.

Level: 2nd level (6-7 years old)	**Topic**: musical instruments

Description:

In previous lessons, students have been learning different types of musical instruments and the family to which they belong (i.e., strings, percussion, brass). The two tasks described subsequently will serve as concluding activities in order to reinforce students' learning about the topic while focusing on oral communication promotion.

Activity 1, Part 1 - Preparation of the poster

In this first part of the task, students are to prepare a poster with the title "My favorite musical instrument" individually. In this poster, they have to glue and color a drawing of their favorite musical instrument (the teacher provides them with the pictures needed). Besides of the title, students have to write the name of the musical instrument, and the family it belongs to.

Activity 1, Part 2 - Presentation of the poster

When the posters are ready, each student presents it in front of their classmates, who, in pairs, have to complete a checklist (Figure 2) about the presentation.

Presentation checklist
"My favourite musical instrument"

The presentation includes...

☐ Name of the musical instrument

☐ Colour

☐ Big-small

☐ Family (strings, percussion, brass)

☐ Coloured drawing

Figure 2. Presentation checklist

Activity 1, Part 3 - Peer feedback

When the presentation finishes, each pair has to give some feedback about it. This feedback is divided into two comments: (1) One thing we like is... and (2) One thing he/she can improve is... In order to help students complete this activity, they could be provided with a work bank with useful expressions.

Activity 2 - Guess who: musical instruments version

Continued on following page

Table 2. Continued

This is a variation of the classic game, and serves to review the features of the instruments that have been shown in the previous presentations. Each student is given a board with the different musical instruments learned. A student selects one of the instruments and the rest of the group has to guess it. To do so, they have to ask yes/no questions based on the features that have been mentioned in the presentations. Some question ideas may be: Is it big? Is it yellow? Is it a string instrument?
Key issues: -Poster preparation is shared in this example because it provides students with the opportunity to create a material to support their oral presentation. Therefore, this first step is basic to scaffold their learning, since it is helpful to prepare oral presentations. In case some students struggle to carry out their presentations, the teacher may provide them with some cues to help them such as: "My favorite instrument is…", "It is… (color)", "It is big/small", "This instrument belongs to the … family".   -The checklist is aimed at making students listen to the person presenting the project, as well as giving them some ideas about the feedback they have to share in the third part of the presentation activity.   -Once the students know how to play "Guess who", the activity may be carried out in small groups or even in pairs to increase even more students' talking time.

Pedagogical Translanguaging

CLIL is a context-led pedagogical approach; therefore, depending on the setting, the way it is implemented may vary. According to Marsh and Langé (1999), CLIL does not necessarily entail the use of the target language 100% of the time if communication is not reached and the learning process is hindered. In some cases, thus, students' first language may play a role in CLIL. The conscious acknowledgement and connection between different languages is called translanguaging, and it is considered an identifiable and planned practice when using CLIL (Liu, 2020), since it may optimize the learning process (Cenoz, 2017).

Pedagogical translanguaging consists of adopting instructional strategies that integrate different languages in order to support and scaffold the learning process. From a pedagogical perspective, thus, the main aim of translanguaging is to enhance students' understanding. Consequently, it may emerge as another interesting and useful strategy to be applied in CLIL contexts. On the one hand, it may develop better comprehension and learning of both, language and content. On the other, it may help accomplish interactive and meaningful communication when the learners are not able to understand or express information. In addition to this, pedagogical translanguaging may act as a lever for activating creative thinking and motivating learning (Lin & He, 2017).

At this point, though, it is worth noting that pedagogical translanguaging in not a synonym of indiscriminate use of the first language nor the mere shift between two languages. It refers to the connection, construction and generation of a complex discourse (García & Wei, 2014), thus acknowledging the capacity of a speaker to interrelate different languages. Therefore, for it to be applied as a pedagogical strategy, conscious planning and careful consideration to when, how and why the first language is used are essential. Bearing in mind the previously mentioned ideas, it seems that pedagogical translanguaging

A Journey Into CLIL-Friendly Pedagogies to Inform Teacher Professional Development

stands as a relevant strategy that CLIL professional development might consider. Given that it may come with some challenges, this training should make sure that CLIL teachers comprehend what pedagogical translanguaging is, the circumstances under which they may apply it, as well as the reflective and planned process it entails.

An Exemplification in the Physical Education Subject

Table 3.

Level: 6th level (11-12 years old)	**Topic**: Australian Rules Football

Description:
This exemplification is again developed within the proposal focused on a team sport in which 6th grade students are learning its rules and how to play this sport. In order to show how pedagogical translanguaging may be applied, subsequently, a set of real excerpts are going to be presented and justified. These examples were developed in CLIL lessons in a Spanish context with English as the target language. Since these are real verbatim transcriptions, they are presented as they took place, and ungrammaticalities, inaccuracies and repetitions have not been eliminated or resolved.

Excerpt 1 – Teacher speech repeating information

> *T: You have to talk about the advices that you would say to play, to do a good attack, ok? What you should do to do a good attack.* Para hacer un buen ataque, *ok? What you have to do to be a very good attacker.*

Excerpt 2 – Teacher speech repeating information

> *T: (...) you should pick up the ball,* recoger la pelota, *in the correct zone.*

In the excerpts 1 and 2 the teacher is sharing information about an activity or the game with the students. In both cases, the teacher repeats a brief sentence she has already said in English using students' first language to ensure the flow of interaction.

Excerpt 3 – Student's translation

> *T: You are a team and you are another team. The goal of the game, the match, is to get ten passes, but doing the exercise that we have been practicing.*
> *S:* Los 10 pases de siempre *[the name of the game in Spanish].*
> *T: Yes, but doing this [showing the technical move they have to carry out].*

Excerpt 4 – Student's translation

> *T: You have to catch a ball and you have to try to get to the other goal. Do you know what's the meaning of goal?*
> *S:* Portería.

In the excerpts 3 and 4 the teacher is sharing information again. In these cases, instead of using students' first language herself, the students engage in the speech to make sure or show their understanding. In excerpt 3, the student understands the game the teacher is explaining and finds it very similar to a game called "los 10 pases". Therefore, he shares with all his classmates the name of this game to make sure he has understood properly the game and to help his classmates understand too. In excerpt 4, the teacher is uncertain about students' knowing the word "goal". Thus, she directly asks them to ensure that all of them are able to follow the message. As a result, a student replies with the translation of the word in Spanish to show that she knows it and helping the rest of her classmates follow the message in case they did not know the word.

Continued on following page

Table 3. Continued

Excerpt 5 – Student completing information

> *S: (...) Eh, you should stay...* atento.
>
> *T: To pay attention.*

Excerpt 6 – Student completing information

> *T: (...) The first who takes the ball starts again.*
>
> *S: But, if you catch the ball and then the ball falls in the ground, ¿*quién la coge? *[who grabs it?]*

In the excerpts 5 and 6 a student is speaking in English but, at some point, they struggle and are unable to express a word or an idea in this language. In order to keep on the flow of interaction, they use the Spanish equivalent.

Key issues:
-It is ok to combine languages since the goal is to learn and avoid losing the flow of the lesson.
-Pedagogical translanguaging should help create a safe atmosphere in which students feel comfortable and are not afraid of using as much English (in this case) as possible.
-It is fine using a first language equivalent or explicitly asking for the translation if students lack a term.

Collaboration Among Teachers

Teachers (including language assistants) should be prone to engage in collaborative practices in any educational setting. However, this teaching practice increases its relevance even more in bilingual contexts, since content specialists might not have native command of the target language or language teachers/assistants might not master non-linguistics subject-specific contents (Marsh, 2012). Therefore, collaboration in CLIL is unique and sometimes intricate because of the specificities of this scenario. This should not be regarded as something negative, but as a strong reason to make the most of each teacher's strengths by encouraging and emphasizing collaborative teaching even more.

According to Pérez-Cañado (2018), CLIL teachers are expected to develop and demonstrate interpersonal and collaborative competencies, because being effective in this respect is key to optimize the teaching and learning process. When effective collaboration is fostered, teachers can engage in discussions, exchange ideas, reflect on the strategies to use, carry out observations, etc. (Lu, 2020); and all these actions improve the teaching practice and facilitate learners' success achievement (Nguyen & Dang, 2020). Yet it is worth sounding a note of caution, since according to Nguyen & Dang (2020), achieving effective collaboration in general, but also in CLIL settings, is not always easy. Consequently,

A Journey Into CLIL-Friendly Pedagogies to Inform Teacher Professional Development

teacher training programs should promote interpersonal and collaborative competencies development (Pappa et al., 2019).

In this sense, teacher development activities may focus on establishing what effective collaboration practices look like in CLIL. Bell and Baecher (2012), for example, suggest that successful collaborative teachers should plan with the students in mind, create unified goals, appreciate other's expertise, be open to share ideas, resources and responsibilities, support each other, and value working with and learning from their colleagues. Only if CLIL teachers are aware of these ideas and ready to put them into practice, will they be enabled to engage in successful collaborative practices.

An Exemplification in the Natural Sciences Subject

Table 4.

Level: 4th level (9-10 years old)	**Topic**: Insects

Description:
This exemplification presents a task in which 4th grade students are to prepare and carry out an oral presentation about an insect, a topic they have been dealing with in the previous sessions. To do so, they will have to design a slide presentation to support their speech. The Natural Sciences teacher and the language assistant will be in charge of monitoring all the process, trying to optimize it through effective collaboration.

Before presenting the task to the students, the Natural Sciences teacher and the language assistant should carefully plan what the activity consists of, the different stages it will have, what students are expected to do, the responsibilities each educator will assume, etc. In this specific example, each pair of students is to carry out a presentation about an insect, therefore, at this first stage, the teachers should discuss and define the linguistic and content objectives, and, as a result, the criteria for both the oral presentations and the written information that students are expected to share in their slide. The following figures present an example of these criteria, which should be clearly described by the teacher. Figure 3 establishes the criteria to carry out peer and self-assessment of the oral presentation, whereas Figure 4 shows the criteria for the slide presentations, which will then be completed as a checklist.

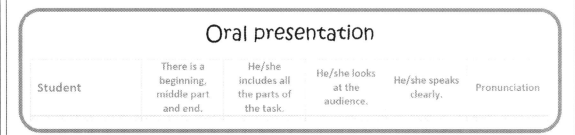

Figure 3. Peer and self-assessment criteria

Continued on following page

Table 4. Continued

Insects

Evaluation criteria:

- Good organization (slides: 1x title, 1x description, 1x place they live in, 1x what they eat, 1x special characteristics, 1x conclusion).
- There is information about an insect (Ex. Name, parts of the body, color, etc.) (3 sentences minimum).
- To use presents simple (at least 3 times).
- To put pictures of the insect.
- Creativity.

Figure 4. Slide presentation criteria

At this stage, the teacher and the language assistant are to establish the phases that the task will consist of as well as their temporal distribution. In addition, they are to decide the (shared) responsibilities each of them will assume during the process. In this specific example, these could be divided into the different steps of the task (although there might be a main responsible, both teachers may interact and take a role at every moment):

Table 1. Sub-tasks and main responsible teacher

Students' task	Main responsible
1. Searching for information	Natural Sciences teacher
2. Writing down information	Language assistant
3. Preparing slide presentation	Natural Sciences teacher
4. Oral presentation preparation	Language assistant
5. Evaluation	Natural Sciences teacher and Language assistant

Key issues:
-At every stage of the process, both teachers should be eager to engage in discussions, willing to exchange ideas and share reflection in order to support each other. This predisposition for working with and learning from each other are key issues to foster effective collaboration.

A Journey Into CLIL-Friendly Pedagogies to Inform Teacher Professional Development

Critical Thinking Promotion

Critical thinking is, according to Kusumoto (2018), the process consisting of purposeful, self-regulatory judgment focused on deciding what to believe or do. And, in fact, this author considers it to be a fundamental skill for 21st Century success. Although human beings are characterized by their ability to reason, consciously think, or even reflect upon thinking; enhancing these skills still represents a major challenge (Romeu et al., 2020). As a result, teachers should be eager to encourage and promote critical thinking among learners. In this sense, CLIL might emerge as an adequate approach to help promote critical thinking, since CLILilized lessons are expected to go beyond developing mere communicative competence and spur students to engage in a continuous process of inquiry and active cognitive engagement. In fact, CLIL learners are expected to create their own knowledge by participating actively in lessons that prompt them to engage in metacognitive reflection through dialogue (Mehisto et al., 2008).

There are two main reasons supporting the close connection between CLIL and critical thinking (Romeu et al., 2020): the first one consists of the fact that bilingualism comes with a set of cognitive benefits, therefore, promoting the development of deeper mental processes. The second one, in addition, is a consequence coming with the use of the pedagogical approach, since CLIL teachers tend to plan and program their lessons paying closer attention to the promotion and development of thinking skills among students in order to enable them to share and communicate knowledge. Furthermore, one of the inherent pillars of CLIL is the cognitive factor (Coyle et al., 2010), and literature asserts that adequate lesson planning when using CLIL should sequence activities to move from low order thinking skills to high order thinking skills following, for example, Bloom's taxonomy (Romeu et al., 2020).

Against this backdrop, therefore, teacher education should give CLIL teachers tools and ideas helping them to plan and sequence CLIL lessons attending to critical thinking and cognition promotion. Besides the use of critical questions, that have already been considered in this chapter, teacher training may rely on promoting active learning techniques such as jigsaw reading, pair work/group discussion, role-play, project-based learning, presentations, etc.; since these may be instrumental to enhance learners' critical thinking skills.

An Exemplification in the Arts and Crafts Subject

Table 5.

Level: 5th level (10-11 years old)	Topic: Paul Klee (artist)
Description: This exemplification presents a task in which 5th grade students discover who the artist Paul Klee is and what his art was. In the first part of the lesson, the teacher could share some information about the artist or tell the students to search about him on the internet to find out some key information as well as a few examples of his art. Afterwards, everyone could engage in group discussion through which students' critical thinking would be promoted. To do so, a number of questions following Bloom's Taxonomy cognitive levels would be posed to prompt discussion among learners (Table 2).	

Table 2. Sequence of questions to promote critical thinking following Bloom's Taxonomy

Remember	Where was he from? In which war did he participate?
Understand	What did he do in World War I?
Apply	Do you know another artist who participated in a war or made art about a war?
Analyze	What problems could he experience during World War I? Why was his task painting planes?
Evaluate	What is your opinion about participating in a war? How was his art influenced by the war?
Create	Create a city landscape inspired by Paul Klee but without the influence of a war.

Through this set of questions, students would be able to think and reflect upon the figure of Paul Klee while tackling the influence that wars might have on one's life and art. In addition, the teacher could guide discussion to help students connect World War I with current wars. The discussion would finish with the last activity, in which students would have to create their own city landscapes, inspired by those of Paul Klee, but trying to inspire a peaceful idea through them.

Key issues:

-CLIL teachers may find it interesting to combine critical thinking with topics related to social justice or other critical pedagogy related ideas (Giroux, 1988), as it is the case of the previous exemplification. In this specific proposal, the discussion involves critical ideas and reflection about war, peace, fights, etc.

-To carry out a group discussion, it is interesting establishing a set of indications so that everyone can participate and share their thought. In addition, it is relevant to ensure respect, active listening and waiting for one's turn to speak.

-The questions presented in this exemplification are open questions, thus, they leave more space to the students to express themselves and engage in the communication process. As a result, these were the type of questions that were aforementioned when tackling oral communication promotion.

Group Learning

This last section is focused on the use of group work to ameliorate the possibilities offered to enhance students' learning regarding both, language and content. Here, group work is presented following the ideas of Johnson and Johnson (2018) of cooperative learning. This means that small groups of students are placed together in order to maximize not only each one's learning, but also that of their groupmates. From this perspective, group work fosters student activeness and engagement, and is expected to promote learning, enhance social skills and increase academic achievement.

This type of group work fits perfectly with the CLIL approach (Casal, 2016) because, for example, both of them approach learning from a socio-constructivist perspective and promote student-centered lessons. In this sense, when learners collaborate and work together on a shared activity, a number of opportunities to learn emerge due to the shared processes in which they are immersed. Consequently, besides being guided by an expert (the teacher or another peer); they may share equal knowledge with their group of peers. This organization grounds a setting which is optimal for CLIL to be applied because group working promotes real language use and interaction among students. Consequently, it may generate a fruitful scenario for students to practice and develop linguistic skills through exchanging information and engaging in discussions about the content worked. Furthermore, group learning usually promotes students' cognitive involvement (Johnson & Johnson, 2018), which, according to the ideas presented in the previous subsection, is another key aspect from a CLIL perspective.

Nevertheless, embedding group activities in CLIL lessons deserves careful thought and planning, as it is more than just placing students together to carry out a shared activity. Thus, teachers are expected to reflect carefully upon the type of tasks and activities to use, in order to facilitate cooperation and communication among students. In addition, teachers are expected to provide proper support (Casal, 2016). As a result, CLIL teacher training should be specific and guide educators to proper planning and use of group activities to make the most of the CLIL teaching and learning process.

An Exemplification in the Math Subject

Table 6.

Level: 1st level (5-6 years old)	**Topic**: Shapes

Description:
This exemplification presents three activities for 1st level students. Each activity is developed with a different type of group (i.e., pair, small group and big group) to enable the reader perceive these three kinds of student distributions.

Activity 1 – What shape am I? (Think Pair Share)
This activity is carried out in pairs, and students are to work together to solve an activity, but they are also prompted to think individually. Basically, it consists of three steps: (1) *Think*, in which learners are expected to reflect independently about the activity that has been presented, in order to generate their own ideas; (2) *Pair*, in which learners are expected to discuss their thoughts with their pairs so that they can articulate their ideas and consider those of their peer; and (3) *Share*, in which pairs are expected to share their final ideas with the whole class.

In this specific example, the problem or activity to be solved would be focused on the topic of shapes. Learners would be shown a prompt similar to Figure 5, displaying a set of characteristics of a shape, and students would have to guess the shape.

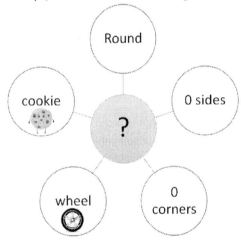

Figure 5. Think Pair Share prompt

Through this activity, students are spurred to interact and communicate because they are given opportunities to talk and use the language meaningfully. This is interesting not only from a linguistic perspective, but also because learners can internally process, organize, and retain ideas, helping them to optimize the learning of the content.

Activity 2 – Remember the sequence (Running dictation)
This activity is carried out using small groups of three to five students. The objective is for one of the learners in each group to walk (or run) to have a look at their groups' paper on the wall or anywhere in the school building (Figure 6). They remember one or some of the shapes and their color and walk (or run) back to their partners. Students dictate what they remember to their group mates, who draw it down. They then swap roles, thus each time a different member of the group goes towards the wall. Over several turns they should have the whole sequence of shapes.

Continued on following page

Table 6. Continued

This means they really do have to run back and forth because students will only remember one, two or three shapes at a time.

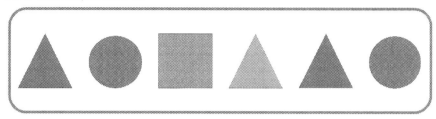

Figure 6. Sequence of shapes of different colors to remember

As it happened with the previous activity, through this one, students are also spurred to interact and communicate, thus, they use the language meaningfully while working with shapes and colors.

Activity 3 – I have, who has…?
This activity is carried out using a big group of students, and each of them is given a card (Figure 7). These cards should be carefully prepared in advance by the teacher, since they have to match each other for the activity to work. Each card should have shapes of different colors on the top without repeating them. In addition, below, each card should ask for another shape that a different student should have. For example, I have and an orange square, who has and a green triangle?. Then the next card would say I have… a green triangle, who has… a yellow circle?. This continues until the last card.

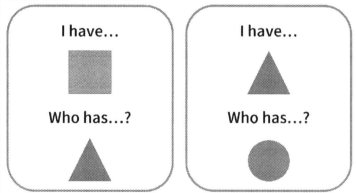

Figure 7. I have, who has card examples

Once every student has a card, the first one should start saying aloud the shape of their card and asking for the following one. After that, they can lay it in a pile in the middle of the class or place it in a basket on a table. Through this activity, students are again pushed to interact and listen to their classmates, using the language and working colors and shapes.
Key issues:

Continued on following page

Table 6. Continued

-It is interesting establishing a set of indications so that everyone can participate. In addition, it is relevant to ensure respect, active listening and waiting for one's turn to speak.
-Once the students know how to effectively carry out this type of group activities, it will be easier to use them in class. The specific content might change, but since students are already used to the dynamics of the activity, it is much easier to use them.

CONCLUSION

This paper has provided a comprehensive overview of a number of CLIL-friendly pedagogies in an attempt to inform, through clear examples, not only current CLIL in-service and pre-service teachers, but also future teacher training programs focused on this approach. It is worth noting that the six strategies depicted may be combined, for example multimodality may be of great help for students to be able to speak among themselves or collaboration among teachers might be a good way to enhance and optimize group learning. To sum up, the present chapter aspires to serve as a starting point to help improve CLIL teaching practices by sharing specific examples that may be adjusted and adapted to different settings.

REFERENCES

Airey, J. (2016, December) *Undergraduate teaching with multiple semiotic resources: Disciplinary affordance vs pedagogical affordance*. Paper presented at the 8th International Conference on Multimodality. Multimodal Landscapes: Designing, changing, shaping. University of Cape Town.

Archer, A. (2014). Power, social justice and multimodal pedagogies. In C. Jewitt (Ed.), *The routledge handbook of multimodal analysis* (2nd ed., pp. 189–197). Routledge.

Attard-Montalto, S., Walter, L., Theodorou, M., & Chrysanthou, K. (2015). *CLIL Book*. Languages. https://www.languages.dk/archive/clil4u/book/CLIL%20Book%20ES.pdf

Bruner, J. S. (1984). *Acción, pensamiento y lenguaje*. Alianza.

Casal, S. (2016). Cooperative assessment for learning in CLIL contexts. *Estudios sobre educación, 31,* 139-157. doi:10.15581/004.31.139-157

Cenoz, J. (2017). Translanguaging in school contexts: International perspectives. *Journal of Language, Identity, and Education, 16*(4), 193–198. doi:10.1080/15348458.2017.1327816

Contero, C., Zayas, F., & Arco-Tirado, J. L. (2018). Addressing CLIL lecturers' needs: reflections on specific methodological training. *Porta Linguarum: Revista internacional de didáctica de las lenguas extranjeras*, (3), 121-135.

A Journey Into CLIL-Friendly Pedagogies to Inform Teacher Professional Development

Coyle, D. (2015). Strengthening integrated learning: Towards a new era for pluriliteracies and intercultural learning. *Latin American Journal of Content and Language Integrated Learning, 8*(2), 84–103. doi:10.5294/laclil.2015.8.2.2

Coyle, D. (2018). The place of CLIL in (bilingual) education. *Theory into Practice, 57*(3), 166–176. doi:10.1080/00405841.2018.1459096

Coyle, D., Hood, P., & Marsh, M. (2010). CLIL. Cambridge University Press.

Coyle, D., & Meyer, O. (2021). *Beyond CLIL: Pluriliteracies Teaching for Deeper Learning.* Cambridge University Press. doi:10.1017/9781108914505

Dalton-Puffer, C. (2016). Cognitive Discourse Functions: Specifying an Integrative Interdisciplinary Construct. In T. Nikula, E. Dafouz, P. Moore, & U. Smit (Eds.), *Conceptualising integration in CLIL and multilingual education* (pp. 29–54). Multilingual Matters. doi:10.21832/9781783096145-005

Estrada, J. L., & Otto, A. (2019). Timing of pedagogical intervention: Oral error treatment in EFL vs. CLIL contexts in primary education in Spain. *Journal of Language and Linguistic Studies, 15*(2), 578–586. doi:10.17263/jlls.586263

Evnitskaya, N., & Jakonen, T. (2017). Multimodal conversation analysis and CLIL classroom practices. In A. Llinares & T. Morton (Eds.), Applied linguistics perspectives on CLIL (pp. 201-220). John Benjamins Publishing Company. doi:10.1075/lllt.47.12evn

Fernández-Fontecha, A., O'Halloran, K. L., Wignell, P., & Tan, S. (2020). Scaffolding CLIL in the science classroom via visual thinking: A systemic functional multimodal approach. *Linguistics and Education, 55,* 100788. doi:10.1016/j.linged.2019.100788

Forey, G., & Polias, J. (2017). Multi-semiotic resources providing maximal input in teaching science through English. In A. Llinares & T. Morton (Eds.), Applied linguistics perspectives on CLIL (pp. 145-164). John Benjamins Publishing Company. doi:10.1075/lllt.47.09for

García, O., & Wei, L. (2014). *Translanguaging: Language, Bilingualism and Education.* Palgrave Macmillan. doi:10.1057/9781137385765

Giroux, H. A. (1988). *Teachers as intellectuals: Toward a critical pedagogy of learning.* Greenwood Publishing Group.

Hu, J., & Gao, X. (2021). Understanding subject teachers' language-related pedagogical practices in content and language integrated learning classrooms. *Language Awareness, 30*(1), 42–61. doi:10.1080/09658416.2020.1768265

Johnson, D. W., & Johnson, R. T. (2018). Cooperative learning: The foundation for active learning. In *Active Learning-Beyond the Future.* IntechOpen.

Kusumoto, Y. (2018). Enhancing critical thinking through active learning. *Language Learning in Higher Education, 8*(1), 45–63. doi:10.1515/cercles-2018-0003

Lasagabaster, D., & Doiz, A. (Eds.). (2016). *CLIL experiences in secondary and tertiary education. In search of good practices.* Peter Lang. doi:10.3726/978-3-0351-0929-0

19

Lin, A. M., & He, P. (2017). Translanguaging as dynamic activity flows in CLIL classrooms. *Journal of Language, Identity, and Education*, *16*(4), 228–244. doi:10.1080/15348458.2017.1328283

Liu, Y. (2020). Translanguaging and trans-semiotizing as planned systematic scaffolding: Examining feeling-meaning in CLIL classrooms. *English Teaching & Learning*, *44*(2), 149–173. doi:10.100742321-020-00057-z

Lu, Y. H. (2020). A Case Study of EMI Teachers' Professional Development: The Impact of Interdisciplinary Teacher Collaboration. *RELC Journal*, *0033688220950888*. doi:10.1177/0033688220950888

Magnusson, P., & Godhe, A. L. (2019). Multimodality in Language Education—Implications for Teaching. *Designs for Learning*, *11*(1), 127–137. doi:10.16993/dfl.127

Marsh, D. (2012). *Content and language integrated (CLIL) A development trajectory*. Servicio de publicaciones de la Universidad de Córdoba.

Marsh, D., & Langé, G. (Eds.). (1999). *Implementing Content and Language Integrated Learning: A Research-Driven Foundation Reader*. University of Jyväskylä.

Martínez-Agudo, J. D. D., & Fielden-Burns, L. V. (2021). What key stakeholders think about CLIL programmes: Commonalities and differences of perspective. *Porta Linguarum: revista internacional de didáctica de las lenguas extranjeras*, (35), 221-237. doi:10.30827/portalin.v0i35.15320

Mehisto, P., Marsh, D., & Frigols, M. J. (2008). *Uncovering CLIL content and language integrated learning in bilingual and multilingual education*. Macmillan.

Meyer, O., & Coyle, D. (2017). Pluriliteracies Teaching for Learning: Conceptualizing progression for deeper learning in literacies development. *European Journal of Applied Linguistics*, *5*(2), 199–222. doi:10.1515/eujal-2017-0006

Nguyen, M. H., & Dang, T. K. A. (2020). Exploring teachers' relational agency in content–language teacher collaboration in secondary science education in Australia. *Australian Educational Researcher*, *48*(4), 1–18. doi:10.100713384-020-00413-9

Pappa, S., Moate, J., Ruohotie-Lyhty, M., & Eteläpelto, A. (2019). Teacher agency within the Finnish CLIL context: Tensions and resources. *International Journal of Bilingual Education and Bilingualism*, *22*(5), 593–613. doi:10.1080/13670050.2017.1286292

Pérez-Cañado, M. L. (2018). Innovations and challenges in CLIL teacher training. *Theory into Practice*, *57*(3), 1–10. doi:10.1080/00405841.2018.1492238

Romeu, M. C., Cerezo, E., & Llamas, E. (2020). Thinking skills in Primary Education: An Analysis of CLIL Textbooks in Spain. *Porta Linguarum: revista internacional de didáctica de las lenguas extranjeras [International Journal of foreign language diadetcs]*, (33), 183-200.

Roussel, S., Joulia, D., Tricot, A., & Sweller, J. (2017). Learning subject content through a foreign language should not ignore human cognitive architecture: A cognitive load theory approach. *Learning and Instruction*, *52*, 69–79. doi:10.1016/j.learninstruc.2017.04.007

Salvador-Garcia, C., & Chiva-Bartoll, Ò. (2017). CLIL in teaching physical education: Views of the teachers in the Spanish context. *Journal of Physical Education and Sport*, *17*(3), 1130–1138.

Siqueira, D. S. P., Landau, J., & Paraná, R. A. (2018). Innovations and challenges in CLIL implementation in South America. *Theory into Practice*, *57*(3), 196–203. doi:10.1080/00405841.2018.1484033

Tagnin, L., & Ríordáin, M. N. (2021). Building science through questions in Content and Language Integrated Learning (CLIL) classrooms. *International Journal of STEM Education*, *8*(1), 1–14. doi:10.118640594-021-00293-0

KEY TERMS AND DEFINITIONS

Collaborative teaching: It is the process of teachers working together to foster a common goal, which is always improved learner outcomes. Collaborative teaching involves: debating, planning, and problem-solving together. inquiring together, etc.

Cooperative learning: This is a learning approach in which students work together in small groups on a structured activity. They are individually accountable for their work and that of the group in general. One of the main aims of this approach is to maximize not only each student's learning, but also that of their groupmates (Johnson & Johnson, 2018).

Critical thinking: It is the process consisting of purposeful, self-regulatory judgment focused on deciding what to believe or do (Kosumoto, 2018).

Multimodal communication: It refers to the fact of conveying meanings thanks to the integration of elements such as language, images, resources, interactions or events.

Oral communication: It entails communication through mouth and the ear, and includes peaople conversing with each other, speeches, presentations, discussions, etc.

Pedagogical affordance: These are the pedagogical characteristics of a learning context that enable learning to occur.

Pedagogical translanguaging: It is the conscious acknowledgement and connection between different languages happening in a teaching-learning process.

Chapter 2
Teachers' Code–Switching in Bilingual Primary Education:
A Literary Review of its Pedagogical Functions

Lidia Mañoso-Pacheco
https://orcid.org/0000-0003-4798-2075
Autonomous University of Madrid, Spain

ABSTRACT

Code-switching is a linguistic phenomenon that is widespread among the bilingual communities of primary school learners. Despite the school administrators' disapproval, teachers commonly resort to this practice as a pedagogical tool to facilitate the dual-focused aim pursued through the content and language integrated learning (CLIL) approach. The present chapter aims to explore the most significant theoretical contributions concerning code-switching in bilingual settings, with an emphasis on its pedagogical functionality in primary education. Data on code-switching were mainly gathered through the bibliographic databases Web of Science (WoS) and Scopus. This literary review categorizes the functions reported by scholars into two broad categories: code-switching as a conceptual-understanding facilitator, focused on mathematics attainment, and code-switching as an interpersonal facilitator, divided into classroom management and affective development. The results point to the need to regulate its use and acknowledge the practicality of code-switching among bilingual school populations.

INTRODUCTION

In the last two decades, there has been progressive implantation of the bilingual education (henceforth, BE) program in various European countries due to the substantial evidence found proving the benefits of this educational instruction (Fortune; 2012; Genesee, 2015; Gómez-Parra et al., 2021; Salomé et al., 2022). The BE in Europe has been conducted through the teaching approach of CLIL (Content and Language Integrated Learning), according to which curricular subjects are taught via an additional language

DOI: 10.4018/978-1-6684-6179-2.ch002

Copyright © 2023, IGI Global. Copying or distributing in print or electronic forms without written permission of IGI Global is prohibited.

that is not the student's mother tongue, mostly English (Coyle, Hood, & Marsh, 2010; Nikula, 2016). This dual-focused approach used for teaching both content and language has implied an adaptation of conventional didactics. Despite its difficulty, CLIL establishes that both content and language be in a (quasi-)equilibrium, i.e., subject knowledge and target language attainment must be produced jointly (Ting, 2010).

CLIL originated in the 1990s, though the acronym was not employed consistently across countries until much time later. It coincided with the proliferation of a series of European movements and language initiatives, such as EMI (English as a Medium of Instruction) or LAL (Learning through an Additional Language). Therefore, CLIL is the 'umbrella' term that comprises all the approaches that emerged in Europe at that time advocating for the promotion of content over form in language teaching. Learning an additional language through content is thus the primary goal of the CLIL approach. The Council of Europe and the European Commission have launched since then successful initiatives to meet the challenges of CLIL in response to European needs, requesting mainly the promotion of second-language education, bilingualism, and internationalization (Darvin et al., 2020; Marsh, 2002). According to the European Commission, CLIL "has a major contribution to make to the Union's language learning goals" (2003, p. 8), and it is the responsibility of the Member States to boost language learning to comply with those European objectives. Thanks to those initiatives, a very high share of primary school children from the EU (European Union) Member States learn English in their educational institutions as this is the main foreign language through which pupils receive bilingual instruction today (Eurostat, 2021). Hence, CLIL has entailed a notable shift from previous teaching approaches with the support of the EU institutions and the formulation of local education policies in the Member States. It has achieved the integration of learning through the English medium instruction, thus promoting bilingualism in the classroom.

Empirical evidence from the literature has shown the effectiveness of CLIL over language-driven tuition, especially concerning EFL (English as a Foreign Language) skills when there is a long exposure of learners to the target language (Jiménez-Catalán, 2016; Lahuerta, 2020; Ruiz de Zarobe, et al., 2011). In addition, it has been confirmed that the CLIL approach has a positive impact on the pre-primary and primary school levels (see Mattheoudakis et al., 2014; Otto & Cortina-Pérez, 2022; van de Craen et al., 2007). Indeed, there is ample research on the outperformance of CLIL students as opposed to their non-CLIL peers concerning their communicative competence in English, as well as their higher motivation toward foreign language acquisition. The relationship between foreign language achievement and motivation has been largely discussed in the field of education (see Lasagabaster, 2011; Navarro-Pablo, 2018; Pfenninger, 2016), and it even plays a more significant role in CLIL settings. According to Navarro-Pablo, CLIL students are "intrinsically more motivated, more instrumentally oriented and showing a higher interest in foreign languages than non-CLIL students" (2018, p. 77). Further, this content-driven approach has proven to be beneficial for the cognitive development of learners, especially when applied during the critical period (0-6 years old) of students (van de Craen et al., 2007). During that time, their brain is being configurated and mirror neurons are actively involved in linking action observation to action execution (Agnew et al., 2008), i.e., connecting the input (motor behavior or sensory recognition) that is received with the corresponding output (motor action or language production). For this reason, those students exposed to two languages during their infancy develop their cognitive flexibility and executive functions to a greater extent than the rest of the learners receiving a monolingual education (Ferjan & Kuhl, 2017).

Notwithstanding the many benefits, the implementation of CLIL has been questioned by many school practitioners in recent years (Alonso-Belmonte & Fernández-Agüero, 2021; Bruton, 2013; Cenoz, Genesee,

& Gorter, 2014; Mañoso-Pacheco & Sánchez-Cabrero, 2022). It has spawned a considerable number of publications reporting the difficulties found in the application of the CLIL tuition in monolingual settings, thus sparking a substantial focus of controversy (Pérez-Cañado, 2020). Since the implementation of the BE plans based on CLIL in Europe, teachers have been systematically insisting on the need to improve their methodological training and provide them with more resources to work under this paradigm (Campillo et al., 2019; Jover, Fleta, & González, 2016). In the case of in-service teachers, they claim to feel unprepared due to their limited linguistic proficiency and/or insufficient subject knowledge skills, resulting in the simplification of the curricular content taught in class (Alonso-Belmonte & Fernández-Agüero, 2021; Coonan, 2007). Stakeholders, parents included, also complain that there is no real immersion in bilingual schools since the CLIL instruction is functional rather than native-like, materials are normally non-authentic, and the curricular content focuses frequently on academic achievement rather than everyday language needs (Pérez-Cañado, 2020). However, as Brüning and Purrmann (2014) indicated, the term 'bilingual' does not necessarily entail gaining target language native-like proficiency, but it pursues partial competence in the additional language.

Despite the numerous publications focused on the difficulties and benefits of its implementation, there is a scarcity of knowledge regarding the positive effects of incorporating the student's mother tongue into the CLIL classroom. In addition, there is no robust analysis assessing the reasons why primary teachers opt for code-switching (CS) in CLIL environments. CS is a linguistic phenomenon widely used in multicultural and BE contexts that can be defined as the alternation of two or more languages with a communicative purpose (Levine, 2011). CS can only occur when both parties share the same mother tongue, emerging as a natural resource from the interactions among the community members. CS can be seen as a tool that promotes language diversity (Sampson, 2012), especially in multilingual communities, since it does not forbid or neglect the use of the student's mother tongue in class. By facilitating its practice, the additional language is no longer perceived as the unique strategy in the teaching-learning process, but as a vehicular language that may be complemented by the L1 when breakdowns in communication appear. CS has mistakenly been labeled in some publications as 'translanguaging', the linguistic phenomenon consisting of mingling languages with the purpose of strategically communicating more effectively (García, 2011). However, the terms CS and translanguaging should not be conflated since they conceptualize the bilingual mind differently. According to Otheguy et al. (2019), translanguaging practices are the result of an additive process from birth that involves the mastery of two or more languages, whereas CS is a by-product of the dual focus of the CLIL approach. Hence, in translanguaging discourse there is only "one underlying system" or unity and, consequently, "the behavior cannot be characterized as switching codes" (2019, p. 640).

Generally, educators are recommended to limit the use of the students' mother tongue to the minimum in order to maximize their foreign language exposure (Sharipova, 2021). However, at the early stages of the BE instruction, both the pre-primary and primary age groups need to be scaffolded by alternating their mother tongue with the additional language. According to Lazăr (2016), it provides them with a more nurturing environment that makes them feel more secure and less anxious. Modupeola (2013) claimed that teachers do not normally code-switch with the deliberate intention of obtaining a specific teaching purpose, but they rather do it subconsciously in their lessons. It is also relevant to note that there are no guiding principles directing its use and, consequently, teachers resort to CS carrying a 'moral burden' because of disrupting the education policies set by their regional authorities, the so-called 'dilemma of CS' (Adler, 1998). Some scholars insist on regulating its use as only if applied systematically and consistently, with a planned and deliberated purpose behind, can it be beneficial for learners (Cahyani, de Courcy, & Barnett, 2018; Then & Ting, 2011; Zhu & Vanek, 2017). According to Maluleke, "all the functions that teachers should achieve through code-switching should be clearly indicated to avoid a situation where the meaning of the subject content becomes complicated due to excessive use of code-switching" (2019, p. 5). The lack of regulation of its use resulting from the general disapproval by the education authorities makes CS a largely controversial issue in the field of education.

This study seeks to offer a literary review of the pedagogical functions of CS at the primary school level. The pedagogical functions, aimed at achieving the dual goal of content and language learning in an integrated way, are categorized into two broad categories: (1) code-switching as a conceptual-understanding facilitator, focused on the learning of mathematics, and (2) code-switching as an interpersonal facilitator, comprising classroom management and affective development. Further, this review aims to showcase the need to design a thorough plan to determine the pedagogical principles that should guide the implementation of CS in the bilingual setting. Curricular integration should go along with solid teaching procedures, and hence, the exploration of why educators switch between languages may help maximize instruction, improving the quality of education under this curricular paradigm.

MATERIALS AND METHOD

To conduct this theoretical review, the main scientific sources available on the Web concerning CS in the field of BE were consulted. The two world-leading bibliographic databases, *Web of Science* (WoS) and *Scopus*, were the main sources accessed, together with the *Education Resources Information Center* (ERIC), the database specialized in education research, and the search engine *Google Scholar*. The literary search carried out via the above-mentioned servers initially limited the selection to scientific peer-reviewed studies published in the last five years (from 2018) with a profound impact on the scientific community. The author regarded 'scientific studies' as any high-quality publication belonging to the field of research, such as journal articles, book chapters, books, conference proceedings, or relevant thesis dissertations. In addition to this criterion, it was established an initial search focused on studies dealing with CS practices with a minimum of i7 (7 or more citations generated) in the *Scopus* and *WoS* databases.

The preliminary selection of publications that complied with the above-mentioned conditions is shown in Figure 1 below, with a total of 17 publications cited 367 times in total according to the selected databases. Works were found using the keywords "code switching" and "bilingual education" contained in "topic", which comprises "article title, Abstract, Keywords". The author tried to narrow down the findings of the searches including the keyword "primary education"; however, no occurrences were found in the scientific databases.

Figure 1. Number of i7 articles on CS in BE published in the last five years compared to total academic articles in the Scopus and WoS databases. The x-axis indicates the year, and the y-axis indicates the number of indexed publications

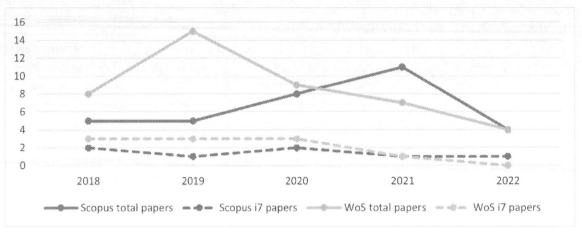

In the case of *ERIC* documents, a total of 32 publications published since 2018 were accessed, all of them peer-reviewed. In this case, the author could restrict the search to the education level "primary education" and the general descriptor "code switching (language)".

The selected studies, from 2018 to today, were reviewed exhaustively in order to limit the selection of definite sources on the basis of their suitability for the subject of study, as well as the relevance and currency of the contents examined. The snowball or chain-referral sampling technique was also applied to gather older but still highly relevant publications departing from the primary data sources accessed. Throughout this complex process, the theoretical foundation of this review study was built.

This literary review comprised a final selection of 94 scientific studies, 25.53% of them published very recently between 2020 and 2022, as can be seen in Figure 2 below.

Figure 2. Publications consulted in the literary review ordered by the decade of publication. The x-axis indicates the time period, and the y-axis indicates the number of publications

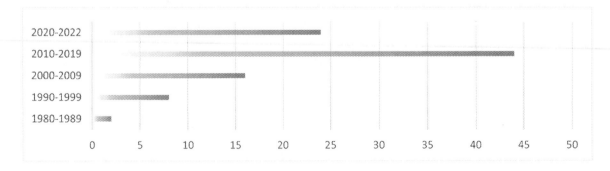

77.66% of the selected publications were academic journal articles, 10.64% correspond to book chapters by top academic publishers, and, finally, 8.51% of the studies consulted were books belonging to the field of education and applied linguistics. The present theoretical review was complemented by other kinds of publications (3.19%), such as conference proceedings or relevant online publications. As for the distribution of studies by the language of publication, 97.87% of the academic works accessed were published in English and 2.13% in Spanish, the author's mother tongue.

In the case of the works not indexed in any of the databases consulted (*WoS, Scopus,* and *ERIC*), the criterion followed to determine their suitability for research purposes concerned their citation impact in *Google Scholar*. This search engine was employed for conducting a separate search to access the secondary sources cited by the primary selected works. The citation factor was also applied to those articles recently published and particularly, the 24 works published between 2020 and 2022 received a total of 153 citations in *Google Scholar*.

RESULTS AND DISCUSSION

Using the methods presented above, a collection of the selected sources and their findings is revised. The review intends to provide a mapping of the teachers' CS in bilingual settings arranged from broad to specific. It particularly aims to assess its pedagogical functions at the primary level based on previous instructional practices. Relevant studies on pedagogical CS, many of which focused on secondary or tertiary education, and the reported students' learning experiences, complemented the topic that is covered in this chapter. As indicated above, the present literary revision analyzes the main pedagogical functions of CS at the primary level by categorizing the studies accessed into two broad categories: (1) code-switching as a conceptual-understanding facilitator, and (2) code-switching as an interpersonal facilitator. For ease of analysis and neatness, the first pedagogical function is focused on the teaching of science, namely mathematics. This field of knowledge commonly poses a difficulty for primary learners, increased by the need to learn it through an additional language. In order to better understand the need for teachers to resort to CS in their CLIL lessons, the revision departs from introducing the complexities of the language of mathematics for primary learners. In the case of the interpersonal function of CS, this pedagogical goal is subdivided into classroom management and affective development. Both subfunctions are assessed through a wider scope, applicable to all fields of knowledge.

Code-Switching as a Conceptual-Understanding Facilitator

There is a common belief that teachers code-switch, i.e., switch from one language to another, against the education policies solely due to their linguistic deficiency in the foreign language (Akindele & Letsoela 2001; Nyati-Ramahobo & Orr, 1993). If this is the reason, this practice will likely harm the students' learning concerning subject content and foreign language acquisition (Nel & Müller, 2010). Nevertheless, the fact that there are also students with learning difficulties in the L2, especially in the lexicon, should not be underestimated by language specialists. For those students, practical work in the classroom is not enough for grasping the meaning of complex concepts via the L2, such as scientific constructs. According to Kenyon (2016), having sufficient vocabulary is key to success in learning mathematics, and the absence of sufficient linguistic proficiency in this area might lead them to feel constrained to share their thoughts in class. Thus, the strict use of the additional language might prevent learners from participating in exploratory talk to comprehend new content knowledge (Arthur, 1994). Primary school students need to learn (and discuss) puzzling new notions and mathematical operations that require a certain degree of critical understanding. If enrolled in bilingual schools, CS can serve them as a successful transition tool or 'conceptual-understanding facilitator' to ensure their understanding and promote curriculum access.

The language used in the BE programs requires a threshold of competence in both BICS (Basic Interpersonal Communication Skills) and CALP (Cognitive Academic Language Proficiency), more demanding for pupils than the former (Cummins, 2000). The language of mathematics is undeniably challenging for students as it is a specialized discourse full of unique symbols and abstracted forms that may obscure the comprehension of subject content, especially when learners have low English language proficiency (Maluleke, 2019). In addition, as Chikiwa and Schäfer (2016) claimed, mathematical texts follow a very formal register that usually forces teachers to code-switch in order to scaffold learners to effectively acquire mathematical knowledge. The literature (Arias de Sanchez et al., 2018; Kotsopoulos, 2007; Pimm, 1991; Resnick, 1989) has identified the main elements that configure the language of mathematics, as follows: the mathematics register, terminology that only exists in the mathematical context (e.g., 'pentahedron'); everyday mathematical terms, common expressions that gain a distinct meaning if embedded within the mathematical work (e.g., 'cancel'); and finally, protoquantitative terms, non-numerical particles that express quantity (e.g., 'little'). According to Arias de Sánchez et al., incorporating everyday terms that are familiar to the learners' reality in the language of instruction allows them to "bridge the outside mathematics with their students' language experiences" (2018, p. 10). Therefore, it is highly recommended that teachers combine the mathematics register with everyday expressions, both in the L2 and L1, to diminish the level of complexity and cognitive demands of the language input. Readers should then note that the presence of those everyday expressions do not necessarily imply CS, as the teacher may resort to less complex expressions in the L2 to facilitate understanding.

Teaching primary school Mathematics in a language distinct from the student's mother tongue is undoubtedly a professional challenge for educators working in bilingual settings. It is even more complicated when they have to teach it to learners coming from non-bilingual nursery schools with limited exposure to English. For those pupils, full immersion is not as effective as desired at the beginning since they require partial or late full immersion in their first years of primary school to allow the natural transition to CLIL (Kasule & Mapolelo, 2005). The difficult decision of whether to code-switch when students fail to understand what is being taught in the Mathematics classroom has been defined as the 'dilemma of code-switching' (Adler, 1998). If teachers opted for CS, this might imply that they would go against the mandate of school administrators and local inspectors of education who firmly insist on using English as the sole medium of instruction. This contradictory position is experienced more intensely in primary education than in the secondary stage (Setati & Adler, 2000) since students are more heterogeneous concerning their level of maturity, which directly affects their class performance (Calsamiglia & Loviglio, 2020).

There is extensive research on the benefits of CS for constructing scientific learning and mathematical knowledge that entails difficult for students (Archila et al., 2021; Arias de Sánchez et al., 2018; Arthur, 1994; Krause & Prinsloo, 2016; Mawela & Mahlambi, 2021; Msimanga, 2015; Shinga & Pillay, 2021). Studies are especially focused on the South African teaching model, in which the dilemma of CS acquires an added significance due to the structural divergence between languages that exists there. Publications have grown exponentially in the last few years centered on distinct sociocultural backgrounds, such as Malaysia or Korea, in which English is the additional language employed for pedagogical purposes. According to Setati and Adler, the practice of CS in Mathematics classrooms from South Africa should be acknowledged in educational planning to legitimize what teachers actually do, i.e., "harness learners' main language as a resource for learning" (2000, p. 266). The literature has long recognized the benefits of CS for mathematical attainment since it encourages a positive attitude toward mathematics learning, provides better learning outcomes, and fosters active participation among school students (Maluleke, 2019; Setati & Adler, 2000). Using terms in the students' L1 permits primary school learners to fill their language when they get stuck or encounter linguistic difficulties responding in English in their CLIL lessons. Kasule and Mapolelo (2005) reported that CS makes the lesson more effective, fostering the students' participation since they are allowed to combine the L2 with the language they are more familiar with in a more natural and meaningful way. Macaro and Lee (2013) studied the effects of teacher CS in South Korea and found that intra-sentential CS was beneficial for primary learners as it allowed them to gradually link their existing lexical concept representations to the ones in the L2. Thus, CS compensates for the students' limited vocabulary in the L2 and helps teachers clarify complex curriculum content by using the learners' mother tongue (Üstünel & Seedhouse, 2005). In order to develop Math competency, Arias de Sánchez et al. (2018) recommended not to underestimate the practicality of the student's mother tongue in the early years of mathematics training. Even though the L1 expressions learners employ may belong to an informal register, they can be a successful tool for the conveyance of mathematical interpretations and the construction of meaning that is challenging for learners. According to Maluleke, CS "promotes active engagement between the teacher and learners who regard their teacher as a mentor and facilitator rather than a custodian who wants to fill the empty vessels with knowledge" (2019, p. 6). Hence, not only can it be a resource for conceptual understanding, but it can also serve as a useful strategy to inspire interest in mathematics and develop a strong bond with students, urging them to abandon the passive role in class.

Although the primary function of CS is to make the mathematical terms more understandable for learners, some teachers mistranslate terms due to their lack of specialist skills in translation, thus posing an added difficulty in the processing of information (Akindele & Letsoela, 2001). On other occasions, teachers code-switch claiming that their students cannot understand the curricular content in English when the real problem is their own linguistic deficiency and poor methodological preparation (Maluleke, 2019). Adriosh and Razi (2019) observed that even though primary students do not insist on translation, teachers frequently code-switch to ascertain whether learning actually took place in the L2 and, in this way, evaluate their own accomplishments in the classroom. As Kasule and Mapolelo claimed, the question that should be addressed is not whether to use the L1 in the classroom to scaffold learners, but "determining how much code-switching is desirable and effective, because if openly condoned, over reliance on it could result in misuse" (2005, p. 604). Keong et al. (2016) stated that educators should not overuse CS as a teaching strategy whenever students do not understand a concept since it might affect the overall learning process and entail significant drawbacks for learners in the long run. Therefore, instructors should not fall into the trap of CS just for translating terms into the student's mother tongue without any systematic pattern. By this, they would distort the basis of CLIL, not fulfilling any pedagogical goal. Although teachers are perfectly aware that they should not code-switch in class, it is also their job to ensure that their students learn what is taught. Hence, CS should be practiced when the rest of the teaching strategies have failed as it might hinder learners' progress in English and trying to comply with a specific pedagogical goal (Davis & Renert, 2013). Further, CS should always be a strategy employed when the instructor has vast disciplinary knowledge in the content subject and her/his linguistic proficiency in English is not limited.

Code-Switching as an Interpersonal Facilitator

The literature (Caballero & Celaya, 2022; Cahyani, de Courcy, & Barnett, 2018; Lin, 1996; May & Abdul, 2020; among others) not only noted that CS can be an effective tool for understanding complex notions in the L2, but it also viewed CS as an interpersonal facilitator. CS is a tool that may enhance the teacher's relationships with learners, especially as concerns classroom behavior and affective development. Classroom behavior management is paramount in the pursuit of academic achievement, and it is one of the greatest concerns reported by primary teachers (Paramita et al., 2020). The students' behavior can be changed by introducing CS in the classroom, which also has a direct impact on their self-esteem, class participation, and linguistic proficiency gains in the L2 (Cahyani, de Courcy, & Barnett, 2018). The kind of organizational strategies adopted by the teacher is determined by class size and, undoubtedly, controlling large classes implies a great professional challenge for any teacher. In the case of primary educators, attending to the students' individual needs and providing them with remedial teaching is complicated due to the mixed-ability levels and the variations in the maturity development of pupils (Kasule & Mapolelo, 2005). Educators should make use of the language that is more effective for their teaching purposes, considering their students' needs and language background. In the case of bilingual programs, CS is configured as a useful strategy that may assist teachers to manage the students' behavior in the classroom. Education scholars argue that it is especially employed as concerns clarifying tasks, providing exam directions, giving instructions, setting homework assignments, and discussing procedures in general (May & Abdul, 2020; Nukuto, 2017). Cahyani, de Courcy, and Barnett (2018) observed that teachers tend to code-switch using the L1 as a disciplinary action aimed at engaging their students, at the same time they reduce the social distance between themselves and learners. In the same vein, Jegede (2011) found that when teachers code-switch and use the students' mother tongue, they generate higher collaboration between them and their primary learners. Indeed, thanks to CS students tend to pay more attention and show more interest and enthusiasm for what is taught, resulting in better retentive memory. When teachers use the L2 in the classroom, on the contrary, the level of formality in the instruction increases (Cahyani, de Courcy, & Barnett, 2018). Educators also reported that they resort to CS to check the students' attendance or remind them not to be late to class, calling for discipline in the classroom. Research findings (Cahyani, de Courcy, & Barnett, 2018; Lin, 2013) also supported the alternation of languages to call for discipline. It was found that teachers tend to code-switch when they want to urge students to be more careful with the submission of the assignments set or when they require them to show a more disciplined attitude in class. Regardless of the language chosen for these goals, it may be derived from these findings that CS is not used carelessly, but it is a marker that is deliberately used to pursue a specific pedagogical purpose.

Further, CS has been proven effective for humanizing the teaching-learning process, i.e., for building rapport with primary learners (Cahyani, de Courcy, & Barnett, 2018; Qian, Tian, & Wang, 2009; among others). The literature has principally focused this affective goal of CS on the following: reducing learners' anxiety, praising students, and finally, conveying humorous effects to lighten the tone of what is being taught. Concerning the reduction of the student's anxiety, Jegede (2011) found that when teachers CS and use their mother tongue, they alleviate the tension and anxiety that primary learners frequently experience with instruction in an English-only medium. Even though students have adequate proficiency in both languages, CS is a "marker of community solidarity since it allows students to have contact with their L1 (Deumert, 2005, p. 116). Teachers should help lower students' anxiety in class especially considering that their levels have increased markedly after the pandemic among primary learners

(Giménez-Dasí et al, 2021). Readers should also note that the L2 may be effective to decrease students' emotional response to a disease outbreak and thus, it can be used to reduce their health-related anxiety (Schroeder & Chen, 2021). In a study conducted by Kamwangamalu and Virasamy (1999), however, it was reported the effectiveness of implementing a kind of CS called "peer-tutoring strategy", through which learners are allowed to use their mother tongue to help other students in the class with learning difficulties in the additional language. In that case, CS was employed for knowledge attainment, as well as a way of building a supportive classroom environment. In any case, the reduction of anxiety, together with fostering motivation and self-confidence, has a very positive impact on the students' learning, mainly in the case of foreign language acquisition (Krashen, 1981). Therefore, as bilingual programs combine content learning with additional language attainment, the reduction of learners' anxiety through CS might help achieve this dual learning goal. In the last few years vast research interest was found concerning not only foreign language anxiety, but also math anxiety among primary learners (Carey et al., 2017, 2021; Deieso & Fraser, 2019; Hill et al., 2016). As indicated above, the area of science, mathematics in particular, provokes feelings of panic, tension, and anxiety among learners (Catlioglu et al., 2009), becoming this field of knowledge one of the most complicated to address through the CLIL approach. In addition, both in math and foreign language anxiety gender seems to play a significant role in shaping the anxiety profile of primary learners, with boys exhibiting higher levels of academic anxiety than their female peers (Carey et al., 2017). According to Krashen (1981), if students are anxious, their affective filter (an imaginary barrier that blocks cognition) is high. That emotional mood state prevents them from perceiving the class as a safe place, impacting negatively on the assimilation of new knowledge. Hence, considering that CS seems to alleviate their anxiety in the BE programs, students are expected to be less prone to experience school segregation by their socioeconomic status, making the most of CLIL tuition.

When the teacher wants to praise a student or tell someone off, a pedagogical strategy that can be effective and is frequently used spontaneously in bilingual settings is CS (Baker, 1993). The schooling experience of primary learners may differ depending on their intrinsic motivation levels, i.e., the extent to which learners consider the class enjoyable and interesting (Buckingham et al., 2022). Praising students in bilingual instruction is key to the success of the teaching activities as it fosters the students' motivation and lowers their anxiety, acting as an external reward. Distinct investigations have delved into the way primary learners perceive praise and positive feedback, and they concluded that in general, students at this stage prefer to be praised for working hard and making effort in class (Burnett, 2001; Merrett & Tang, 1994). However, cultural differences were found regarding whether they prefer to be praised publicly or privately. School practitioners insist on praising students consistently and preferentially, targeted on a learning task or contingent on a particular learner's behavior (Burnett & Mandel, 2010). Although the speech act of praise is culturally bound, the influence of English-speaking countries over bilingual instruction makes educators value the importance of giving praise to students as a learning facilitator (Cahyani, de Courcy, & Barnett, 2018). According to Lin (1996), if praise is given in the L2, learners tend to perceive the social distance between them and the teachers, whereas if praise is provided in their mother tongue, the perceived distance between both parties is shortened. Her finding is in line with the research conducted by Jegede, who found that CS in the primary school classroom "gave room for the teacher to maintain solidarity and express emotional understanding" (2011, p. 50). Therefore, the use of L1 to praise academic behavior helps build rapport with students and, consequently, arouse their intrinsic interest in learning.

Closely connected with the optimization of interpersonal relations between teachers and pupils is the construction of humor. Researchers (Harslett et al., 2000; Lovorn & Holaway, 2015) have defined the sense of humor as one of the main properties of effective teachers that help build higher-order thinking skills and the acquisition of curricular knowledge. The literary review conducted by Sánchez-Cabrero et al. (2021) revealed that the personality traits of teachers, including their sense of humor, are one of the paramount factors that directly affect teaching effectiveness. According to Kim (2021), there is a scarcity of investigations about the pedagogical functions of humor in the primary classroom. When speakers participate in intercultural settings, they normally opt for their most familiar language to convey a hilarious meaning or show a ludic behavior (Cahyani, de Courcy, & Barnett, 2018). CS then plays a significant role in this emotion-focused strategy of humor. As Ladilova and Schröder claimed, "humour is not universal and it needs sufficient local knowledge and understanding to get the meaning" (2022, p. 473). Caballero and Celaya (2022) discovered that humor is closely connected to the maturity level of students. Indeed, they found that the higher the school grade, the more jokes primary learners make in their mother tongue in a CLIL lesson. Regardless of the language chosen in a CLIL class, it is undeniable that a ludic behavior expressed through humor helps build a positive learning atmosphere, thus lowering the students' affective filter and improving the learning experience.

CONCLUSION

This study provided a compilation of research on CS in the field of BE. Specifically, it gave an account of the most relevant findings in this area of inquiry and highlighted the rationale for educators' language choices in CLIL settings. Contrary to previous beliefs, CS is not solely employed to help teachers with limited proficiency in the additional language, but it is used to meet a wide range of pedagogical functions. This study categorized them into two broad areas: (1) CS as a conceptual-understanding facilitator, with an emphasis on the learning of mathematics, and (2) code-switching as an interpersonal facilitator, divided in turn into classroom management and affective development. Despite its benefits, if applied consistently and with precision, CS remains a controversial practice as it is officially disapproved by school administrators. Regardless of the diverse language backgrounds of students, they insist teachers on using English as the sole medium of instruction in BE programs.

Considering that this study did not present an exhaustive review, but rather a scoping revision with a systematic approach that entailed a selection of the existing literature, it should be regarded as incomplete. It might be possible to deepen some of the topics covered in this chapter by analyzing the data and results from the selected publications to a greater extent. Moreover, further research is needed to provide a more comprehensive view of pedagogical CS with substantial evidence and not just based on classroom observation as was the case in most studies consulted. The patterns of CS should also be explored in depth regarding the targeted pedagogical function, whether teachers opt for inter-sentential (within sentence boundaries), intra-sentential (in the middle of a sentence), extra-sentential or tag switching (using a phrase from another language). Despite this and considering that expository clarity was preferred over a more thorough analysis, the present investigation helped to clarify the most relevant pedagogical functions of CS in bilingual schooling with a focus on primary education. This study expects to lay the foundation for the promotion of academic achievement and the incorporation of new pedagogical tools with which to deal with challenging content that requires higher-order thinking.

Based on the findings of this review, a number of implications can be elicited. The first and the most important is showcasing the need to regulate the practice of CS in BE programs. Notwithstanding the resistance posed by school administrators, teachers frequently resort to CS in bilingual schools. However, they frequently code-switch inconsistently, which is not for the benefit of primary learners. A thorough training plan is hence needed to prescribe its rules of implementation. Second, the practicality of CS in the integration of content and language learning must be acknowledged. When there is a deliberate purpose behind and it is applied carefully, CS does not necessarily hamper the students' L2 acquisition. Therefore, CS should not just be conceived in itself as a mere indicator of the low linguistic proficiency of the teacher in the additional language. Having said this, those teaching practices in which educators opt for CS with the sole aim of compensating their own foreign language deficits, should be regulated and even punished by school officials. Third, the teaching-learning process in CLIL must respond to the holistic needs of primary learners. Consequently, this approach should address their cognitive, social, and emotional development. In light of this, CS must be raised to help learners acquire complex content that requires high cognitive abilities, especially curricular knowledge belonging to the field of science, and to strengthen their interpersonal relationships with all class members. Finally, considering that the school's population is predominantly multicultural, CLIL tuition should inspire a positive affection toward the students' L1. This approach should thus reconcile the practice of CS to ensure that the target language is in harmony with the mother tongue as a mediator that reassures young kids and arouses their intrinsic motivation. This new pedagogical orientation expects to be more in line with the essence of the dynamics of current cross-cultural interactions among humans.

FUNDING

This literary review was supported by the Spanish Ministry of Science and Innovation (Ministerio de Ciencia e Innovación, MCIN), grant number PODD, PID2020-119102RB-I00.

REFERENCES

Adler, J. (1998). A language of teaching dilemmas: Unlocking the complex multilingual secondary mathematics classroom. *For the Learning of Mathematics*, *18*(1), 24–33. https://www.jstor.org/stable/40248258

Adriosh, M., & Razi, Ö. (2019). Teacher's Code Switching in EFL Undergraduate Classrooms in Libya: Functions and Perceptions. *SAGE Open*, *9*(2), 1–11. doi:10.1177/2158244019846214

Agnew, Z. K., Brownsett, S., Woodhead, Z., & de Boissezon, X. (2008). A step forward for mirror neurons? Investigating the functional link between action execution and action observation in limb apraxia. *The Journal of Neuroscience: The Official Journal of the Society for Neuroscience*, *28*(31), 7726–7727. doi:10.1523/JNEUROSCI.1818-08.2008 PMID:18667604

Akindele, D., & Letsoela, M. (2001). Code-switching in Lesotho secondary and high schools: Lessons and its effects on teaching and learning. *BOLESWA Educational Research Journal*, *18*, 83–100.

Alonso-Belmonte, I., & Fernández-Agüero, M. (2021). Teachers' narratives of resistance to Madrid's bilingual programme: An exploratory study in secondary education. *Linguistics and Education*, *63*, 100925. doi:10.1016/j.linged.2021.100925

Archila, P. A., Molina, J., & Truscott de Mejía, A. (2021). Fostering bilingual scientific writing through a systematic and purposeful code-switching pedagogical strategy. *International Journal of Bilingual Education and Bilingualism*, *24*(6), 785–803. doi:10.1080/13670050.2018.1516189

Arias de Sánchez, G., Gabriel, M., Anderson, A., & Turnbull, M. (2018). Code-Switching Explorations in Teaching Early Number Sense. *Education in Science*, *8*(38), 785–803. doi:10.3390/educsci8010038

Arthur, J. (1994). English in Botswana primary classrooms: functions and constraints. In C. M. Rubagumya (Ed.), *Teaching & Researching Language in African Classrooms* (pp. 63–78). Multilingual Matters.

Baker, C. (1993). *Foundations of Bilingual Education and Bilingualism*. Multilingual Matters.

Brüning, C. I., & Purrmann, M. S. (2014). CLIL pedagogy in Europe: CLIL teacher education in Germany. *Utrecht Studies in Language and Communication*, *27*, 315–338. doi:10.1163/9789401210485_018

Bruton, A. (2013). CLIL: Some of the reasons why … and why not. *System*, *41*(3), 587–597. doi:10.1016/j.system.2013.07.001

Buckingham, L., Fernández, M., & Halbach, A. (2022). Differences between CLIL and non-CLIL students: Motivation, autonomy and identity. *Journal of Multilingual and Multicultural Development*, 1–15. Advance online publication. doi:10.1080/01434632.2022.2102641

Burnett, P., & Mandel, V. (2010). Praise and Feedback in the Primary Classroom: Teachers' and Students' Perspectives. *Australian Journal of Educational & Developmental Psychology*, *10*, 145–154.

Burnett, P. C. (2001). Elementary students' preferences for teacher praise. *Journal of Classroom Interaction*, *36*(1), 16–23. https://www.jstor.org/stable/23870540

Caballero, N., & Celaya, M. L. (2022). Code-switching by primary school bilingual EFL learners: A study on the effect of proficiency and modality of interaction. *International Journal of Bilingual Education and Bilingualism*, *25*(1), 301–313. doi:10.1080/13670050.2019.1671309

Cahyani, H., de Courcy, M., & Barnett, J. (2018). Teachers' code-switching in bilingual classrooms: Exploring pedagogical and sociocultural functions. *International Journal of Bilingual Education and Bilingualism*, *21*(4), 465–479. doi:10.1080/13670050.2016.1189509

Calsamiglia, C., & Loviglio, A. (2020). Maturity and school outcomes in an inflexible system: Evidence from Catalonia. *SERIEs*, *11*(1), 1–49. doi:10.100713209-019-0196-6 PMID:32226557

Campillo, J. M., Sánchez, R., & Miralles, P. (2019). Primary Teachers' Perceptions of CLIL Implementation in Spain. *English Language Teaching*, *12*(4), 149–156. doi:10.5539/elt.v12n4p149

Carey, E., Devine, A., Hill, F., Dowker, A., McLellan, R., & Szucs, D. (2021). *Understanding mathematics anxiety: investigating the experiences of UK primary and secondary school students*. University of Cambridge.

Carey, E., Devine, A., Hill, F., & Szűcs, D. (2017). Differentiating anxiety forms and their role in academic performance from primary to secondary school. *PLoS One*, *12*(3), e0174418. doi:10.1371/journal.pone.0174418 PMID:28350857

Catlioglu, H., Birgin, O., Costu, S., & Gurbuz, R. (2009). The level of mathematics anxiety among pre-service elementary school teachers. *Procedia: Social and Behavioral Sciences, 1*(1), 1578–1581. doi:10.1016/j.sbspro.2009.01.277

Cenoz, J., Genesee, F., & Gorter, D. (2014). Critical Analysis of CLIL: Taking Stock and Looking Forward. *Applied Linguistics, 35*(3), 243–262. doi:10.1093/applin/amt011

Chikiwa, C., & Schäfer, M. (2016). Teacher code switching consistency and precision in a multilingual mathematics classroom. *African Journal of Research in Mathematics. Science and Technology Education, 20*(3), 244–255. doi:10.1080/18117295.2016.1228823

Coonan, C. M. (2007). Insider views of the CLIL class through teacher self-observation–introspection. *International Journal of Bilingual Education and Bilingualism, 10*(5), 625–646. doi:10.2167/beb463.0

Coyle, D., Hood, P., & Marsh, D. (2010). *CLIL: Content and Language Integrated Learning.* Cambridge University Press. doi:10.1017/9781009024549

Cummins, J. (2000). *Language, power and pedagogy: Bilingual children in the crossfire.* Multilingual Matters Ltd. doi:10.21832/9781853596773

Darvin, R., Lo, Y. Y., & Lin, A. M. (2020). Examining CLIL through a Critical Lens. *English Teaching & Learning, 44*(2), 103–108. doi:10.100742321-020-00062-2

Davis, B., & Renert, M. (2013). Profound understanding of emergent mathematics: Broadening the construct of teachers' disciplinary knowledge. *Educational Studies in Mathematics, 82*(2), 245–265. doi:10.100710649-012-9424-8

Deieso, D., & Fraser, B. J. (2019). Learning environment, attitudes and anxiety across the transition from primary to secondary school mathematics. *Learning Environments Research, 22*(1), 133–152. doi:10.100710984-018-9261-5

Deumert, A. (2005). The unbearable lightness of being bilingual: English–Afrikaans language contact in South Africa. *Language Sciences, 17*(1), 113–135. doi:10.1016/j.langsci.2004.10.002

European Commission. (2003). *Promoting Language Learning and Linguistic Diversity: An Action Plan 2004–2006.* Publications Office of the European Union. https://op.europa.eu/en/publication-detail/-/publication/b3225824-b016-42fa-83f6-43d9fd2ac96d

Eurostat. (2021). *Foreign Language Learning Statistics.* Publications Office of the European Union. https://ec.europa.eu/eurostat/statistics-explained/index.php?title=Foreign_language_learning_statistics

Ferjan, N., & Kuhl, P. K. (2017). The brain science of bilingualism. *Young Children, 72*(2), 38–44.

Fortune, T. (2012). What the research says about immersion. In *Chinese Language Learning in the Early Grades: A handbook of resources and best practices for Mandarin immersion* (pp. 9–13). Asian Society., https://ilabs.uw.edu/sites/default/files/2017_FerjanRamirez_Kuhl_NAEYC.pdf

García, O. (2011). Theorising Translanguaging for Educators. In C. Celic & K. Seltzer (Eds.), *Translanguaging: A CUNY-NYSIEB Guide for Educators* (pp. 1–7). The City University of New York.

Genesee, F. (2015). Myths about early childhood bilingualism. *Canadian Psychology*, *56*(1), 6–15. doi:10.1037/a0038599

Giménez-Dasí, M., Quintanilla, L., & Fernández-Sánchez, M. (2021). Longitudinal Effects of the Pandemic and Confinement on the Anxiety Levels of a Sample of Spanish Children in Primary Education. *International Journal of Environmental Research and Public Health*, *18*(24), 13063. doi:10.3390/ijerph182413063 PMID:34948673

Gómez-Parra, M. E., Huertas-Abril, C. A., & Espejo-Mohedano, R. (2021). Factores clave para la evaluación del impacto de los programas bilingües: Empleabilidad, movilidad y conciencia cultural. *Porta Linguarum. Revista Interuniversitaria De Didáctica De Las Lenguas Extranjeras*, *35*, 93–104. doi:10.30827/portalin.v0i35.15453

Harslett, M., Harrison, B., Godfrey, J., Partington, G., & Richer, K. (2000). Teacher Perceptions of the Characteristics of Effective Teachers of Aboriginal Middle School Students. *The Australian Journal of Teacher Education*, *25*(2). doi:10.14221/ajte.2000v25n2.4

Hill, F., Mammarella, I. C., Devine, A., Caviola, S., Passolunghi, M. C., & Szűcs, D. (2016). Maths anxiety in primary and secondary school students: Gender differences, developmental changes and anxiety specificity. *Learning and Individual Differences*, *48*, 45–53. doi:10.1016/j.lindif.2016.02.006

Jegede, O. (2011). Code Switching and Its Implications for Teaching Mathematics in Primary Schools in Ile-Ife, Nigeria. *Journal of Education and Practice*, *2*(10), 41–54. https://www.iiste.org/Journals/index.php/JEP/article/view/781

Jiménez-Catalán, R. M. (2016). Vocabulary profiles in English as a foreign language at the end of Spanish primary and secondary education. *RLA. Revista de Lingüística Teórica y Aplicada*, *54*(1), 37–50. doi:10.4067/S0718-48832016000100003

Jover, G., Fleta, T., & González, R. (2016). La Formación inicial de los Maestros de Educación Primaria en el contexto de la enseñanza bilingüe en lengua extranjera. *Bordón. Revista de Pedagogía*, *68*(2), 121–135. doi:10.13042/Bordon.2016.68208

Kamwangamalu, N. M., & Virasamy, C. (1999). Zulu peer-tutoring in a multiethnic English-only classroom. *Tydskrif vir Taalonderrig*, *33*(1), 60–71.

Kasule, D., & Mapolelo, D. (2005). Teachers' strategies of teaching primary school mathematics in a second language: A case of Botswana. *International Journal of Educational Development*, *25*(6), 602–617. doi:10.1016/j.ijedudev.2004.11.021

Kenyon, V. (2016). How can we improve mathematical vocabulary comprehension that will allow students develop higher-order levels of learning? *The STeP Journal, 3*(2), 47–61. http://insight.cumbria.ac.uk/id/eprint/2460/

Keong, Y. C., Sardar, S. S., Mahdi, A. A. A., & Husham, I. M. (2016). English-Kurdish Code Switching of Teachers in Iraqi Primary Schools. *Arab World English Journal*, *7*(2), 468–480. doi:10.24093/awej/vol7no2.32

Kim, S. (2021). 'Butter balla here!': The functions of humor in primary English classrooms in Korea. *English Teaching*, *76*(3), 115–137. doi:10.15858/engtea.76.3.202109.115

Kotsopoulos, D. (2007). Mathematics discourse: "It's like hearing a foreign language. *Mathematics Teacher*, *101*(4), 301–305. doi:10.5951/MT.101.4.0301

Krashen, S. (1981). *Second language acquisition and second language learning*. Pergamon Press.

Krause, L. S., & Prinsloo, M. (2016). Translanguaging in a township primary school: Policy and practice. *Southern African Linguistics and Applied Language Studies*, *34*(4), 347–357. doi:10.2989/16073 614.2016.1261039

Ladilova, A., & Schroder, U. (2022). Humor in intercultural interaction: A source for misunderstanding or a common ground builder? A multimodal analysis. *Intercultural Pragmatics*, *19*(1), 71–101. doi:10.1515/ip-2022-0003

Lahuerta, A. (2020). Analysis of accuracy in the writing of EFL students enrolled on CLIL and non-CLIL programmes: The impact of grade and gender. *Language Learning Journal*, *48*(2), 121–132. doi :10.1080/09571736.2017.1303745

Lasagabaster, D. (2011). English achievement and student motivation in CLIL and EFL settings. *Innovation in Language Learning and Teaching*, *5*(1), 3–18. doi:10.1080/17501229.2010.519030

Lazăr, A. (2016). Suggestions on Introducing CLIL in Primary Schools. *2016 8th International Conference on Electronics, Computers and Artificial Intelligence*. 10.1109/ECAI.2016.7861134

Levine, G. S. (2011). *Code Choice in the Language Classroom*. Multilingual Matters. doi:10.21832/9781847693341

Lin, A. (1996). Bilingualism or Linguistic Segregation? Symbolic Domination, Resistance and Code-Switching in Hong Kong Schools. *Linguistics and Education*, *8*(1), 49–84. doi:10.1016/S0898-5898(96)90006-6

Lin, A. (2013). Classroom Code-Switching: Three Decades of Research. *Applied Linguistics Review*, *4*(1), 195–218. doi:10.1515/applirev-2013-0009

Lovorn, M., & Holaway, C. (2015). Teachers' perceptions of humour as a classroom teaching, interaction, and management tool. *The European Journal of Humour Research*, *3*(4), 24–35. doi:10.7592/EJHR2015.3.4.lovorn

Macaro, E., & Lee, J. H. (2013). Teacher Language Background, Codeswitching, and English-only Instruction: Does Age Make a Difference to Learners' Attitudes? *TESOL Quarterly: A Journal for Teachers of English to Speakers of other Languages and of Standard English as a Second Dialect*, *47*(4), 717–742. . doi:10.1002/tesq.74

Maluleke, M. (2019). Using code-switching as an empowerment strategy in teaching mathematics to learners with limited proficiency in English in South African schools. *South African Journal of Education, 39*(3), 1–9. doi:10.15700aje.v39n3a1528

Mañoso-Pacheco, L., & Sánchez-Cabrero, R. (2022). Perspectives on the Effectiveness of Madrid's Regional Bilingual Programme: Exploring the Correlation between English Proficiency Level and Pre-Service Teachers' Beliefs. *Education Sciences, 12*(8), 522. doi:10.3390/educsci12080522

Marsh, D. (Ed.). (2002). *CLIL/EMILE—The European Dimension: Actions, Trends and Foresight Potential*. European Commission.

Mattheoudakis, M., Alexiou, T., & Laskaridou, C. (2014). To CLIL or Not to CLIL? The Case of the 3rd Experimental Primary School in Evosmos. In N. Lavidas, A. Alexiou, & A. Sougari (Eds.), *Major Trends in Theoretical and Applied Linguistics* (Vol. 3, pp. 215–234). De Gruyter Open Poland. doi:10.2478/9788376560915.p13

Mawela, A. S., & Mahlambi, S. B. (2021). Exploring teachers' views on code-switching as a communicative technique to enhance the teaching of mathematics in grade 4. *International Journal of Educational Methodology, 7*(4), 637–648. doi:10.12973/ijem.7.4.637

May, L., & Abdul, A. (2020). Teachers' use of code-switching in ESL classrooms at a Chinese vernacular primary school. *International Journal of English Language and Literature Studies, 9*(1), 41–55. doi:10.18488/journal.23.2020.91.41.55

Merrett, F., & Tang, W. M. (1994). The attitudes of British primary school pupils to praise, rewards, punishments and reprimands. *The British Journal of Educational Psychology, 64*(1), 91–103. doi:10.1111/j.2044-8279.1994.tb01087.x

Modupeola, O. R. (2013). Code-switching as a Teaching Strategy: Implications for English Language Teaching and Learning in a Multilingual Society. *Journal of the Humanities and Social Sciences, 14*(3), 92–94. doi:10.9790/1959-1439294

Msimanga, A. (2015). Code-switching in the Teaching and Learning of Science. In R. Gunstone (Ed.), *Encyclopedia of Science Education* (pp. 160–161). Springer. doi:10.1007/978-94-007-2150-0_408

Navarro-Pablo, M., & Jiménez, E.G. (2018). Are CLIL Students More Motivated?: An Analysis of Affective Factors and their Relation to Language Attainment. *Porta Linguarum: revista internacional de didáctica de las lenguas extranjeras, 29*, 71–90. . doi:10.30827/Digibug.54023

Nel, N., & Müller, H. (2010). The impact of teachers' limited English proficiency on English second language learners in South African schools. *South African Journal of Education, 30*(4), 635–650. doi:10.15700aje.v30n4a393

Nikula, T. (2016). CLIL: A European Approach to Bilingual Education. In N. V. Deusen-Scholl & S. May (Eds.), *Second and Foreign Language Education* (pp. 1–14). Springer International Publishing., doi:10.1007/978-3-319-02323-6_10-1

Nukuto, H. (2017). Code Choice Between L1 and the Target Language in English Learning and Teaching: A Case Study of Japanese EFL Classrooms. *Acta Linguistica Hafniensia*, *49*(1), 85–103. doi:10.1080/03740463.2017.1316631

Nyati-Ramahobo, L., & Orr, J. R. (1993). Primary education and language teaching in Botswana. In K. D. Samway & D. McKeon (Eds.), *Common Threads of Practice: Teaching English to Children Around the World* (pp. 99–109). TESOL.

Otheguy, R., García, O., & Reid, W. (2019). A translanguaging view of the linguistic system of bilinguals. *Applied Linguistics Review*, *10*(4), 625–651. doi:10.1515/applirev-2018-0020

Otto, A., & Cortina-Pérez, B. (2022). *Content and Language Integrated Learning in Pre-primary Education: Moving Towards Developmentally Appropriate Practices*. Springer International.

Paramita, P. P., Anderson, A., & Sharma, U. (2020). Effective Teacher Professional Learning on Classroom Behaviour Management: A Review of Literature. *The Australian Journal of Teacher Education*, *45*(1), 61–81. doi:10.14221/ajte.2020v45n1.5

Pérez-Cañado, M. L. (2020). Common CLIL (Mis)conceptions: Setting the Record Straight. In M. T. Calderón-Quindós, N. Barranco-Izquierdo, & T. Eisenrich (Eds.), *The Manifold Nature of Bilingual Education* (pp. 1–30). Cambridge Scholars Publishing.

Pfenninger, S. (2016). All good things come in threes: Early English learning, CLIL and motivation in Switzerland. *Cahiers de l'ILSL*, *48*(48), 119–147. doi:10.26034/la.cdclsl.2016.429

Pimm, D. (1991). Communicating mathematically. In K. Durkin & B. Shire (Eds.), *Language in Mathematical Education* (pp. 17–23). Open University Press.

Qian, X., Tian, G., & Wang, Q. (2009). Codeswitching in the primary EFL classroom in China – Two case studies. *System*, *37*(4), 719–730. doi:10.1016/j.system.2009.09.015

Resnick, L. B. (1989). Developing mathematical knowledge. *The American Psychologist*, *44*(2), 162–169. doi:10.1037/0003-066X.44.2.162

Ruiz de Zarobe, J. M., Sierra, & F. Gallardo del Puerto (2011). *Content and Foreign Language Integrated Learning. Contributions to multilingualism in European contexts*. Peter Lang.

Salomé, F., Casalis, S., & Commissaire, E. (2022). Bilingual advantage in L3 vocabulary acquisition: Evidence of a generalized learning benefit among classroom-immersion children. *Bilingualism: Language and Cognition*, *25*(2), 242–255. doi:10.1017/S1366728921000687

Sánchez-Cabrero, R., Estrada-Chichón, J. L., Abad-Mancheño, A., & Mañoso-Pacheco, L. (2021). Models on Teaching Effectiveness in Current Scientific Literature. *Education Sciences*, *11*(8), 409. doi:10.3390/educsci11080409

Schroeder, S., & Chen, P. (2021). Bilingualism and COVID-19: Using a second language during a health crisis. *Journal of Communication in Healthcare*, *14*(1), 20–30. doi:10.1080/17538068.2020.1864611

Setati, M., & Adler, J. (2000). Between languages and discourses: Language practices in primary multilingual mathematics classrooms in South Africa. *Educational Studies in Mathematics, 43*(3), 243–269. doi:10.1023/A:1011996002062

Sharipova, I. (2021). Factors effecting friendly atmosphere in application educational technologies in ESP English language classes. *International Journal of Word Art*, 170–176. doi:. doi:10.26739/2181-9297-2021-2-27

Shinga, S., & Pillay, A. (2021). Why do teachers code-switch when teaching English as a second language? *South African Journal of Education, 41*(1, Supplement 1), 1934. Advance online publication. doi:10.15700aje.v41ns1a1934

Then, D. C. O., & Ting, S. H. (2011). Code-switching in English and science classrooms: More than translation. *International Journal of Multilingualism, 8*(4), 299–323. doi:10.1080/14790718.2011.577777

Ting, Y. L. T. (2010). CLIL appeals to how the brain likes its information: examples from CLIL-(Neuro) Science. *International CLIL Research Journal, 1*, 1–18. http://www.icrj.eu/13/article1.html

Üstünel, E., & Seedhouse, P. (2005). Why that, in that language, right now? Code-switching and pedagogical focus. *International Journal of Applied Linguistics, 15*(3), 302–325. doi:10.1111/j.1473-4192.2005.00093.x

Van de Craen, P., Lochtman, K., Ceuleers, E., Mondt, K., & Allain, L. (2007). An interdisciplinary approach to CLIL learning in primary schools in Brussels. In C. Dalton-Puffer & U. Smit (Eds.), *Empirical Perspectives on CLIL Classroom Discourse* (pp. 253–274). Peter Lang.

Zhu, X., & Vanek, N. (2017). Facilitative Effects of Learner-directed Codeswitching: Evidence from Chinese Learners of English. *International Journal of Bilingual Education and Bilingualism, 20*(7), 773–787. doi:10.1080/13670050.2015.1087962

KEY TERMS AND DEFINITIONS

Affective filter: An imaginary barrier or mental block that prevents learners from acquiring the target language.

Code-switching: The act of alternating between two or more languages to overcome language constraints. It can be employed by teachers to perform specific teaching purposes.

Cognitive flexibility: The human capacity to adapt one's cognitive strategies to meet the demands of a new environment.

Foreign language anxiety: A psychological construct whereby foreign language learners experience stress or apprehension about the target language.

Intrinsic motivation: A person's volition to do something. In the case of education, it refers to the students' desire to be engaged in a learning task as it provides an enjoyable experience.

L1: A person's first language, also defined as native language or mother tongue. It is commonly the language learned during childhood, and the one employed to interact with family members.

Translanguaging: The act of utilizing more than one language to communicate more effectively. This is a common practice by speakers who were raised bilingual.

Chapter 3

Let's CLIL!
Pedagogical–Linguistic Reflections Between Teacher Education and Classroom Teaching – A Focus on the Italian Context

Valerio Ferrero
University of Torino, Italy

ABSTRACT

This chapter articulates its reflection on content and language integrated learning (CLIL) methodology in Italian primary schools from a pedagogical-linguistic perspective, emphasising its educational potential for the personal growth of children. Moving between teacher training and didactic action in the classroom, it will highlight how CLIL is useful in making students citizens capable of acting in the globalal world as people in possession of linguistic, cognitive, metacognitive, and emotional tools for analysing reality. An example of a teaching project using CLIL methodology will be proposed to anchor theoretical reflection to educational practice.

INTRODUCTION

In the age of complexity (Morin, 2008), the acquisition of one or more foreign languages turns out to be crucial: schools have a crucial role in promoting educational pathways that allow students to experience linguistic otherness and make a language other than their native tongue (L1) their own (Choi & Ollerhead, 2017; Piccardo et al., 2021). It is about moving beyond transmissive teaching in favor of an educational action in which the teacher brings skills, empathy, and passion into play (Biesta, 2017; Swann, 2011) so that each pupil is deeply involved in a series of mental and cognitive processes and social events that allow for accelerated stages of development of the L2, i.e., the non-native tongue (L2) (Durlak et al., 2015; Gueldner et al., 2020).

CLIL methodology, an acronym for Content and Language Integrated Learning coined in 1994 by David Marsh and Anne Maljers (Marsh, 1994), appears functional in pursuit of this goal. It is a approach aimed at integrated learning of language-communication and disciplinary skills in a foreign language

DOI: 10.4018/978-1-6684-6179-2.ch003

(Marsh et al., 2001). This methodology is becoming increasingly popular both around the world (Hemmi & Banegas, 2021), where it is spreading with incredible rapidity, and in Europe (EC, 2012; EC et al., 2017), as L2 language competence for learning disciplinary content is considered a key dimension for the modernization of European school systems. CLIL, then, is considered an engine for the renewal and improvement of school curricula in an inclusive way, attentive to everyone's needs and to making everyone achieve excellence (Bower et al., 2020; Codó, 2022), in the name of equity. In fact, CLIL was born precisely with the aim of promoting social justice (Fortanet-Gómez, 2013): everyone learns the same language, beyond the socioeconomic and sociocultural conditions of their families, and thanks to schooling they will have the same opportunities to exercise citizenship. Moreover, the *2030 Agenda* (UN, 2015) also emphasized the importance of quality education for all: CLIL certainly represents a means to give everyone a concrete opportunity to open to an increasingly global reality.

This chapter adopts a pedagogical-linguistic perspective to analyse teacher training in CLIL methodology and argue for the need to design CLIL educational pathways that take into account both the linguistic and pedagogical dimensions. For this very reason, it is essential to emphasize the fundamental assumption of this methodology: the acquisition of an L2 is not a goal in itself but is integrated into the teaching and learning process of a discipline (Coyle et al., 2010; Marsh, 2002; Nieto Moreno de Diezmas & Espinar, 2022). In other words, educational and didactic pathways address both L2 and discipline-specific content, since to speak of CLIL means to refer to doubly focused educational contexts in which another language, different from the one habitually spoken by the learner, is used as a means to teach and learn a nonlinguistic content (Mehisto et al., 2008). After specifying the organization of the Italian school system with reference to primary schools and outlining lights and shadows with respect to the spread of CLIL methodology in Italy, we will move on to analyze some essential aspects of their training. In this regard, operational lines will be drawn to highlight the indispensable dimensions of teacher training in CLIL methodology. The design of an educational experience will then be analyzed, to highlight how pedagogical and linguistic aspects must be inseparable within CLIL courses.

BACKGROUND: THE ITALIAN SCHOOL, BETWEEN ORGANIZATION AND CLIL METHODOLOGY

In Italy, school is seen as the key instrument for the development of the country and the exercise of citizenship by all. Creating a more inclusive and fairer society and realizing the democratic project is a task to which schools must contribute as a priority. The Italian school system is organized according to the principles of subsidiarity and autonomy of individual educational institutions (Barberis, 1998; Bracci, 2009). In the 1990s and early 2000s, Law 59/1997, Presidential Decree 275/1999 and Constitutional Law 3/2001 gave legal personality to school institutions, endowing them with organizational, management, financial, teaching and research autonomy. About 15 years later, Law 107/2015 reinforced this arrangement.

The state has exclusive legislative competence for "general rules on education" and to determine the essential levels of services that must be guaranteed throughout the national territory. In addition, the state defines the fundamental principles that the regions must respect in the exercise of their specific competencies. Regions have concurrent legislative competence in education (e.g., they can define the regional school calendar, deciding when classes begin and end, days of suspension of teaching activities) and exclusive competence in vocational education and training (i.e., they can define the training plan

Let's CLIL!

of these courses independently). Thus, educational institutions make autonomous choices based on the educational needs of their student population.

The Italian school system is divided into several segments, as established by Law 53/2003. The first corresponds to the integrated zero-six system and lasts six years: infant education services (crèches, micronides, play spaces and spring sections) welcome children from 3 months to 3 years old, while preschools are open to children between the ages of three and six. Compulsory schooling then begins, from 6 to 16 years old, divided into two different cycles. The first is for students aged 6 to 14 and incorporates primary school (from 6 to 11 years old) and middle school (from 11 to 14 years old). Then it is the turn of the second cycle of education, which bifurcates into two different paths. Then there is the tertiary education offered by universities, High Artistic and Musical Education paths and Higher Technical Institutes. Families can freely decide which school to enroll their children in.

Primary School in Italy: Organization, Pedagogical Principles and Teacher Education

As previously mentioned, Italian primary school lasts five years and involves children aged 6 to 11. It is the first segment of compulsory schooling. Primary school classes can be formed from 15 to 26 pupils. If the number of enrollments does not allow for the formation of a class of 15 pupils, it is possible to activate multi-classes (sections with pupils attending different years of classes), which must accommodate between 8 and 18 pupils. If there are pupils with students with special educational needs, classes cannot accommodate more than 20 pupils.

The *National Indications for the Preschool and the First Cycle of Education Curriculum* (MIUR, 2012) set competence goals and specific learning objectives for each discipline. Elementary school pupils are engaged in the study of Italian, English language, history, geography, math, science, technology, music, art and image, physical education, technology and, thanks to Law 92/2019, civic education. Six years later, the document *National Indications and New Scenarios* (MIUR, 2018) emphasizes the need for interdisciplinary educational action aimed at helping children acquire the habitus of citizens capable of acting in an increasingly globalized reality: although without explicit reference, the pedagogical principles and educational directions in these two documents support the use of CLIL in Italian classrooms, including during the primary school years.

As far as the assessment of learning is concerned, Ministerial Order 172/2020 has revolutionized teachers' practice: for the objectives of each discipline, a descriptive judgment must be assigned, with reference to four levels related to the acquisition of skills (in the process of first acquisition, basic, intermediate, advanced) with respect to specific indicators (autonomy, type of situation, continuity, resources mobilized). Legislative Decree 62/2017 stipulates that the assessment document should also contain a description of the process and overall level of learning development and a summary judgment on behavior, as well as stipulating that at the end of the fifth grade, a competency assessment should be completed for pupils, with reference to the eight European key competencies.

From a pedagogical point of view, the Italian primary school wants to promote the holistic growth of children through non-transmissive but socio-constructivist teaching approaches (Jonnaert, 2009), also because this is the first approach to disciplines for students and it is necessary to put them at the center of the learning process so that they are the ones who construct meanings and knowledge within the different disciplinary fields (Newcombe, 2018). Knowledge construction takes place in the sociocultural context in which the individual acts: interactions and languages play a fundamental function in a learning process, as do the more emotional and emotional aspects (Surhone et al., 2010; Zembylas, 2005). Vygotskji's (1962) work represents an indispensable reference: individual acquisitions always result from interaction with others. Beyond the discipline-specific learning objectives, fitting into the framework of competency-based teaching allows working on educational goals (MIUR, 2012; 2018): learning experiences enhance children's observational and processing skills and allow them to experience their own corporeality, to acquire the habit of shifting from empirical to formal categories, to engage with others to construct new ideas and question their own, including from a cross-cultural perspective (Holmes et al, 2016; Skrefsrud, 2016), to practice civic engagement and solidarity.

Teacher training is also organized to achieve these ends (Mortari & Silva, 2020; Ostinelli et al., 2009). Until 2002, primary school (and kindergarten) teachers were required to attend a secondary school that delved into pedagogical, psychological, anthropological, didactic and sociological subjects (first the four-year institute for teacher education, then the five-year socio-pedagogical and socio-psychopedagogical high schools) (Di Pol, 2000): in fact, even today a lot of people accesses teaching in this school segment by virtue of this degree, which has never lost its enabling value. Since 1998, however, there has been a single-cycle master's degree program in Primary Education (until 2011 four-year, then five-year): through courses, laboratories and internships that deal with pedagogical, didactic, psychological, anthropological and sociological subjects and that are attentive to aspects of disciplinary didactics, students make their own the skills, abilities and knowledge necessary to enter elementary school classrooms and act in the direction indicated so far (Di Pol, 2016; Todeschini, 2003).

CLIL: European Origins and the Italian Situation

Originated in the 1990s, as mentioned above, the CLIL approach has found wide acceptance in Europe, finding its way into several official documents (Breidbach & Viebrock, 2013; Egger & Lechner, 2012). In fact, the idea is that in a united Europe where the intention is to maintain the richness of linguistic diversity but not at the expense of mutual understanding, the task of promoting the learning of multiple non-native languages cannot be entrusted only to teachers specialized in L2 teaching (Danesi et al., 2018). In other words, teachers of non-language disciplines contribute to L2 language education by teaching their subject in a language other than their pupils L1: in this way, L2 enters the curriculum cross-curriculum, not just as an object of learning in itself (Mehisto et al., 2008).

CLIL is rooted in experiences in European bilingual regions and has been gradually promoted and tested in a growing number of states (EC et al., 2017) and, along the lines of European language and school policy, will become a daily practice in all schools. Teachers skilled in a language other than their national language are encouraged to specialize in this approach in order to offer CLIL modules to their students.

Focusing on Italy, the teaching of non-language disciplines in foreign languages is provided for in the school system. The autonomy regulation (Presidential Decree 273/1999) specifies that, also in consideration of the interests of pupils, interdisciplinary educational and didactic paths may be implemented that provide for the teaching of non-linguistic disciplines in a foreign language. The proposal must be submitted to the Teachers' Board and obtain approval; it must be a path organized into a project that describes content, implementation methods, monitoring and evaluation tools.

Before arriving at more normative consistency referring to CLIL, it is necessary to wait until 2010. In the meantime, a lot of schools choose to initiate research-action on foreign language teaching of non-linguistic disciplines (Milito et al., 2015), also driven by the Lingue 2000 Project, promoted by the Ministry of Education and financed with funds allocated by Law 440/1997 for the expansion of the educational offerings of educational institutions.

In fact, the legislative production on CLIL mostly concerns high schools: in 2010 Presidential Decree 88/2010 and 89/2010 were issued, emphasizing the need to align Italian legislation with the good practices present in the European and national territory. In fact, it is stipulated that as of the 2012/2013 school year in the linguistic high school a non-linguistic discipline must be taught in a foreign language in the last three years, and that the same must be done in the other high schools starting in 2014/2015, only in the final year. This mode is referred to in the annexes to the decrees as "CLIL mode" and specific reference is made to English language. Subsequent provisions (Ministerial Decree 49/2010; Ministerial Decree of September 30, 2011) also do not refer specifically to primary school; it is with Law 107/2015 that CLIL is finally indicated as a useful methodology for increasing the language skills of all pupils in every grade.

The analysis of the legislation is useful to understand what characteristics the teaching of nonlanguage disciplines in CLIL mode should take on and what skills CLIL teachers must possess. In this regard, there is provision for the activation at universities of postgraduate or master's courses for the acquisition of the linguistic, didactic and pedagogical skills necessary for the teaching of a non-language discipline in a foreign language, aimed at teaching staff. A teacher who has undergone CLIL training is a teacher with good micro-linguistic competence in a foreign language of his or her teaching discipline, good competence (at least C1 level according to the CEFR) in the foreign language, good knowledge of the fundamentals of the methodology, the ability to collaborate collegially with colleagues, the ability to conduct CLIL lessons by adopting the most suitable teaching approaches to make pupils active experimenters of the language and construction of disciplinary knowledge, and the ability to prepare assessment tools. Pedagogical and linguistic studies also recognize the importance of a professional profile endowed with the skills outlined so far (Aiello et al., 2017), even in reference to the development of educational policies that take into account more purely pedagogical aspects (Leone, 2015).

CLIL pathways qualify as laboratories within primary, middle and high schools, with activities that integrate the curriculum and are intended for pupils from different classes; more specifically, in primary school, CLIL pathways can be carried out within a laboratory by the specialist teacher or by a curricular teacher in the normal classroom hours of a specific discipline (Barbero & Clegg, 2005): the most successful experiences in primary school are those in which English (or, in rarer cases, another foreign language) is included within thematic pathways that involve all or at least many subject areas (Carbonara & Scibetta, 2022). CLIL pathways are also sometimes activated in preschool with reference to specific fields of experience. There are still numerous difficulties in implementing CLIL methodology at the level of good classroom practices and teacher training (Serragiotto, 2017). This is precisely why our reflection on the education of primary school teachers in CLIL methodology is essential: it is not possible to think of quality education for all without adequately trained teachers.

TEACHER EDUCATION FOR EFFECTIVE EDUCATIONAL PRACTICE: INSIGHTS FOR THE ITALIAN CONTEXT FROM THE INTERNATIONAL DEBATE

As we said in the previous paragraphs, CLIL is not compulsory in primary school in Italy. There are few teachers specialized in the use of this methodology and not all teachers of non-linguistic disciplines have enough competence in L2 to allow teaching the subject not in L1 (Aiello ct al., 2017; Leone, 2015; Serragiotto, 2017). When CLIL pathways were implemented in schools, this methodology absolutely represented a resource for L2 learning (Giordano & Maurizio, 2021): the key point is that the teachers promoting these pathways have a good preparation with respect to the linguistic and pedagogical foundations of this approach. Precisely for this reason, it is indispensable that also in Italy the theoretical-practical training of teachers in the use of CLIL methodology considers the international reflections on these dimensions: in this way, quality pathways for L2 learning can be promoted for all students.

As an educational and instructional approach, CLIL aims to foster multilingualism, develop linguistic, metalinguistic and communicative skills in a L2, introduce the teaching of a L2 at an early age through immersion in a linguistic reality different from the L1, promote lifelong and lifewide learning, and link language learning to different subject areas (Coyle & Meyer, 2021).

The communicative interaction taking place in CLIL (both between learners and teacher and between peers) frees pupils from the formal control usually exercised over L2 productions, since the primary goal is the communication of meanings (Ball et al., 2016; Genesee, 2016). In other words, it seeks to have the L2 learned naturally, in a way that mimics the mechanisms through which children experience and acquire their L1. In short, the focus is on language comprehension and production, not on the a priori assimilation of grammatical rules (Llinares et al, 2012); CLIL, in fact, looms as a new learning environment, in which through language use a metalinguistic awareness is elicited with respect to the functioning of the L2 that will facilitate pupils to trace the grammatical rules (morphological, morphosyntactic, syntactic, lexical) underlying the language (Coonan, 2006; Juan-Garau & Salazar-Noguera, 2015).

Teacher education and classroom practice must take these principles into account to produce concrete results in terms of L2 learning. Ensuring that students experience the language with freedom and creativity is the key to success. Strong collegiality among teachers is also required: collaboration both in planning and during teaching action is crucial so that the experience has both linguistic and disciplinary value.

CLIL Education of Teachers in Italy: Pedagogical-Linguistic Guidelines to Improve the Current Situation

As already anticipated, in Italy those teachers who have attained a level of proficiency in the target language of at least C1 according to the CEFR and who have obtained an advanced diploma as a result of attending a master's degree or university advanced course are qualified to use CLIL methodology. There are three types of pathways to qualify for the use of CLIL methodology (Cinganotto, 2016; Serragiotto, 2017):

1. master's program or advanced training courses lasting 1500 hours, with at least 300 hours of internship in classrooms where CLIL methodology is used, which can be accessed by teachers who have acquired certification for the target language at least at C1 level;
2. 1500-hour advanced training courses without internships accessed by teachers who have acquired certification for the target language at least level B2;
3. 3500-hour advanced training courses for tenured teachers who have acquired certification for the target language at least C1 level.

However, the curriculum of these courses is very similar, taking into consideration didactic and linguistic issues; however, it would be desirable to include an internship part for the training courses that currently do not include it, so that teachers can put their acquired skills to use and compare themselves with teachers who are experts in the use of the methodology. Implementing CLIL pathways does not mean teaching lessons in a different language than that of one's students, but it does require the ability to apply certain theoretical principles specific to L2 teaching (Danesi et al., 2018; Nikula et al., 2016). It is precisely by operationalizing these theories that it is possible for pupils to construct and co-construct knowledge autonomously, under the unobtrusive and constant guidance of the teacher who acts as a facilitator in a training setting characterized by didactic approaches capable of enhancing creativity and peer collaboration: a specific focus on these issues during teachers' education courses allows for the development of specific skills for classroom activity (Raud & Orehhova, 2022). The language principles reported here represent inescapable elements of teacher training in the use of CLIL methodology.

The theory of comprehensible language modified and interactive input developed by the American linguist Krashen (1976; 1985) is crucial: the teacher must assess the comprehensibility of the input, adapting his or her own way of speaking, proposed materials and activities to the learners' skills, adding some element of difficulty so as to stimulate the pupils' zone of proximal development and foster new learning. This theory is important because it highlights the cruciality of the educational relationship between learners and teacher as an engine for learning. In this sense, it is important to clarify the concept of the zone of proximal development, introduced by Vygotskji (1962): learning takes place through interaction with others, as new cognitive acquisitions are made thanks to the support of more competent persons (not only adults, but also peers); in other words, in the area in which one can observe what the child is capable of doing alone and what potential learning is possible when supported by competent adults or peers (Hedegaard, 1996).

Input turns out to be important because it represents the trigger of acquisition (Andorno et al., 2017); in other words, the incoming linguistic data feed the learning circuit of the target language (in the case of CLIL, the L2 in which the non-linguistic discipline is taught), so without input, the language acquisition process cannot start. It is important to point out that input is part of a trio of interrelated concepts that are useful in describing how the L2 acquisition process takes place. These are intake, which is the linguistic data processed by the learner and integrated into his or her linguistic knowledge, and output, which is what the learner produces in the target language (Krashen, 1985).

The student moves from input to intake to output through the teaching techniques implemented during guided learning. The input (consisting of oral and written texts to which the student is exposed) is processed in a pathway from its perception to its understanding, to its acceptance (the so-called intake), to the integration of the intake and its transformation into output, that is, the way in which the student, after internalizing it, uses what he or she has learned autonomously (Danesi et al., 2018).

It is evident that in CLIL, input is crucial, in terms of both the teacher's interaction with the class and the L2 materials proposed for disciplinary teaching. It is important, in other words, to engage students in meaningful dialogical exchanges (Long, 1996) and not to understand input only as a model of language, but rather as a useful tool for pupils to make assumptions about how language works as they acquire disciplinary content; it is a matter of fostering on the part of students to relate the content of the input and the language, so as to move toward the acquisition of new knowledge and the reorganization of their cognitive structures.

A second point that deserves careful consideration in teacher training contexts is the difference between acquisition and learning, again theorized by Krashen (1987): language acquisition refers to the phenomenon whereby a human being becomes progressively competent in the use of a language for communication with his or her peers; it is an unconscious process that takes shape through meaningful interactions in an environment in which the use of the L2 is perceived as natural by each speaker and leads to the progressive ability to understand and structure original sentences from what has been acquired (Danesi et al, 2018); learning, on the other hand, is a conscious and rational process and takes place in formal educational settings.

In CLIL, the acquisition of the target language in which the teaching of the non-linguistic discipline takes place is realized (Coyle, 2010). The focus is more on content than on form, as one works in the zone of proximal development of pupils who, from the inputs, learn the L2 almost spontaneously, with lasting outcomes than if one were more focused on the learning dimension, as defined above (Ball et al., 2016). To act in this direction, it is necessary to adopt teaching approaches useful for students to acquire an active role and to create collaborative learning environments through problem solving activities and the techniques of jigsaw, pairing, conversation, discussion, and play (Coyle & Meyer, 2021; Genesee, 2016). A focus on more properly didactic aspects in terms of approaches, ways of working and learning environments is desirable in teacher education courses.

While Krashen theorizes unconscious L2 acquisition, Schmidt (2001) and Swain (1995) emphasize the importance of attention to form (noticing hypotesis). According to this theory, students and learners can gradually construct their own interlanguage, that is, the product of a mental grammar that mixes some rules traceable to the L1, others to the L2, and still others to the universal grammar (Selinker, 1972), increasingly oriented toward the target language, only if they are guided by the teacher in observing the linguistic phenomena emerging from the input and output they themselves produce (Schmidt, 2001; Swain, 1995). It involves initiating metalinguistic reflection with peers in which the teacher plays the role of facilitator, guiding pupils in becoming aware with respect to the functioning of the L2 through negotiating their own meanings, reflecting on their mistakes, and reorienting their assumptions.

Within CLIL pathways, students are called upon to pay attention to both the specific content of the non-linguistic discipline and the form of the target language through which knowledge is conveyed (Mehisto et al., 2008). It is crucial that there be, also in collegial collaboration with the L2 teacher at the center of the CLIL pathway, specific moments in which the teacher facilitates metalinguistic reflection on the functioning of language on the level of vocabulary, morphosyntax, and communication in relation to the non-linguistic discipline.

The theory of interlanguage, mentioned above, also assumes crucial importance: we must not forget that in a CLIL context students are learning a new language, different from the L1, and are thus developing bilingual skills (Danesi et al., 2018). In other words, it is necessary to consider all those mental processes activated by the contact with the L2, such as the comparison of the target language with the L1 (in terms of linguistic structures, functioning...), which in fact remain implicit for the teacher. Selinker (1992) points out that the language production of a native and a non-native learner are different, since the latter's will be characterized by the presence of both L1 and L2 elements. Errors, therefore, are physiological and unavoidable and are valuable to the teacher, who can thus identify the mental processes underlying them and guide pupils toward conscious L2 learning (Corder, 1981).

The iceberg theory and the concepts of BICS and CALP appear important for the structuring and implementation of CLIL pathways. Linguistic competence in one or more languages depends on a single cognitive system (Danesi et al., 2018): for illustrative purposes, Cummins (2000) proposed the image of the iceberg, comparing its emerging tips to the achievements in the different languages available to the subject; all languages, however, are connected to a single source of thought, a kind of control center that orchestrates his cognitive abilities.

Beginning with the experience of multicultural classrooms in Canada, Cummins (2000) noted that newly arrived pupils developed so-called basic communication skills (BICS) in a reasonably short time: in other words, they learned to introduce themselves, talk about their interests, describe, narrate, and interact in everyday verbal exchanges in L2, even with the support of nonverbal language. To continue in school, however, higher cognitive skills are needed so as to access and rework disciplinary content: this involves developing study skills (CALP) in L2. According to Cummins (2000), it may take pupils one or two years to develop BICS in L2, but a much longer period (five to seven years, if not more) is needed to develop CALP. These reflections adhere well to CLIL methodology. To find the most functional teaching strategies for the process of teaching and learning the non-linguistic discipline in L2, the level of cognitive complexity of the task and the degree to which context can be used in the performance of the task must be taken into account (Danesi et al., 2018). Tasks with low cognitive demand require limited use of language and allow support for context, so on the didactic level it is possible to propose tasks of observation, conversation, dramatization, role-playing. Tasks with low cognitive demand that, however, focus on language and, therefore, do not allow contextual support require repetition exercises, sentence or word completion, manipulation, pattern drills. High-cognitive-demand tasks that can rest on context, on the other hand, can be accomplished didactically with techniques such as grid, play on pattern, transcoding, cloze, jigsaw, discussion. High cognitive demand tasks focused on language, where the support that context can provide is limited, defer to didactic techniques such as information research, summaries, writing, translations. In a CLIL course, it is important that the transition from one type of task to another takes place gradually (Ball et al., 2016; Mehisto et al., 2008), so that pupils and students can become familiar with the language tool and approach disciplinary content with confidence. It is, as already pointed out, a matter of gaining metacognitive awareness with respect to both the non-linguistic discipline and L2.

The pluriliteracies approach (Meyer & Coyle, 2017) is a key linguistic and pedagogical reference in this reflection: it is about making visible the connections between content and language learning, creating learning trajectories that take students' abilities as a starting point and track their progress along the way. Acting in this direction means paying attention to the development of students' specific language skills as well as their conceptual understanding and automation of subject-specific procedures, skills and strategies. By communicating their evolving understandings in increasingly sophisticated ways, students internalize these understandings and ways of acting and thinking (Meyer et al., 2015).

From a linguistic perspective, Cognitive Discursive Functions (Dalton-Puffer et al., 2018) is another crucial reference point that teacher training in CLIL approach must take into account. This construct is theoretically grounded in both educational curriculum theory and linguistic pragmatics and consists of a seven-item categorization of verbalizations that express acts of thinking about the subject matter in the classroom (classify, define, describe, evaluate, explain, explore, relate). A specific focus on language is essential to foster learning; with reference to CLIL, this is to emphasize the role of language in shaping the epistemological structure of disciplines. In this sense, work that brings out these language patterns can lead to qualitatively and quantitatively better acquisitions both from a disciplinary perspective and with reference to L2 (Morton, 2020).

These linguistic aspects, which it is important for them to be the focus of teacher education pathways, must be accompanied by a more properly pedagogical reflection as far as the use of CLIL methodology is concerned. It, in addition to embracing the linguistic theories enunciated above (especially the last two, which are more recent, take into account evidence from pedagogical, psychological, and neuroscience research), is characterized by some concepts repeatedly explored in the literature on CLIL. (Ball et al., 2016; Coyle & Meyer, 2021; Danesi et al., 2018; Marsh, 2012). In fact, the communicative interaction taking place in CLIL activates other mental processes than traditional L2 teaching: the primary goal is communication, so students and learners do not exercise total control over the formal aspects of language, thus being able to focus on other dimensions having to do with language learning. In drawing these lines, reference is made to the 4c framework outlined by Coyle et al. (2010), to which the aspect of interculturality is added. These five dimensions, discussed here on a theoretical level, will be operationalized in the following paragraphs with examples referring to educational action in the classroom.

1.   The first concept is the *content*. Disciplinary knowledge, skills and competencies related to a specific area should not be penalized because of L2 enhancement. From the teacher's point of view, it is a matter of adopting those teaching approaches that are useful in making the input comprehensible both linguistically and in terms of disciplinary knowledge, so that the content is not reduced.
2.   The *communication* aspect is crucial. Students must take an active role during lessons, expressing their ideas in L2. The teacher's task is not only to make the inputs accessible, but above all to enhance the interactive, dialogue dimension through the adoption of dialogic and cooperative methodologies (circle time, peer education, brainstorming, cooperative learning, laboratory teaching, role playing, jigsaw, participatory heuristic method...): this encourages the acquisition of the target language and facilitates the reuse of terminology and arguments proper to the non-linguistic discipline.
3.   The *cognitive* side is obviously of essential importance. Disciplinary learning is related to the cognitive skills that pupils and students activate, so the teacher has the task of guiding students in developing the ability to process information in L2, through the provision of gradually more complex tasks (e.g., by providing for complex step-by-step activities in which achieving an end goal depends on completing simpler deliverables) suitable for stimulating their zone of proximal development.
4.   The concept of *culture* is of fundamental value and has to do with intercultural awareness. It is possible to build and stimulate this through text analysis and class discussion (e.g., reading texts related to a specific discipline can lead to a discussion with respect to the terminology used, so as to discover differences between the Italian and English languages with respect to sentence structuring and the nuance of words used for the same concept); in fact, already the transition from L1 to L2 leads to restructuring one's cultural horizons and beliefs, opening to the other in terms of the language and culture associated with the L2.
5.   The intercultural aspect opens to the dimension of citizenship: initiating CLIL pathways means preparing pupils to become European citizens and to confront the possibility of acting in the international context on the level of study and work experiences. Active citizenship is thus exercised in terms of participation in the choices of the European and global community and the possibility of choice with respect to one's education and profession.

In essence, these five dimensions interact with each other and make CLIL a methodology with an extraordinary generative potential, both at the linguistic and disciplinary level and at the level of citizenship (Virdia, 2022). Language, in fact, carries with it cultural implications that confront students with diversity in terms not only of linguistic structures, but also of historical paths, customs, all aspects that have had an influence on language and, in turn, have been influenced by language. CLIL allows learners to increase their awareness of how the L1 works precisely through the discovery of the linguistic structures of the L2: in other words, meeting the other (in terms of vocabulary, grammatical and morphosyntactic structures...) leads to a better definition of one's own language and the way it is used. Deepening and improving in the L2, therefore, always go hand in hand with improving skills in the mother tongue (Coyle

Let's CLIL!

et al., 2010): in general, reflection on the other is always a reflection on oneself, therefore language learning is always played out on two levels, that of the L1 and that of the L2. In this way, oral language skills are worked on, while refining written ones, and interest and curiosity are stimulated, opening to the dimension of multilingualism. This is also crucial on an educational level, as students learn to open to the other with a curious and welcoming gaze.

The inclusion of these pedagogical-linguistic reflections in teachers' education courses is fundamental, as it enables them to acquire useful tools for a classroom practice that is attentive and oriented towards the construction of citizenship and social change. As we will say further on, thinking of apprenticeship courses in which to translate theoretical acquisitions into practice represents an unavoidable pathway.

CLIL Education of Teachers in Italy: Pedagogical-Linguistic Lines

From a methodological point of view, in general, preference should be given to teaching approaches that allow pupils to enter into an interlocutory relationship with knowledge, experiencing language and thus being able to increase their own background (linguistic and cultural) through an active role (Beck & Kosnik, 2021). It is about creating a learning context in which collaboration, cooperation, relationship and interaction are valued. Strategies need to be implemented that involve and place pupils at the center of a process of growth and cultural awareness, which help him or her to reflect not only on language but also with language, to understand its functioning and regularities, in an instructional setting that facilitates the conscious practice of the language tool by virtue of a real purpose (Marsh, 2012).

Metacognition must be the cornerstone of any pathway using the CLIL approach. It is therefore necessary for the teacher to make explicit from the outset the goals that are set, so that they are shared and students and pupils feel they are their own and not imposed, so that there are benefits in terms of interest and motivation (Lord, 2022).

Then, it is necessary to identify goals, establishing concrete intermediate milestones that are adherent to the specific needs of pupils and consistent with their learning styles (Coyle et al., 2010). Increasing opportunities for language contact and practice is crucial to make L2 learning effective and persistent (Danesi et al., 2018): it is about making students and learners aware that the target language is not just a school subject, but something that permeates their existences, allows access to different content such as music, movies, readings, and can increase their study, professional and relational opportunities. In this sense, words encountered in a video game or heard in a song can be an object of reflection and a learning tool.

As has been said many times, children need to be placed at the center of the educational scene and assume the role of protagonists in their own learning process (Ball et al., 2016). It involves working on their metacognitive awareness with respect to how they learn, study, pace and time, and the preconceptions, stereotypes and biases that make them willing to try their hand at one subject area rather than another. Listening to their voice means making them creators of acquired knowledge.

In this perspective, children need to be accustomed to asking questions to become familiar with the attitude of inquiry and discovery (Barbero & Clegg, 2005). This propensity for inquiry should not only concern the non-linguistic discipline and target language, but it needs to invest the processes activated and the linguistic and cultural products produced. Peer comparison (peer review) provides a valuable opportunity to practice language while reflecting on one's own work, learning, and improving one's learning strategies.

Other teaching strategies that enable students to use language are peer tutoring, cooperative learning, and dialogic approaches (Beck & Kosnik, 2021). It is about getting involved in the first person, since explaining a concept, an idea to peers means first and foremost making a clarification to oneself. Pupils and students need to be encouraged to be creative and imaginative, to take unexplored and unexpected paths, to seek the new even in linguistic expression.

It is evident that in reflecting on teaching techniques to support L2 learning and the specific content of the non-linguistic discipline that is the subject of the CLIL pathway, different knowledge needs to be compared, such as discipline didactics, L2 didactics, sectoral language didactics, acquisitional linguistics, neurolinguistics of the bilingual brain, pedagogy, and management of the differentiated ability classroom (Danesi et al., 2018; Lord, 2022). From the teacher's perspective, there is a need to find those strategies that facilitate learning and increase students' autonomy in using L2 and acquiring disciplinary knowledge.

Scaffolding appears to be a useful strategy for supporting the process through which pupils learn (Dale & Tanner, 2012). This concept, developed from Vygotsky's research on the relationship between mind and language (Vygotsky, 1962) and those of Wood, Bruner and Ross (1976), describes the support that students need in their learning journey. Scaffolding in CLIL manifests itself in the form of supportive strategies for greater comprehension of input, nonverbal strategies (images, multimedia materials, concept maps), verbal strategies, and moments of focus on language (glossaries, vocabulary maps) and content (clozes, guiding questions, grids) (Danesi et al., 2018).

Fundamental to CLIL are conceptual mediation strategies. The teacher is an expert and must guide students to discover various disciplinary knowledge using the target language (Genesee, 2016). In CLIL, students are involved in activities of increasing cognitive complexity, so they are more likely to pay attention to content than to linguistic form, with consequent advantages on the level of unconscious L2 acquisition; on the other hand, the teacher has the task of adopting specific strategies to make concepts accessible and reusable by children (Dale & Tanner, 2012). The teacher can ask questions, facilitating dialogue between students through demonstrative questions (for which he or she already knows the answer) or referential questions (for which he or she does not know the answer). Questions can then be asked that stimulate pupils to speak freely (questions-elicitation) or that require searching within a text for implicit information (inferential questions). The question, in essence, represents a crutch for students, who feel supported by the teacher and free to be able to experiment with linguistic possibilities in L2, albeit with some imperfection or error.

Classroom practice can make use of strategies such as pairing (in pairs they compare ideas and opinions), jigsaw (in groups they pool information for the realization of a project), brainstorming and use multimedia and interactive media to initiate shared experiences.

CLIL and Assessment: Perspectives on Action

Assessing in a class that is following a CLIL pathway means taking into consideration both the linguistic plane and the disciplinary content side: it involves understanding how L2 and non-linguistic discipline integrate into a competence or set of competencies (Barbero & Clegg, 2005). Therefore, there is a need for collegial efforts on the part of teachers, as there is an assessment by the L2 teacher, an assessment by the teacher of the nonlanguage discipline, and a joint assessment. The students' voice is of crucial importance and must not be forgotten: thinking of self-assessment modes that promote peer-to-peer comparison allows one to develop that attitude of reflecting on language and one's own learning that is a harbinger of new cognitive acquisitions.

Let's CLIL!

Assessment is useful to understand whether the set learning goals have been achieved, to determine the level of competence achieved by pupils, to measure the results achieved (summative assessment), to monitor the learning process, to improve teaching, to orient and redirect teaching action and learning, and to create positive washback (formative assessment) (deBoer & Leontjev, 2020).

In general, within CLIL, assessment fluctuates between the content of the non-linguistic discipline and L2. It would be appropriate, in this sense, to make judgments that describe separately the results obtained on the linguistic and disciplinary levels, also because a CLIL path within the curriculum involves both the design of the non-linguistic discipline and of the L2, and in the teaching and learning process, in fact, two teachers intervene who, although in the collegiality that CLIL paths require for the achievement of common objectives, can and, to some extent, must diversify their approaches and methodologies in the intermediate stages (Barbero & Clegg, 2005; Coyle et al., 2010). This distinction between performance is necessary to avoid negative effects in terms of motivation on CLIL, thus moving away from the idea that these pathways can only be useful for students and learners who perform well in both the non-language discipline and L2. Pre-service teacher training is crucial: only the acquisition of appropriate docimological and evaluative skills can support the large-scale adoption of the CLIL approach in an inclusive perspective. In other words, the idea is that there is no standard norm that learners should strive for, but that each learner's pathways and the acquisitions he or she makes, starting from different positions and competences, should be evaluated. It is not possible to have a one-size-fits-all measure in mind: training thus plays a key role in fostering a pedagogical-linguistic awareness of this issue on the part of future teachers.

For assessment to be valid, it must be considered that within a CLIL course a specific L2 is used to express a specific content. This presupposes a modular distribution of content and assumes that CLIL refers to a precipitous module, with well-defined cognitive objectives that also incorporate the linguistic demands necessary for their achievement (Hönig, 2010). In terms of assessment tools, it is necessary to think of experiences that put students in the first person and are suitable for stimulating positive washback, going to test those skills whose development is to be encouraged, without creating a disorientation: thinking of group work that promotes the commitment of all components towards a common goal is a strategy that makes explicit the disciplinary content and the linguistic forms being assessed; it is important that the deliverables are clear and unambiguous. The teacher is able to understand the level of disciplinary and linguistic proficiency achieved through observation, without the children being pressured by, for example, a crossword test or a test with open-ended questions.

There are also more traditional assessment tests, which in any case should always be accompanied by experiences that actively bring students into play; we go over them briefly here because they are nonetheless useful tools, especially in terms of diagnostic assessment to understand how to reorient educational pathways. Among the various tests that can be structured, one can choose between mastery tests (proficiency), used to measure the level of competence, diagnostic tests, suitable for identifying strengths and weaknesses of male and female students, placement tests, useful for classifying the level of mastery of students and dividing them into level groups, achievement tests, tests that prove to be the most relevant to assessing a CLIL pathway, since their purpose is to assess the extent to which the specific objectives set out in the pathway have been achieved (Coyle, 2021; deBoer & Leontjev, 2020). The information relates to both individual pupils and the group and promotes positive washback on both teaching and learning.

Generally, there should be a focus on meaning (defining the linguistic forms to be used, leaving pupils and students with the linguistic resources to make use of), promoting real rather than simulated language use, having more than just a linguistic purpose, and focusing on cognitive processes such as selecting, sequencing information, transposing information into different forms of representation, and identifying the appropriate linguistic structures to achieve them (Ellis, 2003). In other words, assessment should focus on problem solving skills, content knowledge, concept processing, language use, communication skills, individual behavior, group behavior, and the attitude and attitude of pupils toward the discipline, the language, and the school.

Given the dual focus inherent in CLIL, it would be good to set up assessment tools at the design stage (Frey & Fisher, 2011), with input from each teacher involved in the pathway. There is a need to evaluate both the linguistic aspects and the disciplinary content in an integrated way, constructing ad hoc tests with respect to what is included in the pathway.

In this sense, the student portfolio (Puspitasari, 2020) is an effective tool for assessment in CLIL (and beyond). By collecting the work and descriptions of the most significant experiences, it is possible to trace the path taken by the individual student by enhancing strengths and critical issues encountered. Thus, assessment can synergistically consider not only linguistic and disciplinary acquisitions, but also attitudes, emotional and motivational aspects that would be lost with an exclusive and unadulterated use of tests.

Structuring tools that facilitate the evaluative task, it might be useful to construct grids that take into account the elements on which the focus is intended to be placed and the observable behaviors of male and female students, with the possibility of assigning each of these scores. Each level can then be made explicit through descriptors, shared with boys and girls so that the assessment is transparent and truly formative.

In assessing language skills more specifically, it is useful to follow this descriptive mode in defining what is expected of boys and girls in terms of language performance. In this sense, it is useful to refer to the *Common European Framework of Reference for Languages* to find those skills and competencies that it is necessary for pupils to activate in their production in L2. In general, oral and written comprehension and production should be assessed in terms of consistency with the task, relevance to the topic, breadth of vocabulary, and correctness of language structures (Barbero & Clegg, 2005).

Assessment, in essence, is a crucial aspect within a CLIL pathway (Coonan, 2006; Coyle & Meyer, 2021; Lord, 2022). It is necessary to define how one intends to measure the progress of pupils, in terms of the characteristics of the tests and their temporal cadence; choosing a suitable format (objective tests, which do not require the judgment of the evaluator, or subjective ones; exercises with a specific focus or requiring both linguistic and disciplinary skills) is essential. It is crucial to define the expected behaviors through descriptors that specify the aspects of the test that are intended to be considered; finally, a measurement scale must be established, which can take different forms: it can be two-level or multilevel, describing more concisely or in more detail the level of competence achieved and any deficiencies (Danesi et al., 2018).

It turns out to be essential to make students open to the self-evaluative dimension, for example, through the portfolio strategy, which allows them to document the experiences they have had as well as the skills they have acquired (Coyle et al., 2010). From the teacher's point of view, the logbook is an extraordinary tool for keeping track of the work done and noting significant moments along the way in terms of strengths, critical issues, strategies implemented by pupils, and collegial collaboration with colleagues.

Teacher education must insist on these assessment aspects so that assessment is a support and guidance for children's learning and not just a certification of acquisitions made. Too often, in fact, teachers are left alone in making assessment choices, without considering that assessment is an essential part of the

Let's CLIL!

design phase of educational pathways. The reflections conducted in this paragraph should find a place in the training paths for future CLIL teachers, so that there is not a specific focus on language or disciplinary content, but a focus on the paths of individual students and their acquisitions over the long term.

AN OPERATIONAL PROPOSAL FOR CLIL ACTIVITIES: AN INSTRUCTIONAL DESIGN FROM A PEDAGOGICAL-LINGUISTIC PERSPECTIVE

The educational path presented in these pages is designed for a fifth-grade elementary school class and relates to the field of science, with references to civic education, mixing CLIL approach to *Philosophy for Children* (P4C) (Lipman, 2003). This is a methodological proposal that presupposes the transformation of the classroom into a community of research in which knowledge is co-constructed and that values dialogue as a tool for an education in critical thinking, creativity and empathy with a view to a school that goes beyond disciplinary knowledge understood as cultural content in its own right and makes pupils capable of making connections, transferring and translating knowledge from narratives capable of provoking reflection with respect to specific issues of philosophical depth. Lipman thus sees the *P4C* curriculum as a tool capable of educating for the improvement of thinking, enhanced in its components (critical, creative and caring thinking), and judgment skills.

The planning of a CLIL course will be proposed in a concise way. It is intended to give a practical example of how teacher training should consider the pedagogical, didactic and linguistic aspects of CLIL practice also from the point of view of educational design and practice, with an enhancement of internship activities even for those training courses that do not include it.

Table 1. Pupils involved, skills and disciplines

Target	Students of fifth-grade of elementary school with an A1/A2 level of English according to the CEFR
Key citizenship skills	- Multilinguistic competence - Competence in science, technology and engineering - Citizenship competence - Personal, social and learning-to-learn competency
Disciplines involved	Science, English, civic education

In defining the disciplinary content involved, knowledge pertaining to the areas of science and civic education is separated from that of language: this allows for greater precision both in planning and in operational and evaluation.

Table 2. Knowledge, skills and expertise involved

Disciplinary content and skills: science and civic education	- Observing, analyzing and describing phenomena belonging to natural reality and aspects of daily life. - Formulate hypotheses and test them, using simple diagrams and models. - Describing and interpreting the functioning of the human body as a complex system located in an environment. - Taking care of one's health, including nutrition and motor skills.
Language content and language and metalinguistic skills	- *Key vocabulary:* learning specific terminology and being able to reuse it. - *Key language* (use of sentences in active form with major verbs, use of interrogative and negative form…) - Acquiring specific language with respect to the human body. - Describing own experiences with the help of pictures. - Learning about the main concepts related to specific vocabulary. - Developing oral and written comprehension and production). - Using L2 to learn.
Transversal knowledge and skills	- Awareness with respect to the importance of L2 as a learning opportunity. - Facilitated learning through the use of new technologies. - Increasing motivation for L2 learning. - Promoting interdisciplinarity. - Foster self-confidence, autonomy, cooperation. - Identify, describe, analyze, compare, explain, create. - Learning to learn. - Using multimedia tools and resources to learn and exchange information.

The path has a duration of twenty hours and is carried out through the collegial collaboration of the science teacher and the L2 teacher. Teachers create the conditions useful for facilitating the learning of the topic through targeted simplification activities, employing strategies to use English language through repetition, rephrasing, asking for confirmation of understanding, use of concrete examples, and illustration of key words through flashcards.

Specific techniques are then used to facilitate pupils' access to disciplinary content, such as reinforcing already acquired language structures, pre-teaching vocabulary, mimic-gestural language, code-switching (switching from one language to another as a natural communication strategy), redundancy, reformulation, simplification, exemplification, problem solving activities, individual activities, pair and group work, role-play, peer tutoring, card completion, cloze.

The last part of the course is devoted to *P4C* sessions, a educational approach already in use in the class in which the CLIL path is initiated, useful for understanding the skills acquired both in L2 and in the disciplinary field and for what concerns civic education. The stimulus texts will cover topics of a scientific nature but open to different possibilities of investigation, as is proper to the Lipman curriculum: arranged in a circle, the chosen pretext is read; from these questions it is decided which topics to investigate. This initiates the actual dialogue, during which members of the class-research community express their ideas freely in a kind of collective argumentation: thinking is structured in the course of hermeneutic inquiry, and everyone's contribution is indispensable for advancing dialogical research; thanks to this setting, each student feels welcomed and can express his or her opinion without fear, even with reference to the formal correctness of the L2 (Lipman, 2003). It ends with a self-assessment, in which metacognitive reflection is made on the research and dialogue methods.

Linguistically, pupils will be invited to express themselves through L2, but still free to use the language code they prefer, with an openness to the possibility of code-switching. In this sense, students can thus

Let's CLIL!

put their acquisitions in terms of disciplinary content and their language skills to good use, experiencing the expressive and creative potential of language.

The assessment rubrics, used by teachers during and at the end of the course to understand how students approach the activity, what skills they have acquired and at what level, of the key competencies focused on in the pathway are proposed below.

Table 3. Multilingual competence assessment rubric

European key competence		Multilinguistic competence	
INDICATORS	LEVELS OF MASTERY		
	TO BE REACHED	PARTIALLY REACHED	REACHED
Access to disciplinary content	The student is not autonomous in accessing disciplinary knowledge.	Only with facilitation does the student access disciplinary knowledge.	The student autonomously accesses disciplinary content.
Communicative exchanges	The student fails to use L2 for communicative exchanges, also through code-switching.	The student can use L2, sometimes code-switching, to participate in communicative exchanges.	The student participates in communicative exchanges with confidence using L2.
Reflection on language	The student fails to model L2.	If supported by the teacher, the student can understand how L2 works.	The student can autonomously understand how L2 works.

Table 4. Competence in science, technology and engineering assessment rubric

European key competence		Competence in science, technology and engineering	
INDICATORS	LEVELS OF MASTERY		
	TO BE REACHED	PARTIALLY REACHED	TO BE REACHED
Human body	The student does not know the different parts of the human body and does not understand that it is a complex system.	Only supported, the student recognizes the body as a complex system composed of multiple interacting organs.	The student understands that the body is a complex system and can make assumptions with respect to its functioning.
Self-care	Pupil fails to discriminate between correct and incorrect acts, behaviors.	Only stimulated by guiding questions, the student recognizes correct and incorrect behaviors.	The student autonomously understands which behaviors are correct and which are not with respect to self-care.

Table 5. Citizenship competence assessment rubric

European key competence		Citizenship competence		
INDICATORS	LEVELS OF MASTERY			
	TO BE REACHED	**PARTIALLY REACHED**	**TO BE REACHED**	
Observance of rules	Even with adult mediation, the student struggles to assume appropriate behavior and language register.	With the mediation of the teacher, the student adapts his/her behavior and language register to the context and interlocutors.	The student adapts his/her behavior and language register to the context and interlocutors.	
Openness to democracy	The student does not seem willing with respect to participating in a discussion process that is democratic, even with the intervention of the adult figure. He/She does not understand the meaning of democracy and the value of being able to express oneself in different languages.	Although autonomously he/she fails to understand the meaning of democracy, with the help of the adult he can converse while keeping a correct attitude. He/She is not always aware of the value of being able to express himself in different languages.	The pupil autonomously participates in the dialogue process, keeping a behavior certainly marked by democracy, a word whose meaning and deep value he knows. He/she is aware of the value of being able to express him/herself in different languages.	

Table 6. Personal, social and learning-to-learn competency assessment rubric

European key competence		Personal, social and learning-to-learn competency		
INDICATORS	LEVELS OF MASTERY			
	TO BE REACHED	**PARTIALLY REACHED**	**TO BE REACHED**	
Self and others	The student is reluctant with respect to different and help toward those in difficulty; does not listen to peers.	If spurred to do so, the student helps those in need and welcomes the different; he/she considers the other's point of view.	The student listens to peers while taking into account their point of view; helps those in difficulty and welcomes the different.	
Metacognition	The student fails to activate strategies for reflection and control over his or her own learning.	Only supported, the student can activate strategies for reflection and control over his or her own learning.	The student can autonomously activate strategies for reflection and control over his or her own learning.	

The educational proposal presented here is not meant to be a universally valid model, but a food for thought for teacher training that considers the more methodological and pedagogical aspects and does not reduce CLIL to acquisition of vocabulary and skills only in L2.

FUTURE RESEARCH DIRECTIONS

The spread of CLIL in Italy proves problematic (Cinganotto, 2016; Serragiotto, 2017) even for the school grades where it is mandatory. It is essential that already during the elementary school years pupils are exposed to L2 through CLIL pathways: at the moment their activation is left to the teaching freedom of teachers. In any case, there is a worrying shortage of adequately trained staff for teaching non-language subjects in L2.

Let's CLIL!

Implementing CLIL in Italian schools still represents a challenge that questions educational policies and teacher education (Mastrorosa, 2018): including specific courses on the teaching of non-linguistic disciplines in L2 in initial teacher training could be useful to broaden the diffusion of the methodology. Enhancing internship activities in CLIL training courses and, in general, in initial teacher training courses represents the way through which they could confront themselves with teachers who are experts in the use of the methodology, use the skills they have acquired and design paths for their classrooms. Educational research should also focus more on how to use CLIL in Italian elementary school, because it has been shown that using this approach facilitates L2 learning not only in terms of cognitive acquisitions, but especially on an emotional level, succeeding in fostering a more serene encounter with the experience of linguistic otherness on the part of students (Held, 2018).

CONCLUSION

In essence, CLIL methodology can be the flywheel for a renewal of teaching practice. It presupposes not only a renewed repertoire of educational and teaching strategies, but above all a new role for language within the school curriculum. Thus, students can practice L2 and use it for a concrete purpose, namely learning a non-linguistic discipline.

In the age of complexity and the globalized world, knowing and speaking multiple languages is crucial, also with a view to greater professional and study opportunities. CLIL, in fact, constitutes a methodology capable of triggering a real renewal of the teaching and learning process, since it overcomes the limits of the frontal lecture and of a compilative and transmissive didactics, leveraging an instrumental use of the foreign language and meanwhile stimulating pupils with learning strategies that aim at the acquisition of meanings elaborated and shared under the guidance of the teacher.

In this sense, this chapter has shown that teachers must acquire pedagogical and linguistic tools to master this methodology and be able to use it in the classroom to its full potential. Careful training in didactic and methodological aspects will enable them to interpret the CLIL approach and adapt it according to the needs of their classrooms. This is especially urgent in the Italian context, where multilingual education based on CLIL methodology is still not widespread, despite the normative dictate.

REFERENCES

Aiello, J., Di Martino, E., & Di Sabato, B. (2017). Preparing teachers in Italy for CLIL: Reflections on assessment, language proficiency and willingness to communicate. *International Journal of Bilingual Education and Bilingualism, 20*(1), 69–83. doi:10.1080/13670050.2015.1041873

Andorno, C., Valentini, A., & Grassi, R. (2017). Verso una nuova lingua. [Towards a new language.] Capire l'acquisizione di L2. Novara: Utet.

Ball, P., Kelly, K., & Clegg, J. (2016). *Putting CLIL into Practice*. Oxford University Press.

Barberis, P. (1998). The New Public Management and a new accountability. *Public Administration, 76*(3), 451–470. doi:10.1111/1467-9299.00111

Barbero, T., & Clegg, J. (2005). *Programmare percorsi CLIL [Program CLIL paths.]*. Carocci.

Beck, C., & Kosnik, C. (2020). *Classroom Teaching in the 21st Century. Directions, Principles and Strategies*. Open University Press.

Biesta, G. J. J. (2017). *The Rediscovery of Teaching*. Routledge. doi:10.4324/9781315617497

Bower, K., Coyle, D., Cross, R., & Chambers, G. N. (Eds.). (2020). *Curriculum Integrated Language Teaching. CLIL in Practice*. Cambridge University Press. doi:10.1017/9781108687867

Bracci, E. (2009). Autonomy, responsibility and accountability in the Italian school system. *Critical Perspectives on Accounting, 20*(3), 293–312. doi:10.1016/j.cpa.2008.09.001

Breidbach, S., & Viebrock, B. (2013). *Content and Language Integrated Learning (CLIL) in Europe; Research Perspectives on Policy and Practice*. Peter Lang. doi:10.3726/978-3-653-02955-0

Carbonara, V., & Scibetta, A. (2022). Integrating translanguaging pedagogy into Italian primary schools: Implications for language practices and children's empowerment. *International Journal of Bilingual Education and Bilingualism, 25*(3), 1049–1069. doi:10.1080/13670050.2020.1742648

Choi, J., & Ollerhead, S. (Eds.). (2017). *Plurilingualism in Teaching and Learning. Complexities Across Contexts*. Routledge.

Cinganotto, L. (2016). CLIL in Italy: A general overview. *LACLIL. Latin American Journal of Content & Language Integrated Learning, 9*(2), 374–400. doi:10.5294/laclil.2016.9.2.6

Codó, E. (Ed.). (2022). *Global CLIL. Critical, Ethnographic and Language Policy Perspectives*. Routledge. doi:10.4324/9781003147374

Coonan, C. M. (Ed.). (2006). *CLIL: un nuovo ambiente di apprendimento. Sviluppi e riflessioni sull'uso veicolare di una lingua seconda/straniera* [*CLIL: a new learning environment. Developments and reflections on the vehicular use of a second/foreign language.*]. Cafoscarina.

Corder, P. S. (1981). *Error analysis and Interlanguage*. Oxford University Press.

Coyle, D., Hood, P., & Marsh, D. (2010). *CLIL. Content and Language Integrated Learning*. Cambridge University Press. doi:10.1017/9781009024549

Coyle, D., & Meyer, O. (2021). *Beyond CLIL. Pluriliteracies Teaching for Deeper Learning*. Cambridge University Press. doi:10.1017/9781108914505

Cummins, J. (2000). *Language, power and pedagogy*. Multilingual Matters. doi:10.21832/9781853596773

Dale, L., & Tanner, R. (2012). *CLIL activities*. Cambridge University Press.

Dalton-Puffer, C., Bauer-Marschallinger, S., Brückl-Mackey, K., Hofmann, V., Hopf, J., Kröss, L., & Lechner, L. (2018). Cognitive discourse functions in Austrian CLIL lessons: Towards an empirical validation of the CDF Construct. *European Journal of Applied Linguistics, 6*(1), 5–29. doi:10.1515/eujal-2017-0028

Danesi, M., Diadori, P., & Semplici, S. (2018). *Tecniche didattiche per la lingua seconda. Strategie e strumenti, anche in contesti CLIL* [*Didactic techniques for the second language. Strategies and tools, also in CLIL contexts.*]. Carocci.

Let's CLIL!

deBoer, M., & Leontjev, D. (2020). *Assessment and Learning in Content and Language Integrated Learning (CLIL) Classrooms: Approaches and Conceptualisations.* Springer. doi:10.1007/978-3-030-54128-6

Di Pol, R. S. (2000). *Cultura pedagogica e professionalità nella formazione del maestro italiano* [*Pedagogical culture and professionalism in the training of the Italian master.*]. Marco Valerio.

Di Pol, R. S. (2016). *La scuola per tutti gli italiani. L'istruzione di base tra Stato e società dal primo Ottocento a oggi* [*The school for all Italians. Basic education between State and society from the early nineteenth century to today.*]. Mondadori Università.

Durlak, J. A., Domitrovich, C. E., Weissberg, R. P., & Gullotta, T. P. (2015). *Handbook of Social and Emotional Learning: Research and Practice.* The Guilford Press.

EC. (2012). *Rethinking Education: investing in skills for better socio-economic outcomes.* EC. https://www.cedefop.europa.eu/files/com669_en.pdf

EC. EACEA, & Eurydice (2017). Key data on teaching languages at school in Europe. Publications Office of European Union.

Egger, G., & Lechner, C. (2012). *Primary CLIL Around Europe: Learning in Two Languages in Primary Education.* Tectum Wissenschaftsverlag.

Ellis, R. (2003). *Task-based language learning and teaching.* Oxford University Press.

Fortanet-Gómez, I. (2013). *CLIL in Higher Education: Towards a Multilingual Language Policy.* Channel View. doi:10.21832/9781847699374

Frey, N., & Fisher, D. (2011). *The Formative Assessment Action Plan: Practical Steps to More Successful Teaching and Learning.* Association for Supervision & Curriculum Development.

Genesee, F. (2016). *CLIL in Context. Practical Guidance for Educators.* Cambridge University Press.

Giordano, C., & Maurizio, C. (2021). *Il CLIL nella scuola primaria e dell'infanzia. Teoria e pratica di una risorsa per l'apprendimento delle lingue* [*CLIL in primary and nursery schools. Theory and practice of a resource for language learning.*]. Carocci.

Gueldner, B. A., Feuerborn, L. L., & Merrel, K. W. (2020). Social and Emotional Learning in the Classroom, Second Edition. Promoting Mental Health and Academic Success. The Guilford Press.

Hedegaard, M. (1996). The zone of proximal development as basis for instruction. In H. Daniels (Ed.), *An Introduction to Vygotsky* (pp. 183–207). Routledge.

Held, G. (2018). *Foreign Language Anxiety and Motivation in CLIL programmes: A Study in Italy.* Edizioni Accademiche Italiane.

Hemmi, C., & Banegas, D. L. (2021). *International Perspectives on CLIL.* Palgrave Macmillan. doi:10.1007/978-3-030-70095-9

Holmes, P., Dooly, M., & O'Regan, J. (Eds.). (2016). *Intercultural Dialogue: Questions of research, theory, and practice.* Routledge.

Hönig, I. (2010). *Assessment in CLIL. Theoretical and empirical research.* VDM Verlag Dr. Müller.

Jonnaert, P. (2009). *Compétences et socioconstructivisme. Un cadre théorique.* [*Skills and socioconstructivism. A theoretical framework.*] Paris: de Boeck.

Juan-Garau, M., & Salazar-Noguera, J. (Eds.). (2015). *Content-based Language Learning in Multilingual Educational Environments.* Springer. doi:10.1007/978-3-319-11496-5

Krashen, S. D. (1976). Formal and Informal linguistic environments in language acquisition and language learning. *TESOL Quarterly, 10,* 157–168.

Krashen, S. D. (1985). *The Input hypothesis: issues and implications.* Longman.

Krashen, S. D. (1987). *Principles and Practice in second language acquisition. Englewood Cliff.* Prentice-Hall International.

Leone, A. R. (2015). Outlooks in Italy: CLIL as Language Education Policy. *Working Papers in Educational Linguistics, 30*(1), pp. 43-63.

Lipman, M. (2003). *Thinking in Education.* Cambridge University Press.

Llinares, A., Morton, T., & Whittaker, R. (2012). *The Roles of Language in CLIL.* Cambridge University Press.

Long, M. (1996). The role of linguistic environment in second language acquisition. In W. C. Ritchie & T. K. Bhatia (Eds.), *Handbook of second language acquisition* (pp. 413–468). Academic Press.

Lord, J. (Ed.). (2022). *Psychology of Education. Theory, Research and Evidence-Based Practice.* Sage.

Marsh, D. (1994). *Bilingual education & content and language integrated learning. International Association for Cross-cultural Communication. Language Teaching in the Member States of the European Union.* University of Sorbonne.

Marsh, D. (2002). *CLIL/ÉMILE. The European dimension.* University of Jyvaskyla.

Marsh, D. (2012). *Content and Language Integrated Learning (CLIL): a development trajectory.* University of Cordoba.

Marsh, D., Maljers, A., & Hartiala, A. K. (2001). *Profiling European CLIL classrooms. Languages open doors.* University of Jyvaskyla.

Mastrorosa, S. (2018). *CLIL methodology in Italian school from origins to the present day.* Lulu.

Mehisto, P., Marsh, D., & Frigols, M. J. (2008). *Uncovering CLIL: Content and Language Integrated Learning and Multilingual Education.* Macmillan.

Meyer, O., & Coyle, D. (2017). Pluriliteracies Teaching for Learning: Conceptualizing progression for deeper learning in literacies development. *European Journal of Applied Linguistics, 5*(2), 199–122.

Meyer, O., Coyle, D., Halbach, A., Schuck, K., & Ting, T. (2015). A pluriliteracies approach to content and language integrated learning–mapping learner progressions in knowledge construction and meaning-making. *Language, Culture and Curriculum, 28*(1), 41–57.

Milito, D., Parise, F. G., & Ting, Y. L. T. (2015). *CLIL. Innovazione metodologico-didattica e apprendimento efficace*. Anicia.

MIUR. (2012). *Indicazioni Nazionali per il curricolo della scuola dell'infanzia e del primo ciclo di istruzione. [National guidelines for the curriculum of kindergarten and first cycle education.]* MIUR. http://www.indicazioninazionali.it/wp-content/uploads/2018/0 8/decreto-ministeriale-254-del-16-novembre-2012-indicazioni-nazionali-curricolo-scuola-infanzia-e-primo-ciclo.pdf

MIUR. (2018). *Indicazioni Nazionali e Nuovi Scenari*. MIUR. http://www.indicazioninazionali.it/wp-content/uploads/2018/0 8/Indicazioni-nazionali-e-nuovi-scenari.pdf

Morin, E. (2008). *On Complexity*. Hampton Press.

Mortari, L., & Silva, R. (2020). Teacher Education in Italy. In K. Pushpanadham (Ed.), *Teacher Education in the Global Era* (pp. 115–132). Springer.

Morton, T. (2020). Cognitive discourse functions: A bridge between content, literacy and language for teaching and assessment in CLIL. *CLIL Journal of Innovation and Research in Plurilingual and Pluricultural Education*, *3*(1), 7–17.

Newcombe, N. (2018). *Europe at School. A Study of Primary and Secondary Schools in France, West Germany, Italy, Portugal & Spain*. Routledge.

Nieto Moreno de Diezmas, E., & Custodio Espinar, M. (2022). *Multilingual Education under Scrutiny. A Critical Analysis on CLIL Implementation and Research on a Global Scale*. Peter Lang.

Nikula, T., Dafouz, E., Moore, P., & Smit, U. (2016). *Conceptualising Integration in CLIL and Multilingual Education*. Multilingual Matters.

Ostinelli, G. (2009). Teacher Education in Italy, Germany, England, Sweden and Finland. *European Journal of Education*, *10*(44), 291–308.

Piccardo, E., Germain-Rutherford, A., & Lawrence, G. (Eds.). (2021). *The Routledge Handbook of Plurilingual Language Education*. Routledge.

Puspitasari, E. (2020). Mind Mapping in CLIL: How It Facilitates Students' Reading Comprehension. *Journal of English Education and Teaching*, *4*(2), 154–169.

Raud, N., & Orehhova, O. (2022). Training teachers for multilingual primary schools in Europe: Key components of teacher education curricula. *International Journal of Multilingualism*, *19*(1), 50–62.

Schmidt, R. (2001). Attention. In P. Robinson (Ed.), *Cognition and Second language instruction* (pp. 3–32). Cambridge University Press.

Selinker, L. (1972). Interlanguage. *IRAL. International Review of Applied Linguistics in Language Teaching*, *10*, 209–231.

Selinker, L. (1992). *Rediscovering interlanguage*. Longman.

Serragiotto, G. (2017). The Problems of Implementing CLIL in Italy. *International Journal of Linguistics*, *9*(5), 82–96.

Skrefsrud, T. A. (2016). *The Intercultural Dialogue. Preparing Teachers for Diversity*. Waxmann.

Surhone, L. M., Tennoe, M. T., & Henssonow, S. F. (Eds.). (2010). *Social Constructivism. Sociological Perspectives, Knowledge, Social constructionism, Social Phenomenon, Social Relation, Continental Philosophy, Phenomenology*. Betascript.

Swain, M. (1995). Three functions of output in second language learning. In B. Seidlhofer, H. Widdow, & G. Cook (Eds.), *Principles and practice in applied linguistics: studies in honour of H. G. Widdowson* (pp. 125–144). Oxford University Press.

Swann, J. (2011). *Learning, Teaching and Education Research in the 21st Century. An Evolutionary Analysis of the Role of Teachers*. Continuum.

Todeschini, M. E. (2003). Teacher Education in Italy. New Trends. In M. Moon, L. Vlasceanu, & L. C. Barrows (Eds.), *Institutional Approaches to Teacher Education within Higher Education in Europe: Current Models and New Developments* (pp. 223–244). UNESCO.

UN (2015). *Transforming Our World: The 2030 Agenda for Sustainable Development*. New York: UN.

Virdia, S. (2022). The (heterogeneous) effect of CLIL on content-subject and cognitive acquisition in primary education: Evidence from a counterfactual analysis in Italy. *International Journal of Bilingual Education and Bilingualism*, *25*(5), 1877–1893.

Vygotskij, L. S. (1962). *Thought and Language*. The MIT Press.

Wood, D., Bruner, J., & Ross, G. (1976). The role of tutoring in problem solving. *Journal of child psicology and psychiatry*, *17*, 89-100.

Woodrow, D., Verma, G. K., Rocha-Trindade, M. B., Campani, G., & Bagley, C. (Eds.). (2020). *Intercultural Education: Theories, Policies and Practices*. Routledge.

Zembylas, M. (2005). Three Perspectives on Linking the Cognitive and the Emotional in Science Learning: Conceptual Change, Socio-Constructivism And Poststructuralism. *Studies in Science Education*, *41*(1), 91–115.

KEY TERMS AND DEFINITIONS

Active Education: Repertoire of non-transmissive teaching strategies that place the student at the center of the educational scene, who experiences and learns through his or her own action and the teacher as facilitator of the processes.

CLIL: Acronym for Content and Language Integrated Learning, it refers to a methodology involving language immersion as a key tool for L2 learning.

Let's CLIL!

Classroom Practice: Educational practice of teachers in the classroom, according to a pedagogical-linguistic perspective useful for understanding how theory is translated into action and how teachers translate the skills and abilities acquired during training courses into practice.

Italian Primary School: School segment involving students aged 6 to 11.

Linguistic: Science that studies language, its formation and evolution, and the mechanisms of acquisition by humans.

Metalinguistic competencies: Learning that concerns reflection on language and how it functions and is organized.

Pedagogy: Human science that studies education to indicate possible courses of action for teachers and educators for the improvement of practice.

Teacher Education: Training courses (initial or in-service) for teachers, in which they acquire skills for classroom practice.

Section 2

Case Studies and Proposals for Teacher Training in Primary Bilingual Education Contexts

Chapter 4

"English in the Kindergarten: Towards Multilingual Education":
Good Practices From a Teacher Training Program in Greece

Anastasia Gkaintartzi
University of Thessaly, Greece

Achilleas Kostoulas
University of Thessaly, Greece

Magda Vitsou
(iD) https://orcid.org/0000-0002-7447-4634
University of Thessaly, Greece

ABSTRACT

This chapter presents a teacher education program that aimed to prepare early childhood educators and English language teachers to collaboratively introduce multilingual learning opportunities in pre-school education in Greece using English as a bridge-language among students' languages and cultures. The program, which was designed to support education policy that introduced the English language into the curriculum of Greek state preschools, had four goals. Firstly, it aimed to approach English as a bridge-language that can help promote multilingual meaning-making. Secondly, it encouraged the use of pedagogical translanguaging in order to support teachers to challenge prevalent monolingual instruction patterns and build upon the children's entire linguistic repertoires. Teachers were also trained in experimenting with and employing arts-based learning and creativity. These learning outcomes are illustrated in the chapter by drawing on teacher training materials and participant output, which provide useful data on the implementation and overall impact of the program.

DOI: 10.4018/978-1-6684-6179-2.ch004

Copyright © 2023, IGI Global. Copying or distributing in print or electronic forms without written permission of IGI Global is prohibited.

INTRODUCTION

Recent years have witnessed an intensification of English language teaching (ELT) across the world, which frequently takes the form of ELT courses in progressively younger ages. Such drives often seem to outpace the capacity of the education systems to prepare teachers for the challenges of language education in very young ages. This chapter describes a teacher education program that was developed to prepare language teachers and early childhood educators in Greece to collaboratively deliver appropriate language courses in the context of pre-school education. The program, entitled 'English in the Kindergarten: Towards multilingual education', was a response to the introduction, in 2020, of English language classes in kindergartens across Greece, while taking into account the changing, and increasingly complex linguistic ecology of schools across the country.

The chapter provides an overview of the teacher education program, and it is structured in four main sections. It begins with a contextualizing section that serves to sketch the background against which the program was developed. Following that, the next section, outlines the theoretical tenets of the program and presents selected examples of activities that were developed to implement these tenets. The subsequent section focuses on the participants' output with a view to illustrating the response to the theoretical tenets and the learning outcomes of the program. The chapter concludes with summative comments and suggestions for research and pedagogy.

THE BACKGROUND OF THE PROGRAM

The intensifying drive towards the early introduction of ELT in education across the world is associated with ongoing globalization processes (Stelma & Kostoulas, 2021) as well as discourses and policies that connect early language learning with multilingualism and intercultural awareness (European Commission, 2011). Early language learning programs are premised on the belief that they can help foster the development of plurilingual awareness and competence as well as to contribute to positive academic and cognitive outcomes (Bland, 2015; Kirsch et al., 2020; Scheffler & Domioska, 2018). However, concerns have been raised about such early language programs, which are often implemented before sufficient empirical evidence has been collected regarding their effectiveness (Pfenninger & Singleton, 2017). Furthermore, the expedience with which such programs are introduced often means that educational systems do not have adequate time to adapt appropriate methodologies, materials and teacher capacities (Enever, 2004). Moreover, the salience of English as the most widely taught language in early language learning programs (Eurydice, 2017) has also attracted critical attention (e.g., Pennycook, 2007; Phillipson, 1992, 2009).

The trend towards intensification of ELT provision is evident in the Greek education system. English was originally introduced in primary education in the early 1990s, and the starting age has been progressively lowered in every successive curricular reform since then (Kostoulas, 2018). In the 2020-2021 school year, a pilot program was implemented for the introduction of English in 58 kindergartens, which are attended by students aged 4-6 as part of compulsory education. Typically, in kindergartens in Greece, all educational activities are part of holistic thematic "cycles", which are designed and implemented by an early education specialist. However, the pilot program stipulated that kindergartens would be visited by an ELT teacher twice a week for an hour of English lessons, co-taught by the two teachers (i.e., the early

"English in the Kindergarten: Towards Multilingual Education"

education specialist and the language teacher). Evaluative data about the program are still emerging, but as of the 2021-2022 school year, ELT was made a compulsory part of the curriculum across the country.

When the policy intention was announced to introduce English in pre-school education in Greece, the authors identified a need to support both early education specialists and language teachers to design and implement teaching activities that were consistent with current understandings of best practice and social justice. This involved raising awareness regarding ongoing debates surrounding the ownership of English (Widdowson, 1994, 2003), language hegemony and linguistic human rights (Phillipson,1992, 2009; Skutnabb-Kangas, 2012), and the 'multilingual turn' in applied linguistics and language education (Conteh &Meyer, 2014; May, 2014). The tension between 'English-only' pedagogical policies that are common in ELT (Kostoulas & Stelma, 2017; Kostoulas, 2018) and the pedagogical and ideological perspective oflinguistic purity (e.g., García & Flores, 2012) was also something that seemed to require problematization. Furthermore, a needs analysis that was carried out by the authors (Gkaintartzi et al., 2021) identified concerns among teachers regarding the potential of cooperation between educators with very different disciplinary backgrounds and experiences and a strong desire to develop competences for creative and art-based education.

OVERVIEW AND FUNDAMENTAL PRINCIPLES OF THE PROGRAM

To address the needs mentioned in the previous section, a professional development program for teachers was created, which was named *English in the Kindergarten: Towards Multilingual Education.* This is a continuing teacher education program that mainly caters to the needs of in-service preschool education and language teachers, but it is also open to pre-service teachers who have an interest in the topic. The program aims at developing the participants' professional competence and readiness in conceptualizing, designing, implementing and evaluating English language learning activities in the kindergarten through a multilingual and inclusive perspective. It builds on a needs analysis that was carried out among early education teachers and language teaching specialists who were involved in the piloting of the new ELT policy in Greek state kindergartens between October and December 2020, and it was first implemented in the Spring Semester of the 2020-2021 academic year.

The program is offered by the 'Centre of Professional Development and Life-Long Learning' of the University of Thessaly using distributed, online teaching, learning and collaboration methods. It lasts 14 weeks which are evenly divided between theoretical knowledge building and activities for teaching practice. The content of the program includes self-study components, individual and group assignments as well as online sessions. Participation fluctuates per cohort, from about 10 to about 35 participants, including both experienced teachers and teachers who are about to start their careers.

The content of the program is divided into 10 modules, presented below:

1. Introduction of the program and exploration of teacher needs (week 1)
2. Multilingualism and Education: languages and cultures in contact and translanguaging (weeks 2-3)
3. The kindergarten as a learning context and space. The Curriculum (weeks 4-5)
4. Early years language development (week 6)
5. Approaches, methods and techniques in multilingual education (week 7)
6. Creative activities, Arts-Based Approach and the Experiential approach (weeks 8-9)
7. Collaboration and co-teaching: workshops and reflection (weeks 10-11)

8. Developing activities and scenarios (weeks 12)
9. Educational material development (week 13)
10. Participant presentations and program evaluation (week 14)

Each module offers multimodal input including PowerPoint presentations with theoretical/methodological content, practical examples, good practices, explanations in English and Greek, videos and additional resources for further practice. Participants are required to study the material, participate in forum discussions, complete quizzes and engage with individual and collaborative activities, with appropriate tutorial support. Regarding assessment, teachers have to submit two written assignments (a short and a final essay on developing teaching scenarios or activity design), individually and collaboratively as well as to participate in the weekly activities (forum-discussions, quizzes and short tasks) in order to successfully complete the program.

Concerning the theoretical principles of its design, the program is informed by a multilingual and inclusive perspective, in which English is approached as *'bridge-language'*, i.e., a language which facilitates cross-linguistic and cross-cultural contact. It is expected that this perspective can facilitate the development of *inclusive, multilingual learning environments,* by making the students' home languages more visible in the class context, and by actively embracing and valuing linguistic diversity in preschool education. In this perspective, English is used to generate 'safe places' in the classroom, by challenging the dominance of the majority language (i.e., Modern Greek), and valorizing a broader range of semiotic resources. In other words, English language activities are not deployed as means for developing language-specific communicative competence in English; rather they are used to destabilize monolingual norms and generate space where additional, minoritized languages and non-standard language varieties may be valued and used without risking stigmatization. Thus, the focus of the program is on helping teachers to make appropriate use of their diverse students' entire linguistic and cultural capitals, and on *'multilingualizing'* teaching.

The theoretical principles of its design draw on a rich, cutting-edge literature base that synthesizes linguistic, identity-based, and pedagogical perspectives (Kostoulas, 2019). Recent developments in the domain of applied linguistics, which inform the program include work on plurilingual and multilingual approaches to education (e.g., Cenoz & Gorter, 2011,2015; Cummins, 2017; García & Flores, 2012; García & LiWei, 2014), which highlight the richness of linguistic ecologies in which students find themselves during and after school. Other relevant work includes perspectives on English as a MultilinguaFranca and on translanguaging (Cenoz & Gorter, 2020; Garcia, 2009; Jenkins, 2015; Seidlhofer, 2007), which draw attention to the fluidity of language use. In addition to the above, the pedagogy that informs the program includes a strong emphasis on pedagogical practices that are appropriate to the education of young students: e.g., art-based learning, drama techniques and creativity. Lastly, the program is premised on the ideal of collaboration among teachers and co-teaching, based on the principles of non-violent communication (Bourdieu, 1999).

The theoretical tenets of the program are analyzed in greater detail in the ensuing paragraphs, and they are illustrated with selected examples of activities that were developed to implement them.

A Multilingual/Plurilingual Approach and English as a 'Bridge' Language

The design and implementation of the program is underpinned by an approach towards very early language education that aims to generate a novel view of languages. At the core of this view is an emphasis

"English in the Kindergarten: Towards Multilingual Education"

on the interconnections between languages, as opposed to the socially constructed boundaries that separate them (see Garcia & Li Wei, 2014; Flores &Rosa,2015), and on the way that these interconnections shape a unitary plurilingual competence (Council of Europe, 2001) that is constantly renegotiated and reconfigured. Seen through this perspective, the language classroom is viewed as a space for softening linguistic boundaries, and for exploring the meaning-making potential of linguistic repertoires that are not confined by monolingual ideologies (Gogolin, 1997). Similarly, the English language is not viewed as a target language, where students must attain specific language-specific competences; rather, it is approached as a vehicle for intercultural encounters in the classroom, as an example of how monolingualism may be challenged, and as a semiotic bridgewhich facilitates the contact and interplay among different linguistic and cultural resources.

In more practical terms, participant teachers are supported to design and implement practices and activities that build on, highlight and explore the relationships between languages and can potentially develop learners' language awareness and multilingual/intercultural awareness (Cenoz & Gorter, 2020), makinguse of students' linguistic and cultural resources cross-linguistically, critically and creatively. Some indicative examples of relevant content, drawn from the program curriculum includethe approach "Awakening to Languages" (Beacco et al., 2016; Candelier, 2017), inclusive, multilingual/plurilingual practices such as 'identity texts'(Cummins & Early, 2011), language portraits (Busch, 2012, 2018; Gkaintartzi & Tsokalidou, 2018; Melo-Pfeifer, 2015; Soares et al., 2020), multilingual/bilingual story books (Ibrahim, 2020), Language Appropriate Practice (LAP) (Chumak-Horbatch, 2012, 2019) and examples of inclusive, plurilingual school approaches (Little & Kirwan, 2019). In addition to theoretical input, participants are expected to engage in an active negotiation of meaning through reflective activities, quizzes and forum discussions.

Moving to examples from the program's curriculum and more specifically from the module *Multilingualism/Pluringualism: Languages and cultures in contact*, below are extracts from the PowerPoint presentations included in the course material concerning multilingual/plurilingual approaches and practices. Figure 1 presents examples of pedagogical activities and good practices that were shared with participants in order to expand their pedagogical repertoire. Figure 2 is a list of myths associated with bilingualism, which was provided as discussion prompts.

Figure 1. Examples of multilingual and pluralistic approaches

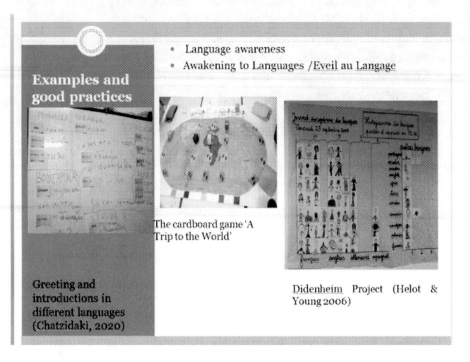

Figure 2. Common myths about bi/multilingualism

Κοινοί μύθοι γύρω από τη διγλωσσία
Common myths about bilingualism

Τροφή για σκέψη - Food for thought

- Bilingualism is a rare phenomenon
- Bilinguals acquire their two or more languages in childhood
- Bilinguals have equal and perfect knowledge of their languages
- Mixing languages is a sign of lack of knowledge in bilinguals, a mistake or a gap in language learning.
- Bilingualism will delay language acquisition in childhood.
- The language spoken in the home will have a negative effect on the acquisition of the school language.
- Parents should use the majority language at home.

adapted from Grosjean (2010)

"English in the Kindergarten: Towards Multilingual Education"

In another course activity teachers were invited to share information in a forum discussion about the sociolinguistic profiles and linguistic repertoires of emergent bilinguals-students, with whom they had worked in class. Such activities were designed to facilitate program participants to engage in an active process of constructing knowledge about their students' linguistic repertoires and cultural backgrounds. By asking participants to outline their learners 'sociolinguistic profiles, and by encouraging a close understanding of what language and cultural "baggage" students bring to class, it is expected that they can embark on a reflective process that involves identifying diverse repertoires and identities and building on them. Furthermore, guided forum discussions are used to encourage participants to become more critically aware of implicit and explicit linguistic beliefs and to take on more active, socially responsible role in challenging and reconstructing them (Stelma& Fay, 2019).

Translanguaging and English as a 'Multilingua Franca'

Translanguaging, the second aspect that underpins the program, is approached as both a theoretical perspective on language, whereby linguistic repertoires are viewed as unitary constructs through a holistic approach (García, 2009), and as an educational approach that can integrate two or more languages in teaching ('pedagogical translanguaging'; Cenoz & Gorter, 2020), i.e., a set of skills and practices which can be strategically planned and activated in class. Furthermore, a useful distinction, especially for teachers is taken into account, between 'Unitary Translanguaging Theory' and the 'Crosslinguistic Translanguaging Theory', of which the latter is argued to facilitate transfer across languages and to encourage approaching languages in an integrated way (Cummins, 2021).

In more concrete terms, program participants are supported in softening the boundaries between named languages, by encouraging the creative use of semiotic resources from all the strata of the linguistic ecology in which a school classroom is embedded. This is done by increasing the participants' competence in moving beyond monolingual types of instruction, and encouraging linguistic meaning-making across languages, using English as necessary as a 'connective tissue', a bridge-language. In other words, English serves the important role of establishing bridges across languages, and bringing the emergent multilingual users, and their expansive repertoires to the fore (Cenoz & Gorter, 2020).

Translanguaging strategies are used in the program aiming to build on relationships between languages and " to maximize the learner's linguistic resources when learning English" (Cenoz, 2019) and thus participant teachers are facilitated in designing and implementing class-based activities which employ translanguaging with English. Good practices such as 'mentor-texts' (García & Kleifgen, 2019), multilingual picture-books (Ibrahim, 2020) and drama techniques (role-play, *kamishibai*) are provided as examples to facilitate teachers to find ways to activate the students' whole linguistic repertoires and encourage plurilingual meaning-making, i.e., the conceptual and linguistic transfer across languages (Cummins, 2008). In this way, 'safe' spaces are constructed in the classroom, in which minoritized students 'linguistic and cultural identities are recognized and valorized.

In addition to translanguaging, the pedagogical potential of plurilingualism is explored through the perspective of English as a Multilingua Franca (Jenkins, 2015). In this perspective, focus is on the learners' pluralistic meaning-making potential, which is placed at the centre of language education. This stands in opposition to a perspective that prioritises the English language as such. Rather, English is understood as a "contact language of choice", which is potentially available but not necessarily chosen and used (Jenkins, 2015, p. 73). In other words, English is "always in the mix" (Jenkins, 2015), along with other languages that are present in the linguistic ecology, including those that are invisible. Pedagogically, it is approached as a bridge, i.e., as a linguistic resource for linking diverse linguistic codes and cultural resources that are present in the school, family and social context. In other words, English is used as a resource to support multilingual communication and translanguaging, drawing on all semiotic resources the children have at their disposal.

At the same time, creative activities that use English as a means for linguistic and cultural inclusion are employed to develop multilingual and intercultural awareness. To illustrate, drawing on examples from the program content, below are extracts from thePowerPoint presentations for the course material (Figures 3, 4, and 5):

Figure 3. Examples of translanguaging

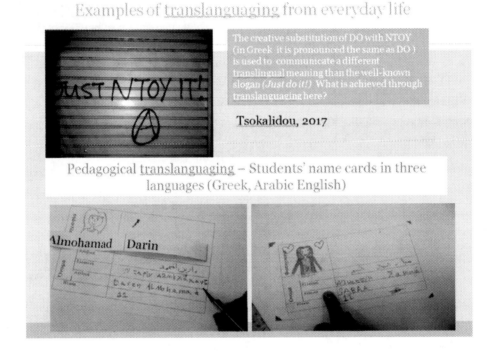

"English in the Kindergarten: Towards Multilingual Education"

Figure 4. Sample identity texts of children with a migrant background in Greece

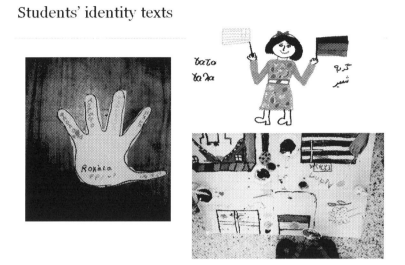

Figure 5. Sample language portraits

Art-based Learning and Creativity

Consistent with the principles of good practice, our program endeavors to help teachers introduce English into the preschool classroom through creative, experiential, and art-based learning activities. This is expected to help pre-school students develop multilingual and cultural awareness and provide a "safe" space to experience diversity and translanguaging (Donley, 2022). Creative activities promote an inclusive and open learning environment that emphasizes the importance and value of linguistic and cultural diversity. These activities are designed with an interdisciplinary perspective to integrate into the preschool curriculum agreeably. By utilizing pedagogical translanguaging, the creative, multilingual activities allow children to encounter, explore, and experiment playfully with English, Greek (the school language), and students' home languages or language varieties. In this way, they contribute to an inclusive ethos that emphasizes the significance and value of linguistic and cultural diversity (Faltis, 2019; Gonzales, 2019).

Music, singing, Drama in Education Techniques, puppetry, Dialogical Drama with Puppets, Animating Objects, Visual Arts, and other creative arts can make English learning more enjoyable and interesting for young learners and encourage pre-school students to communicate during multilingual activities (Al-Jubeh & Vitsou, 2021; Chukueggu, 2012). Art functions as a symbolic system, a second language system, without the fear of academic performance (Krashen, 1998). As a result, communication becomes feasible and straightforward. Through the arts, young learners can express their voices, develop multicultural awareness, take pride in their heritage, and recognize, respond to, and participate in the world at large (De Jesus, 2016; Schröter & Molander Danielsson, 2016; Robinson, 1997).

Especially Drama in Education and puppet theatre have a multimodal dimension in language learning, which has been highlighted by many researchers (Ntelioglou, 2011; Jewitt & Kress, 2008; Kalantzis & Cope, 2008). The acquisition of new knowledge is "unconsciously" constructed through experimental activities and animation. In such a context, students express themselves freely, without the stress of performance, and as a result, the emotional effect filter is reduced (Nicholson, 2009; Vitsou et al., 2020). In addition, puppetry connects children's experiences through language (Cummins, 2005) and helps children to explore the sounds of the language, grammar, and vocabulary through various exercises and communicative events. Students can categorize, explain, ask, analyze, interpret, evaluate a spoken message, and express their experiences through puppets. Furthermore, via drama and puppet activities, the multilingual-plurilingual and pluricultural identities of the students are highlighted, who, interacting on multiple levels, "recognize" themselves and others, overcoming linguistic and cultural borders (Ntelioglou, 2011; Vitsou et al., 2020).

Puppets in the kindergarten (Peyton, 2002) function as a communicative source of economy, which is particularly useful for the teacher and the students. The language children use with the puppets, the perceptions they form and the subsequent interaction results in increased vocabulary, improved communication skills and an increased understanding of the stories. During the play with puppets, the child develops verbal and non-verbal communication, uses new words, and forms sentences and dialogues (Biegler, 2003; Bredikyte, 2002, Zuljevic, 2007). A puppet can translanguage, speak foreign languages, linguistic varieties, dialects or slang, and discover words and expressions for specific communicative needs. The children may not understand all the language used but they will decode the meaning through non-verbal communication (Koshiro, 1990; Maharani, 2016; Remel & Tzuriel, 2015; Sörenson, 2008).

Figure 6. Creative activities, Arts-Based Approach and the Experiential Approach: Kamishibai

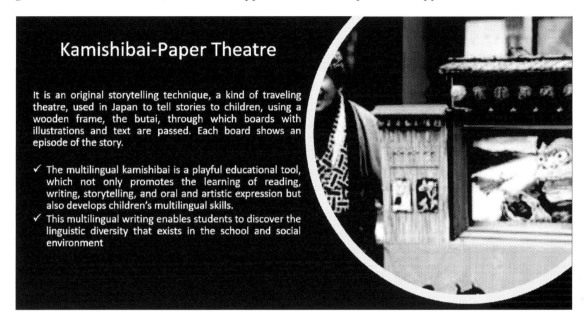

Kamishibai (which is illustrated in Figure 6) is an example of a theatre-based technique to which the participant teachers were introduced and familiarised with. It is considered to be an important tool for multilingual awareness and a gateway to languages through the arts. While creating and performing a multilingual *kamishibai,* it can expose children to linguistic diversity, including home languages and languages learned and spoken at school. The focus is on how a text can be performed theatrically and it involves the participation and interaction of children as active protagonists in the process (Marqués Ibáñez, 2017). Dialogical Drama with Puppets is based on the same rationale: the development of artistic interpretation, the potential value of a text when performed theatrically facilitates children's awareness of multiculturalism and multilingualism. Participants are introduced to these techniques and are encouraged to create activities that include elements of creativity and art-based learning, as well as to discuss and reflect on them in forum discussions (Bredikyte, 2000).

Collaboration and Co-teaching

Within the program, participants are exposed to various co-teaching models and are given numerous opportunities to discuss and reflect on classroom collaboration, with an emphasis on issues such as equal communication, power dynamics between teachers, cultural and other gaps, flexibility, lesson preparation (Schwarz & Gorgatt, 2018). Fostering a collaborative culture among teachers is a fundamental principle of the program, which is informed theoretically by the concept of nonviolent communication (Bourdieu, 1999), thus building on the knowledge, skills, and attitudes required to form relationships based on trust, active listening, a willingness to learn from the other rather than only to teach, and empathy (Gort & Pontier, 2013; Palviainenet al., 2016).

Commonly in most dual language bilingual kindergartens two teachers co-teach programs, with each teacher primarily responsible for instruction in his or her designated language (Palviainen et al., 2016). In this program, collaboration among preschool and English language teachers is crucial for various reasons, including the well documented, in research, challenges in co-teaching and international teacher cooperation (Arkoudis, 2006; Gort & Pontier, 2013; Park, 2014). The English language needs to be included in an integrated manner into the curriculum so that it is not approaches as a separate school subject. Thus, teachers are required to collaborate and teach together, with the organization of kindergarten instruction based on the children's needs, interests, and strengths as a starting point (Friend, 2008; Gately & Hammer, 2005; Hersiet al., 2016).

A successful cooperative teaching model requires effective communication between teachers, the availability of time to prepare and evaluate co-teaching, and the adequate training of teachers for the implementation of the kindergarten curriculum, as well as the provision of logistical resources, and administrative support. Hence, cooperating teachers have full responsibility and mutually contribute to the design and evaluation of instruction, the assessment of the learning progress of all students and use a wide range of teaching approaches (Palviainen et al., 2016; Schwartz & Asli, 2014; Schwartz et al., 2016). As illustrated in Figure 7, the program encourages participants to actively engage teachers in reflective activities and forum discussions concerning collaboration and co-teaching. They are also guided to find meaningful and equal encounters that build on team spirit and collaborative learning/ learning while supporting parent involvement and home-school partnerships.

Figure 7. Sample module content regarding collaboration and co-teaching

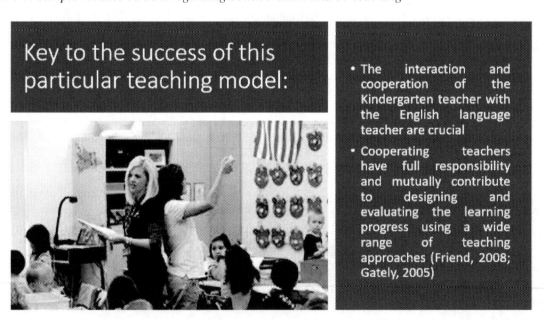

EXAMPLES OF LEARNING OUTCOMES

This section discusses the learning trajectories of the program participants, noting a gradual progression towards increased theoretical competence and readiness to deploy teaching methods that foster plurilingualism. Their progress is illustrated with reference to three forms of input: extracts from forum discussions, a sample lesson planning activity, and extracts from the teachers' output.

Teachers' Theory Construction in Forum Discussions

Drawing on the teachers' learning outcomes through their engagement with the program content and activities, their reflections and interaction in the forum discussions show their progressive awareness and readiness to deal with diversity and multilingualism in class. Extract 1, below, shows a post by one of the participating (English language) teachers. The activity rubric, which prompted these reflections, asked participants to first engage with a corpus of theoretical input (presentations, articles, and multimodal material) about multilingual and plurilingual teaching approaches and encouraged them to connect this input with practices that were already part of their teaching repertoire, and used in their classes or with practices that they planned to incorporate in their teaching in the future.

Extract 1

All the practices presented in the material in this module were really valuable and I found them interesting. I was most impressed by the language portraits, the mapping of languages, parental involvement, and the use of school signs about the different parts of the school in all children's languages. Unfortunately, I have not implemented many of these practices, up to now. However, with my primary school students I often follow techniques that involve both languages (Greek and English), but not other languages. Such practices are, for example, discussing the similarities and differences of words in both languages, comparing the two countries (in terms of customs, school life, types of housing, weather, etc.), the utilization and transfer of information from one language to another (oral and written language), etc. I hope that in the future I will be able to integrate the learning of the English language into a learning environment that is, more and more effectively, multilingual and multicultural.

Another participant, who is a kindergarten teacher, responded to the same prompt by noting the relevance of the practices that had been presented when it came to teaching in her linguistically/culturally diverse classes (Extract 2):

Extract 2

In the kindergarten where I teach, a quarter of the student population is of Albanian origin, and we often use bilingual literature texts and some words within programs concerning diversity and inclusion. However, after such a thorough presentation, we now have many, properly structured good practices to implement. How to implement techniques such as translanguaging, language portraits and of course the effective involvement of the parents. In all these activities, the English language will be introduced as a bridge language.

The teachers' growing awareness of linguistic and cultural diversity in class and of ways to approach it is shown by including the English language as well while recognising the significance of home languages which function in contact and interaction with the languages the children learn and are socialized into the school context.

Growing skills, Confidence and Fostering Collaboration

The sixth week of the program marked the conclusion of participants engagement with the theoretical input, and a shift towards the teaching practice and more activities that encouraged active experimentation with their new knowledge and developing skills. This was the time when they were required to collaboratively design language development activities that could be implemented in a kindergarten context applying multilingual, inclusive, creative approaches. For instance, they were asked in an assignment rubric to develop an activity collaboratively with a colleague so as to bring students in contact with another language and to record their thoughts in a 'planning document'. Thus, they were provided with a 'planning document' including reflection and planning prompts as well as space for recording answers which were later compared and discussed by the whole group of participants. These prompts are listed in Extract 3:

Extract 3

1. Objective: What do you want children to learn / be able to do?
2. Planning: What should you prepare before the lesson?
3. Planning: What kind of classroom layout do you need?
4. Implementation: What will the language teacher do during the activity?
5. Implementation: What will the early education specialist do during the activity?
6. Implementation: What will the children do during the activity?
7. Evaluation: How will you know how well the activity went?
8. Language: What words and phrases you will use to organize the class?
9. Language: What words and phrases will you use when giving instructions?
10. Language: What words and phrases will you use during the actual activity?
11. Anticipated challenges: What might go wrong?
12. Anticipated challenges: How will I deal with this?
13. Linguistic Capital: How will I maximize the use of all the students' linguistic capital?

There are a number of noteworthy points in this activity. Firstly, even though it was expected that most participants would be in contexts were English was taught, a conscious effort was made to use language that did not privilege English hegemony. Their language choice (typically English) was also used as a discussion prompt when sharing feedback on the activity. Additionally, participants were encouraged to reflect on their language choices starting during the planning stage. This was intended to disrupt the normative and contingent ways of using language in class (Stelma & Kostoulas, 2021), such as the spontaneous and/or unplanned tendency to resort to Modern Greek for giving instructions, provide encouragement and deal with disruptions. This was an aspect of the activity that revealed that participants were still struggling with grasping the role of plurilingualism, as many decided to give instructions in English only, even if these were cognitively and linguistically challenging for very young learners (e.g., "*Please use your pencil and crayons and write the seasons and then color the pictures*"). Such examples, and appropriate feedback, helped to raise the participants attention to the normative influence of "English-only" practices often encountered in ELT (Kerr, 2012).

A further way to encourage language diversity was to deliberately plan ways to engage the entire range of the young learners' linguistic resources (see prompt 13, above). The participants' responses to this prompt showed that they were beginning to develop confidence in integrating languages other than Modern Greek and English in their lessons using English as a prompt (e.g., Extract 4).

Extract 4

"English in the Kindergarten: Towards Multilingual Education"

Some children in class [...] could take on a 'teacher' role and ask questions in either [Modern] Greek or English and then the other children might respond in any of the languages they know...

Extract 4 is a good example of how some participants were beginning to visualize the role of languages as 'bridges' and the ways in which meaning can be constructed in short translanguaging exchanges. At this stage, of course, this was still a skill that was being developed: in some cases, participants responded to this prompt by suggesting that they would ask learners about their home countries, or aspects of their culture that were relevant to the lesson –learning activities that were doubtless important in fostering an ethos of acceptance and tolerance, but maybe less consistent with the linguistic aims of this particular activity.

Another point of note is that a deliberate attempt was made to encourage cross-disciplinary collaboration. This was done by designing the activity in ways that required language teachers and early childhood specialists to draw on each other's different sets of skills. For one, participants were grouped in pairs that had different disciplinary backgrounds in order to engage with the activities. Prompt 1, where participants had to specify only one objective was intended to encourage negotiation between the language and early education specialists, and —ideally— lead to aims that integrated input from the national early education curriculum and the language curriculum. An example of such an objective, from one of the assignments, was the following: "*They* [i.e., the young learners] *will learn how to express quantity, from 1 to 5, in Greek and English (numeracy and language)*".

Moreover, the planning document was designed to encourage reflection on many different formats of class collaboration (prompts 4–6). Some examples from the teachers output are presented in Extracts 5and 6, below:

Extract 5

The early education specialist will speak to the children about fruit and colors.

The language teacher will be on his/her side, and will say one-word names for the corresponding fruit and color.

Extract 6

She/he [i.e., the early language specialist] will participate offering assistance to the students and reinforcing students' attention.

She/he [i.e., the language teacher] is going to have the main role of teaching and conducting the activity, interacting with the students and helping them to fully understand the key vocabulary and phrases inferred through the activity, as well as what she/he wants them to do, using gestures, body movement and the pre-prepared material. The English teacher is going to use the CLIL method and TPRin order to fully engage the students as role models asking and answering questions, in the culture of the L2.

In Extract 5, the language specialist is charged with providing linguistic input following the lead of the early education specialist, who will be delivering a content-driven session. In Extract 6, it is the language teacher who has the lead in implementing the activity, with the early language specialist relegated to a role of assisting with language management. These examples illustrate that the participants were beginning to experiment with ways of cooperation, even though the full integration of their lessons had not yet been attained.

The activities that the participants designed in response to this task, set in the middle of the program, provide us with interesting insights into how their pedagogical thinking was developing throughout the program. Using an appropriately scaffolded task, they were beginning to challenge monolingual norms, experiment with linguistic creativity, and explore ways to work together. As seen in the extracts above, their thoughts illustrate ongoing processes, which would eventually lead to more mature thinking, as seen in the following section.

CONCLUSION

The final essay, which the participants were required to submit at the completion of the program, signalled the end of participants' engagement with theoretical input and a shift toward a practicum phase that encouraged active experimentation with their new knowledge and developing skills. Drawing from the content of their final essays, participants seemed able to collaboratively design a series of educational scenarios, which holistically incorporated creative and multimodal activities and fostered multilingual meaning-making among pre-school children. In terms of the linguistic objectives, the participants were able to respond to the challenges associated with plurilingual and pluricultural kindergarten classes, using English as 'a bridge language' connecting and encouraging the use of the children's entire linguistic repertoires. Accordingly, they extended those repertoires, by embracing linguistic and cultural diversity in class, making thus use of their linguistic and cultural resources cross-linguistically, critically, and creatively.

The learning trajectories of the program participants can attest to the fact that supporting multilingualism and using the linguistic and cultural capital of children through English can empower teachers to move towards more open and inclusive ideological stances, beliefs, and practices. This does not suggest that the program's implementation was free of challenges or uniformly unproblematic. For instance, getting the participants to collaborate in designing activities for the course assignments required additional time for the organization of team-work and effort to overcome communication difficulties. Other challenges included finding the time to meet the courses' requirements and completing its activities on the part of the teachers as well as maintaining a consistent contact among them and the course's platform. However, their openness to embrace linguistic diversity in class, challenging the hegemony of Greek and English in the Greek school was progressively developed throughout the program. In the participants' output, there is strong evidence about their positive responses and progressive readiness to leverage multilingualism in class. Doing so addresses needs that have been empirically identified in Greece and elsewhere regarding the students' individual linguistic repertoires, their families' aspirations, and language policy more broadly (Gkaintartzi et al., 2019; Duarte & Günther, 2022; Pulinx& Van Avermaet, 2014). Such learning outcomes seem particularly important when viewing early childhood education in context. While a longitudinal analysis of impact is not in the scope of this chapter, it can reasonably be assumed that awareness of linguistic diversity, the empowerment of students' linguistic repertoires and the development of positive attitudes towards plurilingualism are assets for language education in later years.

The importance of familiarizing teachers with the concepts of creative and experiential learning and their appropriate application in English-language activities was also shown throughout their participation in the program as they were actively engaged in activities which were art-based and employed creativity.

"English in the Kindergarten: Towards Multilingual Education"

Feedback from participants, who stressed their appreciation for the "sharing" culture of the program, the dynamics of 'equal communication' and the opportunities for critical reflection, also suggest the value of supporting teachers in collaboration and co-teaching. Collaborative, appropriate and targeted continuing professional development that engages teachers in active co-learning, discussion and reflection, as well as a wide range of input, can foster their methodological and pedagogical readiness. To borrow the words of one graduating participant teacher, such programs can become 'journeys' in 'knowledge and experience': *"Completing this program, I take with me tools for approaching multilingual education in preschool education and cooperative methods to reinforce the English language in the kindergarten. I started this journey with curiosity and its "end" gave me knowledge and experience".*

REFERENCES

Al-Jubeh, D., & Vitsou, M. (2021). Empowering refugee children with the use of Persona Doll. *International Journal of Progressive Education*, 2(17), 210–227. Advance online publication. doi:10.29329/ijpe.2021.332.13

Arkoudis, S. (2006). Negotiating the rough ground between ESL and mainstream teachers. *International Journal of Bilingual Education and Bilingualism,* 9(4), 415-433. doi:10.2167/beb337.0

Beacco, J.-C., Byram, M., Cavalli, M., Coste, D., Cuenat, M. E., Goullier, F., & Panthier, J. (2016). *Guide for the development and implementation of curricula for plurilingual and intercultural education*. Council of Europe.

Biegler, L. (2003). *Implementing dramatization as an effective storytelling method to increase comprehension*. ERIC Database. http://www.eric.ed.gov

Bland, J. (Ed.). (2015). *Teaching English to young learners: Critical issues in language teaching with 3-12 year-olds*. Bloomsbury.

Bourdieu, P. (1999). Understanding. In P. Bourdieu & G. Balazs (Eds.), *The weight of the world: Social suffering in contemporary society* (pp. 607–626). Stanford University Press.

Bredikyte, M. (2002). Dialogical Drama with puppets (DDP) as a method of fostering children's verbal activity. In E. Majaron & L. Kroflin (Eds.), *The Puppet-What a Miracle!* (pp. 33–60). The UNIMA, Puppets in Education Commission.

Busch, B. (2012). The linguistic repertoire revisited. *Applied Linguistics*, 33(5), 503–523. doi:10.1093/applin/ams056

Busch, B. (2018). The language portrait in multilingualism research: Theoretical and methodological considerations. *Working Papers in Urban Language and Literacies*, 236. King's College London.

Candelier, M. (2017) "Awakening to Languages" and educational language policy. InJ.Cenoz, D. Gorter, & S. May (Eds.),Language awareness and multilingualism: Encyclopedia of language and education (3rd ed.) Springer. doi:10.1007/978-3-319-02240-6_12

Cenoz, J. (2019). Translanguaging pedagogies and English as a lingua franca. *Language Teaching*, 52(1), 71–85. doi:10.1017/S0261444817000246

Cenoz, J. &Gorter, D. (2011). Focus on multilingualism: A study of trilingual writing. *The Modern Language Journal, 95*, 356-369. doi:10.1111/j.1540-4781.2011.01206.x

Cenoz, J., & Gorter, D. (2015). Towards a holistic approach in the study of multilingual education. In J. Cenoz & D. Gorter (Eds.), *Multilingual education: Between language learning and translanguaging* (pp. 1–15). Cambridge University Press. doi:10.1017/9781009024655.002

Cenoz, J., & Gorter, D. (2020). Teaching English through pedagogical translanguaging. *World Englishes, 39*(2), 300–311. doi:10.1111/weng.12462

Chukueggu, C. O. C. (2012). The use of drama and dramatic activities in English language teaching. *The Crab: Journal of Theatre and Media Arts, 1*, 151–150.

Chumak-Horbatsch, R. (2012). *Linguistically appropriate practice: A guide for working with young immigrant children*. University of Toronto Press.

Chumak-Horbatsch, R. (2019). *Using linguistically appropriate practice: A guide for teaching in multilingual classrooms*. Multilingual Matters.

Conteh, J., & Meyer, G. (Eds.), *The multilingual turn in languages education. Opportunities and challenges*. Multilingual Matters.

Council of Europe. (2001). *Common European framework of reference for languages: Learning, teaching, assessment*. Cambridge University Press.

Cummins, J. (2005). Bilingual children's mother tongue: Why is it important for education? *Sprogforum, 19*, 15–20.

Cummins, J. (2008). Teaching for transfer: Challenging the two solitudesassumption inbilingual education. In N. H. Hornberger (Ed.), *Encyclopedia of Language and Education*. Springer. doi:10.1007/978-0-387-30424-3_116

Cummins, J. (2017). Teaching for transfer in multilingual school contexts. In O. García, A. Lin, & S. May (Eds.), *Bilingual education: Encyclopedia of language and education* (pp. 103–115). Springer.

Cummins, J. (2021). *Rethinking the education of multilingual learners: A critical analysis of theoretical concepts*. Multilingual Matters.

Cummins, J., & Early, M. (2011). *Identity texts: The collaborative creation of power in multilingual schools*. Trentham Books.

De Jesus, O. (2016). Integrating the arts to facilitate second language learning. *Open Online Journal for Research and Education, 5*, 1–4.

Donley, D. (2022). Translanguaging as a theory, pedagogy, and qualitative research methodology. *NABE Journal of Research and Practice*, 1–16. doi:10.1080/26390043.2022.2079391

Duarte, J., & Günther-van derMeij, M. (2022). 'Just accept each other,whiletherest of the world doesn't. Teachers' reflections on multilingual education. *Language and Education, 36*(5), 451–466. doi:10.108 0/09500782.2022.2098678

"English in the Kindergarten: Towards Multilingual Education"

Enever, J. (2004). Europeanisation or globalisation in early start EFL trends across Europe. In C. Gnutzmann & F. Intemann (Eds.), *Theglobalisation of English and the English language classroom* (pp. 177–191). Narr.

European Commission. (2011). *Europeanstrategic framework for education and training (ET2020). Language learning at pre-primary school level: Making it efficient and sustainable* (Commission Staff Working Paper). European Commission. https://ec.europa.eu/assets/eac/languages/policy/languagepolicy/documents/early-language-learning-handbook_en.pdf

Eurydice. (2017). *Eurydice Report: Key data on teaching languages at school in Europe.* Publications Office of the European Union.

Faltis, C. (2019). Arts-based pedagogy for teaching English learners. In L. C. Oliveira (Ed.), *The handbook of TESOL in K-12* (pp. 323–337). Wiley., doi:10.1002/9781119421702.ch21

Flores, N., & Rosa, J. (2015). Undoing appropriateness: Raciolinguistic ideologies and language diversity in education. *Harvard Educational Review, 85*(2), 149–171. doi:10.17763/0017-8055.85.2.149

Friend, M. (2008). Co-teaching: A simple solution that isn't that simple after all. *Journal of Curriculum and Instruction, 2*(2), 9-19.https:// doi:10.3776/joci.2008.v2n2p9-19

García, O. (2009). *Bilingual education in the 21st century: A global perspective.* Wiley-Blackwell.

García, O., & Flores, N. (2012). Multilingual pedagogies. In M. Martin-Jones, A. Blackledge, & A. Creese (Eds.), *The Routledge handbook of multilingualism* (pp. 232–246). Routledge.

García, O., & Kleifgen, J. A. (2019). Translanguaging and literacies. *Reading Research Quarterly, 55*(4), 553–571. doi:10.1002/rrq.286

García, O., & Wei, L. (2014). *Translanguaging: Language, bilingualism and education.* Palgrave Macmillan. doi:10.1057/9781137385765

Gately, S., & Hammer, C. (2005). An exploratory case study of the preparation of secondary teachers to meet special education needs in the general classroom. *Teacher Educator, 40*(4), 238–256. doi:10.1080/08878730509555364

Gkaintartzi, A., Mouti, A., Skourtou, E., & Tsokalidou, R. (2019). Language teachers' perceptions of multilingualism and language teaching: The case of the postgraduate programme "LRM". *Language Learning in Higher Education. Journal of the European Confederation of Language Centres in Higher Education (Cercles), 9*(1), 33–54. doi:10.1515/cercles-2019-0002

Gkaintartzi, A., & Tsokalidou, R. (2018). Is translanguaging a possibility in a language class?: Theoretical issues and applications in an EFL class. In V. Kourtis-Kazoullis, T. Aravossitas, E. Skourtou, & P. P. Trifonas (Eds.), *Interdisciplinary research approaches to multilingual education* (pp. 179–196). Routledge. doi:10.4324/9781351170086-15

Gkaintartzi, A., Vitsou, M., & Kostoulas, A. (2021). The design, implementation and evaluation of a teachers' training programme for English in the Kindergarten towards multilingual education. Paper presented at *ENRICH 2021, 1st International Conference on ELF Aware Practices for Multilingual-Classrooms.* Enrich.

Gogolin, I. (1997). The "monolingual habitus" as the common feature in teaching in the language of the majority in different countries. *Per Linguam, 13*(2), 38–49.

Gonzales, G. C. (2019). Review of *Art as a way of talking for emergent bilingual youth: A foundation for literacy in PreK-12 schools* by Berriz, B.R., Wager, A.C., and Poey, V.M. *Bilingual Research Journal, 42*(4), 513–516. doi:10.1080/15235882.2019.1686442

Gort, M., & Pontier, R. W. (2013). Exploring bilingual pedagogies in dual language preschool classrooms. *Language and Education, 27*(3), 223–245. doi:10.1080/09500782.2012.697468

Hersi, A., Horan, D., & Lewis, M. (2016). Redefining 'community' through collaboration and co-teaching: A case study of an ESOL specialist, a literacy specialist, and a fifth-grade teacher. *Teachers and Teaching, 22*(8), 927–946. doi:10.1080/13540602.2016.1200543

Ibrahim, N. (2020). The multilingual picturebook in English language teaching: Linguistic and cultural identity. *Children's Literature in English Language Education, 8*(2), 12–38.

Jenkins, J. (2015). Repositioning English and multilingualism in English as a lingua franca. *English in Practice, 2,* 49-85. doi:10.1515/eip-2015-0003

Jewitt, C., & Kress, G. R. (2008). *Multimodal literacy.* Peter Lang.

Kalantzis, M., & Cope, B. (2012). *Literacies.* Cambridge University Press. doi:10.1017/CBO9781139196581

Kerr, P. (2016). Questioning 'English-only' classrooms: Own-language use in ELT. In G. Hall (Ed.), *The Routledge handbook of English language teaching* (pp. 513–526). Routledge. doi:10.4324/9781315676203-43

Kirsch, C., Aleksić, G., Mortini, S., & Andersen, K. (2020). Developing multilingual practices in early childhood education through professional development in Luxembourg. *International Multilingual Research Journal, 14*(4), 319–337. doi:10.1080/19313152.2020.1730023

Koshiro, U. (1990). 'The Ordinary and the Extraordinary: Language and the Puppet Theatre. In L. R. Komniz & M. Levinson (Eds.), *The Language of the Puppet, Komninz.* The Pacific Puppetry Center Press.

Kostoulas, A. (2018). *A language school as a complex system: Complex systems theory in English language teaching.* PeterLang. doi:10.3726/b11892

Kostoulas, A. (2019). Repositioning language education theory. In A. Kostoulas (Ed.), *Challenging boundaries in language education* (pp. 33–50). Springer. doi:10.1007/978-3-030-17057-8_3

Kostoulas, A., & Stelma, J. (2017). Understanding curriculum change in an ELT school in Greece. *ELT Journal, 71*(3), 354–363. doi:10.1093/elt/ccw087

Krashen, S. (1998). Comprehensible output. *System, 26*(2), 175–182. doi:10.1016/S0346-251X(98)00002-5

Little, D., & Kirwan, D. (2019). *Engaging with linguistic diversity: A study of educational inclusion in an Irish primary school.* Bloomsbury Academic. doi:10.5040/9781350072053

Maharani, S. (2016). The use of puppet: Shifting speaking skill from the perspective of students' self-esteem. *Register Journal, 9*(2), 101–126. doi:10.18326/rgt.v9i2.170-186

Marqués Ibáñez, A. (2017). Kamishibai: An intangible cultural heritage of Japanese culture and its application in Infant Education. *Képzésésgyakorlat: Training and practice, 15*(1-2), 25-44.

May, S. (2014). *The multilingual turn: Implications for SLA, TESOL and bilingual education.* Routledge.

Melo-Pfeifer, S. (2015). Multilingual awareness and heritage language education: Children's multimodal representations of their multilingualism. *Language Awareness, 24*(3), 197–215. doi:10.1080/0965841 6.2015.1072208

Mishina, L., & Wallace, A. (2004). *Relations between the use of puppetry in the classroom, student attention and student involvement.* Brooklyn College.

Nicholson, H. (2005). *Applied drama: The gift of theatre.* Palgrave Macmillan. doi:10.1007/978-0-230-20469-0

Ntelioglou, B. Y. (2011). 'But why do I have to take this class?' The mandatory drama-ESL class and multiliteracies pedagogy. *Research in Drama Education, 16*(4), 595–615. doi:10.1080/13569783.201 1.617108

Palviainen, Å., Protassova, E., Mård-Miettinen, K., & Schwartz, M. (2016). Two languages in the air: A cross-cultural comparison of preschool teachers' reflections on their flexible bilingual practices. *International Journal of Bilingual Education and Bilingualism, 19*(6), 614–630. doi:10.1080/1367005 0.2016.1184615

Park, J.-E. (2014). English co-teaching and teacher collaboration: A microinteractional perspective. *System, 44*, 34–44. doi:10.1016/j.system.2014.02.003

Pennycook, A. (2007). The myth of English as an international language. In P. S. Makoni & A. Pennycook (Eds.), *Disinventing and reconstituting languages* (pp. 90–115). Channel View Publications.

Peyton, J. (2002). The use of puppet. *English Education Journal* (EEJ), 216-228. http://erepository.unsyiah.ac.id/EEJ

Pfenninger, S. E., & Singleton, D. (2017). *Beyond age effects in instructional L2 learning: Revisiting the age factor.* Multilingual Matters.

Phillipson, R. (1992). *Linguistic imperialism.* Oxford University Press.

Phillipson, R. (2009). *Linguistic imperialism continued.* Routledge.

Pulinx, R., & Van Avermaet, P. (2014). Linguistic diversity and education: dynamic interactions between language education policies and teachers' beliefs : a qualitative study in secondary schools in Flanders (Belgium). *Revue Francaisede LinguistiqueAppliquee, 19*(2), 9-27. doi:10.3917/rfla.192.0009

Remer, R., &Tzuriel, D. (2015). "I Teach Better with the Puppet" –Use of Puppet as a Mediating Tool in Kindergarten Education– an Evaluation. *American Journal of Educational Research, 3(*3), 356-365. doi:10.12691/education-3-3-15

Robinson, P. (1997). State-of-the-art: SLA research and language teaching. *The Language Teacher Online, 2*(7), 7–16.

Scheffler, P., &Domioska, A. (2018). Own-language use in teaching English to preschool children. *ELT Journal, 72*(4), 374-83. doi:10.1093/elt/ccy013

Schröter, T., &MolanderDanielsson, K. (2016). English for young learners in Sweden: Activities, materials and language use in the classroom. *Litteraturochspråk, 11*, 47–73.

Schwarz, M., & Gorgatt, N. (2018). "Fortunately, I found a home here that allows me personal expression": Co-teaching in the bilingual Hebrew-Arabic-speaking preschool in Israel. *Teaching and Teacher Education, 71*, 46–56. doi:10.1016/j.tate.2017.12.006

Seidlhofer, B. (2007). Common property: English as a lingua franca in Europe. In J. Cummins & C. Davison (Eds.), *International Handbook of English Language Teaching* (pp. 137–149). Springer. doi:10.1007/978-0-387-46301-8_11

Shaban, M. S., Wahed, A., & Ismail, A. (2013). Exploring the nature of cooperation between teachers usingEnglish and those using Arabic as the medium of instruction in teaching ofclasses in United Arab Emirates. *American International Journal of Contemporary Research, 3*(8), 25–37. doi:10.30845/aijcr

Skutnabb-Kangas, T. (2012). Linguistic human rights. In P. M. Tiersma & L. M. Solan (Eds.), *The Oxford handbook of language and law* (pp. 235–247). Oxford University Press. doi:10.1093/oxfordhb/9780199572120.013.0017

Soares, C. T., Duarte, J., & Günther-van der Meij, M. (2020). 'Red is the colour of the heart': Making young children's multilingualism visible through language portraits. *Language and Education, 35*(1), 22–41. doi:10.1080/09500782.2020.1833911

Sörenson, R. (2008). *Seeing dark things*. Oxford University Press. doi:10.1093/acprof:oso/9780195326574.001.0001

Vitsou, M., Papadopoulou, M., & Gana, E. (2020). Getting them back to class: A project to engage refugee children in school using drama pedagogy. *Scenario, 2*(2), 42–59. doi:10.33178cenario.14.2.3

Widdowson, H. G. (1994). The ownership of English. *TESOL Quarterly, 28*(2), 377–389. doi:10.2307/3587438

Widdowson, H. G. (2003). *Defining issues in English language teaching*. Oxford University Press. Stelma, J. & Kostoulas, A. (2021). *The intentional dynamics of TESOL*. De Gruyter. Stelma, J., & Fay, R. (2019). An ecological perspective for critical action in applied linguistics. In A. Kostoulas (Ed.), *Challenging boundaries in language education* (pp. 51–69). Springer.

Zuljevic, V. (2007). Puppetry *and language development in a first-grade library reading program: a case study*. [Doctoral dissertation, Washington State University]. ProQuest Dissertations and Thesis database. (UMI No. 3268779).

"English in the Kindergarten: Towards Multilingual Education"

KEY TERMS AND DEFINITIONS

A multilingual, inclusive teaching approach: The development of inclusive, multilingual learning environments, by making the students' home languages more visible in the class context, and by actively embracing and valuing linguistic diversity in language education. The focus is on 'multilingualizing' language teaching.

Plurilingual approaches: Approaches that facilitate interconnections between languages in class, by softening linguistic boundaries, aiming to develop a unitary plurilingual competence among learners.

English as a bridge-language: English is approached as a vehicle for multilingual and intercultural encounters in class, as a language that can act as a semiotic bridge to facilitate the contact and interplay among different linguistic and cultural resources (children's home languages, the school, foreign languages as well as 'invisibilised' ones).

Translanguaging: A theoretical concept and a pedagogical approach to integrate languages in teaching through a holistic approach, by encouraging transfer across languages and by bringing the students' linguistic repertoires and identities to the fore.

English as a 'Multilingua Franca': English is introduced as a language that can be used to make links to other languages, especially the children's home languages and minoritized ones in order to support multilingual communication and translanguaging in class, drawing on all linguistic, semiotic resources the children have at their disposal.

Art-based learning: Music, singing, drama in education techniques, puppetry, dialogical drama with puppets, animating objects, visual arts, and other creative arts that can make English learning more enjoyable and interesting for young learners and that students to express themselves creatively during multilingual activities.

Collaborative teaching*:* **This refers to co-teaching models and opportunities for teachers:** i.e. preschool and English language teachers, to jointly plan and implement activities in class thus building on the knowledge, skills, and attitudes required to form relationships based on trust, active listening, and a willingness to learn from each other.

Chapter 5
University and Primary Schools Co–Teaching Together:
Challenges Towards a CLIL Training Program

Cristina Manchado-Nieto
University of Extremadura, Spain

Gemma Delicado-Puerto
University of Extremadura, Spain

Laura Alonso-Díaz
University of Extremadura, Spain

ABSTRACT

Bilingual education is getting great achievements because of the performance of bilingual programs. In Spain, these programs have been developed at the university thanks to the efforts made during the previous decades of their implementation. The autonomous region of Extremadura has been working cooperatively with other institutions since then, and now it is time to look back to recapitulate what has been done and what needs to be done from now on. This chapter aims to gather the main milestones of this process in order to review its internal and external aspects, as well as to reconsider the ways of improving bilingual programs. Final remarks show that bilingual programs have brought benefits, but there are still some aspects that require attention, such as a homogeneous national regulation or minding the methodological qualification of bilingual teachers. These issues need to be addressed in future research for the welfare of bilingual education.

DOI: 10.4018/978-1-6684-6179-2.ch005

Copyright © 2023, IGI Global. Copying or distributing in print or electronic forms without written permission of IGI Global is prohibited.

INTRODUCTION

The sociodemographic scenario in Spain, Europe and the rest of the world has exponentially changed during the last decades due to a series of causes of different nature, and unfortunately most recently because of the Covid-19 pandemic. Add to this, the quick growing of globalization, the use of the English language as a lingua franca (Coleman, 2006; Lasagabaster, 2022), as well as the use of new technologies, make those global changes to be reflected on the educative systems (Barrett et al., 2014). That is the reason why teachers from today and tomorrow need to be trained on certain innovative and interdisciplinary characteristics in order to face the renewed, changing and equalitarian international context (Council of Europe, 2016). Nowadays, schools host a diverse students' profile (Aljure et al., 2014; Julius and Madrid, 2017), whether local or foreign students, and teachers must prepare them to be competent in any part of the world, following the UNESCO's 2014 guideline, as well as they also should be prepared for the after-Covid-19 world (Ramos et al., 2021).

Accordingly, the implementation of CLIL entails a whole revolution referring the way of teaching some non-linguistic subjects of primary and secondary education in Spain. CLIL philosophy, even with its lights and shades, gives response to this new universal outlook where students need to be trained not only on the linguistic dimension, but also on a cultural dimension (Nurutdinova & Bolotnikov, 2018) for a better adaptation to a globalized world. Such implementation represents a reference model to gradually increase the learning of languages (Lasagabaster et al., 2010), since pre-service teachers should be competent to work in the growing number of bilingual[1] schools (Romero-Alfaro & Zayas-Martínez, 2017).

The main learning objective through CLIL approach is to achieve that the students participate actively on their own learning by relating any content with their environment (Marsh, 2002). Therefore, it is essential to strengthen their cognitive development on their metacognitive skills as much as the skills for life. This way, students are prepared to implement what they learn in class into the real world (Coyle et al., 2010; Hu, 2019). Using English as a working language not only helps to improve the students' linguistic competence, but also educates them on the global competence (Deardorff, 2014), what will educate them to take part of international teams and to be able to adapt to those teams in their future professional life. But, above all, having this global competence and knowledge about the real world will make students be aware of their own culture, and this fact will contribute to a better conflict resolution and to live in the basis of equality and democracy. Besides, CLIL depicts a flexible model for universities (Zayas-Martínez & Estrada-Chichón) that might be adapted to any particular context of every region.

These are the reasons why every educator trained at a global scale should wonder whether teachers are well trained and in turn training their students in order to live and work on different changeable societies and cultures (Zabala & Arnau, 2007). Among the diverse ways to give answer to this question, the authors consider that a fundamental solution is bilingual education.

Nonetheless, speaking of language policies in Spain implies to tackle a complex situation because of how bilingual education is seen in the different autonomic communities; this is a matter that hinders establishing a homogeneous training in Spain as a whole. For instance, some autonomous communities began their bilingual programs in the scholar year of 2004-2005 while others, like Extremadura, waited until 2011-2012 so the public centers could hold their bilingual tracks[2] with public funding. The certified linguistic level of the teachers was also a matter of concern because some regions required a C1 level from the Common European Framework of References for Languages (CEFRL) while in other regions it was only necessary to certify a B2 level (Ortega, 2015).

The current situation regarding bilingual education implementation in Spain together with the miscellaneous perspective of the respective autonomous regions of the country to set up the diverse linguistic policies leads the authors to the objective of this work: to review the historical milestones of the linguistic policies in Spain and, more specifically within the autonomous regions of Extremadura.

BACKGROUND

The Role of the Educative Administration and the Linguistic Policies on the Teacher Training

The autonomous region of Extremadura began the bilingual path a few years later than the majority of the regions in Spain. Given to that difference, Extremadura could directly take other regions' experiences into consideration. The autonomic educative law of Extremadura was released in 2011: 4/2011 of 7th March (in Spanish, *Ley 4/2011, de 7 de marzo, de Educación de Extremadura*), where they already committed to fostering multilingualism in the region, boosting the teaching and learning of foreign languages. This idea materialized with the legal regulation of 8th April 2011, which regulates the call to implement bilingual tracks in Extremadura on an experimental basis, in compulsory levels supported by public funding (in Spanish, *ORDEN de 8 de abril de 2011, por la que se regula la convocatoria de secciones bilingües, con carácter experimental, en centros sostenidos con fondos públicos que impartan enseñanzas obligatorias en Exremadura). [ORDER of 8 April 2011, by which regulates the announcement of bilingual sections, with experimental character, in centres sustained with public funds that impart compulsory educations in Exremadura.]*

Despite the different years of implementation and the different regional laws in Spain, Extremadura followed analogous steps to those that other regions did. Such similarities happened because regions normally count on similar resources: the training support from the teachers and resources' centers (abbreviated CPR in Extremadura), the official schools of languages (abbreviated EEOOII in Extremadura), the availability for linguistic and methodological education, language assistants as teaching support, linguistic immersion programs, and European Erasmus+ programs.

It should be considered that the development of one of the key competences in the Spanish curricula, the linguistic communication competence, should not only tackle the acquisition of second languages; according to Trujillo & Rubio (2014), "solo a partir de una visión sistémica se pueden plantear soluciones globales al reto de la competencia comunicativa en el siglo XXI [only from a systemic vision can global solutions be proposed to the challenge of communicative competence in the XXI century] (p. 30). This has been broadly reviewed (Trujillo, 2010; Gómez, 2013; Romero, 2014; Romero & Trigo, 2015; Fábregat, 2016; Lorenzo, 2016; Pavón & Pérez, 2017), which led the corresponding regional governments to take decisions to propel innovation in the educative centers.

Teachers' Centers and Education Colleges

The teaching profession has never been an easy duty. Teachers have been asking and working historically for a quality improvement of the teachers' initial training and permanent training, followed by a greater requirement level on the future teachers' recruitment. According to Fang & Li (2018), "the quality of bilingual teachers is the key to the success of bilingual education" (p. 62). And the required qualification of a foreign language teacher has been an extensively discussed topic (Madrid & Trujillo, 2001). However, since Spain is immersed into educative policies oriented towards multilingualism, there are some difficulties that hinders the bilingual or multilingual programs from flourishing: education degrees with bi(multi)lingual tracks are not enough to properly train a bilingual teacher; plus, education degrees also require the faculty with a bilingual profile to be linguistically qualified, leaving aside the methodological qualification (Ortega, 2015; Madrid & Madrid, 2014).

This kind of difficulties are the reason why several universities started to offer bilingual degrees (one single group receiving training in two languages) or bilingual tracks (one monolingual group and one bilingual group with the same syllabus) to their academic courses. In particular, the education degrees with bilingual tracks are forging agreements, so that pre-service teachers in their initial training on bilingual education could develop their internship periods being supervised by in-service bilingual teachers.

Nevertheless, from the perspective of the authors, if there is not a coordination among the diverse processes of the initial and permanent teachers' training, further advancement will not be granted, since isolated and individual efforts from every agency (including involved teachers) will only unleash a progressive demotivation. Thus, the education institutions of Extremadura built bridges of cooperation together with other regions' institutions, such as the official teachers' center of Andalusia and Extremadura (called CEP and CPR, respectively). This cooperation is feasible starting from Decree 93/2013 of 27th August, which regulates the initial and permanent training of the teaching staff of the autonomous region of Andalusia (in Spanish, Decreto 93/2013, de 27 de agosto, por el que se regula la formación inicial y permanente del profesorado en la Comunidad Autónoma de Andalucía, así como el Sistema Andaluz de Formación Permanente del Profesorado), and the regulation of 25th November 2016, which approves the framework plan on permanent teacher training of the autonomous region of Extremadura (in Spanish, ORDEN de 25 de noviembre de 2016, por la que se aprueba el Plan Marco de Formación Permanente del Profesorado en al Comunidad Autónoma de Extremadura).

Teachers of the 21st century are expected to be qualified enough to properly use a foreign language and develop suitable methodological strategies of bilingual teaching. The internship period is an efficient way to close the gap between knowledge and application (Hu, 2019). To approach this target, one of the main procedures is establishing the internship period as a training activity in which both, ideas and experiences, will converge in order to provide strategies, materials and resources in a real educative context (Romero & Jiménez, 2014). Besides, facilitating the mutual collaboration is addressed by establishing an agreement between the two universities to create working groups composed of faculties, school teaching staff involved into the initial teacher training, and teacher training centers, if applicable.

Challenges and Deficiencies of Bilingual Teachers Training

After several years of implementation and a high-speedy growing of bilingual schools in Spain, society should ask itself where to address with the bilingual and multilingual training that our educative system offers. For that matter and taking into account the lack of a consensus for a national language policy, universities play a fundamental role in analysing the different programs through collaborative working teams. The essence of a working team is to be composed of members with profiles' diversity, like specialists from different autonomous communities, teachers, associate training centers, directive boards, and external experts. All of them should be in charge of settling the guidelines at a national level to seek the improvement of the 21st Century bilingual education.

In this regard, the Teacher Training College of the University of Extremadura (Cáceres, Spain) started to work on a project whose basis were established under the collaboration between different social agents: university administrators, faculty, the regional board of Education, the National Agency of Evaluation and a number of in-service bilingual teachers. The main perspective was to improve the training on bilingual education at both, a linguistic dimension and at a methodological dimension Delicado and Pavón, 2015; Delicado and Pavón, 2016; Alonso et al., 2017, Delicado et al. 2022, Estrada-Chichón & Zayas-Martínez, 2022). This project counted on the regional and national government from the beginning, and it studied the viability of implementing a bilingual track for the primary education degree of the Teacher Training College. The working group for the linguistic and methodological extension also involved international and national experts that assessed and validated the design and the implementation of the degree.

Such a heterogeneous group analysed from different perspectives which were the crossroads between the educative system, from the childhood education until the university, where strengthens and weaknesses of the future bilingual teachers' training were studied, paying special attention to weaknesses. In 2015, after receiving the approval by the quality Spanish agency (ANECA), the bilingual track of the primary education degree at the Teacher Training College got started with a piloting course year.

Therefore, in 2015 a group of 7 primary schoolteachers that were already part of the working group, offered a 15-hour workshop spread all along the different subjects of the first course of the primary education degree. As aforementioned, this first course was considered as a pilot trial.

At the end of the first course, the corresponding results of the whole year were comprehensively analysed and, due to the successful performance, the final decision was to open a new call for the academic year 2016-2017, which received the application (and consequent acceptance) of 30 primary schoolteachers from all around the region of Extremadura, who delivered a total of 20 workshops to university students of the first and second year of the primary education degree. This second-year working dynamics differed a bit from the first year: owing to the raising number of teachers' applications to collaborate with the bilingual program, it was necessary to widen the workshops' offer, so the teachers were asked to deliver a speech of about 2 hours every semester about their field of specialization. The results assessment showed the deeply positive response from every group involved: students, schoolteachers, faculty and janitorial services. That is why the Teacher Training College launched a new call in 2017-2018 in collaboration with the government of Extremadura, where 30 schoolteachers participated.

Nowadays, this collaboration between the regional government of Extremadura and the University of Extremadura is so fruitful that an agreement was signed to establish an official methodological training of 50 hours. The program is delivered by 12 primary and nursery school bilingual teachers and developed annually during the second semester since 2018-2019.

PROJECT PROCEDURE AT THE UNIVERSITY OF EXTREMADURA

Training Global Teachers: Practical Cases

The relationship existing between the education sciences colleges and departments and the educative system is ancestral, because the curricular contents delivered within these entities have a clear professionalizing nature, where the pre-service teachers should pass a number of practical academic credits to obtain the degree certificate. This practical training would not be conceivable without the invaluable collaboration of the primary school centers, which host a large number of pre-service teachers within the annual internship framework.

Nevertheless, there was a noticeable fragile point in this whole process, being that the collaboration of schoolteachers also happened into university subjects, but with a very occasional frequency and because of the willingness and positive intention of the subject's responsible teacher at the university. In other words: it did not exist a specific way nor an effective coordination procedure among courses and working areas.

That is why the intention of this innovation project is to give voice to the true and principal agents of the bilingualism and multilingualism in the primary education schools in Spain: the primary schoolteachers, and also offering them a valuable place by taking part of the early training of the future teachers.

The innovation project is an existing educational reality, since the official document of the bilingual track for the primary education degree (entitled Verifica) validated by ANECA contemplates the option of letting the schoolteachers to participate in such kind of activities at the university. In this context, teachers are allowed to participate in a tangential manner, so they can bring transversal topics to light and expose them, even if these topics are not necessarily related to bilingualism, but to side-related topics, like the role and perception of families whose children are involved in a bilingual track or bilingual center.

This innovation project enabled an offer of 20 workshops to be released in the academic year of 2016-2017. In order to accomplish this step, the whole working group (schoolteachers, faculty, technical staff from the government of Extremadura, and external experts) came to an agreement during a set of meetings, so the workshops could be effective along the first and second semester of that academic year. The methodological procedure to carry out this project consisted of a set of workshops delivered by schoolteachers, who were asked to talk about the topic they were specialists. Once the proposal was elaborated, the working group did a pairing task to match every workshop with the most suitable subject of the syllabus of the primary education degree from the University of Extremadura.

Finally, nine out of the ten subjects from the first year of the syllabus degree were subjected to let the schoolteachers participate; there were also some board team members from schools and one teacher's trade union member. The ultimate pairing and distribution was the following (Table 1):

Table 1. Schoolteachers and university subjects pairing to deploy workshops in 2016-2017

Subject	Workshop title	Schoolteacher collaborator	Topic
Theoretical, Historical and Political Bases of Education	Bilingual miscellany	A board team member of a bilingual center	Bilingual center management, families relationships, and bilingualism light and shadows
Sociology of Education	Labor market	A teacher's trade union member	Entering the labor market related to bilingualism
Sociology of Gender Relations and Family	School-related relationships	A bilingual schoolteacher	Relationships among children of different sex and gender
School Organization	Bilingual tracks genesis	The Head of a bilingual center	Origins of the bilingual tracks in Extremadura
Tutorship and Family Education	Families facing bilingual education	Two bilingual schoolteachers	CLIL guidance for parents
Didactic and Research Technology Resources	ICTs in bilingual centers	ICT advisor and teacher of a bilingual center	eScholarium platform, blogs, webquests, authoring tools, digital board and CLIL resources
Psycho-educational attention to diversity and school coexistence	Functional diversity in bilingual centers	Bilingual schoolteacher	Special educational needs students in bilingual tracks, not adapted curriculum, and training and funding needs on material and human resources
General Didactics	Didactic materials and European projects	Bilingual schoolteacher	Material development to adapt curricular contents. European projects presentation and their didactic use
Psychology of Education	Motivation to face the challenge of bilingual education	Bilingual schoolteacher	Students motivation strategies inside the classroom

Source: Own elaboration.

Professionalizing the Degrees Under a Global Horizon

Considering the abovementioned theoretical framework, in a globalized society constantly adapting to new trends and requirements, more and more intercultural and blurred borders, communication becomes an essential tool to accomplish versatile teachers profile needed by the current labour market.

Besides, the way that teachers handle this task must be considered into the permanent training paradigm, or lifelong learning paradigm, what means that professionals do not end their training once they conclude their academic training, but they are immerse in a permanent training process that will last a life. Continuous training makes real sense when speaking of lifelong learning concept, to which citizens have the right to get access (García-Ruiz & Castro, 2012). This basic assumption applies also for a permanent changing, a renewable criterion, a teacher's reconversion, and a series of wide measures that necessarily addresses to adaptation, renovation and quality that foster the educative community to be willing and ready to keep learning (Bolívar, 2012; González and Cutanda, 2017). This is the way to propel opportunities that give response to knowledge and information society (Imbernón, 2007; Imbernón and Colén, 2015).

In a post pandemic world, it is crucial that universities adapt to a rapidly evolving world. In this challenging context, the learning of languages and cultures are extremely important. Although universities are developing a solid way to internationalization, it is important to get teachers prepared for that, and there is still much to be done in this respect. Specially, for this reason, some years ago universities began to offer bilingual training programs for future teachers, but not without complications. The current rhythm was achieved getting started from the following initial approach: Should the non-bilingual primary schoolteachers be equally trained as the bilingual primary schoolteachers? Initially, the group considered that both tracks, bilingual and non-bilingual, should share the same curriculum. Nevertheless, the bilingual track should have language and methodological domain and fluency. Thus, the group started to work from these two ideas.

Bilingual education teachers not only should work on linguistic competences, but also on methodological competences, and all that requires time, engagement, motivation and collaboration (Doiz et al., 2019). Therefore, universities should offer students a comprehensive and enabling training where the trainees develop specific competences to work in this kind of programs. And in order to achieve that goal, education departments and colleges should get closer to the schools. The case of the University of Extremadura and its innovative training for students and faculty could serve as a reference, not only because of its bilingual syllabus and side activities, but also because of the close collaboration among official entities and educators of all academic levels to co-teach together.

The Bilingual Practicum as a Professionalizing Tool

The syllabus of the primary education degree represents a qualifying opportunity to train future teachers, but there is one subject that is especially interesting and relevant regarding the education of a future bilingual teacher: the Practicum or annual internship. Such Practicum subject consists of 480 hours divided into two periods (2nd and 4th year, respectively) of 240 hours each, where pre-service teachers attend schools as a regular staff member, but without forgetting their role of traineeships. During these two periods pre-service teachers are allowed to become observers and assistants in the classroom, and even they can assume teaching responsibilities if they receive the proper consent of their school mentors.

According to the authors, the Practicum is the most important subject from the whole syllabus of the primary education degree to train the future bilingual teachers. The set of systematized activities in which there is a collaboration between the schools and the university is where its essence lies. The main objective of the Practicum is putting the students into real contexts so they can have professional contact with the teaching reality in which they will subsequently develop their work.

It is about having a teachers' training reference, because it nurtures the use of hybrid spaces in training programs that gathers both, schoolteachers and faculty (Zeichner, 2010). The transcendence of combining academic knowledge and practical experiences for the future teachers shows that their development is carefully planned. Thus, the authors stand that the Practicum is a subject whose main distinguishing marks are the distribution of hours along the degree, the possibility of having feedback from the schoolteacher mentor and from the faculty supervisor, and the organizational viability.

Starting from the idea that Zabala (2011) stated: the universities that have a great collaborating centers network are those that will be able to offer a better Practicum. Accordingly, to develop an effective Practicum for the students of the primary education degree bilingual track, the university community should count on those centers that offer bilingual training, so that is the way to establish a network of collaborating centers within the framework of the bilingual and multilingual education.

Having the possibility of receiving practical training with schoolteachers that deliver bilingual teaching at their schools offers a global perspective and, at the same time, a local, specialized position for the pre-service bilingual teachers. Thanks to the Practicum subject, pre-service teachers can get closer to the professional reality and acquire initial knowledge by means of observation and actual participation in the real school context where they will be taking part. In addition, the theoretical aspects of the professional competences that pre-service teachers study at the university will be represented in their ability to deploy them in real context's specific situations. This ability will show their professionality and skills to reflect about their own practice as well as their school mentor and university supervisor (Díaz & Cuevas, 2015; Villa & Poblete, 2004). The Practicum also allows the pre-service teachers getting started in the use of didactic methodologies and strategies, since they can experience their abilities through controlled and observed realities.

Performing the practical part of the bilingual track of the degree requires that specialized professionals are responsible of the pre-service teacher by mentoring them at university level as much as a school level. This way, the pre-service teacher should count on the support and guidance of the university professorship that need to be aware of the bilingual reality of the school, so they are able to offer a precise coaching. This collaboration amongst all the actors involved would serve to smooth the perennial trouble of having a lack of connection among the teacher training offered at the university, the subject of the corresponding syllabus and the practical experiences of the school (Zeichner, 2010).

There is a series of special moments in which having the support of the university supervisor is meant to be fundamental:

1. At the beginning of Practicum: Before arriving at the school, the university supervisor informs and guides the pre-service teachers about what their role should be as internship students, and about what particularities they may find at their bilingual schools.
2. When the Practicum is in progress: All actors should keep in contact so that the supervisor observes if the pre-service teachers are well adapted and integrated to their schools, so they can be observed and assessed.
3. Specific problem-solving: The supervisor accompanies the pre-service teachers also when they require specific counseling, for instance, when they have difficulties to couple their school mentor, to carry out certain specific activities at their school, to solve questions while emerging situation comes, etc.

Therefore, the authors wonder what teaching competences a Practicum from a bilingual track in the primary education degree should consider. Taking into account the previous exposition, the authors believe that the competences to be developed in a bilingual track should be just similar to those developed in non-bilingual realities, although some of them should be specially reinforced, like the following ones:

*   To expose ideas, problems and solutions publicly, in a logic, structured manner, both, orally and in writing, in either language of study.
*   To reflect about the internship period, and about their class in order to innovate and improve the teaching practice by integrating bilingual methodologies.
*   To acquire practical knowledge about their schools and bilingual classes, and get to know how they are managed.
*   To learn the ways of collaborating with the different sectors of the educative community as well as the social surroundings of the school and the bilingual track or center itself.

Developing these competences in a suitable way requires a specific training with an intercultural perspective.

Particularly, and accordingly to the abovementioned, pre-service teachers that study at the Teacher Training College of the University of Extremadura must attend the Practicum as a compulsory subject. The Practicum is distributed into two parts: Practicum I take place at the first semester of the second year, and the Practicum II takes place at the second semester of the fourth year of the degree. This organization has been a salutary lesson in the region of Extremadura because bilingual schools did not receive CLIL-trained pre-service teachers to their schools so far, what was a difficult first task to solve in their first contact with the real context.

According to the preliminary results that have been collected thus far show that this organization is a success, since, on the one hand, the schoolteacher receives a pre-service teacher completely aware and skilled in this special area of bilingual education and, on the other hand, pre-service teachers have received a CLIL methodological training, what makes them to be more involved and updated to the bilingual education specific strategies and trends. Furthermore, the fact that the university offers internships counting on bilingual specialists has been a collaboration between the University of Extremadura and the Ministry of Education and Employment of the regional government of Extremadura. These actions made possible that the specializations of Music, Physical Education, General itinerary and English were tutored by bilingual school mentors for students of the bilingual track of the degree.

One of the key facts to make this bilingual track succeed is the fact that at the Education College a GID (Teaching Innovation Group) was created. This group was developed under the umbrella of the Vice-chancellor for Studies Plan Office. Its aim is to coordinate courses, agree on evaluation tools, evaluation rubrics, and materials for classes, exams, and BA dissertations in their oral and written spheres (TFGs). Also, the faculties that participates in this group are evaluated and trained annually. One of their best practices is a peer-review evaluation of CLIL lessons. Another one is the training offered by external experts but also by the members of the group on topics like tools for CLIL teaching.

Challenges to Improve Employability

Henceforth, the authors raise a new question: What would need a future graduate of bilingual school programs to know? This sort of professionals should entail professional characteristics related to theoretical academic knowledges as much as practical experiences that allow them to develop their work in the school (Contreras, 2010). The authors observe that the majority of the teacher training programs were focused on non-bilingual realities. It means that the most related contexts were those based on foreign languages specialties, and not on the bilingual approach that this work presents.

In those cases, graduates from the primary education degree that decided to receive the proper qualification or to get enrolled into a bilingual program had to receive their training from out of the university, through training for employment programs, which offered two options: the first option was from the teacher's centers themselves, and the second option was as a complementary training, such as specific courses delivered in academies and teacher's union. For the first option, the teachers' training centers, there were and still are several types of training in-service teachers: training courses offered by the permanent education center (CPR), where contents about specific language teaching methodologies are included; linguistic immersion programs, that entails that a group of students and teachers undergone weekly periods of school coexistence abroad; and also scholar exchanges (stays abroad), which foster coexistence and acquiring knowledge in a different context where a different language is spoken and different cultures exist.

At that point, universities are starting to wake up from their lethargy and they are overcoming the different obstacles and difficulties, like the fears of the unknown, the mistrust of the educative community, or even the university bureaucracy itself. Universities are starting to offer (not being exempt of complications) bilingual training programs for future teachers. The initial approach to achieve this goal is to ask oneself whether if the bilingual primary education teacher should receive the identical degree training as the non-bilingual primary education teachers. The first curricular approach contemplated that they should, effectively, be equal for both, but soon later, their profiles and professional future were confirming that the bilingual teacher needed to be extra-competent in language knowledge and fluency; therefore, universities started to work from that idea.

According to that first idea, bilingual teachers would only need to be trained at the specific language and, consequently, this could be done out of the university (EEOOII or academies, for example). However, recent facts drove the authors to go a step further in this issue because bilingual centers had to receive pre-service teachers when the Practicum subject came into force, and the difficulties emerged. In-service teachers raised several questions about that: Does parents have the same needs when their children are in the bilingual track or not? How does families need to be oriented? What is the syllabus for the specific subjects? How does the schoolchildren with special needs face a bilingual program? etc.

Therefore, that was a key aspect that should be a universities' target (Pavón, 2014; Pérez, 2012; Pérez et al., 2016). That is the reason why (together with several more reasons) universities should offer a comprehensive and qualifying training for future teachers, which allows them to develop specific competences to work on this type of programs. The imminent solution is to work cooperatively with schools, because that is the way of connecting realities and offering the pre-service teachers the best of both entities: necessary knowledge, abilities and attitudes that allow them to be perfectly trained to face the professional emerging reality (Medina & Pérez, 2017).

FINAL REMARKS

According to the objective established in this work, the intention of the authors was to show the milestones of the bilingual education in Spain, above all in the autonomous region of Extremadura, and contributing with ideas and strategies that the University of Extremadura implemented within existent contexts of bilingual education. Bilingual programs at the university seek to bring improvements in the frame of the initial and permanent training of primary education teachers. In order to have an overview of the strongest and weakest aspects about the specific training for primary education teachers and with the aim of fostering debate among the bilingual education community, the authors gathered the main ideas by means of a SWOT (Strengths, Weaknesses, Opportunities and Threatens) overview (Figure 1).

University and Primary Schools Co-Teaching Together

Figure 1. SWOT overview
Source: Own elaboration

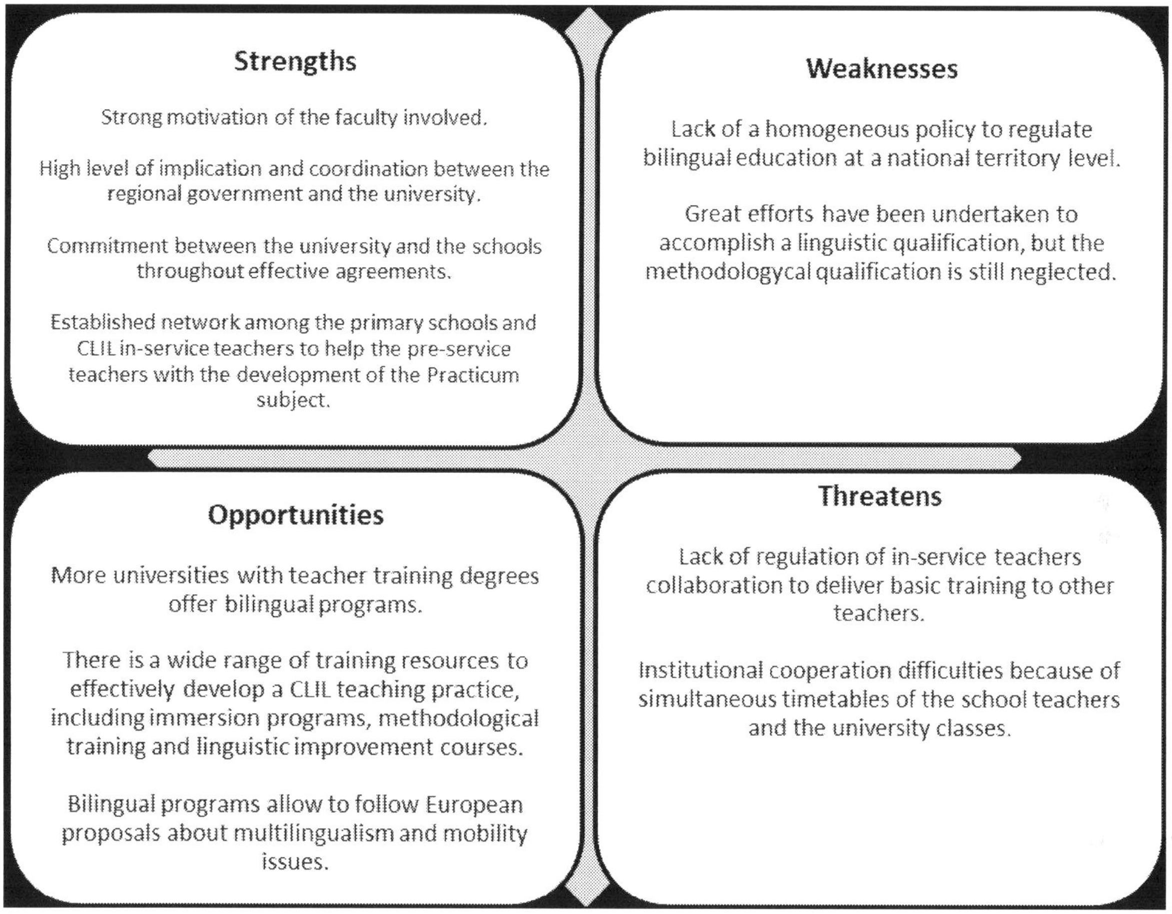

As it can be observed in Figure 1, bilingual programs are attributed with more strengths and opportunities than weaknesses and threatens, what means that the scale seems to tip in favour of these programs, although the bilingual education community should also take care of the internal and external issues to be modified or improved. Consequently, settling the weakest issues and leveraging the strongest ones will contribute to the continuity and the welfare of bilingual programs in the Spanish context.

FUTURE RESEARCH DIRECTIONS

Bilingual programs were implemented in Spanish schools without having properly trained its teachers first, and this is a controversial fact that has generated opposite-end opinions about these programs. Nonetheless, an undeniable truth is that Spanish schools required bilingual programs to be implemented in one way or another, so that the national education system started to be oriented to an international and multilingual perspective. Then, universities in Spain started to design and offer their bilingual programs and bilingual tracks to train the future teachers that would work on those schools, what has implied a breakthrough in the whole educative system.

Nowadays, after several years of implementation of bilingual programs at primary, secondary and university levels, the whole educative community has the duty of caring these programs and their related courses, qualifications, infrastructure, and human capital. For this purpose, it is necessary to provide this structure with continuity by doing research about the different issues that concern and have direct or transversal influence on bilingual education.

Therefore, according to the authors, future research lines should follow the subsequent directions:

- University bilingual programs design and development: How university programs were designed and implemented? What are the development circumstances? Does bilingual programs at the university consider their permanent update in relation to a local, national and international scale?
- Bilingual teaching methodologies: What are the current methodologies and the most suitable and useful ones to apply to a bilingual group? What are the updated trends about that? Are bilingual teachers well trained in the suitable methodologies that give response to the bilingual educational needs? Are these methodologies related to the CLIL approach?
- Global competencies: Are pre-service and in-service teachers receiving a proper training about being global citizens? Are they acquiring the suitable global competencies? Are they trained enough to teach contents taking these global competencies into account?

Given that bilingual programs have been developing for a long time now, it would be viable to get access to all this data, and it is necessary to do it for the welfare of these programs.

CONCLUSION

In spite of the improvable building process of the bilingual education in Spain, the current scenario, as well as the current bilingual programs offer have been established with the intention of conforming a global-oriented education, and with an invaluable human capital. Precisely these two factors contribute to shape the bilingual programs. But thanks to the work hereby presented, the authors can state that one of the key facts to provide quality to bilingual programs is the coordinated activity among the different actors of the educative community.

Firstly, the bilingual education in Spain needs a national policy that regulates the basic and specific aspects homogeneously. This is a fundamental starting point so that every autonomous community of Spain can adapt their bilingual policies to it and the whole country can have a reference to set up abiding bilingual programs, accordingly, related to the national curricular laws.

Secondly, bilingual education regulations should consider what are the specific methodologies that better respond to the needs of a bilingual group, and pre-service and in-service teachers should all be aware of them. In this regard, the educative community should allow for the CLIL approach, being enforced by the methodologies that this approach uses, and also taking the scaffolding technique as the basis of a foreign language learning.

Finally, getting to know the particular context of every autonomous community of Spain would lead to establish or deepen two-tier ties: the first one between the universities and the regional government, and the second one between the university and the schools. The cooperation among all the actors

University and Primary Schools Co-Teaching Together

involved is the undoubted necessary action required for the success of the bilingual programs, since it allows connecting academic knowledge and practical experiences for everyone: schoolteachers, faculty, and pre-service teachers (through the Practicum subject mainly).

This cooperation surely draws from the international knowledge, because it is essential to know about how other educative systems are dealing with the bilingual or multilingual programs. This international action will help universities to be up to date about the current trends, to have the possibility of widening the training exchanges, and to create international networks, apart from working the global competences fostered by the European Union.

REFERENCES

Aljure, L. H., Arciniegas, M. C., & Castillo, M. F. (2014). Bilingüismo y aprendizaje. Un enfoque cognitivo. [Bilingualism and learning. A cognitive approach.] *El astrolabio*, 115–126.

Alonso, L., Delicado, G., & Ramos, F. (2017) A Comparative Study of Bilingual Teacher Preparation Programs in Two Different Contexts: California and Spain, Springer. In production.

Barrett, M., Byram, M., Lázár, I., Mompoint-Gaillard, P., & Philippou, S. (2014). *Developing Intercultural Competence through Education*. Councilof Europe Publishing.

Bolívar, A. (2010). *Competencias básicas y currículo*. Síntesis.

Coleman, J. (2006). English-medium teaching in European Higher Education. *Language Teaching*, *39*(1), 1–14. doi:10.1017/S026144480600320X

Contreras, J. (2010). Ser y saber en la formación didáctica del profesorado: Una visión personal. [Being and knowing in the didactic training of teachers: a personal vision.]. *Revista Interuniversitaria de Formación del Profesorado*, *69*, 61–83.

Council of Europe. (2016). *Competences for Democratic Culture: Living Together as Equals in Culturally Diverse Democratic Societies*. Council of Europe.

Coyle, D., Marsh, D., & Hood, P. (2010). *CLIL: Content and language integrated learning* (1st ed.). Cambridge University Press. doi:10.1017/9781009024549

Deardorff, D. K. (2014). Some thoughts on assessing intercultural competence. [University of Illinois and Indiana University, National Institute for Learning Outcomes Assessment] [NILOA]. *Urbana (Caracas, Venezuela)*, IL.

DECRETO 93/2013, de 27 de agosto, por el que se regula la formación inicial y permanente del profesorado en la Comunidad Autónoma de Extremadura, así como el Sistema Andaluz de Formación Permanente del Profesorado (BOJA, nº 170, 30 de agosto de 2013). [of 27 August, which regulates the initial and permanent training of teachers in the Autonomous Community of Extremadura, as well as the Andalusian System of Permanent Teacher Training (BOJA, nº 170, 30 August 2013).] https://www.juntadeandalucia.es/boja/2013/170/1

Delicado, G. & Pavón V. (2015). La implantación de titulaciones bilingües en la Educación Superior: el caso de la formación didáctica del profesorado bilingüe de primaria en la Universidad de Extremadura, [The implementation of bilingual qualifications in Higher Education: the case of the didactic training of bilingual primary teachers at the University of Extremadura,] *Educación y futuro, 32*, 35-64.

Delicado, G., & Pavón, V. (2016). Training primary student teachers for AICLE: Innovation through collaboration, *Pulso. Review of Education, 39*, 35–57.

Delicado-Puerto, G., Alonso-Díaz, L., & Fielden-Burns, L. V. (2022). Teaching Students, Creating Teachers: Focusing on Future Language Teachers and Their Education for Bilingual Classrooms. *TESL-EJ, 25*(4), 1–31. doi:10.55593/ej.25100a10

Díaz, F., & Cuevas, M. (2013). El Practicum I del Grado de maestro de primaria como materia que contribuye a la formación integral de los futuros maestros. [The Practicum I of the Degree of primary teacher as a subject that contributes to the integral formation of future teachers] In P. C. Muñoz, M. Raposo, M. González, M. E. Martínez, M. Zabalza, & A. Pérez (Eds.), *Un Practicum para la formación integral de los estudiantes* (pp. 231–240). Andavira.

Doiz, A., Lasagabaster, D., & Pavón, V. (2019). The integration of language and content in English-medium instruction courses: Lecturers' beliefs and practices. *Ibérica (New York, N.Y.)*, 38.

Estrada-Chichón, J. L., & Zayas-Martínez, F. (2022). Dual training in language didactics of foreign language/CLIL pre-service primary education teachers in Spain. *Journal of Language and Education. 8*(1), 69-83. Natsional'nyi Issledovatel'skii Universitet "Vysshaya Shkola Ekonomiki", 2022. ISSN 24117390. DOI: , R. & Castro, A. (2012). La formación permanente del profesorado basada en competencias. Estudio exploratorio de la formación del profesorado de Infantil y Primaria, in *Educatio Siglo XXI, 30*(1), 297-322. doi:10.17323/jle.2022.11520García-Ruiz

Gómez, A. (2013). El aprendizaje integrado de la lengua española y los contenidos de áreas no lingüísticas en los proyectos lingüísticos de centro. [The integrated learning of the Spanish language and the contents of non-linguistic areas in the linguistic projects of the center.]. *Porta Linguarum, 20*, 103–115.

González, Mª T. & Cutanda, T. (2017). La formación continua del profesorado de enseñanza obligatoria: incidencia en la práctica docente y el aprendizaje de los estudiantes. [Continuing teacher training in compulsory education: impact on teaching practice and student learning.] *Profesorado. Revista de currículum y formación del profesorado, 21*(2), 103-122.

Hu, Y. C. (2019). Constructing a Bilingual-Education Internship Management Platform to Explore Factors Influencing College Students' Internship Outcome. *Saudi Journal of Humanities and Social Sciences, 4*(1), 21-28. ISSN 2415-6248. Doi:10.21276/sjhss.2019.4.1.3

Imbernón, F. (2007). *Diez ideas clave. La formación permanente del profesorado. Nuevas ideas para formar en la innovación y el cambio* [*Ten key ideas. Ongoing teacher training. New ideas to train in innovation and change*.]. Graó.

Imbernón, F. & Colén, M. T. (2015). Los vaivenes de la formación inicial del profesorado. Una reforma siempre inacabada. [The ups and downs of initial teacher training. A reform always unfinished.] *Tendencias pedagógicas, 25*, 57-76.

Fábregat, S. (2016). El proyecto lingüístico de centro: Aprender más y comunicar mejor. [The language project of the center: learn more and communicate better.]. *Aula de Secundaria, 19*, 25–30.

Fang, H., & Li, M. (2018). A Study on the Training Model of the Bilingual Teachers in Local Universities and Colleges. *Studies in Literature and Language, 17*(2), 62–65. doi:10.3968/10668

Julius, S. M. & Madrid, D. (2017). Diversity of Students in Bilingual University Programs: A Case Study, *The International Journal of Diversity in Education. 17*(2), 17-28. ISSN (print): 2327-0020, (online): 2327-2163.

Lasagabaster, D., & Ruiz de Zarobe, Y. (2010). *AICLE in Spain: Implementation, Results and Teacher Training*. Cambridge Scholars.

Lasagabaster, D. (2022). *English-Medium Instruction in Higher Education (Elements in Language Teaching)*. Cambridge University Press., doi:10.1017/9781108903493

Ley 4/2011 de 7 de marzo, de Educación de Extremadura (BOE nº 70, de 23 de marzo). Mérida, Consejería de Educación y Empleo, Junta de Extremadura.

Lorenzo, F. (2016). Competencia en comunicación lingüística: Claves para el avance de la comprensión lectora en las pruebas PISA. [Competence in linguistic communication: keys to the advancement of reading comprehension in the PISA tests.]. *Review of Education, 374*, 142–158.

Madrid, M., & Madrid, D. (2014). *La formación inicial del profesorado para la educación bilingüe* [*Initial teacher training for bilingual education.*]. Editorial Universidad de Granada.

Madrid, D., & Trujillo, F. (2001). Reflexiones en torno a la formación del profesorado especialista en lenguas extranjeras. [Reflections on the training of teachers specializing in foreign languages.] in Francisco Javier Perales Palacios, Antonio Luis García Ruiz y Luis Rico (eds.) Las didácticas de las áreas curriculares en el siglo XXI. Granada: Grupo Editorial Universitario, 1771-1778.

Marsh, D. (2002). *Integrating language with non-language content, in a dual-focused learning environment*. CLIL/EMILE-The European Dimension: Actions, Trends and Foresight Potential.

Medina, J. L. & Pérez, M. J. (2017). La construcción del conocimiento en el proceso de aprender a ser profesor: la visión de los protagonistas. [The construction of knowledge in the process of learning to be a teacher: the vision of the protagonists.] *Profesorado. Revista de currículum y formación del profesorado, 21*(2), 17-38.

Nurutdinova, A. & Bolotnikov, A. (2018). Study of Foreign Experience in Bilingual Education: Case Study: System of Higher (Professional) Education. *Current Issues of Linguistics and Didactics: The Interdisciplinary Approach in Humanities and Social Sciences* (CILDIAH-2018), 50. doi:10.1051/shsconf/20185001211

Diario Oficial de Extremadura. (2011). *ORDEN de 8 de abril de 2011 por la que se regula la convocatoria de secciones bilingües, con carácter experimental, en centros sostenidos con fondos públicos que impartan enseñanzas obligatorias en Extremadura. [ORDER of 8 April 2011 by which regulates the announcement of bilingual sections, with experimental character, in centres sustained with public funds that impart compulsory educations in Extremadura.]* Junta de Extremadura, Diario Oficial de Extremadura, 77, 9711-9731.

Ortega, J. L. (2015). La realidad de la enseñanza bilingüe. [The reality of bilingual education.] In *Cuadernos de Pedagogía, 458*, 61-68.

Pavón, V. (2014). Perfil y competencia metodológica del profesorado para el Aprendizaje Integrado de Contenidos y Lenguas Extranjeras. [Profile and methodological competence of teachers for Content and Foreign Language Integrated Learning.] *Enclave docente, 5*, 8-13.

Pavón, V., & Pérez, A. (2017). Enhancing disciplinary literacies: Languages of schooling and whole-school language projects in Spain. *European Journal of Applied Lingüistics, 5*, 153–175.

Pérez, A. (2012). *Evaluación de programas bilingües: Análisis de resultados de las secciones experimentales de francés en el marco del Plan de Fomento del Plurilingüismo en Andalucía [Evaluation of bilingual programs: Analysis of results of the experimental sections of French within the framework of the Plan for the Promotion of Multilingualism in Andalusia.].* Servicio de Publicaciones.

Pérez, A., Lorenzo, F., & Pavón, V. (2016). European bilingual models beyond linguafranca: Key findings from AICLE french programs. *Language Policy, 15*, 485–504. https://doi.org/10.1007/s10993-015-9386-7

Ramos, F., Delicado, G., & Alonso, L. (2021, July 25th). Student teaching in Spain in the time of COVID. *Language magazine. Improving Literacy and Communication.* https://www.languagemagazine.com/2021/07/25/student-teaching-in-spain-in-the-time-of-covid/

Romero-Alfaro, E., & Zayas-Martínez, F. (2017). Challenges and opportunities of training teachers for plurilingual education. Integrating Content and Language in Higher Education. Perspectives on Professional Practice, 205 - 226. Peter Lang GmbH, 2017. ISBN 978-3-631-68126-8. doi:10.3726/978-3-653-07263-1

Romero, M. F. (2014). *(Coord.). La escritura académica: diagnóstico y propuesta de actuación. Una visión desde los Grados de Magisterio [Academic writing: diagnosis and proposal for action. A vision from the Degrees of Teaching.].* Octaedro.

Romero, M. F. & Jiménez. (2014). El practicum del MAES y la formación inicial en la enseñanza de lenguas: Entre la realidad y el deseo. [The practicum of the MAES and initial training in language teaching: between reality and desire.]. *Lenguaje y Textos, 39*, 49–58.

Romero, M. F., & Trigo, E. (2015). Herramientas para el éxito. [Tools for success.]. *Cuadernos de Pedagogía, 458*, 16–21.

Trujillo, F. (2010). La competencia lingüística como proyecto de centro: Retos, posibilidades y ejemplificaciones. [Language competence as a school project: challenges, possibilities and exemplifications.]. *Lenguaje y Textos, 32*, 35–40.

UNESCO. (2014). Global Citizenship Education: Preparing learners for the challenges of the 21st century. UNESCO.

Villa, A., & Poblete, M. (2004). Practicum y evaluación de competencias. [Practicum and evaluation of competences.] Profesorado. Revista de currículum y formación del profesorado, 8(2), 1-19.

Zayas-Martínez, F., & Estrada-Chichón, J. L. (2020). Instructed Foreign Language Acquisition (IFLA) at a Faculty of Education: German for Primary Schoolteachers under a CLIL Model. In Innovación Docente e Investigación en Educación. Avanzando en el proceso de enseñanza-aprendizaje, (pp. 1103 – 1113). Dykinson.

Zabala, A., & Arnau, L. (2007). *11 ideas clave: Cómo aprender y enseñar competencias* [*11 key ideas: How to learn and teach competencies*.]. Graó.

Zabalza, M. A. (2011). El practicum en la formación universitaria: Estado de la cuestión. [The practicum in university education: state of the art.]. *Review of Education*, *354*, 21–43.

Zeichner, K. M. (2010). Nuevas epistemologías en formación del profesorado. Repensando las conexiones entre las asignaturas del campus y las experiencias de prácticas en la formación del profesorado en la universidad. [New epistemologies in teacher training. Rethinking the connections between campus subjects and internship experiences in teacher training at the university.] *Revista Interuniversitaria de Formación del Profesorado*, (68), 123-149.

KEY TERMS AND DEFINITIONS

Bilingual program: Educative program whose contents are delivered in two different languages, being the usual distribution around 50% in one language and 50% in another language.

Bilingual track internship: Period of time in which a pre-service teacher receives practical training and gets experience into a real bilingual school context.

CLIL: Educative approach whose acronym stands for Content and Language Integrated Learning, and it makes use of different teaching methodologies and the scaffolding technique.

Co-teaching: Teaching cooperation between schoolteachers and faculty during the internship of the pre-service teachers.

Global teacher: Teacher who has been trained on global competences within an international perspective.

Practicum: Degree subject whose aim is to get the pre-service teachers involved into a real school context, being supervised by a faculty member and mentored by a schoolteacher.

SWOT: Business-coined term that refers to the analysis of the internal (Strengths and Weaknesses) and external factors (Opportunities and Threats) of a specific context.

ENDNOTES

[1] Given the linguistic variety existing in Spain, plus the foreign linguistic offer, the authors consider necessary to specify that the most frequent bilingual situation in the schools of Extremadura refers to English-Spanish.

[2] Bilingual tracks are specific bilingual programs in the Spanish educative system where students receive training in two languages. A *track* implies that there is a monolingual group and a bilingual group sharing the same syllabus. In the Teacher Training College of the University of Extremadura there is a bilingual track for the primary education Bachelor's degree, where the half of the syllabus in taught English and the other half in Spanish, while the non-bilingual group holds the same syllabus completely in Spanish.

Chapter 6
Collaborative Lesson Planning for CLIL Student Teachers of Primary Education

Magdalena Custodio Espinar
iD https://orcid.org/0000-0001-5314-1606
Comillas Pontifical University, Spain

ABSTRACT

The introduction of content and language integrated learning (CLIL) in mainstream education in Spain demands specific teaching competencies. For this, Spanish universities have adapted the design of their degrees in education to meet the challenges of this demanding scenario. However, there is still a heterogeneous scenario among Spanish universities for preparing prospective teachers for CLIL. This chapter aims at exploring the profile of the primary education teacher specialized in CLIL teaching and proposing a collaborative lesson planning task likely to develop some key competencies of this profile in a group of student teachers. The collaborative lesson plannings designed by students are described and discussed in relation to recent literature. Moreover, the answers of 17 of these students to a questionnaire are analyzed to unveil the potential of this type of training for actually developing the collaborative competence of prospective CLIL primary teachers. A final reflection on the need to provide more homogeneous preparation connected to the CLIL classroom is also provided.

INTRODUCTION

Since the beginning of the 21st century, content and language integrated learning (CLIL) has been widely introduced in mainstream education in Spain at pre-primary, primary and secondary education. Simultaneously, different national and regional education authorities have regulated the study of curricular content through a foreign language. A good example of this implementation of bilingual education in mainstream education is the Community of Madrid, where 50.4% of schools (pre-primary and primary) and 63.6% of secondary schools offer CLIL as their bilingual education approach (Comunidad de Madrid, 2021).

DOI: 10.4018/978-1-6684-6179-2.ch006

Copyright © 2023, IGI Global. Copying or distributing in print or electronic forms without written permission of IGI Global is prohibited.

Custodio-Espinar (2019a) and Nieto Moreno de Diezmas and Custodio-Espinar (2022) describe how, in parallel, Spanish universities have been adapting the design of their degrees in education to meet the challenges of this demanding scenario since the Bologna declaration in 1999, which is at the origin of the European Higher Education Area (EHEA). Its Work Plan 2021-24 includes a Working Group on Learning and Teaching, focused on making student-centered learning a reality across the entire EHEA, fostering innovative learning and teaching, and developing international learning environments for the students, among other topics (EHEA, 2022). In particular, Spanish universities have increased the provision of foreign language medium instruction programs, mainly in English (Dafouz & Smit, 2020; Otto & Estrada Chichón, 2021).

As a result, education degrees in Spain cope with a doble challenge. On the one hand, they are supposed to provide student teachers with the necessary skills and competencies to develop bilingual education at schools. On the other hand, universities are expected to offer bilingual education through English Medium Instruction (EMI) courses or CLIL themselves, which has been called ICLHE (Integrating Content and Language in Higher Education) (Pavón-Vázquez & Gaustad, 2013; Smit & Dafouz-Milne, 2012).

However, despite the efforts made to design new teacher education degrees with the aim of aligning them to the EHEA (Order 3857/2007, 27th of December), López-Hernández (2021) unveils the issue of heterogeneity in teacher preparation for bilingual education at university. He explains that universities in Madrid have implemented different itineraries varying the "credit load devoted to English and foreign language pedagogy, which is higher than the national average, and which was found to be particularly noticeable in private universities" (p. 146).

In relation to this situation, this chapter has the following objectives:

1. Describe the profile of the Primary Education teacher specialized in CLIL teaching.
2. Present a student-centered EMI task likely to develop some of the key competencies of prospective CLIL teachers in the Primary Education degree at Comillas Pontifical University.
3. Analyze students' appraisals about the experience and its potential to develop their collaborative competence in the context of CLIL lesson planning.
4. Reflect on the need to provide more homogeneous preparation at university connected to the actual needs of bilingual education.

For this, first, the chapter offers a review of relevant literature about the teacher competency profile, in general, and the primary CLIL teacher, in particular. Next, the CLIL course studied by primary education students at Comillas is described and the collaborative lesson plan they perform as part of the course is discussed in relation to this literature. Then, students' answers to an online questionnaire are analyzed in order to unveil the potential of this type of activities for actually developing the collaborative competence of prospective CLIL primary teachers. Finally, a reflection on the issue of heterogeneity in initial education and its lack of connection with the actual needs of bilingual education contexts is also provided.

BACKGROUND

The European Union (EU) strategy to promote multilingualism and plurilingualism among the EU education systems has been leaded by the European Commission and assisted by different institutions such as the Council of Europe and its European Centre of Modern Languages (ECML) and instruments like the

Common European Framework of Reference for Languages (CEFRL) (Council of Europe, 2001). One of these institutions, Eurydice, was responsible for the first publication aimed at promoting the implementation of CLIL across the EU countries titled "Content and Language Integrated Learning (CLIL) at school in Europe" (European Commission, 2006). Since then, CLIL has become an important thematic area of the ECML to support the implementation of CLIL programs and one of the key components of teacher education (ECML, 2022). However, more than two decades after the Bologna declaration in 1999 and the adaptation of the Education degrees to this scenario, the Education degrees in Spain do not widely prepare student teachers for providing bilingual education in general, nor for teaching CLIL in particular (Custodio-Espinar, 2019a; Custodio-Espinar & García Ramos, 2020; Gutiérrez Gamboa & Custodio-Espinar, 2021).

During this time, there have been many attempts of conceptualizing the key competences of language teachers. One example is the European Portfolio for Language Teacher Education created to propose a profile for teacher initial and in-service education in the twenty-first century, which includes training in CLIL (element 33 in the section describing strategies and skills) and training in team-working, collaboration and networking, inside and outside the immediate school context (element 39 in the section describing values) (Kelly et al., 2004). Similarly, the current regulations for teacher education in Spain (Order 3857/2007, 27th of December) include, in a list of 12 competencies to be developed by student teachers: the competency to design, plan and evaluate teaching and learning processes, both individually and in collaboration with other teachers and professionals from the school; the competency to collaborate with the different stakeholders of the educational community and the social environment, assuming the educational dimension of the teaching function and promoting democratic education for active citizenship; and the competency to effectively address learning situations of languages in multicultural and multilingual contexts.

Therefore, as proposed by Kelly et al. (2004), all teachers should be educated as a CLIL teacher since it will result in an "improved competence in the foreign language, better understanding of language use in CLIL and non-CLIL contexts, improved notion of social, culture and value issues in teaching, and encourages cooperation between teachers" (p. 75). As Wolff (2012) puts it, "CLIL teacher education, if taken seriously, constitutes a fundamental part of all teacher education, that every teacher should be educated, in fact, as a CLIL teacher" (p. 107).

In line with these proposals, authors such as Bentley (2010), Bertaux et al. (2010), Marsh et al. (2010) and Ball et al. (2016) have described CLIL teacher frameworks in which they also emphasize the need to prepare prospective teachers for CLIL, including the competence to design lessons and to work collaboratively. In this sense, Pavón Vázquez and Ellison (2013) highlight the necessary coordination and collaboration between language and content teachers, which is also necessary in primary education even though, a majority of the times, the CLIL teacher is both a language teacher and a generalist teacher.

However, this does not mean that primary teachers of CLIL clearly differentiate between teaching English as a Foreign Language (EFL) and teaching CLIL (Custodio-Espinar, 2017). In this sense, Pavón Vázquez (2014) promotes the idea that the collaboration between the language and content teachers, between the content teachers themselves, and between all the languages present in the curriculum (mother tongue, language of instruction/foreign language, and any other languages) may be beneficial for the students and may provide them with the necessary linguistic support to understand and express the content studied.

Looking at more recent research-based evidence of in-service teachers, Vilkancienė and Rozgienė (2017) proved that the European Framework for CLIL Teacher Education is "a useful tool when designing training courses for specific target groups of qualified content teachers" (pp. 112-113). From the point of view of the competences of CLIL teachers placed in monolingual contexts, Pérez Cañado (2017) signaled that linguistic and methodological competence are a top priority and that collaborative competence has made considerable progress, although difficulties related to teachers' official schedules persist. Likewise, in a plurilingual context of student teachers, Pons Seguí (2020) concludes that the focus should not only be placed on student teachers' communicative and methodological competence but on offering sufficient opportunities for them to develop those competences in practice.

Research conducted in the context of student teachers offers interesting discrepancies between the traditional design of the Education degrees, that promote cognitive and methodological competences over the social and personal ones (Barceló Cerdá & Ruíz-Corbella, 2015). The authors claim for a revision of the education degrees to provide Primary student teachers with an initial education in accordance with the reality in which they are going to work. Similar results from the voices of student teachers are reported in Irie et al. (2018) who explain that the most common mindset among the pre-service teachers is based around a belief in the learnability of the more technical aspects of teaching, while interpersonal skills tend to be related to the individual natural talent.

However, these important competencies cannot depend solely on the personality of the teacher, they must be trained. Placing the focus on the development of the collaborative competence, Santagata and Guarino (2012) summarize three important findings in preparing future teachers to collaborate:

1. Pre-service teachers' initial conceptions of collaboration do not necessarily match with the kind of collaboration expected of them in professional development settings.
2. With support, pre-service teachers can learn to collaborate and find collaboration useful.
3. Collaboration in fieldwork settings can further develop collaboration skills. (p. 67)

Therefore, taking into account these frameworks and the empirical evidence, it seems paramount to include, in undergraduate degrees, this type of learning scenarios that relate the theory to real teaching situations and introduce personal and social skills practice. As Kelly et al. (2004) and Barceló Cerdá and Ruíz-Corbella (2015) state, to ensure effective implementation and application of bilingual education, the courses provided at initial education level have to combine theory and practice. Hence, "academic study of pedagogy and teaching practice need equal status and trainees need to see the link between the two" (Kelly et al., 2004, p. 5). Thus, the challenge for undergraduate degrees in Education is not only to provide bilingual education to students, as in any other degree, but also to prepare them to be bilingual teachers themselves and to do it by combining the theory and the practice.

The following collaborative CLIL lesson planning proposal is aimed at responding to this triple challenge placed at initial teacher education: the acquisition of sufficient knowledge about the foundations of CLIL, its pedagogy and methodological strategies; the development of the key competencies necessary to implement those strategies in the classroom, in particular, collaborative competence and the competence to plan CLIL lessons; and, finally, the improvement of the English proficiency of prospective teachers to be able to cope with teaching in bilingual education contexts.

For this, the six collaborative lesson plannings designed by 21 students (of the total number of 41 students in the Degree of Primary Education at Comillas Pontifical University who took a team-taught CLIL course in 2021-2022) were analyzed. Besides, the opinions of 17 of these students were collected from an online questionnaire to support the analysis.

CLIL LESSON PLANNING AT PRIMARY EDUCATION DEGREES: A COLLABORATIVE APPROACH

The CLIL Course and The Collaborative Competence

At Comillas Pontifical University (Madrid, Spain) all students of the Education degrees (Pre-Primary, Primary and their joint degrees) study the specialization to be English as a Foreign Language (EFL) teachers. This specialization is called *mención en lengua extranjera*. As Lopéz-Hernández (2021) explains, Comillas, which accepts trainees with an A2 level in English according to the CEFRL, offers EMI courses as part of the specialization (Table 1).

Table 1. Overview of the English-taught courses of the "mención" in the education degrees

Year	Course	Type	Credits load
1	English for Education I	English for specific purposes	12 ECTS
2	English for Education II	English for specific purposes	6 ECTS
3	Teaching English as a Foreign Language I	Language pedagogy (EFL)	6 ECTS
4	Teaching English as a Foreign Language II	Language pedagogy (EFL)	6 ECTS
4	Content and Language Integrated Learning	CLIL pedagogy	5 ECTS

This itinerary is likely to enable all potential CLIL teachers to deal effectively with new pedagogical challenges of bilingual education and CLIL, although it is a challenge for professors and students since low proficiency students A2-B1study the same courses imparted in English as their B2, C1 or C2 counterparts.

As part of the *mención*, the CLIL course plays a central role in the attention to diversity of students and the development of student teacher collaborative competence (Custodio-Espinar et al., 2022), one of the key competences included in all CLIL teacher frameworks developed so far (Bentley, 2010; Bertaux et al., 2010; Marsh et al., 2010; Pérez-Cañado, 2017) because it is a team-taught course. However, Custodio-Espinar et al. (2022) confirmed that learning through co-teaching itself did not have an effect on students' general collaborative competence and they found significant differences only in students' learning experience, which students reported to be better in a co-taught course. One of the conclusions of this study was that modelling a collaborative teaching relationship seemed to be insufficient to develop learners collaborative competence.

Hence, in order to boost the modeling effect of learning in a co-teaching context, the team-taught CLIL course was reinforced by introducing a series of collaborative tasks, which explicitly deal with the collaborative competence and co-teaching (Table 2).

Table 2. Structure of the team-taught CLIL course and the collaborative tasks

Module	Content	Students' collaborative task	Assessment load
1	Bilingual education and bilingual schools.	Group jigsaw readings.	5%*
2	The theories behind CLIL.	Group bingo and chunking.	5%*
3	A CLIL Lesson Plan.	Group CLIL lesson planning.	30%
4	Scaffolding learning in CLIL.	Group production scaffolding.	5%
5	Assessment and Evaluation.	Group rubric design.	5%*
6	Skills and resources for the CLIL classroom	Group ICT demonstration.	5%

*This 5% is part of the active participation mark.

As can be seen in the table, in Module 3, students have to complete a collaborative CLIL lesson planning (Appendix 1), which is assessed with a rubric (Appendix 2) to provide formative assessment before they design an individual CLIL lesson planning (Appendix 3). The assessment grid of the whole task is also provided in Appendix 4.

Collaborative Lesson Planning

CLIL in primary education is an excellent context to develop Project Based Learning (PBL) and Task Based Learning (TBL) (Moore & Lorenzo, 2015). This type of learning demands a strong collaboration among CLIL teachers who have to select adequate curricular content, develop subject literacies, set learning goals and outcomes both for content and language, look for and/or design the best materials and activities and assess the learning of students and their own performance (see Dale & Tanner, 2012; Jalongo et al., 2007; Morton, 2010; Leontjev & DeBoer, 2020) .

Therefore, on the basis of this process of teaching and learning curricular content through a foreign language, there must be a detailed lesson plan which includes the pedagogical foundations and methodological principles summarized in Custodio-Espinar (2020). Because proper lesson planning will help prevent most of the problems teachers face in this complex scenario (Bentley et al., 2010; Coyle et al., 2010; Meyer, 2012). As CLIL expert David Marsh says:

There is no doubt that more work is involved in planning lessons that include both content and language. However, teachers that I met years ago in teacher-training sessions have told me that even though planning CLIL lessons is more work, they feel energised. They have an overall satisfaction level which they were lacking before. (Marsh, 2017, p. 10)

These CLIL principles are integrated in the CLIL lesson plan template (Custodio-Espinar, 2019b) (Appendix 3) given to the primary student teachers for developing their individual designs. But before they work individually, students have to work collaboratively, in teams, taking the roles of the different teachers who can teach CLIL in one of the levels of the primary stage. These collaborative planning is actually the starting point of their individual lesson plans, which have to be interconnected among the team members (Appendix 1).

On the collaborative planning worksheet, students have to choose one topic or project or general task for the students of the level they are planning at. Next, they decide who does the lesson plan for each subject, and they all plan for the EFL lesson. Then, they select the content from the curriculum of each subject that best connect to the topic or theme of the project/task, set the learning goals and explain how they will integrate ICT and active methodologies in each lesson plan. Once they complete the group task, they submit the group work worksheet for feedback (Appendix 3) before they start designing the individual lesson plans. After that, they receive the feedback, and finally, they have to submit it again at the end of the task incorporating any necessary changes or improvements, together with the individual lesson plannings of the team (Appendix 3), which are assessed with an assessment grid in which the teamwork assessment mark is incorporated (Appendix 4).

Analysis of Students' Collaborative CLIL Lesson Plannings

Table 3 shows the description of the collaborative CLIL lesson plannings of the six groups and the most relevant general feedback provided.

Table 3. Students' collaborative lesson plannings description and relevant feedback

Group-Members	Topic	Description	Relevant feedback
1-4	Peace	2-week "project" around Nelson Mandela and the objectives for sustainable development (ODS) with focus on the objective "peace and justice" and the role of NGOs. It is actually TBL.	Very good group work! Excellent cognitive development in the design of the learning goals and excellent choose of genres. The metacognition learning goal is not included in all the areas. Revise and improve the ICT resources.
2-3	Body	Content-based cross-curricular proposal. Each area works on the content of body parts but they are not really interconnected.	Very good group work! Excellent selection of content. Some mistakes in the design of the learning goals but good choice of genres. The metacognition learning goal is not included in all the areas. Revise and improve the ICT resources.
3-4	COVID-19	An attempt to develop a cross-curricular proposal.	Good individual work (although some things are missing). Your proposals lack connection among areas, you are not contributing to help children understand a pandemic from different points of view. Review your learning goals, ensure you have all a minimum of 4 learning goals (1 for curricular content at LOTS, 1 for procedural content at HOTS, 1 for metacognition and 1 for language (a genre). Revise and improve the ICT resources.
4-3	The Earth	2-week "project" leaded by the Natural Science area, which is actually TBL.	Excellent performance of the task, good selection of content and very good design of learning goals with a logical cognitive sequence. The metacognition learning goal is not included in all the areas. Revise and improve the ICT resources.
5-4	Egypt	Proper PBL proposal based on Egypt as the thread to learn the different content areas.	Outstanding performance of the task! You have developed an extraordinary cross-curricular design.
6-3	Eco-social awareness	Content-based cross-curricular proposal. Each area works on the content following a sequence: presentation in Natural S., reflection in Social S. and personalization in A&C.	Excellent choice of topic and contents! Very good design of learning goals but a bit too repetitive. You had all selected the same genre! I have given you some ideas... Revise and improve the ICT resources.

In order to analyze the collaborative CLIL lesson plannings of the six groups, the author took a selection of the competencies as defined by Melara Gutiérrez and González López (2016) in their profile of the Primary Education teacher specialized in CLIL teaching and then, it was analyzed to what extent the task was related to those competencies (Table 4).

Table 4. Analysis of students' competencies from their collaborative CLIL lesson plannings

Dimension	Competency	Analysis of students' planning templates
Language	• Linguistic competence in L2 • Ability to use the L2 to transmit the contents of the NLS. • Ability to reflect on the language learning process.	• Some groups combined L1 and L2 in the lesson plans. • In all collaborative plannings there was a strategy in the language learning process based on the final product of each teacher, which they are supposed to connect to a genre. However, not all the members developed proper subject literacies in their individual lesson plans.
Methodology	• Ability to integrate language, content and learning strategies. • Ability to adapt the linguistic component in the preparation of NLS activities. • Ability to use the cultural patterns of the country/countries of the L2. • Pedagogical competence in teaching foreign languages and NLS pedagogy. • Selection, adaptation, elaboration and evaluation of materials. • Ability to design tasks. • Ability to use an active methodology. • Ability to generate in students the ability to learn to learn and critical thinking.	• All groups developed learning goals for content, language and process, although some found it difficult to follow a logical cognitive progression in their design. • Only some students developed proper scaffolding of the language in their lesson plans. • A majority of students demonstrated a clear differentiation between EFL and CLIL and put into practice adequate NLS pedagogy. • Students used a wide variety of materials in their collaborative plannings, although some lacked the integration or use of ICT resources. • All groups designed learner-centered projects although some students did not totally promote this type of learning and the use of active methodologies in their individual lesson plans. • Some members of the groups lacked the learning goal for metacognitive development despite having proper examples in the group.
Personal skills	• Capacity for teamwork. • Empathy. • Flexibility. • Creativity. • Innovation.	• All groups produced a collaborative CLIL lesson planning. • The empathy and flexibility can be inferred from the benefits for the teachers reported by students and collected in Table 6 below. • Creativity was pushed by the need to relate the different content areas. Some groups designed projects based on updated social issues (Table 3). • Three out of the six groups introduced innovative resources and materials.
Attention to diversity	• Ability to adapt and create specific materials for students. • Ability to use specific resources and methodological strategies for students to attend diversity. • Ability to transmit cultural diversity, both local and global, to students.	• This dimension was not considered by any of the groups although all the students planned strategies to change the cognitive demand of the activities from LOTS to HOTS and vice versa. • All the groups dealt with the cultural component and the individual lesson plannings resulted from the group templates adequately included the design of learning goals and outcomes for this C of CLIL.
Evaluation	• Ability to design, select and implement assessment tools. • Ability to develop evaluation criteria in a consensual way (taking into account the content of the NLA and taking into account the linguistic content).	• Currently, the group task does not include this dimension in the template, which seems to be necessary to help students develop a consensual evaluation strategy.
Tools for improving teaching quality	• Use and mastering of ICT.	• Despite being a specific section in the template, explicitly demanding the need to include ICT resources, not all students improved the design of their teaching materials or their implementation/manipulation in the classroom with adequate ICT resources, which were even demonstrated and modelled in class.

Based on Melara Gutiérrez And González López (2016, Pp. 176-178)

Students' Appraisal of the Group Work and its Impact on Their Collaborative Competence

The Primary student teachers also responded to an online questionnaire including three questions:

Collaborative Lesson Planning for CLIL Student Teachers of Primary Education

Q1. Do you like working in group? Why?

Q2. Do you consider collaborative competence an important competence for CLIL teachers? Why?

Q3. Do you think that working in group in the CLIL course has helped you to develop your collaborative competence? Why?

Table 5 shows the comparative of students' answers to questions 1 and 3 on group work.

Table 5. Students' opinions about group work (Q1 and Q3 answers)

	Q1 answers **Do you like group work?**	**Q3 Answers** **Do you think that working in group has helped you to develop your collaborative competence?**
Student 1	Yes, because I have the chance to share my ideas with others and being aware of new perspectives.	Yes, because I have been able to experience what CLIL is and how I will include teamwork in my future classes.
Student 2	Yes, I like it. It is a good way to share ideas and receive help when you need it. Also, it is very important to learn how to treat people.	Yes of course. It helped me to work in group, to ask and provide help to my partners.
Student 3	Yes, I like it a lot due to the multiple applications it has.	Yes, a lot it helped to learn from others in different ways.
Student 4	Yes. I consider that, most of the times, the final product I have created with a group is more complete than when I created one alone. In a group everybody give the best of themselves.	Yes, because when we think with others (for example doing the lesson plan, creating production activities or in the presentation of ICT tools) we developed collaborative competence.
Student 5	Yes, I think it is better to learn from others and to know what the other points of view are. Also it is more dynamic than other ways.	Yes, because you learn how to deal with other perspectives and also how to agree with the others to do the tasks.
Student 6	Yes, because you improve your knowledge with different thinking and points of views.	Of course.
Student 7	The short answer is if there is a good harmony among the group members. In heterogeneous groups, the group members often have an unbalanced load. I have worked with some classmates who didn't work until the last day of the delivery, which made me worry and as I didn't want my grade to decrease, I did the majority of the work. On the other hand, I have had good experiences in homogeneous groups, where all the members show good harmony and dedication. I consider these groups to be cooperative, as everyone contributes the same workload, so the satisfaction is mutual.	I sincerely believe that the collaborative approach has been the right one, as everyone has shown their knowledge, shared it and received feedback to continue learning.
Student 8	Yes. Sometimes because I prefer doing the works or activities with my friends and sometimes because when I think that the activity is difficult, I like to have the support of my group classmates to help me.	Working with people, friends or not friends, always help you to develop the ability to know how to treat people and how to work in a group. If you are always working alone, when you have to work with someone will be more difficult and frustrating than you thought. Simply because you are not used to it.
Student 9	Yes, I love working in group. I like to share my ideas with others and learn from my colleagues.	Yes, we did a lot of group work and by doing that we got to improve our collaborative competence. We worked supporting each other's work.
Student 10	Yes, because it allows to get other perspectives and the final results are better when we work in group. It also gives you more flexibility and allows to do better works than alone.	Yes, because when you work in group, you collaborate with others. For example, hearing their opinions, helping each other during the work...
Student 11	Yes, a lot.	Very good for all students.
Student 12	Yes, because you can learn from your partners and get to see things form different perspectives, it's a chance to be more open minded	Yes, because it has helped me to learn to listen to other people and to balanced everybody's ideas and opinions into a well elaborated final product. Also sometimes when I didn't know how to do something or what was best, having me mates there to explain it to me was helping.
Student 13	Yes, I really like working in a group because we can enrich each other.	Yes, I think that working in groups in our course has helped me to improve my skills and to develop my collaborative competence as we have already worked and learned as if we were real CLIL teachers.
Student 14	Yes, because I can learn from my colleagues as well as increasing the creativity and quality of the project.	Yes, for the same reasons I like working in group.
Student 15	Yes, because we can share different opinions.	Yes! Thanks to that we have learned the importance of working and sharing in group. It is really helpful for all the educational community!
Student 16	No, because I feel like none actually enjoys the task and everyone has to force themselves to do it.	I guess so, but it has not been enjoyable.
Student 17	Yes, because we are more efficient	Not really...

117

All the answers to Q3, except two, were clearly positive towards group work, evidencing that students are aware of the importance of collaborative competence in CLIL teachers. Similarly, students reported a positive experience, except one, from the group work they did in the CLIL course (Q1), which they considered to be suitable to develop their collaborative competence.

Table 6 shows the reasons referred by students to support their positive answers towards the collaborative competence in CLIL teachers, organized by common or repeated areas and for being beneficial to teachers or learners.

Table 6. Students' reasons about the need of collaborative competence for CLIL teachers (taken from Q2 answers)

Area	Benefits for the teachers	Benefits for the learners
Interaction and communication	• To interact and work with other teachers. • To interact with others and practice communication. • To have communication between each other to prepare the lessons, the activities, to improve their teaching, etc. • To work with your colleagues of other subjects, with the language assistant. • To know how to discuss, interact in a good way with others.	
Teaching and learning	• To benefit the teaching of all the teachers, not only the CLIL ones. Sharing ideas and helping and supporting each other. • To work with the other teacher to make sure you all are on the same page. • To collaborate and teach together to help child improve their skills in order to be effective CLIL teachers.	• To ensure the best of learnings and progressions. • To succeed in the learners educational process. • To ensure the students learning.
Transference	• To know how to do it better because at the end it is what we are going to ask for our students in CLIL lessons. • To teach collaborative competence by modeling so if teachers have this competence, they will be able to share it with the students. • To learn things from the other and vice versa. • To enrich our work.	• To develop that competence in your students.
Lesson planning	• To avoid stagnation as collaboration has different phases such as planning, observation and feedback. • To make your own CLIL lesson plan.	

DISCUSSION

This chapter revised the issue of heterogeneity in CLIL teacher education from a double perspective. First, the heterogeneity of itineraries because it is necessary to ensure that all prospective primary teachers have not only a good proficiency in English, but a minimum of knowledge in bilingual education and CLIL. As Jover et al. (2016) affirmed, the role of English in the Education degrees is not only communicative but a vehicle for teaching and learning curricular content. The CLIL course presented in this chapter is an example of how Education degrees can "guarantee that preservice teachers receive sufficient methodological and theoretical grounding on CLIL" (Pérez Cañado, 2018, p. 217). To cope with the second challenge related to the heterogeneity of students' proficiency in the foreign language, it

Collaborative Lesson Planning for CLIL Student Teachers of Primary Education

is necessary to introduce quality EMI instruction and CLIL at universities. Custodio-Espinar and López Hernández (2021) suggest how CLILized EMI instruction can support students' learning in the EMI courses provided at Comillas in the specialization described in this chapter. Finally, both challenges demand, as signaled by Pérez Cañado (2018), "reinforcing CLIL preparation in university teacher trainers" (p. 217). In this sense, as proposed by Pérez Cañado, the centers of Modern Languages can play a central role by assisting in the provision of EMI courses.

From the point of view of students' performance in the collaborative task, it is necessary to remark how important is the coordination between the content studied in the different subjects by student teachers so as to allow them to integrate the theory with the practice. One solution to the fact that some students were unable to design proper subject literacies is the need to reinforce the coordination among the linguistic subjects, to guarantee that students know genres and text types and their role in CLIL to be able to promote primary CLIL students' pluriliteracies development (Meyer et al., 2015).

Student teachers' difficulty in the design of learning goals is in line with Guillén Díaz and Sanz Trigueros (2019) who described the difficulty for CLIL teachers to implement the curricula in practice from the perspective of bilingual education. Specifically, their studies pointed out the difficulties to determine and formulate the objectives of bilingual education. The analysis of the collaborative task also unveiled that there is an unbalanced integration of ICT in students' lesson plannings, despite the explicit study of ICT tools recommended in CLIL, and a lack of coordination in the assessment strategy of the different lesson plannings. This can be interpreted as another evidence of the difficulty to put into practice the content learnt in lectures and seminars reported by Pons Seguí (2020). Therefore, as she suggests, the CLIL course should include more opportunities for students to put what they study in practice similar to the collaborative lesson-planning meetings described by Bauml (2014), in which students have space for on-action reflection.

Concerning the acquisition of the collaborative competence, students' answers clearly valued the opportunity to design CLIL lessons in group. In particular, they valued the experience from the point of view of the support they could give and receive (Table 5, Students 2-9-10-11-12) and the possibility to improve from a real-life situation (Table 5, Students 1-8), "as if we were real CLIL teachers" (Table 5, Student 13). From the answers also transpires the potential of this type of work for transferring (Table 5, Student 1) and developing personal skills such as "learn from others" (Student 3), "think with others" (Student 4), "how to deal with other perspectives" and "how to agree with others" (Student 5), which are not usually developed in the academic context (Barceló Cerdá & Ruíz-Corbella, 2015; Irie et al., 2018). These positive view of collaboration from student teachers can help to overcome the little engagement with aspirations for the future in contexts for collaborative professional development reported by Shavard (2022). There is no doubt that personal skills development is a good starting point to reach the CLIL teacher profile proposed by Melara Gutiérrez and González López (2016) in general, and its personal dimension in particular.

From students' answers to Q2 it is evident that they consider collaborative competence a key competence for CLIL teachers. It is also interesting the emphasis they place on the side of the teacher, reporting a majority of the benefits for the teachers rather than the learners. These benefits reported by students in Q2 (Table 6) are in line with the impact of collaborative lesson planning on student teachers' individual lesson plannings described by Gutierez (2014): (1) continuous learning, (2) improvement of professional practice, and (3) reflective, affective, and professional support.

Finally, the appraisals about the collaborative lesson planning task included in Table 5 are coherent with the benefits of improving the collaborative competence described by students (Table 6) and in line with the real context they will face, described by Pérez Cañado (2018):

...cooperation and collaboration in the elaboration of the integrated curriculum design have been stepped up in more recent studies. Teachers document the heightened use of PBL, which increases coordination and helps attune the programs to specific student needs, of integrated didactic units, and of blogs through which to liaise and give visibility to their outputs. (p. 216)

These identified areas for improvement require further research and study.

FUTURE RESEARCH DIRECTIONS

This initial proposal needs to deepen in teachers' collaborative lesson planning. In this, the scale validated in Mendoza et al. (2022) can serve to assess the student teachers' collaborative lesson planning practices.

With regard to the challenge posed by the different itineraries, future research needs to be focused on examining the differences between Education degrees that provide initial education for CLIL and its impact on prospective bilingual teachers, not only in English but also in other foreign languages such as German or French (Estrada Chichón & Segura Caballero, 2022). Also, it would be necessary to study again if the introduction of collaborative tasks, which explicitly deal with the collaborative competence, in the team-taught CLIL course described in this chapter, have a significant impact on students' collaborative competence (Custodio-Espinar et al., 2022).

It is paramount to continue analyzing the training gaps between university and school, which help to promote reflection and to research on professional skills and key competencies likely to improve the contents of the education offered in the academic plans of the undergraduate degrees in Primary Education. As Barceló Cerdá and Ruíz-Corbella (2015) suggest, the internship can be a period to promote opportunities to experience teaching in action and its relationship with the theory study in class. Another interesting proposal is to analyze students reflections on-action during their collaborative lesson planning (Gutierez, 2021).

CONCLUSION

Although CLIL and non-CLIL teachers share professional competences, CLIL teachers include in their profile a combination of competencies from different teacher profiles (content teacher and language teacher) plus the specific competencies needed to develop bilingual education through CLIL. The experience presented in this chapter is an example of how student teachers can be trained in those specific competencies necessary to achieve what Melara Gutiérrez and González López (2016) call "a competency profile of the Primary Education teacher specialized in CLIL teaching" (p. 359). As Bauml (2014) and Gutierez (2014) confirm, collaborative lesson planning is central to student teachers' knowledge development and it is an excellent context to develop multiple competencies, both technical and personal, necessary to teach CLIL in the classroom and to help student teachers to understand the relationship between the theory and the practice, because "a CLIL approach requires a CLIL professional" (Melara Gutiérrez & González López, 2016, p. 358) and initial education has to cater for this.

APPENDIX A

CLIL LESSON PLAN TEACHING TEAM (age group)	EFL TASK (all members)	Religion TASK (Teacher's name)	A & C TASK (Teacher's name)	Natural S. TASK (Teacher's name)	Social S. TASK (Teacher's name)	TIMING SESSIONS
CONTENT (content from the different content areas in the official curriculum)						
LEARNING GOALS (for content, process and language)						E.g. one week / 2-3 sessions per subject
MATERIALS & RESOURCES (include some ICT resources)						
GENERAL FEEDBACK FOR FORMATIVE ASSESSMENT:						

ACKNOWLEDGMENT

The author would like to thank her students for sharing their work and opinions and allowing the author to use them for the purposes of the article.

This research received no specific grant from any funding agency in the public, commercial, or not-for-profit sectors.

REFERENCES

Ball, P., Kelly, K., & Clegg, J. (2016). *Putting CLIL into practice: Oxford handbooks for language teachers*. Oxford University Press.

Barceló Cerdá, M. L., & Ruiz-Corbella, M. (2015). Las competencias profesionales del maestro de primaria desde la perspectiva del tutor del centro de prácticas [The professional skills of the primary school teacher from the perspective of the tutor of the internship school]. *Revista Fuentes*, (17), 17–39. doi:10.12795/revistafuentes.2015.i17.01

Bauml, M. (2014). Collaborative lesson planning as professional development for beginning primary teachers. *New Educator*, *10*(3), 182–200. doi:10.1080/1547688X.2014.925741

Bentley, K. (2010). *The TKT (teaching knowledge test) course. CLIL module content and language integrated learning*. Cambridge University Press.

Bertaux, P., Coonan, C. M., Frigols-Martín, M. J., & Mehisto, P. (2010). *The CLIL teacher's competences grid. Common constitution and language learning (CCLL)*. Comenius Network.

Comunidad de Madrid. (2021). *Datos y cifras de la educación 2021-2022* [Data and figures of education 2021-2022]. Dirección General de Bilingüismo y Calidad de la Enseñanza de la Consejería de Educación, Universidades, Ciencia y Portavocía. https://www.comunidad.madrid/servicios/educacion/educacion-cifras

Council of Europe. (2001). *Common European framework of reference for languages: Learning, teaching, assessment*. Cambridge University Press.

Custodio-Espinar, M. (2017, September 7). The role of language teaching in the CLIL classroom. Ages and Stages. Pearson. https://www.english.com/blog/clil-classroom/

Custodio-Espinar, M. (2019a). CLIL teacher education in Spain. In In K. Tsuchiya & Pérez-Murillo (Eds.), Content and language integrated learning in Spanish and Japanese contexts (pp. 313-337). Palgrave Macmillan. doi:10.1007/978-3-030-27443-6_13

Custodio-Espinar, M. (2019b). *Los principios metodológicos AICLE (aprendizaje integrado de contenido y lengua)* [The methodological principles CLIL (content and language integrated learning)]. Fundación Universitaria Española.

Custodio-Espinar, M. (2020). Influencing factors on in-service teachers' competence in planning CLIL. *Latin American Journal of Content & Language Integrated Learning, 12*(2), 207–241. doi:10.5294/laclil.2019.12.2.2

Custodio-Espinar, M., & García-Ramos, J. M. (2020). Are accredited teachers equally trained for CLIL? The CLIL teacher paradox. *Porta Linguarum, 33*(1), 9–25.

Custodio-Espinar, M., & López-Hernández, A. (2021). CLILing EMI for Effective Mediation in the L2 in Pre-service Teacher Education: A Case Study at a Spanish University. In L. Escobar & A. Ibáñez Moreno (Eds.), *Mediating Specialized Knowledge and L2 Abilities* (pp. 81–107). Palgrave Macmillan. doi:10.1007/978-3-030-87476-6_5

Custodio-Espinar, M., López-Hernández, A., & Buckingham, L. R. (2022). Effects of co-teaching on CLIL teacher trainees' collaborative competence. *Profesorado. Revista de Currículum y Formación de Profesorado, 26*(1), 87–106. doi:10.30827/profesorado.v26i1.16853

Dafouz, E., & Smit, U. (2020). *ROAD-MAPPING English medium education in the internationalised university*. Palgrave Macmillan. doi:10.1007/978-3-030-23463-8

Dale, L., & Tanner, R. (2012). *CLIL activities with CD-ROM: A resource for subject and language teachers*. Cambridge University Press.

Estrada Chichón, J.L., & Segura Caballero, N. (2022). Análisis de secuencias didácticas AICLE para Educación Primaria. *Revista Interuniversitaria de Formación del Profesorado, 98*(36.2), 275-295. doi:10.47553/rifop.v98i36.2.91999

European Centre of Modern Languages. (August 12, 2022). *Thematic areas of ECML expertise*. ECML. https://www.ecml.at/Thematicareas/Thematicareas-Overview/tabid/1763/language/en-GB/Default.aspx

European Commission, Directorate-General for Education, Youth, Sport and Culture. (2006). *Content and language integrated learning (CLIL) at school in Europe*. Publications Office.

European Higher Education Area (EHEA). (2022, February 19). *Terms of reference of working group on learning and teaching*. Working Group on Learning & Teaching. http://www.ehea.info/Upload/WG_L&T_PT_AD_TORs%20(2).pdf

Gutierez, S. B. (2021). Collaborative lesson planning as a positive 'dissonance' to the teachers' individual planning practices: Characterizing the features through reflections-on-action. *Teacher Development*, *25*(1), 37–52. doi:10.1080/13664530.2020.1856177

Gutiérrez Gamboa, M., & Custodio Espinar, M. (2021). CLIL teacher's initial education: A study of undergraduate and postgraduate student teachers. *Encuentro*, *29*, 104–119. doi:10.37536/ej.2021.29.1927

Irie, K., Ryan, S., & Mercer, S. (2018). Using Q methodology to investigate pre-service EFL teachers' mindsets about teaching competences. *Studies in Second Language Learning and Teaching*, *8*(3), 575–598. doi:10.14746sllt.2018.8.3.3

Jalongo, M. R., Rieg, S. A., & Helterbran, V. R. (2007). *Planning for learning: Collaborative approaches to lesson design and review*. Teachers College Press, Columbia University.

Kelly, M., Grenfell, M., Allan, R., Kriza, C., & McEvoy, W. (2004). *European profile for language teacher education: A frame of reference*. European Commission Brussels.

Leontjev, D., & DeBoer, M. (Eds.). (2020). *Assessment and Learning in Content and Language Integrated Learning (CLIL) Classrooms: Approaches and Conceptualisations*. Springer Nature.

López-Hernández, A. (2021). Initial teacher education of primary English and CLIL teachers: An analysis of the training curricula in the universities of the Madrid Autonomous Community (Spain). *International Journal of Learning. Teaching and Educational Research*, *20*(3), 132–150. doi:10.26803/ijlter.20.3.9

Marsh, D. (2017). Preface. In D. Lee Fields, 101 Scaffolding techniques for language teaching and learning: EMI, ELT, ESL, CLIL, EFL (pp. 9-10). Octaedro S.L.

Marsh, D., Mehisto, P., Wolff, D., & Frigols, M. J. (2010). *European framework for CLIL teacher education: A framework for the professional development of CLIL Teachers*. European Centre for Modern Languages.

Melara Gutiérrez, F. J., & González López, I. (2016). Sketching the figure of a bilingual teacher: Designing a profile of competencies. *Revista Española de Pedagogía*, *74*(264), 357–380.

Mendoza, N. B., Cheng, E. C., & Yan, Z. (2022). Assessing teachers' collaborative lesson planning practices: Instrument development and validation using the SECI knowledge-creation model. *Studies in Educational Evaluation*, *73*, 101–139. doi:10.1016/j.stueduc.2022.101139

Meyer, O. (2012). Introducing the CLIL pyramid: Key strategies and principles for quality CLIL planning and teaching. In M. Eisenmann & T. Summer (Eds.), *Basic issues in EFL teaching and learning* (pp. 265–283). Universitätsverlag WINTER.

Meyer, O., Halbach, A., & Coyle, D. (2015). A pluriliteracies approach to teaching for learning. *ECML-Council of Europe*. https://pluriliteracies. ecml.at/Portals/54/publications/pluriliteracies-Putting-apluriliteracies-approach-into-practice
. pdf

Moore, P., & Lorenzo, F. (2015). Task-based learning and content and language integrated learning materials design: Process and product. *Language Learning Journal, 43*(3), 334–357. doi:10.1080/09571736.2015.1053282

Morton, T. (2010). Using a Genre-Based Approach to Integrating Content and Language in CLIL. In C. Dalton-Puffer, T. Nikula, & U. Smit (Eds.), *Language Use and Language Learning in CLIL Classrooms* (pp. 81–104). John Benjamins., doi:10.1075/aals.7.05mor

Nieto Moreno de Diezmas, E., & Custodio Espinar, M. (2022). *Multilingual education under scrutiny: A critical analysis on CLIL implementation and research on a global scale.* Peter Lang., doi:10.3726/b20079

Otto, A., & Estrada Chichón, J. L. (2021). Analysing EMI assessment in higher education. *Revista Tempos E Espaços Em Educação, 14*(33), e15475. doi:10.20952/revtee.v14i33.15475

Pavón Vázquez, V. (2014). Enhancing the quality of CLIL: Making the best of the collaboration between language teachers and content teachers. *Encuentro, 23*, 115–127.

Pavón Vázquez, V., & Ellison, M. (2013). Examining teacher roles and competences in Content and Language Integrated Learning (CLIL). *Linguarum Arena, 4*, 65–78.

Pavón Vázquez, V., & Gaustad, M. (2013). Designing bilingual programmes for higher education in Spain: Organizational, curricular and methodological decisions. *International CLIL Research Journal, 1*(5), 82–94.

Pérez Cañado, M. L. (2017). CLIL teacher education: Where do we stand and where do we need to go? In M. E. Gómez Parra & R. Johnstone (Eds.), *Educación Bilingüe: tendencias educativas y conceptos claves* (pp. 129–144). Ministerio de Educación Cultura y Deporte.

Pérez Cañado, M. L. (2018). Innovations and challenges in CLIL teacher training. *Theory into Practice, 57*(3), 212–221. doi:10.1080/00405841.2018.1492238

Santagata, R., & Guarino, J. (2012). Preparing future teachers to collaborate. *Issues in Teacher Education, 21*(1), 59–69.

Shavard, G. (2022). Teacher agency in collaborative lesson planning: Stabilising or transforming professional practice? *Teachers and Teaching, 28*(5), 1–13. doi:10.1080/13540602.2022.2062745

Smit, U., & Dafouz-Milne, E. (2012). Integrating content and language in higher education: An introduction to English-medium policies, conceptual issues and research practices across Europe. *AILA Review, 25*(1), 1–12. doi:10.1075/aila.25.01smi

Spain. (2007). Order ECI/3857/2007. *Boletín Oficial del Estado [Official State Bulletin],* No. 312. https://www.boe.es/eli/es/o/2007/12/27/eci3857

Vilkancienė, L., & Rozgienė, I. (2017). CLIL teacher competences and attitudes. *Sustainable Multilingualism, 11*(1), 196–218. doi:10.1515m-2017-0019

Wolff, D. (2012). The European framework for CLIL teacher education. *Synergies Italie,* (8), 105–116.

KEY TERMS AND DEFINITIONS

CLIL training: The efficient design and implementation of academic itineraries and training courses likely to prepare preservice and inservice teachers for CLIL.

Collaborative competence: A personal competence necessary to work in teams in CLIL contexts.

Competency: Specific professional knowledge or skill.

Initial CLIL education: The provision of courses, modules, seminars, etc. on CLIL as part of the Education degrees.

CLIL lesson planning: Integration of the methodological principles of CLIL in the design and implementation of the curriculum by teachers.

PBL: Learner-centered approach in which a task is the focus of a long period of learning, usually combining different content areas.

TBL: Learner-centered approach in which a task is the focus of learning in a specific content area or a combination of them.

Collaborative Lesson Planning for CLIL Student Teachers of Primary Education

APPENDIX B

TEAM TEACHING COLLABORATIVE PLANNING RUBRIC

Teacher Name:

Team members: _____

CRITERIA	EXEMPLARY 2 points	ACCOMPLISHED 1,5 points	DEVELOPING 1 point	BEGINNING 0,5 points
Requirements: a task description per subject, goals and resources are included and are coordinated among them.	All requirements are met and exceeded.	All requirements are met.	One requirement was not completely met.	More than one requirement was not completely met.
Content: performance-based activities based on content of the different subjects included in the official curriculum, learning goals and multimodal input resources are included.	Covers topic in-depth with details and examples. Subject knowledge is excellent.	Includes essential knowledge about the modules. Subject knowledge appears to be good.	Includes essential information about the modules but there are 1-2 factual errors.	Content is minimal OR there are several factual errors.
Language proficiency	Language use is fluent and accurate throughout the team teaching lesson plan.	Language use is generally fluent and accurate, with only minor lexical, grammar and spelling mistakes.	Language use is sometimes fluent and accurate, with some lexical, grammar and spelling mistakes.	Language use includes a significant number of lexical, grammar and spelling errors, which make the lesson plan difficult to follow.
Process: team members work in a coordinated way to program around the same content from different areas including a strategy to develop subject literacies.	The group consistently stays focused on the task and what needs to be done. Very self-directed.	The group focuses on the task and what needs to be done most of the time. Some group members are not engaged.	The group focuses on the task and what needs to be done some of the time.	The group rarely focuses on the task and what needs to be done. There is no group work.
Originality	Product shows a large amount of original thought. Ideas are creative and inventive.	Product shows some original thought. Work shows new ideas and insights.	There is little evidence of original thinking.	Uses other people\'s ideas.

126

Collaborative Lesson Planning for CLIL Student Teachers of Primary Education

APPENDIX C

CLIL LESSON PLAN TEMPLATE*
© *Magdalena Custodio Espinar*

TITLE OF THE PROJECT/TASK:
CONTENT AREA:
Level: Year…
Timing: …sessions
Description (aim):
Final product: (based on a genre)

CONTENT	
Content (subject content from the official curriculum). • CONTENT • LANGUAGE CONTENT (the genre of the final product to develop subject literacies)	**Contribution to key competences** Learning strategies

COGNITION	
(follow a logical cognitive progression from LOTS to HOTS)	
Learning goals 1. To know 2. To compare 3. To peer- assess 4. To (genre)	**Learning outcomes or standards** 1.1 Pupils list 1.2 Pupils match 1.3 Pupils identify 2.1 Pupils classify 2.2 Pupils analyse. 2.3 Pupils compare 3.1 Pupils assess 4.1 Pupils (related to subject literacies)

CULTURE	
(follow a logical cognitive progression from LOTS to HOTS)	
Learning goals (idem) 5. To know/be aware…	**Learning outcomes (standards)** (idem) 5.1 Pupils label … 5.2

COMMUNICATION		
Coyle, Hood, and Marsh (2010)		
Language of learning	**Language for learning**	**Language through learning**
CONTENT-OBLIGATORY LANGUAGE **Key language:** (language specific to content) **Language content (the genre):** e.g., genre/recount = time connectors 'when, later, after…' or time expressions to recount 'used to'. **Academic language:** (linkers)	CONTENT-COMPATIBLE LANGUAGE Speech acts related to content The language necessary to develop the activities you are planning to learn the content Classroom language	New areas of meaning connected to the knowledge

PROCEDURE		
Timing	**Activities (T/ S role)**	**Grouping/spaces**
SESSIONS/Time planned for each activity, in minutes Dale & Tanner (2012) **RECEPTION** (INPUT) Listening/reading **TRANSFORMATION** (INTAKE) Listening/reading /writing/speaking **RODUCTION SCAFFOLDING** (OUTPUT) Writing/speaking	What the teacher (T), language assistant (LA) and students (Ss) are expected to do. **SESSION 1/2** (you plan activities to work the learning goals and standards in COGNITION AND CULTURE= To work the curricular content and its language) 1. ACTIVATION…. (questions, glossaries, brainstorming, rubrics or checklists) 2. XXX (activities to work declarative knowledge such as list, match… look at your learning standards!!) 3. XXX (activities to work procedural knowledge, look at your learning standards!!) VISUAL ORGANIZER, bingo, puzzles, jigsaw readings, … 4. Include the necessary activities for the culture learning outcome(s) in this sequence depending on the *savoir* you are working (Byram's 1997 ICC model). **SESSION 2/3** (to work on the language learning goal of the lesson, connected to the content in the form of a final product that involves a genre). • Reception (genre awareness, formal aspects, language input, modeling) • Transformation (connecting the final product to the content learnt in session 1/2) • Production scaffolding (performance of the final product providing the necessary scaffolds worked and/or produced on the previous activities) • Peer/self-assessment.	How you expect Ss to interact? What are the criteria for choosing groups? Examples: Whole class, pairs, groups of 3, etc.

Materials: (Materials that will be used by teacher and students, including SCAFFOLDING, ICT tools, arts materials, dictionaries, etc., e.g., worksheets, links to videos, audios or websites, printout of MS Ppt slides, sample posters or visual aids, etc.)
  • ICT tools inventory https://www.ecml.at/ECML-Programme/Programme2012-2015/ICT-RE VandmoreDOTS/ICT/tabid/1906/Default.aspx
  •

Continued on following page

Table Continued

CLIL LESSON PLAN TEMPLATE*
© Magdalena Custodio Espinar

Evaluation criteria (To locate, to explain… from official curriculum)
    • To understand, know, explain, describe, identify, respect…
Assessment tools: (Assessment tools that will be used to assess students. Include formative and summative assessment tools to be used by the teacher, the students and/or both).
    • **Of language:** (for interaction, for self/peer-assessment, …)
    • **Of content:** (rubric, checklist, test, quiz …)
Others: a checklist for active observation

ATTENTION TO DIVERSITY (Use a taxonomy to plan some of the activities at lower and higher order cognitive level) **LOTS** **HOTS**

*Taken from Custodio-Espinar (2019b).

APPENDIX D

COLLABORATIVE CLIL LESSON PLAN ASSESSMENT GRID			
STUDENT NAME		**GROUP:**	
ASSESSMENT	**Criteria**	**MAXIMUM SCORE**	**STUDENT SCORE**

CONTENT	The student knows how to integrate content and language in a CLIL lesson.
	    • Content
	    • Cognition
	    • Communication
	    • Culture
		3 points	3 points

	The student is able to plan and develop an integrated assessment strategy of content and language including formative assessment tools (checklists and rubrics).
	    • Connection with learning goals and outcomes
	    • Formative/Summative assessment tools
		3 points	3 points

PROCESS	The student is able to illustrate understanding of the CLIL approach through the analysis of different resources and materials to teach curricular content in different subjects to primary students.
	    • Activities
	    • Scaffolding
	    • ICT resources
		3 points	3 points

	The student is able to develop team teaching awareness and competence to improve the teaching/learning process in the bilingual classroom. (FROM TEAM TEACHING RUBRIC)	1 point	1 point
LANGUAGE	-0.05 points /grammar or spelling mistake -0.10 points/sense mistake	- 0,0	-0,0
FINAL MARK		10 points	**10 points**
FINAL COMMENTS: **Group work planning:** your lesson plans are... **Individual lesson planning:** Your CLIL lesson plan is…			

Chapter 7
CLIL Teachers' Beliefs and Practices:
How Can Teacher Training Help?

Ruth Milla

https://orcid.org/0000-0002-9771-7037
University of the Basque Country (UPV/EHU), Spain

Amaia Aguirregoitia Martínez

https://orcid.org/0000-0003-2465-5768
University of the Basque Country (UPV/EHU), Spain

ABSTRACT

This chapter presents the main aspects of a study conducted to explore existing beliefs and perspectives on CLIL-teaching specific practices and methodological aspects. The study aimed at identifying the educational practices accepted by CLIL experienced teachers and comparing them with prospective primary education teachers' underlying assumptions both before and after explicit instruction on CLIL based on experts' advice. The analysis of the results seems to indicate that instruction has modified students' beliefs and that specific training may contribute to the alignment of in-service teachers' praxis with the suggestions by experts in the field, in areas such as identifying problems in advance, using the learners' mother tongue, correcting language errors, using authentic materials, or presenting content. Interestingly, the answers of both teachers and students acknowledge the effectiveness of CLIL, although they reveal that appropriate qualification and training are a matter of concern that could benefit teachers greatly.

INTRODUCTION

The implementation of content and language integrated learning (CLIL) has widened in the last decades with the aim of creating multilingual and multicultural citizens in Europe, Asia, and South America. At the same time, an ample number of studies have been conducted on various aspects of CLIL, such as methodological issues, learners' language and content results, and stakeholders' perspectives. Results

DOI: 10.4018/978-1-6684-6179-2.ch007

Copyright © 2023, IGI Global. Copying or distributing in print or electronic forms without written permission of IGI Global is prohibited.

have been conflicting due to methodological weaknesses (Pérez Cañado, 2016) and the variations in the manner of implementing the CLIL principles (Cenoz, Genesee & Gorter, 2013). Besides, specific training provided to CLIL teachers has been found to be insufficient, not appropriate or even inexistent, especially before they graduate (Delicado Puerto & Pavón Vázquez, 2016).

The study presented in this chapter aims at exploring CLIL teachers' and teacher trainees' beliefs about how to integrate language in content-oriented lessons. The secondary objective is to look into the effect of training on teachers' beliefs and gain insight into this matter to help researchers in the field of CLIL, teacher trainers, as well as CLIL pre- and in-service teachers. To this aim, two questionnaires have been designed and administered: one of them to a group of 47 students in the Degree of Education both before and after receiving training on CLIL, and the second questionnaire has been completed by 16 in-service CLIL teachers in primary education schools. The answers were analyzed to identify significant differences regarding beliefs and practices after training and years of service.

In the following sections, literature on CLIL teaching and teachers' beliefs about CLIL will be reviewed, followed by a description of the present study and the methodology followed. Then, the results of the investigation will be presented and discussed in light of previous research. The main results point to the positive effects of teacher training on promoting adequate language integration in CLIL lessons. Finally, some implications for CLIL teacher trainers as well as researchers in the field will be discussed. Among others, the conclusions highlight the relevance of raising awareness of the theoretical aspects of the CLIL approach and the benefits of using effective teaching strategies such as scaffolding, communicative tasks or translanguaging. Finally, further research on CLIL teachers' beliefs and practices in CLIL classrooms is suggested.

BACKGROUND

CLIL has been described as "a dual-focused educational approach in which an additional language is used for the learning and teaching of both content and language" (Coyle, Hood, & Marsh, 2010: 1). That is, CLIL teachers have a two-folded aim: to teach a certain content, defined by the official curriculum and the subject itself, and to develop linguistic and communicative competence in a second (typically foreign) language. As Cenoz et al., (2013) put it, CLIL is an umbrella term for varied programs where language and content are taught in an integrated manner but, depending on sociocultural and educational factors, they might take different forms in their realization in the classroom. According to Mehisto, Marsh, and Frigols (2008), CLIL methodology needs to be focused on three types of outcomes: content-related, language-related and general skills related. The integration of these multifaceted goals proves difficult in practice for teachers new to CLIL programs (Villabona & Cenoz, 2022), therefore, teachers resort to their background training, resulting in content-oriented or language-oriented lessons, but without an actual integration of both. Actually, as Pellicer García (2017: 65) explains, "most teachers starting to teach content in the foreign language taught it as they would do in their mother tongue", unless they have been trained with CLIL-specific methodologies, such as the 4C framework: cognition, community, content and communication (Coyle et al., 2010). In this sense, the roles of language in CLIL lessons have been redefined, including academic language for specific subjects and the language of classroom interaction (Llinares, Morton, & Whittaker, 2012).

In spite of the variations pointed out above, CLIL programs should have common principles, methodologies and techniques as well as materials, and certain aspects need to be ensured for the implementation to be successful. Some examples are appropriate input, meaning-focused and form-focused activities, sufficient output production, and communication strategies (de Graaff, Koopman, Anikina, & Westhoff, 2007).

Regarding language, communication is primed, and the main aim is to develop the skills necessary to comprehend and express the content of the subject, such as reading, listening, speaking, writing or vocabulary. To do so, a communicative approach is favoured, the language should be scaffolded, and there is a need for accuracy promotion by the use of corrective feedback. Techniques need to be used, such as using the L1 when necessary but not too often (Costa & D'Angelo, 2011), pre-teaching key vocabulary, and explaining the grammar structures necessary for the lesson (Ioannou-Georgiou & Pavlov, 2011). Language errors are part of the learning process but sometimes attention has to be paid to those occurring more frequently, those which impede communication or understanding of the content, and those which are relevant to the topic. As for the corrective techniques, different types may be used, such as recasts, which do not interrupt the communication flow, or more explicit types such as elicitation, which help learners self-repair their own errors (Lyster & Ranta, 1997). Timing of oral feedback should also be considered, trying to balance the learners' noticing of recent errors and their wellbeing by delaying corrections so as not to put much pressure on them when they are using the foreign language (FL). In what refers to oral language, pronunciation and speaking skills can be promoted by presenting communicative activities with meaningful situations related to the content of the lesson (Richards, 2005). Some authors propose the use of individual and group presentations to promote understanding and participation (Coyle, 2005).

As for content learning, it can be facilitated by means of communicative tasks and the use of scaffolding (Ioannou-Georgiou & Pavlov, 2011). The same as with language, different scaffolding techniques may be used: teachers will find out about learners' previous knowledge on the topic, and spot difficult aspects to identify problems in advance. The content might be presented in different ways to help comprehension, using different formats and resources of varied nature. Additionally, teachers should provide sufficient examples, they can model what they want learners to do, the task may be divided into smaller steps, visual support can be used to illustrate explanations, and content might be graded. Finally, although accuracy is important, sometimes language errors need to be ignored and it is advised to focus on the learning process and consider affective factors (Rea-Dickins, 2020).

The development of cognitive skills such as lower-order thinking skills and higher-order thinking skills (the LOTS and HOTS proposed by Cummins, 1984) is also another essential aim in CLIL lesson planning (Coyle et al., 2010). A technique that teachers are advised to use is grading activities from less to more cognitively demanding, once other aspects such as content and language are gradually mastered.

Besides, collaborative work is an interesting interdisciplinary competence, which may be achieved by means of communicative tasks (Soboleva, 2019) and project-based learning.

In terms of materials, CLIL teachers should be aware of the need to use a variety of materials, not limited to the textbook provided by the school. Teachers may look for authentic materials in the target language, materials adapted to the learners' language level or age, audiovisual resources, and even materials in the learners' first language (L1) to promote translanguaging (Nikula & Moore, 2019) and subsequent learners' engagement with the subject. Materials used in CLIL classrooms nowadays have been found to be too complex in terms of language and content (Aguirregoitia et al., 2021a) and thus insufficient as scaffolding tools (Mahan, 2022), leaving to the teachers the job of adapting the materials to the needs of the students (Lorenzo, 2008), while teachers may or may not be prepared to do so.

Another issue to be considered when addressing CLIL teachers' training is the profile they should have. CLIL teachers need to have strong competence in both the language of instruction as well as in the content taught (Costa & D'Angelo, 2011). However, this is not the case in all CLIL modalities. In some contexts, CLIL teachers are language specialists with sufficient knowledge of the subject they are teaching, but some teachers are subject specialists with a sufficient level of proficiency in the target language but who lack knowledge of how to integrate language in a content-oriented lesson.

Besides specific training, CLIL teachers should coordinate with their language teachers' counterparts so that they can elaborate lesson plans in accordance with the language requirements for the content aims (Costa & D'Angelo, 2011).

Wrapping up, teaching CLIL does not simply consist of transmitting subject content in a language other than the L1, but as explained above, for this approach to be effective, several aspects of lesson planning and teaching itself need to be considered. Results of CLIL in terms of language have not always been positive (Banegas, 2022), even though a general advantage tends to be found in CLIL students over non-CLIL students as far as language proficiency gains. The type of methodology and, particularly, how it is being implemented is one of the main factors affecting the effectiveness of CLIL programmes. As Gutiérrez Gamboa and Custodio Espinar (2021) argue, teachers' training is one of the most influential factors in CLIL effectiveness, together with teachers' linguistic competence. Therefore, CLIL teachers' lack of training may hinder the achievement of the full potential of this approach. For instance, some CLIL teachers are not aware of the fact that CLIL does not just imply using a different language of instruction (Baetens Beardsmore, 1999). Studies investigating CLIL teachers' beliefs and practices have revealed their lack of awareness about the need to integrate language in the CLIL lessons, considering this a duty for their language teacher counterparts (Mariño Avila, 2014; Milla & García Mayo, 2021; Milla & García Mayo, in press; Villabona & Cenoz, 2022). Hence, when asked about teaching techniques to focus on form, CLIL teachers show a welcoming attitude, but then, their practices do not match these beliefs. Conversely, CLIL teachers who are also language teachers (such as Chinese or Spanish primary school teachers) do not present this mismatch between beliefs and practices (Dalton-Puffer, 2007; Guzmán-Alcón, 2019; Llinares & Lyster, 2014; Nguyen, 2018). Therefore, it seems that language teaching training can help in some sense, even though teaching a language and integrating it into a content lesson is not the same thing.

As seen above, teacher training is one of the requirements for a successful CLIL program (Custodio Espinar & García Ramos, 2020). However, training on CLIL is not offered in all teacher education degrees nowadays and it was certainly not provided in the past when many of the in-service teachers graduated. In an attempt to respond to the demands of bilingual education programs, continuous training is now offered to these teachers while CLIL courses are being developed in Education faculties around the world. Based on some research conducted on the effect of training (Banegas, 2015; Delicado Puerto & Pavón Vázquez, 2016; Estrada Chichón & Segura Caballero, 2022; Hillyard, 2011; Pena Díaz & Porto Requejo, 2008; Pérez Cañado, 2015), the aims of teacher training on CLIL should be to develop teachers' skills regarding several competencies such as how to integrate language and content, how to manage two (or more) languages in the lessons, how to include learner-oriented activities and how to select, adapt and assess materials (McDougald & Pissarello, 2020; Pokrivčáková, 2015). In addition to considering official curricula, training can be designed considering teachers' or trainees' beliefs and previous experiences with CLIL as learners and teachers (Banegas, 2015). To do so, insight is needed into pre-service and in-service teachers' perspectives and initial knowledge, as well as studies on the effect of training on those beliefs. To the best of our knowledge, there are no studies comparing the beliefs of experienced and inexperienced CLIL teachers and very few have looked into the impact of training on beliefs about CLIL. With the aim of filling this gap in the literature, the present study was set out to dig into the reported beliefs about CLIL, which will be described in the following sections.

MAIN FOCUS OF THE CHAPTER

Issues, Controversies, Problems

As seen above, and as Setiawan (2013, p. 22) summarizes in his PhD dissertation, "[t]he lack of teacher training, the lack of appropriate and sufficient CLIL material, and teachers' and students' low FL proficiency become some of the contributing factors which diminish CLIL potential." In the present study, the authors aimed to address one of these factors, namely teacher training, as a first step to improving the quality of CLIL teaching. Moreover, teachers' beliefs have a great impact on their pedagogical decisions and their actual behaviour in the classroom (Milla & García Mayo, 2021). Hence, gaining knowledge of CLIL teachers' perspectives is likely to provide insight into which aspects need to be strengthened by means of training. In order to contribute to the existing literature on CLIL beliefs and teachers' training, the questions below were entertained.

Research Questions and Hypotheses

- RQ1: What is the effect of training on the beliefs of pre-service teachers about how to integrate language in CLIL lessons? Does previous experience with CLIL as learners affect the students' perspective about CLIL?
    - ◦ H1: Looking at previous research (Banegas, 2015; 2022; Estrada Chichón & Segura Caballero, 2022; Gutiérrez Gamboa & Custodio Espinar, 2021; Hillyard, 2011; McDougald & Pissarello, 2020; Pérez Cañado, 2015), it was predicted that training would lead trainees' perspectives to be more in line with what literature considers to be effective techniques to integrate language in their CLIL lessons.
    - ◦ H2: Additionally, students with previous experience as CLIL learners were expected to have a positive view of the approach regarding their language gains.
- RQ2: Which are in-service CLIL teachers' beliefs and reported practices to integrate language in CLIL lessons? What effect do teaching experience and training have on teachers' beliefs?
    - ◦ H1: CLIL teachers' beliefs and practices were hypothesized to match previous research on the topic, as long as they had received specific training (McDougald & Pissarello, 2020; Milla & García Mayo, 2021; Pena Díaz & Porto Requejo, 2008).
    - ◦ H2: As for the second question, since there are no previous studies on this comparison, it was hypothesized that there would be differences between teachers and trainees depending on the training as well as the years of experience the teachers had.
- RQ3: What are the concerns of CLIL teachers at primary education level? How can teacher training contribute in relation to these?
    - ◦ H1: CLIL teachers in the present study were expected to have similar concerns to those in previous research: lack of appropriate materials and need for specific training (McDougald

& Pissarello, 2020; Milla & García Mayo, 2021; Pena Díaz & Porto Requejo, 2008; Pérez Cañado, 2016).

- ○ H2: In addition, new ideas related to CLIL implementation or results were hypothesized to have aroused in the last few years.

Instruments

The sample for the research consists of two groups of participants from the Basque Autonomous Community (BAC): sample A, made of 47 students, of which 15 have been students of a CLIL program in the pre-university education and sample B, incorporating a cohort of 16 in-service teachers of which seven have no previous CLIL instruction.

For that purpose, two questionnaires were used, with 5 point-Likert scale items providing five possible answers and a few open questions. Questionnaire 1 (see appendix 1), which was addressed to students in the 4th year of the bachelor's degree in primary education, involved questions covering basic sociodemographic information and previous experience, level of English, and knowledge of CLIL. As to their knowledge of CLIL, they were asked for some definitions, fundamental issues to initiate a CLIL project (training on methodology, language proficiency, materials and resources, learners' motivation), the relevance of some language components (grammar, vocabulary, suitability for content transfer) and the types of activities to be used when planning a CLIL lesson (to work on the different skills, to balance individual and group activities, collaborative tasks). Besides, they were asked about scaffolding practices and their relevance from the respondents' perspective, in which students rated aspects such as modelling, the division of the task into smaller steps and grading them according to their difficulty, presenting the information in different formats, and the use of L1. Another set of twelve questions was devoted to corrective feedback, the type of errors to be corrected and how to address them. The questionnaire also included some questions about how to promote communication and use the CLIL classroom for that purpose (designing communicative activities related to the content, using presentations, and not penalizing the use of L1 when it is necessary, to mention some). The next five questions inquired about the use of authentic material or other types of material (audiovisuals, adapted materials, or content in the student's L1). Furthermore, students were challenged to define the best candidate to be a CLIL teacher based on the candidate's experience, university degree, specific training in CLIL, and English certification level. Finally, the questionnaire included ten questions for students who had attended CLIL lessons during their compulsory education. They were asked to assess, from their previous personal experience, the potential contributions and benefits of CLIL (global improvement in their English proficiency or some specific areas, etc.). This questionnaire was administered twice digitally by means of Google forms before the specific training on CLIL-related topics of the course and after the instruction period (one month). Regarding the training, the students were given reading materials on CLIL principles and theoretical aspects (Escobar Urmeneta, 2019; Ioannoau-Georgiou & Pavlov, 2011), to be analysed before the session when the professor presented the most relevant ideas. Later, a group discussion was opened. In the following session, practical issues were explained by offering information on relevant techniques and strategies along with the design of a lesson plan (Coyle, 2005). Next, students applied their knowledge to design a lesson plan for a specific topic in one of the subjects of primary education. The lesson plans were presented orally and, for each group, one of the activities was used in the classroom to simulate a real learning situation. Finally, feedback was provided on the appropriateness of the pedagogical choices, materials, and performance.

CLIL Teachers' Beliefs and Practices

Regarding the second sample, a cohort of CLIL primary school teachers from the BAC was provided with a Google form containing a very similar questionnaire with minor adjustments. The questionnaire completed by the students was used as a basis for the second questionnaire although a few questions were deleted and replaced by more pertinent ones such as years of experience, previous experience as a CLIL teacher, their viewpoint on the effectiveness of these programs or their concerns on necessities and requirements for a successful experience (see appendix 2). The questionnaire was sent to a high number of schools but only 16 of them agreed to respond to the invitation.

After collecting the data, they were statistically analyzed with the SciPy program, as described in the section below.

Data Analyses

The questionnaire validity was ensured since the items and thematic strands in which the questions were organized stem from the aspects considered in previous research about CLIL methodology and teacher training (Banegas, 2015; Coyle et al., 2011; Pérez Cañado, 2016, among others). In the same line, the face validity of the questionnaire was guaranteed by using Google forms (https://docs.google.com/forms/u/0/), a well-known and user-friendly software which allows easy and efficient answering and analysis of responses.

In order to carry out the statistical analyses, Python 3.8's SciPy version 1.8.1 was used. SciPy is a collection of mathematical algorithms and convenience functions built on the NumPy extension of Python and the numpy 1.23.1 version of the main package. The Wilcoxon signed-rank test, which is the non-parametric univariate test - an alternative to the dependent t-test for samples with non-normal distributions - was used to analyze the significant differences after the specific training course offered in the 4th year of the university degree. Additionally, the Mann-Whitney U test was performed to compare the responses from students with previous CLIL experience and students without previous experience. Finally, the same type of test was also used to detect differences between in-service teachers and prospective teachers (after training). The Mann-Whitney U test is a non-parametric test that can be used in place of an unpaired t-test. It is used to test the null hypothesis that two samples come from the same population or, alternatively, whether observations in one sample tend to be larger than observations in the other. Although it is a non-parametric test it does assume that the two distributions are similar in shape.

Besides the statistical analyses, a descriptive analysis of the data was carried out, searching for common themes in the open questions from both sets of questionnaires. Results will be presented and discussed in the following section.

RESULTS AND DISCUSSION

In what follows, the results of the analyses of the data from the questionnaires are presented and explained.

Significant Differences After Training (RQ1a)

The first question of this research aimed at the identification of the facets or views that have been affected by the training received by the students. For that purpose, a statistical analysis using the Wilcoxon paired test has been carried out to find significant differences between pre-training responses and post-training responses of 47 students. Regarding scaffolding techniques, the analysis has proved that students' awareness of the relevance of dividing the task into small steps and grading the type of activities from less to more cognitively demanding has significantly grown (p=0.00). Students have also scored higher at the use of L1 if necessary and at allowing learners to use it (p=0.02) after instruction. Another aspect that has been significantly affected is their viewpoint on corrective feedback when errors that hinder communication occur (p=0.01). The after-training test shows that the item about the correction of language errors that impede communication scored 4.44 out of 5. Moreover, students will be significantly more inclined to identify problems in advance after the formative period (p=0.02) and therefore, it can be concluded that instruction has also been effective to clarify notions about these practices. Therefore, as predicted, training was effective in making students aware of techniques and teaching strategies on how to integrate language better in the CLIL lessons, as previous studies had found (Banegas, 2015), which confirms the benefits of receiving specific training on CLIL, as mentioned above (Banegas, 2022; Estrada Chichón & Segura Caballero, 2022; Gutiérrez Gamboa & Custodio Espinar, 2021; Hillyard, 2011; McDougald & Pissarello, 2020; Pérez Cañado, 2015).

Table 1 presents the details of the items showing significant differences.

Table 1. Significant differences between the answers of students after and before training

Question	Before training		After training		p value
	Mean value	Standard deviation	Mean value	Standard deviation	
Identify problems in advance	4.21	0.62	4.63	0.54	0.02
Divide the task into small steps	4.36	0.67	4.76	0.43	0.00
Use the L1 if necessary or allow students to use it	3.70	0.78	4.22	0.72	0.02
Grade the type of activities from less to more cognitively demanding	4.00	0.72	4.73	0.59	0.00
Correct language errors that impede communication	3.87	0.80	4.44	0.78	0.01

Significant Differences Between CLIL And Non-CLIL (RQ1b)

To investigate the effect of previous CLIL experience as students, the Mann-Whitney U test has been carried out to compare responses (before training) of students that had previously been taught content through English versus students without previous CLIL experience. The most significant difference is detected in the item "Grade the type of activities from less to more cognitively demanding" (p=0.01), which seems to indicate that learning content through a foreign language makes students acknowledge the need for a careful grading of the activities. Besides, differences have also been found in the items related to the use of the L1 and to the role of motivation in the classroom (p=0.03). This points out that students with prior experience on CLIL do not rely strongly upon the use of the mother tongue for effective transmission of knowledge and that they favour alternative clarification techniques that imply enhancing the use of the L2. Further, students with previous CLIL experience believe that students' motivation is a crucial element to start a CLIL program. Additionally, responses confirm that correcting

CLIL Teachers' Beliefs and Practices

language errors which are relevant to the lesson is perceived as more important by students with prior experience in CLIL (p=0.04). In previous research, CLIL learners have been found to gain motivation toward FL learning (Lasagabaster & Doiz, 2017) and content learning through CLIL (Banegas, 2013). The present study confirms that they might be more aware of effective language teaching techniques, too.

Table 2 presents the details of the items showing significant differences.

Table 2. Significant differences between the answers of students with previous CLIL experience as learners and those without previous experience

Question	CLIL students		Students without previous CLIL exp.		p value
	Mean value	Standard deviation	Mean value	Standard deviation	
Students' motivation	4.89	0.31	4.60	0.49	0.03
Use the L1 if necessary or allow students to use it	3.36	0.68	3.92	0.73	0.03
Grade the type of activities from less to more cognitively demanding	4.31	0.74	3.78	0.61	0.01
Correct language errors which are relevant for the lesson	4.26	0.45	3.85	0.60	0.04

Students' Comments (RQ1c)

The next lines identify the main concerns and contributions made by the fifteen prospective teachers of the Faculty of Education who have previous experience as CLIL students when they attended Primary or Secondary education. Interestingly, all the students affirm that the experience was positive, admit that the methodology is useful and that studying content in a second language has improved their proficiency in English. In particular, one of the students who makes a more accurate identification, observes that vocabulary, listening, and fluency are the most improved areas. Some other students added that CLIL lessons offer a lot of benefits for students and that they only see advantages in this approach.

However, the answers of the students also pose some potential problems to be considered. 37.5% of the students spontaneously address the topic of CLIL teachers' training. Students express their concerns about the specific training and professional capabilities required to be a CLIL teacher with sentences such as "teachers should need to be prepared and well-formed", "teachers should be trained beforehand", and, similarly, they raise the question of which should be the requirements of the perfect candidate to be a CLIL teacher. Moreover, two students support that, to their way of thinking, some students might feel frustrated because grasping the concepts can be more difficult and stressful when learning through a FL. These students object that specifically, it might undermine students who are less proficient in English and cause them anxiety. Another student points out the essential need for coordination among language teachers and CLIL teachers and advises that it is his strong belief that CLIL implementation without this integration seems impossible. It seems clear that pre-service teachers in this study are aware of the need for training and the use of specific methodologies when teaching CLIL, which is in line with previous findings in studies about the positive effect of CLIL training (Banegas, 2015; 2022; Hillyard, 2011; McDougald & Pissarello, 2020; Pérez Cañado, 2015).

Finally, the last issue mentioned in the responses affects particularly the context of the study, the BAC, but might also be extended to other plurilingual contexts. In accordance with the provisions of the European Charter for Regional or Minority Languages (Council of Europe, 1992) and taking into account both that the environmental conditions and social interaction favour the use of Spanish and that evaluations have shown that the use of Basque in the teaching-learning process is essential to acquire sufficient oral and written communicative competence, the multilingual educational system of the BAC has Basque as its axis. The objective is to overcome the current imbalance between the two official languages – currently unfavourable for Basque - and promote social equality of both languages and equal opportunities for students. Being Basque the main axis of education in the BAC, one of the students argues that we should not forget that "Basque language should be the core of public education", which seems to indicate that the introduction of CLIL and its effect might cause concern to some teachers. Nevertheless, achieving multilingual people with sufficient knowledge of at least one foreign language is also among the objectives of education, and that, according to the students' responses, it can be concluded that CLIL seems an effective means to achieve that goal.

Significant Differences Between Students and Teachers (RQ2)

As to the second research question, the study also aimed at interpreting the effect of the professional background as a teacher and comparing the responses of 16 practiced professionals and 47 trained students. As can be seen in table 3, the Mann-Whitney U test pointed out several significant differences. Firstly, students show a greater acknowledgement of the relevance of identifying problems in advance ($p=0.00$) and using the L1 if necessary or allowing learners to use it ($p=0.00$). In contrast, teachers give more importance to correcting learners to prevent the errors from becoming permanent ($p=0.00$). Regarding activities, oral presentations to be done individually and in pairs/groups ($p=0,00$) are graded more highly by experienced teachers. Concerning materials, authentic materials in English (journals, magazines, videos, films, etc.) ($p=0,00$), materials in English adapted to the students' level ($p=0.00$) as well as materials in the students' L1 ($p=0.01$) are also reported to be useful more frequently by students after the training. There is another significant difference regarding the way information is presented, and it is confirmed that students defend more strongly the need for presenting the same content in different formats ($p=0,01$). Regarding error treatment, students also find it more necessary to correct language errors that impede communication ($p=0.02$). Furthermore, another difference is that students identify motivation as a key aspect to starting the implementation of CLIL at schools ($p=0.02$) which is identified as a key aspect to a lesser degree by teachers. As to content, students advocate more enthusiastically for the use of L1 and other techniques to make sure students understand as well as for presenting content in different ways ($p=0.02$). In addition, students defend the use of speaking activities, both individual and collaborative ($p=0.04$), while teachers support more firmly the inclusion of reading activities in the unit, either the ones in the book or self-prepared ones ($p=0.02$). Finally, students without teaching experience seem to be more conscious of the importance of finding out students' previous knowledge about the topic/language of the lesson ($p=0.04$). These findings show that formative actions are helpful in the sense that after receiving instructions students are more aware of effective techniques to integrate language teaching in their CLIL lessons than experienced teachers.

CLIL Teachers' Beliefs and Practices

Table 3. Significant differences between the answers of trained students and in-service experienced teachers

Question	Students		Experienced teachers		p value
	mean value	Standard deviation	mean value	Standard deviation	
Students' motivation	4.73	0.55	4.25	0.86	0.02
CONTENT: use L1 and other techniques to make sure they understand, and present it in different ways	50.24%	16.12%	36.33%	26.69%	0.02
I prepare reading activities if there aren't any and never skip the ones in the book	3.10	1.09	3.88	0.96	0.02
I include speaking activities both individual and collaborative	4.78	0.42	4.25	1.00	0.04
Identify problems in advance	4.63	0.54	3.88	0.89	0.00
Find out students' previous knowledge about the topic/language of the lesson	4.85	0.36	4,.44	0.89	0.04
Use the L1 if necessary or allow students to use it	4,22	0.72	3,13	1.15	0.00
Present the same content in different formats	4.59	0.67	4.13	0.62	0.01
Always correct them to prevent the errors from becoming permanent	2.54	0.90	3.56	1.03	0.00
Correct language errors that impede communication	4.44	0.78	3.69	1.20	0.02
Use of oral presentations to be done individually and in pairs/groups	27.27%	13.54%	48.20%	28.19%	0.00
Authentic materials in English (journals, magazines, videos, films, etc.)	4.93	0.26	4.25	0.86	0.00
Use of materials in the students' L1	2.56	1.05	1.81	1.05	0.01
Materials in English adapted to the students' level	4.83	0.38	4.31	0.70	0.00

Concerns of In-Service Teachers (RQ3)

The next lines will analyze the main concerns of the cohort of 16 in-service teachers that have taken part in the research. Regarding teachers' education, six teachers have a Degree in Primary Education, seven have the said degree but, additionally, they have attended the Foreign Language Minor and only two of them have graduated in different areas of knowledge. Concerning their English level certification, three of them possess the B2 degree, 13 of them are certified at C1 level and only one has obtained the C2 certificate. With respect to their teaching experience, one of the teachers has been teaching for more than 20 years, three of them have more than 10 years of experience and the rest have been on the job between one and four years. When asked about the key aspects to implement CLIL at schools, all the teachers answered that specific CLIL training was required and the mean value for this question was m=4.43 out of 5 points. However, language training (m= 4.62) and materials and resources (4.56) scored slightly higher than specific CLIL instruction, whereas students' motivation is also considered a critical aspect (m= 4.25). The open answers also highlighted the relevance of teachers' motivation, the need for support from administration and families and the time to select the most appropriate material for each session.

When asked about the focus of their sessions, in general, grammar is given less attention (m=25% of the time) than vocabulary (m=39%) or content (m=36%) and only one of the teachers expresses that he devotes more time to grammar. The questionnaire included a question about the use of L1 in the classroom and L2 teachers agreed that the use of L1 should be avoided but they established certain situations where it should be used (for classroom management or to avoid communication problems). However, four of them supported that only English should be used during the CLIL session and, surprisingly, only 12.5% of the participants selected the option of using L1 and integrating the learners' languages in the lessons, with the appropriate planning.

Regarding the perceived effect of CLIL programs, nine teachers (56%) observed that participating in CLIL projects might increase students' motivation toward English, although some others admit that they find it hard to motivate students and add that it depends on the group and also on their level. In the final remarks, one of the teachers was very enthusiastic and held that "We have found CLIL lessons to have greatly improved student participation and motivation in class and it has given them a greater appreciation for learning English". All the teachers recognize that the level of the students increases when participating in a CLIL project and in the open question they subscribe to the need for adaptation of the content in some cases, of the activities in some others, and emphasize that scaffolding and the use of L1 are critical for success.

Teachers were asked to define the perfect candidate to be a CLIL teacher, and 81.3% agreed that the best option would be a teacher who complies with three requirements: a C1 certificate, a degree in primary education and a specific course in CLIL. The second choice, which was made by 12.5% of the participants, is the profile of a teacher who has a Degree in Primary Education, a C1 certificate and teaching experience, so it might be concluded that teachers consider specific education on CLIL more essential than experience. Some of the comments they made to justify their option indeed clarify this idea: "I think C1 is a high level to teach in Primary but it's more important to know how to teach in CLIL", "I think a specific course in CLIL is necessary for teaching in that approach", "I think it is not enough to be a science teacher with a good English level. The teacher with a course in CLIL will know better how to balance language and content teaching because both of them are important".

SOLUTIONS AND RECOMMENDATIONS

The findings of the present study, although limited due to the small size of the samples, call for some implications for teacher training on CLIL. For instance, it seems that some aspects of teachers' knowledge of the CLIL approach are interesting enough to be considered for teacher training programs, such as the use of pedagogical translanguaging, scaffolding techniques, appropriate feedback on language errors and communicative tasks. As teacher trainers, the authors believe that one of their main tasks is to make teachers (and student teachers) aware of the particularities of CLIL as an approach for teaching content as well as language and to offer them the tools to be able to design effective and adequate lessons. Offering them some training in fundamental aspects of CLIL appears to have modified their views, as shown in the results of the present study, which is likely to have an impact on their future teaching. Throughout the chapter, it has been shown that authors in the field of CLIL teacher training agree that teachers perform better when they have been trained and that it seems more appropriate to start this training in the initial formative period at university. Primary school CLIL teachers in the present study appear to be more concerned with the use of communicative tasks and developing oral skills, which might be explained by their linguistic background. However, they admit making scarce use of necessary techniques such as scaffolding or translanguaging in their CLIL lessons, which could be amended by specific training.

The in-service teachers' concerns also call for the administration's help in facilitating adequate materials and training on how to scaffold content and language. Integration of FL and content, together with cognitive and intercultural competencies is a difficult endeavour for these teachers, and it cannot be expected for them to endure the excessive workload of designing lessons and materials without external support.

FUTURE RESEARCH DIRECTIONS

Despite the contributions of the present paper, some limitations are to be acknowledged. First, the sample size, especially in the case of the in-service teachers' group, prevents results from being generalized to other contexts. Nevertheless, general findings are in line with previous research in other settings, both regarding the benefits of CLIL training at undergraduate levels (Banegas, 2022; Estrada Chichón & Segura Caballero, 2022; Gutiérrez Gamboa & Custodio Espinar, 2021; Hillyard, 2011; McDougald & Pissarello, 2020; Pérez Cañado, 2015), and as far as in-service teachers' beliefs about CLIL are concerned (McDougald & Pissarello, 2020; Milla & García Mayo; Pena Díaz & Porto Requejo, 2008; Pérez Cañado, 2016), so it is likely that further research with a larger sample in the context of the BAC would reveal similar results. Besides, nowadays in the BAC, CLIL is beginning to be implemented systematically in primary education, hence, so far there is a limited number of in-service teachers who are currently teaching within this approach, and that explains our limited sample of teachers. However, given the growing interest in multilingualism in the BAC and looking at the rapid spread of CLIL in secondary education in the last few decades, the authors of the present chapter consider it interesting to continue this line of research in the near future with a larger sample of in-service CLIL teachers.

A second limitation is derived from the fact that only reported beliefs and practices have been considered and no direct classroom observations have been carried out to verify if actual practices match what the CLIL teachers reported in the questionnaires, which is not always the case (Milla & García Mayo, 2021). Future studies with in-service teachers would benefit from observations of the participant teachers' lessons as well as from the use of a triangulated methodology with interviews or focus groups to clarify the participants' answers.

Going beyond the scope of the present paper, the authors believe it would be interesting to do research on teachers' beliefs on multilingual education and translanguaging, which also have a significant effect on how languages are used in the classroom, stress, comprehension and on the success of CLIL programs. Moreover, further research should be conducted on students' actual difficulties in CLIL experiences- analyzing and evaluating materials and assessing receptive and productive skills – to identify real obstacles and adapt formative actions to the results.

Lastly, the potential benefits of the use of technology in the CLIL classroom is another issue to be explored in future research, along with the formative needs to ensure that teachers are qualified to apply current technological resources most efficiently. Previous experiences have reported the positive effects of integrating music and video in the CLIL lesson (Aguirregoitia & Etxebarria, 2021b) or using Augmented Reality to learn a second language (Aguirregoitia et al., 2017).

CONCLUSION

In this chapter, insight has been gained into the positive effect of teacher training in CLIL on pre-service teachers' beliefs about the integration of language in CLIL lessons. It seems that in-service teachers might also benefit from specific training since some aspects of the CLIL methodology are reported to be overlooked by these teachers in their everyday practice. CLIL teachers should be made aware of the need for scaffolding of language and content, translanguaging, feedback and focus on forms that are essential for the content, and use of authentic materials and speaking activities.

The findings have also allowed for confirmation of what previous studies had revealed. Teachers in CLIL are concerned with the lack of adequate material available and training to perform efficiently and demand a more active involvement of administrators and families. Given that teachers' behaviour is one of the primary agents for FL learning, further research is encouraged to be conducted on CLIL, particularly with regards to teacher training and learning results.

ACKNOWLEDGMENT

This research received no specific grant from any funding agency in the public, commercial, or not-for-profit sectors.

The authors would like to thank the teachers and university students for their participation in the study.

REFERENCES

Aguirregoitia, A., Bengoetxea, K., & Gonzalez-Dios, I. (2021a). Are CLIL texts too complicated?: A computational analysis of their linguistic characteristics. *Journal of Immersion and Content-Based Language Education, 9*(1), 4–30. doi:10.1075/jicb.19022.agu

Aguirregoitia, A., & Etxebarria, E. G. (2021b). Let's sing this CLIL lesson: Integrating language, content, music and video. In *Innovación e investigación educativa para la formación docente [Innovation and educational research for teacher training]* (pp. 282–296). Dykinson.

Aguirregoitia, A., López Benito, J. R., Artetxe González, E., & Bilbao Ajuria, E. (2017). *Una experiencia de aplicación de Realidad Aumentada para el Aprendizaje del Inglés en Educación Infantil* [An experience of application of Augmented Reality for the Learning of English in Early Childhood Education.]. Atas do XIX Simpósio Internacional de Informática Educativa e VIII Encontro do CIED–III Encontro Internacional [Proceedings of the XIX International Symposium on Educational Informatics and VIII Meeting of CIED–III International Meeting].

Baetens Beardsmore, H. (1999). La consolidation des expériences en éducation plurilingue. [Consolidating experiences in plurilingual education.] In D. Marsh & B. Marsland (Eds.), *CLIL Initiatives for the Millennium*. University of Jyväskylä Continuing Education Centre.

Banegas, D. L. (2013). The integration of content and language as a driving force in the EFL lesson. In E. Ushioda (Ed.), *International perspectives on motivation: Language learning and professional challenges* (pp. 82–97). Palgrave. doi:10.1057/9781137000873_5

Banegas, D. L. (2015). Sharing views of CLIL lesson planning in language teacher education. *Latin American Journal of Content and Language Integrated Learning*, *8*(2), 104–130. doi:10.5294/laclil.2015.8.2.3

Banegas, D. L. (2022). Research into practice: CLIL in South America. *Language Teaching*, *55*(3), 379–391. doi:10.1017/S0261444820000622

Cenoz, J., Genesee, F., & Gorter, D. (2013). Critical analysis of CLIL: Taking stock and looking forward. *Applied Linguistics*, *35*(3), 243–262. doi:10.1093/applin/amt011

Costa, F., & D'Angelo, L. (2011). CLIL: A suit for all seasons? *Latin American Journal of Content & Language Integrated Learning*, *4*(1), 1–13. doi:10.5294/laclil.2011.4.1.1

Council of Europe. (1992). European Charter for Regional or Minority Languages. *European Treaty Series, 148.* https://www.coe.int/en/web/european-charter-regional-or-minority-languages/home

Coyle, D. (2005). *CLIL: Planning tools for teachers*. The University of Nottingham, School of Education.

Coyle, D., Hood, P., & Marsh, D. (2010). *CLIL: Content and language integrated learning*. Cambridge University Press. doi:10.1017/9781009024549

Cummins, J. (1984). *Bilingualism in Special Education. Issues in Assessment and Pedagogy*. Multilingual Matters.

Custodio Espinar, M., & García Ramos, J. M. (2020). Medida de la competencia para programar AICLE y diagnóstico de las necesidades de formación docente. [Measurement of competence to program CLIL and diagnosis of teacher training needs.] *Revista de Pedagogía, 72*(I), 31–48.

Dalton-Puffer, C. (2007). *Discourse in content and language integrated learning (CLIL) classrooms*. John Benjamins. doi:10.1075/lllt.20

de Graaff, R., Koopman, G. J., Anikina, J., & Westhoff, G. (2007). An Observation Tool for Effective L2 Pedagogy in Content and Language Integrated Learning (CLIL). *International Journal of Bilingual Education and Bilingualism, 10*(5), 603–624. doi:10.2167/beb462.0

Delicado Puerto, G., & Pavón Vázquez, V. (2016). Training primary student teachers for CLIL: Innovation through collaboration. *Pulso. Review of Education, 39*, 35–57.

Escobar Urmeneta, C. (2019). An Introduction to Content and Language Integrated Learning (CLIL) for Teachers and Teacher Educators. *CLIL Journal of Innovation and Research in Plurilingual and Pluricultural Education, 2*(1), 7–19. doi:10.5565/rev/clil.21

Estrada Chichón, J. L., & Segura Caballero, N. (2022). Analysis of CLIL teaching sequences for primary education. *Revista Interuniversitaria de Formación del Profesorado, 98*(36.2), 279-299.

Gutiérrez Gamboa, M., & Custodio Espinar, M. (2021). CLIL teachers' initial education: A study of undergraduate and postgraduate student teachers. *Encuentro, 29*, 104–119. doi:10.37536/ej.2021.29.1927

Guzmán-Alcón, I. (2019). Investigating the application of communicative language teaching principles in primary education: A comparison of CLIL and FL classrooms. *English Language Teaching, 12*(2), 88–99. doi:10.5539/elt.v12n2p88

Hillyard, S. (2011). First steps in CLIL: Training the teachers. *Latin American Journal of Content & Language Integrated Learning, 4*(2), 1–12. doi:10.5294/laclil.2011.4.2.1

Ioannou-Georgiou, S., & Pavlou, P. (2011). *Guidelines for CLIL implementation in primary and pre-primary education.* PROCLIL, European Comission.

Lasagabaster, D., & Doiz, A. (2017). A longitudinal study on the impact of CLIL on affective factors. *Applied Linguistics, 38*(5), 688–712.

Llinares, A., & Lyster, R. (2014). The influence of context on patterns of corrective feedback and learner uptake: A comparison of CLIL and immersion classrooms. *Language Learning Journal, 42*(2), 181–194. doi:10.1080/09571736.2014.889509

Llinares, A., Morton, T., & Whittaker, R. (2012). *The roles of language in CLIL.* Cambridge University Press.

Lorenzo, F. (2008). Instructional discourse in bilingual settings: An empirical study of linguistic adjustments in content and language integrated learning. *Language Learning Journal, 36*(1), 21–33. doi:10.1080/09571730801988470

Lyster, R., & Ranta, L. (1997). Corrective feedback and learner uptake: Negotiation of form in communicative classrooms. *Studies in Second Language Acquisition, 19*(1), 37–66. doi:10.1017/S0272263197001034

Mahan, K. R. (2022). The comprehending teacher: Scaffolding in content and language integrated learning (CLIL). *Language Learning Journal, 50*(1), 74–88. doi:10.1080/09571736.2019.1705879

Mariño Avila, C. M. (2014). Towards implementing CLIL at CBS (Tunja, Colombia). *Colombian Applied Linguistics Journal, 16*(2), 151–160. doi:10.14483/udistrital.jour.calj.2014.2.a02

McDougald, J., & Pissarello, D. (2020). Content and language integrated learning: In-service teachers' knowledge and perceptions before and after a professional development program. *Íkala. Revista de Lenguaje y Cultura, 25*(2), 353–372. doi:10.17533/udea.ikala.v25n02a03

Mehisto, P., Marsh, D., & Frigols, M. J. (2008). *Uncovering CLIL: Content and language integrated learning in bilingual education and multilingual education.* MacMillan.

Milla, R., & García Mayo, M. P. (2021). Teachers' and learners' beliefs about corrective feedback compared with classroom behaviour in CLIL and EFL. In K. Talbot, S. Mercer, M.-T. Gruber, & R. Nishida (Eds.), *The psychological experience of integrating language and content* (pp. 112–133). Multilingual Matters. doi:10.21832/9781788924306-012

Milla, R., & García Mayo, M. P. (in press). Feedback in CLIL: Teachers' oral and written choices and learners' response. In *D. Benegas & S. Zappa-Hollman, The Routledge Handbook of Content and Language Integrated Learning.* Routledge.

Nguyen, T. T. (2018). *Interactional corrective feedback: a comparison between primary CLIL in Spain and primary CLIL in Vietnam* [Unpublished doctoral dissertation, Universidad Autónoma de Madrid, Spain].

Nikula, T., & Moore, P. (2019). Exploring translanguaging in CLIL. *International Journal of Bilingual Education and Bilingualism, 22*(2), 237–249. doi:10.1080/13670050.2016.1254151

Pellicer García, M. P. (2017). *Analysis of corrective feedback in a multilingual classroom context from a CLIL perspective.* [Unpublished doctoral dissertation, Universitat de València, Spain].

Pena Díaz, C., & Porto Requejo, M. D. (2008). Teacher beliefs in a CLIL education Project. *Porta Linguarum, 10*, 151–161. doi:10.30827/Digibug.31786

Pérez Cañado, M. L. (2015). Evaluating CLIL programs: Instrument design and validation. *Pulso. Review of Education, 39*, 79–112.

Pérez Cañado, M. L. (2016). Stopping the "pendulum effect" in CLIL research: Finding the balance between Pollyanna and Scrooge. *Applied Linguistics Review, 8*(1), 79–99. doi:10.1515/applirev-2016-2001

Pokrivčáková, S. (2015). CLIL in Slovakia: projects, research, and teacher training (2005-2015). In S. Pokrivčáková, et al. (Eds.), CLIL in foreign language education: e-textbook for foreign language teachers. Nitra, Eslovakia: Constantine the Philosopher University.

Rea-Dickins, P. (2000). Classroom assessment. *Teaching and learning in the language classroom*, 375-401.

Richards, J. C. (2005). *Communicative language teaching today.* SEAMEO Regional Language Centre.

Setiawan, J. E. (2013). *Teacher's Belief and Student's Perception Regarding Content and Language Integrated Learning: A Case Study at SMA YPVDP Bontang* [Unpublished doctoral dissertation, Samarinda, Indonesia: Mulawarman University].

Soboleva, A. V. (2019). A cognitive-style inclusive approach as a means of learner-centered EFL teaching mode implementation. In C. Denman & A. Al-Mahrooqi (Eds.), *Handbook of research on curriculum reform initiatives in English education* (pp. 122–135). IGI Global. doi:10.4018/978-1-5225-5846-0.ch008

Villabona, N., & Cenoz, J. (2022). The integration of content and language in CLIL: A challenge for content-driven and language-driven teachers. *Language, Culture and Curriculum, 35*(1), 36–50. doi:10.1080/07908318.2021.1910703

KEY TERMS AND DEFINITIONS

Communicative Task: It is a goal-oriented activity where learners have to communicate using the target language to reach a specific outcome or result.

Elicitation: Feedback strategies to evoke correct responses from the learners after an error has been made, which are provided with the aim of drawing their attention to the erroneous form and achieving learners' self-repair.

HOTS (Higher Order Thinking Skills): Cognitive operations related to abstract thinking that learners must develop when they are challenged with analytical, creative and evaluative tasks requiring a higher degree of difficulty.

LOTS (Lower Order Thinking Skills): Cognitive operations related to concrete thinking that require a low degree of difficulty, such as defining, describing, classifying or identifying. These skills constitute the base to reach the more complex processing levels or HOTS.

Recast: A widely used pedagogical practice consisting of offering feedback on error to facilitate students' progress in their ability to use a second language. The teacher's correct restatement of a learner's incorrectly formed utterance offers an alternative model of the attempted production of the target form and recognizes the content of the previous turn.

Scaffolding: A variety of instructional techniques used to influence students progressively toward a more profound comprehension and, ultimately, greater independence in the learning process. Teachers use diverse tactics to offer levels of temporary support skill acquisition that they would not be able to achieve otherwise.

Teachers' Beliefs: Ideas teachers hold about what should and should not be done in their practice and that tend to guide their behaviour.

Translanguaging: The deliberate or spontaneous use of two (or more) languages inside the same lesson. Pedagogical translanguaging consists of pre-planned activities or strategies for the inclusion of the learners' native language in the foreign/second language classroom with pedagogical objectives.

APPENDIX 1: STUDENTS' QUESTIONNAIRE

Students' questionnaire on CLIL beliefs

Fill in the questionnaire according to your beliefs about CLIL practices.

Let's start with some personal information:

1./ ID CARD NUMBER

_____

2./ AGE

_____

3./ Studies

_____

4./ English Level (specify CEFR level when certified)

- B2
- C1
- C2
- other

5./ Do you have any previous experience with CLIL as a learner?

- Yes
- No

6./ Do you have any previous experience with CLIL as a teacher/teacher trainee?

- Yes
- No

CLIL methodology

7./ Are you aware of what the CLIL approach is?

- Not at all
- Somehow
- Neutral
- Quite a lot
- Absolutely

8./ How would you define it?

_____

9./ Rate the following things that may be needed to start implementing this approach in a school:
From 1 (not at all necessary) to 5 (Absolutely necessary)

- SPECIFIC TRAINING ON CLIL METHODOLOGY

147

- LANGUAGE TRAINING
- MATERIALS AND RESOURCES
- MOTIVATION
- OTHERS, (specify what)

Focus

10./ When teaching a CLIL lesson, what percentage of the time would you devote to each of these aspects? (SPECIFY PERCENTAGE FOR EACH ONE WITHOUT % SYMBOL)

GRAMMAR: explanations or activities to practise the necessary structures_____

VOCABULARY: pre-teaching the specific terms or practice activities with difficult language_____

CONTENT: use L1 and other techniques to make sure they understand, present it in different ways_____

Type of activities

11./ Rate the following statements from 1 (completely disagree) to 5 (completely agree). When planning activities for a CLIL lesson:

- I prepare reading activities if there aren't any and never skip the ones in the book
- I include both individual and group writing activities. I make sure the lesson involves listening to the teacher as well as from other sources (videos, audios…)
- I include speaking activities both individual and in collaboration
- I pay attention to pronunciation issues and give support or explanations when necessary

Scaffolding

12./ Scaffolding in CLIL is particularly important. To what extent would you do the following?

- Identify problems in advance
- Find out students' previous knowledge about the topic/language of the lesson
- Give examples and model
- Divide the task into small steps
- Use the L1 if necessary or allow students to use it
- Use visual support for difficult content/language
- Present the same content in different formats
- Grade the type of activities from less to more cognitively demanding

Corrective feedback

13./ Rate the following statements from 1 (completely disagree) to 5 (completely agree). If learners make language errors (grammar, vocabulary, pronunciation) in oral interaction in the CLIL lesson, I should…

- Ignore language errors and focus on the content
- Always correct them to prevent the errors from becoming permanent
- Correct language errors that impede communication
- Correct language errors which are relevant to the lesson
- Correct basic language errors or those that appear frequently

CLIL Teachers' Beliefs and Practices

- Correct by reformulating the erroneous utterance
- Give the students hints on how to repair their language errors themselves
- Help learners to repair their errors by giving explanations
- Correct vocabulary errors but not pronunciation or grammar
- Correct errors immediately after it is detected
- Wait until a bit later to give feedback on the errors
- Allow the learner finish the utterance and then give feedback on language and content

Communication in CLIL

14./ Activities in CLIL classes should help students improve their abilities to communicate in English. In what percentage would you use the following? (SPECIFY PERCENTAGE FOR EACH ONE WITHOUT % SYMBOL)

Communicative activities with meaningful situations_____

Communicative activities related to the content_____

Oral presentations to be done individually and in pairs/groups_____

15./ If you had students with problems communicating in the CLIL lesson, which of the following would you do? You can choose more than one.

- Allow the student to use L1
- Ask them to try it in English and give support
- Leave students free not to answer
- Oblige the students to communicate by asking directly

Materials in CLIL

16./ You are a CLIL teacher, and the school has given you a textbook in English, would you supplement with other materials? Rate the following statements from 1 (completely disagree) to 5 (completely agree)

- Authentic materials in English (journals, magazines, videos, films, etc.)
- Audiovisual materials
- Materials in the students' L1
- Materials in English adapted to the students' level
- I wouldn't supplement it and I would stick to the textbook provided
- Other (specify)_____

CLIL learning and teaching

17./ In your opinion, should CLIL teachers avoid using the learners' L1?

- Yes, the CLIL lessons should be completely in English
- Yes, but they could use it for classroom management or when there are communication problems
- No, they may use it and integrate the learners' languages in the lessons, with the appropriate planning
- No, they can use it and allow learners to use it to create a pleasant classroom atmosphere
- No, the content is essential, and the language should not impede teaching it

149

18./ If you had to teach a subject with a CLIL methodology, to what extent would you coordinate with the English teacher? Give examples

_____

____

19./ In your opinion, do students see their motivation towards English learning increased by participating in CLIL programs? What percentage of them? How would you deal with unmotivated students?

_____

_____

20./ In your opinion, does students' proficiency improve in CLIL programs? How would you help less proficient students in CLIL?

_____

_____

21./ You have to hire a teacher for teaching Science in English in a CLIL program. Who would be the best candidate?

- Teacher A has a Degree in Primary Education with a Minor in Foreign Languages and a C1 certificate
- Teacher B has a Degree in Primary Education, a C1 certificate and teaching experience
- Teacher C has a Degree in Primary Education and a C2 certificate in English
- Teacher D has a C1 certificate, a Degree in Primary Education and has completed a specific course in CLIL
- Teacher E has a C1 certificate and two Degrees: in Infant Education and Primary Education with a Minor in FL languages

22./ Give a reason for your choice

_____

_____

ONLY FOR STUDENTS OF A CLIL PROGRAM

23./ Complete the next section if you have studied through English (in a CLIL program or similar) in Primary or Secondary Education. Rate the following statements from 1 (completely disagree) to 5 (completely agree) and explain why:

- In my CLIL lessons, I improved my reading in English more than in the regular English class.
- In my CLIL lessons, I improved my speaking in English more than in the regular English class.
- In my CLIL lessons, I improved my writing in English more than in the regular English class.
- In my CLIL lessons, I improved my listening in English more than in the regular English class.
- In my CLIL lessons, I improved my vocabulary in English more than in the regular English class.
- In my CLIL lessons, I improved my grammar in English more than in the regular English class.
- In my CLIL lessons, I have been more motivated to learn English than in the regular English class
- In my CLIL classes, the language has not been a problem to learn the content in English
- The teaching techniques in my CLIL lessons have been helpful
- The materials used in my CLIL lessons have been appropriate

CLIL Teachers' Beliefs and Practices

Anything left to say?

24./ The space below is for you to elaborate or clarify any of the above as well as to offer your opinions, concerns about teaching CLIL lessons

_____

_____

APPENDIX 2: TEACHERS' QUESTIONNAIRE

Teachers' questionnaire on CLIL beliefs

Please, fill in the questionnaire according to your beliefs about CLIL practices.

Let's start with some personal information:

1./ ID CARD NUMBER

_____

2./ AGE

_____

3./ Studies

_____

4./ English Level (specify CEFR level when certified)

- B2
- C1
- C2
- other

5./ Number of years teaching in CLIL (e.g.: 2)

_____

6./ Have you received training for CLIL teaching? Specify which and approximate duration

_____

CLIL methodology

7./ Are you aware of what the CLIL approach is?

- Not at all
- Somehow
- Neutral
- Quite a lot
- Absolutely

8./ How would you define it?

_____

9./ Rate the following things that may be needed to start implementing this approach in a school:
From 1 (not at all necessary) to 5 (Absolutely necessary)

- TEACHERS' SPECIFIC TRAINING ON CLIL METHODOLOGY
- TEACHERS' LANGUAGE TRAINING
- MATERIALS AND RESOURCES
- STUDENTS' MOTIVATION
- OTHERS, (specify what)_____

Focus

10./ When teaching a CLIL lesson, what percentage of the time do you devote to each of these aspects? (SPECIFY PERCENTAGE FOR EACH ONE WITHOUT % SYMBOL)

GRAMMAR: explanations or activities to practice the necessary structures_____

VOCABULARY: pre-teaching the specific terms or practice activities with difficult language_____

CONTENT: use L1 and other techniques to make sure they understand, present it in different ways_____

Type of activities

11./ Rate the following statements from 1 (completely disagree) to 5 (completely agree). When planning activities for a CLIL lesson:

- I always include reading activities in the unit, either the ones in the book or self-prepared ones
- I include both individual and group writing activities
- I make sure the lesson involves listening to the teacher as well as from other sources (videos, audios…)
- I include speaking activities both individual and in collaboration
- I pay attention to pronunciation issues and give support or explanations when necessary

Scaffolding

12./ Scaffolding in CLIL is particularly important. To what extent do you do the following?

- Identify problems in advance
- Find out students' previous knowledge about the topic/language of the lesson
- Give examples and model
- Divide the task into small steps
- Use the L1 if necessary or allow students to use it
- Use visual support for difficult content/language
- Present the same content in different formats
- Grade the type of activities from less to more cognitively demanding

Corrective feedback

13./ Rate the following statements from 1 (completely disagree) to 5 (completely agree). If learners make language errors (grammar, vocabulary, pronunciation) in oral interaction in the CLIL lesson, I…

- Ignore language errors and focus on the content

CLIL Teachers' Beliefs and Practices

- Always correct them to prevent the errors from becoming permanent
- Correct only language errors that impede communication
- Correct language errors which are relevant to understand or explain the content of the lesson
- Correct basic language errors or those that appear frequently
- Correct mainly by reformulating the erroneous utterance
- Give the students hints on how to repair their language errors themselves
- Help learners repair their errors by giving explanations
- Correct mainly vocabulary errors and leave grammar and pronunciation errors at a second level
- Correct errors immediately after they are detected
- Wait until a bit later to give feedback on the errors
- Allow the learner to finish the utterance and then give feedback on language and content
- Communication in CLIL

14./ Activities in CLIL classes should help students improve their abilities to communicate in English. In what percentage do you use the following? (SPECIFY PERCENTAGE FOR EACH ONE WITHOUT % SYMBOL)

Communicative activities with meaningful situations_____

Communicative activities related to the content_____

Oral presentations to be done individually and in pairs/groups_____

15./ When you have students with problems communicating in the CLIL lesson, which of the following do you do? You can choose more than one.

- Allow the student to use L1
- Ask them to try it in English and give support
- Leave students free not to answer
- Oblige the students to communicate by asking directly

Materials in CLIL

16./ You are a CLIL teacher and the school has given you a textbook in English to teach, would you supplement with other materials? Rate the following statements from 1 (completely disagree) to 5 (completely agree):

- Authentic materials in English (journals, magazines, videos, films, etc.)
- Audio-visual materials
- Materials in the students' L1
- Materials in English adapted to students' level
- I wouldn't supplement it and I would stick to the textbook provided
- Other (specify)_____

CLIL learning and teaching

17./ In your opinion, should CLIL teachers avoid using the learners' L1?

- Yes, the CLIL lessons should be completely in English

- Yes, but they could use it for classroom management or when there are communication problems
- No, they may use it and integrate the learners' languages in the lessons, with the appropriate planning
- No, they can use it and allow learners to use it to create a pleasant classroom atmosphere
- No, the content is essential and the language should not impede teaching it

18./ When you teach a subject with a CLIL methodology, to what extent do you coordinate with the English teacher? Give examples

_____

_____

19./ In your opinion, do students see their motivation towards English learning increased by participating in CLIL programs? What percentage of them? How do you deal with unmotivated students?

_____

_____

20./ In your opinion, does students' proficiency improve in CLIL programs? How do you help less proficient students in CLIL?

_____

_____

21./ The school needs to hire a teacher for teaching Science in English in a CLIL program. Who would be the best candidate?

- Teacher A has a Degree in Primary Education with a Minor in Foreign Languages and a C1 certificate
- Teacher B has a Degree in Primary Education, a C1 certificate and teaching experience
- Teacher C has a Degree in Primary Education and a C2 certificate in English
- Teacher D has a C1 certificate, a Degree in Primary Education and has completed a specific course in CLIL
- Teacher E has a C1 certificate and two Degrees: in Infant Education and Primary Education with a Minor in FL languages

22./ Give a reason for your choice

_____

_____

Anything left to say?

23./ The space below is for you to elaborate or clarify any of the above as well as to offer your opinions, and concerns about teaching CLIL lessons

_____

_____

Chapter 8

Bilingual Education and Attention to Diversity:
Key Issues in Primary Education Teacher Training in Spain

Ramiro Durán-Martínez
University of Salamanca, Spain

Elena Martín-Pastor
University of Salamanca, Spain

ABSTRACT

Inclusive and bilingual education programs are two facets that can define quality education today. This chapter begins by focusing on the convergence between inclusion and bilingual education through a brief analysis of the impact of both in the field of education, and then addresses the principles that define content and language integrated learning (CLIL) and universal design for learning (UDL) approaches. Starting from the aspects shared by CLIL and UDL, five strategies and an example of an educational resource are presented that respond to the needs and characteristics of all students in primary education classrooms. This proposal can serve, in turn, as an element of reflection and analysis for future primary school teachers involved in bilingual programs.

INTRODUCTION: THE CHALLENGE OF ATTENTION TO DIVERSITY IN BILINGUAL EDUCATION

A quality education requires the existence of an educational offering adjusted to the new social demands. If our educational system seeks to respond in consonance with two key elements of today's society, diversity and multilingualism, it needs to face two important challenges: an inclusive approach to education and the promotion of bilingual programs in mainstream education. Various international organizations have highlighted this need by proposing measures, initiatives and action plans aimed at achieving an education in line with the current social reality. A first example is found in the review of

DOI: 10.4018/978-1-6684-6179-2.ch008

Copyright © 2023, IGI Global. Copying or distributing in print or electronic forms without written permission of IGI Global is prohibited.

European policies on language teaching in recent years since, as a way to improve the communicative competence of foreign languages in EU countries, the European educational authorities set out to ensure the supply and to promote the implementation of bilingual programs (Eurydice, 2017; Marsh, 2002). A second example can be seen in the 2030 Agenda for Sustainable Development objectives, where the fourth objective focuses on the need to ensure inclusive, equitable and quality education that promotes lifelong learning opportunities for all students (UNESCO, 2017).

The need for an inclusive educational model, together with the spread of bilingual education throughout compulsory education in European countries such as Spain, have highlighted the need to respond to the needs of all students participating in bilingual programs while following the principles of attention to diversity. The concept of diversity has been frequently narrowed to exclusively refer to Special Educational Needs (SEN) students (Amor et al., 2018; Ritter et al., 2020). However, in this chapter, we share the assumption of diversity as inherent to any human being as a result of developmental traits that cannot but translate into different learning rhythms (Arnáiz, 2003). Thus, from this perspective, the teaching-learning process is designed from the premise that all students naturally differ from one another (Casanova, 2011). Diversity, particularly in bilingual education, should not only cover SEN students but also those with differing learning styles, diverse levels of linguistic competence, varying attainments of knowledge in different subject areas, a wide range of degrees of motivation and ways of engagement as well as different cultural and socioeconomic backgrounds.

Concerns about elitism and discrimination in connection with bilingual education have given rise to controversies in an attempt on the part of the scientific community to address the following thorny question: Does the generalization of bilingual programs, with added linguistic and cognitive challenges, increase rather than decrease segregation of students with learning difficulties? Bruton (2013, 2015, 2019), Gortázar and Taberner (2020), and Paran (2013) take a critical view on the state of bilingual education in Spain as they hold that bilingual programs foster inequalities in education by leaving weaker students behind. However, their critical stance is not shared by authors such as Coyle et al. (2010), Marsh (2002), or Pérez-Cañado (2017, 2019), who acknowledge, as an unprecedented benefit, the fact that when bilingual programs are mainstreamed in every stage of compulsory education they do offer a wider range of students further opportunities to improve their linguistic competence from which they were previously excluded: "bilingual education has officially been advocated as an instrument of social cohesion since it aims to facilitate access to quality education in foreign languages for the whole population which once was the prerogative of the elite" (Barrios 2019, p. 5).

However, there is a general consensus that attending to the diversity of students in a bilingual classroom is a challenge for the educational community in general and for teachers in particular (Durán-Martínez et al., 2020; Lova et al., 2013; Martín-Pastor and Durán-Martínez, 2019; Murillo et al., 2021; Pérez-Cañado, 2017, 2020; Travé, 2013). This situation is the starting point of this chapter, whose main objective is to provide future primary school teachers in bilingual programs with a series of guidelines to help them design and develop educational practices that respond to the diversity of students.

Bilingual programs in Europe mostly adhere to the methodological tenets of Content and Language Integrated Learning (CLIL) (Coyle et al., 2010), and these are fully consistent and compatible with the Universal Design for Learning (UDL) guidelines, which aim to provide a framework for teaching in inclusive learning environments (Alba-Pastor, 2019). Both approaches share a series of methodological principles that allow the design of inclusive didactic practices for teaching content in a foreign language.

After having defined the main elements that characterize CLIL and UDL, this chapter presents a didactic proposal to address the topic of energy sources in the Science classroom taking into consideration

Bilingual Education and Attention to Diversity

the diversity present in a primary education bilingual classroom. Our aim is that this practical proposal may constitute a resource for the training of future elementary school teachers in the field of bilingual and inclusive education.

BACKGROUND: CLIL AND UDL AS INCLUSIVE APPROACHES

Content and Language Integrated Learning

Content and Language Integrated Learning (henceforward CLIL), which has been widely supported by EU institutions, has been defined as "an inclusive term, particularly used in Europe, for bilingual or multilingual education in which a second or later language is used for learning subject content, and where both language learning and content learning occur simultaneously with an emphasis on their integration" (Baker & Wright, 2014, p. 235). CLIL advocates consider that non-linguistic subjects "constitute a reservoir of concepts, topics and meanings which can become the object of 'real communication' where natural use of the target language is possible" (Dalton-Puffer, 2007, p. 3). In this way, CLIL has been regarded as a natural evolution of the communicative approaches to language teaching (Celce-Murcia et al., 2014; Coyle et al., 2010; Richards & Rodgers, 2014), pursuing, through the improvement of the teaching of foreign languages in the classroom, the ultimate goal of increasing the communicative capacity in the different languages of the European population.

For effective CLIL planning, Coyle et al. (2010) establish the "4 Cs Framework" that distinguishes four pillars: Content, Communication, Cognition and Culture. *Content* is worked on through *Communicative* activities and through *Cognitive* processes (such as remembering, classifying, comparing, predicting, evaluating, etc.) that are usually linked to a *Cultural* element (of a historic nature, respect for diversity and the environment, citizenship in a global world, etc.). We will now briefly define each of these four key elements in the CLIL approach and show how all are fully compatible with the principles of an inclusive education.

Figure 1. The 4Cs Framework
Source: Coyle et al. (2010, p. 41)

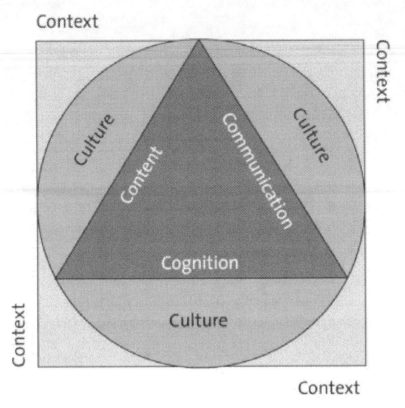

The first C of the Coyle et al. (2010) model refers to *Content*. In line with the principles of personalized learning, the authors qualify that content is "not only about acquiring knowledge and skills, it is about the learners creating their own knowledge and understanding and developing skills" (Coyle et al., 2010, p. 42). Starting from the students' prior knowledge, teachers need to link the contents (conceptual, procedural and linguistic) covered in the classroom with their interests in order to foster their motivation. *Communication* is the second element, since the different learning processes that take place in the classroom are produced through interaction, which is especially beneficial for students in their social environment (Dalton-Puffer, 2007) and with peers (Ball et al., 2015): "CLIL demands a level of talking and interaction that is different to that of traditional language classroom" (Coyle, 2006, p. 11). Learning occurs when the student understands the information received, and it increases exponentially when the learner uses the language to tackle a specific meaningful task. Here a key element of this approach lies in the active role of the learner and the necessary support, provided by the teacher, for this communication to be successful.

Cognition refers to the processes used by our brain when we think and learn and, traditionally, CLIL methodologies have focused on cognition to try to accommodate students with various degrees of knowledge and skills, different levels of competence in the foreign language, and varied degrees of motivation (Marsh, 2013). This ability to respond to the diverse needs of learners enables the CLIL teacher to develop teaching practices that are responsive to the diversity of students and to have strategies for cognitively challenging their students with the level of support necessary for their circumstances. The C of *Culture*

Bilingual Education and Attention to Diversity

deals with issues such as intercultural understanding and global citizenship, which are directly related to the development of tolerance and understanding of the differences inherent in all cultures and all human beings, which can also contribute to knowing ourselves better as individuals: "It could be argued that in the CLIL classroom the use of appropriate authentic materials and intercultural curricular linking can contribute to a deeper understanding of difference and similarities between cultures, which in turn impacts on discovering 'self'"(Coyle et al., 2010, p. 55).

The generalization of bilingual programs is often considered an instrument of social cohesion as it offers a wider range of student's further opportunities to boost their linguistic competence, from which they were previously excluded (Barrios, 2019). Furthermore, authors like Coyle et al. (2010), Marsh (2013), Madrid and Pérez-Cañado (2018), and Pérez-Cañado (2017, 2020) even claim that the main features of the methodological approach associated to bilingual education make it intrinsically inclusive and, if and whenever correctly applied, it indeed works in the most disenfranchised settings: rural contexts, minority groups, and families with low socioeconomic status (Pérez-Cañado, 2020, 2021). In this chapter we also consider that CLIL is fully compatible with the principles of educational inclusion and consequently with the characteristic elements of UDL, which we will analyze below.

Universal Design for Learning

The Universal Design for Learning (henceforward UDL) is an approach created by the Center for Applied Special Technology (CAST) in the early 1990s in the United States, taking as a reference the philosophy of Universal Design in the design and configuration of accessible spaces for any person. When transferred to the educational setting, UDL initially focused on providing access to the curriculum for students with disabilities (Rose, 2001). However, its subsequent application has demonstrated simultaneous benefits for the rest of the students, thereby breaking the "one-size-fits-all" mold of inflexible and rigidly designed curricula. Thus, UDL poses a new approach to teaching, learning and assessment, which contemplates individual student differences (Díez & Sánchez, 2015) and maximizes learning opportunities for all learners (Rose & Meyer, 2002).

The UDL implies, as Alba-Pastor (2019) points out, reformulating education by providing a framework (conceptual and instrumental) that allows the analysis of curricular designs and classroom practices to identify barriers to learning and promote inclusion as a priority teaching model (García-Campos et al., 2018). That is, it involves formulating and working with objectives, content, methodologies, resources and ways of assessing that are flexible so that they respond to each of the students' needs and abilities (Alba-Pastor, 2019; CAST, 2011; Sánchez & Díez, 2013). In addition, the UDL advocates multimodality in the learning environment (Roski et al., 2021).

There are three principles that UDL proposes when planning the teaching-learning process: to provide multiple means of (1) representation, (2) action & expression, and (3) engagement (Alba-Pastor, 2019; Díez & Sánchez, 2015; García-Campos et al., 2018; CAST, 2011; Rose & Meyer, 2002).

The first principle, representation, is based on the fact that students are different in the way they understand and perceive information, so it is essential to identify the strategies and resources with which students will be able to better access new information. Consequently, the information needs to be presented through different media and channels. In addition, each learner has his or her own learning style and, therefore, different strategic, organizational and cognitive skills. From this arises the need to provide multiple forms of expression, the second principle on which UDL is based and which implies that the teacher needs to provide methodological proposals that allow different ways of performing the tasks. The last principle, participation, entails introducing a variety of activities that are consonant with the different interests of the students in order to, firstly, motivate and challenge them in their learning process; secondly, to sustain their effort; and, thirdly, to promote their self-regulation through formative and self-assessment tools that may, in addition, provide immediate feedback.

These three UDL principles are linked to the brain networks that are activated in people simultaneously when faced with a new learning task: the recognition network, responsible for gathering and analyzing information (representation); the strategic network, responsible for planning and executing actions (action and expression); and the affective network related to motivation (engagement) (García-Campos et al., 2018; Sasson et al., 2021).

Table 1 lists a series of guidelines that can be used to implement the UDL principles. In addition to the horizontal division into three columns, responding to the three UDL principles, these guidelines are also organized horizontally so that the "Access" row includes those that suggest ways to increase access to the learning goal. The "Build" row includes guidelines related to different ways to promote effort and persistence, language and expression, and communication and, finally, the "Internalize" row collects actions aimed at empowering learners through self-regulation, comprehension, and executive function (CAST, 2018). All these guidelines are applicable to any area of the curriculum, serving as a guide for the design of accessible and flexible educational practices where all students can participate in meaningful and challenging learning opportunities. In other words, they aim to reduce barriers and maximize learning opportunities to reach students in different ways. Thus, as Roski et al. (2021) point out, it is not the learner who has to adapt to the teaching process, but the curriculum and the way it is delivered.

Table 1. Universal Design for Learning guidelines

	Engagement	**Representation**	**Action & Expression**
Access	Recruiting Interest - Optimize individual choice and autonomy - Optimize relevance, value, and authenticity - Minimize threats and distractions	Perception - Offer ways of customizing the display of information - Offer alternatives for auditory information - Offer alternatives for visual information	Physical Action - Vary the methods for response and navigation - Optimize access to tools and assistive technologies
Build	Sustaining Effort & Persistence - Heighten salience of goals and objectives - Vary demands and resources to optimize challenge - Foster collaboration and community - Increase mastery-oriented feedback	Language & Symbols - Clarify vocabulary and symbols - Clarify syntax and structure - Support decoding of text, mathematical notation, and symbols - Promote understanding across languages - Illustrate through multiple media	Expression & Communication - Use multiple media for communication - Use multiple tools for construction and composition - Build fluencies with graduated levels of support for practice and performance
Internalize	Self-Regulation - Promote expectation and beliefs that optimize motivation - Facilitate personal coping skills and strategies - Develop self-assessment and reflection	Comprehension - Activate or supply background knowledge - Highlight patterns, critical features, big ideas, and relationships - Guide information processing and visualization - Maximize transfer and generalization	Executive Functions - Guide appropriate goal-setting - Support planning and strategy development - Facilitate managing information and resources - Enhance capacity for monitoring progress

Source: CAST (2018)

Bilingual Education and Attention to Diversity

Planning and designing educational practices based on the principles established by the UDL implies having teachers who demonstrate (1) A growth mind-set about learning, (2) Self-Efficacy to implement inclusive practices, and (3) Self-Regulation and motivation for teaching (Griful-Freixenet et al., 2020). These three characteristics will result in teachers developing meaningful and supportive teaching practices for students, using more student-centered approaches and teaching strategies that, in turn, invite them to think, feel, and act.

MAIN FOCUS OF THE CHAPTER

In the previous sections we have seen that both CLIL and UDL bring methodological adaptations that pursue the objective of meeting the diverse needs, skills, expectations and abilities of the students. Both approaches share the following characteristics: they favor a multimodal approach to learning, they advocate for personalizing the learning experience, the two seek to promote students' independence and confidence, both are sensitive to the cognitive development of each student, they aim to scaffold students' responses while giving them an active role in their learning process, and they frame their initiatives within cooperative work and project-based learning styles (Lacar, 2021; Meyer et al, 2016).

Taking the shared features of UDL and CLIL as a starting point, this chapter presents a training scheme designed for prospective primary teachers with a view to equip for diversity in bilingual education programs consisting of the following five strategies: engagement and motivation, scaffolding, multimodality, groupings and student-centered approaches. We will also present the design of an example of a didactic proposal to teach the area of science from an inclusive approach that meets the different needs and abilities of the students present in a classroom.

SOLUTIONS AND RECOMMENDATIONS: A TRAINING PROPOSAL FOR AN INCLUSIVE BILINGUAL TEACHING PROGRAMMING

Five Teaching Strategies for Instructional Practice

The five strategies displayed in Figure 2 should become an element of reflection for future primary education teachers, especially for those who will be involved in bilingual programs, in order to take into account activities to be carried out in the classroom for each proposal.

Figure 2. Teaching strategies for instructional practice

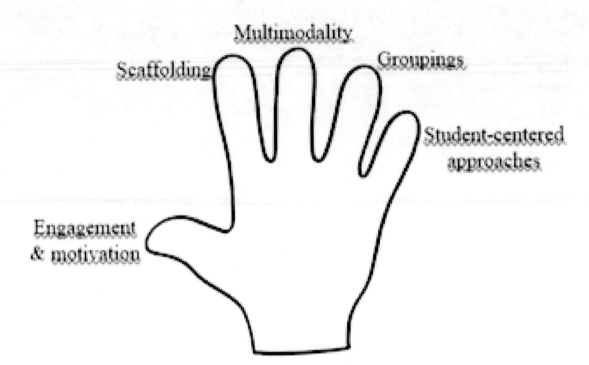

Engagement and Motivation

Motivation is defined as the set of actions that activate, direct and maintain a behavior oriented towards the achievement of a goal (Alonso Tapia, 1997). Therefore, it is a necessary condition for the persistence of learning (Dörneyei, 2001). In order to enhance motivation in the classroom, it is essential to propose a variety of activities that adjust to the different interests of students so as to increase their involvement in the teaching-learning process. Another aspect that contributes to their motivation lies in the need for students to know what they have to do at all times and to accompany them along the way on how to do it, keeping their expectations of success high (Villaescusa, 2021).

Scaffolding

The term scaffolding, from the field of psychology, was first used in the educational field by Bruner in the 1970s and is directly related to Vygotsky's (1978) concepts of mediation and zone of proximal development (ZPD). He described the ZPD as "the kind of learning which is always challenging yet potentially within reach of individual learners on condition that appropriate support, scaffolding and guidance is provided" (Marsh 2013, p. 75). The main goal of scaffolding strategies is to move learners from their prior knowledge to the knowledge that is in their ZPD. Maybin et al. (1992) define scaffolding as: "a type of teacher assistance that helps students learn new skills, concepts, or levels of understanding that leads to the student successfully completing a task" (p. 188). Thus, "Scaffolding enables not only the performance of a more complex task than the learner could handle alone, but also enables learning

Bilingual Education and Attention to Diversity

from that experience" (Reiser and Tabak, 2014, p. 45). Effective Scaffolding practices can be found in Dale & Tanner (2012) and Walqui (2006).

Multimodality

The diversity of learners, as manifested in their different ways of learning, communicating and accessing information, requires a multimodal approach to teaching. This need, linked to the fundamental principles of UDL, has also been highlighted in classrooms that follow bilingual teaching models and is associated with the use of both linguistic and non-linguistic inputs: "Since learners use different ways to take in input, it is useful if input is multimodal at various stages of a lesson or lessons. In the CLIL classroom, it is even more important to exploit as many input modes as possible, both linguistic and non-linguistic, to ensure as many learners as possible understand the input" (Dale et al. 2011, p. 41). Thus, didactic practices based on multimodality integrate different modes of knowledge representation, allowing, in turn, its construction through different means of expression according to the different characteristics of the students (Kress, 2010; Marsh, 2013). Multimodal input also fosters the development of new literacies (Coyle & Meyer, 2021; Meyer, 2013).

Groupings

The organization and grouping of students so that they learn more and better is a fundamental element in any teaching program (Morán et al., 2012). Both the CLIL and UDL approaches are committed to a heterogeneous grouping, in terms of the characteristics of those who are part of them, and flexible, in terms of the number of members -pair, small group, large group-, which adapts to the methodological proposals, as well as to the needs, interests and motivations of the students. Using heterogeneity and flexibility as fundamental criteria provides advantages such as the promotion of collaborative learning where some learn from others and the success of each member depends, in part, on the achievement of the goals set (Calatayud, 2018; Sanahuja et al., 2020).

Student-centered Approaches

Student-centered approaches, such as Project Based Learning (PBL), are considered key elements to address the different learning needs and interests of students as they take an active role in the teaching/learning continuum. PBL is structured around a project in which students work over a certain number of lessons through "activities that contextualize language, integrate skills, and point toward authentic, real-world purposes" (Brown & Lee, 2015, p. 50). Due to its flexibility, PBL can be implemented in many different ways: investigative research, problem-based learning, or project work. However, some general characteristics of PBL can be highlighted: student-centered, hands-on approach to learning, discovery learning, inductive rather than deductive learning, cooperative content driven, cross-curricular, and a vehicle for integrated learning (Alan & Stoller, 2005; Laverick, 2018; Stoller, 2006).

Marsh highlights a key aspect to be taken into account by the mainstream teacher participating in CLIL programs: the need to put into practice pedagogical proposals that, in line with the social-constructivist approaches, provide students with an adequate level of intellectual challenge according to their potential. To this end, collaborative problem-solving is mentioned as "it gives the teacher extra support in identifying specific input needs, and the learners more options for accessing learning" (Marsh 2013, p.

80), and autonomous learning, where learners are encouraged to "develop the capacity to plan, monitor and edit personal progress by way of internalised experiences" (Marsh 2013, p. 80).

Adapting a Didactic Proposal from an Inclusive Approach

This section presents the design of a didactic proposal to teach energy sources from an inclusive approach. For this purpose, the didactic resources offered by the National Center for Curricular Development in Non-Proprietary Systems (Centro Nacional de Desarrollo Curricular en Sistemas no Propietarios) (CEDEC) have been used as a foundation. This organization, under the Ministry of Education and Vocational Training through the National Institute of Educational Technologies and Teacher Training (INTEF) and the Ministry of Education and Employment of the Regional Government of Extremadura, aims to design, promote and develop digital educational materials that are freely available to the entire educational community in order to promote the use of Information and Communication Technologies and facilitate collaborative environments that improve the quality of the teaching-learning processes (Order EDU2341/2009).

Among the various materials offered by CEDEC, the presentation of this proposal is based on the resource "Is our life sustainable?" (Appendices 1 and 2) (freely available at https://descargas.intef.es/cedec/proyectoedia/aicle/contenidos/energy/index.html), which focuses on the learning of contents, in English, related to energy, its types and its sustainable use. It was designed as a set of activities to be carried out over a two-week period in the Science subject by fifth year of primary education students.

This learning proposal will contextualize the aforementioned resource within the Royal Decree 157/2022, of March 1, which establishes the organization and minimum teachings of Primary Education. In this decree, the area of Knowledge of the Natural, Social and Cultural Environment is presented, which organizes the basic information that the students of this stage must acquire in three blocks of content: 1. Scientific culture, 2. Technology and digitalization, and 3. Societies and territories. This proposal focuses on the first of these, as it encompasses the contents of the selected resource: energy.

The design of the suggested activities will be adapted to the CLIL and UDL approaches, considering three main elements: the five teaching strategies defined in the previous section (see Figure 2), Tomlinson´s differentiation model (2014), and the four questions that appear at the end of this section to help teachers adapt their educational practice to their teaching context.

Regarding the five strategies for instructional practice, they are summarized in the following table, which can work as a checklist for pre-service or in-service primary teachers participating in bilingual programs as they help them meet their students' diverse needs:

Bilingual Education and Attention to Diversity

Table 2. Teaching strategies for instructional practice checklist

ENGAGEMENT AND MOTIVATION
✓ Have you used different activities to fit students' diverse interests? ✓ Have you informed students about what they have to do at all times?
SCAFFOLDING
✓ Have you activated student´s previous knowledge? ✓ Have you provided word, sentence and text level support?
MULTIMODALITY
✓ Have you offered multimodal input to cater for student´s diversity? ✓ Have you provided students with the opportunity to create their own multimodal texts?
GROUPINGS
✓ Have you used heterogeneous groupings to foster cooperative learning? ✓ Have you used flexible groupings (pair, small & large group) to adapt to student's needs?
STUDENT-CENTERED APPROACHES
✓ Have you given the students an active role in the learning process? ✓ Have you provided students with the adequate level of intellectual challenge?

As for Tomlinson's differentiation model (2014), it establishes four possibilities of adaptation to meet the different abilities of students: content, process, product and learning environment. Adaptation to the content refers to how the information is presented to the students so that everyone can access it. For this purpose, images, videos, diagrams and linguistic supports can be used. Adaptation of the process involves reflecting on the alternatives for working with this information in the classroom in a way that is adapted to the different ways students learn. This implies reflecting on the most suitable type of grouping and on the necessary support to meet the different needs of the students. Adapting the product brings with it the need to open up the possibilities in which students can show what they have learned according to their learning style, interests and abilities (e.g., preparing an oral and/or visual presentation, making a poster, writing a report, recording a video, etc.). Finally, adapting the learning environment involves configuring the space in such a way that it takes into account the different needs of the learners in the classroom.

Thirdly, any educational practice needs to be accommodated to the reality in which it will be implemented. The following four questions seem essential for teachers to adapt their teaching proposal to their specific school contexts: What am I going to teach?; To whom is my programming directed?; How am I going to teach?; and, How will I monitor what they have learned?

What am I Going to Teach?

First, the teacher must define the objectives and the set of contents and competencies of a given curriculum area on which the teaching-learning process will be centered. It is important to define the minimum knowledge that all students must acquire and, based on this, to specify the methodology and the most suitable activities for the achievement of meaningful learning.

Taking as a reference the curriculum established by the Royal Decree 157/2022, this proposal will cover the contents of the third section of the Scientific Culture block, called Matter, forces and energy which includes the following contents: The forms of energy, sources and transformations; Renewable and non-renewable energy sources and their influence in contributing to the sustainable development of society (p. 24428).

From the model proposed by Tomlinson (2014), when answering the question of what to teach, it is necessary to reflect on how the teacher can differentiate the content to be worked on in the classroom, deciding on the different media, resources and supports to be used so that each student has the same opportunities to access the information. In line with the principle of multimodality advocated by the CLIL and UDL approaches, it is necessary to simultaneously use elements such as the following:

- Text, which should use clear, direct and simple syntax. In addition, the use of color and boldface to highlight certain terms, together with an appropriately sized text, can serve as a visual resource to direct the learner to the most important concepts or to facilitate access to the written document.
- Images, graphs, figures, all with good resolution and with the possibility of contrasting tones, the use of textures to emphasize their differences or reliefs so that they are "visible" to the touch. The possibility of accompanying them with descriptions should also be considered.
- Videos and/or audio to which subtitles or an alternative textual description can be added.

Likewise, it is recommended to incorporate additional resources for those students who want to expand on the information provided by the teacher and for those who need supplementary material to understand the basic content.

As mentioned at the beginning of this section, the adaptation of content involves defining the minimum knowledge that all students should master. To support this idea, we start from the pyramid model of Schumm et al. (1994) (see Figure 3), which makes it possible to adapt the contents to the different abilities, preferences and aptitudes of the students and to prioritize some over others, graduate their difficulty and establish a sequence. Therefore, at the base are those essential contents established by the official curriculum for Primary education that all students must learn while the next levels expand those basic contents in terms of depth and complexity. Thus, the second level includes contents that the majority should learn, but which not everyone will acquire, and the third covers additional and even more complex content, which only a few students are bound to learn.

Figure 3. Organization of the contents according to the model by Schumm et al. (1994)
Source: adapted from Schumm et al. (1994)

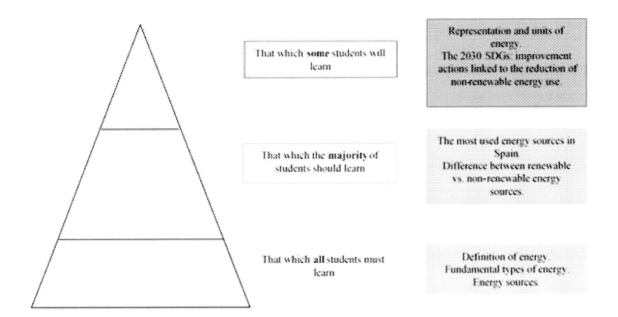

As for the learning objectives, this proposal addresses some of the general objectives that Royal Decree 157/2022 establishes for primary education in article 7, such as: developing individual and team work habits, acquiring a level of basic communicative competence in a foreign language to express and understand simple messages, knowing fundamental aspects of Natural Sciences, developing elementary technological skills and getting started in the construction of visual and audiovisual presentations. In addition, three didactic objectives are closely linked to the contents worked on in the selected resource: to define the concept of energy, identify and describe the different kinds and sources of energy, and promote sustainable routines in our daily life.

With respect to the work on competencies, this proposal reinforces three of the key competencies: multilingual competence, competence in science and digital competence (Royal Decree 157/2022). In addition, the specific competencies of the area that are also used as assessment criteria and must be achieved in accordance with the current legislation, are as follows:

1.1. Use digital resources in a safe and efficient manner, searching for information, reworking, creating simple digital content and communicating and working individually, in teams and in networks.

2.2. Search, select and contrast information from different safe and reliable sources, using the criteria of reliability of sources, acquiring a basic scientific vocabulary, and using it in research related to the natural, social and cultural environment.

5.1. Identify and analyze the characteristics, organization, and properties of the elements of the natural, social, and cultural environment through inquiry using appropriate tools and processes.

6.1. Promote sustainable lifestyles consistent with respect, care, co-responsibility and protection of people and the planet, based on the analysis of human intervention in the environment.

6.2. Participate with an entrepreneurial attitude in the search, contrast and evaluation of proposals to face eco-social problems, seek solutions and act for their resolution, based on the analysis of the causes and consequences of human intervention in the environment (pp.24426-24427).

To Whom is my Programming Directed?

Once the objectives, contents and competencies to be taught have been defined, the focus of attention must now be centered on the students to whom they are addressed. It is necessary to reflect on the characteristics that define each of the students in the classroom, as well as those that define the students as a group. More specifically, it is necessary for the teacher to analyze the needs, tastes and interests of the students, their strengths (skills) and weaknesses (limitations), what they can do on their own and for what type of actions they require support (material, digital or human). All this implies reflection and analysis in order to adapt and individualize the teaching-learning activities, as well as to establish realistic expectations and goals regarding the results to be obtained.

According to Tomlinson's (2014) model, the answer to this question also implies that the teacher should adapt, as far as possible, the learning environment to the characteristics that define the group of students. Thus, it is suggested that the teaching context should ensure physical, sensory, cognitive and emotional accessibility. Here, the classroom should be distributed in such a way that all students can access the necessary information and perform the proposed activities comfortably.

The classroom must be an accessible and versatile space, modifying the layout according to the educational intention and the students who are part of it. Likewise, it is necessary to foster a climate where everyone feels comfortable, welcomed, valued and plays an active role. To this end, it is sometimes advisable to make the times for carrying out tasks more flexible, and to organize the materials and resources to be used in such a way as to facilitate access to them.

How am I Going to Teach?

Once the curriculum (question 1) and the main characteristics of the students (question 2) have been defined, the design of the educational process should focus on the procedure for the acquisition of learning by all students. For this purpose, we start again from Tomlinson's model (2014) as far as process and product adaptation is concerned. Accordingly, we propose the use of different groupings for the development and resolution of tasks, different support resources for the completion of these tasks, as well as different types of activities for the acquisition of the same knowledge. In other words, the design of multilevel activities is presented, where the starting point is the development of the same capacity (objective) in relation to the same content, but with a different acquisition and development process (activities and resources) depending on the different characteristics of the students in the classroom.

Learning menus (Brennan, 2019; Westphal 2013) are an extremely useful resource as they provide different activities grouped in different segments so that the learner may choose one from each group to showcase his or her learning. Through learning menus, tasks with different degrees of complexity will be presented. This difficulty will be defined by both the depth in which the contents are worked and the type of support provided to the students for the resolution of the proposed tasks.

Departing from the educational proposal developed by CEDEC, *Is our life sustainable?,* appendix 1 describes changes to make an inclusive proposal out of it based on the adaptation of the teaching-learning process and product. To do so, we start with a brief description of each of the four parts into which the

Bilingual Education and Attention to Diversity

educational program is divided (Breaking the ice; What is energy?; Sources of energy; Sustainable energy for our lives) and then offer examples of possible adaptations to make the original proposal more inclusive. This, in its turn, may serve to illustrate some adaptation strategies for instructional practice.

The following table shows some of the most frequently used adaptation strategies to cater for diversity in the bilingual classroom. Although they have been distributed in two columns, following Tomlinson's process and product support strategies distinction, some may work for both.

Table 3. Examples of adaptation strategies

PROCESS ADAPTATION STRATEGIES	PRODUCT ADAPTATION STRATEGIES
• Use word level support strategies: highlight key content vocabulary; include labeled images, glossaries, vocabulary clouds, matching terms and definitions activities, partially filled-in graphic organisers, embedded electronic dictionary links, etc. • Use sentence level support strategies: sentence starters, substitution tables, and gap fills; sentences "head and tails" matching activities; provide definitions, short explanations, and examples. • Use text level support strategies: add a diagram, image, or graphic organizer; create a clear layout with useful subheadings; cut down information into manageable chunks; avoid long paragraphs; include matching activities of-headings to paragraphs or paragraphs to pictures; read a text and fill in a table, read a text and sequence sentences.- • Ask concept questions to check that students know what to do at all times • Activate background knowledge: brainstorming, KWL charts, concept maps • Offer multimodal input: infographs, animated descriptions, videos, graphic organisers • Use graphic organisers such as Venn diagrams, timelines, flow charts, or mind maps • Decide on the degree of visual support to be provided through pictures, posters, graphic organisers, etc.	• Give students the opportunity to produce a variety of activities ranging from class presentations, recordings, and posters, to summaries or diaries • Give students the opportunity to produce multimodal texts: presentations, videos, infographs, podcasts, wikis, blogs… • Allow students to choose activities through learning menus or Tic Tac Toes (see appendix 1) • Design pre-task activities for pair work: brainstorming, activating key vocab and previous knowledge… • Assign more specific tasks to some students • Use flexible and heterogeneous groupings to complete the final task: pair, small and large group • Provide students with full scripts, semi-scripts, speaking/writing frames or models • Provide students with sentence starters, substitution tables or annotated visuals

How Will I Monitor What They Have Learned?

Finally, the teacher must define the instruments and procedures to be used to check the degree of student learning and reflect on the evidence to be collected to verify the process of assimilation of the contents, objectives and competencies listed in the first question. A formative assessment based on observation, on the analysis of the tasks, and on the comments made by the students during the teaching-learning process is recommended. All this will allow the teacher to be aware of the difficulties encountered, the main mistakes made, as well as the progress of the students in the learning process.

Below is a proposed observation record (see Table 4) that can be used to collect both general information about the session/unit and specific information about the students in the classroom. In the general observation, the teacher evaluates the degree of satisfaction with the class on a scale of 1 to 5, where 1 corresponds to the lowest score and 5 to the highest. In addition, the teacher should highlight those positive aspects that have worked in the classroom, as well as the difficulties encountered and, based on this, what should be modified for future classes. Regarding the more specific observation, the teacher should collect information about learning, difficulties, support and possible modifications to be made in order to improve the educational response of each of his or her students.

Table 4a. Teacher observation record

Date	Session					
General observation						
		1	2	3	4	5
General assessment of the session						
Positive aspects to highlight						
Main difficulties detected						
Changes to be incorporated for the next session						

Table 4b. Teacher observation record

Specific observation		
Student		
Has the student acquired the required learning established?	Yes	
	No	
Observations:		
Did the student encounter any type of difficulty?	Yes	
	Specify:	
	No	
Did the student receive any kind of support?	Yes	
	Specify:	
	No	
Is it necessary to make any changes for the next session?	Yes	
	Specify:	
	No	

Both the process of solving the activities and the final product delivered by the students provide relevant information to evaluate their learning. The described proposal offers different alternatives for the development of the contents and the achievement of the objectives and competences according to the students' abilities and needs. All the activities, regardless of the degree of difficulty or skill required for their resolution, can be evaluated since they offer different learning opportunities that can be suitable for the particular characteristics of the students in the classroom.

Regarding student self-assessment, the CEDEC resource (see appendix 2) suggests that each student should prepare a learning diary to facilitate reflection on their learning at the end of each of the four sec-

Bilingual Education and Attention to Diversity

tions of the project. Five questions are posed for this purpose: What have I done?; What difficulties have I had and how have I solved them?; What have I learned?; How can I improve my learning for the next session?; Do I want to learn something else? Likewise, at the end of the project, the activity called *The ladder of metacognition*, is presented, where the student must answer another five questions that allow them to carry out a deeper self-evaluation of their learning and thus become more aware of the knowledge acquired: (1) Where, how and when can I use this learning? (2) What do I need to improve? (3) What has been easier, more interesting and more difficult? (4) How have I learned? (5) What have I learned?

In order to answer these questions, different scaffolding strategies can be proposed: offering a glossary of terms that allows the student to construct a simple sentence, providing an incomplete sentence where the student must incorporate the terms they consider appropriate, proposing multiple choice answers, replacing the written text in the different answer options with images or even using the mother tongue to facilitate the answer.

Through the learning diaries the student becomes aware of their own learning and the teacher receives essential information that helps them to better know the students in the classroom as well as to rethink, if necessary, the teaching practice with the search for alternative resources and support that fit the circumstances of their students.

CONCLUSION

This teaching proposal aims to reflect the five dimensions that we have considered key to successfully teaching a specific content through a language other than the mother tongue of the students, taking into special consideration their different characteristics, needs, abilities and interests. In this way, an approach of varied activities where each student knows what to do and how to do it allows us to better respond to their interests and encourage their participation (engagement and motivation). This variety of tasks associated with the same content and the possibility of choice, through strategies such as learning menus, make teaching a more personalized process where the student assumes an active role (student-centered approach). In addition, our proposal also highlights the need to use adequate resources to adapt to different levels of both content mastery and second language proficiency (scaffolding). The contents and activities are presented in different formats in an attempt to accommodate different ways of accessing information and expressing knowledge (multimodality). The fifth and final strategy proposes flexible and heterogeneous groupings in order to encourage collaborative work (groupings).

Through these five core strategies, the proposal presented in this chapter may help pre-service and in-service primary teachers reconsider how to address diversity in bilingual education programs. We believe that the alliance of CLIL and UDL principles is useful in reshaping, analysing, and improving curricular designs and in providing a more flexible approach to education, one in which the needs of all learners can be really met.

ACKNOWLEDGMENT

This research was supported by the *Agencia Estatal de Investigación* of the Spanish *Ministerio de Ciencia e Innovación*. Grant number PID2020-113956RB-I00.

REFERENCES

Alba-Pastor, C. (2019). Diseño universal para el aprendizaje: un modelo teórico-práctico para una educación inclusive de calidad. [Universal design for learning: a theoretical-practical model for inclusive quality education.] *Participación educativa, 6*(9), 64-66.

Alan, B., & Stoller, F. L. (2005). Maximizing the Benefits of Project work in Foreign Language Classrooms. *English Teaching Forum, 43*(4), 10-21.

Alonso Tapia, J. (1997). *Motivar para el aprendizaje. Teorías y Estrategias [Motivate for learning. Theories and Strategies*.]. EDEBE.

Amor, A. M., Hagiwara, M., Shogren, K. A., Thompson, J. R., Verdugo, M. A., Burke, K. M., & Aguayo, V. (2018). International perspectives and trends in research on inclusive education: A systematic review. *International Journal of Inclusive Education, 23*(12), 1277–1295. doi:10.1080/13603116.2018.1445304

Arnáiz, P. (2003). *Educación inclusiva: una escuela para todos [Inclusive education: a school for all*.]. Aljibe.

Baker, C., & Wright, W. E. (2014). *Foundations of Bilingual Education and Bilingualism*. Multilingual Matters.

Ball, P., Kelly, K., & Clegg, J. (2015). *Putting CLIL into Practice*. Oxford University Press.

Barrios, E. (2019). The effect of parental education level on perceptions about CLIL: A study in Andalusia. *International Journal of Bilingual Education and Bilingualism, 25*(1), 183–195. doi:10.1080/13 670050.2019.1646702

Brennan, A. (2019). Differentiation Trough Choice as an Approach to Enhance Inclusive Practice. *Journal of Special Needs Education in Ireland, 32*(1), 11–20.

Brown, H. D., & Lee, H. (2015). *Teaching principles* (Vol. P). Ed Australia.

Bruton, A. (2013). CLIL: Some of the reasons why … and why not. *System, 41*(3), 587–597. doi:10.1016/j. system.2013.07.001

Bruton, A. (2015). CLIL: Detail matters in the whole picture. More than a reply to J. Hüttner and U. Smit (2014). *System, 53*, 119–128. doi:10.1016/j.system.2015.07.005

Bruton, A. (2019). Questions about CLIL which are unfortunately still not outdated: A reply to Pérez-Cañado. *Applied Linguistics Review, 10*(4), 591–602. doi:10.1515/applirev-2017-0059

Calatayud, M. A. (2018). Los agrupamientos escolares a debate. [School groupings for debate.]. *Tendencias Pedagógicas, 32*(32), 5–14. doi:10.15366/tp2018.32.001

Casanova, Mª A. (2011). *Educación inclusiva: un modelo de futuro. [Inclusive education: a model for the future.]* Wolters Kluwer.

CAST. (2018). *Universal Design for Learning Guidelines version 2.2*. CAST. http://udlguidelines.cast.org

Bilingual Education and Attention to Diversity

Celce-Murcia, M., Brinton, D. M., Snow, M. A., & Bohlke, D. (2014). *Teaching English as a Second or Foreign Language* (4th ed.). National Geographic Learning.

Coyle, D. (2006). Content and Language Integrated Learning – Motivating Learners and Teachers. *The Scottish Language Review, 13,* 1–18.

Coyle, D., Hood, P., & Marsh, D. (2010). *Content and Language Integrated Learning.* Cambridge University Press. https://assets.cambridge.org/97805211/30219/frontmatter/9780 521130219_frontmatter.pdf doi:10.1017/9781009024549

Coyle, D., & Meyer, O. (2021). *Beyond CLIL: Pluriliteracies Teaching for Deeper Learning.* Cambridge University Press. doi:10.1017/9781108914505

Dale, L., van der Es, W., & Tanner, R. (2011). *CLIL Skills.* European Platform.

Dale, L., & Tanner, R. (2012). *CLIL Activities. A Resource for Subject and Language Teachers.* Cambridge University Press.

Dalton-Puffer, C. (2007). *Discourse in Content and Language Integrated Learning (CLIL) Classrooms.* John Benjamins. doi:10.1075/lllt.20

Díez, E., & Sánchez, S. (2015). Diseño universal para el aprendizaje como metodología docente para atender a la diversidad en la universidad. [Universal design for learning as a teaching methodology to address diversity in the university.]. *Aula Abierta, 43*(2), 87–93. doi:10.1016/j.aula.2014.12.002

Dörneyei, Z. (2001). *Teaching and researching motivation.* Longman.

Durán-Martínez, R., Martín Pastor, E., & Martínez Abad, F. (2020). ¿Es inclusiva la enseñanza bilingüe? Análisis de la presencia y apoyos en los alumnos con necesidades específicas de apoyo educativo. [Is bilingual education inclusive? Analysis of the presence and supports in students with specific educational support needs.] *Bordón. Revista de Pedagogía, 72*(2), 65–82.

Eurydice (2017). *Key data on teaching languages at school in Europe: 2017 edition.* Publications Office. https://data.europa.eu/doi/10.2797/456818

García-Campos, M. D., Canabal, C., & Alba-Pastor, C. (2018). Executive functions on universal design for learning_ moving towards inclusive education. *International Journal of Inclusive Education.* Advance online publication. doi:10.1080/13603116.2018.1474955

Gortázar, L., & Taberner, P. A. (2020). La incidencia del programa bilingüe en la segregación escolar por origen socioeconómico en la Comunidad Autónoma de Madrid: Evidencia a partir de PISA. [The incidence of the bilingual program in school segregation by socioeconomic origin in the Autonomous Community of Madrid: Evidence from PISA.] *REICE. Revista Electrónica Iberoamericana sobre Calidad, Eficacia y Cambio en Educación, 18*(4), 219–239. doi:10.15366/reice2020.18.4.009

Griful-Freixenet, J., Struyven, K., & Vantieghem, W. (2020). Toward more inclusive education: An empirical test of the universal design for learning conceptual model among preservice teachers. *Journal of Teacher Education.* doi:10.1177/0022487120965525

Lacar, J. B. (2021). Inclusive Education at the Heart of Mainstream Language Pedagogu: Perspectives and Challenges. *International Journal of Linguistics. Literature and Translation*, 4(1), 124–131. doi:10.32996/ijillt

Laverick, E. K. (2018). *Project-based learning*. ELT Development Series. TESOL Press.

Lova, Mª., Bolarín, Mª. J., & Porto, M. (2013). Programas bilingües en Educación Primaria: Valoraciones de docentes. [Bilingual programs in Primary Education: teacher assessments.]. *Porta Linguarum*, *20*, 253–268.

Madrid, D., & Pérez-Cañado, M. L. (2018). Innovations and challenges in attending to diversity through CLIL. *Theory into Practice*, *57*(3), 241–249. doi:10.1080/00405841.2018.1492237

Marsh, D. (Ed.). (2002). *CLIL/EMILE. The European dimension. Actions, trends, and foresight potential*. University of Jyväskylä. http://urn.fi/URN:NBN:fi:jyu-201511093614

Marsh, D. (2013). *Content and Language Integrated Learning (CLIL). A development trajectory*. Servicio de Publicaciones de la Universidad de Córdoba.

Martín Pastor, M. E., & Durán Martínez, R. (2019). La inclusión educativa en los programas bilingües de educación primaria: un análisis documental. [Educational inclusion in bilingual primary education programs: a documentary analysis.] Revista complutense de educación.

Maybin, J., Mercer, N., & Stierer, B. (1992). Scaffolding: learning in the classroom. In K. Norman (Ed.), Thinking Voices. The Work of the National Oracy Project (pp. 186–195). Hodder & Stoughton.

Meyer, O. (2013). Introducing the CLIL-Pyramid: Key Strategies and Principles for CLIL Planning and Teaching. In M. Eisenmann & T. Summer (Eds.), *Basic Issues in EFL Teaching* (pp. 295–313). Universitätverlag Winter.

Meyer, A., Rose, D. H., & Gordon, D. (2016). *Universal design for learning: Theory and practice*. CAST Professional Publishing.

Morán, C., Molina, S., & Sales, G. (2012). Aportaciones científicas a las formas de agrupación del alumnado. [Scientific contributions to the forms of grouping of students.]. *Revista de Organización y Gestión Educativa*, *2*, 13–18.

Murillo, J., Almazán, A., & Martínez Garrido, C. (2021). La elección de centro educativo en un sistema de cuasi-mercado escolar mediado por el programa de bilingüismo. [The choice of educational center in a quasi-school market system mediated by the bilingualism program.] *Revista Complutense de Educación*, *32(*1), 89-97. doi:10.5209/rced.68068

Paran, A. (2013). Content and language integrated learning: Panacea or policy borrowing myth? *Applied Linguistics Review*, *4*(2), 317–342. doi:10.1515/applirev-2013-0014

Pérez-Cañado, M. L. (2017). Stopping the "pendulum effect" in CLIL research: Finding the balance between Pollyanna and Scrooge. *Applied Linguistics Review*, *8*(1), 79–100. doi:10.1515/applirev-2016-2001

Pérez-Cañado, M. L. (2020). CLIL and elitism: Myth or reality? *Language Learning Journal*, *48*(1), 4–17. doi:10.1080/09571736.2019.1645872

Pérez-Cañado, M. L. (2021). Inclusion and diversity in bilingual education: A European comparative study. *International Journal of Bilingual Education and Bilingualism*. doi:10.1080/13670050.2021.2013770

Reiser, B., & Tabak, I. (2014). Scaffolding. In R. Sawyer (Ed.), *The Cambridge Handbook of the Learning Sciences* (pp. 44–62). Cambridge University Press. doi:10.1017/CBO9781139519526.005

Richards, J. C., & Rodgers, T. S. (2014). *Approaches and Methods in Language Teaching* (3rd ed.). Cambridge University Press. doi:10.1017/9781009024532

Ritter, R., Wehner, A., Lohaus, G., & Krämer, P. (2020). Effect of same discipline compared to different-discipline collaboration on teacher trainees 'attitudes towards inclusive education and their collaboration skills. *Teaching and Teacher Education, 87*, 102955. doi:10.1016/j.tate.2019.102955

Rose, D. (2001). Universal Design for Learning. *Journal of Special Education Technology, 16*(4), 64–67. doi:10.1177/016264340101600411

Rose, D. & Meyer, A. (2002). Teaching Every Student in the Digital age: Universal Design for Learning. Harvard Education Press.

Roski, M., Walkowiak, M., & Nehring, A. (2021). Universal Design for Learning: The More, the Better? *Education Sciences, 11*(4), 164. doi:10.3390/educsci11040164

Sanahuja, A., Moliner García, M., & Moliner Miravet, O. (2020). Organización del aula inclusiva: ¿Cómo diferenciar las estructuras para lograr prácticas educativas más efectivas? [Organization of the inclusive classroom: How to differentiate the structures to achieve more effective educational practices?]. *Revista Complutense de Educación, 31*(4), 497–506. doi:10.5209/rced.65774

Sánchez, S., & Díez, E. (2013). La educación inclusiva desde el currículum: el Diseño Universal para el Aprendizaje. [Inclusive education from the curriculum: Universal Design for Learning.] En H. Rodríguez Navarro & L. Torrego Egido, (Coords.), Educación inclusiva, equidad y derecho a la diferencia: transformando la escuela (pp. 107-119). [Inclusive education, equity and the right to difference: transforming the school (pp. 107-119).] Wolters Kluwer.

Sasson, I., Yehuda, I., & Miedijensky, S. (2021). *Innovative learning spaces: class management and universal design for learning*. Learning Enviroments Research. doi:10.100710984-021-09393-8

Schumm, J., Vaughn, S., & Leavell, A. (1994). Planning Pyramid: A framework for planning for diverse students' needs during content instruction. *The Reading Teacher, 47*, 608–615.

Stoller, F. (2006). Establishing a Theoretical Foundation for Project-Based Learning in Second and Foreign Language Contexts. In G. H. Beckett & P. C. Miller (Eds.), *Project-Based Second and Foreign Language Education: Past, Present, and Future* (pp. 19–40). Information Age.

Tomlinson, C. A. (2014). *The differentiated classroom: Responding to the needs of all learners* (2nd ed.). ASCD.

Travé, G. (2013). Un estudio sobre las representaciones del profesorado de Educación Primaria acerca de la enseñanza bilingüe. [A study on the representations of primary education teachers about bilingual education.]. *Review of Education, 361*, 1–14. doi:10.4438/1988-592X-RE-2011-361-149

UNESCO. (2017). *La educación transforma vidas. [Education transforms lives.]* Organización de las Naciones Unidas para la Educación, la Ciencia y la Cultura [United Nations Education, Scientific, and Cultural Center]. https://unesdoc.unesco.org/ark:/48223/pf0000247234_spa

Vygotsky, L. S. (1978). *Mind in society: The development of higher psychological processes.* Harvard University Press.

Villaescusa, M. I. (Coord). (2021). *Diseño Universal y Aprendizaje Accesible. Modelo DUA-A. [Universal Design and Accessible Learning. Model DUA-A.]* Generalitat Valenciana.

Walqui, A. (2006). Scaffolding instruction for English language learners: A conceptual framework. *International Journal of Bilingual Education and Bilingualism, 9*(2), 159–180. doi:10.1080/13670050608668639

Westphal, L. E. (2013). *Differentiating Instruction with Menus for the Inclusive Classroom. Science.* Routledge., doi:10.4324/9781003234296

KEY TERMS AND DEFINITIONS

Bilingual Education: A teaching model in which two languages are used with the objective of improving students' communicative competence in their second language.

Competence: The ability that people have to solve the situations that may arise and that in turn contribute to the development of their intelligences.

Inclusion: The right of all people to receive a quality education adapted to their needs and characteristics.

Diversity: An inherent human condition that makes all people different at different levels (cultural, social, attitudinal, cognitive, physical, etc.).

Learning menu: A collection of different activities grouped in different segments that allow the learner to choose one from each group to showcase his or her learning.

Multimodal learning: Learning based on the use of different stimuli (textual, visual, auditory, kinesthetic...) in order to better adapt to the characteristics of each person.

Scaffolding: The process by which a learner is guided in their own learning by their instructor, who may be the teacher or a more capable peer.

APPENDIX A. HOW AM I GOING TO TEACH? (AN ADAPTATION OF THE CEDEC RESOURCE "IS OUR LIFE SUSTAINABLE?")

freely available at https://descargas.intef.es/cedec/proyectoedia/aicle/contenidos/energy/index.html

Section 1: Breaking the Ice

The first section aims to activate the students' previous knowledge about energy and how to take care of the planet. For this purpose, the *Looking ten times two* activity is proposed in which students are asked to look at a picture of a polluting thermal power plant for 30 seconds and write 10 ideas about it on a list. After sharing them with their classmates, they are asked to look at the photo for another 30 seconds and write 10 new ideas on a second list.

Figure 4. Thinking routine. CEDEC

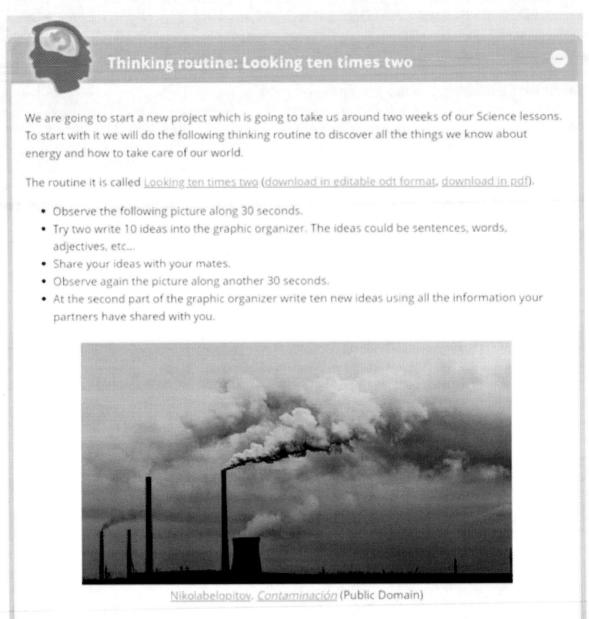

ADAPTATION: To address this activity from an inclusive approach, the process could be adapted by providing some students with a labeled photograph, a card with a glossary of terms accompanied by their corresponding image or an activity in which they have to match key terms with their definition. These resources would serve as lexical support. In addition, in the sharing of ideas phase, the use of heterogeneous groupings is proposed so that students with greater abilities can work together with students who need more support. For the adaptation of the product, the alternative of expressing the ten ideas through a word or short sentence, using the previously described support resources, instead of a long sentence or a paragraph, can be considered.

Section 2: What Is Energy

The second section begins with a brief definition of energy and eight different types of energy are introduced. The main task is to create a mind map about energy and the different types of energy using information from a web page (8 Types of Energy For Kids With Examples - Smartclass4kids.com) and a video (289 Peekaboo Kidz - YouTube). This can be done using pencil, crayons and paper or apps such as Popplet or Bubbl.us.

Figure 5. Task. What is energy? CEDEC

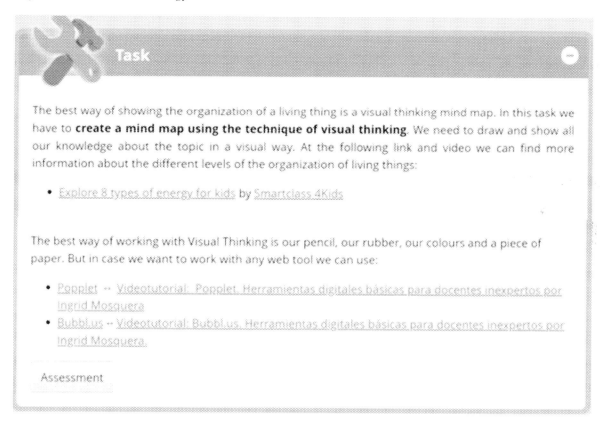

ADAPTATION: The simplest option for adapting the mind mapping process is to provide some students with a partially filled-in model. A more complex strategy would be to use Learning Stations: divide the class into groups and, using different spaces in the classroom, present the same information on types of energy in different formats (video, audio with images, text with images, mind map, outline or teacher-guided presentation). This activity can be done with or without rotation. Without rotation, the presentation of the information could be adapted to the characteristics of each group of students. If the idea of rotation is included, making all students go through the different Learning Stations, a more multimodal activity would be proposed, but the process would be the same for all.

For the adaptation of the product, a Learning Menu type activity based on TIC TAC TOE is presented. Students are divided into groups of four and listen to a short presentation on energy given by the teacher. Subsequently, they are asked to prepare a short oral explanation of their energy type to share with their classmates using the information in the video and on the web page (TIC TAC TOE center box activity) and to carry out two of the following tasks to complete a horizontal, diagonal o vertical line:

Table 5. TIC TAC TOE about energy

Choose a new word and explain it to your classmates	Find five verbs that appear in the text/video	Choose a photo related to your energy type and describe it to your classmates
Search online for three more facts about your energy type	Prepare a brief oral explanation of your energy type to share with your classmates	Write a written summary of your energy type (100 words)
Prepare three questions (with multiple choice answers) about your energy type	Design an outline with basic information about your energy type	Find five adjectives that appear in the text/video

Section 3: Sources of Energy

The third section presents examples of renewable and non-renewable energy sources. Subsequently, the main task is presented, which consists of conducting research on different energy sources and creating a poster including three examples of renewable and three non-renewable energy sources, accompanied by an illustration and a brief explanation.

Bilingual Education and Attention to Diversity

Figure 6. Investigation about energy. CEDEC

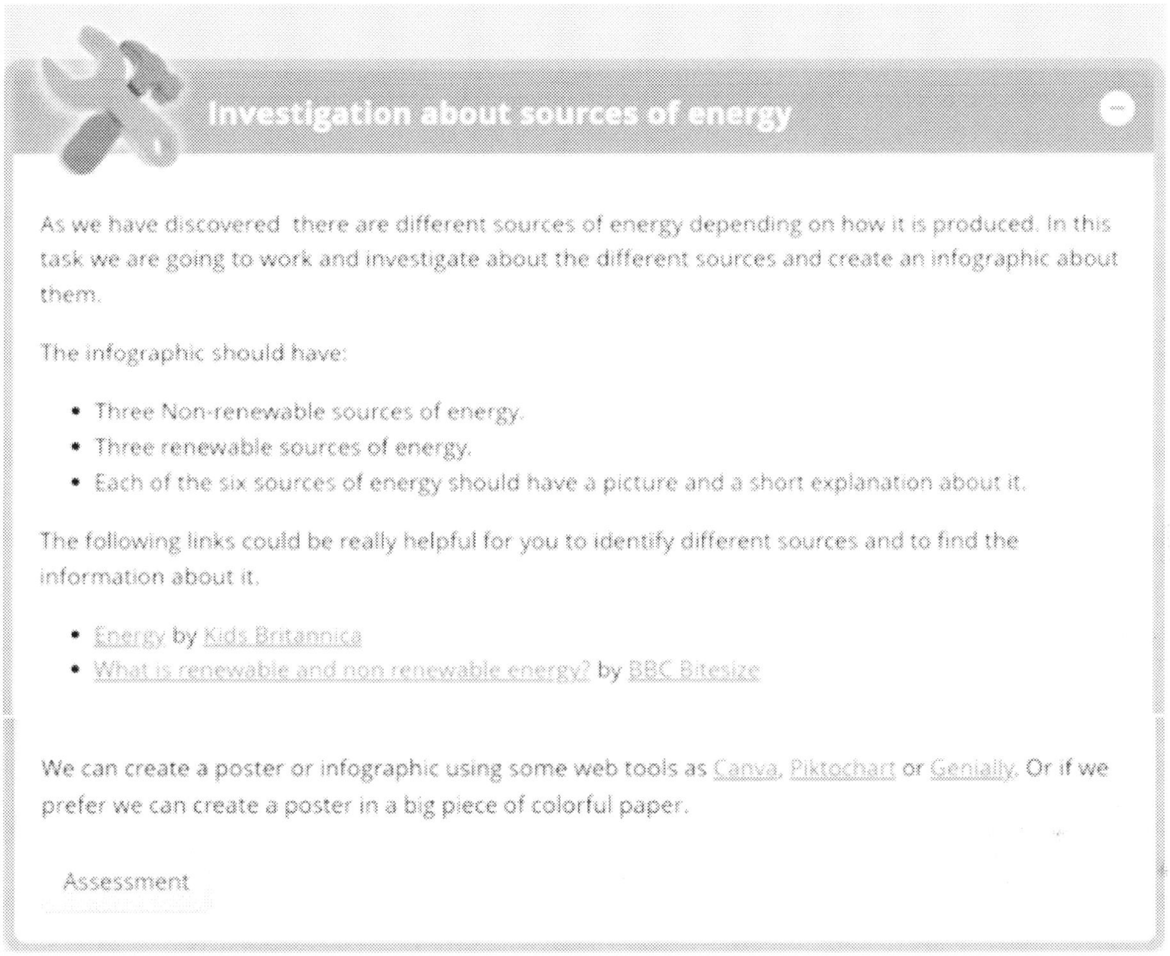

ADAPTATION: In order to adapt the following activity to the diversity of the bilingual classroom, we propose to work through the following *Learning Menu*, in which the students must choose a dish option from each of the groups presented.

Table 6. Learning Menu about sources of energy

Appetizer	Main Course	Dessert
What do you want to know about this topic? Write 2/3 questions.	Complete the graphic organizer (see figure 4) including four sentences on each arrow.	Research the energy sources most used in Spain. Share the information with your classmates through a poster.
Sketch a picture related to this topic and label 6 parts, trying to predict some of the words we will see in this topic.	Write a report on different types of energy including two renewable and one non-renewable energy source (in pairs).	Where can you find more information on this topic? Make a list of resources and share it with your classmates (in pairs).

181

Figure 7. Advantages and disadvantages of an energy source

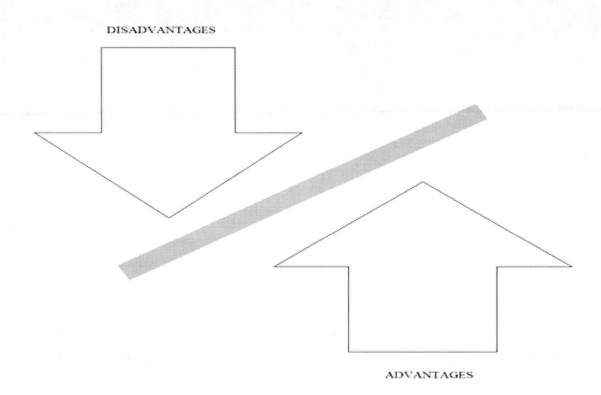

This Learning Menu adapts the process by proposing activities with a greater or lesser degree of visual support, facilitated through posters and graphic organizers, as well as with different types of student grouping. The adaptation of the product is achieved by allowing the choice between different activities that deal with the same basic learning objectives. In all Learning Menu activities, the teacher must persuade the students to choose the option that best reflects what they have learned.

Section 4: Sustanaible Energy for Our Lifes

The fourth section introduces the United Nations Sustainable Development Goals through two videos (*The Global Goals. The World largest lesson* and *What can you do? SDG 11 Sustainable Cities*) and begins by proposing that, as a class effort, students create a word cloud with the key terms of this topic using WordArt. Subsequently, students are asked to choose an energy source from one of the two groups (renewable vs. non-renewable) and compare them with each other using a graphic organizer. Once the graphic organizers have been prepared, students are asked to answer the following question: What do you think is the best source of energy in terms of sustainability of the Earth? Finally, the students are asked to

Bilingual Education and Attention to Diversity

record a short video in which they can choose three actions they can do in their daily life that contribute to energy sustainability. As resources, the procedure for the elaboration of the script is explained to them and they are presented with possible apps to make the recording, such as Flipgrid.

Figure 8. What can I do to be more sustainable? CEDEC

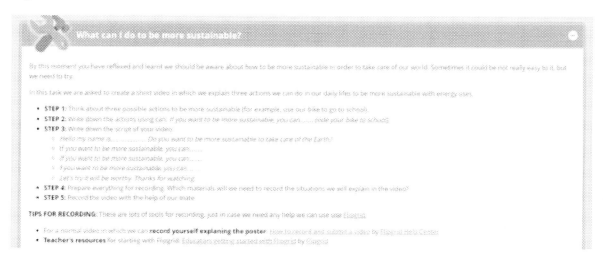

ADAPTATION: In order to provide students with different supports for the recording of the video, regarding the process, the amount of information included in the script presented to the students can be modified or they can be presented with a video sample made by students from previous courses on the topic. The product could be adapted, first of all, by offering the possibility of doing the tasks prior to the recording of the video in pairs (brainstorming, activation of key vocabulary, preparation of the script, etc.). Subsequently, the activity could be adapted by asking them to complement the content of the video by adding more information (What would happen if... type predictions) or by assigning them a more specific task in which they also have a choice, following the Learning Menus approach: Choose five actions to make your school more sustainable in one of these three areas: a) transport, b) heating and lighting, c) waste and equipment.

APPENDIX B. HOW WILL I MONITOR WHAT THEY HAVE LEARNED (AN ADAPTATION OF THE CEDEC RESOURCE "IS OUR LIFE SUSTAINABLE?")

freely available at https://descargas.intef.es/cedec/proyectoedia/aicle/contenidos/energy/index.html

Figure 9. Thinking about my learning

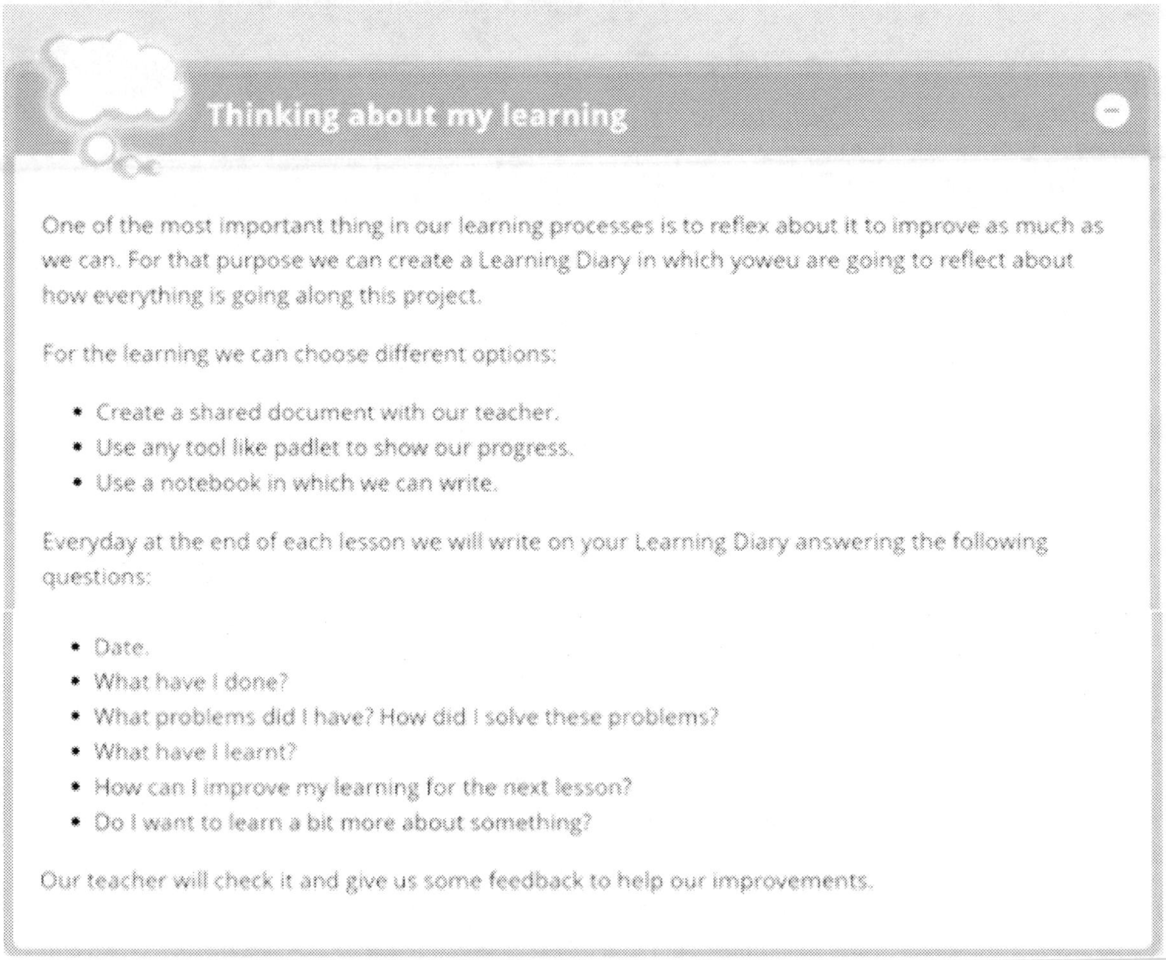

Thinking about my learning

One of the most important thing in our learning processes is to reflex about it to improve as much as we can. For that purpose we can create a Learning Diary in which yoweu are going to reflect about how everything is going along this project.

For the learning we can choose different options:

- Create a shared document with our teacher.
- Use any tool like padlet to show our progress.
- Use a notebook in which we can write.

Everyday at the end of each lesson we will write on your Learning Diary answering the following questions:

- Date.
- What have I done?
- What problems did I have? How did I solve these problems?
- What have I learnt?
- How can I improve my learning for the next lesson?
- Do I want to learn a bit more about something?

Our teacher will check it and give us some feedback to help our improvements.

Figure 10. The ladder of metacognition

Chapter 9
A Service-Learning Program for Multilingual Education at an Early Age:
Tandem Teaching Experiences

Ana Jovanović
https://orcid.org/0000-0001-5006-6006
University of Belgrade, Serbia

ABSTRACT

This chapter explores the effects of a service-learning program on the development of competences for teaching Spanish to young learners during initial teacher education. The framework of action science provides guidelines for the design of participative inquiry in which the student-teachers evaluate their theories of language teaching and embrace opportunities for developing a more efficient, flexible, but also a more critical approach to early language education. By implementing interpretative phenomenology as a research tool, a particular attention is dedicated to the participants' understanding and interpretation of specific pedagogical events of tandem teaching, which marked their positive and negative didactic experiences and influenced reconsideration of their theories of teaching.

INTRODUCTION

Development of multilingualism from early educational stages is recognized as an important task in many countries where different models of multilingual education are being introduced, evaluated, and (re)invented (e.g., Abelio-Contesse et al., 2013; Cenoz & Gorter 2015; Wernicke et al. 2021). Together with the evidence from the relevant scientific research, social, cultural, economic, ideological, and other concerns directly affect language education policies in all its aspects, from the choices of which languages are being learned and taught and at what age, to the ways in which this should be done (Filipović, 2018; Zein & Coady, 2021). While there is ample theoretical and practical evidence to support that languages are efficiently used to teach other content subjects (Mehisto et al., 2008; Naharro, 2019; Nikula et al.,

DOI: 10.4018/978-1-6684-6179-2.ch009

Copyright © 2023, IGI Global. Copying or distributing in print or electronic forms without written permission of IGI Global is prohibited.

A Service-Learning Program for Multilingual Education at an Early Age

2016), traditional perception of the foreign language as a separate subject is still alive in the mind of many language teachers, parents, educational authorities, and other interested parties who influence and define the educational process. Consequently, there is a risk that, when confronted with this traditional approach in the professional environment, beginning teachers will be "less likely to challenge the inherent conservatism in teaching or to advance social reform and social justice agendas" (Hobson et al., 2009, p. 211). Teacher education programs, thus, need to provide adequate support and sufficient positive experience that will empower young professionals to critically evaluate school practices and introduce changes in an informed and creative way while promoting collaboration and professional solidarity.

Programs for initial language teacher education typically include a number of courses that develop professional competences in the field of linguistics, language teaching methodologies, pedagogy, psychology, intercultural studies, etc. Teacher practicum is, additionally, a crucial curricular activity that provides opportunities for experiential learning. While it directly promotes the development of knowledge and skills of pre-service teachers under the guidance of more experienced colleagues, it also facilitates critical practice of self-reflection. Consequently, in those instances where teacher practicum is underrepresented within teacher education programs, alternative modalities for teaching practice must be created, implemented, and continuously evaluated. This is precisely the goal of the service-learning program explored in the present study – to provide necessary additional practice to students, prospective Spanish language teachers, in the realm of early multilingual education.

In order to understand the development of professional knowledge from the perspective of the participants (students-teachers), this research clearly aligns with the qualitative inquiry as epistemological orientation that strives "to better encompass the complexities of human existence and social action" (Filipović, 2015, p. 14; see also Denzin, 2009). It is at the same time an educational activity, based on the need to create learning opportunities for all participants – young language learners, students-teachers, and teacher educators – and guided by the need "to inform action in concrete situations" (Argyris et al., 1985, p. 5) of language teaching while testing general theory on knowledge creation. More specifically, our interest is drawn to the professional knowledge creation from the perspective of the participants themselves. In an attempt to understand the point of view of the students-teachers and their interpretations of the tandem teaching experiences, this research relies on interpretative phenomenological analysis. By providing rich analysis of a limited number of cases, this research method may offer insights into how the participants make meaning of significant occurrences that, in this case, refer to teaching Spanish to young learners. It is assumed that these interpretations will ultimately influence the development of the participants' professional knowledge.

The outline of the chapter is conceived with these goals in mind. Background section addresses several theoretical issues relevant for the topic at hand, that is, the nature of language teachers' epistemologies that are at the core of teachers' professional knowledge and the way these are challenged by the process of (re-)education as understood within the framework of action science; the concept of tandem teaching is introduced to provide necessary argumentation for the choice of educational approach within the explored service-learning project. The section dedicated to the service-learning program, in turn, defines the motivation and the context behind this specific research project that intends to combine practical problem solving with theory building and change. After considering the key aspects of the research methodology, we proceed to the findings from the interpretative phenomenological analysis and discuss its main implications for language teacher education in the final section of the chapter.

BACKGROUND

The development of plurilingual competence is identified as an important goal in language education (see, e.g., Council of Europe, 2001; 2018). An early start is a crucial factor in this respect, given the developmental characteristics of young children (Djigunović, 2011; Pižorn, 2009) and their motivational dispositions that are, in this age, mainly intrinsic (Mihaljević Djigunović, 2012; Páez & Pascual, 2017). Naturally, teaching languages to young children differs significantly from teaching adults, which, in turn, imposes additional challenges for teacher education programs that need to provide opportunities for the development of necessary teachers' competences.

Bleichenbaher et al. (2019) synthesize a substantial work in the field of language teacher education and propose a taxonomy of eight dimensions of professional competences:

1. professional values and principles,
2. language and communicative competences,
3. information technology competences,
4. metalinguistic, meta-discourse and metacultural competences,
5. teaching competences,
6. competences for cooperation,
7. competences for initial education and career-long development and, finally,
8. professional learning opportunities.

In addition to providing a useful tool for an analysis of teacher competences necessary for teaching languages in a variety of contexts, this model is interesting in that it offers a dynamic matrix of interrelated domains that reflect the nature of knowledge, skills, and attitudes for the language teaching profession. While all competences recognized by the model are necessary for successful language teaching, we are particularly interested in its first and eighth dimensions that underline the continuous process of teacher development. Namely, the first dimension involves professional values and principles that represent a foundation for all individual teacher action and development; professional learning opportunities, on the other hand, refer to all activities and opportunities that are conducive to the development of other professional competences (Bleichenbaher et al., 2019, pp. 9–10). In other words, professional learning opportunities might be understood in terms of a temporal axis where each new meaningful activity contributes to the teacher's professional development. Instead, the development in the first domain would imply a reflective movement toward a reconsideration of one's fundamental knowledge that directs all teacher action. Indeed, epistemology represents a central issue in teacher education since any change in one's theory of teaching would imply an evaluation of their basic beliefs and attitudes that constitute the theory in question.

The field of applied linguistics has made important contributions to our understanding of epistemologies in language learning and teaching. The inquiry has been particularly geared by the question of "how beliefs develop, fluctuate and interact with actions, emotions, identities or affordances and how they are constructed within the micro- and macro-political contexts of learning and teaching languages" (Barcelos & Kalaja, 2011, p. 282). The research suggests that learners' beliefs influence the way they approach the learning task (Barcelos, 2012) and that there is a tight relationship between cognition and affect (e.g., Pavlenko & Dewaele, 2004; Barcelos, 2013; Jovanović, 2016). An awareness and understanding of students' epistemologies in teacher education is, then, even more significant for their effect on the

A Service-Learning Program for Multilingual Education at an Early Age

overall educational process: not only will they influence one's language learning, but will affect one's teaching practice with all the implications this may entail for the new generations of students.

People operate guided by their epistemologies that represent repertoires of concepts, ideas, schemas, models, and strategies. The term "theory of action" is used in the action science framework (Argyris & Schön, 1974; Argyris et al., 1985) to underline the intentional nature of human action: theories of action condition one's interpretation of a situation and orient specific actions toward intended consequences (Argyris et al., 1985, p. 81). In this framework, there is always regularity in one's behavior that may be explained by one's theory of action. Much of what constitutes a theory of action is tacit knowledge – routines, beliefs, emotions, and values (Nonaka & Takeuchi, 1995, p. viii) – of which a person may not be truly aware. The basic source of knowledge creation and innovation is, then, the process of externalization of the tacit knowledge which creates a new level of awareness since a person analyzes and evaluates the forces that drive their actions (Nonaka & Takeuchi, 1995; Paavola et al., 2004). The challenge for teacher education is, then, to facilitate this metacognitive activity (Paris & Winograd, 1990; Kuhn, 1999; Hiver et al., 2021) and to create situations that would provoke evaluation of one's tacit knowledge.

Argyris et al. (1985) also draw our attention to the difference between espoused theory and theory-in-use. This distinction emphasizes the fact that human action is not incidental, but consistent with the theory-in-use, which in turn may be consistent or inconsistent with the theory a person declaratively adopts. "Espoused theories are those individuals claim to follow. Theories-in-use are those that can be inferred from action" (Argyris et al., 1985, pp. 81–82). The inconsistency between espoused theories and theories-in-action may possibly explain discrepancies between teachers' declarative adherence with contemporary teaching approaches and their actual practices that reveal incongruent sets of values, as we sometimes witness. While espoused theory is by definition explicit, theory-in-use may easily rely on tacit knowledge which would need to be externalized in order to be evaluated and, ideally, reframed.

This calls for re-education that implies a change in previously well-established patterns of thinking and acting (see Lewin and Grabbe, 1945). Re-education is provoked when people experience the need for change by participating in tasks that challenge their strongly embedded beliefs. Argyris et al. (1985, p. 51) specify that this may happen when the action generates information inconsistent with original theory, when it does not achieve intended consequences or leads to unintended consequences, or when the initial hypothesis is disconfirmed. An inconsistency between one's theory and immediate circumstances is normally experienced as a sense of emotional incoherence that provokes surprise and curiosity (Thagard, 2000; 2006) and stimulates explanatory activity. Importantly, the change is more likely to occur when forces that restrain change are reduced than when there is an increase in the forces driving change (Lewin, 1948/1998, in Coghlan & Jacobs, 2005, p. 445).

Well-established humanistic tradition perceives dialogue as a central resource in knowledge creation (see Mercer et al., 2020). A dialogic exchange facilitates an analysis and consideration of both missing pieces and misconceptions in our theories. Starting from there, the present service-learning program incorporates the strategy of tandem teaching which serves the purpose of providing additional dialogic opportunities for the evaluation of theories in action of tandem partners. It is suggested that close collaboration in co-teaching tasks imposes constant negotiation of meanings and solutions for novice teachers.

Tandem teaching is gaining much importance in the field of inclusive education (Wilson & Blednick, 2011; Honigsfeld & Dove, 2015), higher education (Blanchard, 2012; Ferguson & Wilson, 2011; Graziano & Navarrete, 2012; Liebel et al., 2017; Beaten et al., 2018), as well as in content and language integrated learning (Pavón Vázquez et al., 2015; Custodio-Espinar et al., 2022). Although team teaching is not a new phenomenon in pre-service education, it has not been extensively studied. However, there is a need to implement innovative teacher education strategies that will respond to the needs of contemporary language education. In spite of different disadvantages this teaching strategy may impose (such as, high workload and feelings of unfamiliarity), the research suggests that they are overrun by the opportunities for professional growth. The most salient benefits include scaffold learning experiences, individualized instructions, and diversity in content presentation (Graziano & Navarrete, 2012, p. 109). When students are teamed in tandems, in addition to their mentors, they are also able to provide and rely on emotional and professional peer-support (Tsybulsky, 2019, p. 246). Consequently, it is suggested that this form of professional practice would enhance sense of security, professional solidarity and, most importantly, it would provide additional opportunities for the evaluation of one's teaching theories.

SERVICE-LEARNING PROGRAM FOR EARLY LANGUAGE EDUCATION

Objectives

Language education policies in Serbia reflect an awareness of the importance of plurilingual competence and early language learning: foreign languages are introduced as early as the first grade of primary education (at age seven) and all learners have the obligation to learn at least two foreign languages during their schooling. While these decisions on the state level formally support multilingual education, the school realities paint a somewhat different picture that reflects the lack of flexibility on different levels of the educational system (for critical review of Serbian language education policies, see Filipović et al., 2007; Filipović & Djurić, 2021). Among many other concerns, the crucial question of the purpose of language education and its place in the school curriculum is still hotly debated. While several top-down initiatives have been proposed in order to facilitate interdisciplinary approach though project-based instruction, there is still a general orientation toward separate subjects teaching, foreign languages included. In light of these concerns, there is a clear need to implement innovative educational models that would resolve the breach of linguistic subjects (Djurić, 2017, pp. 408–409) and provide modalities for the development of true plurilingual competence.

In an attempt to respond to the needs of the local educational context, a service-learning program was designed in order to promote multilingual education by introducing Spanish as an additional foreign language at an early age. It represents an experimental project carried out by the Department of Iberian Studies at the Faculty of Philology, University of Belgrade, the Association of Spanish Language Teachers of Serbia, and the primary school "Mihailo Petrovic Alas" in Belgrade. Spanish classes are offered as an optative activity in the duration of four months to the pupils from the first to the fourth grades (age 7 to 10), which means that the Spanish language is the second foreign language (FL) of these children, since English as their first FL, introduced in the first grade, makes part of the compulsory curriculum. Importantly, the program is conceived as a series of workshops whose main objective is the development of plurilingual sensitivity through translingual practices that reflect the linguistic experience of all participating young learners. Having these goals in mind, the adopted teaching approach is task-based language teaching (Ellis et al., 2020) because it offers an efficient platform for active learning and engagement in meaningful open-ended activities, while providing space for authentic language use and multimodal communication. The contents of the program are highly flexible and interdisciplinary, given in the form of a list of suggested topics, so that they may be selected and adapted according to the needs and interests of each particular group.

A Service-Learning Program for Multilingual Education at an Early Age

Another key objective of the proposed service-learning program is to provide professional experience to pre-service Spanish language teachers educated at the University of Belgrade. Namely, teacher education programs for prospective Spanish language teachers are offered at two public universities of the country as a part of the more general curricula of Hispanic Studies. While the program offers ample opportunities for the development of different competences necessary for future language teachers, a detailed examination of the curricula shows an insufficient presence of pedagogical and methodological courses (Jovanović & Mastilo, 2022). Additionally, there is a clear need for more professional practice during the pre-service education, since there is only one mandatory course of teacher practicum offered at the master's degree programs of both universities. While revisions of the curricula are currently being carried out, a number of varied extracurricular activities aimed at promoting students' professional development, activism, and leadership has already been initiated (Jovanović & Filipović, 2013) in order to meliorate deficiencies of the existing programs. This particular service-learning program was designed and implemented so it would provide possibilities for volunteering students-prospective teachers to develop their competences for teaching Spanish to young learners, with the continuous assistance and support of the university faculty.

Design of the Program

The service-learning program was piloted during the academic year 2018/2019 with the pupils of the first grade of the primary school. Since then, it has progressively grown; it currently includes pupils from the first to the fourth grade, so that many of the children, who joined the program in their first grade, have participated for several consecutive years. On the other hand, considering that the program is offered as an additional extracurricular activity, there is certain fluctuation in pupils' attendances, manifested either through their withdrawal or through the inclusion of new pupils at grades other-than-the-first. In the year 2021/2022, which is the focus of our analysis, there was a total of 52 pupils, divided in four groups according to their grades and taught by one teaching tandem each. The classes were organized once a week with each group, in the duration of one school class (45 minutes), from December till May, that is, until the end of the academic semester.

This is a volunteering activity for the students as well. They are all enrolled in one of the language teaching methodologies courses: in 2021/2022 there were eight students – six from undergraduate and two from the master's degree program – teamed up in four tandems. In accordance with the concept of team teaching, the tandems collaborated in the planning, implementation, and evaluation of their teaching activities and taught the same group of young learners simultaneously. Given the amount of shared responsibility among the equals, this teaming model is frequently described as "the most collaborative model of team teaching" (Baeten & Simons, 2014, p. 95).

In order to provide sufficient support to the students-teachers, the program involves several additional activities. Prior to and during the teaching activities, the volunteering students attend a series of workshops tailored to assist novice teachers when working with young children. While some of the topics are covered in teaching methodologies courses, the purpose of the workshops is to approach these issues in a more focused, analytic, and practical way that centers on the characteristics of young language learners. This is particularly important if we have in mind that not a single course of the university curriculum focuses on this topic. In addition to the workshops, several resources serve as a scaffold for students-teachers: a course curriculum for each grade, a collaborative online platform, class observations with a follow-up mentoring session, and less formal means of communication such as emails, *WhatsApp* group, etc.

RESEARCH METHODOLOGY

Research Rationale

Each educational experience interacts with the teacher's theory of teaching in two ways: it either enhances existing beliefs and attitudes by confirming them or it challenges the embedded belief system when the teacher is confronted with new and unexpected. The purpose of the present study is to explore the effect this service-learning program may have on the teaching theories of the participating students-teachers. We are particularly interested in observing which critical events provoke evaluation of one's tacit knowledge relevant for teaching languages to young learners, in which way the participants interpret that experience, and what is the potential of these events for the development of teaching competences. In other words, the goal of this study is to explore the participants' interpretations of the tandem teaching experience with its potential effect on their teaching epistemologies and professional development.

In the attempt to investigate the participants' current teaching theories and to bring to surface their tacit knowledge that directs their actions, the study adheres to the action science as a specific form of participative inquiry. As Friedman (2001) explains, action science represents "social practice which integrates both production and use of knowledge for the purpose of promoting learning with and among individuals and systems whose work is characterized by uniqueness, uncertainty and instability" (p. 159). The guiding idea is to enable transfer of knowledge and skills since its focus is on metacognition: if the participants learn how to engage in the externalization of their tacit knowledge through dialogic learning, they might be able to translate this learning-teaching approach to other domains of their (professional) activity (Jovanović, 2016).

In line with the underlying ideology of the project, grounded in dialogic learning, interviews have a central place in this endeavor. Given their transformative potential, the function of interviews transcends the process of data-collection. They represent "a construction site for knowledge. An interview is literally an *inter-view*, an inter-change of views between two persons conversing about a theme of mutual interest" (Kvale, 1996, p. 14). Hence, in addition to providing data for the following analysis, the interviews create opportunities for common reflection between the researcher-educator and the student-teacher.

This research design imposes a different role on the researcher, as well, since she becomes an interventionist: her activities are not limited to the collection, analysis, and interpretation of data, but imply direct participation in the observed phenomenon through education, support, and reflection. Her goal is to assist change and questioning of the status quo by helping the participants "reflect on the world they create and learn to change it in ways more congruent with the values and theories they espouse" (Argyris et al., 1985, p. 98).

Method

Considering our interest in the participants' interpretation of teaching experiences, we use interpretative phenomenological analysis (IPA) to explore their meaning making related to their significant experiences (Smith et al., 2009; Miller et al., 2018). It is a sort of double hermeneutic since the goal of IPA is "to make sense of the participants making sense of their experiences" (Miller et al., 2018, pp. 247). In other words, it provides detailed accounts on the participants' lived experiences in a way that is not externally imposed but rather created by the participants themselves.

A Service-Learning Program for Multilingual Education at an Early Age

IPA most frequently relies on a limited number of semi-structured individual interviews that enable the participants to engage in real-time, in-depth conversations. This research procedure facilitates "the elicitation of stories, thoughts and feelings about the target phenomenon" (Smith et al., 2009, p. 57) in quite a flexible way. While a specific topic is clearly established prior to the interview, it is possible and even recommended that the interviewee and/or interviewer address other relevant (sub)topics as they arise from the conversation. Thus, although the researcher usually uses an interview schedule to be better prepared for the data collection, the interview itself is not limited by the preset questions. For this study, the interview schedule revolved around the following themes in relation to teaching Spanish as a foreign language to young children: the participants' previous teaching experience, their preferred teaching approach and teaching practices, and tandem teaching experience.

This IPA uses the data from in-depth interviews that were completed with four students-teachers during April and May of 2022. Although at the time there were eight students in the service-learning program, it was essential to limit the analysis to a smaller number of the participants for the sake of richer analysis. It was important, however, that the participants have worked together in the same tandems. Hence, the four participants formed part of two tandems: two master degree students (Milly and Esther, all pseudonyms) and two undergraduate students (Nina and Mia). The average length of the interviews was 65 minutes (Milly – 55 min., Esther – 54 min., Nina – 63 min., and Mia – 91 min.).

After obtaining informed consent, the interviews were conducted in Serbian, the participants' first language. Following act, they were transcribed in totality and hand coded to determine patterns and themes. A particular attention has been given to the explanation of marked teaching occurrences that either reflect commonality or divergence from the common perceptions and interpretations of the discussed phenomenon. Translated citations from the interviews, done by the researcher, play an important part in providing space for the participants to "speak" in their own words. A thorough analysis of individual cases is presented first, so we could move toward discussion of generic themes (Smith & Eatough, 2011) in the final section of the chapter.

Results: The Participants' Perspectives

Milly

Milly is an MA student with an interest for Spanish language teaching. Her experience in teaching is fairly limited, as it might be expected, and consists of teaching Spanish to young learners in short-term programs organized by local communities. Her first professional engagement began during her ultimate year of undergraduate studies when she saw a call for the program announced through the university's social groups. Although prior to this experience Milly had never felt an interest in working with children, she was intrigued by the call and decided to apply. "Since my mom is a primary school teacher, I've always avoided that domain… for some reason, I haven't been inclined to spend time with children, nor have I been around them much… I don't know, in that particular moment, the call sparked my interest." She describes her first teaching experience with young children as "really wonderful". She has been impressed by the uniqueness of every class session and it is precisely this unexpectedness and novelty that made her embrace the activity: "I never know what they'll ask and how they'll put together two words". She strives to be responsive to students' needs and she shows readiness to adapt her teaching approach to children's interests. This is why she explores materials close to the students' realities ("that's when

193

I found out that they watch *The Casagrandes*") and tries to incorporate elements of Hispanic cultures that may provoke their curiosity.

Milly welcomes the singularity of every teaching session and does not fear of straying from her lesson plan. While she engages in thorough preparation of all her classes by reflecting on every segment of the class plan (because this makes her feel more secure), Milly has realized that, during classes, she is being guided by her students. This tendency is rarely observed in inexperienced teachers (Berliner, 1988; Ryan, 1986), though. When asked what makes her improvise, she responds that it is the students' energy that directs her. "Their energy... I think... I'm not a very energetic person... and I'm quiet; but when I see that someone cares, this person motivates me in a way I wouldn't be able to do so by myself".

Indeed, Milly is not a very vociferous individual, but her energy level is strong and balanced as it could be observed in the way she maintains class discipline. In fact, when asked why she believes to have low energy, Milly responded that this was a comment she had received in a private language school when interviewed for a teaching position – she had been told that she lacked energy for maintaining young children animated. She simply did not question this superficial external evaluation until a conversation with her mentor when she received an opposing comment based on the episodes from class observations. The incident underlines the fragility of identity in novice teachers whose insecurities may easily be heightened by unsupportive behavior of more experienced colleagues. On the other hand, it is also true that the comment of another significant colleague, the mentor in this case, may have an opposite effect – under the condition that there is sufficient time and space to identify potential problematic beliefs and establish strings of trust.

This episode is also noteworthy because it points to a misconception in early language education that the goal of the class is to be fun and playful. While playfulness is crucial quality in early language learning, it should not overshadow the educational component of which Milly seems to be aware: "I smile on my way home when I can really feel that they enjoyed the class and that I did something so that they actually learn". The two components are, in fact, inseparable. Milly's quote also brings to our attention another important aspect of teacher identity, that is, the altruistic nature of teacher motivation, which is stimulated by the development and wellbeing of another person.

Milly declares that her teaching goals are directed toward the development of functional competence in the Spanish language in accordance with the students' age: "they should be able to present themselves, to say how old they are, what is their favorite color, animal, and that's it". Later on in the interview, however, she expresses her need to support the intrinsic motivation for learning languages: "that love, that's what's most important for me". This is why she chooses to focus on interesting aspects of Hispanic cultures, to spark students' interest for the Spanish speaking world so that "at least some time, maybe, in the future, they decide to learn Spanish, just for the love of it and not because someone forces them to learn in school". The word choice in defining two types of goals might be indicative of a discrepancy between Milly's teaching theories. While she accepts that the goal *should be* the development of functional competence in the target language, she is driven by the need to nurture their *love* for the language. The contemporary theory on language teaching methodologies insists on the importance of motivation and curiosity in developing communicative competence and it proposes specific techniques to reinforce this conative educational component. However, for some reason, communicative functions contradict with Milly's conception of playful learning. This is of high concern for the teacher educator since it indicates the possibility of erroneous interpretation of the key teaching resources such as the curriculum. Milly explains that she felt limited during the service-learning program: "I wasn't free to introduce the festivals or other cultural aspects and... honestly, even when I wanted to integrate something like that in the class

A Service-Learning Program for Multilingual Education at an Early Age

plan, I didn't know how… because of the learning outcomes". The learning outcomes, specified in the curriculum in terms of a limited number of basic communicative functions, somehow made her shrink her focus to formal aspects of the language teaching and leave aside the cultural aspects she intuitively felt as the most important. An understanding of theoretic principles is necessary for their implementation while the practice in the profession enables teachers to routinize specific actions with which they are able to react without thinking every step of their way (Mitchell & Marland, 1989). The goal of teacher education should then be to create ample opportunities that could facilitate an understanding, analysis and evaluation of the new concepts through both theoretical discussions and professional practice.

This is precisely the case with tandem teaching. "I've always taught individually and I didn't have any idea how I could with someone… it wasn't clear to me at all how this could function with two teachers. Then, I saw it's great." Milly comments on several aspect beneficial for planning, implementation, and evaluation of the teaching process. Their tandem spontaneously acquired a practice of division of work in the planning process: one person would prepare a draft of the lesson plan after which they would meet to analyze and evaluate each proposed segment. As Milly states, these discussion sessions – in the form of face-to-face or online meetings or written exchanges – made them modify the original plan. This was useful for Milly particularly in the domain of time management, since it made her think additionally about the time limitations and class coherence. The collegial communication made this process smooth and pleasant, according to Milly: "we're similar, none of us likes to dominate. So, we worked together, we let the other… she lets me, or I let her, then the other jumps back in, but we were both always present". The fact that they *were letting the other* prepare the drafts might imply that the job division in the planning phase could be evaluated, explicated, and potentially reframed. In fact, Honigsfeld and Dove (2015) defend that planning should be completed in three steps: individual pre-planning, collaborative planning, and individual post-planning. It is quite possible that the explicit analysis of this process early on in the co-teaching process would have provided better understanding of the shared responsibilities within the tandem.

During class sessions, however, the co-teaching ran smoothly and collaboratively. Milly hesitantly comments that her role in maintaining discipline was perhaps somewhat more salient. At the very beginning of the service-learning program, she observed that one boy was particularly impatient and restless, so she made sure to follow him more closely and to assist him in class participation. This seemed to be very important for the overall group dynamics since the boy's vivid energy had a potential to pull the class either toward joint learning or general chaos. No specific disciplinary measures were needed to reach this end, however, as the class observation proved – Milly's steady voice and presence made the whole difference. Esther, on the other hand, was able to provide more individualized attention to the pupils on the other side of the classroom. It seems that the children also enjoyed their co-teaching: "the kids always wanted to have one teacher in each group when we compete. And toward the end, when they've gained more security, they were like 'can we compete against you?' It was really sweet." Milly concludes that the shared responsibility made the overall teaching experience easier since she could rely on Esther in every moment. In spite of this, she prefers individual teaching:

It's true, the pressure is higher, responsibility's greater, but somehow, I don't know, it's different when I'm alone with the children (…) when I can joke, or stray more from the plan… I get to know them better, I can see better what interests them (…) It's not because of Esther, it's just me, I can't when there's someone else, I don't have the same liberty…

Esther

Esther is also an MA student who finds her future vocation in teaching Spanish. Her teaching experience before the service-learning program was quite modest, mainly through individual language classes. At the time she joined the program, she also started a part-time engagement in a private language school where she taught Spanish to two groups of adults. She prefers group classes to individual, even though she believes that the individual lesson provides more opportunities for individualized teaching. She finds advantages of group work in joint learning "they learn from each other, and they hear stories, and so on (…) overall atmosphere, people, communication" is something where she finds an important source of motivation.

Esther loves children and passionately talks about the importance of education and early language learning. However, when the service-learning program was presented in a regular class and students were invited to participate, she raised her hand to volunteer only to quickly withdraw it. Following this incident, the coordinator decided to make an exception and send Esther a separate email. She expressed her belief that Esther would enjoy the program in spite of its challenges and that it would be a valuable experience for her future profession. She accepted the invitation although it was clear that her level of anxiety was far above the optimal. In the interview, however, she talks about this experience with certain pride: "you can't know until you try… it is much better now; absolutely… and I see that I can, of course… I'd change a million things of course, that's the way I am, but I see I can do it, I see that I manage; and I see that the children want to collaborate, which inspires me".

Esther's process of planning has evolved during this experience. As she describes, in the very beginning, she attended more to the formal aspects of the class plan. With time, however, she began to focus on her students' needs and interests during the first stages of planning. "Now I know the children; I choose a topic from the curriculum, then I sit and think about games, because I know they like games; so that's first, what will keep them focused during 45 minutes of class time, what will make them compete and play." This comment makes us deduce that the underlying belief behind Esther's planning is that the class needs to be entertaining. When asked about the expected learning outcomes, she responds that, in line with the students' characteristics, the focus should be on learning vocabulary. And she insists that each student leaves the classroom aware that he or she has learned something. For that reason, she likes to incorporate quizzes and small competitions in her class sessions.

Esther is very satisfied with her co-teaching experience as well. It was particularly important in the beginning of the service-learning program when she struggled with her insecurities. Esther sees their collaboration as an important tool in the learning process: "what I especially appreciate in tandem teaching… of course, if one's willing and wishes to do so… is that you can see where you make mistakes (…) you can look up to your colleague and vice versa, when it comes to ideas as well as actions".

Esther senses that her weak spot is related to class discipline. She tends to be permissive because she focuses on children's vulnerability ("they're still children, they're so little") and finds it difficult to set clear boundaries. She would rather talk with her students, listen to them, try to animate them, but she is not quite sure how to manage discipline when the children lose their focus. Instead, Milly, her tandem partner, has a way of calming the situation and focusing children's attention to the task: "she

A Service-Learning Program for Multilingual Education at an Early Age

does it so smoothly, I really admire it; she's more of an authority". Milly's presence creates favorable circumstances for Esther to be authentic: "In a way I'm more spontaneous than her; I'd rather let the class go with the flow, I wouldn't focus on the plan, I'd rather talk with the children". This proved to be essential for Esther's positive perception of this teaching experience; the fact that she could rely on Milly for class discipline helped her focus on everything she likes in language teaching and become more self-confident. Thus, when she needed to give class alone due to Milly's absence, she was able to do it to her satisfaction.

I think I managed to do everything I wanted. I don't know how, ehm… I don't know how, somehow… I guess I focused on the fact that I was alone and that I needed to take charge of everything, I guess I had to… to organize them, animate them, all by myself… I knew that I was the only responsible, the way the class will turn out… so, I paid more attention to the plan so I'd make sure everything turns out ok.

This was an important lesson in Esther's professional growth since it made her positively evaluate her teaching competences and gain much needed confidence. She resorted to specific resources, such as lesson plan, to maintain structure and fulfill her objectives. It is quite possible that this would have been an overwhelming experience with potentially negative effect on her teaching anxiety if introduced early on in her teaching engagement.

Nina

Nina is enrolled in the last year of the undergraduate program and attends courses in language teaching methodologies. Consequently, her teaching experience is very modest, limited to tutoring sessions with adults. However, she had some experience in working with children: she worked on occasions as a babysitter and was engaged as a part-time animator in child playgrounds. Since she found these activities very fulfilling, she wanted to try herself in teaching language to young children.

Nina and Mia teach second graders, that is, eight-year-olds. Their group is informally famous for being challenging with several very energetic boys. For that reason, when planning the class, Nina's first thought is to identify interesting games that would fully engage the children and particularly the boys. Nina explains that this initial activity needs to capture their attention, for which reason the tandem usually opens the class with a combination of kinetic and verbal activity: for instance, the students play catch and throw with their teachers while pronouncing specific words that were introduced in previous classes. The following activity is usually based on a song selected according to the theme of the class. The children normally listen to the song two or more times, especially if this is what the pupils want. The song usually serves the purpose of introducing the central activity when the children need to draw, color or create something – like when they draw their family tree: "that was the creative part, when they actually got to learn [vocabulary of] family members". The class normally ends with an additional mini-activity that underlines the content introduced during the class. This is usually another game or a competition, the latter being particularly well accepted by the class.

Nina clearly describes class structure that aligns with task-based language teaching approach (TBLT). Although she does not use the TBLT terminology, the function of each class segment is clearly identified and supported by the classroom practice, which indicates the consistency between her espoused and action-in-use teaching theories. It could be assumed that this teaching experience could only reinforce Nina's adherence to TBLT.

Nina believes that the service-learning program instigated a slight change in her approach to class planning that mainly refers to greater flexibility in the use of the curriculum. While at the beginning of the program she tended to strictly follow the proposed schedule, later on she began to combine different functional and lexical contents according to the themes that seemed more important for the children. The teaching methodology is, in fact, where she sees her greatest improvement:

I thought that the most difficult part would be to teach the language, to teach while not using the board, not to turn my back on them... because I remember when you said that we can't turn our back, no writing on the board, teach through games... I was, like, how is that even possible? And this is now my favorite part. And the most difficult part is to keep them calm.

Indeed, it is not easy to keep the group of eight-year-olds completely focused, especially if there is an uncertainty as to the role one may take: "I didn't know what to expect, I didn't know that I must also be a psychologist and, I don't know, a parent... and to teach them how to be friends..." However, different incidents made her accept this role as well, especially instances of misbehavior such as an occasion when a boy called a class friend with names. "I am with this question: am I *the* person who needs to intervene, to dedicate time to the issue or... maybe not... but I came to understand that it *was* my role, I *was* an authority figure there, I was their teacher". This incident should also be considered within the context of the service-learning program which comes with certain fuzziness of roles and responsibilities. The students-teachers are sometimes perceived as "visitors" without clear affiliation with the school. The support from the school community is, consequently, fundamental in helping students-teachers take full advantage of the learning opportunities. In Nina's case, this support came from the class teacher who entered the classroom on one occasion when children were particularly loud and told Nina, in front of the children, that she had every right to put down the names of the children who misbehaved and to later call their parents. "I've never written down a single name, I don't intend to, [I don't plan] to involve the parents... but, they [children] don't know it, so it works. (...) I really didn't know what I can or can't do. I'm with a project, I'm not the school's employee... I didn't know my place." This particular strategy helped Nina take control over the class and, even more importantly, it helped her be more assertive and comfortable in her teacher's shoes.

The process of co-teaching also has a fairly well-established routine, Nina explains. As their first step, the partners identify what will be the focus of the following class meeting. Over the next few days, they brainstorm and share ideas through chat from where they choose the best candidates for the formal lesson plan. Based on this description, one could suppose that the collaboration in the planning phase runs smoothly and according to the best practices. However, it is possible to recognize slight dissatisfaction relative to the tandem's time management: "It [the lesson plan] should be done by Wednesday... however, sometimes it's done, sometimes it isn't, that's all I'll say. I really try to do my part and... of course, we're all very busy..."

For Nina, tandem teaching represents a good initiation strategy. Since she did not have previous teaching experience, it was comforting to know that she would not be alone in the class. However, in spite of the shared enthusiasm for the program, it seems that Nina and Mia had their differences. An illustrative episode occurred during one of the initial classes when Nina raised her voice to try to restore class discipline; Mia disapproved and after the class commented that her teaching style was different, which in turn provoked certain defensiveness in Nina. "I told her, if you have any idea, please, please, take charge, calm them in any way you think it can work". Naturally, the lack of experience in dealing

A Service-Learning Program for Multilingual Education at an Early Age

with the group such as this made them confront new situations that neither of them new how to solve. Although the incident provoked some tension in the tandem, shared experience taught them how to rely on each other. "The relationship improved; I mean, it wasn't bad, but I want to say that we function now; we know that we teach together, we have good time, when we make plans, there's no problem". The word choice in this segment, however, suggests certain ambivalence in Nina, probably provoked by an inaptly formulated criticism from an equally inexperienced partner. However, her overall evaluation of the tandem teaching experience is positive and beneficial for the development of the competence for collaboration.

Mia

Mia, Nina's tandem partner, is the youngest student who volunteered to take part in the service-learning program. She is enrolled in the third year of the undergraduate program and has quite limited knowledge of language teaching methodologies since she has attended only two elective courses on the topic. Her previous teaching experience amounts to tutoring sessions to adults. She loves teaching and sees herself in language teaching profession because "you can reach a person on so many levels".

Mia is well aware of her lack of experience and competence that provokes ambivalent feelings: "I've never had courage to do something if I don't have necessary skills… how can I teach someone Spanish if I don't know how to do it?" Nevertheless, when she heard about the service-learning program, she instantly volunteered, very much in line with her eyes wide open for new experiences and an inclination for community service. The fact is that her enthusiasm and sharp mind camouflaged the lack of competence prior to the initiation of the service-learning program, so she quickly became a member of the team. Quite soon, the amount of challenge showed in its full.

At first, it was like, I don't know, I'll prepare some exercises so we can work, something… but I quickly realized that it wasn't even an option; so, I was stuck, how can I teach them if they don't have any previous knowledge, if they can't write, if there aren't any specific exercises like the ones I used to have…

Although she does not have a clear idea as to what should be content priorities in language learning ("whether they should learn verbs or words, or how to put them together"), Mia shows good teaching intuition: "I look a step further, like, what will they need this for; or how to organize different contents, to make them connect". Even after several months of practice, Mia finds it challenging to set the stage for ludic learning: "it's either game or some kind of exercise". She strongly relies on her language learning experience, which does not offer an optimal model for teaching language to young children. Her predilection for analytic learning which, in turn, has found support in the traditional approach during Mia's previous education, has conditioned her thinking about the teaching process. However, she perceives that this model cannot function with young children and she feels frustrated: "I call it creativity… like I lost my inner child… we're so, so… no games, nothing comes to mind".

Direct experience with young children has made Mia rethink her teaching style. As she explains, she has always felt the need to make an introduction at the beginning of the class in order to emphasize its main objectives. It is through laugh that she comments how this strategy does not make any sense with young children: "they don't listen, they don't hear, because they don't care". She understands that this would probably be an efficient strategy with older students, but it is not efficient with eight-year-olds. This clearly made her change her opening strategy in a way that permits her engage the children in learning tasks from the moment she enters the classroom with her tandem partner. "It's crucial that

199

they know they have a task to do; and when this happens, it's like focusing attention, then it's possible to introduce some... a bit less energetic..." Mia elaborates how this initial *focusing of attention* sets the stage for calmer tasks, but she notes that toward the end of the class the children again become impatient, which calls for another episode of energetic activities.

The described class dynamics demonstrates an evident transformation in Mia's perception of the teaching process. As she explains, while in the beginning she focused on what would be *her* activity, what *she* would say or do, later on she learned to think about the students' activity: "I put an accent on work, in the sense of activity, *their* activity... the focus is on them". She believes that this was the most important change, provoked by her engagement in the program, which helped improve the quality of her teaching style. After the interviewer's observation that this seems like a fundamental change, she enthusiastically responds: "yes, from the roots, absolutely (...) this is a whole new approach". It is not a surprise, then, that she welcomes and highly values the experience with the service-learning program: "this stimulates activity in me; because ... I tend to overthink things and, at the end, I don't do anything (...) so, they [children] motivate me, they make me develop that side, that is less present". However, she also believes that, because of her personality and predilection for abstract thinking, she would probably enjoy more if she worked with older students.

When thinking about the tandem experience, Mia admits that she had her doubts in relation to the effectiveness of co-teaching. "In the beginning, I saw it as a difficulty, in the sense, how could we combine our different styles, in the sense... maybe she wanted or preferred to organize the class differently, because, maybe, she wouldn't like my logic..." The challenge came from their differences, she believes. "She is the creative type, she always has like a million ideas and all, and I come with reason". Hence, Nina would propose a number of different activities and Mia would try to organize them logically in order to reach her very desired coherence. In the process, she would modify some of Nina's proposals to an extent that "could cause some frustration". Mia analyzes how her partner could have felt: "it *is* frustrating; you come up with something and another person tells you 'this is good, this isn't good', I mean... this was never my intention, but it simply... I think I understood soon enough how this could be interpreted; so I, ehm, so, we talked about it". It is possible that the tension in their relationship was provoked precisely by the incongruency between the strengths of the two partners. While Nina thrived in the creative, playful domain, Mia was searching for coherence: "it doesn't matter if something makes sense or not, if there's no [coherence], *nothing* makes sense to me; it paralyzes me; if there's no coherence, I can't... I can't do anything, because, if I don't see a beginning and end, if I don't find sense, I don't know where to start". While Mia dwells on the challenges this personality trait imposes, it is clear that she has strong capacity for finding sense in disparate elements, that is essential for the experience of emotional coherence (Thagard, 2006).

The pronounced differences, in fact, created a fruitful terrain for mutual learning, as Mia concludes, "now I see it as an advantage". It took commitment and patience, however, for both partners to understand each other and to develop more efficient collaborative strategies. Mia also appreciates the possibility to learn by model: "she is a strong person (...) because, I think, she's more experienced than I am; and she motivates me to be, a little bit, I think... she awakens that need in me to work on... not to be too permissive". This is particularly important in the realm of classroom dynamics with young children where it is crucial to establish clear boundaries in order to create constructive learning environment.

A Service-Learning Program for Multilingual Education at an Early Age

POST-REFLECTION

Driven by the immediate need for additional teaching practice in the context of early multilingual education, this service-learning program has provided opportunities for professional development to the participating students, prospective Spanish language teachers. The engagement with the program has had a strong effect on the development of professional identity of the students-teachers. Since they entered the program with fairly limited experience in teaching languages to young learners, it helped them position themselves with respect to the teaching profession. It seems that the four young women had developed a romantic representation of the teacher vocation before they volunteered for the program; this representation stood the test of reality in the case of Milly, Esther and Nina. While Mia also found deep value in this teaching experience, she came to an understanding that her personal traits orient her toward adult learners. This is certainly an important insight for establishing professional identity: timely participation in a variety of opportunities for professional practice might prevent much professional frustration.

Preceding analysis confirms that the close collaboration imposed by co-teaching tasks created favorable circumstances for constant negotiation of different aspects of the teaching process. Although the participants did not have an explicit training in group dynamics and collaboration, they managed to develop functional collaborative strategies that guaranteed positive evaluation of the experience. As the participants themselves reiterated, an intangible but crucial condition for this to happen was to be open for dialog and mutual learning. In tandems with marked differences, the potential for both personal and professional development is possibly even greater – that is, if the partners manage to focus on the common task. It is also imperative that the coordinator develop leadership strategies that might meliorate tensions and reinforce constructive communication.

It is possible that co-teaching is not equally favorable for all participants. While the students-teachers expressed their satisfaction with this teaching strategy and particularly emphasized its importance in the initial period of the program, it is also true that some participants were not able to enjoy the fullness of the teaching experience. Such was the case of our first tandem, in which Milly was more in charge of discipline while Esther was a more spontaneous team member. This division of roles possibly inhibited Milly's capacity to establish closer relationship with the children, which frustrated her need for greater intimacy.

In spite of the complexity of factors that provoked both positive and negative perceptions and interpretations of particular aspects of the service-learning program, it is clear that this scaffolded professional engagement has stimulated the development of a critical and enquiring approach to learning and teaching of future Spanish language teachers. The major positive individual effect was perceived in the realm of teaching competences (that is, pedagogical and methodological competences), as well as of the competences for cooperation. Additionally, the dialogic approach, supported through tandem teaching but also through reflective research interviews, facilitated the process of metacognition. The students-teachers were able to share their thoughts, emotions, fears, and dilemmas, with their peers and mentor, which helped them explore their epistemologies with a more critical eye. This aspect ultimately confirms the sustainability of this action science project, which seeks to promote the life-long learning of the participants.

The success of the project would also need to be evaluated from the point of view of the young learners themselves. While the steady students' attendance and favorable class atmosphere observed during the classes suggest that the young students enjoy their Spanish language workshops, a systematic

201

analysis of the program focused on learning outcomes would provide valuable information for its future implementations.

The engagement with young Spanish language learners during several months of the service-learning program at times appeared to resemble some sort of a shock therapy. The students-teachers approached the task without clearly developed teaching approaches, freshly equipped with different theoretical concepts that maybe contradicted their intimate beliefs on the language teaching process. A reoccurring motive in the four cases is the duality between the playfulness and structure, creativity and coherence, the ludic and the traditional. Encounter with the young children, who only respond to holistic approach that engages them on all levels, shook the pillars of traditional teaching theories in these students-teachers. In this way, opportunities for re-education were created, since they engaged in tasks that challenged some of their strong beliefs. It made them truly reconsider their conceptions of different elements of the teaching process, whether objectives and outcomes, contents, types of activities, class dynamics, or overall teaching styles. It would be interesting to follow later development of these teaching theories, especially if the teachers continue their professional life in different educational contexts. It is particularly intriguing whether Mia, whose teaching experience with young children provoked a fundamental change in her belief system (especially in her understanding of the learner/teacher roles), would implement this new approach with adult learners or would regress to her previous theory of teaching.

The data from the interviews brought our attention to an interesting phenomenon relative to the role of the prescribed curriculum. While its main purpose was to facilitate the planning process for the students-teachers, it seems that it functioned as a restraining force for the transformation of the participants teaching theory. This is particularly the case with Milly who, prior to this teaching activity, had successfully taught small groups of children. Her teaching philosophy was primarily guided by her motivation to awaken interest for the target language cultures and love for the language in young learners. However, when she joined the service-learning program, she felt limited by the curriculum that, to her eyes, underlined the formal aspects of the teaching process and inhibited its potential for creativity. It is, thus, crucial to carefully analyze every element of teaching practice programs such as this in order to try to prevent potential misinterpretation of teaching resources and, consequently, reinforce the status quo. While it is essential to enhance forces that provoke change – which were reinforced through the engagement with young children –, it is particularly important to reduce forces that might prevent change and make the participants fall back to the old habits.

This study also brings to our attention the importance of agents' beliefs for the success of an innovation. While the participants were familiarized with fundamental theoretical concepts during their teaching methodologies courses, their capacity to implement specific teaching actions for students' plurilingual development varied to the extent they had integrated the concept with their teaching theories. As Argyris et al. (1985, p. 19) remind, while implementation of new policies has traditionally been defined as a problem of application, it is quite possible that it depends on theoretical science that needs to establish, test, and evaluate procedures that would facilitate innovation. In the context of this action science project, the results support that innovative teaching practices can only be implemented together with the reconsideration of the participants theories of teaching.

REFERENCES

Abelio-Contesse, C., Chandler, P. M., López-Jiménez, M. D., & Chacón-Beltrán, R. (Eds.). (2013). *Bilingual and multilingual education in the 21st century: Building on experience.* Multilingual Matters. doi:10.21832/9781783090716

Argyris, C., Putnam, R., & McLain Smith, D. (1985). *Action science. Concepts, methods, and skills for research and intervention.* Jossey-Bass Publishers.

Argyris, C., & Schön, D. A. (1974). *Theory in practice: Increasing profesional effectiveness.* Jossey-Bass Publishers.

Baeten, M., & Simons, M. (2014). Student teachers' team teaching: Models, effects, and conditions for implementation. *Teaching and Teacher Education, 41,* 92–110. doi:10.1016/j.tate.2014.03.010

Baeten, M., Simons, M., Schelfhout, W., & Pinxten, R. (2018). Team teaching during field experiences in teacher education: Exploring the assistant teaching model. *European Journal of Teacher Education, 41*(3), 377–397. doi:10.1080/02619768.2018.1448780

Barcelos, A. M. F. (2012). Explorando crenças sobre ensino e aprendizagem de línguas em materiais didácticos. [Exploring beliefs about language teaching and learning in teaching materials.] In D. Scheyerl & S. Siquiera (Eds.), *Materiais didácticos para o ensino de línguas na contemporaneidade: Contestações e proposicões [Didactic materials for language teaching in contemporary times: Challenges and propositions]* (pp. 110–137). EDUFBA.

Barcelos, A. M. F. (2013). Desvelando a relação entre crenças sobre ensino e aprendizahem de línguas, emocões e identidades. [Untandresing the relationship between beliefs about teaching and learning languages, emocões and identities.] In A. F. Lopes Magela Gerhardt, M. Alvaro de Amorim, & A. Monteiro Carvalho (Eds.), *Lingüística aplicada e ensino: Língua e literatura [Applied Linguistics and Teaching: Language and Literature]* (pp. 153–186). Pontes Editores.

Barcelos, A. M. F., & Kalaja, P. (2011). Introduction to beliefs about SLA revisited. *System, 39*(3), 281–289. doi:10.1016/j.system.2011.07.001

Berliner, D. C. (1988). Implications of studies on expertise in pedagogy for teacher education and evaluation. In *New directions for teacher assessment. Proceeding of the ETS Invitational Conference* (pp. 39–68). Princeton Educational Testing Service. https://files.eric.ed.gov/fulltext/ED314432.pdf#page=44

Blanchard, K. D. (2012). Modeling life-long learning: Collaborative teaching across disciplinary lines. *Teaching Theology and Religion, 15*(4), 338–354. doi:10.1111/j.1467-9647.2012.00826.x

Bleichenbacher, L., Goullier, F., Rossner, R., & Schröder Sura, A. (2019). *Teacher competences for languages in education: Conclusions of the project.* Council of Europe, ECML.

Cenoz, J., & Gorter, D. (Eds.). (2015). *Multilingual education: Between language learning and translanguaging.* Cambridge University Press. doi:10.1017/9781009024655

Coghlan, D., & Jacobs, C. (2005). Kurt Lewin on reeducation: Foundations for action research. *The Journal of Applied Behavioral Science, 41*(4), 444–457. doi:10.1177/0021886305277275

Council of Europe. (2001). *Common European framework of reference for languages*. Council of Europe.

Council of Europe. (2018). *Common European framework of reference for languages. Companion volume with descriptors*. Council of Europe.

Custodio-Espinar, M., López-Hernández, A., & Buckingham, L. R. (2022). Effects of co-teaching on CLIL teacher trainees' collaborative competence. *Profesorado. Revista de Currículum y Formación del Profesorado, 26*(1), 87–106. doi:10.30827/profesorado.v26i1.16853

Denzin, L. (2009). The elephant in the living room: Or extending the conversation about the politics of evidence. *Qualitative Research, 9*(2), 139–160. doi:10.1177/1468794108098034

Djurić, Lj. (2017). Minority, foreign and non-native languages in Serbia's linguistic educational policy: Destinies and intersections. *Živi jezici, 37*(1), 397–411.

Ellis, R., Skehan, P., Li, S., Shintani, N., & Lambert, C. (2020). *Task-based language teaching: Theory and practice*. Cambridge University Press.

Ferguson, J., & Wilson, J. C. (2011). The co-teaching professorship: Power ad expertise in the co-taught higher education classroom. *Scholar-Practitioner Quarterly, 5*(1), 52–68.

Filipović, J. (2015). *Transdisciplinary approach to language study: The complexity theory perspective*. Palgrave Macmillan. doi:10.1057/9781137538468

Filipović, J. (2018). *Moć reči: ogledi iz kritičke sociolingvistike* [*The power of words: Essays in critical sociolinguistics.*]. Zadužbina Andrejević.

Filipović, J., & Djurić, Lj. (2021). Early childhood foreign language learning and teaching in Serbia: A critical overview of language education policy and planning in varying historical contexts. In S. Zein & M. R. Coady (Eds.), *Early language learning policy in the 21st century: An international perspective* (pp. 61–84). Springer. doi:10.1007/978-3-030-76251-3_3

Filipović, J., Vučo, J., & Djurić, Lj. (2007). Critical review of language education policies in compulsory primary and secondary education in Serbia. *Current Issues in Language Planning, 8*(2), 222–242. doi:10.2167/cilp103.0

Friedman, V. J. (2001). Action science: Creating communities of inquiry in communities of practice. In P. Reason & H. Bradbury (Eds.), *Handbook of action research: Participative inquiry and practice* (pp. 159–170). Sage Publications Ltd.

Graziano, K. J., & Navarrete, L. A. (2012). Co-teaching in a teacher education classroom: Collaboration, compromise, and creativity. *Issues in Teacher Education, 21*(1), 109–126.

Hiver, P., Whiteside, Z., Sánchez Solarte, A., & Kim, C. J. (2021). Language teacher metacognition: Beyond the mirror. *Innovation in Language Learning and Teaching, 15*(1), 52–65. doi:10.1080/17501229.2019.1675666

Hobson, A. J., Ashby, P., Malderez, A., & Tomlinson, P. D. (2009). Mentoring beginning teachers: What we know and what we don't. *Teaching and Teacher Education, 25*(1), 207–216. doi:10.1016/j.tate.2008.09.001

Honigsfeld, A., & Dove, M. G. (2016). Co-teaching ELLs: Riding a tandem bike. *Educational Leadership*, *73*(4), 56–60.

Jovanović, A. (2016). *Waking up from the university dream. Intersection of educational ideologies and professional identity construction*. Lambert Academic Publishing.

Jovanović, A., & Filipović, J. (2013). Spanish teacher education programs and community engagement. *Hispania*, *96*(2), 283–294. doi:10.1353/hpn.2013.0056

Jovanović, A., & Mastilo, M. (2022). Formación de profesores de ELE para la enseñanza formal de los niños de la edad temprana: el caso de Serbia [Training of ELE teachers for formal teaching of early age children: the case of Serbia.]. *Anali Filološkog fakulteta [Annals of the Faculty of Philology]*, *34*(2), forthcoming.

Kuhn, D. (1999). A developmental model of critical thinking. *Educational Researcher*, *28*(2), 16–26. doi:10.3102/0013189X028002016

Kvale, S. (2007). *InterViews: An introduction to qualitative research interviewing*. SAGE.

Lewin, K., & Grabbe, P. (1945). Conduct, knowledge, and acceptance of new values. *The Journal of Social Issues*, *1*(3), 53–64. doi:10.1111/j.1540-4560.1945.tb02694.x

Liebel, G., Burden, H., & Heldal, R. (2017). For free: Continuity and change by team teaching. *Teaching in Higher Education*, *22*(1), 62–77. doi:10.1080/13562517.2016.1221811

Mehisto, P., Marsh, D., & Frigols, M. J. (2008). *Uncovering CLIL: Content and language integrated learning in bilingual and multilingual education*. Macmillan Education.

Mercer, N., Wegerif, R., & Major, L. (Eds.). (2020). *The Routledge international handbook of research on dialogic education*. Routledge.

Mihaljević Djigunović, J. (2012). Attitudes and motivations in early foreign language learning. *CEPS Journal*, *2*(3), 55–74. doi:10.26529/cepsj.347

Miller, R. M., Chan, C. D., & Farmer, L. B. (2018). Interpretative phenomenological analysis: A contemporary qualitative approach. *Counselor Education and Supervision*, *57*(4), 240–254. doi:10.1002/ceas.12114

Miras Páez, E., & Sancho Pascual, M. (2017). La enseñanza de ELE a niños, adolescentes e inmigrantes. [The teaching of ELE to children, adolescents and immigrants.] In A. M. Cestero & I. Penadés (Eds.), *Manual del profesor de ELE [ELE Professor's Manual]* (pp. 865–912). Servicio de Publicaciones de la Universidad de Alcalá.

Mitchell, J., & Marland, P. (1989). Research on teacher thinking: The next phase. *Teaching and Teacher Education*, *5*(2), 115–128. doi:10.1016/0742-051X(89)90010-3

Naharro, M. (2019). Moving towards a revolutionary change in multilingual education: Does CLIL live up to the Hype? *Journal of e-Learning and Knowledge Society, 15*(1). Italian e-Learning Association. https://www.learntechlib.org/p/207524/

Nikolov, M., & Mihaljević Djigunović, J. (2011). All shades of every color: An overview of early teaching and learning of foreign languages. *Annual Review of Applied Linguistics, 31,* 95–119. doi:10.1017/S0267190511000183

Nikula, T., Dafouz, E., Moore, P., & Smit, U. (2016). *Conceptualizing integration in CLIL and multilingual education.* Multilingual Matters. doi:10.21832/9781783096145

Nonaka, L., & Takeuchi, H. (1995). *The knowledge creating company: How Japanese companies create the dynamics of innovation.* Oxford University Press.

Paavola, S., Lipponen, L., & Hakkarainen, K. (2004). Models of innovative knowledge communities and three metaphors of learning. *Review of Educational Research, 74*(4), 557–576. doi:10.3102/00346543074004557

Paris, S., & Wingrad, P. (1990). How metacognition can promote academic learning and instruction. In B. F. Jones & L. Idoles (Eds.), *Dimensions of thinking and cognitive instruction* (pp. 15–51). Lawrence Erlbaum Associates.

Pavlenko, A., & Dewaele, J.-M. (2004). Language and emotions: A crosslinguistic perspective. *Journal of Multilingual and Multicultural Development, 25*(2-3), 2–3.

Pavón Vázquez, V., Ávila López, J., Gallego Segador, A., & Espejo Mohedano, R. (2015). Strategic and organisational considerations in planning content and language integrated learning: A study on the coordination between content and language teachers. *International Journal of Bilingual Education and Bilingualism, 18*(4), 409–425. doi:10.1080/13670050.2014.909774

Pižorn, K. (2009). *Dodatni tuji jeziki v otroštvu (Pregledna evalvacijska študija)* [*Additional foreign languages in childhood(A critical review)*]. Ljubljana.

Ryan, K. (1986). *The induction of new teachers.* Phi Delta Kappa Educational Foundations.

Smith, J. A., & Eatough, V. (2011). Interpretative phenomenological analysis. In E. Lyons & A. Coyle (Eds.), *Analyzing qualitative data in psychology* (pp. 35–50). SAGE.

Smith, J. A., Flowers, P., & Larkin, M. (2009). *Interpretative phenomenological analysis. Theory, method and research.* SAGE.

Thagard, P. (2000). *Coherence in thought and action.* MIT. doi:10.7551/mitpress/1900.001.0001

Thagard, P. (2006). *Hot thought: Mechanisms and application of emotional cognition.* MIT Press. doi:10.7551/mitpress/3566.001.0001

Tsybulsky, D. (2019). The team teaching experiences of pre-service science teachers implementing PBL in elementary school. *Journal of Education for Teaching, 45*(3), 244–261. doi:10.1080/0958923 6.2019.1599505

Wernicke, M., Hammer, S., Hansen, A., & Schroedler, T. (Eds.). (2021). *Preparing teachers to work with multilingual learners.* Multilingual Matters.

Wilson, G. L., & Blednick, J. (2011). *Teaching in tandem: Effective co-teaching in the inclusive classroom.* ASCD.

Zein, S., & Coady, M. R. (Eds.). (2021). *Early language learning policy in the 21ˢᵗ century: An international perspective*. Springer. doi:10.1007/978-3-030-76251-3

KEY TERMS AND DEFINITIONS

Action Science: An approach to participative inquiry that intends to engage with practical problem solving while elucidating relevant theoretical concepts; it implies re-education of agents through the process of self-reflection.

Action Theory: A set of beliefs, patterns, schemas, and models that direct actions.

Interpretative Phenomenology: A qualitative research approach, grounded in principles of phenomenology, hermeneutics, and idiography, that is used to explore how participants understand and interpret their significant experiences; it originated as a research approach in experiential qualitative psychology.

Metacognition: An ability to engage in cognitive processes of planning, monitoring, and evaluating; a crucial component of metacognition is the capacity of critical thinking that implies an awareness of both the object and the process of thinking.

Plurilingual Competence: The ability to function effectively in more than two languages in a variety of communicative situations and, more importantly, being able to understand and promote interpersonal and intercultural communication for the development of meaningful relationships, whether personal, academic, or professional.

Service-learning: A pedagogy that integrates academically relevant activities with service to the community; it rests on the principals of experiential learning and is motivated by the ideology of solidarity and mutual learning.

Tandem teaching: Co-teaching; a teaching strategy that implies a collaborative participation of two teachers in all or specific stages of the teaching process.

Chapter 10

Learning in Two Languages:
A Long–Term Study at Bavarian Bilingual Elementary Schools

Heiner Böttger

Catholic University of Eichstätt-Ingolstadt, Germany

Tanja Müller

Catholic University of Eichstätt-Ingolstadt, Germany

ABSTRACT

In the school years 2015/2016 and 2018/2019, the authors accompanied and evaluated 21 public elementary schools in Bavaria, Germany, in a research collaboration with the Bildungspakt Bayern Foundation about bilingual (German/English) instruction in German elementary schools. The goal was to investigate how high the potential of implicit teaching and learning in a bilingual primary context is. Altogether, over 900 students, parents, and 42 teachers participated in the empirical long-term study (over 5 years) Learning in Two Languages –Bilingual Elementary School English. The findings not only show that students taught in the bilingual classes have a foreign language advantage and perform at least as well in mathematics and German as students in regular classes do, but also that they have a very positive attitude towards learning English in elementary school. These findings, the study, and its theoretical background are aimed to be portrayed in short in this chapter.

INTRODUCTION

Current research results prove that children and adolescents growing up bilingual or multilingual have considerable competence advantages compared to their peers with regard to concentration, complex thinking, and linguistic creativity (Festman & Schwieter, 2019; Franceschini, 2016)

In 2015, the Bildungspakt Bayern Foundation, together with the Bavarian State Ministry of Education and Cultural Affairs, initiated the school experiment *Learning in Two Languages – Bilingual Elementary School English*. One bilingual class per grade was gradually established at 21 participating model schools. From grades 1 to 4, students receive instruction in the subjects of local history and general stud-

DOI: 10.4018/978-1-6684-6179-2.ch010

Learning in Two Languages

ies, mathematics, art, music, and physical education in two languages (Bayerisches Staatsministerium für Unterricht und Kultus, 2021).

The lessons in the bilingual classes are based on the competency expectations formulated in the subject curricula of the LehrplanPLUS Grundschule, the German curriculum in place (München, 2004). When suitable topics and occasions, e.g., intercultural learning or creative task formats, arise, teaching units or lessons in the above-mentioned subjects are conducted in English. The specific thematic selection for the English language phases is made by the respective teachers based their knowledge of the learning group and is their pedagogical responsibility. The teaching of the English language is implicit. The assurance of the German technical terms as stated in the LehrplanPLUS is guaranteed. The lessons in the bilingual classes are taught according to the given timetable, i.e., without additional time quotas or afternoon classes. Admission to a bilingual class is voluntary upon application by the parent or guardian in accordance with the applicable class formation guidelines.

The first cohort was scientifically monitored from the beginning to the end of primary school (grades 1 to 4), the second cohort from grades 1 to 3. The scientific, comprehensive evaluation included annual surveys with questionnaires (students, teachers, parents, school administrators), standardized tests in English, mathematics and German, classroom documentation, observations, and guided interviews.

The main goal of the project was to investigate how high the potential of implicit teaching and learning in a bilingual primary context is. The subgoals can shortly be outlined as follows:

1. Enhanced foreign language learning without compromising learning success in German and in subject matter:
   a. English proficiency at the end of grade 4 at least at level A1 of the Common European Framework of Reference for Languages (CEFR)
   b. Competencies in German and mathematics that are at least equivalent to the level of students in regular classes
2. Developing a concept of Learning in Two Languages in elementary school:
   a. Development and testing of a suitable concept for bilingual instruction (German/English) in grades 1 to 4, based on the LehrplanPLUS elementary school curriculum
   b. Empowering teachers to design appropriate instructional implementations
   c. Development of suitable profile-building measures for the design of a school profile *Bilingual Elementary School English*
   d. Acceptance of the school profile in the school family (students, parents, school management, teachers)

The school experiment *Bilingual Elementary School English* is unique and not comparable with any research in Germany or pan-European countries as it takes into account the importance of English as an international lingua franca in business and science. In addition to the early promotion of the kids' multilingualism, primary school pupils are supported in the development of their intercultural competence.

Thus, the main focus of this chapter is to present an overview of the school experiment and its results and to introduce the related didactic principles, as these serve as a basis for teacher training regarding bilingual education. The subsequent objectives of this chapter are the elaboration of the didactic concept of Learning in Two Languages against the background of the discussion about bilingual teaching in elementary school, the presentation of the school experiment and the empirical long-term study over

5 years as well as the summary of the most important results and findings with regard to the further development of a general language continuum in elementary school.

BACKGROUND

Concepts of Bilingual Education

The identification of a suitable concept of bilingualism in the school context is significant as a first step. The next step is to develop educational policy standards that define the mandatory framework for bilingual learning.

Currently, bilingual concepts across grades are still characterized by inconsistent terminology and differing didactic procedures as well as varying proportions of the two languages in the classroom.

The four main orientations of so-called bilingual learning include:

1. Content and Language Integrated Learning (CLIL),
2. Bilingual Subject Teaching,
3. Immersion as well as
4. Learning in Two Languages.

A close analysis of the definitions of these concepts in the relevant literature reveals that they show clear overlaps in the essential aspects.

In the following, relevant definitions as well as the description of the essential focuses of the mentioned concepts will serve to identify and locate the concept of *Bilingual Elementary School* in Bavaria.

CLIL and Bilingual Subject Teaching

A special form of foreign language learning at the secondary level in German schools is "bilingual teaching" (Bili, BIU) or "subject teaching in a foreign language". On a European and international level, the term CLIL – Content and Language Integrated Learning – has become established, marking the two reference poles of subject content and foreign language competence (Böttger, 2011, p. 9).

CLIL stands out as the overarching concept of a flexible interplay between language and subject teaching:

CLIL is an umbrella term adopted by the European Network of Administrators, Researchers and Practitioners (EUROCLIC) in the mid 1990s. It encompasses any activity in which a foreign language is used as a tool in the learning of a non-language subject in which both language and subject have a joint role. (Marsh, 2002, p. 58)

The aspect of the lifelong, dynamic language continuum plays a crucial role in CLIL:

CLIL is a lifelong concept that embraces all sectors of education from primary to adults, from a few hours per week to intensive modules lasting several months. [...] In short, CLIL is flexible and dynamic, where topics and subjects – foreign languages and non-language subjects – are integrated in some kind

Learning in Two Languages

of mutually beneficial way so as to provide value-added educational outcomes for the widest possible range of learners. (Coyle et al., 2010, p. 3)

CLIL does not simply mean teaching a subject in a foreign language, but requires its own didactics:

It is obvious that teaching a subject in a foreign language is not the same as an integration of language and content... language teachers and subject teachers need to work together... [to] formulate the new didactics needed for a real integration of form and function in language teaching. (Marsh, 2002, p. 32)

The "new" CLIL didactics works against a paradox: The students usually do not have sufficient knowledge of the foreign language, which would be necessary for a productive examination of the respective subject content.

[CLIL is] ... an approach to bilingual education in which both curriculum content (such as science or geography) and English are taught together. It differs from simple English-medium education in that the learner is not necessarily expected to have the English proficiency required to cope with the subject before beginning study. (Graddol, 2006, p. 86).

In the native language, however, the subject content can be imparted and processed at a high level appropriate to the age. In relation to early bilingual instruction, such an effect is reinforced.

To counter this, various slightly modified and less time-consuming and less didactically complex concepts have already been proposed, for example, so-called "CLIL showers" (Ioannou-Georgiou, 2011, p. 16): these are temporary (up to 50% of the teaching time in the subject) teaching units in the CLIL target language, based on the immersion concept or the idea of a language bath, which includes authentic, but manageable language situations. Since other contents of the same subject are taught in another language, the basic bilingual idea is still visible here.

Bilingual teaching, or so-called Bilingual Subject Teaching, is an established concept at the national level in Germany, especially in high schools:

In German states, bilingual instruction is basically understood as subject instruction in the non-language subjects in which a foreign language is predominantly used for the subject discourse. (Kultusminister-konferenz [KMK], 2006, p. 3)

Bilingual Subject Teaching excludes the explicit teaching of the foreign language:

Bilingual teaching refers to a form of second language teaching in the school environment in which the subjects are taught in the foreign language (L2) as the language of instruction [...]. In concrete terms, this means that subjects such as mathematics, subject teaching, music, etc. are taught exclusively in the foreign language. The foreign language itself is no longer the subject of the instruction. (Kersten, 2005, p. 22)

The foreign language serves as the working language in Bilingual Subject Teaching:

Bilingual education means the use of foreign languages as working languages in non-language subjects. (Christ, 2003, p. 108)

In some cases, the terms CLIL and Bilingual Subject Teaching are also used synonymously in academic discourse, although the acronym CLIL is broader in scope and more common internationally. In CLIL models, the emphasis is placed on application and the teaching of intercultural competencies.

In elementary school, for example, topics are dealt with in foreign language lessons that do not exclusively serve language acquisition, but at the same time aim at the acquisition of knowledge and skills in non-language teaching areas. This can be supplemented and deepened in German-language lessons.

Both concepts, CLIL and Bilingual Subject Teaching, contain not insignificant structural weaknesses. Although language acquisition is a completely individual, non-linear and a largely uncontrollable process, the CLIL concept is based on a static theoretical framework. The basic principle for any language teaching is to teach language with authentic and relevant content. A contentless language or language use is meaningless. The artificial separation of content and language (Content/Language) in the term CLIL is therefore illogical and not remedied by the fact that the term seems to actively connect two concepts that relate to each other anyway and quite naturally. An artificial separation of language and content is also inaccurate from the point of view of language acquisition theory; it cannot be automatically generalized and is unnecessary. The so-called Bilingual Subject Teaching, too, is inconsistent and contradictory conceptually; however, it is usually conducted monolingually in English or in the respective foreign language.

Immersion

Following the Canadian model of immersion education, all subjects, except the mother tongue, are taught in the foreign language for four years. In a weakened form, there is the so-called "parity model", half of all subjects are offered in the native language and half in the foreign language.

The mental image associated with immersion is usually that of the language bath:

'Immersion' has its origin in the word 'to immerse', such that this concept is generally understood as a 'language bath' in which the children are immersed. (Kersten, 2010, p. 4)

Immersion is often described as a form of bilingual education, e.g.:

[Immersion is] a form of bilingual education that aims for additive bilingualism by providing students with a sheltered classroom environment in which they receive at least half of their subject-matter instruction through the medium of a language that they are learning as a second, foreign, heritage, or indigenous language. In addition, they receive some instruction through the medium of ... [the majority language] in the community. (Lyster, 2007, p. 8)

It is precisely the image of the language bath that mistakenly leads one to view the concept as monolingual instruction in the foreign language. Viewed in a more differentiated way, it reads as follows:

The term immersion is used as a subcategory of bilingual education in Canadian literature. A concept is called immersion when at least 50% of the instruction is in the second language (Genesee 1987: 1). This

Learning in Two Languages

therefore corresponds to a particularly intensive form of bilingual education. Immersion [...] is used in this context as 'immersion in the language bath of the foreign language'. In this context, the lessons follow exactly the curriculum of the respective mainstream school (Zydatiß 2000: 27 f.). (Kersten, 2005, p. 22)

The immersion concept is based on intuitive, implicit foreign language learning:

In practice, immersion means that as many subjects as possible are taught in the target language in order to generate an approximately natural language acquisition of an L2 'along the way', so to speak. (Burmeister, 2006, p. 197)

Immersion programs, similar to CLIL programs, are flexible:

On the one hand, there are programs in which sporadic foreign language units, called CLIL modules, are taught in subject teaching. On the other hand, there are programs with immersion, in which a substantial part of the subject lessons is taught in a foreign language during the entire elementary school period. (Massler & Burmeister, 2010, p. 7-8)

There are positive findings from accompanying scientific research on immersive English instruction in elementary schools (Kersten, 2010, p. 6). Nevertheless, immersion teaching in its fully comprehensive form is not feasible in Germany at present or will be in the near future, whether looking at day care centers or elementary schools. Among other things, this is because of a lack of institutionalized follow-ups in secondary schools and the shortage of trained educators or teachers. Less dogmatic immersion approaches, especially with targeted explicit inclusion of systematically taught literacy, are also significant in developing bilingualism in the school classroom (Pliatsikas et al., 2014).

The concept "Learning in Two Languages" (Böttger, 2011), which is also the name giver and first concept template for the school experiment *Learning in Two Languages - Bilingual Elementary School English* on which this article is based, has a much lower threshold than CLIL, Bilingual Subject Teaching and Immersion. However, combines important, age-appropriate aspects of these approaches: Here, subject content is identified that is appropriate for the target group as well as in accordance with the subject-specific training of the teachers. This can, on the one hand, be taught concretely and can thus also be easily visualized, and on the other hand, it can be taught implicitly in the foreign language with little language capabilities needed. The concept is not only suitable for the primary level, but also as a basis for a bilingual program in preschool institutions.

This approach is often implemented across all types of schools, even without comprehensive conceptual support, since it is open and overall has a low threshold didactically: the only foreign language didactic requirement is the implicit approach without explicit teaching of linguistic content, such as vocabulary and grammar. The didactic focus is on the following aspects, among others:

- Explicit explanations move into the background, while independent and individual meaning identifications of facts and linguistic rules move into the foreground
- In particular, vocabulary and grammatical structures are taught implicitly
- Relevant content that can be implemented in foreign languages is specifically selected
- Targeted feedback and feedforward is included to support language development

- Language activation and language reception are balanced, communicative competencies that develop in parallel manners
- Native/first languages are specifically promoted and developed

At its core, the Learning in Two Languages concept is about designing modularized foreign language learning opportunities that take individual circumstances into account and are tailored to local conditions. The teachers decide in which phases of the lesson they will teach in English and in which phases in German. In doing so, they can always keep the individual framework conditions of the class in mind.

A Brief Overview of the State of Research

The state of research on bilingual learning and its impact in elementary school is generally deficient. However, representative studies from secondary school support the assumption that students who participate in bilingual subject instruction generally have a demonstrably better foreign language proficiency level than their peers who did not attend bilingual subject instruction (Bredenbröker, 2002; Burmeister, 1998; Wode et al., 1996; Zydatiß, 2004). The largest study to date in this area is the DESI study (Deutsch-Englische Schülerleistungen International, translated: German-English Student Achievement International) from 2006, which certified that ninth graders in the bilingual classes examined were up to one and a half years ahead of those taught monolingually regarding communicative competence (Deutsches Institut für Internationale Pädagogische Forschung [DIPF], 2006, p. 60). The result of the study is summed up in the report of the German Institute for International Educational Research: "Students in bilingual classes have a very clear competence advantage in all areas. In particular, they progress almost twice as fast as other classes in listening comprehension" (DIPF, 2006, p. 60).

Similar evidence is available for the pilot project *Bilinguale Züge* at Bavarian secondary schools: The students in the bilingual classes acquired significant gains in knowledge and competence in English as a foreign language compared to their regularly taught peers. In a comparison of performance, the bilingual classes were even able to recall knowledge content in the subject areas more soundly and over a longer period of time. In addition, the bilingual classes performed significantly better in English than their Bavarian peers in the centrally set final exams (Böttger & Rischawy, 2016; Rischawy, 2016).

Considering a language acquisition perspective, significant assertions regarding growing up bilingual are available (Böttger, 2017). In summary, the picture is positive:

Two languages can be efficiently processed by the child's brain at an early age (Pierce et al., 2014). In particular, measurably increased and faster partial brain maturation and early cognitive decision-making abilities (Poulin-Dubois et al., 2011) show this. In addition, significantly higher concentration abilities when blocking out interfering factors are, too, particularly pronounced and consequently (Antón et al., 2014). In addition, rapidly developing, clear advantages in school performance, more precisely in linguistic learning performance, emerge in 8- to 11-year-old multilingual school children compared to monolingual peers (Poarch & Bialystock, 2015). Another added value of early bilingualism for further language learning in higher grades is: Newly added foreign languages are processed at the same neural location in the brain and thus arguably seem to be integrated and learned more easily, quickly, and efficiently (Nitsch, 2007; Wattendorf et al., 2001).

Learning in two languages is therefore possible and advantageous for elementary school students and takes into account important child potentials and predispositions (Franceschini, 2008). These lie in cognitive potentials such as early learning strategies, also in other learning areas such as mathematics,

Learning in Two Languages

early parallel alphabetization even at preschool age (Böttger, 2013), as well as early language awareness and the associated qualitative processing of language in pronunciation and sentence structure.

Didactical Project Principles

The following principles form the basis of the Learning in Two Languages teaching concept and form both an elementary basis for teacher training. The didactic principles were presented, explained and supported with practical examples within regular training sessions for teachers at all model schools participating in order to establish a comparable teaching concept and to create the prerequisites for fulfilling the goals of the school experiment as well as for the comparability and validity of the results. In order to ensure that the study is comprehensible and that the principles can also be used in future teacher training courses, they are described in more detail below.

Contextualization and Scaffolding Support Independent Understanding and Meaning Identification

The contextualization of content through extensive use of gestures, facial expressions, and body language leads to implicit, independent identification of semantic content when, for example, absorbing and processing vocabulary and structures. Such "Negotiation of Meaning" is also supported by child-friendly media, such as realia, picture books, films or the activation of the students' background knowledge in German or English.

Contextualization is supported by targeted scaffolding. This can, for example, be realized through linguistic redundancies and many repetitions in the subject lessons in English. In addition, this can be supported by repetition of certain routines in specific subjects as well as the structuring of everyday school life in English.

Aesthetics Increase Linguistic Receptive Capacities

Multisensory learning or learning with all senses has been known as a concept for a long time. Successful learning in two languages goes beyond this: The identification of subject content is not only done with a view to linguistic "feasibility", but via possible positive sensory experiences. Such an aesthetic is created through constant exposure to things relevant to the subject that can be discovered, labeled, and commented upon. Things that are perceived as "beautiful" are interesting, motivating, and easier or longer to retain.

Positive Feedback / Feedforward Sustainably Supports Individual Language Development

The psychological-pedagogical concept of positive reinforcement through feedback is supplemented by a targeted feedforward. This is realized through indirect but concrete and constructive corrections and additions to children's speech production. This is preferably done using the correct speech model in comments on the content of the utterances or through paraphrasing.

Differentiate, Individualize, Include Means Cooperate and Participate

Participation in *Learning in Two Languages – Bilingual Elementary School English* is best realized through inclusive, cooperative, and skill-balancing forms of learning. Tutoring and peer-teaching, for example, are efficient differentiation methods.

A Balance Between Language Activation and Language Reception Requires New Foreign Language Didactic Planning Patterns

An overriding goal of *Learning in Two Languages – Bilingual Elementary School English* is learner activation. Progression in this regard is made possible primarily by providing enriched foreign language input with a great deal of linguistic redundancy and repetition.

Subject-specific authentic but manageable language situations (an "educational language bath") as well as diverse classroom situations with intensive communication in and about the subject form the basis for interactions, linguistic actions and an orientation towards the learning product.

The language requirements are ideally just above the individual language ability of the students (N + 1), a quasi-calculated challenge. Task formats and learning level assessments are based on this.

As many language aids (scaffolding; method tools) are correct as are needed for the endeavor for successful, but not necessarily error-free, mastery of the language situations.

Teaching Vocabulary and Grammar Implicitly is Natural Language Acquisition

Targeted language work with explicit vocabulary work (e.g., pronunciation practice and correction) and grammar explanations remains the domain of regular English classes beginning in grade 3. When learning in two languages, the acquisition of linguistic competence happens implicitly, quasi "in passing". For an increasingly communicative orientation, verb forms in particular are necessary for intuitive sentence formation. Special technical terms from the subject content are processed more effectively in English if the meaning or the accompanying concept has been grasped in the school language German. This means that the English-language part of learning in two languages should be located primarily in immersion phases. Introductory phases are appropriate when the concept formation can be extraordinarily "supported". As a general rule, unknown vocabulary is taught when the content is known.

Communicative Competencies Develop in Parallel, Do Not Form a Separate Focus

Linguistic and intercultural competencies develop naturally and implicitly when learning in two languages. The strong progression of listening comprehension makes clearly challenging texts possible, including, for example, communicative, less order-oriented classroom management.

In interactive task formats based on dialogization, reproductive and increasingly "free" speech develops rapidly beyond language switching and interlanguage.

Reading and writing form an important area of competence for subject teaching. The transition from *learning to read* to *reading to learn* is pointedly developed through reading and writing exercises beginning in grade 3. For grades 1 and 2, examples include labeling, concrete poetry, hand-eye coordination exercises, or fine motor skills exercises. Students quickly form their own hypotheses regarding linguistic orthography. These are best countered by offering correct writing implicitly or with individual, targeted

Learning in Two Languages

cues as needed. Intercultural learning is implicit in the choice of topics and texts, as well as in the specific choice of language (e.g., forms of politeness). In addition, communicating in a foreign language offers an implicit intercultural learning situation as students need to rightly decode the language input and apply their knowledge of or experience with cultural features themselves (e.g. directness).

An English-language Subject Lesson is Language-sensitive

The goal of teaching subject matter in English is to understand concepts of subject content. In order to create authentic language situations at the appropriate language and subject level for these learning situations, which at the same time promote the acquisition of subject-specific and linguistic competence, tasks are designed and learning materials or methodological procedures are created (e.g. change of presentation forms, standard language situations, language aids).

Educational language, technical language and everyday language form the language(s) of instruction. The students' formulations are to be evaluated primarily as the language of the comprehension process, not of what is understood. An understood statement cannot be formulated more precisely than the respective linguistic competence of the speaker allows (bilingual paradox). The formulations become more technical with increasing expertise (also via meta-reflection).

Gamification is Not Language-oriented, but Subject-oriented

When learning in two languages, playing is not done for the sake of playing, but serves the acquisition of subject-specific, linguistic competencies. The focus is on subject-specific content. Especially when speaking about the subject matter in playful forms of dialogue, role plays, discussions, expressions of opinion, etc., the subject matter is effectively processed.

Learning in Two Languages Requires the Full Development of the Native / First Languages

Learning in two languages takes place with the school language German, which is also usually the mother tongue, and the English language. Other first/native/second and, if necessary, other languages are taken into account in an appropriate form depending on the individual context. Cooperation in lesson planning, involvement of parents, etc. ensures that the bilingual students have further access to possible, already developed linguistic references. If these are missing, for example, in the case of students with a migration background, an important cognitive basis for the acquisition of further languages is missing.

METHODS

The evaluation measures described below were implemented in different formats and rhythms during the first 4 years of the project (school year 2015/2016 to school year 2018/2019):

Documentation of the English-language Proportion of Instruction by Teachers

Teachers volunteered to document the proportion (minutes) of English-language instruction over several weeks. The implementation took place annually.

Observations/Work Shadowing

Classroom visits were conducted by the Catholic University of Eichstaett-Ingolstadt in the first and second year of the project and were carried out with the help of already validated questionnaires for classroom observation and input quality of instruction (ELIAS study 2008-2010) (Kersten, 2010).

Reflective Conversation

Qualitative interviews were conducted, in conjunction with the above observations: Teachers were interviewed regarding their experiences in the classroom; students, parents and principals were also interviewed with regard to their experiences. The interviews were conducted by the Catholic University of Eichstaett-Ingolstadt in the first and second year of the project.

Written Language Tests

The areas tested were listening comprehension, reading comprehension, communicative competence (speaking) and writing (only from grade 2). The test formats show progressions in the requirements. Selected parts of the *Cambridge English Tests For Young Learners* (STARTERS, adapted) were used to test English language skills in Year 1; these have already been validated and thus offer the possibility of comparison with students outside the school experiment. In grades 2 and 3, an adapted form of the BIG test (ELEK 4) was used, which has been validated several times and offers nationwide comparative data (Böttger, 2009).

The test areas of listening comprehension and reading comprehension were taken in abbreviated form from the EVENING study (Engel, 2009), which has also been validated several times, while the tasks in the subareas writing and speaking were newly constructed for the BIG test. The BIG test is based on the language competence level A1, which should be reached by all students by the end of primary school. For the school experiment, the test had already been used two and one year earlier (in grades 2 and 3, respectively); it provides evidence that the relevant competency targets have been met. At the end of the project, an adapted Cambridge test was used again in grade 4, consisting of the MOVERS and FLYERS test formats. Thus, at the end of grade 4, the test was taken at the A1 to A2 competence level, which exceeds the competence target to be achieved in elementary school.

Oral Language Tests

Five pairs of students per class, which were chosen randomly, took part in the communicative competence (speaking) tests, what amounts to a total of approximately 200 children per school year or approximately 100 pairs. The survey took place in grades 1, 2, and 4 in the first cohort and in grade 1 in the second cohort. Testing was done using an adaptation of the BIG tests and the *Cambridge* tests for each grade.

Learning in Two Languages

Elicitation of Competencies in the Subjects German and Mathematics

Tests in German (VERA 3, Hamburger Schreib-Probe 4/5) and Mathematics (VERA 3, DEMAT 2 and 4) were conducted with all students, which were made available to the university for the evaluation of the school experiment. All students completed these tests. The VERA data were provided to the Catholic University of Eichstaett-Ingolstadt by the State Institute for School Quality and Educational Research (ISB) for evaluation. The DEMAT 2 and 4 surveys and the Hamburg Schreib-Probe (writing test) were conducted separately and submitted to the university by the schools in the form of anonymized results.

Surveys (Quantitative)

In addition, surveys of all groups of people involved (teachers, parents, students and school administrators) were conducted at annual intervals. These were conducted as online surveys (teachers and school administrators) or as pen & paper surveys (parents, children). The number of subjects varied by group and by project year. The content and objectives of the surveys depended on the particular group of people. One the one hand, the questionnaire for students included questions about teaching in general, questions about bilingual teaching, questions about English teaching, and questions about family background. The questionnaire for teachers, on the other hand, dealt with experiences from the school trial in general, didactic experiences, or suggestions for optimization, and the questionnaire for school administrators covered experiences from the school trial (implementation, realization, reactions). Finally, the questionnaire for parents addressed experiences from the school experiment in general, experiences with learning in two languages, experiences from teaching English, conclusions about the school experiment as well as background of the parents (language use, English skills).

MAIN FINDINGS

In the following, the most important research results of the accompanying evaluation of the school experiment are presented. A large part of the data, its analysis and interpretation must remain unmentioned at this point due to the available space.

The Foreign Language Advantage of Bilingually Taught Students IN ENGLISH is Comparatively Very Clear

In the competence areas listening comprehension English, reading comprehension English and writing English, the students examined already show impressive performances at the end of grade 3, which corresponds to or even exceeds those of non-bilingually taught students in a nationwide comparison at the end of grade 4 (c.f. results of BIG test, BIG-Kreis, 2015). At the top, we can speak of performance competencies of the 6th grade of secondary schools, especially in listening comprehension and reading comprehension (receptive competencies).

Across all project years, the students' performance in the English language tests – especially in the receptive areas – exceeded the expected targets. Two particularly outstanding results in listening comprehension tasks at the end of grade 4 serve as examples here. Both tasks test at CEFR language proficiency level A2 and thus exceed the requirements of elementary school. Figure 1 and 2 show a right-

219

skewed distribution and illustrate that the majority of the students mastered the tasks well to very well. In addition, a so-called ceiling effect occurred among the very good students, who could have handled even more challenging tasks. Some tasks were unexpectedly too easy for them despite the standardized specifications.

Figure 1. Listening comprehension part 4 (total score)

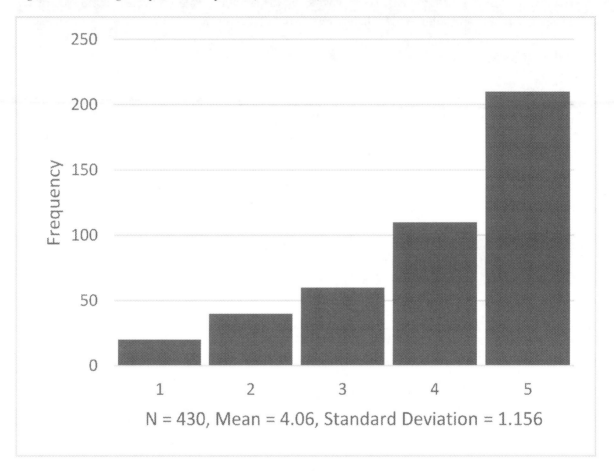

Figure 2. Listening comprehension part 5 (total score)

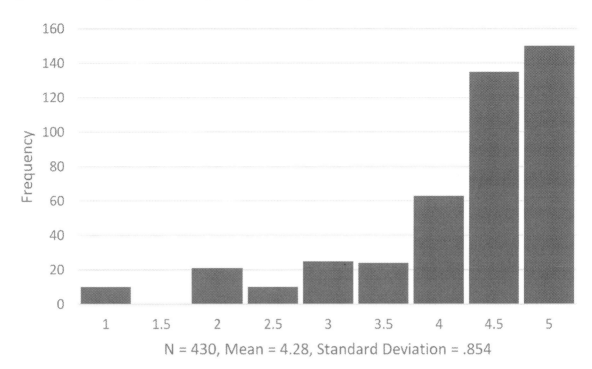

N = 430, Mean = 4.28, Standard Deviation = .854

On a very positive note, it did not matter how well the guardians/parents mastered the German language in any area for the results in the English test (no significant values).

All the same, the educational level of the guardians/parents seems to have a minimally greater influence on the students' performance in English. The higher the educational level of the respondents, the better the children perform in writing. However, the correlation is only weak, as can be seen in the detailed final report of the study (Böttger & Müller, 2020).

Students in Bilingual Classes Perform at Least as Well in Mathematics and German as Students in Regular Classes

The results of the Hamburger Schreib-Probe (HSP) do not show any disadvantages for the students in the area of German: All schools are in the average range with percentile ranks between 39 and 78. No class shows below-average performance, all classes reach the required level of competence in German at the end of grade 4. Around 25% of the students show above-average knowledge, and another 5.5% even show well above-average knowledge of German (correctly spelled words according to the HSP standard at the end of grade 4).

The DEMAT 2 and 4 tests were used to assess the mathematics performance of the students in the bilingual classes. Figure 3 shows the performance (average values) of the students in grade 4 from the project in comparison to average performance in Bavaria and Germany as a whole: The average value of all students in the model classes in DEMAT 4 is 24.50 points with a dispersion of 6.9 points. The comparative value (norm value Germany) is 22.70 points (almost 2 points less). In comparison with the 18 Bavarian school classes, which achieve an average of 20.89 points, the students from the project classes actually score more than 3 points higher.

Figure 3. Comparison of DEMAT4 results

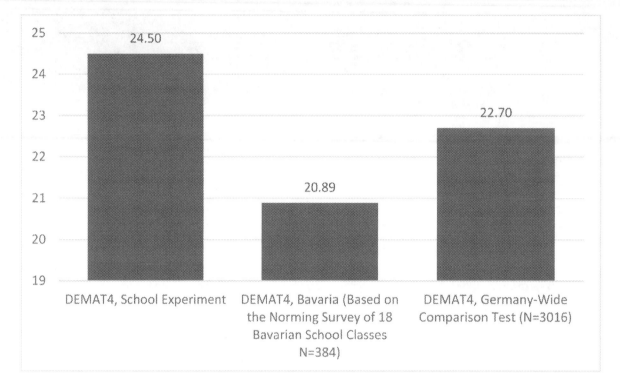

Already in DEMAT 2 at the end of grade 2, the students from the school experiment performed significantly better than the Germany-wide comparison group (federal republic of Germany, BRD). In grade 4, the girls in the project again outperform the boys from the Germany-wide comparison and come even closer to the boys in the project classes; the latter also again perform better in DEMAT 4 than the boys in the Germany-wide comparison group (Figure 4).

Learning in Two Languages

Figure 4. DEMAT results: Comparison of points achieved in mathematics by cohort and gender

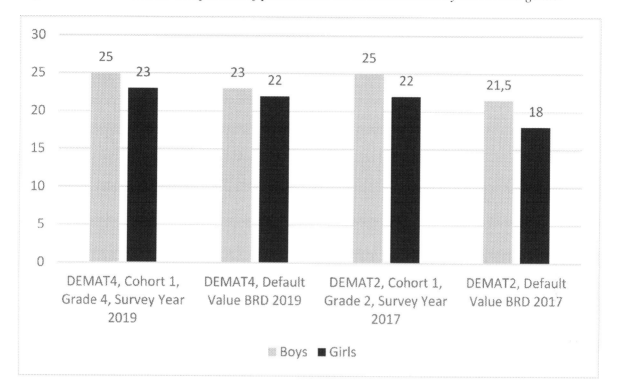

The quality agency at ISB (State Institute for School Quality and Educational Research) draws the following conclusions from the comparison of the model classes with the Bavarian data from the standardized Germany-wide school achievement tests VERA (IQB, 2019):

The results of the comparison in the school year 2018/19 provide no indication that students are disadvantaged by participating in the bilingual instruction. This finding also emerged from the analysis of the data for the 2017/18 school year. Similarly, there is no evidence of performance superiority in the model classes. Overall, therefore, there is no evidence for the 2018/19 school year that the performance of students in model and regular classes differs significantly from one another in the third grade (in the subject areas of German and mathematics).

The Students Participating in the Project have a Very Positive Attitude toward Learning English in Elementary School

Students are, for the most part, very satisfied with being able to learn in the bilingual classes and consider themselves as having an advantage over learners in parallel classes or their own siblings without bilingual education. All of the students in grade 4 (ten per school) interviewed consider English from grade 1 to be very useful and are convinced of the project and bilingual classes. The majority of the students think that English from grade 1 is suitable for all children. The questionnaire survey, in which over 800 students from the bilingual classes (grades 3 and 4) participated in the 2018/2019 school year, also paints an extremely positive picture in this regard (Figure 5).

Figure 5. Attitudes of students towards being in the Bili-class

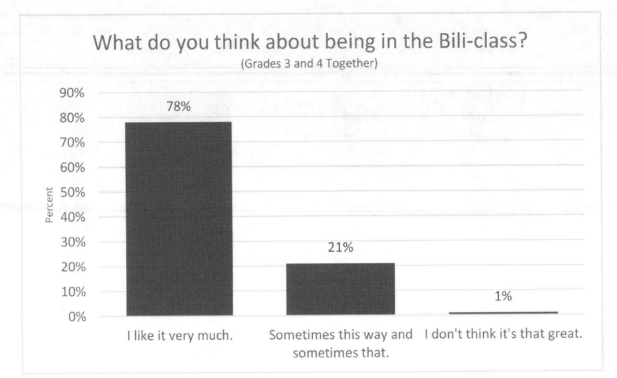

Parents Want Their Children to Attend a Bilingual Elementary School

95% of the parents surveyed who participated in the 2018/2019 school year would continue to have their children taught bilingually if they had the choice in the future. Approximately 800 guardians participated in the survey. In addition, 97% were found to have a very positive or positive attitude towards the project (Figure 6).

Learning in Two Languages

Figure 6. Attitudes towards the project

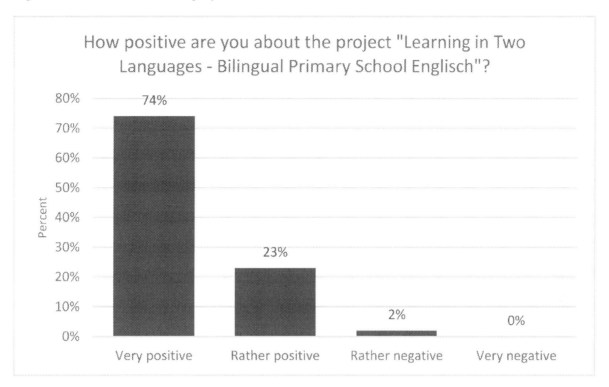

According to statements by parents, students, and school administrators at the bilingual elementary schools, a continuation of bilingual instruction is definitely desired. The justifications reflect the project's results: The performance of the students in English is above the language competence level A1 of the CEFR and thus exceeds the target competence level of the elementary school. The performance in German and mathematics is at least at the level of the regular classes and, in the opinion of those involved, is not harmed by learning in two languages (Figure 7).

Figure 7. Rating of the influence of English on the German language development

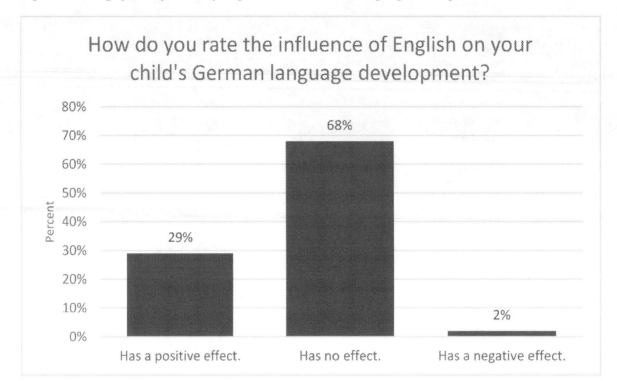

According to the parents, the English language in the classroom tends not to have an impact on German: 68% see no influence of the English language of instruction on the German language. 29% note a positive influence, only 2% a negative one.

A Meaningful Continuation of the Project is Desired and Considered Necessary by All Sides

100% of the school administrators are satisfied with the school trial. All school administrators note that many parents of new children request enrollment in the bilingual project class. At some schools, an additional bilingual class could be created in view of the enrollment figures. In addition, many schools have received an increasing number of applications from other schools with the aim of being accepted into the bilingual class. A continuation of the bilingual elementary school is strongly desired by the principals of the model schools.

School administrators and teachers have a very positive attitude to the project overall and are very satisfied with its progress and results, as Figure 8.

Figure 8. Satisfaction with the progress of the school experiment

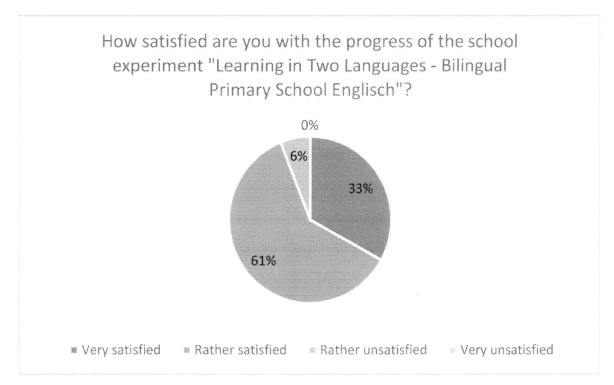

DISCUSSION

English Language Development

The expectations were exceeded in the receptive competence areas listening comprehension and reading comprehension. In the absence of comparisons with similar research projects in bilingual learning, the selected task formats were tested in advance in all competence areas and found to be adequate. According to the test results, the listening comprehension development in the real test context is in a much more positive range than could be presented. The increased English language input (e.g. vocabulary, phrases) is efficiently implicitly received, processed and memorized. This logically leads to higher comprehension performance.

The structure of reading comprehension in English follows the general literacy development of first graders in German. It can be observed that the early development of reading literacy in English does not fundamentally differ from that in German for the students tested. However, dealing with the written word has to be learned explicitly. Unlike in listening comprehension, intuitive learning processes are possible only to a limited extent. The selected test formats were on average again mastered well by the students, a clear indication of the early cognitive potential of the first graders in this respect; this was also considered to be likely in advance.

The development of elementary speaking is individually rapid and an unexpectedly steep progression was observable especially in the first two years of the project. Already after a short time - normally still in the course of grade 1 - the one-word stage is left (similar to the development of the mother tongue).

The well-developed imitation potential for short dialogic utterances, applied in the right situational context, was to be expected. Further information on this can be found in the detailed final report of the study (Böttger & Müller, 2020)

Only the best-performing students usually make their first longer free speech attempts at such an early stage; at the lower end of the performance spectrum, "*language switching*" into English is often still blocked by a lack of language self-confidence. The project classes, however, showed a willingness to experiment in communication and English from Year 1 onwards. Fluent, coherent utterances were consistently observable from the end of grade 1, with a steep, positive development curve in the further course (c.f. Böttger & Müller, 2020).

In direct comparison with regular classes, speaking readiness, speaking ability and speaking competence are on average significantly increased in the bilingual classes from grade 3 onwards.

Acceptance

The positive attitude toward the English language was to be expected. As an omnipresent lingua franca with many high-frequency words and a genuine component of everyday and youth culture, English is accepted as a "natural" language of instruction. This correlates strongly with extensive experience at bilingual schools in Vienna. The students are aware of the special situation due to comparison with non-bilingual parallel classes and recognize the attractive added value for themselves early on. Therefore, initial comprehension difficulties do not seem to be significant on average. This needs to be followed up when the subject content becomes more complicated and abstract.

Trilingualism

At the same time, the, at least systematically, new access to the English language for all students in the project means a new opportunity for all and to the same extent – regardless of mother tongues. This is especially true for learners with a migration background: the fact that an integrative element based on the early access to the acquisition of knowledge and skills in subject areas with the help of English and German is not only significant in terms of language policy.

Pupils with a migrant background also seem to develop their cognitive potential advantageously by processing three or more languages. This must be explicitly addressed again in further tests. This evaluation could not prove this but could hypothetically state it on the basis of the results.

Language Learning Strategies

Building initial conscious language learning strategies of inquiry supports the assumption that much of language learning involves self-construction. The students in the project wanted to learn and acquire knowledge. This argues against excessive explication, e.g., in establishing semantic knowledge. 75% of the learners eliminate possible comprehension difficulties on their own, a highly remarkable finding, as can be seen in the detailed final report of the study (Böttger & Müller, 2020). It goes hand in hand with the comparatively faster cognitive development of the students in the project due to the processing of at least two or more languages.

Self-Assessment

The students' self-assessments of their own language competence in grade 4, which were obtained by means of the aforementioned surveys, indirectly but clearly lean towards the CEFR language competence level A2. Whereas, this still needs to be verified by further tests, simple self-evaluations already make sense at school entry age. Thus, the results can be taken as a serious indication of early cognitive development.

Methodology

Systematic language work is usually occasion-oriented – especially in pronunciation and literacy – and is practiced as such by teachers. This does not contradict the concept of implicit, intuitive learning; it additionally takes highly professional cognitive needs of students into account. For the further development of reading and writing skills, a balance between implicit and explicit task formats are still needed to be defined. This is especially true from Year 3 onwards, with the start of regular English lessons in German elementary schools as well as the fact that writing skills largely need to be developed systematically.

However, language teaching patterns appear to be questionable in case vocabulary is explicitly introduced or language content, rather than subject content, is preserved in writing (on worksheets or similar). This aspect must be readjusted in the future: According to their own statements, an alarming percentage of teachers still fall into patterns of a standard English instruction. Among others, this is one reason why, especially in the evaluation of year 3 and 4, when teacher turnover increased in the project classes, the students' development curve flattened visibly in almost all measured areas after an initially steep progression. In contrast, scaffolding measures and associated professional, comprehensive visualization (including through extralinguistic signs) significantly enable students' comprehension, bilingual semantic knowledge, and language production. Conscious, targeted language switching also has a constructive effect. Taken together, the findings point to a need for a bilingual teacher training manual.

Advanced Training

In the future, there will be an increasing proportion of bilingual or multilingual children in Bavaria and Germany in a united Europe. With the *Bilingual Elementary School English*, English-speaking children are provided with a state school offer and German-speaking children are in turn provided with a bilingual learning offer. Thus, the authors of this paper see the implementation of bilingual instruction as a promising solution and therefore, future training needs of teachers participating in bilingual instruction in elementary and secondary schools are necessary: The focal points must be collegial exchange in terms of content and media, reflection of teaching best/good practice, as well as further conceptual control. In particular, the concept of implicit Learning in Two Languages requires permanent, sustainable and continuous professionalization. The success of the *Bilingual Elementary School English* in Bavaria depends on it to a large extent.

FUTURE RESEARCH DIRECTIONS

A first, obvious need for research arises from the discussion about the transition from preprimary to primary schools. The transition to the primary level usually remains unstructured in the case of preschool bilingual programs. Examples of mutual preparatory visits of kindergarten groups to elementary school with the aim of getting to know each other beyond temporary shadowing remain singular, not institutionalized and dependent on the commitment of local and regional institutions. The same applies to the teachers involved in elementary schools. An exchange at the conceptual, didactic and pedagogical level is therefore still usually arbitrary and subject to the discretion of the individual institutions involved. Then, however, it is highly intensive and successful.

A second, future area of research is the acceptance of multilingualism. "Multilingualism is an enrichment for society and for every individual. There is no reason to fear, to fear loss of language and identity" (Ehlich, 2015). All collected and evaluated data of the school experiment *Learning in Two Languages - Bilingual Elementary School English* show very clearly that Learning in Two Languages means a win-win situation for all involved, for the children, the parents, the teachers, the schools as well as for science.

Early education in bilingualism brings decisive economic, social and professional advantages for children. In addition, there are considerable cognitive advantages (Böttger, 2016), which are, for example, particularly evident in comparative tests in mathematics. Nevertheless, the concerns of teachers' associations and parents must be taken seriously. Convincing, comprehensible evaluation results are the first duty in the development of an early bilingual education concept. So far, the school infrastructure is not yet sufficient for a comprehensive offer and a seamless transition and continuation in secondary schools. In the future, bilingual teacher training and continuing education must be promoted in order to develop sustainable, easily communicable and "natural" learning in two languages from a language acquisition point of view. In addition, steps towards a continuous language continuum must be taken (Böttger, 2009).

In the federalist education system of the Federal Republic of Germany, the transition from primary school to secondary schools in particular remains an unresolved need for nationwide coordination and harmonization, with a focus on transition phases and the development of a language teaching and learning continuum.

A neuralgic point for the educational biography of students, who were taught according to the Learning in Two Languages concept during their primary school years, is the transition to secondary school. The Bavarian State Ministry of Education and Cultural Affairs has commissioned a follow-up study to the *Learning in Two Languages - Bilingual Elementary School English* school experiment in order to gain scientific insights into how the transition can be optimally organized and how the foreign language skills of the learners concerned develop further at middle schools, intermediate schools and high schools. The results, which are expected to be available by the end of 2022, can provide further impetus for shaping the Bavarian educational landscape.

CONCLUSION

After five years of intensive work, all those involved in the project have successfully completed the *Bilingual Elementary School English* school experiment, according to the preliminary objectives. The concept is well received by school authorities, primary schools, parents, teachers and the pupils. The scientific evaluation has shown that children can successfully learn in two languages from the first grade

Learning in Two Languages

onwards and acquire more languages easily and implicitly. At the same time, they perform just as well in other subjects as pupils in comparison to regular classes without bilingual instruction. Therefore, the *Bilingual Elementary School English* as an official concept has been and will be continued as a regular offer from the school year 2020/2021 onwards. The school experiment further provides an insight into what is possible when teachers are trained to teach bilingually. The didactic principles that played a key role within this trial have been the focus of this chapter and offer starting points for further practical applications.

ACKNOWLEDGMENT

This research was supported by the Bildungspakt Bayern Foundation.

REFERENCES

Antón, E., Duñabeitia, J. A., Estévez, A., Hernández, J. A., Castillo, A., Fuentes, L. J., & Carreiras, M. (2014). Is there a bilingual advantage in the ANT task? Evidence from children. *Frontiers in Psychology*, *5*, 398. PMID:24847298

Böttger, H. (2011). *In zwei Sprachen lernen: die Fremdsprache in den Lernbereichen der Grundschule.* Empfehlungen des BIG-Kreises in der Stiftung LERNEN. [*Learning in two languages: the foreign language in the learning areas of primary school.* Recommendations of the BIG circle in the LEARNING Foundation.]

Böttger, H. (2009). *Fremdsprachenunterricht als Kontinuum: der Übergang von der Grundschule in die weiterführenden Schulen.* Empfehlungen des BIG-Kreises in der Stiftung LERNEN. [*Foreign language teaching as a continuum: the transition from primary to secondary school.* Recommendations of the BIG circle in the LEARNING Foundation.]

Böttger, H., & Müller, T. (2020). *Schulversuch Lernen in zwei Sprachen - Bilinguale Grundschule Englisch. [Abschlussbericht der wissenschaftlichen Evaluation, Katholische Universität Eichstätt-Ingolstadt].* [*School experiment Learning in two languages - Bilingual primary school English.* [*Final report of the scientific evaluation, Catholic University of Eichstätt-Ingolstadt].*] Stiftung Bildungspakt Bayern. https://bildungspakt-bayern.de/wp- content/uploads/2020/07/A bschlussbericht.pdf

Böttger, H., Festman, J., & Müller, T. (Eds.). (2019). Language Education and Acquisition Research: Focusing Early Language Learning. Verlag Julius Klinkhardt, 82-116.BIG-Kreis (Ed.) (2015). Der Lernstand im Englischunterricht am Ende von Klasse 4. Ergebnisse der BIG-Studie [The level of learning in English lessons at the end of grade 4. Results of the BIG study]. München: Domino.

Böttger, H. (2017). Early foreign language learning - predispositions and potentials. In H. Böttger (Ed.), *Early foreign language learning. FLuL - Fremdsprachen Lehren und Lernen 46/2 (2017) [FLuL - Teaching and Learning Foreign Languages].* Narr/Francke/Attempto.

Böttger, H. (2016). Neurodidactics of early language learning. *Where language is at home.* Stuttgart: utb GmbH.

Böttger, H., & Rischawy, N. (2016). Bilingual classes at Realschulen in Bavaria. Final report on the accompanying scientific research. Catholic University of Eichstätt-Ingolstadt.

Bayerisches Staatsministerium für Unterricht und Kultus [Bavarian State Ministry for Education and Culture]. (2021). *Projekte Bilinguale Grundschule.* Stiftung Bildungspakt Bayern [*Projects bilingual primary school.* Bavaria Education Pact Foundation]. https://www.bildungspakt-bayern.de/projekte_bilinguale_grund schule/

Böttger, H. (2013). Was Kinder wirklich können: Ein Plädoyer für die Entfaltung kindlicher (Sprachen-) Potenziale. [What children can really do: a plea for the development of children's (language) potential.]. *Grundschule Englisch*, (34), 44–46.

Bredenbröker, W. (2002). Förderung der fremdsprachlichen Kompetenz durch bilingualen Unterricht. Empirische Untersuchungen. [Promotion of foreign language competence through bilingual teaching. Empirische Untersuchungen.] In S. Breidbach, G. Bach, & D. Wolff (Eds.), *Bilingualer Sachfachunterricht: Didaktik, Lehrer- und Lernerforschung und Bildungspolitik zwischen Theorie und Empirie [Bilingual subject teaching: didactics, teacher and learner research and educational policy between theory and empiricism.],* (pp. 141–149). Lang.

Burmeister, P. (2006). Immersion und Sprachunterricht im Vergleich. [Immersion and language teaching in comparison.] In M. Pienemann (Ed.), *Englischerwerb in der Grundschule. Ein Studien- und Arbeitsbuch [English acquisition in elementary school. A study and workbook].* Schöningh.

Burmeister, P. (1998). Zur Entwicklung der Fremdsprachenkenntnisse im bilingualen Unterricht: Ergebnisse aus fünf Jahren Forschung. [On the development of foreign language skills in bilingual teaching: Results from five years of research.] In G. Hermann-Brennecke & W. Geisler (Eds.), *Zur Theorie und Praxis & Praxis der Theorie des Fremdsprachenerwerbs [On the theory and practice & practice of the theory of foreign language acquisition]* (pp. 101–116). LIT Verlag.

Coyle, D., Hood, P., & Marsh, D. (2010). *CLIL. Content and language integrated learning.* Cambridge Univ. Press. doi:10.1017/9781009024549

Christ, H. (2003). Sprachenpolitik und das Lehren und Lernen fremder Sprachen. [Language policy and the teaching and learning of foreign languages.] In Bausch, K.-R./ Christ; H./ Krumm; H.J. (Ed.) (20034) Handbuch Fremdsprachenunterricht, 102-111 [Foreign language teaching handbook]. Tübingen und Basel: Francke.

Deutsches Institut für Internationale Pädagogische Forschung [DIPF] (Ed.) (2006). *Unterricht und Kompetenzerwerb in Deutsch und Englisch. [Teaching and competence acquisition in German and English.]* Zentrale Befunde der Studie Deutsch-Englisch-Schülerleistungen-International (DESI) [Central findings of the German-English student performance study]. Frankfurt am Main.

Ehlich, K. (2015). *Deutschlands Zukunft ist mehrsprachig. [Germany's future is multilingual.]* Unter. http://www.tagesspiegel.de/wissen/position-deutschlands-zukunft-ist-mehrsprachig/11183286.html

Learning in Two Languages

Engel, G. (2009). EVENING – Konsequenzen für die Weiterentwicklung des Englischunterrichts in der Grundschule. [EVENING – Consequences for the further development of English teaching in primary school.] In G. Engel, B. Groot-Wilken, & E. Thürmann (Eds.), *Englisch in der Primarstufe – Chancen und Herausforderungen. Evaluation und Erfahrungen aus der Praxis [English in primary school - Opportunities and challenges. Evaluation and practical experience]* (pp. 197–221). Cornelsen.

Festman, J., & Schwieter, J. W. (2019). Self-Concepts in Reading and Spelling among Mono- and Multilingual Children: Extending the Bilingual Advantage. *Behavioral Sciences (Basel, Switzerland)*, *9*(4), 39. doi:10.3390/bs9040039 PMID:31013920

Franceschini, R. (2016). Multilingualism and multicompetence. In V. Cook & L. Wei (Eds.), *The Cambridge Handbook of Linguistic Multi-Competence* (pp. 97–124). Cambridge University Press. doi:10.1017/CBO9781107425965.005

Franceschini, R. (2008). Früher Spracherwerb und frühes Lernen: Wie nutzen wir die Chancen? [Early language acquisition and early learning: How do we take advantage of the opportunities?] In Ministerium für Bildung, Familie, Frauen und Kultur des Saarlandes (Ed.). Mehrsprachiges Aufwachsen in der frühen Kindheit. Band 1. Weimar: Verlag das Netz [Saarland Ministry for Education, Family, Women and Culture (ed.). Multilingual growing up in early childhood. Volume 1 Weimar: Publisher the network], 13-20.

Genesee, F. (1987). *Learning Through Two Languages: Studies of Immersion and Bilingual Education*. Newbury House.

Graddol, D. (2006). *English next. Why global English may mean the end of 'English as a foreign language*. British Council.

Ioannou Georgiou, S. (2011). Guidelines for CLIL Implementation in Primary and Preprimary Education. Unter. http://www.academia.edu/15067157/Guidelines_for_CLIL_Implementation_in_Primary_and_Preprimary_Education

Institut zur Qualitätsentwicklung im Bildungswesen [Institute for quality development in education] [IQB]. (2019). *VERA VER gleichs Arbeiten in der 3. und 8 [VERA comparative work in the 3rd and 8th grades]*. IQB

Kersten, K. (2010). DOs and DONT's bei der Einrichtung immersiver Schulprogramme. [DOs and DONT's in setting up immersive school programs.] In Bongartz, C.M.; Rymarczyk, J. (Eds.). Languages Across the Curriculum, 71-92. Peter Lang.

Kersten, K. (Ed.). (2010). *ELIAS – Early Language and Intercultural Acquisition Studies: Final Report*. Magdeburg University: ELIAS.

Kersten, K. (2005). Bilinguale Kindergärten und Grundschulen: Wissenschaft und Praxis im Kieler Immersionsprojekt. [Bilingual kindergartens and primary schools: Science and practice in the Kiel immersion project.] In P. Baron (Ed.), *Bilingualität im Kindergarten und in der Primarstufe. Zukunftschancen für unsere Kinder [Bilingualism in kindergarten and primary school. future prospects for our children]* (pp. 22–33). Niemieckie Towarzystwo Oswiatowe.

Kultusministerkonferenz [KMK]. (2006). *Konzepte für den bilingualen Unterricht – Erfahrungsbericht und Vorschläge zur Weiterentwicklung [Concepts for bilingual teaching - field report and suggestions for further development].* KMK. https://www.kmk.org/fileadmin/Dateien/veroeffentlichungen_beschluesse/2006/2006_04_10-Konzepte-bilingualer-Unterricht.pdf

Lyster, R. (2007). *Learning and teaching languages through content. A counterbalanced approach.* Benjamins. doi:10.1075/lllt.18

Marsh, D. (2002). CLIL/EMILE. The European dimension: actions, trends and foresight potential. Jyväskylä: UniCOM.

Massler, U., & Burmeister, P. (2010). *CLIL und Immersion. Fremdsprachlicher Sachfachunterricht in der Grundschule [Concepts for bilingual teaching - field report and suggestions for further development].* Westermann.

Nitsch, C. (2007). Mehrsprachigkeit: eine neurowissenschaftliche Perspektive. [Multilingualism: a neuroscientific perspective.] In T. Anstatt (Ed.), *Mehrsprachigkeit bei Kindern und Erwachsenen. Erwerb, Formen, Förderung [Multilingualism among children and adults. Acquisition, forms, promotion]* (pp. 47–68). Attempto.

Pierce, L. J., Klein, D., Chen, J. K., Delcenserie, A., & Genesee, F. (2014). Mapping the unconscious maintenance of a lost first language. *Proceedings of the National Academy of Sciences of the United States of America, 111*(48), 17314–17319. doi:10.1073/pnas.1409411111 PMID:25404336

Pliatsikas, C., Johnstone, T., & Marinis, T. (2014). Grey matter volume in the cerebellum is related to the processing of grammatical rules in a second language: A structural voxel-based morphometry study. *Cerebellum (London, England), 13*(1), 55–63. doi:10.100712311-013-0515-6 PMID:23990323

Poarch, G.J., & Bialystok, E. (2015). Bilingualism as a Model for Multitasking. *Developmental review, 35*, 113–124.

Poulin-Dubois, D., Blaye, A., Coutya, J., & Bialystok, E. (2011). The effects of bilingualism on toddlers' executive functioning. *Journal of Experimental Child Psychology, 108*(3), 567–579. doi:10.1016/j.jecp.2010.10.009 PMID:21122877

Rischawy, N. (2016). *Bilinguale Züge an Realschulen in Bayern. Vergleichsstudien zum Zuwachs englischsprachiger Fertigkeiten und Kompetenzen im Rahmen des Modellversuchs. [Bilingual traits at secondary schools in Bavaria. Comparative studies on the increase in English-language skills and competences within the framework of the pilot project.]* [Dissertation, Katholische Universität Eichstätt-Ingolstadt].

München, S. (2004). *Staatsinstitut für Schulqualität und Bildungsforschung München 2004: Lehrplan Sozialkunde [State Institute for School Quality and Educational Research Munich 2004: Social studies curriculum.]* ISB. http://www. isb-gym8-lehrplan. de/contentserv/3.1. neu/g8. de/index. php

Wattendorf, E., Westermann, B., Zappatore, D., Franceschini, R., Lüdi, G., Radü, E. W., & Nitsch, C. (2001). Different languages activate different subfields in Broca area. *NeuroImage, 6*(13), 624. doi:10.1016/S1053-8119(01)91967-6

Learning in Two Languages

Wode, H., Burmeister, P., Daniel, A., & Rhode, A. (1996). Die Erprobung von deutsch-englisch bilingualem Unterricht in Schleswig-Holstein: Ein erster Zwischenbericht. [The testing of german-English bilingual teaching in Schleswig-Holstein: A first interim report.]. *Zeitschrift für Fremdsprachenforschung, 7*(1), 15–42.

Zydatiß, W. (2004). Sachfachlicher Kompetenzerwerb im bilingualen Sachfachunterricht. [Subject-related competence acquisition in bilingual subject teaching.] In A. Bonnet (Ed.), *Didaktiken im Dialog. Konzepte des Lehrens und Wege des Lernens im bilingualen Sachfachunterricht [Didactics in dialogue. Concepts of teaching and ways of learning in bilingual subject teaching]* (pp. 89–90). Lang.

Zydatiß, W. (2000). Bilingualer Unterricht in der Grundschule. [Bilingual education in primary school.] Ismaning: Hueber.

ADDITIONAL READING

Bürvenich, P. (2017). *Zur Qualität kommerzieller Angebote frühen Fremdsprachenlernens. [On the quality of commercial offers of early foreign language learning.]* [Dissertation Katholische Universität Eichstätt-Ingolstadt].

Dämon, K. (2014). Mehrsprachige Kitas: Was bringt eine bilinguale Früherziehung? [Multilingual day-care centres: What are the benefits of bilingual early education?]. WIWO.https://www.wiwo.de/erfolg/trends/mehrsprachige-kitas-was-bringt-eine-bilinguale-frueherziehung/10316226.html

EURYDICE. (2006). *Content and Language Integrated Learning (CLIL) at School in Europe*. Brüssel.

Gölitz, D., Roick, T., & Hasselhorn, M. (2006). *Deutscher Mathematiktest für vierte Klassen* [German mathematics test for fourth grades.]. Hogrefe.

Kersten, K., Fischer, U., Burmeister, P., Lommel, A. (2009). *Immersion in der Grundschule – Ein Leitfaden.* Kiel: Verein für frühe Mehrsprachigkeit an Kindertageseinrichtungen und Schulen FMKS e.V. [*Immersion in elementary school – A guide.* Kiel: Association for early multilingualism in day-care centers and schools FMKS e.V]

Lübke, F. (2014). Wenn Zweijährige mit drei Sprachen aufwachsen. [When two-year-olds grow up with three languages.] *Welt.* https://www.welt.de/wirtschaft/karriere/bildung/article131069044/Wenn-Zweijaehrige-mit-drei-Sprachen-aufwachsen.html

Pienemann, M. (Ed.). (2006). Englischerwerb in der Grundschule. [English acquisition in primary school.] Ein Studien- und Arbeitsbuch. Paderborn: Schöningh.

Verein für frühe Mehrsprachigkeit an Kindertageseinrichtungen und Schulen. [Association for Early Multilingualism at Day Care Centres and Schools.] (2014a). Bilinguale Kitas in Deutschland [Bilingual daycare centers in Germany]. www.fmks.eu

Verein für frühe Mehrsprachigkeit an Kindertageseinrichtungen und Schulen. [Association for Early Multilingualism at Day Care Centres and Schools.] (2014b). Bilinguale Grundschulen in Deutschland 2014 [Bilingual Primary Schools in Germany]. https://www.goethe.de /resources/files/pdf92/fmks_bilinguale -grundschulen-studie2014.pdf

KEYTERMS AND DEFINITIONS

Bilingual Education: Bilingual education involves two languages as a means of instruction for students, either embedded in individual subjects or the entire school curriculum. The respective subjects, however, are taught monolingually in one of these languages.

Learning in Two Languages: In dual-language education, subjects are taught in two languages during one lesson.

Language Development: The developmental process through which children acquire the ability to communicate in a language.

Language Acquisition: The process by which humans acquire (their native) language(s). It occurs naturally and differs from most institutionalized language education due to implicit learning processes.

Immersion: The process of learning a language implicitly by being surrounded by the foreign language itself.

Implicit Learning and Teaching: A natural and unconscious form of learning in which students are exposed to a large amount of highly comprehensible and compelling input as well as respective teaching approaches.

Chapter 11
Teaching Physical Education Through English:
Promoting Pre-Service Teachers Effective Personality Through a Learning-Practice Approach

Teresa Valverde-Esteve
University of Valencia, Spain

Celina Salvador-García
iD https://orcid.org/0000-0003-0776-8760
Jaume I University, Castellón, Spain

María Noelia Ruiz-Madrid
Jaume I University, Castellón, Spain

ABSTRACT

Applying a learning-practice approach to CLIL in teacher education may be instrumental not only to promote the development of CLIL professional skills, but also to improve pre-service teachers' 'effective personality.' This chapter provides, first, a detailed description of a specific course of physical education teacher education that has been successfully applied for three years, in which pre-service teachers are required to implement CLIL through a learning-practice approach. Subsequently, it presents an explanatory mixed-methods study to examine how pre-service teachers' effective personality was influenced by the learning-practice approach to CLIL used. Informed by the results obtained, the chapter finishes by sharing some clues on how to foster effective personality through CLIL teacher training to help lecturers design and develop proper CLIL teacher development activities.

DOI: 10.4018/978-1-6684-6179-2.ch011

Copyright © 2023, IGI Global. Copying or distributing in print or electronic forms without written permission of IGI Global is prohibited.

INTRODUCTION

Higher education must face the challenge of attending to the demands of the 21st century by renewing the methodological approaches used, among other fields, in teacher education (Calvo-Bernardino & Mingorance-Arnáiz, 2009). To do so, the educational process should foster the development of competences instead of being limited to the mere transmission of knowledge (Álvarez-Rojo et al., 2011). Against this backdrop, increasing pre-service teachers' effective personality and the four dimensions that compose it (i.e., Academic Self-Realization, Resolute Self-Efficacy, Self-esteem and Social self-realization) emerges as an indisputable goal of 21st century education (Martín del Buey et al., 2000), since this hallmark relates personality traits with behavior in professional or academic contexts.

In accordance with these requirements, applying a learning-practice approach in teacher education (Strom & Viesca, 2021) may be instrumental in order to promote the development of professional skills, improve 'effective personality' and enhance citizenship among pre-service teachers. According to Strom and Viesca (2021), learning and practice are not separate things, but rather intertwined processes that co-constitute, or co-make, each other. In addition, adopting a learning-practice approach promotes affirmative attitudes towards pluralism of language, culture, and ways of knowing and being, since it considers that teaching should not be considered linear and 'process-product' driven anymore (Strom & Martin, 2017).

During the last two decades, Spain has been involved in a mass adoption of Content Language Integrated Learning (CLIL) programs in order to respond to the European Union's multilingualism goals (Custodio, 2019). Nevertheless, their rapid expansion has exceeded the provision of teachers who are able to face the challenge of adopting pedagogical approaches such as CLIL (Pérez-Cañado, 2016). This means that, nowadays, CLIL teacher training is essential (Estrada & Otto, 2019), and it may be approached from a learning-practice approach so that pre-service teachers are enabled to experience CLIL and connect learning and practice while reflecting and articulating how they are capable of enacting their learning. Likewise, pre-service teachers should develop a range of personal and professional competences among which we may find their effective personality (Chiva-Bartoll et al., 2018).

This chapter provides, first, a detailed description of a specific course of Physical Education teacher education that has been successfully applied for three years, in which pre-service teachers are required to implement CLIL. In addition, we present a study developed in this context, aimed at examining how pre-service teachers' effective personality could be influenced by this learning-practice-approach to CLIL. Informed by the results obtained, the chapter finishes by sharing some clues on how to foster effective personality through CLIL teacher training to help lecturers design and develop proper CLIL teacher development activities (Contero et al., 2018).

THE PHYSICAL EDUCATION COURSE

The subject of Didactics of Physical Education in Primary Teaching is a compulsory subject developed in the second year of the degree of Primary Teaching. However, students in this degree are able to decide whether they want to carry it out through the bilingual option or not. In any case, the contents are always the same and include: the Physical Education and its educational value, the historical evolution and trends in Physical Education, the curriculum of Physical Education in Primary Education, the elements included in the Didactics of Physical Education, Programming in Physical Education, as well as the Teaching-learning of the different blocks of contents of Physical Education in Primary Education.

Several active methodologies are used when dealing with these topics. Therefore, the subject uses a learning-practice approach (Strom & Viesca, 2021), since pre-service teachers are to teach their peers through experiential learning, and embodied cognition (Wilson, 2022). This is to say that, according to Dewey's (1938) theory, students 'learn by doing', since during the subject they act as both teachers and students, and they are required to reflect upon their practices in order to be critical and find ways to improve them.

One of the essential characteristics of the subject in the bilingual itinerary is the fact that pre-service teachers are to develop the sessions and presentations through the English language, therefore challenging their language communication skills (Villabona & Cenoz, 2022). For example, among other tasks, pre-service teachers are to design and perform a Didactic Unit addressed to Primary school students using CLIL. Thus, they have to base it on the 4c's framework (Coyle et al., 2010) considering how to properly use and embed a language that students are not expected to master, which means that they think about how to develop the following dimensions for their future students:

- **Contents:** starting from the students' previous knowledge and looking for a significant learning acquisition.
- **Cognition:** developing different ways of thinking or innovative approaches to reach the successful strategies that better suit the students' demands.
- **Communication:** by acquiring new ways of interacting through verbal and non-verbal strategies and adapting to the different practical and theoretical situations.
- **Culture:** moving towards a multicultural understanding, including national and international students, as well as their specific backgrounds.

This subject consists of 60 teaching hours and the methodological sequence moves from a more guided teaching (lower cognitive demand) towards a more creative style that pursues pre-service teachers' autonomy and initiative (higher cognitive demand). As a guide, the organizational planning of the subject is shown in table 1. The specific example presented in this section will focus on sessions 22 to 29, dealing with the design and application of a Didactic Unit using CLIL.

Table 1. Schedule followed along the course

Sessions	Issue	Contents	Thinking skills
Sessions 1-3	Introduction to the subject	The professor present the contents, methods, assessment criteria and performs games and activities in order for pre-service teachers to introduce themselves and decide the groups of 3-4 people in which they will work during the subject.	Remember Understand
Sessions 4-21	Role playing and project learning theoretical and practical activities	During the 17 sessions, the professor teaches the contents through different active and participatory methodologies, so that the pre-service teachers acquire the contents from an active approach. Some examples are: the content of traditional games with recycled materials through 'learning stations', or attention to diversity through Service Learning. During these sessions, the importance of the interdependence between content and cooperation is shown (Lewis & Tsuchida, 1998).	Apply Analyze
Sessions 22-29	Performance and presentation of the DU designed by the pre-service teachers	During these sessions, the different groups perform their presentations, using material resources and methodologies previously agreed upon during the three tutorials with the teacher, in order to achieve maximum variety in the different proposals. It is at this point when pre-service teachers take up the role of teachers and really engage in a learning-practice approach.	Analyze Evaluate Create
Session 30	Assessment of the subject	During the last session of the course, pre-service teachers write down and share with their peers the best moments during the course. The whole group discusses about what improvements we can all make in our future lectures, including the pre-service teachers and the professor of the subject.	Evaluate

Source: self-elaborated by the authors.

According to Meyer (2010), there are seven principles that might be included for the CLIL implementation to be successful, which did take part in the Physical Education subject as follows:

- 1st, Rich input: considering the appropriate choice of materials in order to contribute to a meaningful foreign language acquisition (e.g., presentations, videos).
- 2nd, Scaffolding learning: adapting the cognitive load by guiding the learning acquisition process through a supportive structure and by providing specific vocabulary.
- 3rd, Rich Interaction and Pushed Output: providing feedback after interaction. In this principle, Meyer (2010) states that the communication gaps are the moments in which the authentic communication is produced:
  - *Information gap*: by transferring information among peers.
  - *Reasoning gap*: teaching their peers (pre-service teachers) or their future students.
  - *Opinion gaps*: starting a story with different endings and comparing them.
- 4th, Adding the Inter-cultural dimension: learning from their national and international peers' cultural backgrounds and respecting the differences among everyone.
- 5th, Making it H.O.T.: including Higher Order Thinking skills, starting from a meaningful input, facilitating authentic communication, students' active participation in the tasks, and obtaining a complex output that includes cross cultural communication.
- 6th, Sustainable Learning: in order to obtain output that facilitates the expression of the specific contents of the subject in the second language.
- 7th, Introducing the CLIL Pyramid: which can be applied once the 4 c's are established, and provides a systematical guidance to perform CLIL:

Teaching Physical Education Through English

- ◦ *Topic selection*, this is the base of the pyramid and the beginning of the process.
- ◦ *Choice of media*, learning styles, and how the second language skills are going to be developed.
- ◦ *Task-design*, indicating which skills will be practiced and how the cognition is going to be included in the communication process in order to pursue the Higher Order Thinking skills and authentic communication.
- ◦ *CLIL-workout*, in the ways of the desired product.

All in all, in the course of Didactics of Physical Education, the professor guides the pre-service teachers following the CLIL pyramid (Meyer, 2010). Table 2 shows the roles of the professor and the pre-service teachers when CLIL is applied regarding the four phases mentioned on the seventh principle of this pyramid.

Table 2. CLIL pyramid progression displaying the professor and pre-service teachers' roles

Phase	Professor's role	Pre-service teachers' role
1st: *topic selection*	The professor asks pre-service teachers about their Physical Activity and Sports background in order to design the task progression and contents that better suits their demands during the course.	Pre-service teachers write down an essay about their experience with Physical Education, so that the professor can design a scaffolding process. Also, pre-service teachers decide what is the topic that they want to design their Didactic Unit for during the last sessions.
2nd: *choice of media*	The professor provides pre-service teachers with the different materials and resources in order to encourage the active methodologies (e.g., specific Physical Education materials and videos).	Pre-service teachers provide their peers with the materials and resources needed, according to the topic of the Didactic Unit (e.g., powerpoint presentation, Physical Education materials).
3rd: *task-design*	The professor starts from Lower Order Thinking Skills (Remember, Understand, Apply), moving towards Higher Order Thinking skills (Analyze, Evaluate, Create) in order to make sure that pre-service teachers acquire the significant learning through scaffolding process.	Pre-service teachers apply the basic Lower Order Thinking during the theoretical part of their presentations, moving towards Higher Order Thinking, during the practical part. At the end of the session, all pre-service teachers perform the peer assessment.
4th: *CLIL-workout*	The professor designs activities that encourage the active participation and communication of pre-service teachers (e.g., representation of the history of Physical Education)	Presentation of a Didactic Unit, including a theoretical and a practical section.

Source: self-elaborated by the authors.

Along these practices, pre-service teachers were also engaged in peer-assessment (Topping, 2009), self-assessment (Ross, 2006) and shared discussions and reflection through 'lesson study' (Lewis et al., 2004; McMillan & Jess, 2021), as they were invited not only to improve their Physical Education lessons but also the way they were carrying out the teaching and learning process through CLIL. Indeed, "Lesson study" was performed during the presentation sessions, since all issues were initially presented by the professor and continued by the pre-service teachers acting as teachers.

Subsequently, we are going to focus only on a specific block of sessions because of the limited length of the chapter. Specifically, we will share how sessions 22 to 29 worked, since these sessions allowed pre-service teachers to engage in a learning-practice approach to CLIL, as they were to design and apply a lesson a Didactic Unit using CLIL. Before these sessions, pre-service teachers attended a minimum of three meetings with the professor to design the Didactic Unit, and a post-lesson discussion, mainly addressed to share the observations during the teaching process (Kihara et al., 2021). Table 3 shows an example of the tasks that the students were to prepare for each meeting.

Table 3. Contents during the three follow-up meetings among the pre-service teachers and the professor

Number of meeting	Tasks to be prepared in advance
1st	Main topic, literature review, work planning and members' roles during the elaboration process
2nd	Structure of the Didactic Unit: objectives, competences, methodology, and assessment criteria; all of them linked to the 4c's of CLIL.
3rd	Specific activities, materials, members' roles during the theoretical and practical performances, and complementary information for their peers in order to follow the presentations.

Source: self-elaborated by the authors.

CLIL Implementation

Table 4 shows a typical session scheduled when the pre-service teachers were to adopt a learning-practice approach to present and implement a Didactic Unit. This table shows the contents to be worked, the pre-service teachers' roles and how they were expected to implement CLIL, as well as a specific example of one of the sessions implemented to provide a clear idea about the organization of a typical session.

Table 4. Example of a session of didactics of physical education performed during the presentations

Part of the session	Contents	Pre-service teachers' roles	Example
Beginning	Presentation of the theoretical framework of the Didactic Unit that the students are about to develop (e.g., Games and sports, body expression, outdoor activities), including the context it is designed for.	Students take notes in order to respond to some questions that will be addressed along the session and that can be included in the final test of the subject.	The professor introduces the contents such as the History of Physical Education, as well as the cognition, communication and culture resources that are needed to: 1) explore the theoretical framework and 2) to present, through role playing activities, the Physical Education during the Ancient Greece, Rome, the Renaissance or the Enlightenment periods.
Main part	Practical presentation of a typical session included in the Didactic Unit (e.g., working in corners, students follow the brief explanations of each activity and, through a guided discovery, they perform the game, sport or choreography).	Pre-service teachers acting as teachers develop the practical contents and pay attention to the elements that are included in the rubric in order to provide a constructive feedback after this section.	Pre-service teachers acting as teachers play their respective roles whilst they explain their peers how was the Physical Education during the mentioned dates or the Olympic Games. The professor encourages the active participation and provides supportive feedback
Discussion and conclusion	'Lesson study': after the observation and practice of the students' theoretical and practical presentations, a rubric is given, in order to encourage the students' group processing.	Students fill the rubric of the practical part of the session, according to the following items: contextualization of the DU, Organization of the group, presentation flow, originality of the activities, adequacy of the activities and the curriculum of Primary Education, and adaptation to the special needs.	Pre-service teachers acting as teachers prepare a game to ask interactive questions regarding the theoretical and practical presentations. After this, students provide a constructive feedback with their peers in order to improve their future presentations and activities design.

Source: self-elaborated by the authors.

242

Teaching Physical Education Through English

The Assessment Process in the Physical Education Course

Evaluation consists of collecting information and analyzing it, thus monitoring the student learning process. During this time, feedback was given by both the professor and other students. After this, a mark was given, aiming at reflecting the students' knowledge acquisition process (Hamodi et al., 2015). In this context, formative and shared evaluation allowed the democratization and negotiation of the evaluation process (López-Pastor, 2011), positively influencing the teaching-learning processes in higher education, while promoting responsibility and autonomy.

Following the classification of Hamodi et al., (2015) to carry out the evaluation process in the described subject, evidence was collected through: 1) means of student production, 2) information collection techniques used by the professor and 3) instruments that the professor and students used to evaluate the students (Table 5).

Table 5. Evaluation means and techniques used in the subject

Mediums	Written	Didactic Unit: written presentation (15%) Written test (20%)
	Oral	Didactic Unit: oral presentation (10%)
	Practical mediation	Projects with role-playing (40%)
Techniques	Observation	Didactic Unit: Self-assessment (5%) Didactic Unit: Peer assessment (10%)

Source: adapted from Hamodi et al. (2015)

Focusing specifically on the assessment of the Didactic Units, students used a rubric to evaluate their peers and their own Didactic Unit (Table 6). In addition, at the end of the sessions, the professor gave a mark for the oral presentation as well as for the written presentation of the Didactic Unit. Likewise, additional comments were shared among peers, in a respectful and constructive atmosphere, guided by the professor, and aiming at improving future presentations.

Teaching Physical Education Through English

Table 6. Peer-assessment rubric used by the professor and peers to assess the presentations

	C's	Excellent (4)	Very well (3)	Well (2)	Poor (1)	Additional comments
Contextualization of the DU	Content, Cognition, Culture	The context is understandable and reflect the contents of the DU and culture of the area in which it is implemented	The context is quite understandable, but there is missing some information regarding on element of: contents, cognition or culture.	The context is incomplete and there is missing information of more than two elements of: contents, cognition or culture.	The contents are not clear and the group doesn't show the contents, cognition or culture at all.	
Organization of the group	Communication	The verbal and nonverbal communication among the members of the group is very clear and understandable.	The verbal information is not complete but they compensate it with the nonverbal information.	The verbal and nonverbal information are difficult to follow.	The verbal and nonverbal communication are not clear at all.	
Presentation flow	Communication	The group communication flows very clearly.	The group communication flows quite clearly.	The group communication flows not very clearly.	The group communication's flow is not clear at all.	
Originality of the activities	Content, Cognition, Culture	The proposal of the activities is highlighted by their originality and includes contents, cognition and culture.	The proposal of the activities is quite original and includes two elements of: contents, cognition and culture.	The originality of the activities could be improved and more than two elements of: contents, cognition and culture do not appear.	The proposal does not include original activities, contents, cognition or culture.	
Adequacy of the activities and the curriculum of Primary Education	Content, Cognition, Culture	The activities are very appropriate to the curriculum of Primary Education, including specific contents, cognition and culture.	The activities are quite suitable to the curriculum of Primary Education, but they miss one element of: contents, cognition and culture.	The activities are appropriate to the curriculum of Primary Education, but they miss two elements of: contents, cognition and culture.	The activities are not at all appropriate to the curriculum of Primary Education, and do not include specific contents, cognition and culture.	
Inclusion of all students	Content, Communication	The proposal includes the adaptation to special needs and the transmission of the contents are perfectly understandable.	The adaptation to special needs and the transmission of the contents are quite understandable.	The adaptation to special needs and the transmission of the contents are not clear enough.	The proposal does not include the adaptation to special needs and the transmission of the contents are not clear at all.	

Source: adapted from the Didactic guide provided to the students.

Teaching Physical Education Through English

Effective Personality in Teacher Education

The positive influence of effective personality in the educational field has been widely described. The concept of 'effective personality', is divided into four interacting dimensions that may be promoted through some educational practices (Gómez, 2012): Academic Self-Realization, Resolute Self-Efficacy, Self-esteem and Social self-realization. Academic Self-Realization is related to knowledge about the self and success achievement. Resolute Self-Efficacy refers to skills related to decision-making and facing problematic situations. Self-esteem is mainly focused on variables stressing self-strengths. And finally, Social self-realization refers to skills concerning communication, empathy and assertiveness.

Authors such as Fueyo-Gutiérrez et al. (2010) found that some dimensions of the effective personality construct could influence students' academic performance. Whereas, Pizarro et al. (2014), identified that effective personality traits could work as protective factor against the burnout syndrome. Bearing in mind these ideas, it seems that effective personality and the dimensions it comprises should be promoted among students (Gómez, 2012). In this sense, Chiva-Bartoll et al. (2018) assert that active and participatory methodologies such as Service Learning could be instrumental to promote participants' effective personality in the teacher education scenario. Therefore, the study presented in this chapter aspires to examine how pre-service teachers' effective personality could be influenced by a learning-practice-approach to CLIL in the subject previously described.

THE STUDY

Design

This study used an explanatory mixed-methods approach to tackle the objective established. The quantitative part of the study used a survey-based technique to collect data (Mean, Standard Deviation, Median and Interquartile Ranges). With regard to the qualitative part, the aim was to examine in detail the perspectives of the participants in order to understand, according to the pre-service teachers' opinions, how their effective personality could have been developed (or not) thanks to the learning-practice approach to CLIL used (Denzin, 2017). This design lets gather qualitative and quantitative data to examine the phenomenon at multiple levels, to combine the strengths of both approaches, and develop a more comprehensive understanding of it (Creswell & Plano-Clark, 2017).

Participants

Since 2018-2019, 145 pre-service teachers have carried out the abovementioned Physical Education course. From all, 48 of them volunteered to take part in this study, representing 33.10% of the total sample. Since the course in which the study is contextualized is developed through a hard-CLIL approach, international students enrolled in the Primary Education Degree tend to opt for the bilingual itinerary. In Table 7, we show the level of English reported by the participants. Particularly, 9 of the participants of this study were Erasmus students. They were from Norway, Germany, Czech Republic, Italy and Hungary. 4 of them were enrolled in their last year of their Primary degree in their universities.

245

Table 7. Participants' reported level of English

Level of English	Percentage of national students	Percentage of International students
A2	4.17%	-
B1	14.58%	11.11%
B2	60.42%	50%
C1	20.83%	33.33%

Source: self-elaborated by the authors.

Instruments

Quantitative evidence was gathered at the beginning of the subject through the Effective Personality Questionnaire for University Students (Gómez, 2012). This validated questionnaire shows a high reliability (α=.87) and is a tool specific for the higher education stage. Its 30 items are divided into four different dimensions: Social Self-Realization, Academic Self-Realization, Self Esteem and Resolute Self-Efficacy. Participants had to answer a 5-point Likert scale for each item, ranging from completely disagree (1) to completely agree (5).

Qualitative data consisted of a survey through which pre-service teachers were to explain how the effective personality constructs were (or not) developed through the Physical Education subject. The design of this instrument allowed us to triangulate and integrate both types of data (Plano-Clark, 2019). Specifically, pre-service teachers had to answer the following questions regarding each of the four dimensions of the Effective Personality questionnaire:

- How has my participation in the subject through CLIL helped me to acquire academic self-realization (motivation, expectation and attributions of academic performance)?
- How has my participation in the subject through CLIL helped me to acquire social self-realization (link between the self-perception of ability to establish and maintain relationships with others and the expectations of success in those future social relationships)?
- How has my participation in the subject through CLIL helped me improve my self-esteem (knowledge and appreciation of oneself, high valuation and confidence in one's own cognitive-motivational and social resources, and recognition of limitations)?
- How has participation in the subject through CLIL helped me to improve my resolute self-efficacy (effective coping with challenges and decision making)?

Data Analysis

For the quantitative part of the study, the statistical analysis was performed through the SPSS (Version 26, Chicago, IL, USA). We obtained descriptive data, such as the mean, standard deviation, median and Interquartile Range (IQ). We also assessed the questionnaire reliability through Alpha's Cronbach, considering moderate reliability when values ranged between 0.5 and 0.80 (Ekolu & Quainoo, 2019). Therefore, the values obtained for the present study were α=0.663.

Teaching Physical Education Through English

Regarding the qualitative part of the study, an interpretative approach to data analysis was used. We followed accepted recommendations for qualitative analysis, and applied a double procedure from inductive to deductive and back again (Yin, 2003). Thematic areas used to perform the qualitative analysis were defined by Gomez's (2012) dimensions on effective personality (social self-realization-SSR, academic self-realization-ASR, self-esteem-SE and resolute self-efficacy-RSE). We carried out a multi-phase analysis consisting of an initial open-coding phase and a second axial coding phase (Patton, 2002). First, relevant information related to the four aforementioned dimensions was identified. Subsequently, we looked for additional data that could be relevant to foster the objective of the study. Therefore, we moved between inductive and deductive reasoning, and two iterations were developed. The results section presents a selection of extracts as examples. All these extracts include a reference code (acronym of the dimension + number of student). The selection of these quotes is related to their importance and depth to highlight the students' perceptions regarding each dimension.

RESULTS

This section presents the findings obtained in our study in an integrated way (Plano-Clark, 2019). Therefore, it presents the four dimensions conforming the Effective Personality Questionnaire for University Students and shows both the descriptive findings for each item as well as the related qualitative data.

Academic Self-Realization

Regarding the dimension focused on academic self-realization, quantitative results are displayed in Table 8.

Table 8. Academic self-realization results

Academic Self-Realization	M (SD)	Median (IQ)
1. My success in studies is due to my effort and dedication	4.25 (0.98)	5 (1)
5. My success in a subject is because I do my best to do a good job	4.27 (0.79)	4 (1)
9. I have a good ability to study at the University	4.00 (1.03)	4 (2)
13. I consider myself a good student	4.21 (0.74)	4 (1)
17. I study because I like to overcome the challenges presented by the subjects	3.64 (1.07)	4 (2)
21. My success in studies is due to my personal capacity	4.02 (0.70)	4 (0)
24. When I have a problem, I spend time and make an effort to solve it	3.96 (0.82)	4 (1)
27. I am convinced that I will succeed when I work	4.17 (0.66)	4 (1)
Total	4.01 (0.52)	4.00 (0.78)

Source: self-elaborated by the authors.

From a general perspective, this is the category that has been developed to the higher extent according to the scores obtained from participant pre-service teachers. In particular, students seem to consider their own effort to be critical to succeed in the subject and studies (items 1 and 9). Furthermore, qualitative results point to a number of pre-service teachers emphasizing high levels of self-realization in terms of

247

language improvement and teaching skills. Subsequently, we present three representative quotes that evince these ideas:

My participation in the subject through CLIL has really improved my language skills and my ability to express myself and communicate properly. The fact that I feel more comfortable with the language has increased my motivation to learn. In addition, it has also increased my confidence to teach in another language in the future, since I have been able to experience and know in depth this methodology and I feel capable of developing it when I become a teacher. (ASR-S29)

This subject has helped me to feel fulfilled because I have had a constant motivation and we have participated in different ways, being the teachers and the students of the different sessions that we have carried out. (ASR-S17)

I have managed to develop both my instructional skills to be a teacher and know how to manage myself within a classroom as well as my ability to use English. (ASR-S39)

According to these results, it seems that pre-service teachers were able to develop a better understanding of themselves and their capacity to be successful regarding language skills, self-confidence, motivation, among other aspects.

Resolute Self-Efficacy

Moving now to the resolute self-efficacy dimension, quantitative results point to students considering it to be sufficiently developed (Table 9).

Table 9. Resolute self-efficacy results

Resolute Self-Efficacy	M (SD)	Median (IQ)
4. When I have to make a decision, I plan carefully what I'm going to do	3.58 (0.92)	3.5 (1)
8. When I have a problem, I try to see its positive side	3.31 (1.11)	3 (2)
12. To make a decision, I gather all the information that I can find	3.88 (0.91)	4 (2)
16. I control my emotions well	3.44 (1.01)	3 (1)
20. When I experience a failure, I try to learn from that experience	4.35 (0.73)	4,5 (1)
Total	3.71 (0.51)	3.60 (0.65)

Source: self-elaborated by the authors.

Pre-service teachers emphasize their capacity of learning from unsuccessful experiences (item 20) or gathering sufficient information in order to make proper decisions (item 12). Furthermore, through qualitative data they specified that the Physical Education subject through CLIL let them improve this dimension in terms of both language and teaching skills. The following quotes are representative ideas shared by three pre-service teachers:

Teaching Physical Education Through English

It (the subject) helped me a lot because I needed to think very quickly in English and know what words I should choose to use at every moment of the class. (RSE-S32)

I think I have had the opportunity to see how a class works and how many times you have to put alternatives and solutions to things that are happening. I have realized that things can be modified and that everything does not always go as planned, and that nothing happens if that occurs, you just have to act quickly and calmly to continue with the class. (RSE-S31)

When we had to perform a class, sometimes there was not enough material for everyone, or we had too many students and we had to think of a solution to solve the problem. We talked as a team to see how to solve the problem and we took decisions. This way of learning was useful to help us develop our decision making and to deal with problems. (RSE-S21)

Bearing in mind these results, students were able to acknowledge their improvement in skills related to decision-making and facing problematic situations. In this sense, they could relate them to language use, facing unexpected events, or using problem-solving skills in order to face the different situations that emerged in the lessons through CLIL.

Self-Esteem

Self-esteem dimension was the third most developed construct of effective personality according to pre-service teachers' responses (Table 10).

Table 10. Self-esteem results

Self-esteem	M (SD)	Median (IQ)
3. I feel very good about my physical appearance	3.29 (0.99)	3 (1)
7. There are many things about myself that I would like to change if I could	2.90 (1.02)	3 (1)
11. In general, I am satisfied with myself	3.85 (0.85)	4 (1)
15. I accept myself as I am, with my qualities, limitations and defects	3.67 (1.10)	4 (2)
19. I have many qualities to be proud and satisfied with myself	4.13 (0.73)	4 (1)
23. I almost make everything work well	3.71 (0.71)	4 (1)
26. I believe that I am a valuable person for others	3.98 (0.73)	4 (0)
29. I think I have the talent to make things work	3.88 (0.76)	4 (1)
Total	3.26 (0.46)	3.25 (0.50)

Source: self-elaborated by the authors.

Specifically, pre-service teachers highly value the many personal qualities they can feel proud of (item 19) and they consider themselves to be a valuable person for other people (item 26). In addition, the least valued item (7) refers to the things about themselves they would like to change. Therefore, most of the participants would not change many of their characteristics. Regarding qualitative findings, the majority of the pre-service teachers consider that their self-esteem has increased due to their participation in the

Physical Education subject. In particular, they highlight an improvement in terms of English language and their teaching skills. As some of them put it:

When you are speaking a foreign language and you see that people try to understand what you are trying to say and they do not judge you because of your pronunciation or your level, you feel gratified and happy, which leads to an improvement of self-esteem. (SE-S21)

It (the subject) has helped me to be more confident in my conflict resolution skills. It has also improved my self-esteem as I feel that I am becoming more capable of speaking in public without panicking or getting too stuck. Moreover, doing it in English has also given me the opportunity to improve my fluency in this language, which gives me more self-confidence. (SE-S30)

(This subject has helped me) By improving my self-esteem at the time of leading the way and creating sessions and content. (SE-S35)

Considering the results found related to the dimension of self-esteem, students stressed that in the Physical Education subject through CLIL their efforts when using a language they did not master were being considered. In addition, they also mention that their self-confidence increased in terms of teaching skills considering both the content itself as well as language. Therefore, it seems that students were able to increase these areas as well as strengthen them.

Social Self-Realization

Finally, we present the social self-realization dimension. According to the participant pre-service teachers, this was the least relevant of the four dimensions from a general perspective (Table 11).

Table 11. Social self-realization results

Social self-realization	M (SD)	Median (IQ)
2. I have few friends because it takes me a while to deal with others	1.81 (1.02)	1.5 (1)
6. I make friends easily	3.96 (0.92)	4 (2)
10. My failures in relationships with others are due to my lack of ability to make friends	1.77 (1.08)	1 (1)
14. I believe that, knowing myself as I am, I will have problems in my relationships with others	1.07 (0.7)	2 (1)
18. I believe, for sure, that I will succeed in my relationships with others	3.77 (0.88)	4 (1)
22. My success in relationships with others are due to my ability to make friends	3.75 (0.96)	4 (1)
25. My success in relationships with others come as a result of the fact that they take the initiative	2.65 (0.98)	2.5 (1)
28. I think my failure in relationships with others are because most people do not like me	1.85 (0.95)	2 (1)
30. I feel comfortable sharing things with other people	4.35 (0.79)	5 (1)
Total	3.25 (0.25)	3.22 (0.22)

Source: self-elaborated by the authors.

Teaching Physical Education Through English

Although pre-service teachers tend to feel comfortable sharing things with others (item 30), there are items with very low scores (items 14 and 28), which are related to problematic relationships. This means that pre-service teachers consider their social relationships to be good. Qualitative findings, in fact, show that the majority of the participants stress that applying CLIL let them establish tighter bonds between national and international students that would have not been achieved if they had not been required to speak in English in the lessons. The following quotes display the ideas shared by three participants:

In this case, it has also helped me to have a greater capacity and ability to communicate with the Erasmus students and to relate more with them. (SSR-S30)

I think that it has encouraged me to participate and to feel very comfortable with the Erasmus people. (SSR-S31)

Especially as an Erasmus student, it helped me to find Spanish speaking friends. I learned a lot in this subject and I am glad that I went to Valencia. (SSR-S23)

According to these qualitative results, students were able to identify some aspects related to social self-realization that they could develop such as communication, empathy and assertiveness skills. In this sense, they acknowledged that the Physical Education subject through CLIL triggered them to interact more with other classmates, to participate more in the lessons and therefore, it encouraged building relationships among classmates, even between national and foreign students.

DISCUSSION

The development of skills linked to effective personality has become one of the most important missions for higher education in the 21st century (Chiva-Bartoll et al., 2019). As a result, the aim of this study was to examine how the effective personality of pre-service teachers' participating in the bilingual Physical Education course could be influenced by engaging in a learning-practice-approach to CLIL. A mixed methods approach was used, and results lead us to suggest that the experience came with some benefits related to effective personality development. These positive outcomes are aligned with previous investigations in the teacher education area, when active methodologies such as Service-Learning are applied (Chiva-Bartoll et al., 2020; Chiva-Bartoll et al., 2019; Chiva-Bartoll et al., 2018).

Regarding the different constructs that compose effective personality, our quantitative results show that these were developed at differing levels. However, the unequal development of these constructs has also been reported in previous studies (Chiva-Bartoll et al., 2020). In our case, academic self-realization and resolute self-efficacy were the most developed, in accordance with the results of Chiva-Bartoll et al. (2018). Qualitative findings, though, let us better understand why (or why not) the four constructs were promoted according to the participant pre-service teachers.

Academic self-realization is often times related to motivation on the part of students. In this study, this motivation could be related to the fact that pre-service teachers acknowledged an improvement in terms of language and teaching skills. In this sense, Kao (2020) examined the effect of a CLIL module in a Taiwanese teacher education program, concluding that it was instrumental to boost learners' motivation and L2 learning, among other aspects. Furthermore, authors such as Banegas and del Pozo (2022) assert that CLIL may contribute to learning both curricular content and an additional language while increasing pre-service teachers' motivation. This is relevant because pre-service teachers may identify target language proficiency and language awareness as a barrier when using CLIL (Lo, 2020).

Regarding resolute self-efficacy, some of the participant pre-service teachers highlighted that, thanks to the experience, they were able to learn and make proper decisions related to both teaching skills and language use. In a similar vein, Otwinowska and Foryś (2017) consider CLIL to be an approach in which learners develop linguistic competence and problem-solving abilities. These abilities are essential for future teachers, even more if they are to apply CLIL with their own students, since they will have to use the target language properly and cope with a number of pedagogical issues and the continuous constraints that the teaching-learning process comes with. Therefore, increasing their perceived self-efficacy might be useful to overcome possible barriers that pre-service teachers may encounter to using CLIL (Lo, 2020).

Several pre-service teachers considered that participating in the Physical Education subject through CLIL had boosted their self-esteem regarding both English language and teaching skills. Similar results were found by Kossybayeva et al. (2022), although their study used CLIL in distance education through ICT. Anyway, they assert that students' self-esteem was promoted as they improved their perception of learning and themselves. However, Cortina and Pino (2021) warn that, despite a subject being taught according to a CLIL approach, pre-service teachers might not yet feel prepared to become CLIL practitioners. Therefore, continuous support seems to be necessary at the intersection of theoretical knowledge and implementation (Banegas & del Pozo, 2022).

Finally, social self-realization, which refers to communication, assertiveness and empathy, seems to be the least developed construct according to quantitative results. This finding is similar to that of Chiva-Bartoll et al. (2018) and could be related to the fact that pre-service teachers may need to contextualize their answers and directly relate them to their experiences. Consequently, from a qualitative perspective, participants still were able to identify how this construct was promoted. In this vein, some of them acknowledged that using CLIL let them establish bonds between national and international students which, at the same time, helped them to improve spoken interaction and fluency (Pérez-Cañado & Lancaster, 2017).

All in all, the learning-practice approach to CLIL seems to have been instrumental for pre-service teachers to develop their effective personality by promoting their language and teaching skills from a 'learning by doing' perspective (Dewey, 1938). In this vein, Klein et al. (2013) assert that pre-service teachers need to be offered ongoing, recursive experiences that more tightly connect learning and practice; and the approach used in the Physical Education subject presented in this text seems to have been helpful in this sense. Learning ideas and practicing them are not separate activities. Learning is bound up in practice (Strom, 2015), therefore being able to put learning into practice and reflect upon what they did, how they did it, when they did it or why they it will shape the way they become teachers. A teacher is a multiplicity themselves (encompassing background experiences, previous learning, beliefs and attitudes, etc.) (Strom & Viesca, 2021); therefore, all the experiences they live related to teaching and learning will inevitably influence and shape their teacher identities when applying CLIL. In other words, if pre-service teachers engage in a learning-practice approach to CLIL as students, two main benefits may be identified: (1) they may see their language and teaching skills improved, and (2) they may better understand what their future students will feel when they apply CLIL as teachers.

CONCLUSION

The results of our study allow us to conclude that using the CLIL approach in Didactics of Physical Education subject may come with a positive influence on the effective personality of the students. In this sense, through the mixed methods approach used, pre-service teachers reported that their most notable improvement in the dimensions referred to self-realization and self-efficacy. These results were closely related to motivation towards the integrated learning of Didactics of Physical Education and an additional language through a learning-practice approach to CLIL. Likewise, social self-realization is the dimension that improves to a lesser extent from a quantitative perspective. For this reason, more studies that examine in depth this dimension are required.

FUTURE IMPLICATIONS

Bearing in mind the experience of the three academic years in which this subject has been applied through a learning-practice approach to CLIL and the results derived from this study, there are some practical implications that teachers could consider in order to foster the effective personality of pre-service teachers. In other words, informed by the results obtained, the chapter finishes by sharing some clues on how to foster effective personality and its four basic dimensions through CLIL teacher training to help lecturers design and develop proper CLIL teacher development activities (Contero et al., 2018):

- To promote Social Self-realization a learning practice approach to CLIL may be really useful, since CLIL is tightly connected to culture. As the results of our study suggest, CLIL enabled national and international students to be closer. Therefore, emphasizing the cultural aspect in CLIL teacher training may be instrumental to increase cultural awareness of future teachers regarding not only their peers, but also better understanding their future international students.
- To promote Academic Self-Realization, one should remember that CLIL is based on a specific content. In the case of the example shared in the present chapter, it dealt with didactics of Physical Education. Therefore, in this specific context, educators may consider combining CLIL with other active pedagogical models, since they are also part of the curricular elements to be learned. Through a learning-practice approach, pre-service teachers will be able to perceive the entanglements between different pedagogical approaches (including CLIL), how synergies may be created between them and thus, better understand how they work; which is critical if they are to apply them in their future teaching practices.
- To promote Self-esteem it is important to build a safe atmosphere in the lessons so that pre-service teachers boost their confidence regarding their teaching and language skills. In this sense, for example, pre-service teachers may create a guide with specific vocabulary to use in the lessons. This may have a two-fold objective. On the one hand, this reflection upon language will help perceive the connection among the contents, cognitive skills needed and communication that are to be tackled in the lesson. Therefore, they will feel more secure and better understand the basics of the session they are to implement. On the other hand, it may serve as a scaffolding tool, thus facilitating language use for both pre-service teachers acting as teachers and those acting as students.
- Finally, to promote Resolute Self-Efficacy CLIL teacher training may encourage pre-service teachers' involvement in the observation process. In this sense, a possibility may be using 'lesson

study' (Banegas & Hemmi, 2021). This may help develop the ability to plan, design, reflect and improve the sessions, based on the constructive dialogue that it establishes. The results of our study suggest that this shared discussion may be useful for pre-service teachers to see themselves as more capable to apply CLIL successfully and raise their confidence towards using this pedagogical approach in their future teaching practices.

ACKNOWLEDGMENT

This research was supported by the University of Valencia [grant number UV-SFPIE_PID-1638998] and the Generalitat Valenciana, Conselleria d'Innovació, Universitats, Ciència i Societat Digital [grant number CIGE/2021/019]. Also, projects: CIGE/2021/019 and UV-SFPIE_PID-2076400.

REFERENCES

Álvarez Rojo, V., Romero Rodríguez, S., Gil Flores, J., Rodríguez Santero, J., Clares López, J., Asensio Muñoz, I. I., & Salmerón Vílchez, P. (2011). *Necesidades de formación del profesorado universitario para la adaptación de su docencia al Espacio Europeo de Educación Superior (EEES)* [Training needs of university teachers for the adaptation of their teaching to the European Higher Education Area (EHEA).]. Revista Electrónica de Investigación y Evaluación Educativa [Electronic Journal of Educational Research and Evaluation].

Banegas, D. L., & del Pozo Beamud, M. (2022). Content and language integrated learning: A duoethnographic study about CLIL pre-service teacher education in Argentina and Spain. *RELC Journal, 53*(1), 151–164. doi:10.1177/0033688220930442

Banegas, D. L., & Hemmi, C. (2021). CLIL: Present and Future. In International Perspectives on CLIL (pp. 281-295). Palgrave Macmillan.

Calvo-Bernardino, A., & Mingorance-Arnáiz, A. C. (2009). La estrategia de las universidades frente al Espacio Europeo de Educación Superior. [The strategy of universities against the European Higher Education Area.]. *Revista Complutense de Educación, 20*(2), 319–342.

Chiva-Bartoll, O., Baena-Extremera, A., Hortiguela-Alcalá, D., & Ruiz-Montero, P. J. (2020). Contributions of service-learning on PETE Students' effective personality: A mixed methods research. *International Journal of Environmental Research and Public Health, 17*(23), 8756. doi:10.3390/ijerph17238756 PMID:33255718

Chiva-Bartoll, Ó., Gil-Gómez, J., & Zorrilla-Silvestre, L. (2019). Improving the effective personality of pre-service teachers through service-learning: A physical education approach. *Revista de Investigación Educacional, 37*(2), 327–343. doi:10.6018/rie.37.2.303331

Chiva-Bartoll, O., Pallarés-Piquer, M., & Gil-Gómez, J. (2018). Aprendizaje-servicio y mejora de la Personalidad Eficaz en futuros docentes de Educación Física. [Service-learning and improvement of the Effective Personality in future teachers of Physical Education.]. *Revista Complutense de Educación*, *29*(1), 181–197. doi:10.5209/RCED.52164

Contero, C., Zayas, F., & Tirado, J. L. (2018). Addressing CLIL lecturers' needs: reflections on specific methodological training. *Porta Linguarum: Revista internacional de didáctica de las lenguas extranjeras [Porta Linguarum: International magazine on the teaching of foreign languages]*, (3), 121-135. doi:10.30827/Digibug.54305

Cortina-Pérez, B., & Pino Rodríguez, A. M. (2021). Analysing CLIL teacher competences in pre-service preschool education. A case study at the University of Granada. *European Journal of Teacher Education*, 1–19. doi:10.1080/02619768.2021.1890021

Coyle, D., Hood, P., & Marsh, D. (2010). CLIL. Cambridge.

Creswell, J. W., & Clark, V. L. P. (2017). *Designing and conducting mixed methods research*. Sage publications.

Custodio Espinar, M. (2019). CLIL teacher education in Spain. In *Content and language integrated learning in Spanish and Japanese contexts* (pp. 313–337). Palgrave Macmillan. doi:10.1007/978-3-030-27443-6_13

Del Buey, F. D. A. M., Zapico, A. F., Palacio, E. M., Pellerano, B. D., Trigo, R. M., & Urban, P. G. (2008). Cuestionario de personalidad eficaz para la formación profesional. *Psicothema*, *20*(2), 224–228. PMID:18413082

Denzin, N. K. (2017). *The research act: A theoretical introduction to sociological methods*. Routledge. doi:10.4324/9781315134543

Dewey, J. (1938). *Experience and education*. Macmillan.

Ekolu, S. O., & Quainoo, H. (2019). Reliability of assessments in engineering education using Cronbach's alpha, KR, and split-half methods. *Global journal of engineering education, 21*(1), 24-29.

Estrada, J. L., & Otto, A. (2019). Timing of pedagogical intervention: Oral error treatment in EFL vs. CLIL contexts in primary education in Spain. *Journal of Language and Linguistic Studies*, *15*(2), 578–586. doi:10.17263/jlls.586263

Fueyo-Gutiérrez, E. F., Palacio, M. E. M., & Pellerano, B. D. (2010). Personalidad eficaz y rendimiento académico: Una aproximación integrada. [Effective personality and academic performance: an integrated approach.]. *Revista de Orientación Educacional*, *24*(46), 57–70.

Gómez, R. (2012). *Evaluación de la personalidad eficaz en población universitaria. [Evaluation of the effective personality in university population.]* [Doctoral Thesis, Universidad de Huelva].

Hamodi, C., López Pastor, V. M., & López Pastor, A. T. (2015). Medios, técnicas e instrumentos de evaluación formativa y compartida del aprendizaje en educación superior. [Means, techniques and instruments of formative and shared assessment of learning in higher education.]. *Perfiles Educativos*, *37*(147), 146–161. doi:10.22201/iisue.24486167e.2015.147.47271

Kao, Y. T. (2022). Understanding and addressing the challenges of teaching an online CLIL course: A teacher education study. *International Journal of Bilingual Education and Bilingualism, 25*(2), 656–675. doi:10.1080/13670050.2020.1713723

Kihara, S., Jess, M., McMillan, P., Osedo, K., Kubo, K., & Nakanishi, H. (2021). The potential of Lesson Study in primary physical education: Messages from a longitudinal study in Japan. *European Physical Education Review, 27*(2), 223–239. doi:10.1177/1356336X20932950

Klein, E. J., Taylor, M., Onore, C., Strom, K., & Abrams, L. (2013). Finding a third space in teacher education: Creating an urban teacher residency. *Teaching Education, 24*(1), 27–57. doi:10.1080/1047 6210.2012.711305

Kossybayeva, U., Shaldykova, B., Akhmanova, D., & Kulanina, S. (2022). Improving teaching in different disciplines of natural science and mathematics with innovative technologies. *Education and Information Technologies, 27*(6), 1–23. doi:10.100710639-022-10955-3 PMID:35233175

Lewis, C., Perry, R., & Hurd, J. (2004). A deeper look at lesson study. *Educational Leadership, 61*(5), 18–22.

Lewis, C., & Tsuchida, I. (1998). The basics in Japan: The 3 C's. *Educational Leadership, 55*(6), 32–37.

Lo, Y. (2020). *Professional Development of CLIL Teachers*. Springer. doi:10.1007/978-981-15-2425-7

López-Pastor, V. M. (2011). Best practices in academic assessment in higher education: A Case in formative and shared assessment. *Journal of Technology and Science Education, 1*(2), 25–39.

Martín del Buey, F., Granados, P.; Martín, Mª E., Juárez, A., García, A. & Álvarez, M. (2000). *Desarrollo de la Personalidad Eficaz en Contextos Educativos.* [*Effective Personality Development in Educational Contexts.*] Marco Conceptual. FMB.

McMillan, P., & Jess, M. (2021). Embracing complex adaptive practice: The potential of lesson study. *Professional Development in Education, 47*(2-3), 273–288. doi:10.1080/19415257.2021.1884588

Meyer, O. (2010). Introducing the CLIL-pyramid: Key strategies and principles for quality CLIL planning and teaching. *Basic issues in EFL-teaching and learning*, 11-29.

Otwinowska, A., & Foryś, M. (2017). They learn the CLIL way, but do they like it? Affectivity and cognition in upper-primary CLIL classes. *International Journal of Bilingual Education and Bilingualism, 20*(5), 457–480. doi:10.1080/13670050.2015.1051944

Patton, M. Q. (2002). Two decades of developments in qualitative inquiry: A personal, experiential perspective. *Qualitative Social Work: Research and Practice, 1*(3), 261–283. doi:10.1177/1473325002001003636

Pérez Cañado, M. L. (2016). Teacher training needs for bilingual education: In-service teacher perceptions. *International Journal of Bilingual Education and Bilingualism, 19*(3), 266–295. doi:10.1080/13 670050.2014.980778

Pérez Cañado, M. L., & Lancaster, N. K. (2017). The effects of CLIL on oral comprehension and production: A longitudinal case study. *Language, Culture and Curriculum, 30*(3), 300–316. doi:10.1080/ 07908318.2017.1338717

Pizarro Ruiz, J. P., Raya, J. J., Castellanos, S., & Ordóñez, N. (2014). La personalidad eficaz como factor protector frente al Burnout. [Effective personality as a protective factor against Burnout.] *Revista Iberoamericana de educación*, *66*, 143-158.

Plano-Clark, V. L. (2019). Meaningful integration within mixed methods studies: Identifying why, what, when, and how. *Contemporary Educational Psychology*, *57*, 106–111. doi:10.1016/j.cedpsych.2019.01.007

Ross, J. A. (2006). The reliability, validity, and utility of self-assessment. *Practical Assessment, Research & Evaluation*, *11*(1), 10. doi:10.7275/9wph-vv65

Strom, K. J. (2015). Teaching as assemblage: Negotiating learning and practice in the first year of teaching. *Journal of Teacher Education*, *66*(4), 321–333. doi:10.1177/0022487115589990

Strom, K. J., & Martin, A. D. (2017). *Becoming-teacher: a rhizomatic look at first-year teaching*. Springer. doi:10.1007/978-94-6300-872-3

Strom, K. J., & Viesca, K. M. (2021). Towards a complex framework of teacher learning-practice. *Professional Development in Education*, *47*(2-3), 209–224. doi:10.1080/19415257.2020.1827449

Topping, K. J. (2009). Peer assessment. *Theory into Practice*, *48*(1), 20–27. doi:10.1080/00405840802577569

Villabona, N., & Cenoz, J. (2022). The integration of content and language in CLIL: A challenge for content-driven and language-driven teachers. *Language, Culture and Curriculum*, *35*(1), 36–50. doi:10.1080/07908318.2021.1910703

Wilson, M. (2002). Six views of embodied cognition. *Psychonomic Bulletin & Review*, *9*(4), 625–636. doi:10.3758/BF03196322 PMID:12613670

Yin, R. (2003). *Case study research*. Sage Publications.

KEY TERMS AND DEFINITIONS

Input: A message (oral or written) received by the students.
Lesson study: A process through which both students and teachers analyze and discuss the elements and procedures of a specific teaching practice.
Output: A message (oral or written) produced by the students.
Peer assessment: An evaluation among equals of the teaching practice.
Self-efficacy: A student's capacity to perform successfully a given task.
Self-esteem: A concept related to the students' perception of themselves.
Self-realization: A concept related to the sense of developing one's potentials.
Social self-realization: A sense of realization with others.

Section 3

Innovative Techniques, Resources, and Materials for Bilingual Teaching in Primary School Contexts

Chapter 12

CLIL:
Towards a Transdisciplinary and Literacy–Focused Approach to Language–Learning

Y. L. Teresa Ting
iD https://orcid.org/0000-0003-2901-8194
The University of Calabria, Italy

ABSTRACT

By integrating content and language learning-objectives, one gains a transdisciplinary literacy-focused perspective that brings into focus the thinking skills, literacies, and soft skills that all children need to succeed. This proposition is grounded in two sets of CLIL-materials. For preschoolers, this transdisciplinary literacy-focused perspective transformed must-learn vocabulary and grammar into tasks for cultivating early numeracy, logical thinking, and self-regulatory behaviours. For primary-level learners, this approach recognized the cognitive maturity and reasoning abilities of 8-year-olds: age-appropriate disciplinary concepts regarding natural history were presented through materials using age-matched academic language, thus providing children whole complex discourses for thinking whole complex thoughts. To help readers incorporate such a perspective into their own practice, a workshop format presents some cognitive-neuroscience principles guiding the development of these materials alongside specific design considerations, implementation processes, and classroom observations.

INTRODUCTION

In a call for a special issue regarding "Teaching English to Young Learners", *English Language Teaching Journal* (ELTJ: 2013) stated: "As both parents and educational authorities seek to increase young learners' English language skills, we cannot assume that an earlier start to learning English is automatically better." Indeed, although most of the incoming students at the local university in Italy where I teach have had at least eight, if not 12, years of EFL-instruction, the majority reach an underwhelming B1-lower (Tucci, 2019). This reflects the fact that Italy, with its strong dubbing industry, is among the least multilingual countries in Europe (Eurobarometer, 2012). To this, we can add that the national primary-level EFL-curriculum does not get learners off to a good start: rather than encouraging a "naturalistic whole

DOI: 10.4018/978-1-6684-6179-2.ch012

Copyright © 2023, IGI Global. Copying or distributing in print or electronic forms without written permission of IGI Global is prohibited.

language" approach to learning English, the curriculum (1) emphasizes "vocabulary-lists" of everyday items for many years and (2) delineates a "grammar-sequence" which restrains children's communicative range to very simple-minded exchanges (details below). The upward-cascade is that our University Language Centre must organize intensive "70-hour refresher courses" to help incoming students move from A2 to B1 in preparation for more discipline-relevant EFL coursework offered in students' chosen departments. Not surprisingly, to date, no short-term refresher course has been able to recuperate years of what should have been learnt better. The result is that students may not get the most from discipline-relevant tertiary-level EFL coursework and many struggle to achieve certified intermediate/B2-level EFL-competence required by today's international job market (e.g. Cambridge English, 2016).

More concerning might be the fact that incoming students who do have B1-Level EFL competence, if not even B2 and C1, are usually from families with resources for securing private extracurricular EFL-tuition plus short-term summer-abroad programmes, etc. English, being a *lingua franca,* has turned EFL into a lucrative business which, in turn, risks turning "English" into a "divisive-factor" that further differentiates the *haves* from the *have-nots* (Bruton, 2013; Dioz, Lasagabaster and Sierra, 2014). In addition, given its position as today's *lingua franca*, English is increasingly being mainstreamed to "do schooling" in non-Anglophone realities (Macaro, 2018). Experts in tertiary-level English Medium Instruction (EMI) equate EMI to "an unstoppable train which has already left the station" (see Hultgren & Lasagabaster, 2019, p. 232). The same might be said about the EFL-Train for young learners: it too has left the station. However, on this train of young learners, there is a very serious concern: while some children are comfortably seated, others are hanging on, if not limping behind this train. This chapter suggests that, although some passengers will continue to sit comfortably from the start, we who teach English must be cognizant of the hegemonic position of English: If almost all children in non-Anglophone countries are "learning English", we in EFL-instruction are in the position to "optimize English" so that our lessons contribute to reducing existent socio-economic and cultural gaps (Rowe 2012; Bakken & Brevik 2022). One way forward is for EFL teacher-training to help aspiring teachers move beyond "English as subject" to see "English as opportunity", showing future teachers how "learning English" can become moments to *also* cultivate age-appropriate academic literacies, critical-thinking abilities, logical-reasoning, soft-skills, etc., that *all* children need to succeed in school today, and in society tomorrow (OECD, 2018).

The notion that *Foreign Language*-instruction can be optimized so to also learn something else, such as *Content*, is of course the premise of CLIL (Coyle, Hood & Marsh, 2010). Since its inception in the early 1990s, CLIL has garnered immense interest, especially from the perspective of second and foreign language learning and acquisition, generating an immense body of theories, materials and classroom research which delineate both the challenges as well as potentials of CLIL, particularly with regard to lexical range, accuracy, form and fluency (Llinares, Morton & Whittaker 2012; Dalton-Puffer 2008; Ruiz de Zarobe 2011; Perez-Vidal & Roquet 2015). See also and Suggested Readings at the end of this chapter for thorough reviews and discussions regarding CLIL/bilingual teacher-education and the potential of early CLIL from the stance of language instruction and learning theories in early ages.

This chapter wishes to discuss the immense potential of early CLIL from two different but complementary perspectives which together might guide us towards more effectively designed early CLIL-instruction which go beyond language-learning. The first perspective is founded upon established notions from cognitive neuroscience research while the second perspective regards transdisciplinary and literacy-focused instruction. However, to render this information concrete, useful and usable for early CLIL/bilingual teacher-development, these perspectives are presented through CLIL-instructional-materials. This creates a "virtual teacher-training workshop" within which we can understand, step-by-step, what

CLIL

a transdisciplinary, literacy-focused approach to early bilingual education might look like in practice, and also identify, analyse and reflect upon the neurocognitive processes needed to work through these materials. Classroom observations from our own experiences using these materials are also included to help readers "participate" in the reflection process and consider how such CLIL-instruction might be adopted and adapted to their own contexts.

Section 1 commences with a brief look at *Learning*, the last but most important construct in the CLIL acronym and discusses limitations facing young brains "doing CLIL". Section 2 presents instructional materials for preschoolers, illustrating how the simple objective of "teaching English words" can easily be up-scaled into tasks for nurturing early numeracy skills, logical reasoning and even cultivating self-efficacy behaviours. In Section 3, instructional materials developed to teach 8-year-old Italian children notions of Natural Sciences will illustrate how bilingual-instruction can provide the context for developing age-appropriate disciplinary literacy and thinking skills, while using complex age-appropriate academic English.

Contextualizing *Learning* from the perspective of "cognitive science research" reflects my own training in neuroscience and my belief that, since teachers teach to brains, there are some notions from the field of cognitive neuroscience that all teachers should be familiar with and keep in mind while designing instruction and "doing teaching" (see also Roussel, Joulia, Tricot & Sweller, 2017). Some of these principles were used to develop CLIL-materials which have received, or been nominated for, international awards for innovative EFL-learning materials (Ting, 2013; Ting, Stillo and Barci, 2022) and guided the design of CLIL-materials presented in Sections 2 and 3. In particular, this chapter discusses the notions of *working memory*, *attentional flow through problem-solving* and the *haptics of writing*. The principles of *working memory* and *attention through problem-solving* were deployed in both sets of materials and are therefore discussed in Section 1 and, where relevant, highlighted in brackets in Sections 2 and 3. Cognitive processes underlying the *haptics of writing* and how this can be harnessed to support learning is illustrated in Section 3, contextualized within CLIL-materials for 8-year-olds. By linking these neuroscience notions to analyses of the CLIL-materials and our classroom observations, we hope aspiring teachers can "virtually participate in the learning" and thus understand how materials might be designed to optimize cognitive processes which are conducive to learning.

As already stated, the purpose of presenting the materials in Sections 2 and 3 is to create a context for analysing the pedagogic and didactic strategies behind the CLIL-tasks and learning processes so that aspiring teachers also learn to "critically observe learning" and hopefully "plan for learning." Subsections entitled *"The process: observations and instructions for use"* contribute to this by describing how the materials were implemented, reporting classroom observations of children working with the materials, and providing a few suggestions regarding materials-design, should readers wish to create similar materials or adopt and adapt these to their own instructional contexts. It should be noted that, although these CLIL-materials were developed for the highly monolingual context in southern Italy and regard English foreign language instruction, they can easily be adapted for different contents and contexts, and for other target FL situations. Finally, it should be clear that the use of instructional-materials does not intend to suggest that teachers should become materials developers, which is a profession in its own right. The materials are intended to provide readers a concrete context for *seeing theories at work*. We hope aspiring teachers can then use the notions discussed here to evaluate commercial materials and/or adapt them for their own "transdisciplinary and literacy-focused" initiatives. The final Conclusions, together with the Conclusions at the end of Sections 2 and 3, summarize and suggest ways forward.

CLIL

SECTION 1. *LEARNING* IN YOUNG BRAINS: LIMITATIONS AND A "SIMPLE" SOLUTION

Any attempt to link "education" to "the brain" must be read critically:

Since teachers teach to brains, teacher-training should offer aspiring teachers some basic notions regarding how the brain processes information, or not. Not doing so is akin to training epidemiologists to recognize symptoms and treat infectious diseases without understanding basic notions about how the immune system works. That said, we must guard against the "seductive allure of neuroscience" (Skolnick Weisberg, Keil, Goodstein, Rawson & Gray, 2008) and "neuromyths" (Della Sala, 2009) which reduce the immense complexity of "learning" into one-liner-panacea, leading well-meaning teachers astray by drawing "this-means-that arrows" between reproducible research undertaken in well-controlled laboratory conditions, and irreproducible classrooms where no two learners are alike (Ting, forthcoming).

With that forewarning, it is undeniable that the education enterprise and our teaching profession are based on the fact that our brain not only *can*, but actually *enjoys* paying attention, being challenged, understanding novelty, and thus learning (Smith, 1976; Csikszentmihalyi, 2011). In fact, our long-term-memory seems to have an infinite capacity for storing a versatile array of information and thanks to stored knowledge, we can make sense of most incoming-information (Sweller, 1998; Ericsson and Kintsch, 1995; Cowan, 2008), even if it is non-sense, as illustrated in Figure 1.

Figure 1. This orphaned meme, although of dubious verity (Davis), nonetheless clearly demonstrates our ability to use stored knowledge to quickly process and make sense of input, even if it is non-sense

Aoccdrnig to rscheearch at Cmabrigde uinervtisy, it deosn't mttaer waht oredr the ltteers in a wrod are, the olny iprmoentnt tihing is taht the frist and lsat ltteres are at the rghit pclae. The rset can be a tatol mses and you can sitll raed it wouthit a porbelm. Tihs is bcuseae we do not raed ervey lteter by itslef but the wrod as a wlohe.

Figure 1 illustrates how our brain comprehends incoming information through an "inside-out" process, using what we already know (inside) to make sense of input from the outside. However, what if our brains have little by way of stored-information inside because we, being children, have had only very limited "life-experiences" which have made enough sense to have become stored knowledge? To understand this limitation for young brains in concrete terms, we might consider an example from EFL-instruction for young learners, the word "*pineapple*". Listed as a "should-know" word for A2-level English certification (Cambridge, 2018), this tropical fruit is certainly not a daily occurrence in the life of children living in Italy. Since local Italian foods and produce are so infamously good, imported pineapples might appear as an extravagance around Christmas time, which means that many Italian preschoolers might not be able to rely on well-consolidated knowledge of *ananas* as conceptual-scaffold towards the English word *pineapple*. As such, for young Italian learners of English, even a simple word as "*pineapple*" becomes not only new *Language*, but also new and rather unfamiliar "object/*Concept*". Therefore, while adults can harness stored knowledge to quickly process and make sense of most incoming information, even

262

non-sense related to "Cmabrigde uinervtisy rscheearch", young children are working with a more limited database of stored information.

In addition, what if, before being stored in long-term-memory, all incoming information must first be processed through our working memory, and what if the working memory of young children is still under construction? (Bjorklund & Pellegrini, 2000). Box 1 describes a scenario to help readers appreciate the limits of working memory in adults' brains. Basically, contrary to the infinite capacity of long-term-memory, working memory can only process approximately 4-6 pieces of new information at any one time, i.e., working memory is *limited in capacity*. In addition, working memory can only "keep in mind" new information for approximately 20 seconds, i.e., it is *limited in duration*. Add to this the fact that working memory is also easily disrupted, i.e., *volatile,* so that new incoming-information easy distracts us, overriding whatever progress we have made with processing preceding pieces of information (Smith, 1976; Miller, 1956; Cowan, 2008). Such limitations of working memory limit the quantity of information passing into long-term-memory (Figure 2).

Figure 2. All input passes through working memory. While long-term memory has infinite storage capacity, working memory is limited in capacity and duration, and is also highly volatile, resulting in only a relatively small amount of information passing through working memory into long term memory

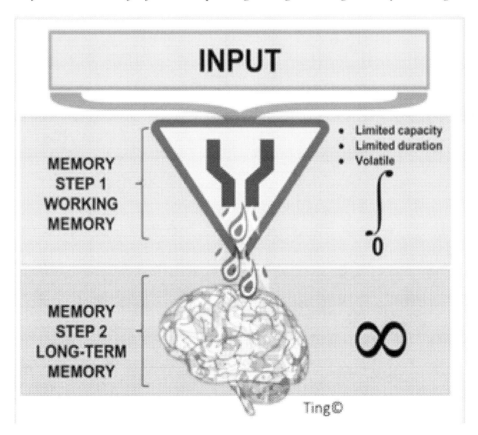

Therefore, while we teachers hope that students assimilate most, if not all, of our instruction into their long-term memory, working memory, and its limitations, stands between our instruction and long-term-memory. Like it or not, working memory is in the brain we have and in the brain that our learners bring to their learning. In addition, those in early CLIL/bilingual instruction should note that, the younger our learners, the "weaker" their working memory is (Ferguson, Brunsdon & Bradford, 2021). That said, anyone who has watched young children at play realize that, despite limited working memory and store of life-experiences with which to make sense of incoming-input, children can pay attention for a significant amount of time, entering into what Csikszentmihalyi calls "flow" (2014). The notion of "flow" derives from Csikszentmihalyi's observations of artists who, once in the full attentional-state of flow could paint non-stop for days. Most of us have personally experienced and also observed "flow" that, although not lasting for days, is nonetheless intense and all-absorbing: from children (or ourselves) playing video games to surgeons at work to engineering students discussing their robot designs. The question for aspiring bilingual teachers is "how can we design CLIL/bilingual instruction so as to draw young learners into flow" so that they attend to the language we want them to learn for a long enough amount of time to hopefully learn it, i.e., form new long-term memories. And, in light of literacy-development, can we also design the tasks so that, whilst "in flow with the language", children also acquire discipline-relevant skills?

One of the key ingredients for luring individuals into a sustained state of flow is engagement with "challenging but solvable problems" (Ulrich, Keller, Hoenig, Waller & Grön, 2014). The pleasure gained from "solving solvable problems" is probably what keeps video-gamers gaming, surgeons operating, engineering students negotiating, and why the Sudoku and crossword puzzle industry remains popular, even among busy individuals. Indeed, researchers monitoring brain activity of volunteers "solving problems" noted that "Aha-moments" were associated with increased activity in brain dopaminergic circuitry (Tic et al., 2018), suggesting that this may explain the pleasure state incurred when solving Sudokus and crossword puzzles. Monitoring pupil-diameter in the eyes of volunteers, Kahneman (2011), observed that, when volunteers were presented with solvable math problems, volunteers not only entered a heightened attentional state, but their pupils also increased in diameter. Upon finding solutions, i.e., the "Aha-moment", pupil diameters increased slightly more before resuming normal size. However, as the math problems became too difficult, "pupils stopped dilating, or actually shrank" (*ibid*: 33).

The question for aspiring teachers is therefore, "if the brain enjoys solving challenging-but-solvable problems, can we design instruction that harnesses this?" (Ting, *forthcoming*). Sections 2 and 3 will illustrate how "solving challenging but solvable problems" was a key ingredient for creating CLIL-materials which transform "learning English" into one which also cultivates thinking skills, soft-skills and age-appropriate discipline-specific literacies.

SECTION 2. DISCIPLINARY LITERACY WITH PRE-SCHOOLERS: "PINEAPPLE PLEASE!"

Age-group: 4-5 years of age.

CLIL strategy: Explicit focus on new vocabulary supports implicit cognitive focus on logical sequences and patterns.

Language Learning: vocabulary; formation of plurals; pronunciation of plurals ('s', 'z'); preliminary "reading".

Competences, Cognition & Soft-skills: logical deduction & sequence and pattern-recognition; training working memory; following social rules; reinforcing self-regulatory behaviours.

CLIL

Preschoolers: Specific Issues to Overcome

Among the numerous challenges facing FL-instruction in preschoolers, six are particularly relevant to the design of the materials presented below: the challenges of limited quantity, restricted modality, incompletely crystallized L1, weak working memory, lack of life-experiences, and lack of schooling-experience.

In many pre-school kindergarten contexts around the world, "foreign language lessons" expose children to the target foreign language (tFL) for only a few hours per week, very different from the very constant and authentically purposeful language experience that characterizes children's learning of their mother tongue (L1). "*Limited Quantity*" is therefore Challenge Number 1. "*Restricted Modality*" is Challenge 2: Contrary to teaching older learners who can already read and write, teaching a FL to pre-literate children is challenged by that very fact, they don't yet read or write. As such, we can neither "show the language" through the receptive medium of *reading* nor can we consolidate preschoolers' learning of new language through *writing*. As such, receptive input for preschoolers relies on solely *aurality,* and productive output, which is essential for consolidating learning, can only mainly rely on *orality*.

The challenge posed as "incompletely crystalized L1" draws on Cummins' dual-iceberg analogy which suggests that extant language skills related to literacy and vocabulary as well as thinking skills in L1 support their formation in the tFL and maybe even vice-versa, i.e., thinking skills developed through a tFL can cultivate thinking processes in L1 (Cummins et al., 1984). An important challenge facing foreign language instruction with very young learners is that the most basic of tools for learning, "*an L1*", is rather underdeveloped: there is very little by way of even Cummins' metaphoric "L1-iceberg" upon which to form the tFL-iceberg. Since it is quite amazing how such helpless neonates have become children who can fluently express themselves in L1, it is easy to forget that, at such a young age, children are still honing their language-skills and consolidating linguistic-notions in L1: e.g. notions of *plurality, gender-agreement,* etc. In addition, L1-fluency is not founded on formalized instruction but reflects implicitly acquired functional fluency. Such "naturalness" is indeed the beauty of L1(s). However, when L1 is still "very much under construction" and not yet a "fully-formed and crystalized iceberg", as in the case of preschoolers, FL-instruction becomes more reliant on input that makes sense in and of itself, even in the absence of any equivalent on the underlying "L1-iceberg".

This challenge of "incompletely crystalized L1" ties in directly with two more challenges: the fact that children's "working memory" is still very much "under construction" (Ferguson et al., 2021) and that young children have limited "life-experiences and memories". As discussed in Section 1, working memory in adults is already challenged by being limited in both capacity and duration, plus being highly volatile, easily interrupted. Using age-appropriate Stroop tests, researchers have shown that the working memory of 4–5-year-olds is even more "limited" (Diamond, Kirkham & Amso, 2002; Richland, Morrison & Holyoak, 2006), maturing and reaching full average adult capacity around the age of 30 (Ferguson et al., 2021). As such, young working memories can only engage with and process a very limited amount of new information at any one moment. Add to this the fact that preschoolers have limited life-experiences and thus limited understandings already stored in their long-term-memories, during learning, their working memory may often have little by way of "already-known" to make sense of and understand incoming-unknowns: e.g. the example of "*pineapple*" discussed above. Finally, the last challenge is that preschoolers are *not yet schooled*. As such, classroom groupings and interactional strategies which work with older learners may not be effective for preschoolers.

Transdisciplinary, Literacy-focused CLIL-Materials at Preschool

We were tasked to design an intensive 12-hour English course which, through eight 90-minute lessons over two months, would teach a group of 18 kindergarten-aged children (1) approximately 40 words chosen from various "must know" lists for A2-level leaners (Cambridge, 2018: Table 1); (2) the concept of how English regular plurals are formed and (3) the '*s*', '*z*' and '*ez*' pronunciation of English regular plural nouns (Ting, 2010).

Table 1. List of English vocabulary and grammar words organized by category. Note that only words which are not L1-cognates are listed here: e.g., words such as "banana" and "kiwi" which are similar in Italian, the children's L1, were used but not shown here, as also "pizza" and "pasta"

Food items
- Strawberry
- Banana
- Pineapple
- Apple
- Orange
- Lemon
- Watermelon
- Egg
- Cake
- Bread

Parts of the body
- Eye
- Nose
- Head
- Hair
- Hand
- Knee
- Mouth
- Arm
- Leg

Clothes
- Shoe
- Boot
- Glove
- Shirt
- Skirt
- Sweater
- Pants
- Shorts
- Socks

Articulation:
- Shirt / Skirt
- Hat / Head
- Leg / Egg

Regular Plurals:
- eye / eyes (z)
- sock / socks (s)
- shoe / shoes (z)
- glove / gloves (z)
- orange /oranges (ez)

Given (1) the number of words to be learnt in a rather limited time, alongside the grammatical notion of regular plurals and their pronunciation; (2) the impossibility of providing preschoolers formal direct instruction such as "*regular English plurals can be pronounced in three different ways*"; plus (3) the fact that learning and consolidation at this age is limited to *aural* input and *oral* output, the challenge was to design instruction that would not only expose *all* children to maximum amounts of aural input, but also prompt *all* children to orally produce *all* words in *all* forms of plurality and at *a very high frequency* throughout a 90-min lesson. While teacher-directed instruction have been reported to be promising for young learners (Griva & Sivropoulou, 2009) and even older children (Nash & Snowling, 2006; Harme, Pianta, Downer, De Coster, Mashburn, Jones, Brown, Cappella, Atkins, Rivers, Brackett

& Hamagami, 2013), we felt that, with a class of 18 preschoolers, teacher-led interactions based on IRF (*Initiate* (Teacher: "*Carlo, what is this?*"), *Response* (Carlo: "*apple*"), *Feedback* (Teacher: "*good*")) for 90 minutes would not be ideal, as also any "teacher-pointing and children-repeating" methods, regardless of whether the repeating would be individual or choral. Such considerations prompted the instructional-design question, "what else can children learn while they are learning English words?" This question regarding instructional design moves us towards a more transdisciplinary approach to FL-instruction.

Preschool-CLIL: Doing more than "English words"

By re-imagining the FL-classroom as a context for developing literacies, thinking-skills and soft-skills, the 40-plus vocabulary words were organized into worksheets, three of which are illustrated in Figure 4. Each worksheet is based on 3-4 vocabulary items (RESPECTING WORKING MEMORY LIMITATIONS), organized in repeating sequences along a "clothesline". The *basic repeating set* is shown at the start of the worksheet. For example, the basic 4-item repeating set in Figure 3A would be "strawberry-strawberry-pineapple-apple", repeated 7 times; the 3-item sequence in Figure 3B would be "scarf-sweater-jacket" repeated 8 times; the sequence in Figure 3C would be "head-finger-eye-eyes" repeated 6 times.

The objective is for preschoolers to complete their clotheslines by asking for missing items (SOLVING A CHALLENGING BUT SOLVABLE PROBLEM). To do this, the children must first recognize that single items can be united into "*sets*" (i.e. the basic repeating set), and, strung together, repeating sets form "*patterns*" which implies the existence of *boundaries*. However, such boundaries are not explicitly indicated on these clotheslines, requiring children to understand the concrete concept of "*set boundaries*" that is, however, not visible. Once the children have identified the pattern of items forming a set, they must *solve a solvable problem:* identify which missing item they need to complete sets along their clothesline. As such they are drawn into a problem-solving state, which contributes to their staying focused throughout the task (ATTENTION & FLOW). "Learning English" is thus transformed into a process which cultivates young children's *observation-skills*, *logical reasoning*, *pattern-recognition*, etc., all of which, as will be explained below, support *proto-algebraic thinking skills* and subsequent development of *numeracy*.

Figure 3. Example of three worksheets which optimize English-language learning for the cultivation of logical-reasoning skills in pre-literate children. See text for a detailed analysis of the learning strategies behind each sequence

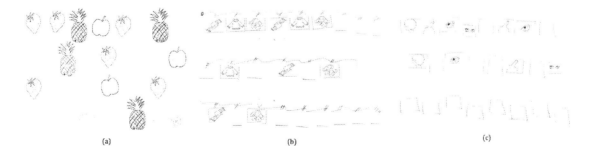

The Process: Observations and Instructions for Use

To start, in plenary, the teacher shows the worksheet and "reads" the *basic repeating set* that starts the clothesline, modelling the syllabic-rhythm of this basic repeating set (e.g. *straw*-ber-ry●*straw*-ber-ry●*pine*-app-le●*app*-le; use QR-Code-1 to access an audio recording of the spoken rhythm). Rhythmic chants have been shown to help children learn their L1 (Kenney, 2005) and foreign languages (Albaladejo, Coyle & Roca de Larios, 2018). To help preschoolers learn a string of foreign words, the teacher should model a rhythm when reading the basic repeating set before asking the children to do likewise, echoing and familiarizing themselves with this rhythm since this aural mnemonic will help children "recall" otherwise unknown foreign words. After this choral rhythmic chanting of the *basic repeating set*, each child gets a copy of the worksheet, and the activity can begin. The teacher, positioned in the classroom so to encourage queuing rather than crowding, has a tray of items the children will need. The children queue up and wait their turn to request the item they need for completing their clothesline: only one item can be requested each time.

Figure 4 illustrates how the task establishes a very learner-centered classroom dynamic where *every* preschooler becomes both information-recipient as well as information-provider, regardless of prior familiarity with the items on the worksheet or with English. Briefly, children must use the visual cues on the worksheet to figure out which item they need (moment 1); here, they would be assisted by the rhythmic aural-mnemonic from the plenary-reading of the *basic repeating set* at the head of the "clothesline" (moment 2a). While weaker students may still be trying to recall the sound of the item they need, more confident children will already have recalled what they need (moment 3) and thus be queuing in front of the teacher to get their missing items. Studies report that, before the age of 7, children tend to not use goal-directed verbalization as a strategy to improve memory performance, but that 5- to 6-year-olds who do verbalize recall more than those who did not (Registered Replication Report, 2021). Interestingly, although the children here were between the age of 4 and 5, they all tended to verbalize and repeat what they needed to ask for whilst waiting in line. This may have been because the few who used this strategy to help themselves keep in mind what they needed, prompted others to do the same. As such, those waiting in the queue loudly repeated "strawberry please", "eyes please", etc. By loudly

CLIL

and constantly repeating "X-please" to themselves, children in the queue inadvertently provided their less confident peers audio cues, thus helping weaker students "recall" what they needed to ask for to complete their sequences (moment 2b → moment 3). Although everyone is solving their own "solvable clothesline problem", the *perceptions and cognitions* of stronger learners supported the *thinking and learning* of less confident learners (i.e., GROUP DYNAMICS HELP OVERCOME INDIVIDUAL WORKING MEMORY LIMITATIONS).

Figure 4. Possible cognitive processes children might be engaged in during the task and how peer-generated audio cues provide an inclusive learning environment for even weak students. Use QR-Code-2 to access this image in color

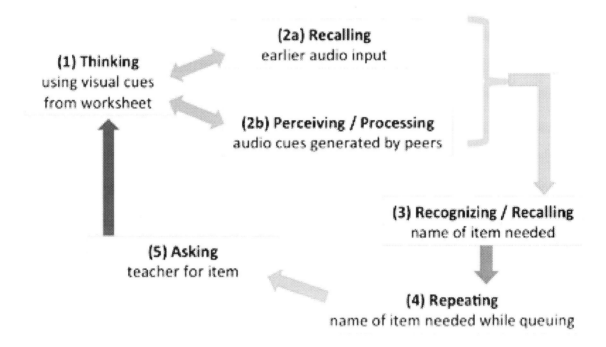

In addition, while all the children start into the first few missing items together, in phase, since each child progresses at their own pace along their own clothesline, children's needs soon become de-phased, with each queuing for a different item. Therefore, even if weaker learners still need input to support their recall of the item they need, it becomes necessary for them to identify, within the loud cacophony of "X-please!", which incoming cue corresponds to the item they need: as such, the learners themselves establish a sort of "auditory multiple choice" (i.e., GRADUALLY INCREASING THE "CHALLENGE" FACTOR IN THE PROBLEM-SOLVING PARADIGM). This very learner-centered and learner-generated learning-process allows *all* learners to recognize and/or recall the name of the item(s) needed to complete their own clothesline (turquoise arrow). In this way, even weak learners are able to join the queue and request what they need (purple arrow): while waiting, they too also loudly repeat "X-please" (moment 4: speaking) before finally attaining the item from the teacher (moment 5). After gluing an item onto their clothesline (blue arrow) children can start thinking about (and listening for) the next item (moment 1); if necessary, children can "choose from" the aural clues and cues generated by their peers who are "waiting loudly" (again, GROUP DYNAMICS HELP OVERCOME INDIVIDUAL WORKING MEMORY LIMITATIONS).

Suggestions for Materials Design

Since each queue-up is valid for only one item and since each child will need to say/yell the English word of each item innumerable times in an effort to keep in mind the item they are queuing for, the end result is the creation of a "purposeful speaking-task", with each child saying loudly what he/she needs, numerous times. This in turn becomes an "inadvertent multiple-choice listening-task" which helps those in doubt "recall" the English words of items on their clothesline. By the end of each worksheet, with so much oral-output and aural-input, children easily secure all the vocabulary and grammatical notions presented on their clothesline. It should be noted that, the process of queuing not only allows children to stand up and move about, it also provides children the context for learning the social skill of respecting queues and turn-taking. Finally, Box 2 lists some of the design considerations when setting up such "clotheslines".

CLIL

BOX 2. Some design considerations regarding the choice of words for these "clotheslines":

Consideration 1: Since "apple" appears early on in most primary-level EFL textbooks, and is not too difficult to pronounce, this word, where used, was not used frequently so to not detract from any sense of novelty these children might have when encountering "apple" in elementary school. By contrast, items which are a mouthful to pronounce and appear later on in EFL-textbooks, were strategically used more frequently (e.g. strawberry). Thus the sequence "strawberry-strawberry-pineapple-apple".

Consideration 2: L1-cognates were strategically used to lighten cognitive load: For example, "kiwi" is rather familiar to Italian children and is pronounced identically in English and Italian and thus used adjacent to less familiar items, such as "coconut".

Consideration 3: Familiar items which have quasi-L1-cognate pronunciations are very interesting as these provide "object-familiarity" and thus potentially lightens the cognitive load needed to define the sequence of items, but are challenging when it comes to pronunciation, e.g. "lemon", which in Italian is "limone" (IPA: liˈmo.ne); "jacket" and "giacca" (IPA: d͡ʒak.ka) in Italian. It is therefore especially important to correct the pronunciation of quasi-L1-cognates when children ask for these items.

Consideration 4: When establishing sequences to "teach the notion of plurals", single-items were positioned before their plurals to ensure children see, hear and hopefully grasp the notion of "plurality" e.g. eye → eyez (see Figure 3C).

Additional suggestions:

• Upon finishing their worksheet, each child brought their worksheet to the teacher and "read" it to the teacher since ''reading pictures is reading, too'' and contributes to the learning of a foreign language (Griva & Sivropoulou, 2009).

• Since children work at different speeds, while waiting for others to finish their worksheets, those finishing first coloured-in the items on their worksheets. It is therefore crucial that the images are line-drawings and not already in colour.

Conclusion to Section 2

On an explicit level, preschoolers are "simply" using target foreign words to ask their teacher for items they need to complete a clothesline upon which repeating item-sets are organized. Implicitly, however, the completion of these clotheslines requires children to engage in deep-level logical reasoning: firstly, children must recognize that singular items form *sets;* although no visible boundaries are seen along the clothesline, these *sets* form *repeating sets* that follow a rule regarding *item-sequencing* within the set, resulting in the formation of *patterns*. *Pattern-recognition* is at the base of *subitizing*, the ability to accurately gauge the number of elements within a set, such as the number of dots on the face of a die (Kaufman, Lord, Reese & Volkmann, 1949). Reporting on the relation between pattern-recognition and children's ability to subitize small numbers, Jansen et al. (2014) eloquently explain that:

...subitizing "is a component of number sense, which is essential for proficient math performance (Jordan, Kaplan, Locuniak and Ramineni, 2007; Kroesbergen, van Luit, van Lieshout, van Loosbroek and van de Rijt, 2009). Deficient subitizing is suggested to underlie lagging math skills of children with dyscalculia (Schleifer and Landerl, 2011)" (p. 178), concluding that "Training of pattern recognition (see Fischer, Kongeter and Hartnegg, 2008; Wilson, Revkin, Cohen, Cohen and Dehaene, 2006) and presenting elements in fixed patterns may ease number recognition and encourage insight into simple addition and subtraction. After all, enumeration is an important requisite for later math skills (Jordan et al., 2007; Kroesbergen et al., 2009) (p. 192).

Pattern recognition, and the ability to complete patterns with missing items, as the clotheslines here, thus involves, among other abilities, *careful observation*, *logical reasoning* and *prediction*, and has been identified as one of four foundational skills at the core of *computational thinking*, along with understanding *decomposition*, *abstraction* and *algorithms* (Lee, Joswich & Pole, 2022). With preschoolers, opportunities to cultivate pattern-recognition skills thus contributes to developing age-appropriate thinking skills, which become crucial "not only for later math achievement but also for achievement in other content areas" (Classens & Engle, 2013).

In addition, since children must queue up for each item they need, the context becomes an occasion for teaching children to respect turn-taking. Again, on a more implicit level, obliging preschoolers to wait their turn establishes a moment for reinforcing their ability to *delay gratification*. Studies have shown that children who can delay gratification, such as not eating one sweet at this moment in exchange for more sweets later on, show more *self-regulation* and *impulse-control* as adults and that weak impulse control is associated with poor management of finances, drug addiction and alcoholism (Mischel, Shoda and Rodriguez, 1989; Steelandt et al., 2012; Madden, Petry, Badger & Bickel, 1997).

In conclusion, by looking beyond the "list of English words" that preschoolers must learn, and adopting a more transdisciplinary, literacy-focused approach to bilingual instruction, "foreign-language instruction" can be transformed and expanded into a context for doing much more, developing not only age-matched discipline-relevant literacies and thinking skills, but also soft-skills, and even becoming a context for cultivating beneficial behavioural-habits.

CLIL

SECTION 3. DISCIPLINARY LITERACY AT PRIMARY-LEVEL: "DINOSAURS AND MAMMOTHS CANNOT EXIST TOGETHER!"

Age-group: 8-9 year olds.

CLIL strategy: Age-appropriate complex discipline-specific concepts plus age-appropriate academic language needed to communicate disciplinary understanding.

Language Learning: Function-focused language-use: necessary tenses, lexis and whole discourses needed to address content at an age-appropriate level and complexity.

Competences & Cognition: Formulation of complex thoughts via a foreign language; using logical reasoning skills to sequence events.

Primary-Level: Specific Issues to Overcome

As already mentioned earlier, most Italian youth start learning English as a foreign language in primary school, so that by the time they enter universities, they will have been studying English for almost 12 years; yet most do not achieve a solid B1-level competence. One reason for this may be a national primary-level EFL-curriculum which seems to ignore the fact that language, be it L1 or a tFL, is learnt best when it is used to "do something meaningful". Indeed, the suggested national curriculum (MUR, 2012), interpreted by schools into concrete scholastic content (e.g., see Verdello and Cazzago San Martino) focuses on vocabulary (colors, body parts, animals in zoos, weather, time, etc.), "simple exchanges about familiar everyday events", and is very grammar restricted. In fact, the most complicated verb forms appearing only around the final years of primary school (year 4-5; ca. 9-10 years of age) are, *to be, to have got* (sic), *to like, can*, *present continuous (e.g., I'm wearing), possessive* and *demonstrative adjectives*. Basically, while content in most other school subjects grow in synch with children's cognitive development, engaging them in age-appropriate complex thinking, the EFL-curriculum does not "mature with the learners". An example pertinent to this Section is the fact that the Italian curriculum introduces children to the *English simple past* only in middle-school (age 11-13). As such, before 11-years-of-age, Italian youth have "no English" to speak about "what they did and who they saw last weekend". This means that the English these children learn in school is not very useful for speaking about their exciting pre-adolescent life.

In addition, by exposing Italian children to only the English *present simple* and the *imperative* through very simple verbs (*to be, like, can*) for 5 years of primary-level EFL-instruction (*I like red; we have a cat; do you have a dog; sit down,* etc.), we inadvertently transmit the gravely incorrect notion that the *English present simple* is comparable to the very ubiquitous Italian "*presente indicativo*" which, as shown in Table 2, can be used for almost any and all events, "now, future, and ongoing". Indeed, such mis-learning is evident in how older Italian learners of English commonly misuse and overuse the *English present simple* when another tense is required in English (see Table 2). Thus the impetus for designing FL-instruction which matures alongside the cognitive abilities of young learners.

Table 2. The Italian "presente indicativo" is structurally similar to the English present simple, leading to common errors made by Italian learners of English

Acceptable uses of the *"presente indicativo"*:	Errors in English commonly made by adult Italian learners of English:
• Oggi non piove.	- It does not rain today.
• Che fai stasera?	- What do you do this evening?
• La settimana prossima vado a Roma.	- Next week I go to Rome.

Transdisciplinary, Literacy-focused CLIL-Materials at Primary-Level

As has been explained extensively elsewhere (Coyle et al., 2010), since CLIL regards the learning of also scholastically relevant Content, language-instruction in CLIL must inevitably set aside vocabulary lists and "grammar chronology" to adopt an "as needed" approach to FL-use and thus FL-learning. Therefore, in the case of this set of CLIL-materials designed to teach "The History of the Earth", it was of course necessary to use the simple past tense, trusting that 8-year-old children have enough life-experience to notice we no longer live amongst "Dinosaurs" on a "Big Ball of Fire".

Primary-level CLIL: Providing Age-matched English Instruction

To create CLIL-instructional materials regarding "The History of the Earth", a Natural Science expert at the local university was asked to organize Natural History into approximately 10 "concrete Episodes" which 8-year-olds could appreciate, starting from "The Big Bang" and ending with "Big Mammals", without necessarily delimiting information within geological or natural history timelines (e.g. prokaryotes, eukaryotes, Precambrian Time, Paleozoic Era, etc.). After several iterations, the result is a timeline with the 13 Episodes listed in Figure 5. From the point of view of Content, this emphasized several discipline-specific concepts, such as the notion that "water as essential for life" and "dinosaurs and large mammals existed at very different moments", contrary to popular media showing humans riding mammoths and fighting dinosaurs. Another important related concept is that, on the grand scheme of things, dinosaurs, despite their popularity with young children, made only a very minor appearance on Earth. And likewise, humans: we too are a very small happening within the entire process, and thus only mentioned very briefly at the end of the 13 Episodes.

From the point of view of Language, the main objective was to engage children with more age-appropriate yet academic and complex English. Therefore, as illustrated by the texts explaining each of the 13 Episodes (Figure 5), verbs in the simple past were used as needed, be they regular or irregular. In addition, whole complex sentences were used for supporting "whole, academically relevant thoughts". As discussed below regarding task-design, where possible, L1-cognates were used to lighten cognitive-processing (ACKNOWLEDGING WORKING MEMORY LIMITATIONS). Interestingly, since many English academic words are derived from Latinate equivalents, in the case of Italian, L1-cognates were not only the more academic English choices but also the more academic Italian equivalents. For example, instead of *"the seas became full of fish"*, the more academic English equivalent *"the oceans became populated with fish"* embodied many L1-cognates *"Gli oceani si popolarono di pesci"*. As such, in the case of Italian, our wish to target English academic language also contributed to increasing students' exposure to their

CLIL

L1-academic language. Finally, an important objective was to increase children's appreciation of this foreign language as gateway to information that is interesting and new: Basically, English can be more interesting than "red, yellow, blue" "twelve, twenty, twenty-two" and "my name is".

Figure 5. The History of the Earth divided into 13 Episodes

1) The Big Bang: a long, long time ago, there was a big explosion.

2) Earth: The big explosion produced a very big ball of fire. This big ball of fire was EARTH! The Earth was very very very hot!

3) Moon: A small ball emerged from the planet Earth. This small ball detached - this became The Moon!

4) Water: Gradually, The Earth became less hot. Small pools of water appeared.

5) The First Signs of Life: Very small and very primitive organisms appeared in these pools of water.

6) Life Inside Water: When the Earth cooled, the small pools of water became big pools of water – oceans! In the oceans, primitive life became algae and fish! The oceans became populated with fish!

7) Life Outside Water: Outside water, green plants started to grow.

8) Animals on Land: With time, some of the fish in the water became amphibians. Amphibians can live in the water and on the land. Some of these amphibians became reptiles (snakes, crocodiles) and also very very small mammals. Reptiles can swim but they prefer to live on land. Reptiles are small animals.

9) Then Big Animals - Dinosaurs!: In time, generation after generation, some small reptiles became bigger and bigger and became dinosaurs. Some dinosaurs were very very big. The Earth was populated by dinosaurs, small dinosaurs and big dinosaurs!

10) Then Flying Animals - Birds: In time, generation after generation, some of the reptiles became birds! The Earth was full of life: algae, fish and amphibians in the water - and plants, reptiles, very very small mammals and dinosaurs on the land - and birds in the air!

11) All the Dinosaurs Died!: One day, a very very big meteorite crashed onto the Earth. There was fire and dust! This fire and dust killed all the creatures outside the water who could not escape. Birds can fly so they escaped but all the dinosaurs died. With no dinosaurs on the Earth, life was very quiet for a long time…

12) Mammals: Many many years after the big meteorite, some amphibians became mammals. So now the Earth had new life – mammals! For example, mammoths and monkeys.

13) Man: In time, generation after generation, Man appeared! Man has now populated the Earth!

It should be noted that this set of materials had been designed to meet the needs of an aspiring CLIL teacher-trainee who, graduating in Natural Sciences and with C1-Level English competence, had intended to use English to explain these 13 episodes to 8-year-olds Italian children, believing that, thanks to professional commercial images plus her good English, she would be "doing CLIL", helping the children appreciate all the concepts and acquire age-appropriate academic discourse. Understanding the limits of working memory makes clear that a teacher explaining (lecturing about) unfamiliar content through foreign language is unlikely to work well, regardless of how professional the images. Below, we see how, by designing instruction through a transdisciplinary literacy-focused approach to language learning children easily learnt both complex new concepts and age-appropriate academic English, even with non-professional images coloured in by the children themselves.

275

The Process: Observations and Instructions for Use

The 13 Episodes were organized into two 120-minute lessons separated by 2 days, with each preceded by "art-related preparatory homework". A third 45-minute encounter was organized a week following the second lesson for evaluating children's learning. Line-drawings were created to illustrate the first six Episodes, from *The Big Bang* to *Life Inside Water* and children were invited to make their own drawings for any one the remaining Episodes, agreeing as a class so that each of the Episodes 7-13 were illustrated by at least two students. Here, for sake of space, we will detail the learning process involving the first six Episodes and report observations from the first lesson, alongside some learning outcomes attained during the final evaluation.

The first six Episodes were represented through simple line-drawings on A4-sized paper with zones numbered from 1 to 20 (Figure 6A). A week prior to the first lesson, each child received a packet of these six line-drawings plus a number-colour key (Figure 6B) which they were instructed to follow for colouring the drawings. Note that the numbers ranged from 1 to 20, in line with the EFL curriculum, presented as words rather than Arabic numbers; in addition, the colour spectrum included *light* and *dark* shades of the pure primary colours usually found in primary-level textbooks. In this way, the CLIL-task fully harnesses what 8-year-olds already know about numbers and colour-shades in their L1-life and provides the children an opportunity to master these in spelt-out English words. Note that an "information box" was positioned at the bottom of each drawing; Being an L1-cognate (*informazione*), children were instructed to ignore this space as they would be receiving information about the drawings at Lesson-1.

Figure 6. (A-C) Line drawings representing Episodes 1, 2 and 6 in Figure 5; (D) the colour key children used to colour in the set of six line-drawings

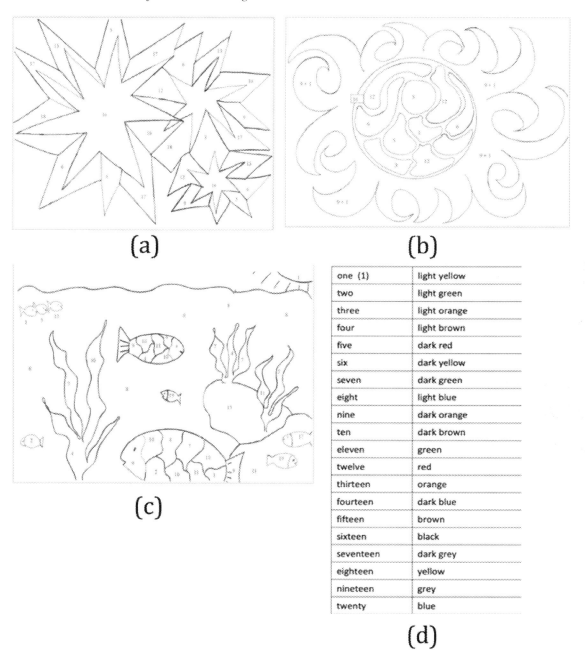

Children brought their fully coloured drawings to Lesson 1. Since the children had a week's time to undertake this preparatory work and colour-in the six drawings, they had time to fully digest the spelling of the number-words in the colour-key and learn that, unlike Italian, the adjectives *dark* and *light* precede their colours. In addition, and more importantly, as children spent time colouring, they gradually took ownership of their drawings, which now deserve some "information" in those boxes below. As shown in Figure 7, once coloured-in following the colour-key, the drawings provided "clues" and scaffold into the textual information of the first six Episodes (SETTING UP A "PROBLEM" THAT NEEDS RESOLUTION: "I HAVE COLOURED IN THESE IMAGES, BUT WHAT DOES EACH IMAGE REPRESENT"?). Below, we explain each learning-moment of Lesson-1, provide a brief explanation of the pedagogic and didactic intentions behind each learning-moment and share exchanges which we overheard between the children.

Figure 7. Example of drawings completed by different children, along with the information texts from Figure 5. Coloured images can be accessed via the QR-Code-3

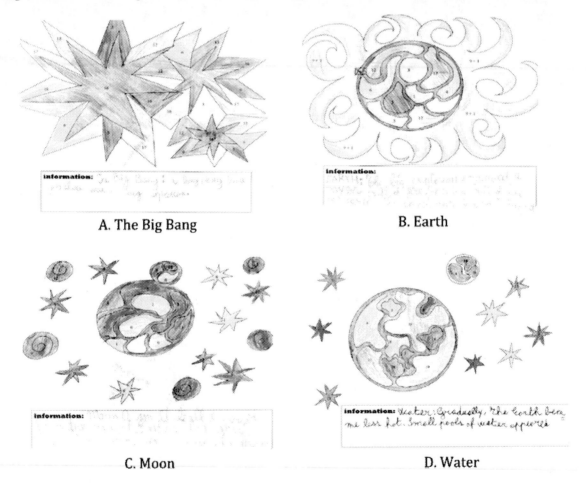

Moment 1: Children were instructed to place their fully-coloured drawings on their desks and go around the class to admire and compliment each other's work.

- The purpose for this was, of course, to cultivate children's social skills in favour of positive attitudes towards other's effort and work.
- Secondly, by seeing that others had produced very comparable drawings, this moment confirmed to children their ability to understand the English colouring-key.
- Finally, and very implicitly, seeing numerous drawings depicting the same Episode prepared children for the next moment which involved listening to foreign language input, the explanatory information about Episodes 1 to 6 in Figure 5. Therefore, comprehensible visual input provided a scaffold for potentially difficult FL-audio input. (ATTENTION TO WORKING MEMORY LIMITATIONS).
- Exchanges between the children were of course in only L1 as they had not yet received any English to speak about the Episodes:
  - Pointing to drawing 1: "*Questa è una grande esplosione!*" (This is a big explosion!).
  - Pointing to drawing 6: "*E qui ci sono i pesci*" (Here, there are fish)
  - Pointing to the moon in drawing 3: "*Che cos'è?*" (What is this?)

(STARTING TO "SOLVE THE PROBLEM" OF WHAT EACH IMAGE "MEANS").

Moment 2: Children were then instructed to organize their own drawings into what they believed would be the chronological order of events. Not surprisingly, Episodes 1, 2, 5 and 6 were ordered correctly by almost all the children. Then, sitting at their desks, with their own drawings in front of them, children listened to an audio-recording which explained the first six Episodes in the correct order: i.e., reading of the information in Figure 5. The children were told that the audio would be played twice: they were therefore instructed to only listen and to not touch their drawings during the first listening. They were assured that, if they wished, they would be free to move their drawings around during the second listening.

- The purpose of the audio-input was of course to provide children the English language needed to explain the drawings they had worked hard to produced.
- The purpose of blocking children from moving their drawings during the first listening was to ensure they paid full attention to the entire audio-input; In light of the limited resources available to

WORKING MEMORY, we should realize that, if we want children to listen for information, they should not be busy repositioning drawings as that may absorb attentional focus away from listening to, and thus understanding, the foreign language input.

- It was equally important to ensure the children that they would have a chance during the second listening to reorganize their drawings. Knowing that they would be hearing the information again and thus "correct" any incorrect sequences, reduced learning-anxiety (Nilsson, 2019), allowing the children to listened attentively to the information of each Episode without worrying about trying to retain information.

  - Since the children were sitting at their desks and listening, extensive verbal exchanges were limited. However, we observed that, at the first listening, children started looking at and sometimes also pointing to the drawing they believed the audio-explanation was referring to and nodding in each other's direction. They were "**SOLVING A SOLVABLE PROBLEM**" together. At the second listening, all the children moved their drawings into the sequence they thought correctly corresponded to the audio-input and looked to each other for confirmation.

Moment 3: This is the subject-literacy moment when learners acquire the language of the discipline. Even if learners have organized their drawings into the correct order and thus understand the chronological sequence of events, we must nonetheless provide them with the discipline-appropriate *Language* needed for formulating their thoughts into discipline-appropriate understandings. In STEM subjects, such as the case of "the History of the Earth" here, "creative thinking" may be entertaining (what if humans co-existed with dinosaurs? Could we ride them?), it is not the main objective of STEM Content-instruction. We therefore need to provide learners the *academic language* they need to think about the content in *academic ways*. Here, we needed to provide children age-appropriate and discipline-acceptable *discourses* they would need to describe their drawings correctly. Children were given the information-texts regarding Episodes 1-6 (Figure 5) on individual and randomly organized strips of paper. They were instructed to first work individually to decide which image each text was explaining (placing the strip in the "information box" below the corresponding drawing) and then, when instructed by the teacher, they could form groups of 2 to 4 children and work together to reach an agreement. Children were fully attentive since they were tasked with solving a solvable problem. Once an agreement was reached, they called the teacher to check on their collaborative decision.

- This represents an important learning moment for both Content and Language: inklings of Content-related ideas (e.g. *explosion, fish*, etc.) that the children had gleaned through the visual input they themselves "produced", became *integrated* with the Language they needed to concretize these inklings into proper discipline-appropriate content-understandings.
- Thus the importance of some thinking time for themselves, yet also the reassurance that they would then be able to work with peers to collaboratively decipher the foreign language.
- To help students easily understand the English texts, the information referred to the children's colourful drawings and, as shown in Figure 8, the texts optimized the use of L1-cognates and English words which children were familiar with through their regular EFL-coursework: e.g., *big, ball, water*. The words *Earth* and *Moon* were explained explicitly (i.e., "Earth means "la Terra"; "Moon means "la luna"), although some children were already familiar with these.
- By intepreting their drawings through the English texts, the children were able to collaboratively deduce the meaning of the words *detached, emerged, cooled, appeared, less* and *pools* and were

CLIL

able to ask their teacher to confirm these guesses. Interestingly, children did not seem to need confirmation for their understanding of *was* and *became:* both were used numerous times, occupying equivalent syntactic positions in Italian, thus reinforcing children's identification and learning of these two irregular verbs.

*Figure 8. The texts explaining Episodes 1 to 6 used not only words children had already learnt through regular EFL-instruction (**bold**) but also maximized the use of L1-Cognates (italics)*

1) The **Big** Bang: a long, long time ago, **there** was a **big** *explosion.*

2) Earth: The **big** *explosion produced* a **very big ball** of fire. This **big ball** of fire was EARTH! The Earth was **very very very hot**!

3) Moon: A **small ball** *emerged* from the *planet* Earth. This **small ball** detached - this became The Moon!

4) **Water**: *Gradually*, The Earth became less **hot**. **Small** pools of **water** *appeared.*

5) The First *Signs* of Life: **Very small** and **very** *primitive* organisms *appeared* in these pools of **water**.

6) Life Inside **Water**: When the Earth cooled, the **small** pools of water became **big** pools of water – *oceans*! In the *oceans*, *primitive* life became *algae* and **fish**! The **oceans** became *populated* with **fish**!

- Children realized that the drawings they themselves had produced were of immense help for identifying the Episodes. Observing the children, we heard them seamlessly code-switch between L1 and familiar English words they now had in front of them:

  ◦ Pointing to drawings of Episode 1 and Episode 2: "questo è il *Big Bang*, una grande esplosione" and "questo è *Earth*, la Terra, che è un *big ball of fire*…una grande palla di fuoco che era *very very hot*, molto molto calda" (pointing to Episode 2) [IT: this is the Big Bang, a big explosion and this is the Earth, la Terra which is a big ball of fire… a big ball of fire that was very very hot, very very hot].
  ◦ Pointing to the light-blue area in Episode 4, which is the first time the colour light-blue appeared in their drawings, children immediately intuited that this colour represented water: "E questo è *water*, l'acqua" [IT: and this is water].
  ◦ Children had no problems reasoning through the fact that Episode 5 came before Episode 6: "*primitive organisms*…qui ci sono gli organismi primitivi"; "*fish* sono negli oceani, *oceans*"; "*fish* non sono *primitive organisms*, organismi primitivi, quindi vengono dopo" [IT: primitive organisms, here are some primitive organisms; fish are in oceans, oceans; fish are not primitive organisms, so they come later].

Moment 4: As each working group received confirmation from the teacher that their proposed sequence of events was correct, they were instructed to work individually to copy the description into corresponding information boxes under each drawing. This moment deployed the process of HAPTICS. Children were happy to copy the English "*informazione*" into the *information boxes* as they werer able to give meaning to the drawings that they had produced. As explained in Box 3, HAPTICS is an invaluable strategy for both *Language* as well as *Content* learning since this seemingly simple act of writing/copying by hand actually involves a cognitively complex, co-ordinated process.

Box 3. The importance of "haptics" for learning complex Content and whole Language

• The apparently simple act of copying a text by hand is actually a cognitively complex process: first, the visual system is engaged for deciphering the orthography forming letters, words and phrases; this visual information then undergoes cross-modal co-processing with phonological information generated in auditory and speech centres of the brain (Bonte et al., 2017): it is as if we "hear" and "say" the letters, words or phrases we "are seeing". This information then reaches the motor cortex which in turn coordinates our hands and body so that we can produce the finely controlled motor movements needed to write out the words and phrases we have seen.

• Some have classified this intricate act of writing by hand under "haptics", which, strictly speaking, involves "touch" (see Wikipedia). Although the term *haptics* has rapidly become popularized within digital technology for other equally interesting but more "modern" digitalized constructs, scholars discussing the *haptics of writing* by hand versus typing on the keyboard alert us to the complex cognitive control behind a seemingly simple act: "[…], the visual attention of the writer is strongly concentrated during handwriting; the attentional focus of the writer is dedicated to the tip of the pen…" (Mangen & Velay, 2010).

• The act of "writing out" increased the success of learning foreign language words in adults (Thomas & Dieter, 1987; for overview see Candry Deconinck & Eyckmans, 2018). To understand the importance of writing out by hand for the learning of a foreign language, consider the word "with". Since "with" ranks around the 15th most frequent word in the English language (see Wikipedia "most common words in English"), there is little doubt most of our university students have seen this word several times, yet many often write "whit". It would be interesting to conduct a longitudinal study to compare university students' ability to properly spell "with", or any word, when learnt through simply reading the word, circling it, dragging-and-dropping, cutting-and-pasting it, or "copying it out by hand".

Continued on following page

CLIL

Box 3. Continued

• In addition, and very importantly, given the slower and more cognitively involved process of copying complete texts by hand, as the case here, learners
also have more time to engage with the Content-notions we want them to understand and learn. As such, this process ensures that *all* children are sharply
focusing on the exact information they should learn, from the point of view of
both Language and Content.

• Finally, while copying in L1 would undoubtedly also be useful in many circumstances, it would seem tedious: the advantage of CLIL is that learners see
more sense in such "copying/writing by hand" when they are learning a foreign
language. This is one example of when "learning a foreign *Language*" benefits
the "learning of *Content*".

Final Evaluation and Conclusion to Section 3

The final evaluation took place a week after the second CLIL lesson. The teacher projected pairs of items written in English (e.g., "Big Bang – Fish"; "Oceans – Primitive Life"; etc.), one pair at a time, and children were asked if these pairs of items could "co-exist". Many excellent discussions ensued which clearly demonstrated that the children had, in only two lessons, comprehended both disciplinary-Concepts and also the Language, as evidenced by their ability to choose appropriate English words and phrases and respect English syntactic norms while code-switching. An example of this regards the animated response of two children when shown the pair "Mammoths – Dinosaurs".

S1: *oi maè, non potevano esistere insieme perchè i* **mammoths** *erano* **very very primitive elephants...**
     erano **very big**
[hey maè (affectionate slang for *maestra (teacher)*) they could not exist together because **mammoths**
     were **very very primitive elephants** … they were **very big**]
S2: *si, quando c'erano i* **dinosaurs**, *i* **mammals** *erano* **very small** *proprio perchè potevano nascondersi*
     dai dinosauri…
[Yes, when there were **dinosaurs**, the **mammals** were **very small** so they could hide from the dinosaurs.]

The understanding that only very small mammals coexisted with dinosaurs was addressed in Lesson 2, so it is not surprising that the children were able to generate this reasoning. However, what was surprising was children's ability to code-switch swiftly and correctly to discuss disciplinary-notions. For example, the phrase "*very very primitive elephants*" reflects the correct language combination of the following input in the CLIL materials:

(1)   "*very very very hot*", referring to the Earth being a *Big Ball of Fire* in Episode 2;
(2)   "*primitive life*" in Episode 5.

Note that, in Italian, while *very very hot* would be *molto molto calda*, *primitive life* would be *vita primitiva*. In addition, although the word *elephant* was not in the CLIL materials, it is an L1-cognate (*elefante*) and was probably familiar to students through their EFL-coursework. By unifying meaningful, albeit complex language input from different inputs, the children were able to correctly sequence English words to communicate their understanding that mammoths are *"very very primitive elephants"*. This ability to describe the link between modern elephants and mammoths by first positioning the English adjective before the noun, contrary to L1, and then prefixing this correct adjective-noun pair with a double-dose of the adverbial modifier *very,* shows that young learners had deeply processed and internalized the complex English input; they were able to *think in* and *reason through* complex foreign language text. By using English to access age-appropriate and challenging new Content, this way of learning English becomes relevant, and more importantly, benefits *all* learners.

CONCLUSION

This chapter has sought to contribute to early CLIL/bilingual instruction through two perspectives, that of cognitive neuroscience and that of transdisciplinary literacy-focused language instruction. Regardless of "the language of instruction" being used, pre-school and primary-level teachers are, without a doubt, in the position to shape and ready malleable young minds for the academic and social habitat ahead. With this important social responsibility comes important professional responsibilities, not least of which is the ability to design instruction that contributes to cultivating literacies, disciplinary understandings, critical-thinking, logical-reasoning, interpersonal-communication, etc., basically, the knowledge, skills and competences today's young children will need to succeed in school and society tomorrow. This means adopting a transdisciplinary literacy-focused perspective towards foreign language instruction. However, such instruction should be designed so to not only respect the natural cognitive limits of young brains (e.g. working memory), but also harness its natural cognitive tendencies (e.g. enjoy solving solvable problems), and optimize certain cognitive processes for CLIL/bilingual contexts (e.g. haptics of writing).

To help aspiring CLIL/bilingual teachers understand how to apply these theoretical perspectives to their own practice, we presented, dissected, and discussed two sets of CLIL-instructional materials which provided for transdisciplinary literacy-focused early CLIL/bilingual-instruction, while keeping the brain in mind. When *foreign language objectives* are integrated with *content-learning objectives*, FL-classrooms can be transformed into contexts which also attend to the development of disciplinary literacies, competences, and soft-skills, which all children need for both academic as well as social success. In the case of pre-schoolers, a transdisciplinary and literacy-focused CLIL-perspective allowed us to organize a list of must-learn vocabulary and grammar into tasks which also cultivated early numeracy skills, logical reasoning, and children's ability to respect turn-taking and delay gratification. For primary-level children, materials developed through a transdisciplinary and literacy-focused CLIL-mindset respects children's cognitive maturity and ability to engage with, think though and learn from age-matched yet complex disciplinary information, even when presented through a foreign language. Indeed, when we expand our "language-instruction-schema" to include age-appropriate *Content*, language-instruction naturally moves beyond vocabulary-lists and grammar-confined curricula so to engage more complex age-matched *Thinking*. Only with *purpose-driven language-use*, can we merge *vocabulary* and *grammar* into *whole disciplinary discourses,* the "whole language" learners need for communicating meaningful "whole thoughts". In the case of primary-level learners, since CLIL-instruction involves age-appropriate *complex and academic* content, children are naturally required to engage with and learn the *complex and academic* discourse needed for speaking about those complex disciplinary notions: CLIL thus provides *receptive literacy as input*, but also expects *productive disciplinary literacy at output.* Cummins et al. (1984) have shown that "literacy skills" are transferable between languages, and classroom research with older learners have found that even weak learners who gain academic discourse awareness through a FL via CLIL-instruction subsequently show productive academic competence when writing in L1 (Grandinetti, Langellotti and Ting, 2013).

Finally, since learning happens in the brain, the three simple cognitive neuroscience notions (*working memory, attention through solving solvable problems* and *the haptics of writing*) presented here would be pertinent to any learning, of anything, be it CLIL or not, and for whatever age-group of learners. However, by linking these notions to the CLIL-materials for young learners, and by explicitly delineating how these informed various CLIL-learning-moments, we hope to have provided aspiring CLIL/bilingual teachers another way to "observe bilingual learning", i.e., through a more cognitive neuroscience perspective. Consequently, we hope that such a perspective might then inform how these teachers design instruction: maybe teachers will recognize the potential of "haptics" for learning complex language; support young children's very limited working memory resources through non-textual modalities (drawings, graphs, etc.); understand to maintain students' attention by enticing them with "challenging but solvable problems". We hope that aspiring CLIL/bilingual teachers will recognize the potential of a transdisciplinary literacy-focused approach to language learning and merge this with theories on second language learning and acquisition to design even more effective instructional materials and learning environments which not only respect, but also optimize, the cognitive resources in young brains.

REFERENCES

Albaladejo, S. A., Coyle, Y., & Roca de Larios, J. (2018). Songs, Stories, and Vocabulary Acquisition in Preschool Learners of English as a Foreign Language. *System, 76,* 116–128. doi:10.1016/j.system.2018.05.002

Bakken, J., & Brevik, L. M. (2022). Challenging the notion of CLIL elitism: A study of secondary school students' motivation for choosing CLIL in Norway. *TESOL Quarterly,* tesq.3173. doi:10.1002/tesq.3173

Bjorklund, D. F., & Pellegrini, A. D. (2000). Child development and evolutionary psychology. *Child Development, 71*(6), 1687–1708. doi:10.1111/1467-8624.00258 PMID:11194266

Bonte, M., Correia, J. M., Keetels, M., Vroomen, J., & Formisano, E. (2017). Reading-induced shifts of perceptual speech representations in auditory cortex. *Nature, 7,* 5143–5154. PMID:28698606

Bruton, A. (2013). CLIL: Some of the reasons why ... and why not. *System, 41*(3), 587–597. doi:10.1016/j.system.2013.07.001

Cambridge (2018). *Assessment Wordlist For Exams From 2018.* Cambridge https://www.cambridgeenglish.org/images/149681-yle-flyers-word-list.pdf

Candry, S., Deconinck, J., & Eyckmans, J. (2018). Written repetition vs. oral repetition: Which is more conducive to L2 vocbulary learning? *Journal of European Second language Association, 2,* 72-82.

Cazzago San Martino Primary School. (2016). *Cazzago San Martino Primary School Curriulum*. Cazzago San Martino Primary School. https://www.icverdello.edu.it/wp-content/uploads/2016/10/INGLESE-1.pdf

Classens, A., & Engel, M. (2013). How important is where you start? Early mathematics knowledge and later school success. *Teachers College Record*, *115*(6), 1–29. doi:10.1177/016146811311500603

Cowan, N. (2008). What are the differences between long-term, short-term, and working memory? *Progress in Brain Research*, *169*, 323–338. doi:10.1016/S0079-6123(07)00020-9 PMID:18394484

Coyle, D., Hood, P., & Marsh, D. (2010). *CLIL*. Cambridge University Press. doi:10.1017/9781009024549

Csikszentmihalyi, M. (2011). *Flow: The Psychology of Optimal Experience*. Harper Collins.

Csikszentmihalyi, M. (2014). Toward a psychology of optimal experience. In M. Csikszentmihalyi (Ed.), *Flow and The Foundations of Positive Psychology* (pp. 209–226). Springer.

Cummins, J., Swain, M., Nakajima, K., Handscombe, J., Green, D., & Tran, C. (1984). Linguistic interdependence among Japanese and Vietnamese immigrant students. In C. Rivera (Ed.), *Communicate Competence Approaches to Language Proficiency Assessment: Research and Application* (pp. 60–81). Multilingual Matters.

Dalton-Puffer, C. (2008). Outcomes and processes in content and language integrated learning (CLIL): current research from Europe. In W. Delanoy and L. Wolkmann, (eds.) *Future Perspectives for English Language Teaching*, 139–57. Heidelberg: https://balancedreading.com/cambridge/ https://www.mrc-cbu.cam.ac.uk/people/matt.davis/cmabridge/

Della Sala, S. (2009). The use and misuse of neuroscience in education. *Cortex*, *45*(4), 443. doi:10.1016/j.cortex.2008.11.012 PMID:19103447

Diamond, A., Kirkham, N., & Amso, D. (2002). Conditions under which young children can hold two rules in mind and inhibit a prepotent response. *Developmental Psychology*, *38*(3), 352–362. doi:10.1037/0012-1649.38.3.352 PMID:12005379

Doiz, A., Lasagabaster, D., & Sierra, J. M. (2014). CLIL and motivation: The effect of individual and contextual variables. *Language Learning Journal*, *42*(2), 209–224. doi:10.1080/09571736.2014.889508

English, C. (2016). English at Work: Global analysis of language skills in the workplace. Cambridge. https://www.cambridgeenglish.org/images/335794-english-at-work-executive-summary.pdf; https://eflmagazine.com/prove-youre-a-pro-with-the-communication-skills-for-business-english-for-it-exam/

Oxford Academic. (2013) *Call for Papers*. English Language Teaching Journal. (https://academic.oup.com/eltj/article-abstract/67/2/NP/532236

Ericsson, K. A., & Kintsch, W. (1955). Long-term working memory. *Psychological Review*, *102*(2), 211–245. doi:10.1037/0033-295X.102.2.211 PMID:7740089

Eurobarometer (2012). *Europeans and Their Languages. Special Eurobarometer 368.* European Commission.

Ferguson, H. J., Brunsdon, V. E. A., & Bradford, E. E. F. (2021). The developmental trajectories of executive function from adolescence to old age. *Nature, 11*, 1382–1399. PMID:33446798

Fischer, B., Kongeter, A., & Hartnegg, K. (2008). Effects of daily practice on subitizing, visual counting and basic arithmetic skills. *Optometry and Vision Development, 39*, 30–34.

Grandinetti, M., Langellotti, M., & Ting, Y. L. T. (2013). How CLIL can provide a pragmatic means to renovate science education – even in a sub-optimally bilingual context. *International Journal of Bilingual Education and Bilingualism, 16*(3), 354–374. doi:10.1080/13670050.2013.777390

Griva, E., & Sivropoulou, R. (2009). Implementation and evaluation of an early foreign language learning project in lindergarten. *Early Childhood Education Journal, 37*(1), 79–87. doi:10.100710643-009-0314-3

Harme, B. K., Pianta, R. C., Downer, J. T., DeCoster, J., Mashburn, A. J., Jones, S. M., Brown, J. L., Cappella, E., Atkins, M., Rivers, S. E., Brackett, M. A., & Hamagami, A. (2013). Teaching through interactions: Testing a developmental framework of teacher effectiveness in over 4,000 classrooms. *The Elementary School Journal, 113*(4), 461–487. doi:10.1086/669616 PMID:34497425

Hultgren, A. K., & Lasagabaster, D. (2019). Plenary speeches English medium instruction: Global views and countries in focus. *Language Teaching, 52*(02), 231–248. doi:10.1017/S0261444816000380

Jansen, B. R. J., Hofman, A. D., Straatemeier, M., van Bers, B. M. C. W., Raijmakers, M. E. J., & van der Maas, H. L. J. (2014). The role of pattern recognition in children's exact enumeration of small numbers. *British Journal of Developmental Psychology, 32*(2), 178–194. doi:10.1111/bjdp.12032 PMID:24862903

Jordan, N. C., Kaplan, D., Locuniak, M. N., & Ramineni, C. (2007). Predicting first-grade math achievement from developmental number sense trajectories. *Learning Disabilities Research & Practice, 22*(1), 36–46. doi:10.1111/j.1540-5826.2007.00229.x

Kaufman, E. L., Lord, M. W., Reese, T. W., & Volkmann, J. (1949). The discrimination of visual number. *The American Journal of Psychology, 62*(4), 498–525. doi:10.2307/1418556 PMID:15392567

Kenney, S. (2005). Nursery Rhymes: Foundation for Learning (pp. 28-31). *General Music Today, 19*, 28–31. doi:10.1177/10483713050190010108

Kroesbergen, E. H., van Luit, J. E. H., van Lieshout, E. C. D. M., van Loosbroek, E., & van de Rijt, B. A. M. (2009). Individual differences in early numeracy: The role of executive functions and subitizing. *Journal of Psychoeducational Assessment, 27*(3), 226–236. doi:10.1177/0734282908330586

Lee, J., Joswick, C., & Pole, K. (2022). Classroom play and activities to support computational thinking development in early childhood. *Early Childhood Education Journal.* doi:10.100710643-022-01319-0

Llinares, A., Morton, T., & Whittaker, R. (2012). *The Roles of Language in CLIL.* Cambridge University Press.

Macaro, E. (2018). *English Medium Instruction: Content and Language in Policy and Practice.* Oxford University Press. doi:10.30687/978-88-6969-227-7/001

Madden, G. J., Petry, N. M., Badger, G. J., & Bickel, W. K. (1997). Impulsive and self-control choices in opioid-dependent patients and non-drug- using control participants: Drug and monetary rewards. *Experimental and Clinical Psychopharmacology*, *5*(3), 256–262. doi:10.1037/1064-1297.5.3.256 PMID:9260073

Mangen, A., & Velay, J.-L. (2010). Digitizing literacy: reflections on the haptics of writing. *Advances in Haptics*. https://www.intechopen.com/articles/show/title/digitizing-li teracy-reflections-on-the-haptics-of-writing

Miller, G. A. (1956). The magical number seven, plus or minus two: Some limits on our capacity for processing information. *Psychological Review*, *63*(2), 81–97. doi:10.1037/h0043158 PMID:13310704

Mischel, W., Shoda, Y., & Rodriguez, M. L. (1989). Delay of gratification in children. *Science*, *244*(4907), 933–938. doi:10.1126cience.2658056 PMID:2658056

MUR. (Ministero Università della Ricerca (Italian Ministry of Education). (2012). Indicazioni Nazionalie Nuovi Scenari [National Indicators and New Scanarios]. MUR. Https://Www.Miur.Gov.It/Documents/20182/0/Indicazioni+Nazionali+E+Nuovi+Scenari/

Nash, H., & Snowling, M. (2006). Teaching new words to children with poor existing vocabulary knowledge: A controlled evaluation of the definition and context methods. *International Journal of Language & Communication Disorders*, *41*(3), 335–354. doi:10.1080/13682820600602295 PMID:16702097

Nilsson, M. (2019). Foreign language anxiety: The case of young learners of English in Swedish primary classrooms. *Apples. Journal of Applied Language Studies*, *13*(2), 1–21. doi:10.17011/apples/urn.201902191584

OECD. (2018). The Future of Education and Skills. *Education, 2030.* https://www.oecd.org/education/2030-project/contact/E2030%20 Position%20Paper%20(05.04.2018).pdf

Perez-Vidal, C., & Roquet, H. (2015). The linguistic impact of a CLIL Science programme: An analysis measuring relative gains. *System*, *54*, 80–90. doi:10.1016/j.system.2015.05.004

Report, R. R. (2021). Multilab direct replication of Flavell, Beach and Chinsky (1966): Spontaneous verbal rehearsal in a memory task as a function of age. *Advances in Methods and Practices in Psychological Science*, *4*, 1–20.

Richland, L. E., Morrison, R. G., & Holyoak, K. J. (2006). Children's development of analogical reasoning: Insights from scene analogy problems. *Journal of Experimental Child Psychology*, *94*(3), 249–273. doi:10.1016/j.jecp.2006.02.002 PMID:16620867

Roussel, S., Joulia, D., Tricot, A., & Sweller, J. (2017). Learning subject content through a foreign language should not ignore human cognitive architecture: A cognitive load theory approach. *Learning and Instruction*, *52*, 69–79. doi:10.1016/j.learninstruc.2017.04.007

Rowe, M. L. (2012, September). A longitudinal invetigation of the role of quantity and quality of child-directed speech in vocabulary developent. *Child Development*, *83*(5), 1762–1774. doi:10.1111/j.1467-8624.2012.01805.x PMID:22716950

Ruiz de Zarobe, Y. (2011). Which language competencies benefit from CLIL? An insight into applied linguistics research. In Y. Ruiz de Zarobe, J. M. Sierra, & F. Gallardo del Puerto (Eds.), *Content and Foreign Language Learning. Contributions to Multilingualism in European Contexts* (pp. 129–153). Peter Lang. doi:10.3726/978-3-0351-0171-3

Schleifer, P., & Landerl, K. (2011). Subitizing and counting in typical and atypical development. *Developmental Science, 14*(2), 280–291. doi:10.1111/j.1467-7687.2010.00976.x PMID:22213901

Skolnick Weisberg, D. (2008). The seductive allure of neuroscience explanation. *Journal of Cognitive Neuroscience, 20*(3), 470–477. doi:10.1162/jocn.2008.20040 PMID:18004955

Smith, F. (1976). *Comprehension and Learning: A conceptual Framework for Teachers.* Richard C. Owen Publishers.

Steelandt, S., Thierry, B., Boihanne, M. H., & Dufour, V. (2012). The ability of children to delay gratification in an exchange task. *Cognition, 122*(3), 416–425. doi:10.1016/j.cognition.2011.11.009 PMID:22153324

Sweller, J. (1998). Cognitive load during problem solving: Effects on learning. *Cognitive Science, 12*(2), 257–285. doi:10.120715516709cog1202_4

Thomas, M. H., & Dieter, J. N. (1987). The positive effects of writing practice on integration of foreign words in memory. *Journal of Educational Psychology, 79*(3), 249–253. doi:10.1037/0022-0663.79.3.249

Ting, Y. L. T. (2010). Pineapple please! *English Teaching Professional, 71,* 24–26.

Ting, Y. L. T. (2013). CLIL-Biology Towards IGCSE: Content and Language Integrated Learning Towards International Science Standards. *ELTons 2013 Award for Innovative Writing.* https://www.britishcouncil.org/contact/press/eltons-2013-winners

Ting, Y. L. T. (2022). Tertiary-level STEM and EMI: Where EFL and content meet to potentiate each other. *English Language Teaching Journal, 76*(2), 194–207. doi:10.1093/elt/ccab093

Ting, Y. L. T. (n.d.). Preparing teachers for CLIL. In M. L. Pérez Cañado & P. Romanowski (Eds.), *The Cambridge Handbook of Multilingual Education.* Cambridge University Press.

Ting, Y. L. T., Stillo, L., & Barci, G. (2022). Helping Mother Nature Compost Faster: Using Chemistry to Transform Trash into Treasure. *ELTons 2022 Award for Innovative in Learner Resources.* https://www.teachingenglish.org.uk/article/eltons-innovation-awards-2022-finalists

Tucci, C. (2019). Inglese, dopo 13 anni di scuola solo uno studente su tre capisce ciò che ascolta. *Sole 24 Ore* [English, after 13 years of school only one in three students understand what they hear. *Only 24 Hours.*].

Ulrich, M., Keller, J., Hoenig, K., Waller, C., & Grön, G. (2014). Neural correlates of experimentally induced flow experiences. *NeuroImage, 86,* 194–202. doi:10.1016/j.neuroimage.2013.08.019 PMID:23959200

Verdello Primary School. (2016). Verdello Primary School Curriculum. Verdello Primary School. https://www.icverdello.edu.it/wp-content/uploads/2016/10/INGLESE-1.pdf

ADDITIONAL READING

Baddeley, A. (2012). Working memory: Theories, models and controversies. *Annual Review of Psychology*, *63*(1), 1–29. doi:10.1146/annurev-psych-120710-100422 PMID:21961947

Cowan, N. (2022). Working memory development: A 50-year assessment of research and underlying theories. *Cognition*, *224*, 1–19. doi:10.1016/j.cognition.2022.105075 PMID:35247864

Doolittle, P. (2914). How your "working memory" makes sense of the world. TED TALK. [Video} Youtbe. https://youtu.be/UWKvpFZJwcE)

Elis Research Digest. (2017). Enhancing the subject literacy competencies and pedagogic practices of English-medium subject teachers. *ELiS Research Digest*, *4*, 33–45.

Greenes, C., Ginsburg, H. P., & Balfanz, R. (2004). Big maths for little kids. *Early Childhood Research Quarterly*, *19*(1), 159–166. doi:10.1016/j.ecresq.2004.01.010

Moore, P. (2007). Enhancing classroom discourse: A modelling potential for content teachers. *Volumen Monografico*, *2007*, 141–152.

Morton, T. (2020). Cognitive Discourse Functions: A Bridge between Content, Literacy and Language for Teaching and Assessment in CLIL. *CLIL Journal of Innovation and Research in Plurilingual and Pluricultural Education*, *3*(1), 7–17. doi:10.5565/rev/clil.33

Rosli, R., & Lin, T. W. (2018). Children early mathematics development based on a free play activity. *Creative Education*, *9*(07), 1174–1185. doi:10.4236/ce.2018.97087

San Isidro, X. (2019). The multi-faceted effects of CLIL: A literature review. *Nexus Aedean Journal*, *1*, 33–49.

Ting, Y. L. T. (2015). Video: A pluriliteracies approach to learning: The Graz Group Model (European Centre for Modern Languages (ECML) Project on CLIL and Literacies: https://youtu.be/_YJ5ja-TfOc) .

KEY TERMS AND DEFINITIONS

Age-Appropriate Disciplinary and Academic Thinking Skills and Literacies: Even preschoolers can acquire age-appropriate academic thinking skills and discipline-specific literacies. For example, Section 2 illustrates how it was possible to cultivate, in preschoolers, the discipline-specific mathematics cognitive skill of *pattern-recognition*. Likewise, if we show a 4-year-old a beach ball and a bucket, we can ask "how are these similar?" (we take them to the beach) and "how are these different" (the ball floats on water but the bucket carries water") and thus develop age-appropriate *cognitive discourse functions* (see works of Dalton-Puffer) and proto-academic thinking skills of "compare and contrast", "explain similarities and differences", etc.

CLIL/Bi-lingual Teacher Development: Professional development which helps foreign language teachers see themselves as professionals who are in the position to *also*, through the use of age-appropriate *content*, help their students develop academic language competences and thinking skills as well as social skills and beneficial personal life-skills.

Functional-Language: When language instruction prioritizes "what notions do learners need to understand", thus using whatever language is necessary for achieving such understandings, rather worrying about "what grammar and words have these learners already learnt to use".

Instructional Materials for Student-Centered Classroom Dynamics: Materials which consist of a series of tasks, each of which reflects how one or more learning/teaching theories "looks like in practice". As students work through the progression of tasks, we can observe learning as it happens in real time, monitor students' collaborative efforts and provide individualized guidance where necessary.

Literacy-Focused Instruction: When teaching goes beyond "textual literacy" (reading and writing) and surface elements related to "a topic" such as "epidemics (topic: what epidemics means; historical examples; how epidemics come about, are treated, controlled, etc.)", and *optimizes the topic for cultivating adjunct literacies skills*, such as (1) using graphs to show how epidemiological cases rise and fall, thus cultivating students' "*graphic literacy skills*"; (2) using infographics regarding the recognition and subsequent management of epidemic cases, thus cultivating students' "*visual literacy skills*".

Literacy-Focused Language-Instruction: Expanding "language-instruction" so to also attend to the cultivation of age-appropriate disciplinary literacies and academic language proficiency

Virtual Teacher-Training Workshop: An attempt to provide teachers concrete examples of how various "theories of teaching/learning" might look like as "instructional input" when put into practice. This can be achieved by presenting a set of learning-materials students have used and providing teachers a detailed analysis of the pedagogic and didactic principles behind various "learning moments", alongside classroom observations (e.g. non-verbal and verbal actions), learning outcomes (e.g. what students said), etc.

Chapter 13
Benefits of the Application of Task-Based Learning Within the Bilingual Field in Primary Education

Antonio Daniel Juan Rubio
https://orcid.org/0000-0003-3416-0021
University of Granada, Spain

Isabel Maria García Conesa
https://orcid.org/0000-0001-7005-2509
University Defense Center in San Javier, Spain

ABSTRACT

Over the last two decades, the second language acquisition field has been influenced by new pedagogical approaches and innovative trends, which have reframed the principles of how foreign languages should be taught. The emergence of the task-based language teaching (TBLT) since the late nineties, and its increasing implementation, transformed it into one of the trendiest pedagogical approaches. Later, the dual-focused vision of the content and language integrated learning (CLIL) approach gained momentum in European countries, and it was included as an essential part of schools' curricula. Nowadays, although CLIL and task-based instruction are well established in educational contexts, the combined use of the two still produces doubts among teachers. In this chapter, a thorough exploration of the main pedagogical constituents of CLIL and TBLT is carried out to analyse their commonalities and set relationships between them. To sum up, this paper will convince bilingual teachers about implementing authentic and meaningful task-based experiences within their CLIL curricula.

DOI: 10.4018/978-1-6684-6179-2.ch013

Benefits of the Application of Task-Based Learning Within the Bilingual Field in Primary Education

INTRODUCTION

Over the past two decades, with the advent of globalisation the world has witnessed numerous geographical, socio-economical and sociocultural variations, which have had huge implications on the way people live, communicate, travel and entertain themselves worldwide. Naturally, this big phenomenon has also strongly influenced the educational field implying changes in the way people read, write, study languages, search for information and approach knowledge. Furthermore, new pedagogical approaches and methods emerged so as to adjust the educational processes to the new sociocultural settings. This is the case of the two main approaches that will be dealt with in this chapter: CLIL instruction and Task-Based Learning and Teaching.

Nowadays, educational institutions have to adapt their curricula to the current social needs of the 21st century, in which mastering several languages and acquiring key competences applicable in real world contexts are a necessity. Indeed, educational agents must ensure the provision of an integral formation to turn young FL students into citizens capable to function in a globalised word. For that reason, both CLIL and task-based instruction gained a huge momentum in educational contexts. According to Nunan (2004), the influence of TBLT on educational policy-making and its combination with English teaching made it a keystone of educational centres.

Along the last decades, many experts have studied the pedagogical possibilities of implementing CLIL and TBLT in education, but there are still many lines of study related to them which should be addressed from a broader perspective to provide a deeper insight on both pedagogical approaches. Therefore, in this chapter both learning approaches will be analysed from a practical standpoint in order to provide CLIL educators with a variety of learning strategies, instructional techniques and classroom procedures in relation to task design. The tasks will generate their language and create an opportunity for language acquisition (Krashen, 2015; Lao & Krashen, 2014; Saville-Troike & Barto, 2016).

With regard to the exploration of CLIL instruction and the principles of integrated learning, it is worthy to mention that this research project is based on the 4Cs framework set by Coyle, but especially on the extended analysis of Coyle's work carried out by Meyer. Meyer claimed that for an effective implementation of CLIL, teachers need to fully comprehend its constituents and embrace its paradigm (Meyer, 2010). Therefore, considering the relevance of making sense of these key aspects for CLIL educators, this study aims to develop an exhaustive discussion of the quality principles established by Meyer from a practical and contextualised standpoint.

Moreover, many investigations of task-based instruction have focused their research of tasks' features in one-dimensional manner. Hence, this limited vision of TBLT could be mistaken, since for taking full advantage of tasks' potential it is essential to combine them with other pedagogical approaches. Therefore, this work will look into the benefits of designing tasks in conjunction with other learning perspectives like Communicative Language Teaching (CLT) and CLIL.

Last but not least, Meyer stressed the importance integrating the four Cs from Coyle's framework (content, communication, cognition and culture) within CLIL settings. Meyer's depiction of these four cornerstones of CLIL instruction is really detailed and instructive (Meyer, 2010). However, he analyses the four Cs in a theoretical and isolated way. Hence, it would be helpful to establish connections between the four Cs and illustrate these relationships within contextualised examples. Moreover, it is advisable to describe the implementation of these four variables in task-based experiences, since setting connections between diverse topics and disciplines is more achievable within sequences of tasks

When it comes to the object of this paper, it should be noted first that it is the result of a thorough investigation on the existing literature related to CLIL features and all the pedagogical aspects related to task-based instruction. Considering that both educational approaches have similar natures and share numerous principles, one of the main targets of this research paper is to examine all these common points. Furthermore, a deep analysis of the educational potential of combining both approaches will be carried out, so as to identify the benefits, but also the limitations of implementing a task-based instruction within the bilingual field.

LITERATURE REVIEW

CLIL Approach and Principles of Bilingual Education

CLIL refers to a dual-focused approach to bilingual education in which a target language (TL) is used as a medium to teach and learn non-linguistic content. As learning a language is not the objective, CLIL fosters the acquisition of L2 and then is more focused on the development of fluency rather than on accuracy. According to Tardieu and Doltisky "The CEFR offers a vision of language learning that enhances the social dimension of the individual through and action-based approach whereby human communication is not to be restricted to a performance in a given situation" (Tardieu and Doltisky, 2012, p. 2).

The European Commission of Languages established the following general objectives of CLIL in the Common European Framework of Reference for Languages (CEFRL, 2001): to allow students to broaden their knowledge of a subject; to improve student's abilities in a foreign language; and to give students an intercultural perspective of the subject, thus stimulating their interest and shaping new attitudes towards other cultures.

Teachers need clear methodological guidelines for complying with the dual-focused nature of CLIL so as to integrate successfully content and language. In this context of a lack of practical guidance, Coyle devised a theoretical but flexible framework consisting of 4 basic interrelated principles of CLIL: content, cognition, communication, and culture. Thus, CLIL teachers, textbook writers and material developers can utilize it as a reference for designing quality, rich and authentic materials aimed at teaching contents through language (Coyle, 2007). Hereunder are listed and briefly defined the main components of Coyle's 4Cs framework:

- *Content* is not only focused on knowledge and skills, since it also refers to how learners build their own personalized learning through strategies and understanding the way they develop their skills.
- *Cognition* is closely related to the thinking skills that were studied and classified in Bloom's taxonomy into "Lower Order and Higher Order Thinking Skills". When learners interpret contents and are faced with learning experiences which involve some linguistic demands, they need to put into practice cognitive strategies. In CLIL design and implementation our learner thinking skills have to be born in mind, to ensure that they can perform activities successfully and provide scaffolding and support if necessary.
- *Communication* is paramount when learning content through a FL, since learners have to interpret and reconstruct content and meanings in specific learning contexts. For that reason, language has to be clear and accessible and has to foster rich interactions among FL students.

- *Culture* can be seen as the combination of "self" and "other" awareness, identity and citizenship towards a global understanding. Intercultural awareness is one of the pillars of CLIL and culture is connected to the creation of learning communities worldwide by means of digital means.

Task-Based Learning and Teaching (TBLT)

To begin with, it is necessary to delve into the meaning of the term "task" and analyse its main constituents and characteristics. The concept of task has been defined on many occasions by numerous authors, who have taken diverse perspectives. However, they have also reached a consensus on numerous common features of the nature of tasks. The CEFR defined a task "as any purposeful action considered by an individual as necessary in order to achieve a given result in the context of a problem to be solved, an obligation to fulfil or an objective to be achieved" (CEFR, 2001, p. 10).

Prabhu described tasks as activities that require students to utilize the information they are provided with so as to arrive to an outcome by means of thought processes. Moreover, he added that TBLT approaches are ideal to practice a FL, since tasks have specific targets and the L2 is used as a medium for attaining them and the full engagement of students in task completion makes them learn the TL unconsciously. Similarly, Dave and Willis pinpointed the difference between tasks and grammatical exercises, owing to the fact that in tasks learners can make use of a wide range of linguistic structures, which are not specified and provided beforehand, so as to realize the task outcome (Willis and Willis, 2001, 2007).

According to Nunan a pedagogical task is a "piece of classroom work that involves learners in comprehending, manipulating, producing or interacting in the target language while their attention is focused on mobilizing their grammatical knowledge in order to express meaning, and in which the intention is to convey meaning rather than to manipulate form" (Nunan, 2004, p. 4).

According to Ellis, a pedagogical task is "a workplan that requires learners to process language pragmatically in order to achieve an outcome that can be evaluated in terms of whether the correct or appropriate propositional content has been conveyed" (Ellis, 2003, p. 16). He also suggested that any task-based course involves the following variables: the nature of the task input, the way information is provided to the students, both cognitive demands and discourse necessary to perform the task and the expected product of the task.

In their work "Integrating the task-based approach to CLIL teaching", Tardieu and Doltisky described language learners as social agents in a social-communicative perspective. They quoted the CEFR to describe language users and learners as "members of society who have tasks to accomplish a given set of circumstances in a specific environment and within a particular field of action." (CEFR, 2001, p. 9, in Tardieu and Doltisky, 2012, p. 7).

Figure 1. Kolb's experiential learning theory diagram
Source: McLeod, S. (2017)

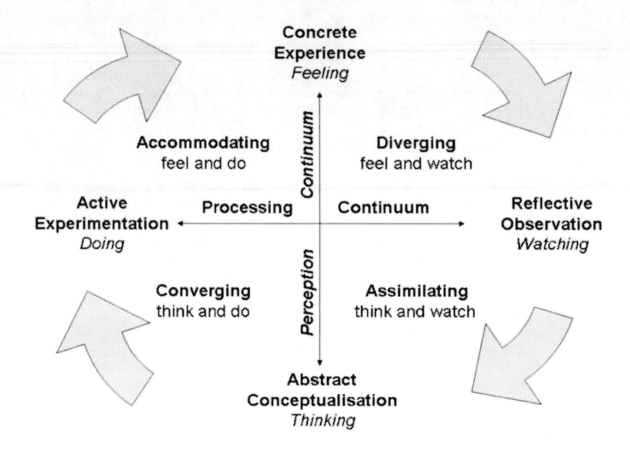

TBLT is based on the concept of experiential learning because it requires the involvement of students to learn by doing and their personal experiences are utilized as starting points. According to Nunan,

learners move from what they already know and can do to the incorporation of new knowledge and skills. They do this by immediate experience, and then going beyond the immediate experience through a process of reflection and transformation (2004, p. 12).

Communicative Language Teaching and TBLT

Since the emergence of Communicative Language Teaching (CLT) during the 1970s, diverse opposing views on how this approach needed to be integrated along with the FL curriculum have arisen. On the one hand, "methodologists" believed that focusing exclusively on form was not necessary for acquiring an L2. According to these linguists, learning how to utilize the FL could be developed automatically and spontaneously by completing tasks. On the other hand, "syllabus designers" challenged that view, since they considered that grammar is an essential resource for meaning making. As for Nunan: "the

Benefits of the Application of Task-Based Learning Within the Bilingual Field in Primary Education

development of CLT has had a profound effect on both methodology and syllabus design, and has greatly enhanced the status of the concept of 'task' within the curriculum" (Nunan, 2004, p. 10).

Regarding the relationship between TBLT and Communicative Language Teaching, Nunan defines CLT as a broad approach to the FL curriculum. Moreover, he affirms that: "Task-based language teaching represents a realization of this philosophy at the levels of syllabus design and methodology" (2004, p. 10). He also suggested that after the rise of CLT, the approaching to curriculum became broader, since the differentiation between syllabus design and methodology was not substantial anymore. In fact, he claimed that when programming contents, tasks and learning procedures had to be specified in an integrated way.

Breen (2001) suggested the solution to resolve the dichotomy between language product and learning. The process was to join both perspectives and see them as one. Besides, he defended that communication had to be the main goal of language curriculum and that language process had to be prioritized over language content. In other words: "prioritize the route itself; a focusing upon the means towards the learning of a new language. Here the designer would give priority to the changing process of learning and the potential of the classroom" (Breen, 2001, p. 52, in Nunan, 2004, p. 8).

Advantages and Disadvantages of Task-Based Instruction

Education researchers have been deeply analysing the positive effects of Task-Based Instruction over the last decades. Many of these investigations have focused on the benefits of applying tasks within the field of SLA. One of the forerunners of TBLT study, Prabhu, noticed that students learn the FL better when its use is embedded in a task (Prabhu, 1987). Willis (1996), established four key conditions for a successful FL acquisition through the development of tasks:

1. Willis pointed out the high interaction with the teacher in pre-task phases and between peers during the performance of tasks. Besides, she highlighted the richness and authenticity of language input utilized when learners try to make themselves understood in dynamic communication settings. In tasks, FL input is not limited to simple and isolated sentences.
2. Willis also praised the opportunities that TBLT framework offered for language learners so as to experiment with TL in various circumstances. Students are provided with practical contexts for using the L2 to express their ideas or opinions, interact spontaneously with other classmates, take turns or planning and carrying out a presentation to an audience.
3. Regarding motivation, Willis explained that the goal-oriented nature of tasks is a highly motivating factor for students, because they need to use the FL to complete the task or solve the problem. Moreover, pupils are more willing to listen and read materials through the L2.
4. Lastly, she stresses the necessity to focus on language form after the task cycle. This analysis of language accuracy makes students reflect on language items that they have employed to systematize them and allows them to consolidate new language. Then, leaners control their own linguistic improvement and we prevent the fossilisation of some mistakes.

Even though this chapter aims to provide the beneficial effects of applying TBLT, it is also essential to analyse its shortcomings. Swan (2005) examined the drawbacks of only applying meaning-centred tasks along a whole year and rejecting other complementary approaches when designing a syllabus.

Swan points out some of the drawbacks of applying narrow form-centred approaches and critics some of the following misconceptions associated to TBI:

1. The lack of convincing empirical theoretical and practical evidences for supporting the superiority and adequacy of TBLT over other more traditional ESL approaches.
2. The ill-founded rejection of complementary traditional approaches for the sake of supporting a new teaching approach. Swan warns about the negative effects that this subtractive change of focus could have in ESL.
3. If the learning perspective is excessively focused on students in TBI this may downgrade the role and influence of the teacher. According to Swan (2005), a balance between teacher- centred and learner-centred approaches needs to be struck so as to get build a multi-faceted syllabus.
4. The exclusive application of TBI with a naturalistic and communication-based pedagogy is not suitable for teaching new linguistic materials and is rather limited and poor when it comes to expose students with contexts.
5. TBLT approaches are inappropriate to the learning contexts of a vast majority of learners. Swan criticizes the fact that naturalistic tasks do not take into consideration key factors of educational contexts such as the actual learner's FL level and the available resources.

DISCUSSION

Classification of Different Types of Tasks

In order to understand the relationships between TBLT and CLIL and establish how tasks could be applied in within CLIL lessons it is paramount to discuss several tasks classifications. To begin with, Ellis distinguished between task-supported language teaching, which refers to the traditional utilization of tasks in an isolated way during the course and the task-based language teaching, which considers tasks as a central part of the course design (Ellis, 2003).

Similarly, Nunan explained that individual tasks are often part of larger sequences of tasks. Nunan (2004) divided tasks into two main types: real-world tasks and pedagogical tasks. While real-world or target tasks refer to language use outside the classroom, pedagogical tasks are transformed from the real world to the classroom and become pedagogical in nature.

Authors like Richards, Platt, and Weber, Breen and Nunan embraced the concept of pedagogical task, since it contemplated linguistic and non-linguistic outcomes. According to the authors, a pedagogical task could be defined as:

(…) an activity or action which is carried out as the result of processing or understanding language. For example, drawing a map while listening to a tape, listening to an instruction and performing a command may be referred to as tasks (Richards, Platt, and Weber, 1986, p 289).

Tardieu and Doltisky made another distinction that should be taken into account by teachers when designing tasks by considering how tasks will be performed and how their goals will be achieved by learners (Tardieu and Doltisky, 2012). Then we have to distinguish between final tasks, which are guided by intermediary exercises and are the outcome attained as a result of several lessons; micro tasks, which only focus on one linguistic aspect of the task; and macro tasks, which are compilations of other tasks, including micro tasks.

In 1993, Teresa Pica and her fellow researchers studied tasks: interaction relationships, requirements, goals and possible outcomes, so as to determine the nature of the task itself and of learners' behaviours. As a result, they distinguished these types of tasks (Pica et al., 1993):

- *Jigsaw tasks* are collaborative activities where participants have information that has to be shared through interaction with their classmates to successfully complete a task. Pica describes jigsaw tasks as: "the type of task most likely to generate opportunities for interactants to work toward comprehension, feedback, and interlanguage modification processes related to successful SLA" (Pica et al., 1993, p. 21, in Jackson, 2022).
- *Information gap tasks* share various commonalities with jigsaw tasks, but the main difference is that only one of the participants has the information required to complete the task. Therefore, it is essential to make students alternate their roles to allow them to have the same amount of feedback and to make use of the L2 to fulfil the goal of the activity.
- In *problem-solving tasks* all interactants have access to information, so interaction is not needed. However, students can help each other to achieve the tasks completion. These tasks only have one possible outcome and the whole performance is aimed at reaching it.
- With regard to *decision-making tasks*, participants work together to choose between several solutions. Although interaction between learners is necessary to agree the most suitable outcome, they may not equally participate in the task. Pica claims that in these tasks: "comprehension, feedback, and production become reduced" (Pica et al., 1993, p. 21).
- Finally, *opinion exchange tasks* are based on discussion and have a very flexible nature, because participants can have different communicative goals. As there are numerous possible outcomes, interactants can negotiate. Then, there is more room for students practicing production and understanding skills and for developing their own interlanguages.

TBLT Pedagogical Connection with CLIL Principles

Meyer deeply examined CLIL's integrative nature and its main constituents in his articles. He established six quality principles and strategies that need to be considered by all CLIL teachers when planning their lessons and designing materials for their students. Then, these underpinnings of CLIL instruction will be briefly examined in order to set relationships between them and TBLT. Furthermore, a thorough analysis of all the pedagogical possibilities and benefits of applying tasks to put CLIL principles into practice will be carried out.

Figure 2. Core elements of CLIL instruction
Source: Meyer (2010)

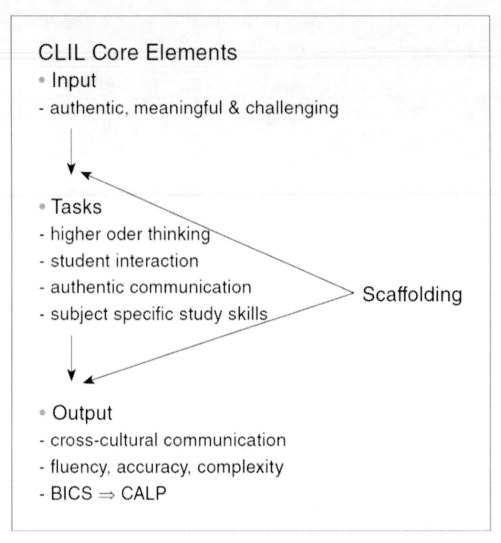

Principle 1: Rich Input

In his first quality principle named "Rich Input" Meyer pointed out the importance of providing learners with meaningful and challenging inputs so as to foster their L2 acquisition. Teachers must make connections between classroom contents and learners' areas of interest, because if topics are closer to students' real-life experiences, we enhance their curiosity and motivation for learning through the FL. Besides, learners can link new subject contents to their previous knowledge developing a more contextualised and solid learning.

In addition, for providing learners with genuine TL input it is paramount to make use of digital and interactive materials, like videos and web-quests, since these materials are challenging and motivating for learners. This essential principle of CLIL instruction is closely related to the TBLT, owing to the multimodal characteristics of tasks. Task-based instruction provides bilingual students with a great variety of authentic materials and resources, which are ideal for working subject contents through a TL in dynamic and challenging tasks. Therefore, when children apply their knowledge to answer complex questions, solve problems or create products in tasks, they are bringing the real world to their classroom.

Principle 2: Scaffolding Learning

The second quality principle "Scaffolding Learning" is focused on the need of applying scaffolding strategies when working with authentic FL and content specific materials. In this way, we guide our students' learning and maximise their intake of content. On the one hand, Meyer emphasizes the key role of teachers for a successful CLIL instruction when providing a scaffolding model, feedback and a systematic error treatment. On the other hand, he explains the relevance of scaffolding for helping learners to construct their own learning, which requires meaningful and systematic practices in CLIL settings.

Leaners need constant feedback and continuous practice to develop declarative knowledge, so as to comprehend authentic materials and FL contents. However, they should perform cognitive activities to develop their learning skills and strategies, which represent procedural knowledge. According to Lyster, instructional activities have to "set up contexts in which these skills can be displayed, monitored, and appropriate feedback given to the shape of their acquisition" (Lyster, 2007, p. 149, in Meyer, 2010, p. 16).

Principle 3: Rich interaction and Pushed Output

Meyer named his third quality principle "Rich interaction and pushed output" for expressing the way interlanguage is developed by FL students and how they improve their language production through conversational interactions and by exchanging feedback. Learners apply their linguistic resources and reflective strategies to express their output in a clear and comprehensible way. He highlights Dalton-Puffer's and Vollmer's findings, since they revealed that in CLIL classrooms speaking and writing skills are scarcely promoted. Thus, the lack of development of productive language skills limits their capacity to verbalize subject-specific aspects, promotes a misuse of argumentation patterns and has a negative impact on their writing skills. Therefore, Communicative Language Teaching is instrumental for contributing to the development of interlanguage by students. In fact, TBLT is based on the idea that genuine communication is produced when there are communication gaps.

In 2008, Vollmer carried out a comparative study in several CLIL classrooms that brought concerns about some lacks of CLIL students in their FL academic use. Considering Vollmer's findings, tasks offer ideal learning contexts where learners could not only improve their mastery of Cognitive Academic Language Proficiency (CALP), but also increase their Basic Interpersonal Communication Skills (BICS), which are essential to encourage learners' participation in CLIL lessons.

Figure 3. Exchange models for oral interaction within CLIL group tasks
Source: Meyer (2010)

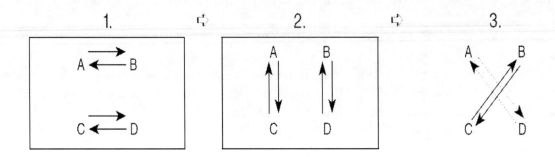

Principle 4: Addition of Intercultural Dimension

The fourth quality principle set by Meyer stands for the C of Culture in Coyle's CLIL framework. In 2006, Grimalda studied the process of globalization and how interaction among individuals and knowing better each other in a group foster a higher predisposition for cooperating. Owing to that fact, understanding the target language culture is essential for developing a satisfactory intercultural communication. Therefore, learners need to be aware of the cultural differences between their own culture and the foreign one, by means of knowing the FL sociocultural perception of time and the singularities of verbal and non-verbal communication styles.

Meyer pointed out that CLIL has the potential to provide learners with rich cultural learning experiences, in which topics can be analysed from diverse cultural angles by applying different values and beliefs. "They need to become aware of the hidden cultural codes and the appropriate linguistic and non-linguistic means and strategies to address them and they need to be taught how to keep the flow of communication going without offending the partner" (Meyer, 2010, p. 20). As for Nunan, language plays a key role in students' learning processes due to its cognitive and sociocultural nature:

Although it is not always immediately apparent, everything we do in the classroom is underpinned by beliefs about the nature of language, the nature of the learning process and the nature of the teaching act (Nunan, 2004, p. 6).

Principle 5: Promotion of Higher Order Thinking Skills

In his fifth strategy entitled "Make it H.O.T.", Meyer refers to higher order thinking skills, a concept which belongs to Bloom's Taxonomy. Bloom devised this method for classifying educational goals for student performance evaluation. The original Taxonomy contained six major cognitive categories and in 2001 the six categories were changed to verbs by Anderson and Krathwohl (2001), since thinking skills involve action and engagement. Bloom's Taxonomy establishes a progression from Lower Order Thinking Skills (LOTS) to Higher Order Thinking Skills (HOTS).

Figure 4. Bloom's Taxonomy revisited
Source: Wilson, L. O. (2001)

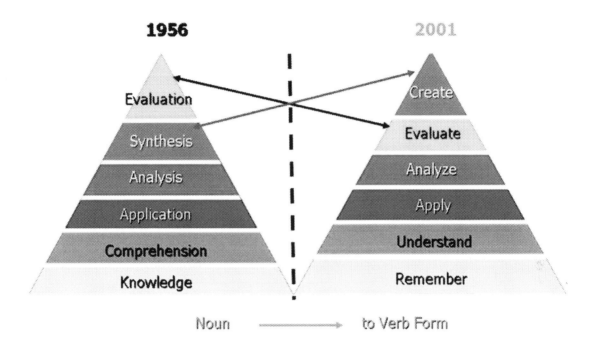

Along the lines set in Bloom's Taxonomy, Meyer claims that learners need systematic instruction for applying complex thought processes: "Students need to be shown how to express their thoughts in an increasingly complex manner" (Meyer, 2010, p. 21). He also emphasizes the necessity of providing learners with a high variety of cognitive activities within challenging and organized learning environments. Besides, teachers should follow the guidelines set in Bloom's taxonomy so as to adjust the cognitive level of activities to learners' actual skills.

Task-based experiences have a clear and organised structure and scaffolding frames which encourage learners to apply diverse scaffolding techniques. Tasks also offer rich and authentic input to the students and challenge them to implement personal strategies and diverse cognitive processes. Therefore, they are perfectly suitable for making pupils develop their multiple intelligences and develop their higher cognitive skills. Furthermore, the problem-solving nature of tasks involves employing different types of intelligences at the same time.

Principle 6: Sustainable Learning

Finally, Meyer adopted "Sustainable Learning" as his sixth quality principle, which he defines as the active knowledge that becomes ingrained in learners' long-term memory. For achieving a spontaneous and precise knowledge usage, students need to develop several skills and reach a high level of automatization by means of meaningful practice through rich and challenging learning experiences. He also describes competent learners as: "those who can deliberately retrieve knowledge and apply it to solve problems or complete tasks" (Meyer, 2010, p. 22).

In other words, teachers can only try to predict how learners are going to react to the tasks and perform them. For these reasons, Breen urges to train students to be active task designers and then agents of their own learning processes, by making their own choices on what to do and how to do it (Breen, 2001). Nunan affirms that in Task-based experiences learners are involved in all the steps of the process of curriculum creation, from the planning and content selection, through methodology implementation, to assessment and evaluation (Nunan, 2010).

Task Designing and Programming in Bilingual Education

Considering that CLIL is mainly focused on the fusion of different contents, strategies and languages, integration has to be a basic principle in its planning and implementation. In fact, CLIL could be defined as a net of connections among the different subjects, topics, languages and projects. Moreover, all the new skills and literacies that citizens of the 21st century need to acquire to live in highly complex and interrelated societies cannot be taught and learnt in isolated content areas.

Integration has to be implemented through cross-curricular connections between diverse subjects, topics and subtopics, but especially in the CLIL field where the development of subject-related pluriliteracies is aimed at employing the L2 to express knowledge and content. The TBLT approach is suitable to ensure a successful transition from an integrated CLIL curriculum planning to its implementation, since task-based experiences set ideal contexts for developing integrated learning in a natural and unconscious way.

According to San Isidro, task-based instruction makes it easier to align curriculum design and its implementation in CLIL settings, leading to creative outcomes. However, bilingual teachers must provide preparatory and scaffolding input by means of pre-tasks and micro-tasks so as to ensure pupils are able to perform the final task. In addition, programming task-based experiences permits different levels of performance in mixed-ability groups and thus caters for students' diverse learning styles and needs (San Isidro, 2017).

Lastly, Jensen emphasized learners' need for developing HOTS in cognitively significant and rich learning contexts. To that effect, he formulated the following key factors to ensure meaningful learning and content acquisition by students (Jensen, 1998):

- Engagement in learning experiences is necessary for promoting unconscious and meaningful learning by our students. Tasks are highly motivating for pupils because they establish dynamic contexts in which learners' commitment and responsibility are essential.
- The repetition of key concepts is vital to ensure learners internalize them, especially when dealing with CLIL subject contents. Task-based experiences prove to be useful because pupils can employ these terms on numerous occasions and in a purposeful way.
- Input quality allows learners to cope with all the linguistic and cognitive demands of learning experiences. This concept is closely linked to scaffolding. Regarding TBLT, the structured and gradual nature of tasks makes them really suitable to guide children acquisition of contents through the L2.
- Coherence is also needed when the teacher selects and plans the instruction approach. In other words, coherence stands for taking consistent methodological decisions and setting realistic learning goals to cater for our students' learning styles and real needs.
- Timing must also be considered when programming task-based learning experiences since authentic tasks are cognitively demanding and require students to show high levels of attention. As

the aim is to maximize students' readiness for working, teachers have to choose the moment of the day when the children feel more energetic and are more attentive.
- Error correction and feedback are fundamental in any learning process. Tasks provide safe and stress-free settings, where students feel more confident and less anxious and are more willing to participate and make contributions to answer complex questions.
- Emotional states have a great impact on students' performances in tasks, since some feelings can hinder FL learning, such as anxiety or the lack of motivation and self-confidence. Thus, teachers need to establish relaxed and stress-free task environments in order to encourage positive attitudes by learners towards learning.

Figure 5. Requirements for a meaningful content acquisition
Source: Own elaboration (from Jensen)

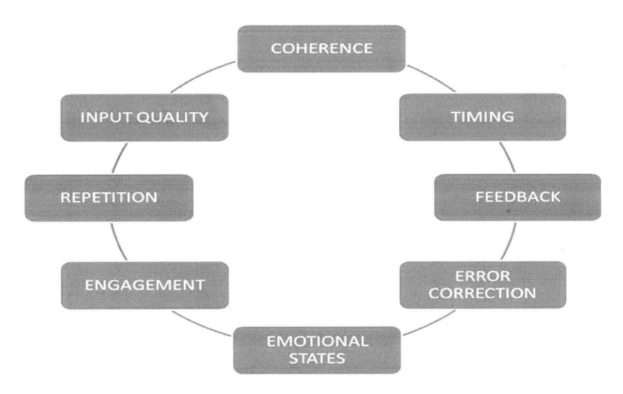

Practical Tools and Resources for Planning and Designing CLIL Tasks

As it has been dealt within the literature review section, integration in CLIL can be carried out through Coyle's 4Cs framework. Indeed, Meyer employed this framework as a reference so as to generate the CLIL pyramid, which is a systematic and tested approach aimed at planning and implementing CLIL-oriented tasks. The CLIL pyramid is a practical tool devised to help CLIL teachers to program lessons and units and to adapt materials by providing them with templates. Although content and language integration are the basis of CLIL instruction, it is essential to note that it is extremely difficult to integrate all quality principles and strategies in one single task or lesson. Thus, when designing tasks, it is necessary to embed them in a sequenced way by organising tasks around a central topic or unit. Meyer's CLIL pyramid outline can be observed in Figure 6, along with some brief explanations of every step of the Pyramid needed to plan CLIL units and to design CLIL-oriented tasks (Meyer, 2010).

Figure 6. The CLIL Pyramid
Source: Meyer, O. (2010)

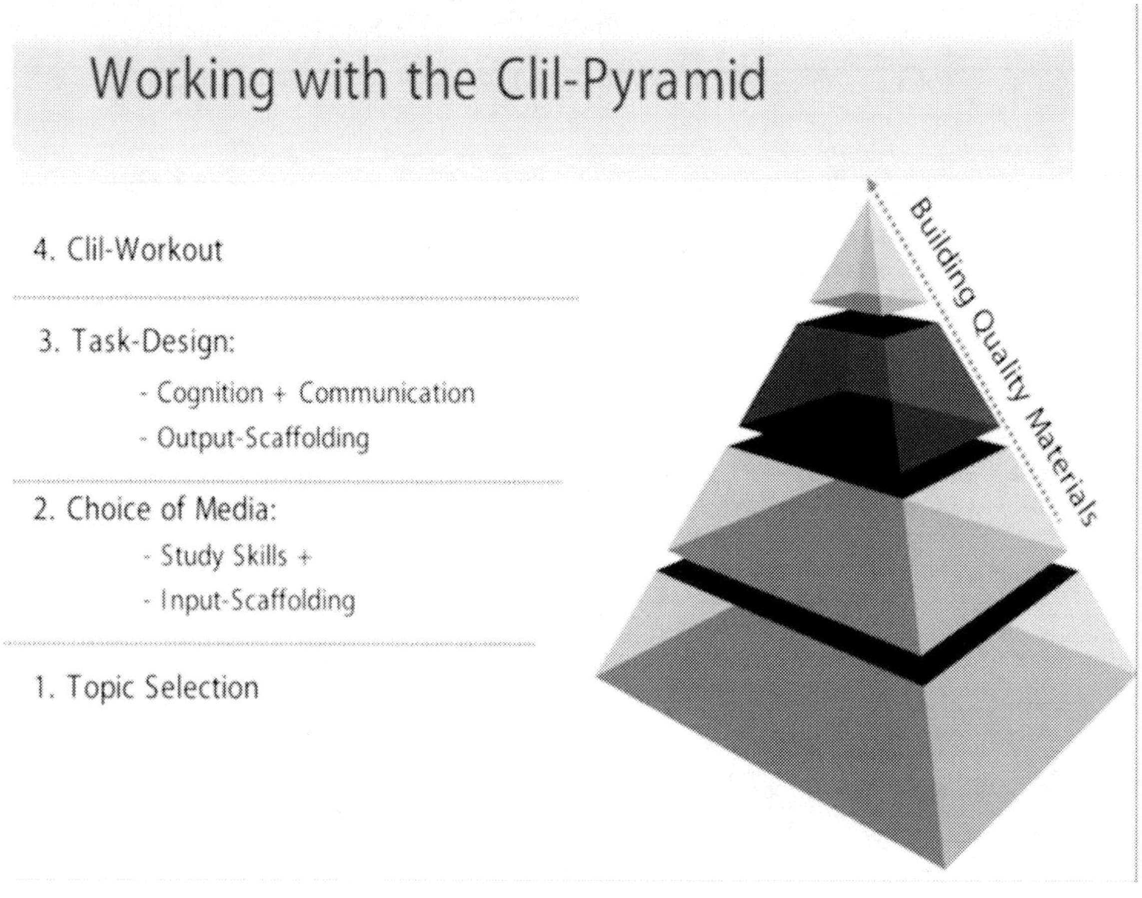

- TOPIC SELECTION can be seen as a starting point dedicated to consider the specific characteristics and requirements of the subject matter.
- CHOICE OF MEDIA covers the provision and the distribution of multimodal input. In other words, this step stands for the utilization of a wide variety of materials across CLIL units; the activation of FL skills and improvement of new literacies by our pupils
- TASK-DESIGN leads teachers to take into account the type of selected input so as to decide what type of scaffolding will be necessary and how much students need to deal with the selected input. Teachers have to apply various interaction models and group arrangements to encourage students to develop individual and collaborative skills.
- CLIL WORKOUT defines the nature of the output that teacher wants learners to generate. For instance, pupils can create a map, an infographic or a digital presentation, among other products.

Meyer also developed a model of template designed to guide the process of CLIL task-design, which can be seen in Figure 7 "to help students and teachers plan their lessons with the CLIL pyramid, we have developed a template for CLIL units" (Meyer, 2010, p. 24). In order to apply this practical tool, designers have to select a main topic or a driving question as starting point for structuring sub-topics around it. Then, interrelationship is developed in-between topics and sub-topics, but also with regard to the tasks, the language and thinking skills and the media employed.

Figure 7. Template sample for CLIL unit tasks
Source: Meyer, O. (2010)

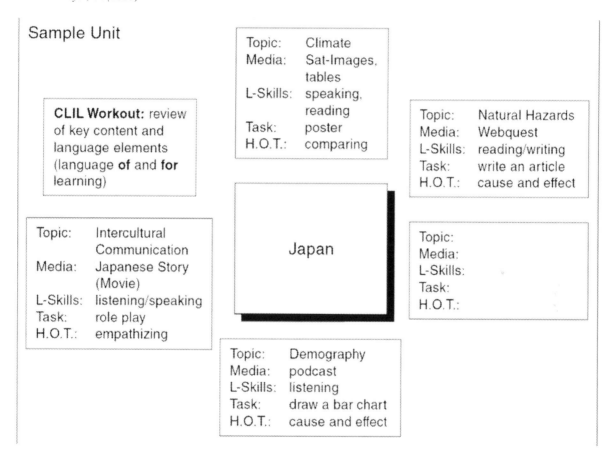

DISCUSSION OF RESULTS

Analysis of the Template Model for Task Design in CLIL

In the field of CLIL education, teachers have always pointed out the need for being provided with more learning materials and extra resources to be able to provide a quality and integral instruction. However, the application of various supports and tools aimed at programming CLIL units in a structured and systematic manner is as relevant and essential as material provision. Therefore, templates must be the cornerstone in the process of design of CLIL tasks, since they are useful and suitable tools to align learning experiences with the CLIL curriculum and foster integrated learning among all learning areas.

Meyer's template has been taken as a reference to create a more detailed version of a CLIL template aimed at designing sequences of task-based experiences. Regarding the structure of the adapted sequence of tasks, it is clearly inspired by the one provided by Meyer because both templates contain several tasks related with each other and designed around a main topic, not a final task. In the case of this adapted version of Meyer's template the central topic is "Ecosystems and Biomes" and there are five tasks about diverse subtopics linked to the main one.

As it can be observed in the simplified outline presented in Figure 8, this sequence of tasks sets a progression between tasks with regard to their sub-topics and contents, but also from cognitive and linguistic standpoints. Besides, all task titles are driving questions or inquiries that have to be answered or solved out by learners by means of performing the tasks. The level of interrelation among the tasks is high since they are planned to be developed as a continuum. However, each one could also be treated independently and adjustments could be made by the teacher according to students' circumstances or the desired learning objectives.

As for the age group to which this sequenced CLIL tasks are targeted to, it is relevant to note that they are intended to be performed by 5th graders of Primary Education. Nevertheless, it is a flexible tool and the same template model could be adapted to other school levels by making changes like adjusting the content and language demands, offering more or less input scaffolding, choosing different materials or grading the level of learning objectives. In addition, the subject in which this sequence of tasks will be carried out is Natural Science, but as integration is paramount in CLIL instruction this sequence will be connected directly and indirectly to other areas by embedding contents and subtopics from other disciplines.

Figure 8. Outline of the sequence of CLIL tasks
Source: Own elaboration

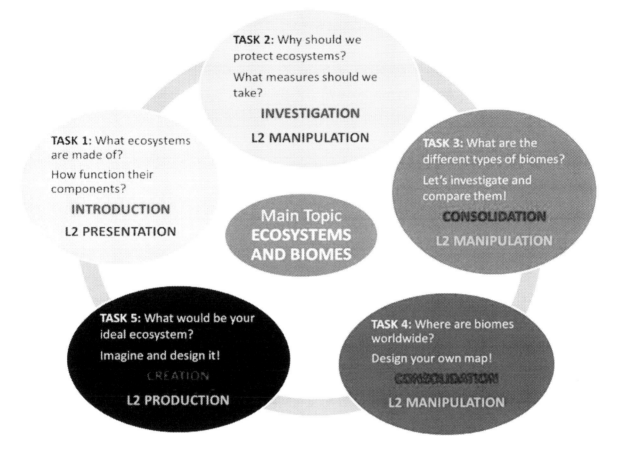

Even though the template model that will be analysed hereafter is a flexible tool which could be adjusted to carry out either multidisciplinary, transdisciplinary or interdisciplinary curriculum integration, in this case its utilization is based on a transdisciplinary curriculum integration approach. Within the context of this sequence of planned tasks CLIL learners establish relationships among disciplines and topics, but also develop autonomous learning and cooperative strategies in group tasks. Moreover, considering that the curriculum is organized around a unifying topic, students are encouraged to acquire meaningful knowledge and develop interdisciplinary skills in authentic contexts. Lastly, San Isidro highlighted the fact that diverse types of intelligences are developed when completing a single task (San Isidro, 2017). This is due to the fact that for performing successfully every task, pupils need to develop several of Gardner's Multiple Intelligences in an integrated way.

Figure 9. Legend of the adapted template model for CLIL tasks
Source: Own elaboration

TASK nº – TITLE (driving question)
➢ **DESCR.** → task Description and Topic - <u>pre-task:</u> topic and task introduction - <u>post-task:</u> desired final output and its utilization
➢ **OBJ.** → Objectives (including Cross Curricular goals)
➢ **ORG.** → Organization (groupings/arrangements)
➢ **M.** → Media (physical / digital)
➢ **Lang. Skills.** → Language Skills involved
➢ **Cog. Skills** → Cognitive Skills developed
➢ **M. I.** → Gardner's Multiple Intelligences
➢ **C for** Content, Communication, Cognition, Culture
➢ **BICS** → Basic Interpersonal Communication Skills
➢ **CALP** → Cognitive Academic Language Proficiency subject specific content *"examples"*

Figure 9 shows the template model that has been used for planning and designing every task of the previously described sequence of tasks. The legend also lists the meanings behind the acronyms and abbreviations of all the items of the template. With regard to this enlarged adaptation of Meyer's template, it is relevant to highlight that it is a more complex and detailed version because it includes specific items for describing the characteristics of each task and analysing each aspect in a more accurate way. In addition, as this template has a flexible nature, teachers can decide on the level of precision and detail that they want to implement when completing each point during task design.

Unlike Meyer's template model, the adapted version that can be observed in Figure 9 has a more complex structure including items that will be discussed below. The inclusion of these new elements of task analysis is clearly beneficial for CLIL teachers because they can enlarge on more task variables and enhance the usefulness of their task design.

- In the <u>description</u> of the task teachers identify the topic of the task and summarize the steps that pupils need to take to perform it. Task designers can also expand these explanations and highlight

some key terms in order to clarify task completion. Moreover, pre-task and post-task guidelines are also added for providing a complete picture of the task.
- The item dedicated to the <u>objectives</u> of the task can be utilized by bilingual educators for listing the main objectives that learners are expected to attain during task implementation and the goals they have to achieve at the end.
- As for the <u>organization</u>, task designers can briefly note down the types of groupings, number of pupils per group and aspects of the class arrangement that are intended to be utilized in each task, along with keywords related to the organizational choices.
- Regarding <u>cognitive skills</u>, their relevance in the process of task design is indisputable, since adjusting the cognitive level of a task determines how successful CLIL learners can be when performing it. Hence, for planning the level of cognitive demand of a task, teachers can complete this item on the template by employing the verbs of Figure 10, which resulted from the revisited version of Bloom's taxonomy carried out by Anderson and Krathwohl (2001).

Figure 10. Cognitive verbs for task design
Source: Armstrong, P. (2010)

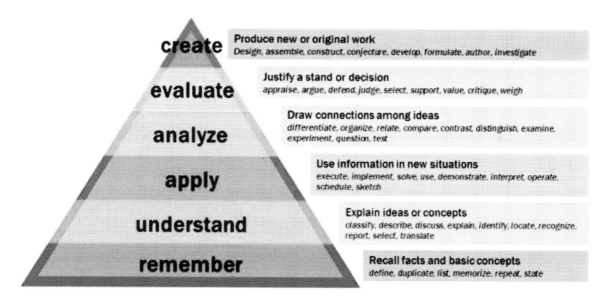

- The function of the <u>multiple intelligences</u> point is to identify the types of intelligences that are involved in the completion of each task, relying on Gardner's theory of multiple intelligences. Indeed, all the tasks illustrate the integration of numerous intelligences because they require learners to apply several of them.
- The item <u>C for</u> serves for noting down the four Cs (Content, Communication, Cognition and Culture) developed within each task. Although Coyle established in the 4Cs framework that all four Cs are inherently present in CLIL educational experiences, it is really complicated to integrate all of them in one single task.

- Last by not least, the points devoted to the treatment of <u>BICS and CALP</u> language features are highly relevant in the bilingual field, since CLIL teachers need to take into consideration both language for classroom interaction and content specific language. Therefore, when planning tasks, it is useful to describe what type of academic vocabulary and linguistic expressions students are expected to employ while performing tasks.

Analysis of the Stages for Task Development and Implementation

Cano created two different structures containing the necessary stages which have to be followed when developing and implementing tasks. On the one hand, Cano's first model for task designing is based on Bloom's taxonomy because it aims to ensure the cognitive progression in tasks planning and implementation (Cano, 2013). He separated the following cognitive stages, whose goals are deeply linked to the cognitive evolution:

1. The **Introduction stage** has a brainstorming function through tasks which provide learners with feedback about what they know about the topic. There are numerous types of introductory tasks, such as brainstorming games or the visualisation of multimedia materials.
2. The **Investigation stage** fosters students' research about a particular topic so as to get familiar with it. Manipulation is also fundamental within this stage because students have to carry out matching, classifying and reading tasks to discover the topic in a deeper way.
3. The **Consolidation stage** allows students to gather all the contents they have learnt and the skills they have acquired, in a structured manner. To that effect, learners make use of graphic organizers and mind maps in order to perform organizing tasks.
4. The **Creation stage** learners develop higher thinking skills (analyse, evaluate, create) for generating a final product, like a digital presentation, an infographic or a video. Therefore, they apply what they have learnt in a practical and creative way.

With regard to the previously analysed outline in Figure 8, it is relevant to note that the sequence of tasks presents a sequenced cognitive evolution from task 1 to task 5 following the four stages established by Cano. The first task has an introductory function since learners activate their previous knowledge on the components of ecosystems and also have to elicit the main contents of the task to organize their own theoretical base. Then, task 2 belongs to the investigation stage because students carry out research about environmental topics and have to select information to prepare their arguments for a debate and eventually summarize their conclusions in an infographic. As for tasks 3 and 4, both of them fit into the consolidation stage owing to the fact that learners collaborate for gathering relevant information and selecting data related to world biomes. Then, they reformulate key contents visually in mind maps and posters. Finally, the creation stage is developed in task 5 in which pupils have to put together the knowledge and skills they have acquired during the previous tasks so as to create and describe the characteristics of their own ideal ecosystem.

Hereafter, Figure 11 represents the cognitive progression that occurs throughout the five tasks, by classifying them into a pyramid based on Bloom taxonomy's categories, according to the level of cognitive demand of every task. Moreover, the main cognitive skills required to carry out each task are disposed in the form of cognitive verbs, like the ones that were presented in Figure 10. As for the organization and sequencing of the five tasks they show a gradual cognitive evolution from LOTS to HOTS.

Figure 11. Pyramid of cognitive progression in tasks
Source: Own elaboration

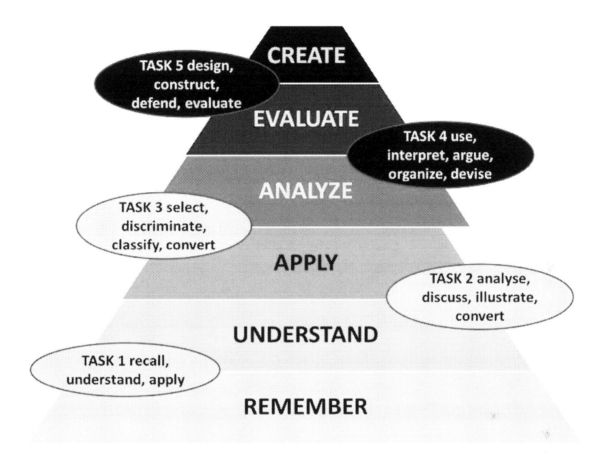

Regarding the sequenced tasks analysed in the previous section, it is worthy to note that the model of linguistic phases set by Cano has been taken as a reference to plan the tasks and to design the adapted template version. The first task has an introductory function since it aims at activating learners' previous knowledge and enlarging their vocabulary about the components of ecosystems. Then, the manipulation phase is mainly carried out during the second, third and fourth tasks, in which pupils are provided with a great variety of scientific documents and materials containing authentic language. For performing these tasks students need to apply linguistic strategies, in order to interpret and reformulate all this information. Even though these tasks are clearly manipulative they also share some elements with the production stage. Lastly, the fifth task has a clear productive nature since learners need to make usage of their English repertoire with a clear communicative purpose. Thus, they have to apply all their linguistic skills and strategies for setting about their own short projects and for assessing their classmates' creations.

Practical Application of the TBLT Framework in CLIL Tasks

Considering that Willis' TBLT framework has a functional nature, it would not be possible to fully understand its usefulness for designing CLIL tasks without analysing all the pedagogical possibilities that this model entails. Thus, it is necessary to carry out a thorough analysis of the practical variables present within each part and subsection of this model. In addition, all the main guidelines set by Willis (2016) will be discussed from a practical standpoint, including specific indications related to groupings and class arrangements, diverse pedagogical strategies, the roles of teachers and students within every stage and some examples of tasks and activities.

When it comes to the flexibility of the TBLT framework, Willis claims that "depending on the needs and backgrounds of the students, the components of the framework can be weighted differently" (2016, p. 7). Lastly, taking into account that the task sequence described in the previous sections has been conceived along the lines of the TBLT framework, the third task will be taken as a reference in order to illustrate how the framework could be implemented within a CLIL task. Then, the following table outlines some brief explanations of how TBLT framework elements are integrated in task 3.

1. When starting the PRE-TASK phase, the teacher is in charge of introducing the topic and outlining the main themes of the task. To that effect, students can use pictures, relate to their personal experiences or play diverse types of games, such as memory or vocabulary games and role plays. For example, the third task of the sequence starts with a brainstorming activity intended to activate learners' previous knowledge for recalling what a biome is. Students can make their contributions about biomes' characteristics and note this information on a shared document which is projected on the whiteboard. Then, the whole group will select the most significant comments and include them in an infographic that will serve as theoretical base for students when performing the task.

2. Then, it is time to go into the TASK CYCLE which is the most extensive of the TBLT framework. To begin with, this stage starts with the task itself which has a communicative nature and is aimed at authentic interactions. According to Willis, collaborative tasks are more suitable in TBLT because they give students opportunities for spontaneous interaction in the L2. Moreover, group work also raises learners' self-confidence and motivation levels. For instance, task 3 requires learners to collaborate in pairs to research the components of several biomes in websites, select key concepts and additional materials and summarize this information in digital concept maps. Hence, meaning negotiation and the effective communication in the L2 are essential to perform the task correctly. Moreover, when working in pairs, pupils collaborate and assist each other for making a successful use of both BICS and CALP languages during task completion. When it comes to the planning, it is a stage dedicated to reflect on the task outcome. During this planning phase, the teacher should monitor groups and advise them by solving their doubts related to the L2 or making suggestions for enhancing their linguistic production. Finally, after planning their report, learners have to share it with the rest of the class either in written form or by means of oral presentation. Then, taking as a reference task 3, all the concept maps that each pair have created to represent the characteristics of biomes can be considered a report in digital written form. However, concept maps could also be employed for performing oral reports since they could be used as visual supports in oral presentations displayed to the whole class.

3. Lastly, the last stage of the TBLT framework is dedicated to the LANGUAGE FOCUS. According to Willis, the function of this phase is to encourage the exploration of the FL by pupils and enhance students' awareness of linguistic features for getting a deeper comprehension of key concepts. Therefore, this phase is instrumental in CLIL settings because students improve their understanding of subject contents. Within the analysis stage, the CLIL teacher prepares tasks aimed at working with specific linguistic features to raise learners' FL consciousness. In addition, students should

Benefits of the Application of Task-Based Learning Within the Bilingual Field in Primary Education

take notes and extract useful language features to put these words and expressions together with their classmates and discuss their form and their meaning. On the other hand, to finish this stage students perform a controlled <u>practice</u> which consists of hands-on activities based on the FL aspects discussed during the analysis stage. Learners are intended to make use of the FL correctly in directed and structured activities, such as words substitution drills, sentences completion or matching verbs to their subjects. To finish up the third task and foster students' internalization of linguistic aspects, they could play memory games with the names of all biomes or complete descriptive sentences with information about the characteristics of each biome.

Table 1. Practical application of TBLT Framework within a CLIL task

PHASE	STAGE	TASK ELEMENTS	AIM
PRE-TASK	**Introduction to topic and task**	- Brainstorm vocabulary of biomes (components). - Create a document with the theory of reference.	- Activate previous knowledge - Select key concepts
TASK CYCLE	**Task**	- Research information about the types of biomes in pairs. - Select relevant vocabulary and create concept maps.	- Collaborate in web research - Meaning negotiation - Summarize content
	Planning	- Design concept maps in digital format. - Prepare oral presentation. - Employ visual supports.	- Accurate writing - Structure a clear oral presentation
	Report	- Share the concept maps in the classroom and read them. - Display the oral presentation. - Whole class topic discussion.	- Clarity and fluency in oral presentation - Provide feedback. - Discuss the outcomes.
LANGUAGE FOCUS	**Analysis**	- Examine concept maps with a variety of key terms. - Visualize native speaker speech. - Discuss words form and meaning.	- Focus on L2 aspects - Improve CALP language
	Practice	- Practice linguistic features in guided settings.	- Internalize FL terms - Unconscious acquisition

Source: Own elaboration

CONCLUSION

By way of conclusion, it is time for recapitulating and gathering the main findings of this research in order to discuss and truly understand its pedagogical contributions. Before starting any analysis, it is necessary to recall that the main object of this investigation was to explore the similarities between CLIL fundamentals and task-based instruction features, so as to establish relationships between both approaches and assess the usefulness of utilizing tasks in bilingual settings. Furthermore, it also relevant to mention that this study has a practical focus, because it aims to provide a functional insight into how tasks can be programmed in CLIL contexts. In other words, this research work intends to instruct CLIL teachers on functional strategies and classroom procedures for applying TBLT but also provides them with practical tools and instruments to design bilingual tasks.

With regards to the characteristics of CLIL instruction and of the TBLT, it must be noted that setting connections between both approaches was a seamless process. This is due to the fact that both learning perspectives have holistic approaches and share numerous principles, like their student-centred perspective, their communicative focus, their learning contexts linked to the real world, as well as their need for providing L2 students with rich, authentic and meaningful input and materials. Finally, after an extensive review of Meyer's work it can be concluded that implementing the 4Cs of Coyle's framework is achievable by means of contextualized CLIL tasks and that the six quality principles for CLIL instruction can be put into practice within task-based experiences.

As for the pedagogical benefits of carrying out bilingual instruction through tasks, this work has supplied the following significant insights. Firstly, tasks are ideal learning experiences so as to promote students' development of all linguistic skills, while employing them in a purposeful way when working CLIL topics. This is especially true within sequences of tasks which really allow encompassing the implementation of all the four skills.

Secondly, TBLT enables to provide learners with lots of exposure to rich input and authentic language. Besides, well-designed tasks are really suitable for scaffolding both cognitive and linguistic demands ensuring the acquisition of subject contents and CALP language by children. However, as CLIL tasks are mainly focused on meaning and are inserted in genuine and real contexts, they also foster an unconscious acquisition of L2 by students.

Thirdly, the highly communicative nature of tasks within CLIL and the need for oral and written interaction in the L2 to perform them encourage pupils' development of BICS language. In addition, group tasks require collaboration and meaning negotiation and as a consequence students improve their teamwork strategies.

Lastly, when it comes to the analysis of the instruments for designing CLIL tasks, the scarcity of studies providing practical insights into the application of tasks in bilingual learning contexts should be born in mind. Nevertheless, after examining the functionality of several practical tools and frameworks aimed at TBLT design, it has been proven that they could perfectly be adapted for sequencing bilingual tasks. This is the case of the TBLT framework, whose structure has successfully been adjusted to the planning of a sequence of CLIL tasks.

Furthermore, this research also intended to refine the existing practical tools for task design, so as to provide CLIL educators with comprehensive instruments for sequencing and programming bilingual tasks. Hence, the structures of some task designing instruments, such as Meyer's CLIL template model, have been taken as a reference to create a more detailed and enlarged template version. This adaptation has been successful since the resulting template model could help bilingual teachers to contextualize and systematize the programming of task sequences.

When dealing with bilingual tasks, pupils make decisions about the task itself and about the processes involved in its implementation. In addition, in order to provide them with opportunities for assessing their performance in CLIL tasks and the outcomes they have produced, it is essential to employ systematic designing instruments. For instance, the TBLT framework is an extremely useful tool because it encourages the use of self-assessment techniques by pupils and guarantees a comprehensive bilingual instruction.

Then, this investigation has also brought several useful findings on the application of TBLT in CLIL contexts from a functional standpoint. Owing to the analysis of other task designing tools, it has been possible to create a new streamlined template version which has a more complex and detailed structure. This template model includes more variables for adding extra information, like an item to reflect cognitive evolution or items to describe classroom management and grouping features. Therefore, the integration of new elements in templates results in obtaining more systematic and specific instruments for programming CLIL tasks, which ensure setting cognitive progressions from LOTS to HOTS in tasks sequences and allow scaffolding both subject and linguistic contents within CLIL task.

REFERENCES

Anderson, L. W., & Krathwohl, D. R. (2001). A Taxonomy for Learning, Teaching and Assessing (Abridged Edition). New York: Longman-Pearson Education.

Armstrong, P. (2010). *Bloom's Taxonomy*. Vanderbilt University Center for Teaching.

Breen, M. (2001). *Learner contributions to language learning: New directions in research*. Routledge.

Cano, W. (2013). *Manual CLIL para centros bilingües*. UNIR Ediciones.

Council of Europe. (2001). *Common European framework of reference for languages: Learning, teaching, assessment*. Press Syndicate of the University of Cambridge.

Coyle, D. (2007). Content and Language Integrated Learning: Towards a Connected Research Agenda for CLIL Pedagogies. *International Journal of Bilingual Education and Bilingualism*.

Ellis, R. (2003). *Task-Based Language Learning and Teaching*. Applied Linguistics. Oxford University Press.

Jackson, O. (2022). *Task-Based Language Teaching*. Cambridge University Press. doi:10.1017/9781009067973

Jensen, E. (1998). *Teaching with the brain in mind*. Association for Supervision and Curriculum Development.

Krashen, S. D. (2015). Remarks on language acquisition and literacy: Language acquisition and teaching, free reading, and its consequences, the use of the first language, writing, and the great native speaker teacher debate. *Indonesian JELT*, *10*(1), 1–17.

Lao, C., & Krashen, S. (2014). Language acquisition without speaking and without study. *Journal of Bilingual Education Research and Instruction*, *16*(1), 215–221.

McLeod, S. (2017). Kolb's learning styles and experiential learning cycle. *Simply psychology, 5*.

Meyer, O. (2010). *Towards quality-CLIL: successful planning and teaching strategies*. Pulso.

Nunan, D. (2004). *Task-based Language Teaching*. Cambridge University Press. doi:10.1017/CBO9780511667336

Pica, T., Kanagy, R., & Falodun, J. (1993). Choosing and using communication tasks for second language instruction and research. In S. Crookes & S. M. Gass (Eds.), *Tasks and Language Learning: Integrating Theory and Practice* (pp. 9–34). Multilingual Matters.

Prabhu, N. S. (1987). *Second language pedagogy* (Vol. 20). Oxford University Press.

Richards, J., Platt, J., & Weber, H. (1986). *Longman Dictionary of Applied Linguistics*. Longman. doi:10.1177/003368828601700208

San Isidro, X. (2017). *CLIL in a multilingual setting: a longitudinal study on students, families and teachers*. University of the Basque Country.

Saville-Troike, M., & Barto, K. (2016). *Introducing second language acquisition*. Cambridge University Press. doi:10.1017/9781316569832

Swan, M. (2005). *Legislation by Hypothesis: The Case of Task-Based Instruction*. Applied Linguistics. Oxford University Press.

Tardieu, C., & Dolitsky, M. (2012). *Integrating the task-based approach to CLIL teaching*. Cambridge Scholars Publishing.

Willis, D., & Willis, J. (2007). *Doing Task-Based Teaching*. Oxford University Press.

ADDITIONAL READING

Ahmadian, M. J., & García Mayo, M. P. (2018). *Recent Perspectives on Task-Based Language Learning and Teaching*. De Gruyter.

Baharun, R., Awang, Z., & Padlee, S. F. (2011). International students' choice criteria for selection of higher learning in Malaysian private universities. *African Journal of Business Management*, 5(12), 4704–4714.

Bygate, M., Skehan, P., & Swaim, M. (2001). *Researching Pedagogic Tasks. Second Language Learning, Teaching and Testing*. Routledge.

Coyle, D., Hood, P., & Marsh, D. (2010). *CLIL—Content and Language Integrated Learning*. Cambridge University Press. doi:10.1017/9781009024549

Hazleena B., Hanson, M.S., Mohd, M.I., Noor, M.S. (2016). Task-based language learning: investigating the dynamics of learners' oral interaction. *IJASOS- International E-journal of Advances in Social Sciences, 2*(5), 570-580.

Lackman, K. (n.d.). *Introduction to Task-based Learning: The Willis model and variations. Methods and activities for more effective teaching with less preparation*. Ken Lackman & Associates Educational Consultants.

Meyer, O. (2012). *Introducing the CLIL-Pyramid: Key Strategies and Principles for Quality CLIL Planning and Teaching*. Heidelberg, Germany: Winter.

Norris, J. (2016). Current uses for task-based language assessment. *Annual Review of Applied Linguistics*, *36*, 230–244. doi:10.1017/S0267190516000027

Nunan, D. (2016). Language teacher identity in teacher education. *Reflections on Language Teacher Identity Research*, 164.

Nunan, D. (2018). Teaching Speaking to Young Learners. The TESOL Encyclopedia of English Language Teaching, 1–8.

Panavelil, A. (2015). Teaching and Learning to Write: Using a Task-based approach in an EFL Class. In *Al-Mahrooqi, R., Singh V., Roscoe, A. Methodologies for Effective Writing Instruction in EFL and ESL Class Rooms Edition*. IGI Global.

Seals, C. A., & Olsen-Reeder, V. I. (Eds.). (2019). *Embracing multilingualism across educational contexts*. Victoria University Press.

Viet Hung, N. (2012). *Mother Tongue Use in Task-Based Language Teaching Model*. Canadian Center of Science and Education. doi:10.5539/elt.v5n8p23

APPENDIX

Task 1: What are ecosystems made of?
Task 2: Why should be protect ecosystems?
Task 3: What are the different types of biomes?
Task 4: Where are biomes worldwide?
Task 5: What would be your ideal ecosystem?

	Task 1	Task 2	Task 3	Task 4	Task 5
Description	Watch a video about ecosystems and its components and take notes	Students read articles from environmental organisations' magazines in groups	Research characteristics of world biomes in websites	Students search territories occupied by 1 biome	Students combine elements of real ecosystems to create their ideal one
Objective	Activate previous knowledge and vocabulary. Encourage autonomous learning. Develop learning to learn	Interpret contents from authentic documents. Develop research & negotiation skills. Employ information to build real products	Deal with specific content on different supports. Classify & compare the features of diverse biomes	Revise & elaborate specific scientific content. Apply geographical research. Develop artistic skills	Practice oral expression and presentation skills. Apply digital skills to create a presentation
Organization	Individual task	Small interactive groups (4-5)	In pairs	In pairs	Individual
Material	Video, note taking worksheet	Articles, digital whiteboard, computers	Computers, conceptual map, websites	Computers, digital maps	Art materials, computers, presentation programs
Skills	Listening, reading, writing	Reading, speaking, listening, writing	Reading, speaking, writing	Reading, listening, writing, speaking	Reading, listening, writing, speaking
Cognitive skills	Recall, understand, apply	Analyse, discuss, illustrate	Select, discriminate, classify	Use, interpret, argue, organise	Design, construct, defend, evaluate
M.I.	Naturalistic, linguistic-verbal, intrapersonal	Naturalistic, interpersonal, linguistic-verbal	Naturalistic, linguistic-verbal, visual-spatial	Naturalistic, linguistic-verbal, interpersonal, visual-spatial	Naturalistic, linguistic-verbal, intrapersonal, visual-spatial
C for	Content & Cognition	Content, Communication, Culture	Content, Communication, Cognition	Content, Communication, Cognition, Culture	Content, Communication, Cognition, Culture
BICS	Exchanges with the teacher	Oran expressions & strategies to defend positions	Meaning negotiation & oral collaboration	Communicative skills to organise & perform a common task	Employ linguistic strategies to provide a clear presentation
CALP	Living & non-living ecosystem components, function of elements	Main threats to nature, vocabulary to express solutions	World biomes glossary	Geographical location	Combine scientific vocabulary to describe ideal ecosystem

Chapter 14

Augmented Reality as an Innovative Tool for the Training of Bilingual Education Teachers in Primary Schools

Gerardo Reyes Ruiz

ⓘ https://orcid.org/0000-0003-0212-2952

Center for Higher Naval Studies (CESNAV), Mexico

ABSTRACT

Children know a language when they associate words with images and sounds—this facilitates the assimilation of knowledge. This research uses applications based on augmented reality, which are designed to help teachers who want to teach another language, particularly English. The set of useful terms for the student to learn is defined in various categories such as animals, colors, and things. These terms are stored in a database with different formats such as text, 3D image, audio, and video which are associated with items that contain, in turn, a vocabulary which represents abstract entities, which are necessary to complement the learning of a language. The words are associated with the images and with the corresponding audio so that the students learn to read, write, listen, and, consequently, pronounce the words correctly. This research is projected as an innovative technological support that helps primary school teachers in the process of teaching the English language, and it is expected that in the short term it will become an indispensable basis for this educational dynamic.

INTRODUCTION

Globalization has resulted in the need for people with knowledge of several languages to enter an increasingly competitive world in labor, economic and cultural terms (Marlina, 2013; Cummins, 2021). Learning different languages is one of the most frequent activities in elementary schools, especially in their first years of learning (The Curriculum Development Council, 2017; Rao and Yu, 2019). This last perspective has the premise that children make better use of their cognitive system than they have

DOI: 10.4018/978-1-6684-6179-2.ch014

Copyright © 2023, IGI Global. Copying or distributing in print or electronic forms without written permission of IGI Global is prohibited.

at those ages (Williams et al, 2021). Children who begin to know a language other than their mother tongue normally associate words with images and sounds, facilitating the assimilation of knowledge and increasing their educational interest (Roberts et al, 2018; Garton & Copland, 2019). In this context, educational technology has shown multiple advances to offer various tools related to language learning, which have been implemented in basic education because, as already mentioned, their purpose is to take advantage of the cognitive system and the plasticity so powerful that children of these ages have (Pliatsikas, 2020; Birdsong, 2018). The technological tools that are used for learning a language can facilitate a series of skills, which should be useful so that children at the basic level can communicate effectively and, if possible, develop and facilitate new educational contexts whose characteristics promote their learning (Llevot-Calvet, 2018). In this sense, it makes sense to generate new educational contexts whose implementation characteristics are not expensive, rather they are easy to implement and manage (Valverde-Berrocoso et al, 2021). That is, its costs are measured in low monetary terms, while its educational benefits are as high as possible (Kayapinar, 2021).

Technological development has shown multiple advances, which have strengthened strategies focused on the teaching-learning process (Sailer et al, 2021; da Silva et al, 2019). This progress is surpassed every day by more efficient technologies that aim to help students in their learning and support teachers in their educational process (Huang et al, 2019). Some of the new educational technologies are embedded with various devices and media such as the Internet, mobile devices, the cybernetic cloud, and various technological objects (Llevot-Calvet, 2018; Dengel et al, 2019). This is to more efficiently support the task of teaching and learning (Tzima et al, 2019). However, the new technology called Augmented Reality (AR) has emerged as an innovative and efficient tool that both supports and creates new educational environments (Rohrbach et al, 2021; Karagozlu, 2021). In addition, one of the most outstanding characteristics of AR is the interactive and dynamic way in which it helps students and supports teachers so that abstract educational content is easier to understand (Buchner & Zumbach, 2020). Therefore, it is currently required to generate educational contexts whose characteristics strengthen both the learning process and build new ways of transmitting knowledge with quality (Roopa, 2021; Muhammad, 2021). In this sense, it has been observed that AR is an ideal complement for creating various educational applications. In particular, it has also been shown to be quite useful for teaching a language (Redondo, 2020; Bensetti-Benbader & Brown, 2019). This is mainly because the basic characteristics of AR are defined as a technology through which the visualization of the real environment is augmented by elements or objects generated by a computer or mobile device (Yildiz, 2021; Abad -Segura et al, 2020).

Any language is used as a means of communication in different parts or regions of the world, so students must learn that language with the perspective that, when they need it, it will be easier for them to enter an increasingly globalized context (Mayilyan, 2019; Kessler, 2018). To complement this task, new but, above all, innovative technological tools are required that contribute first so that these students easily acquire new skills for learning a language and, subsequently, that this learning, being innovative and attractive for students, motivates teachers to learn to build new environments/learning environments, which are of interest to their students who want to learn a language in an innovative, efficient and continuous way (Marrahí-Gómez & Belda-Medina, 2020; Kessler, 2018). Undoubtedly, this last point commits basic-level teachers to be able to understand and empower themselves with these new technologies so that they can generate more innovative, interesting, and entertaining environments for their basic-level students (Palamar, 2021; Petrovych et al, 2021). With the background that children generally require games or activities that motivate them to want to learn, then AR is being proposed to be used by these students who study at preschool or primary levels (Nezhyva et al, 2020; Lai and Chang,

Augmented Reality as an Innovative Tool

2021). Furthermore, AR contemplates any person who wishes to learn a particular vocabulary, since this new technology aims to develop and implement the greatest possible number of tools that serve as a complement and support in the teaching-learning process of a language. at any age and educational level (Simonova & Kolesnichenko, 2022; Majid & Salam, 2021; Isaeva, 2021). In addition, the low cost of AR makes it possible to encapsulate suitable characteristics so that students, even of any age, assimilate another language using different learning styles during the teaching-learning process (Fan, Antle, & Warren, 2020).

The present work was carried out taking as a premise the previous precepts, which will be developed to describe how a system, based on AR, can work as training for basic-level students who want to learn or are motivated to learn a language and who are supported by their teachers interested in creating new and innovative educational environments based on AR (Alharbi, 2022). In particular, and as an example, reference is made to the English language (Altun & Lee, 2020), since if it is not the most widely spoken language worldwide, it is the most used in the main countries that generate avant-garde knowledge and, consequently, the results of their research are published in this type of language (Di Bitetti & Ferreras, 2017).

BACKGROUND

Globalization requires the training of teachers with knowledge in different subjects and, mainly, with suitable communication skills towards people with other lifestyles and, more than anything, with different communication languages (Hamid & Nguyen, 2016; Brock-Utne, 2022; Altan, 2017). All this is to allow entering a world of work that is as competitive as it is functional worldwide (Sun, 2013; Adawiyah & Gumartifa, 2022). Information and communication technologies provide guidelines for this to be achieved and for people to understand each other, regardless of the variety of their ideological and cultural areas (Lee & Daiute, 2019). The learning of another language different from the one that each individual has in their native environment is a constant need every day and on which schools are based so that students begin to be taught a language, preferably English, at an earlier age (Williams et al, 2021). The learning of different languages is one of the activities that are done more frequently in elementary schools, this is a consequence of studies where it is affirmed that the younger the age of the individuals for the learning of other different languages, the greater it is the cognitive plasticity of the individual to assimilate a foreign language (Pliatsikas, 2020; Birdsong, 2018).

The English language is the predominant language in the developed world in both reading, writing, and speaking. This is perceived mainly because, in addition to the people whose main language is English, this language is studied at different levels of the educational systems of multiple countries (Education First, 2020). The reason for this second choice of language is that the English language is used in more than 60 countries and is used for writing books, newspapers, airports and air traffic control, international business and academic conferences, science, technology, medicine, diplomacy, sports, international competitions, music, and advertising, in addition, scientific research is written, for the most part, in English (Di Bitetti & Ferreras, 2017). This dynamic results in millions of children studying, thanks to their school plans, the English language at different educational levels (National Academies of Sciences, Engineering, and Medicine, 2017; Council of Europe, 2018).

Consequently, the knowledge that is found in libraries, repositories or knowledge centers around the world, and that is available for teachers to make use of, is embodied in various languages, but mainly in the English language (Banegas and Consoli, 2021). This generates the need for teachers to be able to innovate strategies that help the learning process of this language and to generate educational tools that are supported by the various current technologies, such as free translators (Jubran & Arabiat, 2021; Al-Amri et al, 2014), which have evolved over the years and have been increasingly perfected, becoming a daily consultation software. In this context, the Google Translator tool is a freely accessible program designed for all types of people who already know how to read and write fluently. However, it is important to mention that this tool also has the option of voice search and is becoming more accessible, even with AR, for people who have some limitations, such as sight (The Economic Times, 2018; Disability Awareness Training, 2022).

The thematic contents of the schools referring to the English language contain helpful tools for teachers in their teaching and training (Guzmán, 2019). In addition, multiple tools have been designed to support learning in this language, which is offered to students from preschool, basic and professional levels, and even to anyone who wishes to obtain this knowledge (Sailer, Murböck, & Fischer, 2021; Llevat-Calvet, 2018; Huang, Spector, & Yang, 2019). A language can be learned at any age or situation of people and various materials have been developed to help both teachers and students in this task; In the same way, there are various technological tools to help people in this task of learning new vocabulary that make it easier for them to move through different countries smoothly (Cummins, 2021). From this perspective, educational technologies have constantly worked to offer various language learning tools, which are recommended to be used in preschool education and to take advantage of the powerful cognitive system that children have at that age (Williams et al, 2021). Therefore, the technological tools for learning the English language must be composed of a series of skills that allow teachers, students, and, in general, anyone to communicate effectively and develop in diverse educational contexts (Garton & Copland, 2019).

Times change along with the way of communicating, the way of obtaining information and learning has changed and, therefore, educational contexts have to be modified as well (Kayapinar, 2021). These changes must combine elements that promote learning in students of this century, who are restless and who have been born in a digital age where technological resources fill their space and life (Hugill, 2016; Elsobeihi & Abu Naser, 2017). For this reason, the traditional way of teaching and learning must migrate to new educational approaches, based on the fact that true learning requires experience and that the more senses are involved (sound, sight, touch, emotions, etc.), then more it will be more powerful and favorable for learning a language (Pérez-López & Contero, 2013). Furthermore, mobile devices, particularly through the new Apps, have become an extremely important and sensitive means of giving continuity to the educational process of schools at all educational levels (Saadeh et al, 2021). The multiple uses of these innovative applications have not been ignored by educational institutions and by those teachers who are looking for new and novel but above all efficient, ways to continue with the teaching-learning process. In this way, AR can be an essential part of the task of teaching and help create new educational environments that must be designed to motivate students to use their visual, auditory, and kinesthetic senses to learn (Petrov & Atanasova, 2020; Karagozlu, 2021). Peaceful students listening to lectures or exhibitions are a thing of the past, mainly because new ways of teaching and learning are now needed (Roopa, Prabha & Senthil, 2021). In other words, teachers require new ways of teaching a language, which require inserting knowledge into students, making them feel it, live it and enjoy it. Perhaps this sounds a bit poetic, but now there are technologies with which these goals can be achieved such as AR, VR, or mixed reality (MR) (Farshid et al, 2018).

In this context, AR is a tool that has gradually entered the educational option with various tools that strengthen the task of teachers to transmit their knowledge and help their students in the learning process

Augmented Reality as an Innovative Tool

(Roopa, Prabha & Senthil, 2021). This help is reflected in the fact that students develop skills such as spatial, practical skills, and conceptual understanding that are provided by image-based AR with mobile devices (Lv, Lloret, & Song, 2021). This technology aims to show students abstract elements in a virtual way that are superimposed on real physical reality, in addition, AR provides an interactive and attractive interface for students to reinforce their learning using 3D images or other multimedia resources (Rohrbach et al, 2021; Karagozlu, 2021). All this has shown that the implementation or development of activities in the classroom, based on AR, helps improve the learning process, increase motivation, and facilitate the work of the teacher (Sharma & Mantri, 2020; Gargrish, Mantri & PritKaur, 2020).

AR has been used to translate texts, as is the case with Google's Word Lens App, which bases its operation on positioning the camera over the text and its translation will automatically be displayed. Word Lens translates English, Spanish, French, German, Italian, Portuguese, and Russian languages with AR, plus it has additional features like erasing and reversing words and searching using a dictionary module (Word Lens, 2022). Another tool that AR uses to help teachers in the transmission of their knowledge of the English language is Wordbook, which bases its operation on markers that allow the selection of correctly written words in English so that the student trains the reading of that language (WordBook, 2022).

AR has not only served to teach English but systems have also been designed that help the learning of other types of languages, such as the Mayo Lottery App, which facilitates the learning of the Mayan language and is based on a Mayan lottery game. In other words, this App bases its operation on the interaction between images and audio that are used together to implement and present the AR. This App is a game that works with 89 images that are used as markers for the student to learn, as a game, interact with other classmates, and integrate various teams that make up the game. The way of understanding and interacting with abstract elements, shown through images, means that both the words that are shown as well as their meaning are recorded in the student's repertoire of knowledge (Miranda et al, 2016).

MAIN FOCUS OF THE CHAPTER

Issues, Controversies, Problems

In a globalized world, new ways of learning are currently needed, and, consequently, new and innovative technological tools that support emerging processes to transmit the learning of a language other than the mother tongue (Valverde-Berrocoso et al., 2021). In this sense, new technologies help to create innovative teaching-learning environments through which people can learn or train their skills acquired in various fields of knowledge and, in particular, in learning a language. (Sailer, Murböck, & Fischer, 2021). This dynamic has created an evident need for the new generations to learn another language, different from their mother tongue, through the use of current technology means that promote constant training (Kessler, 2018), which must be implemented in schools or be accessible from individually so that interested people train constantly (Abuhassna et al., 2020). The learning of new languages is one of the activities that is carried out most frequently in basic level schools, this is mainly due to the following result: the younger the age of the individuals for the learning of languages other than the Therefore, the cognitive plasticity of the individual to assimilate a foreign language is greater (Pliatsikas, 2020; Birdsong, 2018). For this reason, it is important to have teaching staff who can understand the use of new technologies so that, through them, they can transmit knowledge of a new language with more innovative and interesting tools to young students. Otherwise, the transmission of knowledge, including learning a new language, will continue to be unattractive to students and the paradigm of new technologies will continue to be just an educational proposal.

The importance of the English language cannot currently be denied or ignored (Nishanthi, 2018). In addition to being one of the most common languages spoken in the world, the benefits or advantages of a person learning this language are multiple, among them the following can be mentioned: it is the language of the academy; gives you access to a large number of written, online or print media; it comes in handy when traveling; it is essential if you want to work in an international company among many others (Srinivas Rao, 2019). However, something very important is associated with this language: knowledge of English is necessary if a person wants to progress and succeed in life (OECD, 2020; Butler & Le, 2018). Undoubtedly, this is why a large number of schools around the world have considered the teaching of the English language in their study plans, especially in the first years of learning children (National Academies of Sciences, Engineering, and Medicine, 2017; Council of Europe, 2018). Thus, throughout the world learning this language is an activity that is carried out more frequently in basic-level schools (The Curriculum Development Council, 2017; Rao & Yu, 2019). This last perspective is based on the premise that children take better advantage of their cognitive system than they have at these ages (Williams, Parthasarathy & Molnar, 2021). Children who are beginning to learn the English language normally associate words with images and sounds, this makes it easier for them to assimilate knowledge and increases their educational interest (Roberts, Vadas & Sanders, 2018; Garton & Copland, 2019).

The need to have increasingly younger and better-prepared human resources motivate teachers and researchers to create new educational environments or learning techniques so that children assimilate the English language as quickly and effectively as possible so that, when they need it, it is easier for them to enter a highly competitive globalized context. In this context, it makes sense to create and provide a new way of learning for a specific group of students, in particular for children who have the opportunity to learn the English language at their school. It is clear that the transfer of knowledge has gradually evolved, and it is also logical that the process of educating has also shown changes (Kayapinar, 2021). Thus, the new generations of students have a lot to do with the so-called new technologies, mainly because they have grown up with them and are prepared to use them and adapted to quickly assimilate them. Undoubtedly, the challenge is for academics and developers of these technologies, since they must create new contexts and innovative, efficient, and interesting technological tools to capture the greatest possible attention of children but, above all, prepare them as soon as possible for the challenges that a globalized world holds for them in the future.

In this scenario, it is important for teachers, particularly those teaching a new language, to be aware of the new technologies currently available (Ha Bui, 2022). This with the purpose of first, helping and facilitating the teaching-learning process with their students, second, being at the forefront of the learning environments that take place in a globalized world, and, third, transmitting their knowledge in an innovative, efficient and interesting to its students so that, in turn, they feel motivated to continue learning in a more interesting and cutting-edge way (Knezek & Christensen, 2002). For this reason, a system based on AR is presented below, which has the purpose of supporting the teacher in teaching the English language in a new and interesting way for their students at the basic level who begin their life with the knowledge of a language other than the mother tongue.

In a world where everyday life encompasses the management of new technologies focused on making people's lives easier and having the knowledge that individuals must be equipped with skills to face problems and provide solutions in contexts where, simultaneously, knowledge revolves around To different topics that are written by various researchers in various languages, learning environments are

Augmented Reality as an Innovative Tool

required that prepare students with suitable skills that involve them in the dialectic between the real and the virtual with tools based on cutting-edge educational technology (Hernandez de Menendez, Escobar Díaz & Morales-Menendez, 2020.

The English language is used as a means of communication in different parts of the world (Education First, 2020), so children and young people must learn this language so that, when they need it, it is easier to enter a globalized context (Valverde-Berrocoso et al., 2021). Under this approach, students whose first language is other than English must learn it, although it is important to mention that this language can be learned at any age and/or educational level (Pennycook, 2017). However, and as has already been mentioned above, it is of greater benefit than this learning to be as early as possible to take advantage of the student's cognitive flexibility and, with it, facilitate the creation of a teaching process different from the traditional one, in which, with the support of didactic and technological elements, their learning is highly effective (Pliatsikas, 2020; Birdsong, 2018). This is based on the experience that during the teaching-learning process, younger students are easily distracted. For this reason, they require games or activities that motivate them to want to learn, and, derived from that, they need technological tools that contribute to their academic training so that it is easy, pleasant, and, consequently, motivating (National Academies of Sciences, Engineering, and Medicine, 2017; Council of Europe, 2018). To achieve this dynamic, tools/technologies are needed to help teachers in the teaching process, strategies in the classroom that encourage the acquisition of knowledge and that provoke joy in learning in students; in addition it inductees them to make learning be for them a praiseworthy opportunity rather than a hardy necessity (Roberts et al., 2018; Garton & Copland, 2019. Undoubtedly, cutting-edge technology is also required that allows the construction of educational contexts whose implementation characteristics are not high costs, but with tools that are easy to manage and implement, but above all, their costs are measured in low monetary terms and, on the other hand, with the highest possible cognitive benefits (Huang et al., 2019; Llevot-Calvet, 2018; Redondo et al., 2020; Abad-Segura et al., 2020).

SOLUTIONS AND RECOMMENDATIONS

This document describes a software engineering methodology based on the 4+1 views model (Kruchten, Nord, & Ozkaya, 2019; Kurniawan & Luhukay, 2014), which describes step by step, and with diagrams, how this application has been developed and the UML (Unified Modeling Language) (UML, 2022) diagrams with which the system is described and which are used to clarify its concepts. In addition, the types of software and hardware that should be used for its development are described, the cost-benefit of this educational technology is emphasized and this technology is promoted for future research.

AR has been an ideal complement for various educational applications and for teaching English it is also useful due to the basic characteristics that define it as a technology through which the visualization of the real environment is augmented by elements or objects generated by a computer. or mobile device (Rohrbachet al, 2021). To demonstrate this idea, applications are required that encapsulate the elements based on an AR system and join with the design of systems that interact with students so that, together, they allow visualizing the real world associated with the physical world (Karagozlu, 2021).

A system is developed using a software engineering methodology that allows you to create, step by step, each part of the system so that in the end it encapsulates them and emits a result. An Information System (IS) is a set of interrelated components that collect, process, store and disseminate data and information. In addition, it provides monitors with "feedback" mechanisms and control of operations that result in the objectives for which were designed being achieved. In other words, good systems produce great results (Sommerville, 2016; Pressman, 2010; Leach, 2016). The main parts of an IS are people, who during the use of the software increase the productivity of their work, groups of these same people, and, in turn, companies that interrelate these groups of people. In this context, an IS based on AR would be an analogy (see Figure 1).

Figure 1. Result of an Information System (IS) whit Augmented Reality
Source: Author's elaboration

It is necessary to develop educational systems that generate contexts whose implementation characteristics are not high cost, but rather the opposite, that is, that contain tools that are easy to manage and implement but, above all, that their cost is measured in low monetary terms. And your profits are high. Various studies indicate that AR can improve the academic performance of students (Chiu, DeJaegher, & Chao, 2015), so it is important to continue creating systems that use this technique although numerous tools have already been made that enrich educational contexts, always there are ways to improve what has already been invented since it is important to mention that AR has been implemented in different fields such as the military, medicine, engineering design, robotics, manufacturing, maintenance and repair applications, teaching and learning, entertainment, psychological treatments, etc. (Cipresso et al, 2018; Azuma, 2015).

Phase I. System Analysis

Currently, teacher and apprentice educators should not take a passive and contemplative attitude toward new technologies. On the contrary, they must assume an open attitude and delve, to the extent of their possibilities and interests, into the internal context of the new technological tools and even the creation

Augmented Reality as an Innovative Tool

of new ideas that serve to innovate or implement precisely new tools. technologies to enrich the teaching-learning process. Undoubtedly, the following sections serve as support to understanding, roughly, how a system based on augmented reality works. And perhaps most importantly, it is intended that teachers interested in topics of this nature get excited and, consequently, become a little more involved in the design of these educational environments and collaborate, in the not-too-distant future, in multidisciplinary projects. which, in turn, provides a better quality during the transmission of their knowledge. Therefore, this book chapter is focused, in addition to teachers interested in the use of new technologies, on all those teachers who dare to explore issues related to new technologies from an amateur perspective. In this way, the analysis phase seeks in the learning environments how and where the English language training system can fit, which makes it a necessity that must be addressed from different types of technologies but, in our case, the context will be designed. of learning using AR as the main element. This requirement or need may consist of a way of doing training that is based on capturing and processing data to later produce desirable information. Under this sequence of activities, the identification of the requirements includes researching the case study and analyzing the information to find out what those requirements are. Therefore, an outline must be drawn up for what the procedures involved in the project are required to do, determining and allocating the time required for each of these activities, which need to be reflected in a work program.

Reyes et al (2016), observed that the identification of the time requirements for each of the activities of a project allows for knowing the number of days, weeks, or months that are necessary to integrate the "time program". It is also essential, as in any type of project, to allocate a margin of time to counteract any event that implies a delay in the completion of the project, for which, it is necessary to allocate a margin of time, precisely, for setbacks, as well as point out all the policies, regulations, rules and restrictions to which the development and operation of the AR system must be subject and define the functional bases of the system. For all this, it is necessary to establish the information flows, documents to be used, reports to be produced, controls, times, and responsibilities within the areas of the organization that are involved in some way with the system that is being built.

Therefore, before starting with the design of the system, it is necessary to investigate how the way of teaching and learning the English language is currently carried out, what methods are used for said activity, in addition, how educational technology is involved in them, how AR is used with those methods, if at all, and how they relate to each other. It is also necessary to know the benefits that one and the other bring (technological and non-technological) and compare these results in such a way as to show, as clearly as possible, the needs and functions that this system, based on AR, will add to regarding this field of knowledge. Once the previous results have been investigated, discussed, and reflected, we proceed with the design of the system; In this stage, the functions that the system will perform are defined, and how these functions will stimulate and impact the cognitive process of the students, and not only that, the sequence of operation is also determined, that is, the information required and the characteristics on which these requirements are based. Subsequently, the idea of the software that satisfies these requirements, the feasibility of carrying out the system as well as the necessary resources are determined, and, from this, it is defined which is the most appropriate. Also, according to the specialized resources that are available, the programming language that will be used for the construction of the system is chosen, in such a way that the selected tools will have an important impact on the process and cost of the development of the system with AR.

As an important part of the development and implementation of the English language learning system with AR, it is essential to consider a cost-benefit analysis, which will determine if there is financial feasibility to carry out the selected system. This will be done taking into account that the development of a system is not only based on its coding, since software licenses, hardware tools, and qualified personnel are also required to carry out the corresponding tasks. In addition, the cost-benefit analysis does not only involve monetary terms, rather, and in this case of abstract benefits, it refers to the fact that large terms could help students in their academic development and, of course, to more efficient achievements and not only at the level of the student as a person because these benefits could also be measured at the level of the prestige of the educational institution, its teaching staff and, of course. to student achievement at the state, national, or international levels. The cost-benefit is complex to analyze, there will always be variants to take into account and the results that each information system provides are perceived by its usefulness in the institutions, which are measured by the degree to which it improves the performance of the person or the quality of the information system (ease of use, reliability, flexibility) and the type of information it provides (relevant, understandable, complete and timely), which can be measured by the use of the information system and user satisfaction (Bravo, Santana, & Rondon, 2015).

After the analysis of the system as a whole, the activities that must be carried out are listed, organizing them in a general way depending on the methodology to be used for the abstract and physical design, the coding and creation of the software, the preparation of the files to create data test and, of course, the test itself, testing and integrating the software and ordering, purchasing and installing the equipment and, where appropriate, "implementation" and "release". Applications must be organized in a way that allows for scalability, security, and robust execution under stressful conditions, and their structure, or architecture, as it is commonly called, must be clearly defined so that a later bug is quickly found and fixed. A correctly designed architecture benefits any program regardless of the complexity of the system or the company, it must work excellently well during scalability, and it must also be reusable to facilitate the restructuring of the system and the reuse of the code, which is stored in libraries for use in later projects (UML, 2022).

Based on what has been explained above, the first mission is to find the way the current system works, this is done by representing the system through diagrams, which use their symbols to explain the system's operation in a very understandable way. A recommended practice due to the simplicity of its symbology is the diagrams of the Unified Modeling Language (UML), which is a universal language where software systems are modeled and which is backed by one of the most important certification companies worldwide. Software: Object Management Group (2022). This language is used to visualize, specify, build and document a system, offering standardized diagrams that describe a model of the system where concepts, processes, functions, and specific aspects of the system are described, in addition, to expressions of programming languages, schemes of databases and recycled compounds.

Software engineering methodologies make use of various diagrams, which adapt to the paradigm, that is, not necessarily all the diagrams have to be used, only some are used and they are very necessary to show the architecture of the software system software. The symbology of these models is simple and easy to understand; There are diagrams with specific objectives that, depending on the perspective of the system that is required to be modeled, then the diagrams will complement various methodologies, such as the diagrams described in OMG and UML described below: 1) Class diagram; 2) Component diagram; 3) Deployment diagram; 4) Object diagram; 5) Package diagram; 6) Activities diagram; 7) Use case diagram; 8) State diagram; 9) Global diagram of interactions and; 10) Timing diagram.

Augmented Reality as an Innovative Tool

PRESENTATION OF THE AR-BASED SYSTEM

Continuing with the development of the AR-based system that serves for the training of bilingual primary school teachers, it is important to mention that this system begins with its design, which is defined as the determination of the system architecture. This means that it will start with the hierarchical structure of the program modules and it will be shown visually as well as the way of interacting between its components and the structure of the data used by the corresponding modules (van den Berg et al, 2019; Montilva, Barrios, & Besembel, 2014). Due to the nature of the system, its design is based on the proposal of Kruchten, Nord & Ozkaya (2019), who shows the architecture of a system from the perspective of the software from "4+1 types of views" (Kurniawan & Luhukay, 2014) that are defined below.

1. **Logical view**. It refers to the organization and functionality of the system and is what can be seen in this view, that is, it refers to the structure and functionality of the system. To represent it, UML diagrams are used, which are specified through representations with Class Diagrams or Sequence Diagrams.
2. **Development view**. In this view, a Component Diagram is used that is used to appreciate the programmer's view, that is, it shows the programmer what each part of the code does.
3. **Process view**. This view uses, in turn, dynamic views where the system processes are shown and explained. In addition, this view details how these processes are communicated and where aspects such as concurrency, distribution, performance, and scalability are considered, which are represented by Activity Diagrams.
4. **Physical view**. It represents the topology of the software components and the Deployment Diagram is used to represent it.
5. **Scenarios**. In addition to the aforementioned views, the Scenarios are also contemplated, which are represented by use cases. These Scenarios describe the sequences and interactions between objects and processes. In addition, they are used as a starting point to test the prototype of the system.

Phase II. System Requirements

As we have already observed, the details for the elaboration of the system have been carried out and gathered, which are integrated, in turn, into the analysis of the system, where it is sought to understand why and how a system of this nature works to learn the English language with AR. After this, we proceed to develop its design and construction under the actions described in subsequent paragraphs. Pressman (2010) defines the design of a system as the establishment of data structures, the general software architecture, and the representations of interfaces and algorithms. In other words, he describes the process that translates requirements into software specifications. The objective of the design phase is to make known the behavior of the proposed solution. This is conceived taking into account that design is a pre-phase that begins the construction of programs and/or activity processes that are normally carried out by users, which seek to improve by adding speed, efficiency, effectiveness, savings, and visual design.

System Architecture

The first action that begins with the design is the determination of the system architecture, which is the hierarchical structure of the program modules, the way its components interact, and the structure of the data used by these modules (Sommerville, 2016; Leach, 2016). Of the multiple software architectural systems that exist, as mentioned above, the "4+1 views" methodology was chosen for its development. Since each view has already been described, then now it is time to note the development of each stage.

Logical View

In this view, the actions that the system performs sequentially are appreciated, in which all the entities that interact for the proper functioning of the system are immersed. For the system developed in this work, the entities are the teachers and students, the camera, the system, and the database. This view is represented with a sequential diagram and shows the actions that the system performs during the interaction with the entities; From the moment the camera focuses on the student so that, through pattern recognition, it detects his face, then the system asks him to write a word in English to awaken the desire in the student to learn to write, recognize and speak in English. Subsequently, the system shows the three-dimensional image (3D) of the abstraction associated with the written word, if it is correct, as well as the audio of its pronunciation in English (these digital files are superimposed on the physical reality, which in this case is the which is known as AR). If the word has not been written correctly, the system will show the student some options where it will ask him what the word he wants to write is, then the student writes it in Spanish and the system shows it in English. With this suggestion, the student tests the training of writing the word in English again (Figure 2). This phase notes the requirements of the proposed system and the way to address them, that is, it searches among various hardware and software elements for the most suitable and viable for its execution.

Figure 2. Sequence diagram of the AR system
Source: Author's elaboration

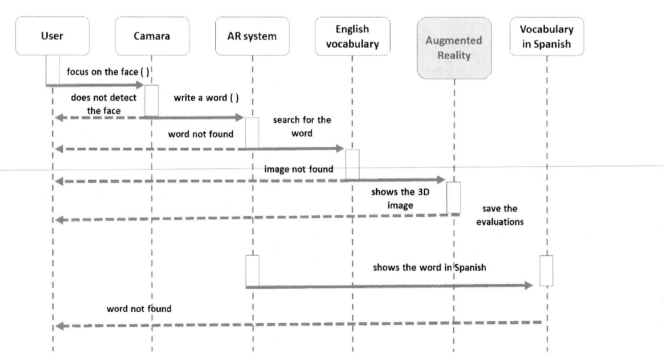

Augmented Reality as an Innovative Tool

Hardware

The hardware required to visualize the system with AR is described as follows:

- **Photo camera**: With this camera the AR is "triggered/detonated", it is essential to superimpose virtual elements on the user's real face. Every cutting-edge device has one, both on a computer and a mobile device.
- **Device screen**: It is contained in any computing device (computer or mobile) and this AR system, is used to display virtual elements, messages, the user's face, and, in general, the entire environment of this educational technology system.
- **Keyboard**: It is provided in any of the aforementioned devices, although they can also be added as accessories and used in the system to interact with it when you write the words you want to search for in the database, both in English and in Spanish.
- **Audio**: Also provided on mobile devices, including in computers or as an accessory. This audio is very useful since the system's AR also incorporates sounds with the words spoken in English so that the student not only associates the image with the writing but also associates them with the diction.

The above elements are included or acquired but are basic and common in everyday life. The recent evolution of mobile hardware has allowed AR to be played on small units such as smartphones or tablets, which contain all the necessary components to generate it; high-resolution cameras, screens, accelerometers, GPS, wireless connectivity via WLAN and radio links (Liou et al, 2017; Honkamaa, Jäppinen, & Woodward, 2007).

Software

The software required for the implementation of the AR system must be selected taking into account cost, feasibility, access, and even ease of use. For three-dimensional (3D) images to be clear, design software is needed, although there are free downloadable images on the internet that can be used to save time, however, this requires time and patience to find the one that suits you. search. For audio, where the words are heard, the sounds must be recorded with good diction. For its part, to display the AR, a variety of browsers have been implemented, some free to use and others paid to acquire.

AR Browser

There are various types of software dedicated to the construction and development of AR. Among them, the following can be mentioned: Aurasma, Vuforia, ArToolKit, Layar, Total Immersion, Mixare, ARPA, Unity3D, and ARCore. Some others were designed to show AR on more specific topics, such as LearnAR, WordLens, Wikitude World Browser, TAT Augmented ID, Point & Find, TwittARound, Lookator, Yelp Monocle, Google Goggles, and Google Sky Map.

Development View

The system components will serve to guide the programming that is conceived from the programmer's view and serves to implement the software through the component diagram. The diagram that represents this AR system shows as components of the processes that the system will perform. These processes are the recognition of the image before the camera, an association of the word written in English with the database, the search for the word written in Spanish and the messages generated when issuing the correct answer, as well as the deployment of the AR displayed with multimedia elements (in this case 3D images and audio). In addition, a counter of the progress and achievements that the students have accumulated through the use of the App is added, which in the end provides the score obtained and a motivational message to the student (Figure 3).

Figure 3. Diagram of components of the AR system
Source: Author's elaboration

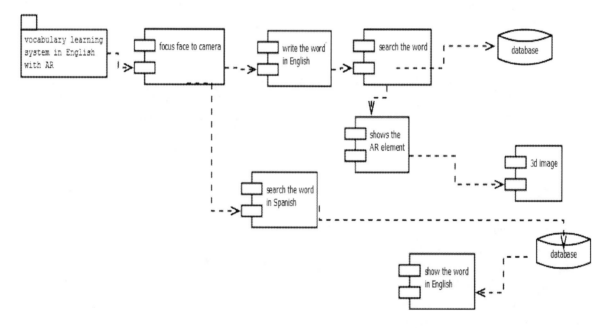

Process View

The model of the system with AR, to learn the English language, proposes that in its process view the design of the images, the design of the programming, the searches in the database, and the "trigger" of the AR (Figure 4). In the activity diagram, the programming paradigms require a structure that integrates modules and that are interconnected but, simultaneously, they are required to operate individually. The latter can be shown graphically in the architecture of the system by showing a diagram that integrates its operation, which starts from the precise moment in which the student stands in front of the computer or mobile device to start the system and ends up at the moment in which the same student wishes to conclude with the training.

Augmented Reality as an Innovative Tool

Figure 4. Activity diagram of the AR system
Source: Author's elaboration

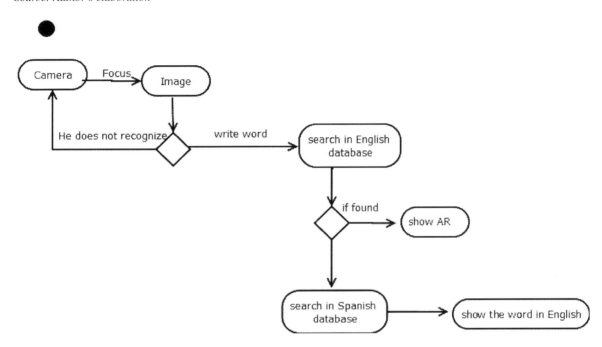

In this context, and for the design of three-dimensional (3D) images, the SketchUp Make program was used, as it is a free version, although images can also be downloaded from other sites with free access, such as 3D Warehouse. These images are stored in a database and are associated with the correct words that the user enters into the system if the words, which are captured by the students, are not located in the list of stored words, then the system will ask the user to enter the word, which he wants to learn to write in English, in the Spanish language. Thus, the system locates the word in Spanish and associates it with the word in English, which is shown to the student in a message like the following: "the word you want to know is spelled as follows <correct word>", so the system concludes by displaying the correctly spelled English word.

The system procedures can work separately, since if the student wishes from the beginning to know how a word is written in Spanish, then he will select the corresponding Menu, which will ask him to write the word to start the process described above. Otherwise, if the student starts her training without wanting to know how to write the word she captured in English, to motivate her to remember the way that word is written, then she can do it without choosing the second option. Thus, this view shows the programming, the association of words with images, and the search for words in Spanish to show their translation into English.

Physical View

As mentioned above, this view represents the topology of the software components and the deployment diagram is used to represent it. In the case of the vocabulary writing system with AR, the components are a camera, databases, and interaction. The interaction will be applied using the keyboard of the computer or mobile device and superimposing the AR in digital format through 3D images, audio, and text, which will be displayed according to the point of interaction of the student with the system. The language that performs the interaction is JavaScript with Html5, which handles the programming with events, that is, through these programming tools, it is possible to "trigger" the AR through the previously designed buttons and Menus (Figure 5).

Figure 5. Use a case diagram of the AR system
Source: Author's elaboration

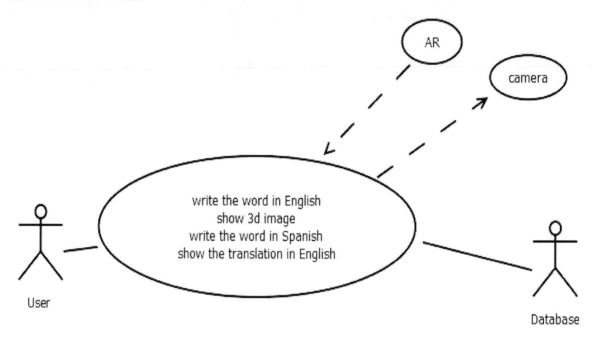

Additional View

This view is based on the methodology that, in turn, is referred to and represented by the use case diagram, that is, it represents the general operation of the system from the user's point of view (Figure 6) and where how the user interacts with the system in the cases of translation and search of the words as well as the superposition of the AR.

Prototype Construction

To finalize the design and construction, a prototype of the system is made. That is, it shows what the system would be like in a more approximate way than the final system. In this case, the sequence of actions necessary to reproduce the AR is shown, starting from the image of the user in front of the webcam (Figure 6). It is important to mention that the following images are the result of the system that the teacher will show the student for learning the English language.

Augmented Reality as an Innovative Tool

Figure 6. Image triggered by the AR system
Source: Author's elaboration

When the student selects the option to write in English, the system requests that they type the word in English and if the search in the database is successful, then the system sends the three-dimensional (3D) image and the audio that corresponds to that word (Figure 7).

Augmented Reality as an Innovative Tool

Figure 7. The system displays the AR if the word is found in the database
Source: Author's elaboration

The student has the option of writing the word in Spanish and the system searches for it in the database, if the word is found then the system returns that word translated into English (Figure 8).

Figure 8. The system receives the word in Spanish and returns it in English
Source: Author's elaboration

FUTURE RESEARCH DIRECTIONS

For future research, AR is an element that, as a complement to educational technology, turns out to be of multiple benefits. Improvements to this system could be investigated and even adapted to new languages, where its pedagogical characteristics would promote the training of those languages, which would allow the generation and construction of more useful and efficient knowledge that would serve as support for teachers.

This type of system works with classes and objects, where their reuse is a highly useful resource for building new systems. In addition, the interaction promoted by this type of system means that it can be applied to any discipline. In future research, it could be complemented with a tactile interaction, which, although it is in the initial phase, could be added so that the student achieves the sensation of a more physical virtual reality (Figure 9).

Figure 9.
Source: Author's elaboration

The system presented in this work is a means of training for teachers to train their students in the English language and exercise it, both teachers and students, learning the names of animals, things, food, means of transportation, stars, and multiple categories displayed using AR (database figures can be incremented by multiple categories). That is, this system works by associating various resources with words written by the student and is modeled with various Menus (animals, stars, food, objects, transportation, etc.). Of course, these Menus can also be increased gradually, in addition, a Test Module can be added to the system to monitor the training of each student since its design allows analyzing the results through their answers (it even generates a history of their progress), which allows and facilitates the creation of new learning approaches from previously established premises. Of course, this supervision must be carried out by teachers with specific bilingual skills, knowledge of pedagogy, with an open attitude to the knowledge of new technologies, and, above all, the aim of creating new learning environments.

CONCLUSION

The traditional teaching model was put to the test with the global pandemic of Covid19 and while human being accepted the changes caused by this pandemic, new teaching methodologies emerged and many others showed their viability and efficiency in these times of change: The traditional classroom had to be transformed into a virtual classroom and the teacher became "something" very similar to a hologram. Of course, the functions of the teacher had to adapt to these new educational needs. Above all, he was forced to transmit his knowledge through new technologies that, most likely, he did not know and did not know how to operate them. However, the demands of a world immersed in mobile devices led them to immerse themselves in innovative educational environments and totally oriented to the new generations,

Augmented Reality as an Innovative Tool

which did not have any mishap with these new technologies. Simply because they grew and continue to evolve with them. The challey, was for the academics and researchers who decided not to be simply a hologram but to become a guide for their students on the long path of learning.

The use of AR implies an educational technological task that uses various virtual reality scenarios to simulate the operation of abstract elements, in such a way that, through various visual and multimedia effects, both teachers and students can abstract meaningful learning and relate it to their prior knowledge; all to make learning and identify words in English more innovative and interesting. By using AR in the educational processes of children, and more specifically in the teaching of another language, it shows that if it is possible to encapsulate certain suitable characteristics, then they will be able to learn through different learning styles such as auditory, kinesthetic and visual that, used in Together, it will allow them to develop their cognitive potential to the maximum.

The present work focused on presenting an AR system to learn the English language with the premise that it will be used by teachers and students with Spanish as their mother tongue. Of course, this system can be modified for learning a language other than English and with a mother tongue other than Spanish. In this way, through the present work it was verified that AR is an innovative, efficient and accessible tool that serves as support for bilingual teaching staff because the following is true: 1) AR is a useful and easy-to-use tool, that works to build suitable learning environments, which allow students to feel motivated, encouraged and with the desire to continue learning; 2) With the support of AR, systems can be generated that help the learning of abstract or difficult-to-perceive knowledge; 3) In learning English, models are handled where appearance and shape help and strengthen learning, which can be represented with three-dimensional objects; 4) Interaction with AR and multimedia materials that are added to physical reality allow students' sensory senses to be stimulated, particularly at the basic level, which in turn allows these students to learn auditorily, visual and kinesthetic; 5) The cost of the design will depend on how much you invest in the accessories and plugins to display the AR, but the programming and design of the virtual reality (3D design, simulation and web page) are generally not very expensive.

The use of AR implies an educational technological task that uses various VR scenarios to simulate the operation of abstract elements, in such a way that through various visual and multimedia effects, basic-level students can abstract meaningful learning and relate it to their prior knowledge: All this with the purpose of learning and identifying words in English. The use of AR in the educational processes of children and young people, specifically in the teaching of a second language, shows that it is possible to encapsulate suitable characteristics for these students to learn through different ways of learning, such as auditory, kinesthetic, and visual that each individual has, then when used jointly it would be possible to develop their cognitive potential to the maximum.

The times of the digital age, which are lived day by day, make education professionals require other more innovative and efficient ways to focus and maximize the teaching-learning process. These innovative ways of transmitting knowledge must be focused on technological tools that help and motivate, in turn, the basic level of students' language learning process. These students need virtual tools with which they can interact to make their learning more meaningful. Information and communication technologies help these students to function better in their different learning styles. AR is a virtual tool that is easy to manipulate and, with its peculiar way of overcoming real things, it allows young students at the basic level to create environments that are sufficiently motivating and fun. Furthermore, AR allows these students to turn the process of learning a new language into a task that encourages them to continue studying.

AR is a motivating tool since teachers like their students to feel motivated to reinforce their educational tasks. The system developed in this work, based on AR, is an instrument that has several real characteristics, which allow and facilitate effective learning due to how real objects are related to words that have a fairly abstract meaning. This educational tool creates in the student the desire to continue training in her learning and, at the same time, makes this student know, in a real and immediate way, her learning achievements. This dynamic will surely make students remember and learn more easily. Under this premise of AR and the approach that was given to the system designed in this work, it can be affirmed that AR can work as part of the tools of educational technologies, supplying and providing useful tools as a support for the teaching of all kinds. of disciplines, which intend to generate a similar approach to the one achieved with this technological tool.

In the end, it concludes by pointing out the use of AR as an educational technological task that uses various Virtual Reality (VR) scenarios to simulate the operation of abstract elements in such a way that, through various visual and multimedia effects, students can abstract significant learning, transmitted by their teachers, and relate it to their previous knowledge (Nikolaidis, 2022). All this is for them to learn and identify both the words in English and their correct pronunciation through an AR-based system. Thus, the use of AR in the educational processes of basic level students, and more specifically in the teaching of a second language, manages to demonstrate that if the characteristics of the different learning styles are encapsulated, such as auditory, kinesthetic, and visual, which turn out to be suitable when used together, then students from an early age will be able to develop their cognitive potential to the maximum (Stecker, 2019; Sigrist et al, 2013; Jeřábek, Rambousek, & Wildová, 2014; Iqbal, Mangina, & Campbell, 2019).

REFERENCES

Abad-Segura, E., González-Zamar, M. D., Luque-de la Rosa, A., & Morales, C. (2020). Sustainability of Educational Technologies: An Approach to Augmented Reality Research. *Sustainability*, *12*(10), 4091. doi:10.3390u12104091

Abuhassna, H., Al-Rahmi, W. M., Yahya, N., Zakaria, M. A. Z. M., Kosnin, A. B. M., & Darwish, M. (2020). Development of a new model on utilizing online learning platforms to improve students' academic achievements and satisfaction. *International Journal of Educational Technology in Higher Education*, *17*(1), 38. doi:10.118641239-020-00216-z

Adawiyah, D., & Gumartifa, A. (2022). English language teaching and globalization: To support economic growth. *Premise: Journal of English Education and Applied Linguistics*, *11*(1), 228–242. doi:10.24127/pj.v11i1.4114

Al-Amri, W. B. (2014). Translation in teaching and learning a foreign language: A methodological approach. *International Journal of Humanities and Cultural Studies*, *1*(2), 1–20.

Alharbi, W. H. (2022). The Affordances of Augmented Reality Technology in the English for Specific Purposes Classroom: It's Impact on vocabulary learning and students motivation in a Saudi Higher Education Institution. *Journal of Positive School Psychology*, *6*(3), 6588–6602. https://journalppw.com/index.php/jpsp/article/view/3849

Altan, M. Z. (2017). Globalization, English Language Teaching and Turkey. *International Journal of Languages Education and Teaching*, *5*(4), 764–776. doi:10.18298/ijlet.2238

Altun, H. K., & Lee, J. (2020). Immersive Learning Technologies in English Language Teaching: A Meta-Analysis. *International Journal of Contents*, *16*(3), 18–32. doi:10.5392/IJOC.2020.16.3.018

Azuma, R. (2015). Location-Based Mixed and Augmented Reality Storytelling. In Woodrow Barfield Fundamentals of Wearable Computers and Augmented Reality, pp. 259-276.

Banegas, D. L., & Consoli, S. (2021). Initial English language teacher education: The effects of a module on teacher research. *Cambridge Journal of Education*, *51*(4), 491–507. doi:10.1080/030576 4X.2021.1876840

Bensetti-Benbader, H., & Brown, D. (2019). Language Acquisition With Augmented and Virtual Reality. In K. Graziano (Ed.), *Proceedings of Society for Information Technology & Teacher Education International Conference*, pp. 1730-1734. Association for the Advancement of Computing in Education (AACE). https://www.learntechlib.org/primary/p/207876/

Birdsong, D. (2018). Plasticity, Variability and Age in Second Language Acquisition and Bilingualism. *Frontiers in Psychology*, *9*, 81. doi:10.3389/fpsyg.2018.00081 PMID:29593590

Bland, B. (2019). Teaching English to Young Learners: More Teacher Education and More Children's Literature! *CLELE Journal, 7*(2), 79-103. https://eric.ed.gov/?id=ED608240

Bravo, E., Santana, M., & Rodon, J. (2015). Information systems and performance: The role of technology, the task and the individual. *Journal Behaviour & Information Technology*, *1*(3), 247–260. doi:10.1080/0144929X.2014.934287

Brock-Utne, B. (2022). Globalization and the Issue of Language of Instruction: Examples from Tanzania and Norway. In: Zajda, J., Vissing, Y., Majhanovich, S. (Eds.) Globalisation, Ideology and Social Justice Discourses, Globalization, Comparative Education and Policy Research, 30. Springer. doi:10.1007/978-3-030-92774-5_3

Buchner, J., & Zumbach, J. (2020). Augmented reality in teacher education. A framework to support teachers' technological pedagogical content knowledge. *Italian Journal of Educational Technology*, *28*(2), 106–120. doi:10.17471/2499-4324/1151

Butler, Y. G., & Le, V. N. (2018). A Longitudinal Investigation of Parental Social-Economic Status (SES) and Young Students' Learning of English as a Foreign Language. *System*, *73*, 4–15. doi:10.1016/j.system.2017.07.005

Chiu, J. L., De Jaegher, C. J., & Chao, J. (2015). The effects of augmented virtual science laboratories on middle school-students' understanding of gas properties. *Computers & Education*, *85*, 59–73. doi:10.1016/j.compedu.2015.02.007

Cipresso, P., Giglioli, I. A. C., Raya, M. A., & Riva, G. (2018). The Past, Present, and Future of Virtual and Augmented Reality Research: A Network and Cluster Analysis of the Literature. *Frontiers in Psychology*, *9*, 2086. doi:10.3389/fpsyg.2018.02086 PMID:30459681

Council of Europe. (2018). *Common European Framework of Reference for Languages: Learning, Teaching, Assessment.* European Commission. https://www.coe.int/en/web/common-european-framework-reference-languages

Cummins, F. (2021). Language as a problem. *Language Sciences*, *88*, 101433. doi:10.1016/j.lang-sci.2021.101433

da Silva, M., Teixeira, J., Cavalcante, P., & Teichrieb, V. (2019). Perspectives on how to evaluate augmented reality technology tools for education: A systematic review. *Journal of the Brazilian Computer Society*, *25*(1), 3. doi:10.118613173-019-0084-8

Dengel, A., Iqbal, M. Z., Grafe, S., & Mangina, E. (2022). A Review on Augmented Reality Authoring Toolkits for Education. *Frontiers Virtual Real.*, *3*, 798032. doi:10.3389/frvir.2022.798032

Di Bitetti, M. S., & Ferreras, J. A. (2017). Publish (in English) or perish: The effect on citation rate of using languages other than English in scientific publications. *Ambio*, *46*(1), 121–127. doi:10.100713280-016-0820-7 PMID:27686730

Disability Awareness Training. (2022). *Homepage.* DA. https://disabilityawarenesstraining.com

Education First. (2020). *EF EPI. Índice del Dominio del Inglés de EF. Una clasificación de 100 países y regiones por sus habilidades de inglés [EF EPI extension. Index of the English Domain of EF. A classification of 100 countries and regions by your English skills].* EF. https://www.ef.com.mx/epi/

Elsobeihi, M. M., & Abu Naser, S. S. (2017). Effects of Mobile Technology on Human Relationships. *International Journal of Engineering and Information Systems*, *1*(5), 110–125.

Fan, M., Antle, A. N., & Warren, J. L. (2020). Augmented Reality for Early Language Learning: A Systematic Review of Augmented Reality Application Design, Instructional Strategies, and Evaluation Outcomes. *Journal of Educational Computing Research*, *58*(6), 1059–1100. doi:10.1177/0735633120927489

Farshid, M., Paschen, J., Eriksson, T., & Kietzmann, J. (2018). Go boldly! Explore augmented reality (AR), virtual reality (VR), and mixed reality (MR) for business. *Business Horizons*, *61*(5), 657–663. doi:10.1016/j.bushor.2018.05.009

Gargrish, S., Mantri, A., & Kaur, D. P. (2020). Augmented Reality-Based Learning Environment to Enhance Teaching-Learning Experience in Geometry Education. *Procedia Computer Science*, *172*, 1039–1046. doi:10.1016/j.procs.2020.05.152

Garton, S., & Copland, F. (2019). *The Routledge Handbook to Teaching English to Young Learners.* Taylor & Francis group.

Guzmán, D. B. (2019). Technology Integration for the Professional Development of English Teachers. *Tecné, Episteme y Didaxis: TED, 46,* 157-168. http://www.scielo.org.co/scielo.php?script=sci_arttext&pid=S0121-38142019000200157

Ha Bui, T. (2022). English teachers' integration of digital technologies in the classroom. *International Journal of Educational Research Open, 3,* 100204.

Hamid, M. O., & Nguyen, H. T. M. (2016). Globalization, English language policy, and teacher agency: Focus on Asia. *The International Education Journal: Comparative Perspectives, 15(1),* 26-44. http://openjournals.library.usyd.edu.au/index.php/IEJ/index

Hernandez de Menendez, M., Escobar Díaz, C., & Morales-Menendez, R. (2020). Technologies for the future of learning: State of the art. *International Journal on Interactive Design and Manufacturing, 14*(2), 683–695. doi:10.100712008-019-00640-0

Honkamaa, P., Jäppinen, J., & Woodward, C. (2007). A Lightweight Approach for Augmented Reality on Camera Phones using 2D Images to Simulate in 3D. *MUM '07: Proceedings of the 6th international conference on Mobile and ubiquitous multimedia*, (pp. 155-159). ACM. 10.1145/1329469.1329490

Huang, R., Spector, J. M., & Yang, J. (2019). *Educational Technology a Primer for the 21st Century*. Springer Nature. doi:10.1007/978-981-13-6643-7

Hugill, P. J. (2016). The Power of Knowledge: How Information and Technology Made the Modern World. *Journal of Historical Geography, 52*, 123–124. doi:10.1016/j.jhg.2015.06.007

Iqbal, M. Z., Mangina, E., & Campbell, A. G. (2019). Exploring the use of Augmented Reality in a Kinesthetic Learning Application Integrated with an Intelligent Virtual Embodied Agent. *2019 IEEE International Symposium on Mixed and Augmented Reality Adjunct (ISMAR-Adjunct)*, (pp. 12-16). IEEE. 10.1109/ISMAR-Adjunct.2019.00018

Isaeva, A., Semenova, G., Nesterova, Y., & Gudkova, O. (2021). Augmented reality technology in the foreign language classroom in a non-linguistic university. *XIV International Scientific and Practical Conference State and Prospects for the Development of Agribusiness-INTERAGROMASH 2021, (Vol. 273*, Article 12119). 10.1051/e3sconf/202127312119

Jeřábek, T., Rambousek, V., & Wildová, R. (2014). Specifics of Visual Perception of The Augmented Reality in The Context of Education. *Procedia: Social and Behavioral Sciences, 159*, 598–604. doi:10.1016/j.sbspro.2014.12.432

Jubran, S. M., & Arabiat, R. M. (2021). Using Translation in the Framework of Learning a Foreign Language from Learners' Perspectives. *Multicultural Education, 7*(8). doi:10.5281/zenodo.5167622

Karagozlu, D. (2021). Creating a Sustainable Education Environment with Augmented Reality Technology. *Sustainability, 13*(11), 5851. doi:10.3390u13115851

Kayapinar, U. (2021). *Teacher Education. New Perspectives*. IntechOpen Book Series. doi:10.5772/intechopen.94952

Kessler, G. (2018). Technology and the future of language teaching. *Foreign Language Annals, 51*(1), 205–218. doi:10.1111/flan.12318

Khan, T., Johnston, K., & Ophoff, J. (2019). The Impact of an Augmented Reality Application on Learning Motivation of Students. *Advances in Human-Computer Interaction, 2019*, Article 7208494. doi:10.1155/2019/7208494

Knezek, G., & Christensen, R. (2002). Impact of New Information Technologies on Teachers and Students. *Education and Information Technologies, 7*(4), 369–376. doi:10.1023/A:1020921807131

Kruchten, P., Nord, R., & Ozkaya, I. (2019). *Managing Technical Debt-Reducing Friction in Software Development*. Addison-Wesley Professional.

Kurniawan, Y., & Luhukay, D. (2014). ERP Conceptual Model for School Using 4+1 View Model of Architecture. *International Journal of Information and Electronics Engineering*, *4*(3), 201–208. doi:10.7763/IJIEE.2014.V4.435

Lai, J. Y., & Chang, L. T. (2021). Impacts of Augmented Reality Apps on First Graders' Motivation and Performance in English Vocabulary Learning. *SAGE Open*, *11*(4), 1–13. doi:10.1177/21582440211047549

Leach, R. J. (2016). *Introduction to Software Engineering* (2nd ed.). Taylor & Francis Group.

Lee, C. D., & Daiute, C. (2019). Introduction to Developmental Digital Technologies in Human History, Culture, and Well-Being. *Human Development*, *62*(1-2), 5–13. doi:10.1159/000496072

Liou, H. H. (2017). The Influences of the 2D Image-Based Augmented Reality and Virtual Reality on Student Learning. *Journal of Educational Technology & Society*, *20*(3), 110–121. https://www.jstor.org/stable/26196123

Llevot-Calvet, N. (2018). *Advanced Learning and Teaching Environments. Innovation, Contents and Methods*. Intech Open Book Series. doi:10.5772/intechopen.68354

Lv, Z., Lloret, J., & Song, H. (2021). Real-time image processing for augmented reality on mobile devices. *Journal of Real-Time Image Processing*, *18*(2), 245–248. doi:10.100711554-021-01097-9

Majid, S. N. A., & Salam, A. R. (2021). A Systematic Review of Augmented Reality Applications in Language Learning. *International Journal of Emerging Technologies in Learning*, *16*(10), 18–34. doi:10.3991/ijet.v16i10.17273

Marlina, R. (2013). Globalization, internationalization, and language education: An academic program for global citizens. *Multilingual Education*, *3*(1), 5. doi:10.1186/2191-5059-3-5

Marrahí-Gómez, M., & Belda-Medina, J. (2020). The Application of Augmented Reality (AR) to Language Learning and its Impact on Student Motivation. *International Journal of Linguistics Studies*, *2*(2), 7–14. doi:10.32996/ijls.2022.2.2.2

Mayilyan, H. (2019). Implementation of Augmented Reality Globe in Teaching-Learning Environment. *2019 IEEE Conference on Multimedia Information Processing and Retrieval (MIPR)*, (pp. 389-390). IEEE. 10.1109/MIPR.2019.00078

Miranda, E., Vergara, O. O., Cruz, V. G., García-Alcaraz, J. L., & Favela, J. (2016). Study on Mobile Augmented Reality Adoption for Mayo Language Learning. *Mobile Information Systems*, *2016*, 1069581. doi:10.1155/2016/1069581

Montilva, J., Barrios, J., Besembel, I., & Montilva, W. (2014). A Business Process Model for IT Management Based on Enterprise Architecture. *CLEI Electronic Journal*, *17*(2), 3. doi:10.19153/cleiej.17.2.3

Muhammad, A., Khan, K., Lee, N., Imran, M. Y., & Sajjad, A. S. (2021). School of the Future: A Comprehensive Study on the Effectiveness of Augmented Reality as a Tool for Primary School Children's Education. *Applied Sciences (Basel, Switzerland)*, *11*(11), 5277. Advance online publication. doi:10.3390/app11115277

National Academies of Sciences, Engineering, and Medicine (2017). Promoting the Educational Success of Children and Youth Learning English: Promising Futures. *The National Academies Press.* doi:10.17226/24677

Nezhyva, L. L. (2020). Perspectives on the use of augmented reality within the linguistic and literary field of primary education. *CEUR Workshop Proceedings, 2731,* 297–311. https://ceur-ws.org/Vol-2731/paper17.pdf

Nikolaidis, A. (2022). What is Significant in Modern Augmented Reality: A Systematic Analysis of Existing Reviews. *Journal of Imaging, 8*(5), 145. doi:10.3390/jimaging8050145 PMID:35621909

Nishanthi, R. (2018). The importance of Learning English in Today World. *The International Journal of Trend in Scientific Research and Development, 3*(1), 871–874. doi:10.31142/ijtsrd19061

Object Management Group. (2022). *Web site.* OMG. https://www.omg.org

OECD. (2020). *How language learning opens doors.* OECD. https://www.oecd.org/pisa/foreign-language/opens-doors.pdf

Palamar, S. P. (2021). *Formation of readiness of future teachers to use augmented reality in the educational process of preschool and primary education.* AREdu 2021: 4th International Workshop on Augmented Reality in Education, Kryvyi Rih, Ukraine. https://ceur-ws.org/Vol-2898/paper18.pdf

Pennycook, A. (2017). *The Cultural Politics of English as an International Language.* Routledge. doi:10.4324/9781315225593

Pérez-López, D., & Contero, M. (2013). Delivering educational multimedia contents through an augmented reality application: A case study on its impact on knowledge acquisition and retention. *The Turkish Online Journal of Educational Technology, 12*(4), 19–28. http://www.tojet.net

Petrov, P. D., & Atanasova, T. V. (2020). The Effect of Augmented Reality on Students' Learning Performance in Stem Education. *Information (Basel), 11*(4), 209. doi:10.3390/info11040209

Petrovych, O. B. (2021). The usage of augmented reality technologies in professional training of future teachers of Ukrainian language and literature. Proceedings of the 4th International Workshop on Augmented Reality in Education (AREdu 2021). Kryvyi Rih, Ukraine. May 11, 2021. *CEUR Workshop Proceedings, 2898,* 315–333. https://ceur-ws.org/Vol-2898/paper17.pdf

Pliatsikas, C. (2020). Understanding structural plasticity in the bilingual brain: The Dynamic Restructuring Model. *Bilingualism: Language and Cognition, 23*(2), 459–471. doi:10.1017/S1366728919000130

Pressman, R. (2010). *Software Engineering, A practitioner's approach.* McGraw-Hill Companies, Inc.

Rao, Z., & Yu, P. (2019). Teaching English as a foreign language to primary school students in East Asia: Challenges and future prospects. *English Today, 35*(3), 16–21. doi:10.1017/S0266078418000378

Redondo, B., Cózar-Gutiérrez, R., González-Calero, J. A., & Sánchez Ruiz, R. (2020). Integration of Augmented Reality in the Teaching of English as a Foreign Language in Early Childhood Education. *Early Childhood Education Journal, 48*(2), 147–155. doi:10.100710643-019-00999-5

Reyes, R. G., Olmos, S. & Hernández, M. (2016). Private Label Sales through Catalogs with Augmented Reality. In Handbook of Research on Strategic Retailing of Private Label Products in a Recovering Economy (Coord. Mónica Gómez-Suárez y María Pilar Martínez-Ruiz) (pp. 275–305). Business Science Reference (An imprint of IGI Global).

Roberts, T. A., Vadas, P. F., & Sanders, E. A. (2018). Preschoolers' alphabet learning: Letter name and sound instruction, cognitive processes, and English proficiency. *Early Childhood Research Quarterly*, *44*, 257–274. doi:10.1016/j.ecresq.2018.04.011

Rohrbach, N., Hermsdörfer, J., Huber, L. M., Thierfelder, A., & Buckingham, G. (2021). Fooling the size-weight illusion-Using augmented reality to eliminate the effect of size on perceptions of heaviness and sensorimotor prediction. *Virtual Reality (Waltham Cross)*, *25*(4), 1061–1070. doi:10.100710055-021-00508-3

Romano, M., Díaz, P., & Aedo, I. (2020). Empowering teachers to create augmented reality experiences: The effects on the educational experience. *Interactive Learning Environments*, 1–18. doi:10.1080/104 94820.2020.1851727

Roopa, D., Prabha, R., & Senthil, G. A. (2021). Revolutionizing education system with interactive augmented reality for quality education. *Materials Today: Proceedings*, *46*(9), 3860–3863. doi:10.1016/j.matpr.2021.02.294

Saadeh, H., Al Fayez, R. Q., Al Refaei, A., Shewaikani, N., Khawaldah, H., Abu-Shanab, S., & Al-Hussaini, M. (2021). Smartphone Use Among University Students During COVID-19 Quarantine: An Ethical Trigger. *Frontiers in Public Health*, *9*, 600134. doi:10.3389/fpubh.2021.600134 PMID:34381747

Sailer, M., Murböck, J., & Fischer, F. (2021). Digital learning in schools: What does it take beyond digital technology? *Teaching and Teacher Education*, *103*, 103346. doi:10.1016/j.tate.2021.103346

Sharma, B., & Mantri, A. (2020). Assimilating Disruptive Technology: A New Approach of Learning Science in Engineering Education. *Procedia Computer Science*, *172*, 915–921. doi:10.1016/j.procs.2020.05.132

Sigrist, R., Rauter, G., Riener, R., & Wolf, P. (2013). Augmented visual, auditory, haptic, and multimodal feedback in motor learning: A review. *Psychonomic Bulletin & Review*, *20*(1), 21–53. doi:10.375813423-012-0333-8 PMID:23132605

Simonova, O., & Kolesnichenko, A. (2022). The effectiveness of the augmented reality application in foreign language teaching in higher school. *SHS Web of Conferences*, *137*, 01025. 10.1051hsconf/202213701025

Sommerville, I. (2016). *Software Engineering* (10th ed.). Pearson Education Limited.

Srinivas Rao, P. (2019). The Role of English as a Global Language. *Research Journal of English*, *4*(1), 65–79.

Stecker, G. C. (2019). Using Virtual Reality to Assess Auditory Performance. *The Hearing Journal*, *72*(6), 20–23. doi:10.1097/01.HJ.0000558464.75151.52 PMID:34113058

Sun, J. (2013). Globalization and language teaching and learning in China. *International Journal on Integrating Technology in Education*, *2*(4), 35–42. doi:10.5121/ijite.2013.2404

The Curriculum Development Council. (2017). *English Language Education. Key Learning Area Curriculum Guide (Primary 1-Secondary 6).* Curriculum Development Council. https://www.edb.gov.hk/en/index.html

The Economic Times. (2018). Meet the new Google translator: An AI app that converts sign language into text, speech. *The Economic Times.* https://economictimes.indiatimes.com/magazines/panache/meet-the-new-google-translator-an-ai-app-that-converts-sign-language-into-text-speech/articleshow/66379450.cms?from=mdr

Tzima, S., Styliaras, G., & Bassounas, A. (2019). Augmented Reality Applications in Education: Teachers Point of View. *Education Sciences*, *9*(2), 99. doi:10.3390/educsci9020099

UML. (2022). *Web site to Unified Modeling Language.* UML. http://www.uml.org/what-is-uml.htm

Valverde-Berrocoso, J., Fernández-Sánchez, M. R., Revuelta Dominguez, F. I., & Sosa-Díaz, M. J. (2021). The educational integration of digital technologies preCovid-19: Lessons for teacher education. *PLoS One*, *16*(8), e0256283. doi:10.1371/journal.pone.0256283 PMID:34411161

van den Berg, M., Slot, R., van Steenbergen, M., Faasse, P., & van Vliet, H. (2019). How enterprise architecture improves the quality of IT investment decisions. *Journal of Systems and Software*, *152*, 134–150. doi:10.1016/j.jss.2019.02.053

Williams, L., Parthasarathy, P., & Molnar, M. (2021). Measures of Bilingual Cognition-From Infancy to Adolescence. *Journal of Cognition*, *4*(1), 45. doi:10.5334/joc.184 PMID:34514316

Word Book (Universal). (2022). *Web site.* Apple. https://apps.apple.com/us/app/wordbook-universal/id364030280

Word Lens. (2022). *Web site.* WL. https://universoabierto.org/2016/06/24/word-lens-traductor-de-realidad-aumentada/

Yildiz, E. P. (2021). Augmented Reality Research and Applications in Education. In D. Cvetković (Ed.), *Augmented Reality and Its Application.* Intech Open., doi:10.5772/intechopen.99356

KEY TERMS AND DEFINITIONS

Augmented reality: It is a technological resource that offers interactive experiences to the user from the combination of the virtual and the physical dimension, with the use of digital devices.

Computer system: A computer system is a basic, complete, and functional computer or computer, including all the hardware and software necessary to make it functional for a user.

Hardware: It is the physical part of the computer. Set of boards, integrated circuits, chips, cables, printers, monitors, etc. (what we can touch).

Information system (IS): It is a set of interrelated elements or components to collect, manipulate and disseminate data into information and to provide a feedback mechanism towards the fulfillment of an objective.

New technologies: They are those technological currents that are marking a change in the industrial, social, educational model, the global economy and in multiple disciplines that are currently in force.

Software: They are the programs, that is, the instructions to communicate with the computer and that make its use possible (we cannot touch it).

UML diagrams (Unified Modeling Language): They represent the design, architecture, and implementation of complicated software systems.

Virtual reality: It is an environment of scenes and objects of real appearance that is generated by computer technology and serves to create in the user the sensation of being immersed in it.

Chapter 15

Example of a CLIL Teaching–Learning Sequence About Geology and Evolution for Pre–Service Teachers

Sila Pla-Pueyo

https://orcid.org/0000-0003-4884-4096

University of Granada, Spain

Francisco González-García

https://orcid.org/0000-0001-8127-9792

University of Granada, Spain

Ana María Ramos-García

University of Granada, Spain

Laura Torres-Zúñiga

https://orcid.org/0000-0001-8434-2021

Autonomous University of Madrid, Spain

ABSTRACT

The present chapter describes in detail a teaching-learning sequence using the CLIL approach to teach contents related to sedimentary rocks, fossils, and evolution to pre-service primary education teachers. The sequence was designed and implemented during two consecutive semesters of the academic year 2021-2022. The target students belong to the bilingual strand of the courses 'Didactics of Experimental Sciences' I and II, dealing with physics, chemistry, geology, and astronomy contents (course I) and life sciences contents (course II). The courses are taught mainly in Spanish, but this particular sequence was delivered, produced, and assessed in English. Students' performance was assessed by means of self-evaluation, peer-evaluation, as well as immediate or delayed feedback from the lecturer.

DOI: 10.4018/978-1-6684-6179-2.ch015

Copyright © 2023, IGI Global. Copying or distributing in print or electronic forms without written permission of IGI Global is prohibited.

INTRODUCTION

The current chapter describes in detail a teaching-learning sequence (TLS) using the CLIL approach to teach contents related to sedimentary rocks and fossils to pre-service Primary Education Teachers. English as a Medium of Instruction (EMI) and Content and Language Integrated Learning (CLIL) approaches are used throughout the sequence. The TLS was designed and implemented at two different stages during the academic year 2021-2022, within the discipline of Didactics of Experimental Sciences. The main results of the implementation are discussed. Then, a SWOT analysis, evaluating the Strengths, Weaknesses, Opportunities and Threats of the TLS, is provided at the end of the chapter, in order to assess its usefulness and potential.

The main objectives of the chapter are as follows:

- To present a case study of a CLIL TLS implemented at the University of Granada with pre-service Primary Education teachers of a bilingual group, highlighting their initial lack of familiarity with the CLIL approach.
- To provide core materials that may be modified and adapted by other Secondary Education and University teachers to use CLIL in the science classroom.
- To show the positive outcome of introducing the CLIL approach to pre-service teachers.

BACKGROUND

Bilingual science teaching has become the norm in most bilingual schools in Spain, where *Conocimiento del Medio Natural, Social y Cultural* is usually the first of the Non-Linguistic Areas (NLAs) to be included in bilingual programmes from primary education onwards. In Andalusia, the southern-most region of Spain, 695 bilingual Primary schools (as in 2021/22; Consejería de Educación y Deporte, 2022) teach that subject of Science in English. They follow the regional government's Order of 28th of June of 2011 that regulates bilingual education in Andalusia (Orden de 28 de junio de 2011) and establishes Science as its priority area and Content and Language Integrated Learning (CLIL, or in Spanish *AICLE: Aprendizaje Integrado de Contenidos y Lengua Extranjera*) as the preferred methodological approach (Barrios & Milla, 2020; Fernández-Viciana, Barrios & Ramos, 2019; Ruiz, 2019).

Mehisto, Marsh & Frigols (2008) define CLIL as "a dual-focused educational approach in which an additional language is used for the learning and teaching of both content and language" (p. 9).

Therefore, to be adequately prepared for teaching Science in a bilingual classroom, Science teachers need to develop a wide range of competences that define the CLIL teacher profile, such as proficient linguistic communication in the foreign language, familiarity with a variety of pedagogical approaches and resources, depth of scientific knowledge about the theory of learning and language underlying CLIL, organisational competence to manage different groupings and learning modalities, interpersonal and collaborative skills, and reflective and developmental competences (Coyle, Hood & Marsh, 2010); the training these teachers are receiving, however, does not yet make the grade (Pérez, 2018; Custodio-Espinar, 2019; Pavón & Rubio, 2010; Ramos-García & Fernández-Viciana, 2022).

Numerous studies in the last decade have been dedicated to both examining the scope and quality of teacher training programmes in providing preparation for CLIL teachers (Banegas, 2012; Barrios & Milla 2020; Calle-Casado, 2015; Custodio-Espinar, 2019; De la Maya & Luengo, 2015; Delicado & Pavón,

Example of a CLIL Teaching-Learning Sequence

2016; Estrada, 2021; Jover, Fleta, & González, 2016; Lasagabaster & Ruiz de Zarobe, 2010; Palacios, Gómez, & Huertas, 2018; Pérez Cañado, 2015; Pavón & Ellison, 2013; Porcedda & González-Martínez, 2020; Romero & Zayas, 2017) and to gathering the practitioners' opinions and beliefs in relation to their satisfaction with their training and their perceived needs (Alcaraz-Mármol, 2018; Campillo, Sánchez, & Miralles, 2019; Durán-Martínez & Beltrán-Llavador, 2020; Milla & Casas, 2018). As regards the former, the systematic review of European studies carried out by Porcedda and González-Martínez (2020) sheds some light on the challenges that CLIL teacher training still faces. One is the scarcity of pre-service training (or, at least, of studies about its implementation): although most of the training is set at universities, only 16% of the courses are addressed exclusively to pre-service teachers through specific Degree or Master programmes (almost all located in Spain), whereas 52% of the courses are for in-service teachers and 32% for both pre- and in-service. Porcedda and González-Martínez (2020) conclude that there is the need to improve Initial Teacher Education because most of the focus so far has been placed on the access of in-service teachers to Continuous Professional Development and Lifelong Learning opportunities for their methodological training.

Also, teachers and researchers in Porcedda and González-Martínez's review (2020) perceive that the most relevant lacks in their training are, in order of importance, prior CLIL training, experience or knowledge; pedagogical/educational preparation (about educational strategies, students' cognitive and intercultural development, or evidence-based research) and instructional/planning problems. This distribution varies when considering only pre-service teachers, for whom the main lacks are foreign language competence, instructional/planning problems, and availability/management of ICTs (Porcedda and González-Martínez, 2020). The suggestions and good practices mentioned by the authors of the reviewed articles highlight the need to offer CLIL methodological courses and pedagogical-educational training as well as the teaching of collaborative learning/practices, among others.

Other studies confirm that, although pre-service teachers' self-evaluations show their lower consideration of their linguistic competence (Cortina-Pérez & Pino-Rodríguez, 2021), it is the methodological training, including materials design (Durán-Martínez & Beltrán-Llavador, 2016), or theoretical underpinnings of CLIL (Pérez, 2016), that consistently concerns in-service teachers (Melara & González, 2016), even those who in fact show a high level of satisfaction with their training. These practitioners acknowledge the need for teacher training *before* starting to work in any CLIL programme (San Isidro & Lasagabaster, 2019). As Custodio-Espinar (2019) affirms:

training programmes for CLIL teachers are not as effective as might be expected, and they do not satisfy these teachers' training needs. We have seen that this is connected with two main factors: the fact that CLIL training is not well integrated into university teacher education programmes, and the emphasis placed by educational authorities on language proficiency at the expense of methodological expertise (p. 328).

This second factor is repeatedly mentioned as one of the main reasons for the scarcity of pre-service methodological training (Alcaraz-Mármol, 2018), since only a limited number of regions in Spain, such as Canarias, Extremadura and La Rioja, demand some number of hours of prior methodological training in order for a teacher to be qualified to participate in bilingual programmes (Guadamillas & Alcaraz, 2017). Linguistic certification of at least a B2 level of English, on the other hand, is a must all over Spain, with many regions following the lead of Madrid and Navarra in intensifying the requirement up to a C1 level.

As regards content teachers –i.e. teachers of NLAs, in contrast to teachers of English as a Foreign Language (EFL)– the need for training seems to be greater, since they acknowledge the largest gaps in both areas, "linguistic and intercultural competence and materials and resources" (Pérez, 2016, p. 285): for example, content teachers are more pessimistic in their perception regarding the quality of CLIL materials than foreign language teachers (Milla & Casas, 2018). In particular, the training of Primary Education CLIL science teachers requires an in-depth reconsideration because they will be involved in "procesos de enseñanza y aprendizaje distintos a los de las didácticas de la lengua extranjera y de las ciencias por separado" [teaching-learning processes different from those of foreign language teaching and those of science teaching considered separately, own translation] (Amat, Vallborna, & Martí, 2017, p. 4932). It is the role of universities to include in their academic programmes subjects, units, or learning experiences that introduce future science teachers to the fundamentals of CLIL education (Estrada, 2021; Ramos-García & Fernández-Viciana, 2022) because, although some experiences in this regard have been carried out in programmes for pre-service English teachers (Ramos & Espinet, 2013; Amat et al., 2017), this revision of the syllabus to incorporate compulsory CLIL courses should be extended to all general Primary Education teacher training programmes so that "all future teachers, regardless they decide to teach bilingual education or not, acquire the methodological foundations of this approach" (Gutiérrez & Custodio, 2021, p. 113-14). As a result, a subject like Didactics of Experimental Sciences should be formulated not simply as "una asignatura en la que la lengua vehicular sea el inglés, sino de forma que sirva para reflexionar sobre los enfoques AICLE" [A subject taught in English, but a subject that reflects on the CLIL approaches"; own translation.] (Amat et al., 2017, p. 4936).

The other basic component of science teacher-training is the knowledge of scientific content, as Primary teachers need solid foundations in the areas included in the national legislation establishing the curriculum for Primary Education studies (Real Decreto 126/2014 and Real Decreto 157/2022). As regards the area of *Conocimiento del Medio Natural, Social y Cultural* [Kowledge of the Natural, Social, and Cultural Environment, own translation], the curriculum contemplates competences and content knowledge (so-called *basic knowledge* or '*saberes básicos*' in the new law) related to the adaptation of living beings to their environment, the human impact on nature and the preservation of ecosystems and species, as well as the features of the natural environment, including types of rocks and natural resources (that include fossil fuels). There is also recurrent mention to climate change stemming from human activities. Large-scale changes such as adaptation to the environment and evolution, extinction of species or climate change cannot be fully comprehended within the restricted span of a human lifetime. Thus, in order to understand all the above-mentioned contents and develop the corresponding competences, a basic geological knowledge about history of life and geological time is needed (Dodick, 2007; Gómez-Loarces, Ferrer & González-García, 2019; Trend, 2000).

MAIN FOCUS OF THE CHAPTER

Issues, Controversies, Problems

By looking at the official curriculum for Primary Education and at the corresponding textbooks (Pla-Pueyo, González-García, & Ramos-García, in preparation), it is evident that the responsibility for teaching about geological time, palaeontology and evolution falls on the Primary Education teachers because, although Primary Education children show certain familiarity with the concept of fossil, they

Example of a CLIL Teaching-Learning Sequence

mostly learn about it through non-formal or even informal education (Ceballos, Vílchez, & Reina, 2019). Nonetheless, even when pre-service Primary Education teachers may be familiar with fossils as well (Pla-Pueyo, González-García & Ramos García, 2021), misconceptions about the concept of fossil and the process of fossilisation have been identified in students from the Primary Education level to the university level, including pre-service and in-service teachers (Calonge, Bercial, García, & López, 2003; Calonge & López, 2005; Ceballos et al., 2019; Gómez-Loarces et al., 2019; Lillo, 1995; Pedrinaci, 1996). The understanding of geological time seems difficult for all education levels as well (Pedrinaci & Berjillos, 1994; Trend, 1998, 2000; Dodick & Orion, 2003, 2006; Libarkin, Kurdziel, & Anderson, 2007, Teed & Slattery, 2011; Corrochano & Gómez-Gonçalves, 2020). Geological time is the framework in which evolutionary change happens, so this lack of understanding may also affect the ability to place events related to history of life in a timeline and to order them (Libarkin, Anderson, Beilfuss, & Boone, 2005; Dodick, 2007). Finally, evolution in itself presents many problems for students of all ages around the world (see Kuschmierz, Meneganzin, Pinxten, Pievani, Cvetković, Mavrikaki, Gra, & Beniermann, 2020 and references within).

As a result, most pre-service and in-service Primary Education teachers lack the confidence on their knowledge or understanding about the history of life to teach about geological time, palaeontology and evolution (Corrochano & Gómez-Gonçalves, 2020; Teed & Slattery, 2011). This low level of scientific knowledge can cause these science teachers to have difficulties in carrying out educational changes and to depend more on ready-made materials such as textbooks (Mellado, Blanco, & Ruiz, 1998), when it is precisely the creation of new, personal CLIL materials that is the main task of the CLIL teacher (Consejería de Educación y Deporte, 2013, p. 97).

Thus, as Jover et al. (2016, p. 130) and others affirm, university bilingual teacher training degrees should not merely offer lessons in English on science didactics or other curricular areas, but they should combine bilingual instruction, designed to improve the pre-service teachers' linguistic competence, with specialised training in methodological aspects of CLIL and language teaching and, it may be added, lessons on the necessary scientific knowledge. There is, therefore, a need to adopt a holistic approach (Pérez & Steele, 2017) and design teaching-learning situations through which pre-service Primary Education teachers may acquire, on the one hand, sufficient basic knowledge and skills and, on the other, the required pedagogical competence and tools to be able to teach about geological time, palaeontology and evolution to their future students (Vázquez-Ben & Bugallo-Rodríguez, 2020), and to do so in English in their future bilingual classrooms.

In order to design such a holistic teaching-learning experience, the authors have adopted a constructivist perspective of 'learning by doing' based on proposals such as Delicado & Pavón (2016) and Cortina-Pérez & Pino-Rodríguez (2021), which advocate for an approach where pre-service teachers are introduced to CLIL by experimenting that very methodology as students themselves. This type of experiential learning would first begin with a tutor-centred introduction to the main tenets of CLIL, followed by a CLIL lesson or teaching-learning sequence (TLS) through which students revise or learn about certain geological concepts. The TLS includes a series of activities to promote reflection, discussion, and the design of CLIL activities by students themselves (Banegas, 2012). The teaching-learning sequence (TLS) or *secuencia didáctica* is the preferred planning unit in Spanish CLIL contexts for "organizing and distributing the contents of the NLA and, therefore, structuring their [the students'] learning processes" (Campillo et al. 2019, p. 151). As mentioned above, the Andalusian guidelines for bilingual schools establish that CLIL teachers must create their own adapted materials in the form of those TLS (Consejería de Educación y Deporte, 2013, p. 97), although they can initially resort to a databank of sample sequences in an official repository (Dirección General de Participación e Innovación Educativa, Consejería de Educación, Junta de Andalucía, 2011). Consequently, it is by means of the pre-service teachers' own experience in learning about geological concepts through a CLIL TLS that they gain first-hand knowledge about the processes and contents of CLIL and they subsequently can reflect on them and try to put them into practice in their own planning and design of a TLS. This complex learning environment does not only foster the integrated learning of science and foreign language by the student teachers (Ramos & Espinet, 2013, p. 45), but also their understanding and practice of CLIL pedagogy.

METHODOLOGY

Sample

The sample involved in the CLIL TLS sequence consists of students of the third year of the Primary Education Teacher Training degree at the University of Granada, specifically those enrolled in the bilingual group. Although a total of 60 students were enrolled in the target course in the first semester, only 37 of the students fully participated in the two stages of the sequence and answered the final questionnaire about the experience with CLIL, so in this chapter, the authors will consider those 37 students as the sample. All presented data derive from the student's questionnaires.

The sampled students are 18-25 years old and an 86.5% of the group are females. Regarding their scientific background, it is remarkable that a majority of the students (62.2%) took the optional subject of biology and geology in the 4th year of compulsory Secondary Education. This is the first course in their schooling years in which evolution contents are officially included in the curriculum, meaning that most of the students should already have some background knowledge about evolution previous to their university studies. However, only a 24.3% continued their geological education in the two years prior to their university degree. These numbers are slightly higher than the general results obtained for a larger sample including both bilingual and non-bilingual groups for the academic years 2020-2022 (Pla-Pueyo, González-García, Ramos-García, & Ramón-Ballesta, 2022a).

In terms of their English level, an 8.1% of the students had not received any official certificate. Only one student (2.1%) had an A2 level at the beginning of the academic year, but by the end of the second semester obtained a higher one (B2). Most of the students (43.7%) had a B1 level at the beginning of semester 1, which was reduced to a 37.8% when some of them obtained their B2 or even C1 certificate in the second semester. The second most frequent certificate is the B2 (35.1% at the beginning, increased to a 37.8% at the end of semester 2), while only 5 students (16.2%) had obtained a C1 certificate by the end of the academic year. These data, similar to the ones obtained for previous academic years (Pla-Pueyo, González-García & Ramos-García, 2022), show the generally low level of English presented by the students, which is remarkable when the 56.8% considers bilingual schools as their first option and the 40.5% considers it a possibility, with just a 2.7% stating that they would not teach at a bilingual school if they can help it.

Intervention

The didactic intervention started with a questionnaire in English, focusing on three main aspects: prior students' education to the degree, knowledge and understanding of target geological and palaeontological

Example of a CLIL Teaching-Learning Sequence

contents and attitude towards bilingual education and CLIL. A TLS, detailed in the following section, was then implemented, and two questionnaires were passed to the students at the end of the TSL. One of them was the post-test for the geological contents, basically identical to the first one, and the other one focused on the students' personal reflection on their whole experience with the CLIL approach.

Teaching-Learning Sequence Design

As it has been mentioned above, the TLS presented in this chapter is designed for pre-service Primary Education teachers studying Didactics of Experimental Sciences. At the University of Granada, this discipline is divided into two courses taught in consecutive semesters. During the first semester, the course is called 'Didactics of Experimental Sciences I' and it covers physics, chemistry, geology and astronomy contents, while during the second semester, the course is named 'Didactics of Experimental Sciences II' and focuses on life sciences, including one topic about evolution, fossils and fossilisation, that also tackles the organisation of living beings. Thus, the TLS was divided accordingly into two stages, each one carried on in a different semester. However, if it were to be implemented at a different university, it would be possible to combine both parts and to use the TLS presented here as one continuous sequence. As the sequence is designed for future Primary Education teachers, the content level is slightly higher than the required by Primary Education students. This means that this TLS could be easily adapted for Secondary Education students of Biology and Geology courses as well. For further details on the TLS contents, please see next section.

The CLIL part of the TLS was designed according to two criteria: a scientific criterion and a linguistic one.

On the one hand, the scientific design included:

- the selection of the target content, based both on the current legislation for Primary Education studies and on the course syllabus (Didactics of Experimental Sciences I and II), in which the target students were enrolled.
- the definition of the scientific learning objectives for the TLS.
- the identification of the competences and skills to be developed, related to the scientific content.
- the design of a questionnaire, using questions and activities either selected from specialised literature or designed to cover the scientific contents and including a first set of questions about their English background and experience with CLIL.
- the sequencing of contents and activities following a scaffolding approach, from simpler to more complex ones.

On the other hand, the linguistic design included:

- the identification of target language used to teach each scientific content, including specific vocabulary and grammar.
- the definition of the linguistic learning objectives for the TLS.
- the identification of linguistic competences and skills to be developed during the sequence.
- the design of activities related to each content that integrated both scientific and language content.
- sequencing of activities starting with controlled-practice activities followed by free-practice activities (combined with the scaffolding scientific sequencing).

Example of a CLIL Teaching-Learning Sequence

- the preparation of a document with basic guidelines and a set of instructions for the students to design their own CLIL sequence as a final outcome.
- the design of a final questionnaire about the whole CLIL experience.

In order to assess the degree of achievement of the learning objectives and competences by the students, different evaluation approaches were applied for each activity in the sequence, including self-evaluation, peer-evaluation, as well as immediate or delayed feedback from the teacher.

At the end of each stage of the TLS, the relevant questions of the initial questionnaire regarding the scientific contents were passed again to the students, in order to assess the changes in their answers before and after the intervention.

At the end of the whole sequence, an online questionnaire adapting questions from Guadamillas (2017) and Cortina-Pérez & Pino-Rodríguez (2021) was used to evaluate the perception of the instruction process and the willingness to apply the CLIL approach in their future bilingual teaching after their personal experience. The questionnaire is available at: https://forms.gle/ywigT5h3i3Z66HLd9

CLIL TEACHING-LEARNING SEQUENCE ON GEOLOGICAL TIME, PALAEONTOLOGY AND EVOLUTION

As mentioned in the previous section, due to organisational reasons, the TLS was divided into two stages, each one carried on in a different semester. A detailed description of each stage of the TLS is provided below. It is important to mention that in the present chapter, the focus will be on the sessions in which the CLIL approach has been applied.

CLIL Session TLS-Stage 1

The first stage of the designed TLS (Table 1) deals with geological contents (Earth's formation, plate tectonics, rocks and minerals, etc) and includes a CLIL session focusing on the concepts of sedimentary rock and strata, the basic principles of stratigraphy (superposition and actualism) and dating (relative and absolute dating of fossils and evolutionary events). In terms of geological time, it stresses how fossils can be useful to date rocks and vice versa, providing an invaluable tool to reconstruct history of life through them. From this point of view, one of the learning objectives of this session is to emphasise the connection between fossils and the rocks bearing them, as there seems to be a problem understanding the synchronicity between fossils and the containing rocks identified in previous studies (Pedrinaci, 1996; Gómez-Loarces et al., 2019). A detailed description of the first stage of the TLS is shown in table 1.

Example of a CLIL Teaching-Learning Sequence

Table 1. First stage of the TLS, taught during the first semester, as part of the course 'Didactics of Experimental Sciences I'

Date	Timing	Teaching strategy	Contents
Week 10	25 minutes	EMI	Questionnaire (pre-test) about: • Formal and non-formal education related to geology and palaeontology • Knowledge and skills related to geological time, absolute and relative dating of fossils and main evolutionary events, the concept of fossil and fossilisation, macroevolution and history of life on Earth. • Bilingual education received previously to the degree • Level and use of English • Degree of familiarity with CLIL
Week 11	Session 1 (1.5h)	EMI	• Concept of geosphere • Internal structure of planet Earth • Plate tectonics and plate boundaries
Week 12	Session 2 (3h)	EMI	• Plate tectonics, earthquakes and vulcanism • Rocks and minerals. The rock cycle • Agents that change the landscape: water, ice, wind • Meteorisation/erosion/dissolution, transport and deposition/precipitation • Earth surface processes, sedimentary rocks and resulting landscapes • Soil formation
Week 13	Session 3 (1.5h)	CLIL	• Basics on CLIL approach • Review of sediment cycle and sedimentary rocks • Concept of stratum/bed • Principles of stratigraphy • How to date geological events (relative vs absolute dating) • Synchronicity between fossils and rock that contains them
Week 14	Session 4 (15 min)	EMI	Questionnaire (post-test) about: • **Knowledge and skills related to geological time, absolute and relative dating of fossils**

Regarding the CLIL session (1.5h), that took place during Week 13 of the first semester, the scientific topic to be covered was geological time (Table 2). Upon completion of the topic on geological time, students should be able to:

- Apply the basic principles of stratigraphy
- Explain the difference between relative and absolute age
- Order events by their relative age
- Provide the absolute age of the formation of Earth and the main events that mark the history of life
- Carry out simple stratigraphical correlations
- Order events from a correlation panel by their relative age

Regarding the target language related to the topic, eight key terms were identified (bed, stratum, relative age, absolute age, correlation, extinction, appearance, fossil record) and the following linguistic elements were selected in relation to the scientific contents:

- comparative adjectives (older, younger, the most recent...)
- numbers (billions, millions, thousands of years)
- prepositions of time (since, from, ago, ...)

Example of a CLIL Teaching-Learning Sequence

- expressions related to telling the time (12h clock)
- past verbal tenses
- possible false friends

Table 2. Description of the CLIL session within the first stage of the TLS

Activity	Content	Target language
Lecture by teacher	Earth's formation Concept of stratum Principles of stratigraphy How to date geological events	Key terms, past verbal tenses, prepositions of time
Activity 1. Ordering beds (individually) (Fig. 1) Activity 2. Ordering fossils (individually)	Application of basic principles of stratigraphy Relative dating	Vocabulary (bed, stratum, strata, relative age) Controlled practice of comparative adjectives
Lecture by teacher	Concept of absolute age History of life and main extinction events	Vocabulary (absolute age, extinctions)
Activity 3. How old are the fossils (individually)	Concept of absolute age	Free practice of comparative adjectives
Activity 4. Fill in a table, then fill in the gaps (individually)	Absolute ages of main events related to Earth's formation and history of life	Controlled practice of the use of time prepositions
Activity 5. Speaking (in pairs)	12-hour clock analogy for geological time	Telling the time in English Free practice of the use of time prepositions and simple past tense
Activity 6. Lithological correlation (individually)	Basic correlation and relative age using lithology	Vocabulary (correlation)
Activity 7. Correlation using fossils (individually)	Basic correlation and relative age using fossils	Free practice of comparative adjectives
Evaluation	Questionnaire in English on geological time	All the new content

Each complete activity from Table 2 is provided below as it was presented to the students.

Activity 1

- Number the beds in Figure 1 from 1 to 6, being 1 the first that was deposited and 6 the one which deposited most recently.
- Fill in the gaps using the correct comparative or superlative form (younger, older, the youngest, the oldest):
  - Bed 1 is _____.
  - Bed 6 is _____.
  - Bed 2 is _____ than bed 4.
  - Bed 5 is _____ than bed 3.

360

Example of a CLIL Teaching-Learning Sequence

Figure 1. Figure for activity 1, modified from Dodick and Orion (2003) by S. Pla-Pueyo

Activity 2

- In Figure 2, order the fossils from the oldest to the youngest.
- Which fossil is younger, the coral or the ammonite?

Figure 2. Figure for activity 2, modified from Dodick and Orion (2003) by S. Pla-Pueyo

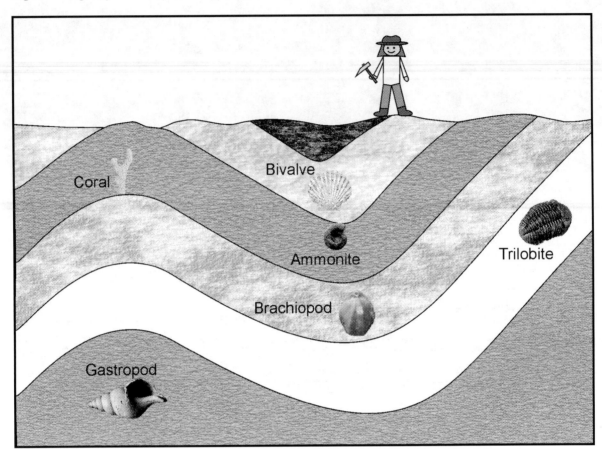

Activity 3

We know that the two volcanic layers (marked with the symbols v v v in Figure 3) have been dated by the scientists, obtaining an absolute age for each one.

- Number the beds from the oldest (1) to the youngest (5)
- What would be the absolute age for each fossil? Use comparative adjectives when needed to answer the question.

Example of a CLIL Teaching-Learning Sequence

Figure 3. Figure for activity 3, modified from Dodick and Orion (2003) by S. Pla-Pueyo

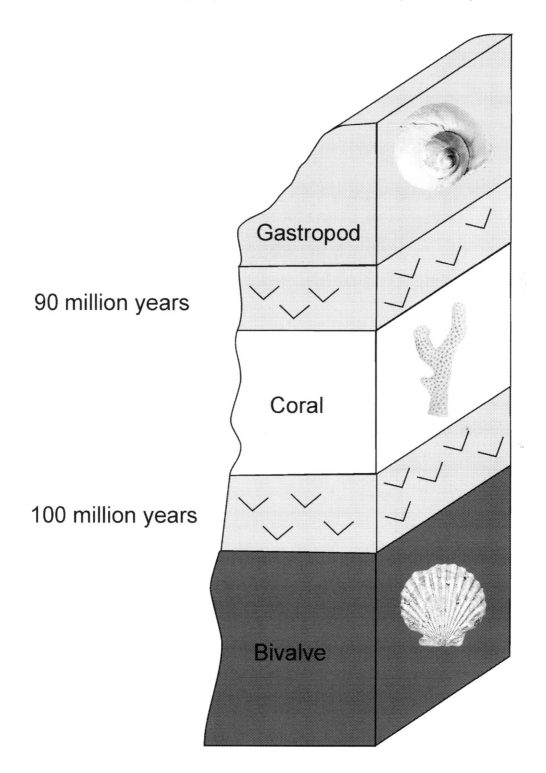

Example of a CLIL Teaching-Learning Sequence

Activity 4

- Fill in the following table (Table 3), adding the absolute age for the events listed. Then order them by giving them a number from 1 (the oldest event) to 5 (the most recent event).

Table 3. Table for activity 4

Age (in Ma*)	Event	Order of event
	Extinction of dinosaurs	
	Formation of Earth	
	Appearance of life on Earth	
	Appearance of dinosaurs	
	Appearance of modern humans *(Homo sapiens)*	

Ma means Mega annum, a million years

* The information may be provided by the teacher, or they may have to look it up in the textbook or the internet.

- Fill in the gaps in the following sentences using the time prepositions provided below:

After ago before for from_to since until

- The Earth was formed 4.6 million years _____.
- The dinosaurs lived on Earth _____ 230 ___ 65 million years ____.
- Humans (genus homo) have inhabited the Earth ____ 200,000 years.
- There was no life on Earth ___ the first bacteria appeared 3,500 million years ____.
- Dinosaurs are extinct ____ the end of the Cretaceous, 65 million years _____.

Activity 5

- Using the analogy that represents the history of life on Earth in a 12h-clock*, discuss with your partner at what time did the main events listed in activity 4 occurred, and to which absolute age (in Ma) does that time corresponds.

*There are many available images in the internet representing the geological timescale in a 12h- or a 24h-clock. The teacher should select the one that better fits their needs.

364

Example of a CLIL Teaching-Learning Sequence

Figure 4. Figure for activity 5 (by S. Pla-Pueyo)

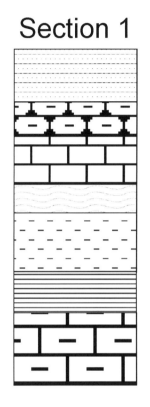
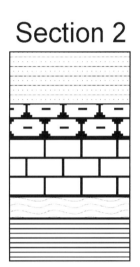

Activity 6

- Draw lines in Figure 4 to correlate the following sections by their lithology
- After correlating the sections, assign the correct numbers to Section 2 beds
- Is layer 3 present in both sections?
- Use complete sentences and compare beds 1 and 3, and beds 6 and 2, using comparative adjectives of age.

Activity 7

- Draw lines to correlate the following sections in Figure 5 by their fossil content.
- After correlating the sections, assign the correct numbers to Section 2 beds
- Which fossil is older, the ammonites or the trilobite?
- What is the relative age of bed 5 in regards to bed 2?

Figure 5. Figure for activity 7 by S. Pla-Pueyo

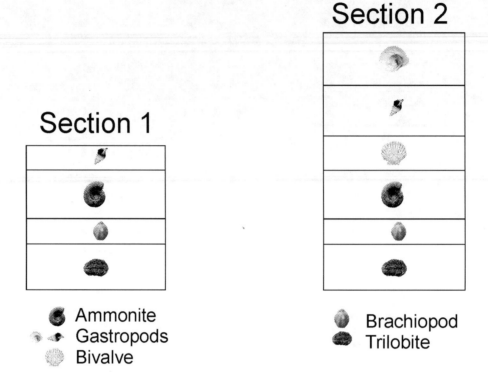

CLIL Session TLS-Stage 2

The second stage of the TLS sequence (Table 4) focuses on fossils themselves, fossilisation and evolution contents. The geological timescale is used to locate events related with macroevolution and history of life on Earth, and the students learn some analogies to use with Primary Education students to improve the understanding of the immensity of geological time. The different evolutionary theories are discussed, focussing on misconceptions about evolution, Lamarckism and teleological thinking. During the practical session (for which the group is divided into two smaller groups), they also have to identify fossils using hand samples and sections on the ornamental rocks of the building (Pla-Pueyo, González-García, Ramos-García, & Ramón-Ballesta, 2022b), and to associate them with the different fossilisation processes.

Example of a CLIL Teaching-Learning Sequence

Table 4. Second stage of the TLS, taught during the second semester, as part of the course 'Didactics of Experimental Sciences I'

Date	Timing	Teaching strategy	Contents
Week 11	Session 2.1. (Theory) (2h)	EMI	• Origin of life on Earth • Evolutionary hypothesis and theories (Cuvier, Lamarck, Darwin-Wallace, Neo-Darwinism) • Fossils and fossilisation • Classification of living and extinct organisms following cladograms showing main evolutionary anatomical changes
	Session 2.2a (Practical session for half the students) (2h)	EMI	• Identification and dating of fossil hand samples and fossils on ornamental rocks of the building • Geological time scale • Analogies for geological time • Main evolutionary events in history of life on Earth (absolute dates) • Vertebrates' evolution (absolute and relative dates) (Based on the activities in González-García et al. 2021)
Week 12	Session 2.2b. (Practical session for the remaining students)	EMI	Idem to session 2.2a.
Week 13		EMI	Written instructions provided online through learning platform on how to develop a CLIL TLS on human evolution
Week 14	Session 3 (1.5h)	EMI	Explanation of CLIL activity and Q&A session about it
Week 15	25 min	EMI	Questionnaire (post-test) about: • Knowledge and skills related to geological time, absolute and relative dating of fossils and main evolutionary events, the concept of fossil and fossilisation, macroevolution and history of life on Earth. • Final online questionnaire about: • Changes in level and use of English throughout the academic year • Evaluation of the CLIL sequences and activities • Appreciation of CLIL • Willingness to use CLIL in their future teaching

During this second stage of the TLS, the sessions were taught using EMI and it was the students who had to develop a CLIL session, in order to improve their pedagogical competence.

They worked in groups of 3-4 students, and they received a set of written instructions in order to guide them through the process.

They students were asked to prepare a 50 minutes-1h session for Primary Education students, focusing on the contents of vertebrate evolution and human evolution. In order to simplify the activity, a set of materials were provided including all the contents, so they could focus on the design of the CLIL activities themselves.

In order to help them, a template was provided, including all the compulsory sections that they needed to fill and a brief explanation for what was expected in each of them. All of these sections represented each of the items in the rubric that was later used to evaluate their work. This rubric was provided as well to the students with the starting set of materials and evaluated the following aspects:

1.   Length of session vs. content of session: Timing of session and activities specified and realistic.

2. Structure and organisation: Template used and session organised and structured after the instructions given.
3. Didactic transposition of contents for 6th grade Primary Education: Contents and/or language perfectly suitable for the target teaching level.
4. Learning objectives: Contents and focus of session coherent with learning objectives.
5. Competences: Competences correctly expressed and coherent with the design of the session. Scientific and linguistic competences mentioned.
6. Teaching methodology: Use of CLIL approach in all activities and active role of student fully promoted.
7. Contents:
    a. Contents about vertebrate evolution completely covered and the presentation is correct and clear.
    b. Contents about human evolution completely covered and the presentation is correct and clear.
    c. English contents completely covered and the presentation is correct and clear.
    d. Conceptual errors and misconceptions: Concepts correctly understood and explained, no misconceptions or conceptual errors present.
    e. Correct use of English language in written original materials: Correct vocabulary/expressions. No use of teleological nor lamarkist expressions.
8. Activities:
    a. Final session ready to use: Session provided as it will be presented to students, including complete instructions and resources, ready to use.
    b. Clarity of instructions: Instructions clear and comprehensible for the target level.
    c. Full description of activity and needed resources provided.
9. Sequencing of contents and activities:
    a. Sequence of scientific contents and activities: Sequencing of contents and activities based on pedagogical criteria.
    b. Sequence of English contents and activities.
10. Evaluation: Different forms of evaluation proposed, all appropriate for the contents and competencies to be evaluated.

Although the instructions were given in written form, a 1.5h session was devoted to orally explain them and for the students to start working on the design of their sequence, so they could ask any questions that arose during the initial stages of the process.

For those teachers interested in using this TLS, the materials are available for downloading at the following Google Drive folder: https://drive.google.com/drive/folders/1ZVKiX_LO9yhRXHhImD2O1Jqpj7MUm7z3?usp=sharing

RESULTS OF THE TLS IMPLEMENTATION

Based on the student's answers to the different questionnaires and the evaluation of the activities they have handed in throughout the TLS, the sequence has been effective to improve the student's knowledge about some geological and biological aspects (preliminary results have already been published in Pla-Pueyo et al. 2021).

Example of a CLIL Teaching-Learning Sequence

Regarding the marks they obtained for the design of their own CLIL session, the majority of the students (55.3%) obtained a mark between 7-8.9 over a full score of 10, while a 17% obtained a mark between 5 and 6.9 a 12.8% a mark over 9. The 14.9% of the students failed the activity with a mark below 5.

Unexpected problems arose related to the pedagogical competence of the pre-service teachers performing the TLS that affected their design of the CLIL sequence, such as their difficulty sequencing activities by their level of complexity. However, these problems seem to have no negative impact on their perception of the CLIL approach. An 81.1% of the students had never heard of CLIL at the beginning of the TLS in the first semester, for a 10.8% the term rung a bell but had no meaning, and only an 8.1% was familiar with it, but just a 5.4% would apply it in their future teaching. After completing the TLS, an 89.2% of the students would apply the CLIL methodology in their future bilingual teaching, which may be considered a success. Moreover, most of the students (62.2%) agree that the TLS sessions were satisfactory to understand and practice on CLIL as an innovative and useful approach, with a 32.4% of neutral students and only a 5.4% in disagreement.

CLIL TLS SWOT ANALYSIS

SWOT analyses are a commonly used tool in education (Al Marwani, 2020; Longhurst et al., 2020; Resnawati et al., 2020), consisting of an internal and external analysis of the proposal. The internal analysis focuses on the identification of organisational strengths and weaknesses, while the external analysis helps understanding the advantages (opportunities) that the proposal may offer, and the threats that may affect the implementation of the proposal (Gürel &Tat, 2017). There are some aspects to be taken into account when performing a SWOT analysis on the CLIL TLS that has been designed and applied to pre-service Primary Education teachers at the University of Granada:

11. As it has been explained above, due to both academic and organisational reasons, the TLS has been divided into two different courses (Table 5). Although most students were enrolled in both (47 students), some were enrolled only in one of the two subjects, either because they failed the course in the past and were retaking it, or they were exchange students and they left for an Erasmus stay abroad during the second semester. Moreover, occasional absence due to covid-19 also affected the number of students participating in each session. As a result, only 37 students have fully participated in the two stages of the TLS. A summary of the number of students performing each part of the TLS is shown in table 5.

Example of a CLIL Teaching-Learning Sequence

Table 5. Number of students performing each activity in each semester

Semester and course	Activity	Number of students	Participation
Semester 1 DES1	Total of students enrolled in the course	60	
	Stage 1 Pre-test questionnaire (1st semester)	59	98,3%
	Stage 1 CLIL session	54	90%
	Stage 1 Post-test questionnaire	45	75%
Semester 2 DES2	Total of students enrolled in the course	49	
	Stage 2 Attendance to Q&A session about CLIL sequence design	46	93,9%
	Stage 2 Hand in of CLIL sequence design	47	95,9%
	Stage 2 Post-test questionnaire	38	77,6%
	Stage 2 CLIL questionnaire	38	77,6%

12. As it has been shown when characterising the sample, the certified level of English is low to medium, with only a 35.1% of the students holding a B2 certificate and just a 10.8% holding a C1.

13. At the beginning of the academic year, most of the students (81.1%) had never heard about CLIL. Thus, this TLS is the first contact they have with the CLIL approach in their academic life. However, as the courses involved were focused on science and not in English, there was no time to include specific sessions about the foundations of the CLIL approach, just a few brief remarks within science-based lessons.

14. Taking into account that most of the students consider teaching in bilingual schools as their future job, that many bilingual schools are embracing the CLIL approach and that the students are in the third year of the degree (they graduate in the fourth year), this TLS is the only formal and practical experience on CLIL they have acquired during their degree.

Bearing those aspects in mind, we will proceed with the SWOT analysis.

Internal Aspects: Strengths and Weaknesses

Regarding the participation of students in the TLS (aspect 1), taking into account the results in Table 5, the high percentage of participation in the different stages should be considered a strength, with more than 60% of the students having performed the complete sequence.

On the other hand, this is a unique study in our faculty, representing a founding stone for future studies on practical training on CLIL. The students in the bilingual group are a strong asset for our faculty and the continuation of this strand; if lecturers involved do not fail in transmitting the importance of this TLS in their training, it may appeal to future students as an important part of their training in bilingual teaching methodology, thus promoting a higher participation in the sequence.

The second aspect is definitely a weakness, due to the low English level qualifications of the students, that translate into teaching and learning difficulties in the bilingual classroom. However, this is something out of our control, as the University of Granada has no entry requirements regarding the English level for this specific strand, so anyone may access the bilingual modality of the Primary Teacher Training degree, independently of their English level. Moreover, only a B1 is required to graduate, which is a

370

Example of a CLIL Teaching-Learning Sequence

general requirement for every student at the University of Granada or any other Andalusian university up to the present moment. A potential solution would be to establish an entry level of B1 or even B2 for the bilingual strand of the Primary Teacher Training degree, ensuring that the students have a minimum linguistic competence, as it is the case in some other Spanish universities. Thus, by tackling this problem, this internal weakness could become an opportunity to improve the degree and to increase its prestige.

The third aspect, the students' low pedagogical competence, is also an internal weakness of the strand itself, related to contents that the students should have learnt in previous courses. Although it does directly affect the TLS results, experimental science courses are not supposed to focus on general pedagogical aspects, but on science, so this is not associated with the TLS itself and should be tackled by degree coordinators by distributing courses and contents differently and/or adding a new course dealing with the CLIL approach, its foundations and practical aspects.

The fourth and last aspect is a strength of the TLS, as after their first contact with the CLIL approach through this experiment, most of the students (62.2%) have developed a positive attitude towards the CLIL approach and its usefulness.

External Aspects: Opportunities and Threats

Based on their personal experience, the authors have perceived a general apathy in our students towards innovative approaches in the bilingual classroom, especially when a bit of extra work is involved. However, as it is a subjective perception, it may be worth to obtain direct evidence of this attitude in future interventions. The authors believe that this lack of motivation may be related to their uncertainty about their professional future and because they feel they are in a position of disadvantage when compared to their colleagues in the regular (monolingual) stream, because in their opinion they have to work less than them. From this point of view, as it may affect the level of participation (aspect 1), it would be interesting to present this TLS in years to come as a unique opportunity for them to improve their professional training.

Regarding aspects 2 to 5, the improvement of the TLS regarding content knowledge, linguistic and pedagogical competences is considered a great opportunity for pre-service teachers, not only at a scientific level, but as a means to help them acquire a higher English level and/or certificate and professional training for bilingual teaching.

CONCLUSION

A CLIL TLS has been designed and implemented with positive results for the bilingual strand of the Primary Education Training degree at the University of Granada during the academic year 2021-2022. For most of the students, the TLS has been the first contact with the CLIL approach and it has been a satisfactory experience. The authors intend to continue improving and applying the sequence in the future, and it might prove to be useful for other bilingual science teaching contexts.

REFERENCES

Alcaraz-Mármol, G. (2018). Trained and Non-Trained Language Teachers on CLIL Methodology: Teachers' Facts and Opinions about the CLIL Approach in the Primary Education Context in Spain. *Latin American Journal of Content and Language Integrated Learning, 11*(1), 39-64. https://files.eric. ed.gov/fulltext/EJ1190982.pdf

AlMarwani, M. (2020). Pedagogical potential of SWOT analysis: An approach to teaching critical thinking. *Thinking Skills and Creativity, 38*, 100741. doi:10.1016/j.tsc.2020.100741

Amat, A., Vallborna, A., & Martí, J. (2017). Percepciones de futuros maestros de infantil y primaria sobre la enseñanza y el aprendizaje de las ciencias en inglés. *Enseñanza de las Ciencias*, (Special Issue), 4931–4936. https://ddd.uab.cat/pub/edlc/edlc_a2017nEXTRA/27._percepcion es_de_futuros_maestros_de_infantil_y_primaria.pdf

Banegas, D. L. (2012). CLIL teacher development: Challenges and experiences. *Latin American Journal of Content & Language Integrated Learning, 5*(1), 46–56. doi:10.5294/laclil.2012.5.1.4

Barrios, E., & Milla Lara, M. D. (2020). CLIL methodology, materials and resources, and assessment in a monolingual context: An analysis of stakeholders' perceptions in Andalusia. *Language Learning Journal, 48*(1), 60–80. doi:10.1080/09571736.2018.1544269

BOE. (2014). *Boletín Oficial del Estado, 52*, de 1 de Marzo de 2014, 19349-19420. https://www.boe. es/eli/es/rd/2014/02/28/126

Calle-Casado, J. J. (2015). *Teacher training for CLIL: Lessons learned and ways forward* [unpublished Masters' Thesis, Universidad de Jaén, Jaén]. https://tauja.ujaen.es/bitstream/10953.1/2285/1/Calle_Casado _Juan_Jos_TFG_Estudios_Ingleses.pdf

Calonge, A., Bercial, M. T., García, J., & López, M. O. (2003). El uso didáctico de los fósiles en la enseñanza de las Ciencias de la Tierra. [The didactic use of fossils in the teaching of Earth Sciences.] *Pulso, 26*, 117-128. https://revistas.cardenalcisneros.es/index.php/PULSO/article /view/38/239

Calonge, A., & López, M. D. (2005). Una propuesta práctica para acercarse a la noción de fósil y fosilización. [A practical proposal to approach the notion of fossil and fossilization.] *Alambique: Didáctica de las ciencias experimentales [Alembic: Didactics of experimental sciences], 44*, 49-56. http://cmap.unavarra.es/rid=1R3Q206R7-1STX7W6-12PBB/una-prop uesta-practica-para-acercarse-a-la-nocion-de-fosil-y-fosiliz acion.pdf

Campillo, J. M., Sánchez, R., & Miralles, P. (2019). Primary Teachers' Perceptions of CLIL Implementation in Spain. *English Language Teaching, 12*(4), 149–156. https://files.eric.ed.gov/fulltext/EJ1210453. pdf. doi:10.5539/elt.v12n4p149

Ceballos, M., Vílchez, J. E., & Reina, M. (2019). Concepto de fósil en niños de primero a cuarto de Educación Primaria: ¿cómo lo adquieren? [Concept of fossil in children from first to fourth of Primary Education: how do they acquire it?] *Enseñanza de las Ciencias de la Tierra [Teaching Earth Sciences], 27*(2), 210-218. https://raco.cat/index.php/ECT/article/view/367145

Example of a CLIL Teaching-Learning Sequence

Consejería de Educación y Deporte. (2013). *Guía informativa para centros de enseñanza bilingüe*. [*Informative guide for bilingual schools*.] (2nd ed.). Junta de Andalucía. https://www.juntadeandalucia.es/export/drupaljda/Guia_informativa_centros_ense%C3%B1anza_bilingue_.pdf

Consejería de Educación y Deporte. (2022). *Cuadro resumen centros bilingües en Andalucía*. [*Informative guide for bilingual schools*.] Junta de Andalucía. https://www.juntadeandalucia.es/educacion/portals/web/plurilinguismo/centros-bilingues

Corrochano, D., & Gómez-Gonçalves, A. (2020). Analysis of Spanish pre-service teachers' mental models of geologic time. *International Journal of Science Education*, *42*(10), 1653–1672. doi:10.1080/09500693.2020.1774093

Cortina-Pérez, B., & Pino-Rodríguez, A. M. (2021). Analysing CLIL Teacher Competences in Pre-service Preschool Education. A Case Study at the University of Granada. *European Journal of Teacher Education*. doi:10.1080/02619768.2021.1890021

Coyle, D., Hood, P., & Marsh, D. (2010). *CLIL: Content and Language Integrated Learning*. Cambridge University Press. doi:10.1017/9781009024549

Custodio-Espinar, M. (2019). CLIL Teacher Education in Spain. In K. Tsuchiya & M. D. Pérez-Murillo (Eds.), *Content and Language Integrated Learning in Spanish and Japanese Contexts. Policy, Practice and Pedagogy* (pp. 313–337). Palgrave Macmillan. doi:10.1007/978-3-030-27443-6_13

De la Maya Retamar, G., & Luengo González, R. (2015). Teacher training programs and development of plurilingual competence. In D. Marsh, M. L. Pérez Cañado, & J. Ráez Padilla (Eds.), *CLIL in Action: Voices from the Classroom* (pp. 114–129). Cambridge Scholars Publishing.

Delicado Puerto, G., & Pavón Vázquez, V. (2016). Training primary student teachers for CLIL: innovation through collaboration. *Pulso, 39*, 35-57. https://ebuah.uah.es/dspace/handle/10017/28243

Dodick, J. (2007). Understanding evolutionary change within the framework of geological time. *McGill Journal of Education*, *42*(2), 245–264. https://mje.mcgill.ca/article/view/2222

Dodick, J., & Orion, N. (2003). Cognitive Factors Affecting Student Understanding of Geologic Time. *Journal of Research in Science Teaching*, *40*(4), 415–442. doi:10.1002/tea.10083

Dodick, J. T., & Orion, N. (2006). Building an understanding of geological time: A cognitive synthesis of the "macro" and "micro" scales of time. *Geological Society of America. Special Paper*, *413*, 77–93. doi:10.1130/2006.2413(06)

Durán-Martínez, R., & Beltrán-Llavador, F. (2016). A Regional Assessment of Bilingual Programmes in Primary and Secondary Schools: The Teachers' Views. *Porta Linguarum*, *25*, 79–92. https://digibug.ugr.es/handle/10481/53890. doi:10.30827/Digibug.53890

Durán-Martínez, R., & Beltrán-Llavador, F. (2020). Key issues in teachers' assessment of primary education bilingual programs in Spain. *International Journal of Bilingual Education and Bilingualism*, *23*(2), 170–183. doi:10.1080/13670050.2017.1345851

Estrada, J. L. (2021). Diagnóstico de necesidades formativas entre maestros AICLE en formación inicial. *European Journal of Child Development. Education and Psychopathology*, *9*(1), 1–16. doi:10.32457/ejpad.v9i1.1402

García-González, F., Ruiz Rodríguez, L., Jiménez de Tejada, M.P., Romero López, M.C., Rams Sánchez, S., Fernández Oliveras, A., Vázquez Vílchez, M., Pla Pueyo, S., Barón López, S. D. (2021). *Didáctica de las Ciencias Experimentales II: Prácticas de Laboratorio* (3ª edición). [*Didactics of Experimental Sciences II: Laboratory Practices* (3rd edition).] Ediciones Pirámide (Grupo Anaya, S.A.).

General de Participación, D., Educativa, I., de Educación, C., & de Andalucía, J. (2011). *AICLE Secuencias didácticas. Educación Primaria y Secundaria.* https://www.juntadeandalucia.es/educacion/descargas/recursos/aicle/html/inicio.html

Gómez-Loarces, R., Ferrer G. F. & González-García F. (2019) Evolución de los modelos mentales sobre fosilización tras el proceso de enseñanza-aprendizaje [Evolution of mental models about fossilisation after the teaching-learning process]. *Revista Eureka sobre Enseñanza y Divulgación de las Ciencias [Eureka Magazine on Teaching and Dissemination of Sciences]*, *6*(2), 1-14. doi:10.25267/Rev_Eureka_ensen_divulg_cienc.2019.v16.i2.2102

Guadamillas, V. (2017). Trainee primary-school teachers' perceptions on CLIL instruction and assessment in universities: A case study. *Acta Scientiarum. Education. Maringá, 39*(1), 41-53. https://dialnet.unirioja.es/servlet/articulo?codigo=5827650

Guadamillas, V. & Alcaraz, G. (2017). Legislación en enseñanza bilingüe: análisis en el marco de Educación Primaria en España. [Legislation in bilingual education: analysis in the framework of Primary Education in Spain.] *Multiárea. Revista de didáctica, 9,* 82-103. doi:10.18239/mard.v0i9.1528

Gürel, E., & Tat, M. (2017). SWOT analysis: A theoretical review. *The Journal of International Social Research*, *10*(51), 994–1006. doi:10.17719/jisr.2017.1832

Gutiérrez Gamboa, M., & Custodio Espinar, M. (2021). CLIL teacher's initial education: a study of undergraduate and postgraduate student teachers. *Encuentro, 29*, 104-119. https://ebuah.uah.es/dspace/handle/10017/47069

Jover, G., Fleta, T., & González, R. (2016). La formación inicial de los maestros de Educación Primaria en el contexto de la enseñanza bilingüe en lengua extranjera. [Initial training of primary school teachers in the context of bilingual education in a foreign language.] *Bordón. Revista De Pedagogía*, *68*(2), 121–135. doi:10.13042/Bordon.2016.68208

Junta de Andalucia. (2011). *Boletín Oficial de la Junta de Andalucía, 135,* de 12 de Julio de 2011, 6-19. https://www.juntadeandalucia.es/boja/2011/135/boletin.135.pdf

Junta de Andalucia. (2015). *Boletín Oficial de la Junta de Andalucía, 60*, de 23 de Marzo de 2015, 9-696. https://www.juntadeandalucia.es/boja/2015/60/BOJA15-060-00831.pdf

Example of a CLIL Teaching-Learning Sequence

Kuschmierz, P., Meneganzin, A., Pinxten, R., Pievani, T., Cvetković, D., Mavrikaki, E., Gra, D., & Beniermann, A. (2020). Towards common ground in measuring acceptance of evolution and knowledge about evolution across Europe: A systematic review of the state of research. *Evolution (New York)*, *13*(18), 1–24. doi:10.118612052-020-00132-w

Lasagabaster, D., & Ruiz de Zarobe, Y. (Eds.). (2010). *CLIL in Spain: Implementation, Results and Teacher Training*. Cambridge Scholars Publishing.

Libarkin, J. C., Anderson, S. W., Beilfuss, M., & Boone, W. (2005). Qualitative Analysis of College Students' Ideas about the Earth: Interviews and Open-Ended Questionnaires. *Journal of Geoscience Education*, *53*(1), 17–26. doi:10.5408/1089-9995-53.1.17

Libarkin, J. C., Kurdziel, J. P., & Anderson, S. W. (2007). College student conceptions of geological time and the disconnect between ordering and scale. *Journal of Geoscience Education*, *55*(5), 413–422. doi:10.5408/1089-9995-55.5.413

Lillo, J. (1995). Ideas de los alumnos y obstáculos epistemológicos en la construcción de los conceptos fósil y fosilización. [Students' ideas and epistemological obstacles in the construction of fossil concepts and fossilization.] *Enseñanza de las Ciencias de la Tierra 3*(3), 149-153. https://raco.cat/index.php/ECT/article/view/88245

Longhurst, G. J., Stone, D. M., Dulohery, K., Scully, D., Campbell, T., & Smith, C. F. (2020). Strength, Weakness, Opportunity, Threat (SWOT) Analysis of the Adaptations to Anatomical Education in the United Kingdom and Republic of Ireland in Response to the Covid-19 Pandemic. *Anatomical Sciences Education*, *13*(3), 301–311. doi:10.1002/ase.1967 PMID:32306550

Mehisto, P., Marsh, D., & Frigols, M. J. (2008). *Uncovering CLIL, Content and Language Integrated learning in Bilingual and Multilingual Education*. Macmillan.

Melara Gutiérrez, F. J., & González López, I. (2016). Trazos para el diseño del perfil competencial de la figura del maestro bilingüe. *Revista Española de Pedagogía*, *264*, 357–380. https://revistadepedagogia.org/lxxiv/no-264/trazos-para-el-diseno-del-perfil-competencial-de-la-figura-del-maestro-bilingue/101400001955/

Mellado, V., Blanco, L., & Ruiz, C. (1998). A framework for learning to teach science in initial primary teacher education. *Journal of Science Teacher Education*, *9*(3), 195–219. https://www.jstor.org/stable/43156195. doi:10.1023/A:1009449922079

Milla Lara, M. D., & Casas Pedrosa, A. V. (2018). Teacher Perspectives on CLIL Implementation: A Within-Group Comparison of Key Variables. *Porta Linguarum*, *29*, 159–180. https://www.ugr.es/~portalin/articulos/PL_numero29/8_MARIA%20DOLORES%20MILLA.pdf. doi:10.30827/Digibug.54032

Ministerio de Educación y Formación Profesional (2022). *Boletín Oficial del Estado, 52*, 24386-24504. https://www.boe.es/eli/es/rd/2022/03/01/157

Palacios, F. J., Gómez, M. E., & Huertas, C. (2018). Formación inicial del docente de AICLE en España: Retos y claves. [Initial CLIL teacher training in Spain: Challenges and keys.] *Estudios Franco-Alemanes 10*, 141-161. https://dialnet.unirioja.es/servlet/articulo?codigo=8019873

Pavón, V., & Ellison, M. (2013). Examining teacher roles and competences in content and language integrated learning (CLIL). *Linguarum Arena*, 4, 65-78. https://ojs.letras.up.pt/index.php/LinguarumArena/issue/view/293

Pavón, V., & Rubio, F. D. (2010). Teachers concerns and uncertainties about the introduction of CLIL programmes. *Porta Linguarum, 14*, 45–58.

Pedrinaci, E. (1996). Sobre la persistencia o no de las ideas del alumnado en geología. [On the persistence or not of the ideas of the students in geology.] *Alambique*, 7, 27-36. http://hdl.handle.net/11162/25350

Pedrinaci, E., & Berjillos, P. (1994) Concepto de tiempo geológico: orientaciones para su tratamiento en la educación secundaria. [Concept of geological time: orientations for its treatment in secondary education.] *Enseñanza de las Ciencias de la Tierra, 2* (1), 240-251. https://raco.cat/index.php/ECT/article/view/88138

Pérez Cañado, M. L. (2015). Training Teachers for plurilingual education: a Spanish case study. In D. Marsh, M. L. Pérez Cañado, & J. Ráez Padilla (Eds.), *CLIL in Action: Voices from the Classroom* (pp. 165–187). Cambridge Scholars Publishing.

Pérez Cañado, M. L. (2016). Teacher training needs for bilingual education: In-service teacher perceptions. *International Journal of Bilingual Education and Bilingualism, 19*(3), 266–295. doi:10.1080/13670050.2014.980778

Pérez Cañado, M. L. (2018). Innovations and Challenges in CLIL Teacher Training. *Theory into Practice, 57*(3), 212–221. doi:10.1080/00405841.2018.1492238

Pérez Murillo, M. D., & Steele, A. J. (2017). Initial Teacher Education for CLIL at Primary Education Level in Madrid: Key Issues and Challenges. In M. E. Gómez Parra & R. Johnstone (Eds.), *Educación Bilingüe: Tendencias Educativas y Conceptos Clave. Bilingual Education: Educational Trends and Key Concepts* (pp. 221-233). Ministerio de Educación. https://sede.educacion.gob.es/publiventa/educacion-bilinge-tendencias-educativas-y-conceptos-claves--bilingual-education al-trends-and-key-concepts/educacion-investigacion-educativa-lenguas/22107

Pla-Pueyo, S., González-García, F., & Ramos-García, A. M. (2021). Los fósiles y el profesorado en formación de Educación Primaria en la Universidad de Granada [Fossils and Primary Education pre-service teachers at the University of Granada]. *Lucas Mallada, Revista de Ciencias, 23*, 125-126. https://dialnet.unirioja.es/servlet/articulo?codigo=8166799

Pla-Pueyo, S., González-García, F., & Ramos-García, A.M. (in preparation). ¿Cómo tratan los libros de Educación Primaria los contenidos sobre tiempo geológico, fósiles y evolución? [How do primary school books deal with content on geological time, fossils and evolution?] *Enseñanza de las Ciencias. Revista de investigación y experiencias didácticas [Science Teaching. Magazine of investigation and didactic experiences].*

Example of a CLIL Teaching-Learning Sequence

Pla-Pueyo, S., González-García, F., Ramos-García, A. M., & Ramón-Ballesta, A. (2022a). *Educación geológica formal y no formal de los estudiantes del Grado en Educación Primaria en la Universidad de Granada (España) [Formal and non-formal geological education of the students of Primary Education Teacher Training at the University of Granada (Spain)].* Paper presented at the XXI Simposio sobre Enseñanza de la Geología, Guadix, Granada.

Pla-Pueyo, S., González-García, F., Ramos-García, A. M., & Ramón-Ballesta, A. (2022b). *Gymkhana paleontológica por la Facultad de Ciencias de la Educación (Universidad de Granada, España) [Palaeontological gymkhana at the Faculty of Educational Sciences (University of Granada, Spain)].* Paper presented at the XXI Simposio sobre Enseñanza de la Geología, Guadix, Granada.

Pla-Pueyo, S., Ramos-García, A. M., & González-García, F. (2022). *Are future Primary Education teachers ready for bilingual education?* Paper presented at the meeting CIEB VIII 2022, Jaén, Spain.

Porcedda, M. E., & González-Martínez, J. (2020). CLIL Teacher Training: Lacks and Suggestions from a Systematic Literature Review. *Enseñanza & Teaching: Revista Interuniversitaria de Didáctica*, *38*(1), 49–68. doi:10.14201/et20203814968

Ramos de Robles, S. L., & Espinet, M. (2013). Una propuesta fundamentada para analizar la interacción de contextos AICLE en la formación inicial del profesorado de ciencias. [A well-founded proposal to analyze the interaction of CLIL contexts in the initial training of science teachers.]. *Enseñanza de las Ciencias*, *31*(3), 27–48. https://ensciencias.uab.cat/article/view/v31-n3-ramos-espine t. doi:10.5565/rev/ec/v31n3.777

Ramos-García, A. M., & Fernández-Viciana, A. (2022). La formación en AICLE de los futuros docentes de Educación Primaria. [CLIL training for future primary school teachers.] In J. R. Guijarro Ojeda & R. Ruiz Cecilia (Eds.), *Investigación e innovación en lengua extranjera: una perspectiva global. Research and innovation in foreign language teaching: A global perspective* (pp. 477–493). Tirant lo Blanch.

Resnawati, A., Kristiawan, M., & Puspita Sari, A. (2020). Swot Analysis of Teacher's Professional Competency. *International Journal of Progressive Sciences and Technologies*, *20*(1), 17–25. https://ijpsat.org/index.php/ijpsat/article/view/1704/924

Romero Alfaro, E., & Zayas Martínez, F. (2017). Challenges and opportunities of training teachers for plurilingual education. In J. Valcke & R. Wilkinson. Integrating content and language in higher education. Perspectives on professional practice, (pp. 205-225). Frankfurt am Main, Peter Lang.

Ruiz Pérez, M. C. (2019). The Practice of Bilingualism in Andalusia, Spain. *International Journal for Infonomics*, *12*(4), 1916–1919. doi:10.20533/iji.1742.4712.2019.0197

San Isidro, X., & Lasagabaster, D. (2019). Monitoring of Teachers' Views on Both CLIL and the Development of Pluriliteracies: A Longitudinal Qualitative Study. *English Language Teaching*, *12*(2), 1–16. https://files.eric.ed.gov/fulltext/EJ1202200.pdf. doi:10.5539/elt.v12n2p1

Teed, R., & Slattery, W. (2011). Changes in Geologic Time Understanding in a Class for Preservice Teachers. *Journal of Geoscience Education*, *59*(3), 151–162. doi:10.5408/1.3604829

Trend, R. D. (1998). An investigation into understanding of geological time among 10- and 11-year-old children. *International Journal of Science Education*, *20*(8), 973–988. doi:10.1080/0950069980200805

Trend, R. D. (2000). Conceptions of geological time among primary teacher trainees, with reference to their engagement with geosciences, history and science. *International Journal of Science Education*, *22*(5), 539–555. doi:10.1080/095006900289778

Vázquez-Ben, L., & Bugallo-Rodríguez, A. (2020). Teaching to teach the model of evolution in Primary Education: an experience with preservice teachers. In B. Puig, P. Blanco Anaya, M. J. Gil Quílez, & M. Grace (Eds.), *Biology Education Research. Contemporary topics and directions* (pp. 323–334). Servicio de Publicaciones de la Universidad de Zaragoza. https://zaguan.unizar.es/record/89959/files/BOOK-2020-124.pdf#page=323

KEY TERMS AND DEFINITIONS

Bilingual Program: A program of study which has been designed to be developed in a bilingual stream. This means that a set percentage of the total number of courses are delivered in another language.

Bilingual Science Teaching: Teaching Science in a bilingual stream.

CLIL: Content and language integrated learning refers to the teaching of both language and content at the same time. It can be done either by language teachers or by content teachers, i.e., those who master content and also include language-driven activities to tackle language issues.

EMI: English as a Medium of Instruction. This term is used when referring to a course which is delivered in English, without any other methodological change but the language of instruction.

Methodological Training: This is any kind of training devoted to methodological issues, that is, referring to teaching methodology.

NLA: Non-linguistic areas, those which are included in bilingual programmes.

Teacher Training: Any activity or program devoted to the instruction of pre-service teachers.

University of Granada: A public university in Granada, Andalusia, Spain.

Chapter 16
Training the BE Trainee Teacher in Drama:
A Focus on English and Science

Francesca Costa
Università Cattolica del Sacro Cuore, Italy

ABSTRACT

This paper presents a teacher training experience for bilingual education (BE) using drama activities and techniques within a university degree in primary education. Many studies have underlined the similarities between teachers and actors, seeing teachers as performers, especially in regard to the correct and effective use of the voice, body language, and involvement of the audience. The type of training described here has a twofold objective: to make trainee-teachers participate as learners of drama techniques, and to help them use these techniques with their pupils. This paper will investigate studies on teacher training and BE and on BE and drama, describe the Italian context, and show the activities carried out in the teacher training. It will also analyze the script of a science play in English from a lexical point of view and show one of the lesson plans produced by the trainees. This study is theoretical-descriptive and has no research-based aims.

All the world's a stage,

And all the men and women merely players;

They have their exits and their entrances;

And one man in his time plays many parts,

His acts being seven ages. At first the infant,

DOI: 10.4018/978-1-6684-6179-2.ch016

Training the BE Trainee Teacher in Drama

Mewling and puking in the nurse's arms;

And then the whining school-boy, with his satchel

And shining morning face, creeping like snail

Unwillingly to school. And then the lover,

Sighing like furnace, with a woeful ballad

Made to his mistress' eyebrow. Then a soldier,

Full of strange oaths, and bearded like the pard,

Jealous in honour, sudden and quick in quarrel,

Seeking the bubble reputation

Even in the cannon's mouth. And then the justice,

In fair round belly with good capon lin'd,

With eyes severe and beard of formal cut,

Full of wise saws and modern instances;

And so he plays his part. The sixth age shifts

Into the lean and slipper'd pantaloon,

With spectacles on nose and pouch on side;

His youthful hose, well sav'd, a world too wide

For his shrunk shank; and his big manly voice,

Turning again toward childish treble, pipes

And whistles in his sound. Last scene of all,

That ends this strange eventful history,

Is second childishness and mere oblivion;

Training the BE Trainee Teacher in Drama

Sans teeth, sans eyes, sans taste, sans everything.

- William Shakespeare, As You Like It

INTRODUCTION

This paper presents a teacher training course for bilingual education (BE) based on the use of drama. For the purpose of this chapter BE is "about the teaching/learning a subject through an additional language" (Costa, 2021, p.93). In the case of this chapter, the language is English and the subject is science.

There are many points of contact between drama and the classroom, which can be seen from many points of view and have been the subject of study for many years. A whole line of research views the teacher as a performer (Giggs, 2001), and therefore tends to try to develop in the teacher skills and competences similar to those of an actor (correct and effective use of the voice and body language, the involvement of the audience, learning how to be on center stage, etc.). There are obviously also some differences between the two contexts, for example, the audience (see also Horning, 1979). For teachers, the audience remains the same for a long period of time and is called on to intervene, while for actors the audience is usually passive and different every time.

This paper starts from and shares these premises, focusing on the description of a teacher training activity within a university degree in Primary Education for BE trainee-teachers in Italy based on drama activities and techniques, which sees trainees both as future educators and as learners themselves. This type of training is based on the belief that future teachers must be able to experience first-hand the techniques they will then develop with their classes. Therefore, the training has a twofold objective: to make trainees participate as learners of drama activities for BE and to make them aware as teachers of how to use these techniques with their future students. As part of their final assessment trainees could choose between two types of activities. They either had to write the script of a science play and perform it or they had to prepare a lesson plan with a drama activity and present it to their class. Both the script and the lesson plan had to be in English and had to be 'reusable' with primary school students.

This paper will illustrate studies on teacher training and BE and on BE and drama, and then move on to describe the Italian context in terms of BE, the activities carried out in the teacher training, and provide examples of a script and a lesson plan prepared by the trainees. Finally, it will analyze one of the plays created by the trainees from a lexical point of view. This study is theoretical-descriptive in nature and has no research-based aims.

TEACHER TRAINING IN BILINGUAL EDUCATION

This section will discuss previous studies on training for BE. Within the context of BE, content and language integrated learning (CLIL) studies will also be included since, for the purposes of this paper, these two concepts are considered as strictly related (see Costa, 2021; Murphy, 2014). Only studies in primary education will be referred to since this is the focus of the book and the paper. It must be noted that there has been a paucity of studies on BE at the primary school level and that the vast majority of studies on this topic have been based on the Spanish context (described below), even if there are two papers referring to Italy that underline the extent to which teacher training for CLIL is crucial in primary schools (Catenaccio & Giglioni, 2016) as well as in secondary schools (Di Martino & Di Sabato, 2012).

Delicado Puerto and Pavón Vázquez (2016), Pavón Vázquez et al. (2020) and Ioannou-Georgiou and Ramírez Verdugo (2011), highlighted how fundamental a bilingual teacher training program is in which there is both a linguistic and methodological focus. Drama activities encompass both these aspects.

Pérez Cañado (2018) identified some cornerstones in CLIL training: linguistic competence, pedagogical competence, scientific knowledge, organizational competence, interpersonal and collaborative competence, and reflective and developmental competence. Here, too, the use of drama activities certainly refers to the linguistic, pedagogical, and interpersonal fields.

Two very recent papers highlight a lack of training in CLIL (Porcedda & González-Martínez, 2020) and the importance of training (Lancaster & Bretones Callejas, 2020, in their article on training in Andalusia).

BE AND DRAMA

It is generally recognized that drama as a form of teacher training for English teachers is a good practice (Mages, 2020). This section will illustrate studies that have dealt with BE or CLIL and the use of drama. The first to deal with the topic was by Costa & Mariani in 2007 (see also Costa, 2019), which highlights the link between drama and CLIL and how the two approaches can be integrated to make learners better understand both the content and the language. The article focuses expressly on science plays as a way of processing subject-matter concepts and linguistic elements at the same time. Meeting points between the two approaches are identified: the fact that they both focus on learning by doing, use authentic materials not created for language learning, and focus on meaning with an incidental learning of the linguistic form.

The article also explains some techniques to use and provides suggestions for teachers. The advantages of the approach (which are intended both for trainee teachers and their future students) mainly entail the development of the lexis and the acquisition of phraseological structures that take place through the memorization of the assigned parts. Another advantage is certainly an implementation of the correct pronunciation, intonation, rhythm, and stress with both segmental and supra-segmental elements. Moreover, communicative oral skills are clearly developed together with writing skills in the case of the writing of the script of a play (both for teachers and learners).

As for the content, the fact of expressing concepts with and using the body to express ideas lead to a deep processing of the subject matter (in the case of this article science), in part through the engagement and involvement from being in front of an audience.

About 10 years later, in 2015, Peter Lang dedicated an entire book to drama and CLIL. The work underlines various ways in which the two approaches can be integrated: "The versatility of bilingual education enables teachers to adopt a more holistic and inclusive approach to classroom practice. This book proposes articles on the possibilities of drama as a challenging learning experience from primary to higher education" (Nicolás, 2015, p. 21) and "[...] develop[s] the performance-related competences of teachers, such as effective use of voice and body language and nonverbal awareness, just to name few. Nevertheless, there is still a need for practical and doable tasks and activities for trainers' classroom use" (Özmen & Balçıkanlı, 2015, p. 78).

Regarding the need for training in drama activities for CLIL and BE teachers, Pérez Cañado (2016) investigated the needs for teacher training in BE, where an analysis of 706 European teachers showed

Training the BE Trainee Teacher in Drama

that materials are of great concern; in this sense, drama can help by enriching the types of materials through the production of scripts or entire plays.

In their article, Muszyńska, et al. (2017) found that training primary school teachers in drama for CLIL works. They state that: "drama integrates four contextualized building blocks: content (subject matter), communication (language learning and using), cognition (learning and thinking processes) and culture, and acknowledges the symbiotic relationship that exists between these elements" (2017, p. 184). CLIL and drama have also been explored as a topic in a study on teachers conducted by Breidbach and Medina-Suárez (2016).

THE ITALIAN CONTEXT

Italy is the focus of study in this paper. Primary school lasts five years and begins at about five and a half to six years of age. There are public primary schools and legally recognized private ones. English is taught throughout the five years of primary school.

Primary school teachers are trained to be competent in all the subjects that are taught. They must complete a five-year Primary Education university degree, which can be undertaken only after passing an entry test since the number of openings are determined from year to year by the Ministry of Education according to national needs.

During their university studies, students of Primary Education must reach a B2 level of English and attend English language courses (formally called labs) for all five years, with varying amounts of focus on teaching methodologies or linguistic aspects.

Recent legislation on primary schools refers to the Moratti law 53/2003, the Gelmini law 240/2010, and the so-called Buona Scuola law 107/2015. Drama is not a school subject as in many other European countries, and so drama activities, if used by teachers, are embedded in other subject-matters. The present article will present examples of drama activities for science in English.

As mentioned, the CLIL methodological approach is practiced in Italian primary schools, but there is yet to be an updated survey of these experiences, which are often left to the discretion of individual teachers. At this level, CLIL is taught by teachers who have language and subject-matter competences (Costa, 2004; Costa, 2019). At the time of writing, a Departmental Decree (n. 1511, 23/6/2022) was issued in which CLIL training courses for in-service primary school teachers are regulated.

There has clearly been a growth in bilingual primary schools in Italy, especially in the private sector. Among the existing projects is the BEI (Bilingual Education Italy) project, which follows a memorandum of understanding between the Ministry of Education and the British Council that initiated the BEI as a pilot project in 2009 in some state schools in Lombardy (Costa, 2023), where part of the curriculum is taught in English (Cavalieri & Stermieri, 2016).

DESCRIPTION OF THE COURSE

The activity described in this paper took place during the third year of the university degree in Primary Education. The title of the course was English lab with 2 credits and 18 hours of teaching. It is a compulsory lab with a cohort of 15 trainees. The course was taught entirely in English. Trainees were expected to have nearly an B1 English proficiency level, according to the CEFR.

383

The objectives of the course were that trainees:

- practiced the various drama techniques to develop their performing persona and to be able to use them with their future classes
- learned how to prepare a lesson plan or a script of a play that included a drama activity for BE with a specific focus on science topics and English
- acquired tools to use in organizing or writing a science play for BE to be used as a show in the end-of-course evaluation.

All of these activities were designed so as to be 'reused' for real primary school pupils. After an initial theoretical part on the teacher as a performer and the importance of drama in BE, the course continued with practical activities. At the beginning, some warm-up activities normally used in drama courses were proposed. Group improvisations were implemented giving the trainees a context for the activity: e.g., a phone call between friends, buying a dress, etc., to familiarize themselves with the use of English. Later, the trainees were asked to perform various sketches on science topics in various settings and situations written by the trainer.

Alongside this type of activity, role plays were organized in which trainees had to imagine already being in service and struggling with various situations, such as a child who does not want to participate in the activities or a parent to whom they have to explain a given evaluation. The tableau technique was also used by asking the trainees to use their body to express a given situation, usually related to some science topic, in order to create a link with the BE (e.g. sunrise). Always with the same purpose in mind, the narration technique was used where the trainer would explain some science topics (for example, the water cycle) and the trainees would represent it using both their bodies and words.

The course then moved on to a more theoretical phase in which some techniques were examined on how to stage a play starting from a brainstorming about science topics by using realia, photographs, or visuals. Trainees were told that when staging a play it is always a good idea to allocate roles to the students without penalizing those who may be shyer or speak less in English. They were also told that it is always a good idea to be repeating and rehearsing each scene until science themes or concepts have been understood and internalized. Trainees were instructed on how to behave like directors and show students how each part can be played. Trainees were advised on the fact that as for costumes, scenery, and props, teachers can indulge the students and ask for the participation of parents, if the conditions so permit.

At this point, the trainees were asked to work in groups and to prepare either: 1. a lesson plan describing a science drama activity for BE (to be presented to the class), or 2. a short script of a play on a science topic suitable for BE at primary school (to be staged to the class). The trainees were left free to decide the composition of the groups. The trainers acted as facilitators by following the groups and providing advice on how to perform tasks but they did not correct mistakes because this was part of the final evaluation. The trainees were free to choose the science content even if they were advised to look for topics which are part of the syllabus of primary schools in Italy. Among the topics chosen by the trainees were: photosynthesis, the five senses, the water cycle and the solar system.

As for the lesson plan the trainees teachers were given a sample format. For the writing of the play, the trainees had to imagine a plot involving characters and their relationships. Finally, a storyboard was developed followed by the actual writing phase. The trainers pointed out that it was very important to check that the language used in the play was realistic and contained colloquial elements as well as spe-

Training the BE Trainee Teacher in Drama

cific lexis related to the chosen science topics but trainees were left free to choose how many of these lexical items they wanted to include in their plays or their lesson plans.

Both tasks (lesson plan or script) were the subject of a final evaluation, which was performed by a panel of lecturers. Trainees were evaluated on their competence in English, on the appropriateness of the science topics chosen and on how they designed their drama activities. Their presentation and writing skills (in the case of the lesson plan) and their performing and writing skills (in the case of the script of the play) were evaluated. In the case of the script the trainees were allowed to read the script if they could not remember it by heart.

In addition to describing the course activities, an analysis of the scientific lexis used in the script of one of the science plays is presented below, together with the text of one of the science plays, and a drama activity lesson plan created by the trainees.

ILLUSTRATION OF THE PRESENCE OF SCIENTIFIC LEXIS IN SAVED BY THE SKIN OF OUR TEETH!

The script of the play analyzed here concerns the scientific topic of tooth care. The play was imagined for a hypothetical third-year primary school class and is titled *Saved by the Skin of Our Teeth*!

The plot of the play concerns a community of teeth, one of whom gets sick with cavities but is cheated by some bad bacteria and does not understand that it must go quickly to the dentist. In the end, the diseased tooth decides to go to the dentist and is very happy, since it no longer has any pain.

Below is a purely qualitative and descriptive illustration of the scientific lexis used in the script play and some of its phraseological forms.

Table 1. Type of lexis in the Saved by the Skin of Our Teeth! play

	Scientific lexis	Phraseological structures
Saved by the Skin of Our Teeth	Deciduous teeth, root, wisdom tooth, incisors, canines, bacterium, streptococcus mutans, gram positive, plaque, cavity	Saved by the skin of our teeth, we fight tooth and nails to keep you healthy, you've got a sweet tooth

As evidenced above, many scientific terms related to the specific topic of tooth care are present in the text to varying degrees. Their presence in the play helps the actors / learners remember them and learn their pronunciation, which, in the case of cognate forms from Latin and Greek, can be particularly difficult in English (for example, the term canine). Alongside these forms are phraseological elements that can be learned as chunks by the actors/learners. These phrases mostly involve sayings or proverbs. The play and the lesson plan are presented exactly as were written by the trainees.

Training the BE Trainee Teacher in Drama

EXAMPLE OF THE SCRIPT OF A PLAY (SAVED BY THE SKIN OF OUR TEETH!)

Characters

20 deciduous teeth (one of them is sick molar)

6 bacteria

3 wisdom teeth

Props and scenes

The inside of a mouth (cardboard?)

White t-shirts, one with a black spot

Old toothbrushes

Chairs

Fake beard for wisdom tooth

Brownish Sheet

Script

Enter all teeth

Teeth: Hi we are teeth and we live inside a mouth. Actually we're deciduous teeth… that is why there are only 20 of us. That means that sooner or later we are going to fall out but new teeth are going to take over. We are all kins. Some of us have one root some others have two or three.

Enters wisdom tooth

WT: Yes, for example I can have up to three roots. I am wisdom tooth. But I will appear later on when this mouth is 18 years old. In total there are 4 of us but my brothers are not here at the moment.

Incisors: Hi we are incisors! 2 bottom and top central and two bottom and top lateral. So in total there are 8 of us. We are very useful to cut food (top ones will be on a chair. When the word food is pronounced they do the movement with their mouth making an evident sound).

Canines: Hi we are canines and there are 2 of us at the top and 2 at the bottom. So in total there are 4 of us. We are useful to tear food (same as above + make the movement of tearing food).

Training the BE Trainee Teacher in Drama

Molars: Hi we are molars and there are 4 of us at the top and 4 at the bottom. So in total there are 8 of us. We grind food, that's what we do! (same as above).

All teeth leave apart from WTs, sick molar and enter all bacteria.

Sick molar: I am not well today. I have got this little black spot that won't go away.

Bacterium 1: Oh hello! I am streptococcus mutans. I come from the gram positive species of bacteria. Do you live around here?

Sick molar: Yes, and you?

Bacterium 2: Of course. I live here! I am actually very useful around here because I create a thin layer (covers tooth with a brown sheet) around you teeth. It's called plaque and it is very useful because it protects you all from being attacked by acids. We fight tooth and nail to keep you healthy! Did you not know?

Sick molar: No, sorry, I am a newcomer and I did not know. Well thank you for your help then. Maybe you could help me a bit more. Today I am not very well. I have got this small black dot.

Bacterium 2: It's only a small dot! Don't you see? It's gonna go. Things are not all black and white! And I must admit it really suits you…

WT 2: Molar, this bacterium is lying through his teeth! Don't trust him. This black spot is not gonna go. It is called cavity and it's not gonna go. You have to go to the dentist's and have it fixed otherwise it's gonna grow and hurt and you'll have to be pulled out! Please believe me, I am called wisdom tooth for a reason!

Sick molar: I don't know. I do not feel bad… it's just a little bit strange but I do not want to go to the dentist's. Everyone says it hurts!

WT 3: Do you know why this happened to you? You've got a sweet tooth! You keep on eating sweets and this is too bad for you. You're gonna be attacked by bacteria if you do not brush yourself regularly!

Sick molar: Oh come on. All little ones like sweets (he shows sweets inside pockets).

All leave apart from bacteria

Bacterium 3: We've just told him a white lie… nothing too serious! (all laugh). At the end of the day some of us are good and some bad… Unfortunately for teeth we are the bad ones!!!

Bacterium 4: Yes, that's right. If we start with one deciduous tooth we'll conquer them all in no time.

Bacterium 5: By the end of the year all teeth in this mouth will have cavities and we'll have a great party!

Bacterium 6: Sure, but we need to keep focussed. We need to keep on getting sugars otherwise we cannot do our job.

All bacteria leave. Enter all teeth!

Sick molar: Oh gosh. I am not well at all now. I feel very weak and all my parts are aching.

Teeth 2, 3, 4, 5: Come on. I think we need to go to the dentist's. Don't you see that your hole has become bigger?

Sick molar: Yes, I know but luckily, streptococcus mutans will help me with plaque.

Teeth 6, 7, 8, 9: Plaque??? Are you serious? It's one of the worst things that could happen to us. It creates a favorable habitat for cavities to develop. And this, my friend, is a cavity!!!

Sick molar: Oh dear. I have heard about cavities. They are really bad for us. What can I do???

All molars: Go to the dentist's!!!

All leave

All teeth back

Sick molar: Hi guys I am back (all cheerful with new t-shirt).

Teeth 10, 11, 12, 13: Are you OK? Did you go to the dentist's? Was it horrible?

Sick molar: Not at all. I did not feel anything. And look now I am perfectly fine. The doctor was very nice and he taught me a lot of interesting things… First of all. Sugars are OK but not too many. And if we eat sugars then we should brush our teeth after about 20 minutes.

Teeth 14, 15, 16, 17: We knew that! And I also know that milk and cheese are very good for our health so who cares about sweets if we can have some parmesan sticks???

Teeth 18, 19, 20: Oh, fantastic so all we have to do to be healthy is to eat cheese and milk?

Tooth: No! We also need to brush our teeth after every meal! And we need to brush them the right way!

Sick molar: Look this is what the dentist gave me (shows the poster and does the correct movements all follow).

Training the BE Trainee Teacher in Drama

EXAMPLE OF THE LESSON PLAN ON THE FIVE SENSES

BE Class: first form of primary school
  Subject: Science + Drama in English + Arts and Crafts
  Topic: The Five Senses
  Time: two hours
  Aims (both language and subject related):

- Revise the 5 senses
- Identify the organs of the 5 senses
- Be able to remember what the 5 senses are needed for
- Recognise and correctly pronounce the terminology related to the 5 senses
- Stimulate retention of content

Activities:

Background: this lesson is devised as the final activity of a whole project on the Five Senses. The project has explored the senses from a Science point of view (an experiment has previously been performed), from a Literacy/English language point of view (through the use of flashcards to recognize and correctly pronounce the specific terminology) and from an Arts point of view (with the construction of a sensory poster). The use of drama has been chosen for this final activity because it is known to work well to gain a deeper processing of science topics. Drama is strictly connected to learning by doing and it allows for an incidental acquisition of both language and content. It allows the internalisation of both linguistic structures (by means of repetition) and content processes since mind and body are involved in a holistic way. The whole activity can be video recorded for three reasons: to have an archive of the activities, to help the teachers evaluate the project and to show the children (and the other stakeholders) their own performances.

Procedure: The teachers bring the children to a space outside the classroom where the class can fit and where the children can move around freely. The first task is a warm-up revision of what has been carried out on the topic of the Five Senses. The teachers may use flashcards and a sensory poster (original materials prepared ad hoc) to elicit prior knowledge. For the second task the teachers tell their children that they are going to do a casting to look for actors performing the various characters related to the five senses (see vocabulary). The teachers ask some children to become *mouths* or *noses* etc and the others (the audience) will be judging by applauding them and deciding the best ones for each character. The children who are assigned the character start working on props and preparing a drawing to represent their characters. Every character will learn to introduce him/herself by using scaffolding structures elicited by the teachers. E.g. *I am a nose. I can smell things*. Depending on how the children react teachers might think of further developing the lesson with a proper drama activity which might entail even a small dramatisation/play on the Five Senses.

Vocabulary: *taste, mouth, tongue, hearing, ears, hands, skin, touch, soft, hard, nose, smell, sour, bitter, sweet, salty*

Material needed: flashcards, paper, pencils

CONCLUSION

This paper has dealt with drama activities and techniques for teacher training for pre-service primary school teachers doing a Primary Education degree in Italy. The paper highlighted how useful the use of drama techniques can be for BE or CLIL courses at primary school level. The paper illustrates in a completely descriptive way the type of activity that can be carried out in a BE teacher training context focused on drama, illustrating some output from the trainees during these types of courses and describing the type of English vocabulary used for science topics. Given the purely descriptive and theoretical nature of the paper, the description of the activities can only be seen as an ongoing process, an example, or a starting point to be adapted to other contexts. It would be interesting in the future to enter the classrooms and observe the extent to which the trainee-teachers are able to put into practice with real students the drama skills acquired during the course. Unfortunately, this part of the study will have to be postponed to when the Covid pandemic has passed and researchers can return to schools to make observations.

REFERENCES

Breidbach, S., & Medina-Suárez, J. (2016). Teachers' perspectives on CLIL and classroom innovation in a method based on drama games. La perspectiva de los profesores acerca de CLIL y la innovación en clase en un método basado en juegos teatrales. *Estudios Sobre Educación, 31*, 97–116. doi:10.15581/004.31.97-116

Catenaccio, P., & Giglioni, C. (2016). CLIL teaching at primary school level and the academia/practice interface: some preliminary considerations. In G. Garzone, D. Heaney, & G. Riboni (Eds.), *Focus on LSP teaching: developments and issues* (pp. 211–244). LED. doi:10.7359/791-2016-cate

Cavalieri, S., & Stermieri, A. (2016). The BEI/IBI Project: A study on the best practices in integrating Language and Content Learning in primary schools. In G. Garzone, D. Heaney, & G. Riboni (Eds.), *Focus on LSP teaching: developments and issues* (pp. 211–244). LED. doi:10.7359/791-2016-cava

Costa, F. (2004). Il CLIL (Content and Language Integrated Learning). In C. Bianchi, P. Corasaniti, & N. Panzarasa (Eds.), L'inglese nella scuola primaria (122-138). Carocci.

Costa, F. (2019). *Enjoy teaching English. Insegnare inglese nella scuola primaria*. Giunti Scuola.

Costa, F. (2021). What does research tell us about experiences and forms of bilingual education? In M. L. Maggioni & A. Murphy (Eds.), *Back to the future* (pp. 91–112). Peter Lang.

Costa, F. (2023). Mediation and mode continuum in primary bilingual (English and Italian) education. In L. Lopriore (Ed.), *Engaging research: Transforming practices for the English as a foreign language classroom* (pp. 9–21). TESOL Press.

Costa, F., & Mariani, M. (2007). Drama and CLIL (Content and Language Integrated Learning. In D. Marsh & D. Wolff (Eds.), *Diverse contexts – converging goals: CLIL in Europe* (pp. 297–308). Peter Lang.

Delicado Puerto, G., & Pavón Vázquez, V. (2016). Training primary student teachers for CLIL: innovation through collaboration La formación del profesorado de educación primaria para CLIL: innovación por medio de la colaboración. *Pulso: revista de educación, 39*, 35-57.

Training the BE Trainee Teacher in Drama

Di Martino, E., & Di Sabato, B. (2012). CLIL implementation in Italian schools: Can long-serving teachers be retrained effectively? The Italian protagonists' voice. *Latin American Journal of Content and Language Integrated Learning*, *5*(2), 73–105. doi:10.5294/laclil.2012.5.2.9

Griggs, T. (2001). Teaching as acting: considering acting as epistemology and its use in teaching and teacher preparation. *Teacher Education Quarterly*, 23-37.

Horning, A. (1979). Teaching as performance. *The Journal of General Education*, *31*(3), 185–194.

Ioannou-Georgiou, S., & Ramírez Verdugo, M. D. (2011). Stories as a tool for teaching and learning in CLIL. In S. Ioannou-Georgiou & P. Pavlou (Eds.), *Guidelines for CLIL implementation in primary and pre-primary education* (pp. 137–155). European Commission.

Mages, W. (2020). Educational drama and theatre pedagogy: An integral part of training English-as-a-foreign-language teachers. *Scenario*, *1*(1), 12–24. doi:10.33178cenario.14.1.2

Murphy, V. (2014). *Second language learning in the early school years trends and contexts*. Oxford University Press.

Muszyńska, A., Urpí, C., & Gałązka, A. (2017). Teacher education through drama. CLIL practice in the Spanish context. Formación del profesorado a través de la dramatización: Práctica en el Aprendizaje Integrado de Lengua y Contenido en el contexto español. *Estudios Sobre Educación*, *32*, 179–195.

Nicolás, S. (2015). Introduction. In S. Nicolás Román & J. J. Torres Núñez (Eds.), *Drama and CLIL. A new challenge for the teaching approaches in Bilingual Education* (pp. 21–23). Peter Lang. doi:10.3726/978-3-0351-0832-3/11

Özmen, K. S., & Balçıkanlı, C. (2015). Theatre acting in second language teacher education. In S. Nicolás Román & J. J. Torres Núñez (Eds.), *Drama and CLIL. A new challenge for the teaching approaches in Bilingual Education* (pp. 77–106). Peter Lang.

Pavón Vázquez, V., Lancaster, N., & Bretones Callejas, C. (2020). Keys issues in developing teachers' competences for CLIL in Andalusia: Training, mobility and coordination. *Language Learning Journal*, *48*(1), 81–98. doi:10.1080/09571736.2019.1642940

Pérez Cañado, M. L. (2016). Teacher training needs for Bilingual Education: In-service teacher perceptions. *International Journal of Bilingual Education and Bilingualism*, *19*(3), 266–295. doi:10.1080/13670050.2014.980778

Pérez Cañado, M. L. (2018). Innovations and challenges in CLIL teacher training. *Theory into Practice*, *57*(3), 212–221. doi:10.1080/00405841.2018.1492238

Porcedda, M. E., & González-Martínez, J. (2020). CLIL teacher training: Lacks and suggestions from a systematic literature review. *Enseñanza & Teaching*, *38*(1), 49–68. doi:10.14201/et20203814968

KEY TERMS AND DEFINITIONS

BE (Bilingual education): Teaching/learning a subject through an additional language.

Drama: A technique or a text telling a story that involves theatrical performance and acting.

Incidental learning: This happens when the attention of the learner is not focused on the learning itself.

Play: A text that is constructed to be staged.

Plot: The story of a play.

Primary school in Italy: A school period lasting 5 years.

Science play: A play that is about a science topic.

Sketch: A very short play constructed around a topic or a situation.

Compilation of References

Abad-Segura, E., González-Zamar, M. D., Luque-de la Rosa, A., & Morales, C. (2020). Sustainability of Educational Technologies: An Approach to Augmented Reality Research. *Sustainability*, *12*(10), 4091. doi:10.3390u12104091

Abelio-Contesse, C., Chandler, P. M., López-Jiménez, M. D., & Chacón-Beltrán, R. (Eds.). (2013). *Bilingual and multilingual education in the 21ˢᵗ century: Building on experience*. Multilingual Matters. doi:10.21832/9781783090716

Abuhassna, H., Al-Rahmi, W. M., Yahya, N., Zakaria, M. A. Z. M., Kosnin, A. B. M., & Darwish, M. (2020). Development of a new model on utilizing online learning platforms to improve students' academic achievements and satisfaction. *International Journal of Educational Technology in Higher Education*, *17*(1), 38. doi:10.118641239-020-00216-z

Adawiyah, D., & Gumartifa, A. (2022). English language teaching and globalization: To support economic growth. *Premise: Journal of English Education and Applied Linguistics*, *11*(1), 228–242. doi:10.24127/pj.v11i1.4114

Adler, J. (1998). A language of teaching dilemmas: Unlocking the complex multilingual secondary mathematics classroom. *For the Learning of Mathematics*, *18*(1), 24–33. https://www.jstor.org/stable/40248258

Adriosh, M., & Razi, Ö. (2019). Teacher's Code Switching in EFL Undergraduate Classrooms in Libya: Functions and Perceptions. *SAGE Open*, *9*(2), 1–11. doi:10.1177/2158244019846214

Agnew, Z. K., Brownsett, S., Woodhead, Z., & de Boissezon, X. (2008). A step forward for mirror neurons? Investigating the functional link between action execution and action observation in limb apraxia. *The Journal of Neuroscience: The Official Journal of the Society for Neuroscience*, *28*(31), 7726–7727. doi:10.1523/JNEUROSCI.1818-08.2008 PMID:18667604

Aguirregoitia, A., Bengoetxea, K., & Gonzalez-Dios, I. (2021a). Are CLIL texts too complicated?: A computational analysis of their linguistic characteristics. *Journal of Immersion and Content-Based Language Education*, *9*(1), 4–30. doi:10.1075/jicb.19022.agu

Aguirregoitia, A., & Etxebarria, E. G. (2021b). Let's sing this CLIL lesson: Integrating language, content, music and video. In *Innovación e investigación educativa para la formación docente [Innovation and educational research for teacher training]* (pp. 282–296). Dykinson.

Aguirregoitia, A., López Benito, J. R., Artetxe González, E., & Bilbao Ajuria, E. (2017). *Una experiencia de aplicación de Realidad Aumentada para el Aprendizaje del Inglés en Educación Infantil* [An experience of application of Augmented Reality for the Learning of English in Early Childhood Education.]. Atas do XIX Simpósio Internacional de Informática Educativa e VIII Encontro do CIED–III Encontro Internacional [Proceedings of the XIX International Symposium on Educational Informatics and VIII Meeting of CIED–III International Meeting].

Airey, J. (2016, December) *Undergraduate teaching with multiple semiotic resources: Disciplinary affordance vs pedagogical affordance.* Paper presented at the 8th International Conference on Multimodality. Multimodal Landscapes: Designing, changing, shaping. University of Cape Town.

Akindele, D., & Letsoela, M. (2001). Code-switching in Lesotho secondary and high schools: Lessons and its effects on teaching and learning. *BOLESWA Educational Research Journal, 18,* 83–100.

Al-Amri, W. B. (2014). Translation in teaching and learning a foreign language: A methodological approach. *International Journal of Humanities and Cultural Studies, 1*(2), 1–20.

Alan, B., & Stoller, F. L. (2005). Maximizing the Benefits of Project work in Foreign Language Classrooms. *English Teaching Forum, 43*(4), 10-21.

Albaladejo, S. A., Coyle, Y., & Roca de Larios, J. (2018). Songs, Stories, and Vocabulary Acquisition in Preschool Learners of English as a Foreign Language. *System, 76,* 116–128. doi:10.1016/j.system.2018.05.002

Alba-Pastor, C. (2019). Diseño universal para el aprendizaje: un modelo teórico-práctico para una educación inclusive de calidad. [Universal design for learning: a theoretical-practical model for inclusive quality education.] *Participación educativa, 6*(9), 64-66.

Alcaraz-Mármol, G. (2018). Trained and Non-Trained Language Teachers on CLIL Methodology: Teachers' Facts and Opinions about the CLIL Approach in the Primary Education Context in Spain. *Latin American Journal of Content and Language Integrated Learning, 11*(1), 39-64. https://files.eric.ed.gov/fulltext/EJ1190982.pdf

Alharbi, W. H. (2022). The Affordances of Augmented Reality Technology in the English for Specific Purposes Classroom: It's Impact on vocabulary learning and students motivation in a Saudi Higher Education Institution. *Journal of Positive School Psychology, 6*(3), 6588–6602. https://journalppw.com/index.php/jpsp/article/view/3849

Al-Jubeh, D., & Vitsou, M. (2021). Empowering refugee children with the use of Persona Doll. *International Journal of Progressive Education, 2*(17), 210–227. Advance online publication. doi:10.29329/ijpe.2021.332.13

Aljure, L. H., Arciniegas, M. C., & Castillo, M. F. (2014). Bilingüismo y aprendizaje. Un enfoque cognitivo. [Bilingualism and learning. A cognitive approach.] *El astrolabio,* 115–126.

AlMarwani, M. (2020). Pedagogical potential of SWOT analysis: An approach to teaching critical thinking. *Thinking Skills and Creativity, 38,* 100741. doi:10.1016/j.tsc.2020.100741

Alonso Tapia, J. (1997). *Motivar para el aprendizaje. Teorías y Estrategias [Motivate for learning. Theories and Strategies].* EDEBE.

Alonso, L., Delicado, G., & Ramos, F. (2017) A Comparative Study of Bilingual Teacher Preparation Programs in Two Different Contexts: California and Spain, Springer. In production.

Alonso-Belmonte, I., & Fernández-Agüero, M. (2021). Teachers' narratives of resistance to Madrid's bilingual programme: An exploratory study in secondary education. *Linguistics and Education, 63,* 100925. doi:10.1016/j.linged.2021.100925

Altan, M. Z. (2017). Globalization, English Language Teaching and Turkey. *International Journal of Languages Education and Teaching, 5*(4), 764–776. doi:10.18298/ijlet.2238

Altun, H. K., & Lee, J. (2020). Immersive Learning Technologies in English Language Teaching: A Meta-Analysis. *International Journal of Contents, 16*(3), 18–32. doi:10.5392/IJOC.2020.16.3.018

Compilation of References

Álvarez Rojo, V., Romero Rodríguez, S., Gil Flores, J., Rodríguez Santero, J., Clares López, J., Asensio Muñoz, I. I., & Salmerón Vílchez, P. (2011). *Necesidades de formación del profesorado universitario para la adaptación de su docencia al Espacio Europeo de Educación Superior (EEES)* [Training needs of university teachers for the adaptation of their teaching to the European Higher Education Area (EHEA).]. Revista Electrónica de Investigación y Evaluación Educativa [Electronic Journal of Educational Research and Evaluation].

Amat, A., Vallborna, A., & Martí, J. (2017). Percepciones de futuros maestros de infantil y primaria sobre la enseñanza y el aprendizaje de las ciencias en inglés. *Enseñanza de las Ciencias*, (Special Issue), 4931–4936. https://ddd.uab.cat/pub/edlc/edlc_a2017nEXTRA/27._percepcion es_de_futuros_maestros_de_infantil_y_primaria.pdf

Amor, A. M., Hagiwara, M., Shogren, K. A., Thompson, J. R., Verdugo, M. A., Burke, K. M., & Aguayo, V. (2018). International perspectives and trends in research on inclusive education: A systematic review. *International Journal of Inclusive Education*, 23(12), 1277–1295. doi:10.1080/13603116.2018.1445304

Anderson, L. W., & Krathwohl, D. R. (2001). A Taxonomy for Learning, Teaching and Assessing (Abridged Edition). New York: Longman-Pearson Education.

Antón, E., Duñabeitia, J. A., Estévez, A., Hernández, J. A., Castillo, A., Fuentes, L. J., & Carreiras, M. (2014). Is there a bilingual advantage in the ANT task? Evidence from children. *Frontiers in Psychology*, 5, 398. PMID:24847298

Archer, A. (2014). Power, social justice and multimodal pedagogies. In C. Jewitt (Ed.), *The routledge handbook of multimodal analysis* (2nd ed., pp. 189–197). Routledge.

Archila, P. A., Molina, J., & Truscott de Mejía, A. (2021). Fostering bilingual scientific writing through a systematic and purposeful code-switching pedagogical strategy. *International Journal of Bilingual Education and Bilingualism*, 24(6), 785–803. doi:10.1080/13670050.2018.1516189

Argyris, C., Putnam, R., & McLain Smith, D. (1985). *Action science. Concepts, methods, and skills for research and intervention*. Jossey-Bass Publishers.

Argyris, C., & Schön, D. A. (1974). *Theory in practice: Increasing profesional effectiveness*. Jossey-Bass Publishers.

Arias de Sánchez, G., Gabriel, M., Anderson, A., & Turnbull, M. (2018). Code-Switching Explorations in Teaching Early Number Sense. *Education in Science*, 8(38), 785–803. doi:10.3390/educsci8010038

Arkoudis, S. (2006). Negotiating the rough ground between ESL and mainstream teachers. *International Journal of Bilingual Education and Bilingualism,* 9(4), 415-433. doi:10.2167/beb337.0

Armstrong, P. (2010). *Bloom's Taxonomy*. Vanderbilt University Center for Teaching.

Arnáiz, P. (2003). *Educación inclusiva: una escuela para todos* [*Inclusive education: a school for all.*]. Aljibe.

Arthur, J. (1994). English in Botswana primary classrooms: functions and constraints. In C. M. Rubagumya (Ed.), *Teaching & Researching Language in African Classrooms* (pp. 63–78). Multilingual Matters.

Attard-Montalto, S., Walter, L., Theodorou, M., & Chrysanthou, K. (2015). *CLIL Book*. Languages. https://www.languages.dk/archive/clil4u/book/CLIL%20Book%20E S.pdf

Azuma, R. (2015). Location-Based Mixed and Augmented Reality Storytelling. In Woodrow Barfield Fundamentals of Wearable Computers and Augmented Reality, pp. 259-276.

Baeten, M., & Simons, M. (2014). Student teachers' team teaching: Models, effects, and conditions for implementation. *Teaching and Teacher Education*, *41*, 92–110. doi:10.1016/j.tate.2014.03.010

Baeten, M., Simons, M., Schelfhout, W., & Pinxten, R. (2018). Team teaching during field experiences in teacher education: Exploring the assistant teaching model. *European Journal of Teacher Education*, *41*(3), 377–397. doi:10.1080/02619768.2018.1448780

Baetens Beardsmore, H. (1999). La consolidation des expériences en éducation plurilingue. [Consolidating experiences in plurilingual education.] In D. Marsh & B. Marsland (Eds.), *CLIL Initiatives for the Millennium*. University of Jyväskylä Continuing Education Centre.

Baker, C. (1993). *Foundations of Bilingual Education and Bilingualism*. Multilingual Matters.

Bakken, J., & Brevik, L. M. (2022). Challenging the notion of CLIL elitism: A study of secondary school students' motivation for choosing CLIL in Norway. *TESOL Quarterly*, tesq.3173. doi:10.1002/tesq.3173

Ball, P., Kelly, K., & Clegg, J. (2015). *Putting CLIL into Practice*. Oxford University Press.

Ball, P., Kelly, K., & Clegg, J. (2016). *Putting CLIL into practice: Oxford handbooks for language teachers*. Oxford University Press.

Banegas, D. L., & Hemmi, C. (2021). CLIL: Present and Future. In International Perspectives on CLIL (pp. 281-295). Palgrave Macmillan.

Banegas, D. L. (2012). CLIL teacher development: Challenges and experiences. *Latin American Journal of Content & Language Integrated Learning*, *5*(1), 46–56. doi:10.5294/laclil.2012.5.1.4

Banegas, D. L. (2013). The integration of content and language as a driving force in the EFL lesson. In E. Ushioda (Ed.), *International perspectives on motivation: Language learning and professional challenges* (pp. 82–97). Palgrave. doi:10.1057/9781137000873_5

Banegas, D. L. (2015). Sharing views of CLIL lesson planning in language teacher education. *Latin American Journal of Content and Language Integrated Learning*, *8*(2), 104–130. doi:10.5294/laclil.2015.8.2.3

Banegas, D. L. (2022). Research into practice: CLIL in South America. *Language Teaching*, *55*(3), 379–391. doi:10.1017/S0261444820000622

Banegas, D. L., & Consoli, S. (2021). Initial English language teacher education: The effects of a module on teacher research. *Cambridge Journal of Education*, *51*(4), 491–507. doi:10.1080/0305764X.2021.1876840

Banegas, D. L., & del Pozo Beamud, M. (2022). Content and language integrated learning: A duoethnographic study about CLIL pre-service teacher education in Argentina and Spain. *RELC Journal*, *53*(1), 151–164. doi:10.1177/0033688220930442

Barceló Cerdá, M. L., & Ruiz-Corbella, M. (2015). Las competencias profesionales del maestro de primaria desde la perspectiva del tutor del centro de prácticas [The professional skills of the primary school teacher from the perspective of the tutor of the internship school]. *Revista Fuentes*, (17), 17–39. doi:10.12795/revistafuentes.2015.i17.01

Barcelos, A. M. F. (2012). Explorando crenças sobre ensino e aprendizagem de línguas em materiais didácticos. [Exploring beliefs about language teaching and learning in teaching materials.] In D. Scheyerl & S. Siquiera (Eds.), *Materiais didácticos para o ensino de línguas na contemporaneidade: Contestações e proposicões [Didactic materials for language teaching in contemporary times: Challenges and propositions]* (pp. 110–137). EDUFBA.

Compilation of References

Barcelos, A. M. F. (2013). Desvelando a relação entre crenças sobre ensino e aprendizahem de línguas, emocões e identidades. [Untandresing the relationship between beliefs about teaching and learning languages, emocões and identities.] In A. F. Lopes Magela Gerhardt, M. Alvaro de Amorim, & A. Monteiro Carvalho (Eds.), *Lingüística aplicada e ensino: Língua e literature [Applied Linguistics and Teaching: Language and Literature]* (pp. 153–186). Pontes Editores.

Barcelos, A. M. F., & Kalaja, P. (2011). Introduction to beliefs about SLA revisited. *System, 39*(3), 281–289. doi:10.1016/j.system.2011.07.001

Barrett, M., Byram, M., Lázár, I., Mompoint-Gaillard, P., & Philippou, S. (2014). *Developing Intercultural Competence through Education.* Councilof Europe Publishing.

Barrios, E. (2019). The effect of parental education level on perceptions about CLIL: A study in Andalusia. *International Journal of Bilingual Education and Bilingualism, 25*(1), 183–195. doi:10.1080/13670050.2019.1646702

Barrios, E., & Milla Lara, M. D. (2020). CLIL methodology, materials and resources, and assessment in a monolingual context: An analysis of stakeholders' perceptions in Andalusia. *Language Learning Journal, 48*(1), 60–80. doi:10.108 0/09571736.2018.1544269

Bauml, M. (2014). Collaborative lesson planning as professional development for beginning primary teachers. *New Educator, 10*(3), 182–200. doi:10.1080/1547688X.2014.925741

Bayerisches Staatsministerium für Unterricht und Kultus [Bavarian State Ministry for Education and Culture]. (2021). *Projekte Bilinguale Grundschule.* Stiftung Bildungspakt Bayern [*Projects bilingual primary school.* Bavaria Education Pact Foundation]. https://www.bildungspakt-bayern.de/projekte_bilinguale_grund schule/

Beacco, J.-C., Byram, M., Cavalli, M., Coste, D., Cuenat, M. E., Goullier, F., & Panthier, J. (2016). *Guide for the development and implementation of curricula for plurilingual and intercultural education.* Council of Europe.

Bensetti-Benbader, H., & Brown, D. (2019). Language Acquisition With Augmented and Virtual Reality. In K. Graziano (Ed.), *Proceedings of Society for Information Technology & Teacher Education International Conference,* pp. 1730-1734. Association for the Advancement of Computing in Education (AACE). https://www.learntechlib.org/primary/p/207876/

Bentley, K. (2010). *The TKT (teaching knowledge test) course. CLIL module content and language integrated learning.* Cambridge University Press.

Berliner, D. C. (1988). Implications of studies on expertise in pedagogy for teacher education and evaluation. In *New directions for teacher assessment. Proceeding of the ETS Invitational Conference* (pp. 39–68). Princeton Educational Testing Service. https://files.eric.ed.gov/fulltext/ED314432.pdf#page=44

Bertaux, P., Coonan, C. M., Frigols-Martín, M. J., & Mehisto, P. (2010). *The CLIL teacher's competences grid. Common constitution and language learning (CCLL).* Comenius Network.

Biegler, L. (2003). *Implementing dramatization as an effective storytelling method to increase comprehension.* ERIC Database. http://www.eric.ed.gov

Birdsong, D. (2018). Plasticity, Variability and Age in Second Language Acquisition and Bilingualism. *Frontiers in Psychology, 9*, 81. doi:10.3389/fpsyg.2018.00081 PMID:29593590

Bjorklund, D. F., & Pellegrini, A. D. (2000). Child development and evolutionary psychology. *Child Development, 71*(6), 1687–1708. doi:10.1111/1467-8624.00258 PMID:11194266

Blanchard, K. D. (2012). Modeling life-long learning: Collaborative teaching across disciplinary lines. *Teaching Theology and Religion, 15*(4), 338–354. doi:10.1111/j.1467-9647.2012.00826.x

Bland, B. (2019). Teaching English to Young Learners: More Teacher Education and More Children's Literature! *CLELE Journal, 7*(2), 79-103. https://eric.ed.gov/?id=ED608240

Bland, J. (Ed.). (2015). *Teaching English to young learners: Critical issues in language teaching with 3-12 year-olds.* Bloomsbury.

Bleichenbacher, L., Goullier, F., Rossner, R., & Schröder Sura, A. (2019). *Teacher competences for languages in education: Conclusions of the project.* Council of Europe, ECML.

BOE. (2014). *Boletín Oficial del Estado, 52*, de 1 de Marzo de 2014, 19349-19420. https://www.boe.es/eli/es/rd/2014/02/28/126

Bolívar, A. (2010). *Competencias básicas y currículo.* Síntesis.

Bonte, M., Correia, J. M., Keetels, M., Vroomen, J., & Formisano, E. (2017). Reading-induced shifts of perceptual speech representations in auditory cortex. *Nature, 7*, 5143–5154. PMID:28698606

Böttger, H. (2016). Neurodidactics of early language learning. *Where language is at home.* Stuttgart: utb GmbH.

Böttger, H., & Müller, T. (2020). *Schulversuch Lernen in zwei Sprachen - Bilinguale Grundschule Englisch. [Abschlussbericht der wissenschaftlichen Evaluation, Katholische Universität Eichstätt-Ingolstadt]. [School experiment Learning in two languages - Bilingual primary school English. [Final report of the scientific evaluation, Catholic University of Eichstätt-Ingolstadt].]* Stiftung Bildungspakt Bayern. https://bildungspakt-bayern.de/wp- content/uploads/2020/07/Abschlussbericht.pdf

Böttger, H., & Rischawy, N. (2016). Bilingual classes at Realschulen in Bavaria. Final report on the accompanying scientific research. Catholic University of Eichstätt-Ingolstadt.

Böttger, H., Festman, J., & Müller, T. (Eds.). (2019). Language Education and Acquisition Research: Focusing Early Language Learning. Verlag Julius Klinkhardt, 82-116.BIG-Kreis (Ed.) (2015). Der Lernstand im Englischunterricht am Ende von Klasse 4. Ergebnisse der BIG-Studie [The level of learning in English lessons at the end of grade 4. Results of the BIG study]. München: Domino.

Böttger, H. (2009). *Fremdsprachenunterricht als Kontinuum: der Übergang von der Grundschule in die weiterführenden Schulen.* Empfehlungen des BIG-Kreises in der Stiftung LERNEN. [*Foreign language teaching as a continuum: the transition from primary to secondary school.* Recommendations of the BIG circle in the LEARNING Foundation.]

Böttger, H. (2011). *In zwei Sprachen lernen: die Fremdsprache in den Lernbereichen der Grundschule.* Empfehlungen des BIG-Kreises in der Stiftung LERNEN. [*Learning in two languages: the foreign language in the learning areas of primary school.* Recommendations of the BIG circle in the LEARNING Foundation.]

Böttger, H. (2013). Was Kinder wirklich können: Ein Plädoyer für die Entfaltung kindlicher (Sprachen-) Potenziale. [What children can really do: a plea for the development of children's (language) potential.]. *Grundschule Englisch,* (34), 44–46.

Böttger, H. (2017). Early foreign language learning - predispositions and potentials. In H. Böttger (Ed.), *Early foreign language learning. FLuL - Fremdsprachen Lehren und Lernen 46/2 (2017) [FLuL - Teaching and Learning Foreign Languages].* Narr/Francke/Attempto.

Bourdieu, P. (1999). Understanding. In P. Bourdieu & G. Balazs (Eds.), *The weight of the world: Social suffering in contemporary society* (pp. 607–626). Stanford University Press.

Bravo, E., Santana, M., & Rodon, J. (2015). Information systems and performance: The role of technology, the task and the individual. *Journal Behaviour & Information Technology, 1*(3), 247–260. doi:10.1080/0144929X.2014.934287

Compilation of References

Bredenbröker, W. (2002). Förderung der fremdsprachlichen Kompetenz durch bilingualen Unterricht. Empirische Untersuchungen. [Promotion of foreign language competence through bilingual teaching. Empirische Untersuchungen.] In S. Breidbach, G. Bach, & D. Wolff (Eds.), *Bilingualer Sachfachunterricht: Didaktik, Lehrer- und Lernerforschung und Bildungspolitik zwischen Theorie und Empirie [Bilingual subject teaching: didactics, teacher and learner research and educational policy between theory and empiricism.],* (pp. 141–149). Lang.

Bredikyte, M. (2002). Dialogical Drama with puppets (DDP) as a method of fostering children's verbal activity. In E. Majaron & L. Kroflin (Eds.), *The Puppet-What a Miracle!* (pp. 33–60). The UNIMA, Puppets in Education Commission.

Breen, M. (2001). *Learner contributions to language learning: New directions in research.* Routledge.

Breidbach, S., & Medina-Suárez, J. (2016). Teachers' perspectives on CLIL and classroom innovation in a method based on drama games. La perspectiva de los profesores acerca de CLIL y la innovación en clase en un método basado en juegos teatrales. *Estudios Sobre Educación, 31,* 97–116. doi:10.15581/004.31.97-116

Brennan, A. (2019). Differentiation Trough Choice as an Approach to Enhance Inclusive Practice. *Journal of Special Needs Education in Ireland, 32*(1), 11–20.

Brock-Utne, B. (2022). Globalization and the Issue of Language of Instruction: Examples from Tanzania and Norway. In: Zajda, J., Vissing, Y., Majhanovich, S. (Eds.) Globalisation, Ideology and Social Justice Discourses, Globalization, Comparative Education and Policy Research, 30. Springer. doi:10.1007/978-3-030-92774-5_3

Brown, H. D., & Lee, H. (2015). *Teaching principles* (Vol. P). Ed Australia.

Bruner, J. S. (1984). *Acción, pensamiento y lenguaje.* Alianza.

Brüning, C. I., & Purrmann, M. S. (2014). CLIL pedagogy in Europe: CLIL teacher education in Germany. *Utrecht Studies in Language and Communication, 27,* 315–338. doi:10.1163/9789401210485_018

Bruton, A. (2013). CLIL: Some of the reasons why ... and why not. *System, 41*(3), 587–597. doi:10.1016/j.system.2013.07.001

Bruton, A. (2015). CLIL: Detail matters in the whole picture. More than a reply to J. Hüttner and U. Smit (2014). *System, 53,* 119–128. doi:10.1016/j.system.2015.07.005

Bruton, A. (2019). Questions about CLIL which are unfortunately still not outdated: A reply to Pérez-Cañado. *Applied Linguistics Review, 10*(4), 591–602. doi:10.1515/applirev-2017-0059

Buchner, J., & Zumbach, J. (2020). Augmented reality in teacher education. A framework to support teachers' technological pedagogical content knowledge. *Italian Journal of Educational Technology, 28*(2), 106–120. doi:10.17471/2499-4324/1151

Buckingham, L., Fernández, M., & Halbach, A. (2022). Differences between CLIL and non-CLIL students: Motivation, autonomy and identity. *Journal of Multilingual and Multicultural Development,* 1–15. Advance online publication. doi:10.1080/01434632.2022.2102641

Burmeister, P. (1998). Zur Entwicklung der Fremdsprachenkenntnisse im bilingualen Unterricht: Ergebnisse aus fünf Jahren Forschung. [On the development of foreign language skills in bilingual teaching: Results from five years of research.] In G. Hermann-Brennecke & W. Geisler (Eds.), *Zur Theorie und Praxis & Praxis der Theorie des Fremdsprachenerwerbs [On the theory and practice & practice of the theory of foreign language acquisition]* (pp. 101–116). LIT Verlag.

Burmeister, P. (2006). Immersion und Sprachunterricht im Vergleich. [Immersion and language teaching in comparison.] In M. Pienemann (Ed.), *Englischerwerb in der Grundschule. Ein Studien- und Arbeitsbuch [English acquisition in elementary school. A study and workbook].* Schöningh.

Burnett, P. C. (2001). Elementary students' preferences for teacher praise. *Journal of Classroom Interaction*, *36*(1), 16–23. https://www.jstor.org/stable/23870540

Burnett, P., & Mandel, V. (2010). Praise and Feedback in the Primary Classroom: Teachers' and Students' Perspectives. *Australian Journal of Educational & Developmental Psychology*, *10*, 145–154.

Busch, B. (2018). The language portrait in multilingualism research: Theoretical and methodological considerations. *Working Papers in Urban Language and Literacies*, *236*. King's College London.

Busch, B. (2012). The linguistic repertoire revisited. *Applied Linguistics*, *33*(5), 503–523. doi:10.1093/applin/ams056

Butler, Y. G., & Le, V. N. (2018). A Longitudinal Investigation of Parental Social-Economic Status (SES) and Young Students' Learning of English as a Foreign Language. *System*, *73*, 4–15. doi:10.1016/j.system.2017.07.005

Caballero, N., & Celaya, M. L. (2022). Code-switching by primary school bilingual EFL learners: A study on the effect of proficiency and modality of interaction. *International Journal of Bilingual Education and Bilingualism*, *25*(1), 301–313. doi:10.1080/13670050.2019.1671309

Cahyani, H., de Courcy, M., & Barnett, J. (2018). Teachers' code-switching in bilingual classrooms: Exploring pedagogical and sociocultural functions. *International Journal of Bilingual Education and Bilingualism*, *21*(4), 465–479. doi:10.1080/13670050.2016.1189509

Calatayud, M. A. (2018). Los agrupamientos escolares a debate. [School groupings for debate.]. *Tendencias Pedagógicas*, *32*(32), 5–14. doi:10.15366/tp2018.32.001

Calle-Casado, J. J. (2015). *Teacher training for CLIL: Lessons learned and ways forward* [unpublished Masters' Thesis, Universidad de Jaén, Jaén]. https://tauja.ujaen.es/bitstream/10953.1/2285/1/Calle_Casado_Juan_Jos_TFG_Estudios_Ingleses.pdf

Calonge, A., & López, M. D. (2005). Una propuesta práctica para acercarse a la noción de fósil y fosilización. [A practical proposal to approach the notion of fossil and fossilization.] *Alambique: Didáctica de las ciencias experimentales [Alembic: Didactics of experimental sciences]*, *44*, 49-56. http://cmap.unavarra.es/rid=1R3Q206R7-1STX7W6-12PBB/una-propuesta-practica-para-acercarse-a-la-nocion-de-fosil-y-fosiliz
acion.pdf

Calonge, A., Bercial, M. T., García, J., & López, M. O. (2003). El uso didáctico de los fósiles en la enseñanza de las Ciencias de la Tierra. [The didactic use of fossils in the teaching of Earth Sciences.] *Pulso*, *26*, 117-128. https://revistas.cardenalcisneros.es/index.php/PULSO/article/view/38/239

Calsamiglia, C., & Loviglio, A. (2020). Maturity and school outcomes in an inflexible system: Evidence from Catalonia. *SERIEs*, *11*(1), 1–49. doi:10.100713209-019-0196-6 PMID:32226557

Calvo-Bernardino, A., & Mingorance-Arnáiz, A. C. (2009). La estrategia de las universidades frente al Espacio Europeo de Educación Superior. [The strategy of universities against the European Higher Education Area.]. *Revista Complutense de Educación*, *20*(2), 319–342.

Cambridge (2018). *Assessment Wordlist For Exams From 2018*. Cambridge https://www.cambridgeenglish.org/images/149681-yle-flyers-word-list.pdf

Campillo, J. M., Sánchez, R., & Miralles, P. (2019). Primary Teachers' Perceptions of CLIL Implementation in Spain. *English Language Teaching*, *12*(4), 149–156. doi:10.5539/elt.v12n4p149

Compilation of References

Candelier, M. (2017) "Awakening to Languages" and educational language policy. InJ.Cenoz, D. Gorter, & S. May (Eds.),Language awareness and multilingualism: Encyclopedia of language and education (3rd ed.) Springer. doi:10.1007/978-3-319-02240-6_12

Candry, S., Deconinck, J., & Eyckmans, J. (2018). Written repetition vs. oral repetition: Which is more conducive to L2 vocbulary learning? *Journal of European Second language Association, 2*, 72-82.

Cano, W. (2013). *Manual CLIL para centros bilingües*. UNIR Ediciones.

Carey, E., Devine, A., Hill, F., Dowker, A., McLellan, R., & Szucs, D. (2021). *Understanding mathematics anxiety: investigating the experiences of UK primary and secondary school students*. University of Cambridge.

Carey, E., Devine, A., Hill, F., & Szűcs, D. (2017). Differentiating anxiety forms and their role in academic performance from primary to secondary school. *PLoS One, 12*(3), e0174418. doi:10.1371/journal.pone.0174418 PMID:28350857

Casal, S. (2016). Cooperative assessment for learning in CLIL contexts. *Estudios sobre educación, 31*, 139-157. doi:10.15581/004.31.139-157

Casanova, Mª A. (2011). *Educación inclusiva: un modelo de futuro*. [*Inclusive education: a model for the future.*] Wolters Kluwer.

CAST. (2018). *Universal Design for Learning Guidelines version 2.2*. CAST. http: //udlguidelines.cast.org

Catenaccio, P., & Giglioni, C. (2016). CLIL teaching at primary school level and the academia/practice interface: some preliminary considerations. In G. Garzone, D. Heaney, & G. Riboni (Eds.), *Focus on LSP teaching: developments and issues* (pp. 211–244). LED. doi:10.7359/791-2016-cate

Catlioglu, H., Birgin, O., Costu, S., & Gurbuz, R. (2009). The level of mathematics anxiety among pre-service elementary school teachers. *Procedia: Social and Behavioral Sciences, 1*(1), 1578–1581. doi:10.1016/j.sbspro.2009.01.277

Cavalieri, S., & Stermieri, A. (2016). The BEI/IBI Project: A study on the best practices in integrating Language and Content Learning in primary schools. In G. Garzone, D. Heaney, & G. Riboni (Eds.), *Focus on LSP teaching: developments and issues* (pp. 211–244). LED. doi:10.7359/791-2016-cava

Cazzago San Martino Primary School. (2016). *Cazzago San Martino Primary School Curriulum*. Cazzago San Martino Primary School. https://www.icverdello.edu.it/wp-content/uploads/2016/10/INGLESE-1.pdf

Ceballos, M., Vílchez, J. E., & Reina, M. (2019). Concepto de fósil en niños de primero a cuarto de Educación Primaria: ¿cómo lo adquieren? [Concept of fossil in children from first to fourth of Primary Education: how do they acquire it?] *Enseñanza de las Ciencias de la Tierra [Teaching Earth Sciences], 27*(2), 210-218. https://raco.cat/index.php/ECT/article/view/367145

Celce-Murcia, M., Brinton, D. M., Snow, M. A., & Bohlke, D. (2014). *Teaching English as a Second or Foreign Language* (4th ed.). National Geographic Learning.

Cenoz, J. &Gorter, D. (2011). Focus on multilingualism: A study of trilingual writing. *The Modern Language Journal, 95*, 356-369. doi:10.1111/j.1540-4781.2011.01206.x

Cenoz, J. (2017). Translanguaging in school contexts: International perspectives. *Journal of Language, Identity, and Education, 16*(4), 193–198. doi:10.1080/15348458.2017.1327816

Cenoz, J. (2019). Translanguaging pedagogies and English as a lingua franca. *Language Teaching, 52*(1), 71–85. doi:10.1017/S0261444817000246

Cenoz, J., Genesee, F., & Gorter, D. (2014). Critical Analysis of CLIL: Taking Stock and Looking Forward. *Applied Linguistics*, *35*(3), 243–262. doi:10.1093/applin/amt011

Cenoz, J., & Gorter, D. (2015). Towards a holistic approach in the study of multilingual education. In J. Cenoz & D. Gorter (Eds.), *Multilingual education: Between language learning and translanguaging* (pp. 1–15). Cambridge University Press. doi:10.1017/9781009024655.002

Cenoz, J., & Gorter, D. (2020). Teaching English through pedagogical translanguaging. *World Englishes*, *39*(2), 300–311. doi:10.1111/weng.12462

Cenoz, J., & Gorter, D. (Eds.). (2015). *Multilingual education: Between language learning and translanguaging*. Cambridge University Press. doi:10.1017/9781009024655

Chikiwa, C., & Schäfer, M. (2016). Teacher code switching consistency and precision in a multilingual mathematics classroom. *African Journal of Research in Mathematics. Science and Technology Education*, *20*(3), 244–255. doi:10.1 080/18117295.2016.1228823

Chiu, J. L., De Jaegher, C. J., & Chao, J. (2015). The effects of augmented virtual science laboratories on middle school students' understanding of gas properties. *Computers & Education*, *85*, 59–73. doi:10.1016/j.compedu.2015.02.007

Chiva-Bartoll, O., Baena-Extremera, A., Hortiguela-Alcalá, D., & Ruiz-Montero, P. J. (2020). Contributions of service-learning on PETE Students' effective personality: A mixed methods research. *International Journal of Environmental Research and Public Health*, *17*(23), 8756. doi:10.3390/ijerph17238756 PMID:33255718

Chiva-Bartoll, Ó., Gil-Gómez, J., & Zorrilla-Silvestre, L. (2019). Improving the effective personality of pre-service teachers through service-learning: A physical education approach. *Revista de Investigación Educacional*, *37*(2), 327–343. doi:10.6018/rie.37.2.303331

Chiva-Bartoll, O., Pallarés-Piquer, M., & Gil-Gómez, J. (2018). Aprendizaje-servicio y mejora de la Personalidad Eficaz en futuros docentes de Educación Física. [Service-learning and improvement of the Effective Personality in future teachers of Physical Education.]. *Revista Complutense de Educación*, *29*(1), 181–197. doi:10.5209/RCED.52164

Christ, H. (2003). Sprachenpolitik und das Lehren und Lernen fremder Sprachen. [Language policy and the teaching and learning of foreign languages.] In Bausch, K.-R./ Christ; H./ Krumm; H.J. (Ed.) (20034) Handbuch Fremdsprachenunterricht, 102- 111 [Foreign language teaching handbook]. Tübingen und Basel: Francke.

Chukueggu, C. O. C. (2012). The use of drama and dramatic activities in English language teaching. *The Crab: Journal of Theatre and Media Arts*, *1*, 151–150.

Chumak-Horbatsch, R. (2012). *Linguistically appropriate practice: A guide for working with young immigrant children*. University of Toronto Press.

Chumak-Horbatsch, R. (2019). *Using linguistically appropriate practice: A guide for teaching in multilingual classrooms*. Multilingual Matters.

Cipresso, P., Giglioli, I. A. C., Raya, M. A., & Riva, G. (2018). The Past, Present, and Future of Virtual and Augmented Reality Research: A Network and Cluster Analysis of the Literature. *Frontiers in Psychology*, *9*, 2086. doi:10.3389/fpsyg.2018.02086 PMID:30459681

Classens, A., & Engel, M. (2013). How important is where you start? Early mathematics knowledge and later school success. *Teachers College Record*, *115*(6), 1–29. doi:10.1177/016146811311500603

Coghlan, D., & Jacobs, C. (2005). Kurt Lewin on reeducation: Foundations for action research. *The Journal of Applied Behavioral Science*, *41*(4), 444–457. doi:10.1177/0021886305277275

Compilation of References

Coleman, J. (2006). English-medium teaching in European Higher Education. *Language Teaching*, *39*(1), 1–14. doi:10.1017/S026144480600320X

Comunidad de Madrid. (2021). *Datos y cifras de la educación 2021-2022* [Data and figures of education 2021-2022]. Dirección General de Bilingüismo y Calidad de la Enseñanza de la Consejería de Educación, Universidades, Ciencia y Portavocía. https://www.comunidad.madrid/servicios/educacion/educacion-cifras

Consejería de Educación y Deporte. (2013). *Guía informativa para centros de enseñanza bilingüe.* [*Informative guide for bilingual schools.*] (2nd ed.). Junta de Andalucía. https://www.juntadeandalucia.es/export/drupaljda/Guia_inform ativa_centros_ense%C3%B1anza_bilingue_.pdf

Consejería de Educación y Deporte. (2022). *Cuadro resumen centros bilingües en Andalucía.* [*Informative guide for bilingual schools.*] Junta de Andalucía. https://www.juntadeandalucia.es/educacion/portals/web/pluril inguismo/centros-bilingues

Conteh, J., & Meyer, G. (Eds.), *The multilingual turn in languages education. Opportunities and challenges.* Multilingual Matters.

Contero, C., Zayas, F., & Arco-Tirado, J. L. (2018). Addressing CLIL lecturers' needs: reflections on specific methodological training. *Porta Linguarum: Revista internacional de didáctica de las lenguas extranjeras*, (3), 121-135.

Contero, C., Zayas, F., & Tirado, J. L. (2018). Addressing CLIL lecturers' needs: reflections on specific methodological training. *Porta Linguarum: Revista internacional de didáctica de las lenguas extranjeras [Porta Linguarum: International magazine on the teaching of foreign languages]*, (3), 121-135. doi:10.30827/Digibug.54305

Contreras, J. (2010). Ser y saber en la formación didáctica del profesorado: Una visión personal. [Being and knowing in the didactic training of teachers: a personal vision.]. *Revista Interuniversitaria de Formación del Profesorado*, *69*, 61–83.

Coonan, C. M. (2007). Insider views of the CLIL class through teacher self-observation–introspection. *International Journal of Bilingual Education and Bilingualism*, *10*(5), 625–646. doi:10.2167/beb463.0

Corrochano, D., & Gómez-Gonçalves, A. (2020). Analysis of Spanish pre-service teachers' mental models of geologic time. *International Journal of Science Education*, *42*(10), 1653–1672. doi:10.1080/09500693.2020.1774093

Cortina-Pérez, B., & Pino Rodríguez, A. M. (2021). Analysing CLIL teacher competences in pre-service preschool education. A case study at the University of Granada. *European Journal of Teacher Education*, 1–19. doi:10.1080/026 19768.2021.1890021

Costa, F. (2004). CLIL (Content and Language Integrated Learning) - esempi di monitoraggio e valutazione per scienze in inglese. *LEND*, (September), 36–41.

Costa, F. (2019). *Enjoy teaching English. Insegnare inglese nella scuola primaria [English teacher in the primary school]*. Giunti Scuola.

Costa, F. (2021). What does research tell us about experiences and forms of bilingual education? In M. L. Maggioni & A. Murphy (Eds.), *Back to the future* (pp. 91–112). Peter Lang.

Costa, F. (2023). Mediation and mode continuum in primary bilingual (English and Italian) education. In L. Lopriore (Ed.), *Engaging research: Transforming practices for the English as a foreign language classroom* (pp. 9–21). TESOL Press.

Costa, F., & D'Angelo, L. (2011). CLIL: A suit for all seasons? *Latin American Journal of Content & Language Integrated Learning*, *4*(1), 1–13. doi:10.5294/laclil.2011.4.1.1

Costa, F., & Mariani, M. (2007). Drama and CLIL (Content and Language Integrated Learning. In D. Marsh & D. Wolff (Eds.), *Diverse contexts – converging goals: CLIL in Europe* (pp. 297–308). Peter Lang.

Council of Europe. (1992). European Charter for Regional or Minority Languages. *European Treaty Series, 148.* https://www.coe.int/en/web/european-charter-regional-or-minority-languages/home

Council of Europe. (2001). *Common European framework of reference for languages.* Council of Europe.

Council of Europe. (2001). *Common European framework of reference for languages: Learning, teaching, assessment.* Cambridge University Press.

Council of Europe. (2016). *Competences for Democratic Culture: Living Together as Equals in Culturally Diverse Democratic Societies.* Council of Europe.

Council of Europe. (2018). *Common European framework of reference for languages. Companion volume with descriptors.* Council of Europe.

Council of Europe. (2018). *Common European Framework of Reference for Languages: Learning, Teaching, Assessment.* European Commission. https://www.coe.int/en/web/common-european-framework-reference-languages

Cowan, N. (2008). What are the differences between long-term, short-term, and working memory? *Progress in Brain Research, 169,* 323–338. doi:10.1016/S0079-6123(07)00020-9 PMID:18394484

Coyle, D. (2007). Content and Language Integrated Learning: Towards a Connected Research Agenda for CLIL Pedagogies. *International Journal of Bilingual Education and Bilingualism.*

Coyle, D., Hood, P., & Marsh, D. (2010). CLIL. Cambridge.

Coyle, D., Hood, P., & Marsh, M. (2010). CLIL. Cambridge University Press.

Coyle, D. (2005). *CLIL: Planning tools for teachers.* The University of Nottingham, School of Education.

Coyle, D. (2006). Content and Language Integrated Learning – Motivating Learners and Teachers. *The Scottish Language Review, 13,* 1–18.

Coyle, D. (2015). Strengthening integrated learning: Towards a new era for pluriliteracies and intercultural learning. *Latin American Journal of Content and Language Integrated Learning, 8*(2), 84–103. doi:10.5294/laclil.2015.8.2.2

Coyle, D. (2018). The place of CLIL in (bilingual) education. *Theory into Practice, 57*(3), 166–176. doi:10.1080/00405841.2018.1459096

Coyle, D., Hood, P., & Marsh, D. (2010). *CLIL: Content and Language Integrated Learning.* Cambridge University Press. doi:10.1017/9781009024549

Coyle, D., & Meyer, O. (2021). *Beyond CLIL: Pluriliteracies Teaching for Deeper Learning.* Cambridge University Press. doi:10.1017/9781108914505

Creswell, J. W., & Clark, V. L. P. (2017). *Designing and conducting mixed methods research.* Sage publications.

Csikszentmihalyi, M. (2011). *Flow: The Psychology of Optimal Experience.* Harper Collins.

Csikszentmihalyi, M. (2014). Toward a psychology of optimal experience. In M. Csikszentmihalyi (Ed.), *Flow and The Foundations of Positive Psychology* (pp. 209–226). Springer.

Compilation of References

Cummins, F. (2021). Language as a problem. *Language Sciences*, *88*, 101433. doi:10.1016/j.langsci.2021.101433

Cummins, J. (1984). *Bilingualism in Special Education. Issues in Assessment and Pedagogy*. Multilingual Matters.

Cummins, J. (2000). *Language, power and pedagogy: Bilingual children in the crossfire*. Multilingual Matters Ltd. doi:10.21832/9781853596773

Cummins, J. (2005). Bilingual children's mother tongue: Why is it important for education? *Sprogforum*, *19*, 15–20.

Cummins, J. (2008). Teaching for transfer: Challenging the two solitudesassumption inbilingual education. In N. H. Hornberger (Ed.), *Encyclopedia of Language and Education*. Springer. doi:10.1007/978-0-387-30424-3_116

Cummins, J. (2017). Teaching for transfer in multilingual school contexts. In O. García, A. Lin, & S. May (Eds.), *Bilingual education: Encyclopedia of language and education* (pp. 103–115). Springer.

Cummins, J. (2021). *Rethinking the education of multilingual learners: A critical analysis of theoretical concepts*. Multilingual Matters.

Cummins, J., & Early, M. (2011). *Identity texts: The collaborative creation of power in multilingual schools*. Trentham Books.

Cummins, J., Swain, M., Nakajima, K., Handscombe, J., Green, D., & Tran, C. (1984). Linguistic interdependence among Japanese and Vietnamese immigrant students. In C. Rivera (Ed.), *Communicate Competence Approaches to Language Proficiency Assessment: Research and Application* (pp. 60–81). Multilingual Matters.

Custodio Espinar, M., & García Ramos, J. M. (2020). Medida de la competencia para programar AICLE y diagnóstico de las necesidades de formación docente. [Measurement of competence to program CLIL and diagnosis of teacher training needs.] *Revista de Pedagogía*, *72*(I), 31–48.

Custodio-Espinar, M. (2017, September 7). The role of language teaching in the CLIL classroom. Ages and Stages. Pearson. https://www.english.com/blog/clil-classroom/

Custodio-Espinar, M. (2019a). CLIL teacher education in Spain. In In K. Tsuchiya & Pérez-Murillo (Eds.), Content and language integrated learning in Spanish and Japanese contexts (pp. 313-337). Palgrave Macmillan. doi:10.1007/978-3-030-27443-6_13

Custodio-Espinar, M. (2019b). *Los principios metodológicos AICLE (aprendizaje integrado de contenido y lengua)* [The methodological principles CLIL (content and language integrated learning)]. Fundación Universitaria Española.

Custodio-Espinar, M. (2020). Influencing factors on in-service teachers' competence in planning CLIL. *Latin American Journal of Content & Language Integrated Learning*, *12*(2), 207–241. doi:10.5294/laclil.2019.12.2.2

Custodio-Espinar, M., & García-Ramos, J. M. (2020). Are accredited teachers equally trained for CLIL? The CLIL teacher paradox. *Porta Linguarum*, *33*(1), 9–25.

Custodio-Espinar, M., & López-Hernández, A. (2021). CLILing EMI for Effective Mediation in the L2 in Pre-service Teacher Education: A Case Study at a Spanish University. In L. Escobar & A. Ibáñez Moreno (Eds.), *Mediating Specialized Knowledge and L2 Abilities* (pp. 81–107). Palgrave Macmillan. doi:10.1007/978-3-030-87476-6_5

Custodio-Espinar, M., López-Hernández, A., & Buckingham, L. R. (2022). Effects of co-teaching on CLIL teacher trainees' collaborative competence. *Profesorado. Revista de Currículum y Formación de Profesorado*, *26*(1), 87–106. doi:10.30827/profesorado.v26i1.16853 da Silva, M., Teixeira, J., Cavalcante, P., & Teichrieb, V. (2019). Perspectives on how to evaluate augmented reality technology tools for education: A systematic review. *Journal of the Brazilian Computer Society*, 25(1), 3. doi:10.118613173-019-0084-8

Dafouz, E., & Smit, U. (2020). *ROAD-MAPPING English medium education in the internationalised university*. Palgrave Macmillan. doi:10.1007/978-3-030-23463-8

Dale, L., & Tanner, R. (2012). *CLIL activities with CD-ROM: A resource for subject and language teachers*. Cambridge University Press.

Dale, L., & Tanner, R. (2012). *CLIL Activities. A Resource for Subject and Language Teachers*. Cambridge University Press.

Dale, L., van der Es, W., & Tanner, R. (2011). *CLIL Skills*. European Platform.

Dalton-Puffer, C. (2008). Outcomes and processes in content and language integrated learning (CLIL): current research from Europe. In W. Delanoy and L. Wolkmann, (eds.) *Future Perspectives for English Language Teaching*, 139–57. Heidelberg: https://balancedreading.com/cambridge/ https://www.mrc-cbu.cam.ac.uk/people/matt.davis/cmabridge/

Dalton-Puffer, C. (2007). *Discourse in content and language integrated learning (CLIL) classrooms*. John Benjamins. doi:10.1075/lllt.20

Dalton-Puffer, C. (2016). Cognitive Discourse Functions: Specifying an Integrative Interdisciplinary Construct. In T. Nikula, E. Dafouz, P. Moore, & U. Smit (Eds.), *Conceptualising integration in CLIL and multilingual education* (pp. 29–54). Multilingual Matters. doi:10.21832/9781783096145-005

Darvin, R., Lo, Y. Y., & Lin, A. M. (2020). Examining CLIL through a Critical Lens. *English Teaching & Learning*, 44(2), 103–108. doi:10.100742321-020-00062-2

Davis, B., & Renert, M. (2013). Profound understanding of emergent mathematics: Broadening the construct of teachers' disciplinary knowledge. *Educational Studies in Mathematics*, 82(2), 245–265. doi:10.100710649-012-9424-8

de Graaff, R., Koopman, G. J., Anikina, J., & Westhoff, G. (2007). An Observation Tool for Effective L2 Pedagogy in Content and Language Integrated Learning (CLIL). *International Journal of Bilingual Education and Bilingualism*, 10(5), 603–624. doi:10.2167/beb462.0

De Jesus, O. (2016). Integrating the arts to facilitate second language learning. *Open Online Journal for Research and Education*, 5, 1–4.

De la Maya Retamar, G., & Luengo González, R. (2015). Teacher training programs and development of plurilingual competence. In D. Marsh, M. L. Pérez Cañado, & J. Ráez Padilla (Eds.), *CLIL in Action: Voices from the Classroom* (pp. 114–129). Cambridge Scholars Publishing.

Deardorff, D. K. (2014). Some thoughts on assessing intercultural competence. [University of Illinois and Indiana University, National Institute for Learning Outcomes Assessment] [NILOA]. *Urbana (Caracas, Venezuela)*, IL.

DECRETO 93/2013, de 27 de agosto, por el que se regula la formación inicial y permanente del profesorado en la Comunidad Autónoma de Extremadura, así como el Sistema Andaluz de Formación Permanente del Profesorado (BOJA, n° 170, 30 de agosto de 2013). [of 27 August, which regulates the initial and permanent training of teachers in the Autonomous Community of Extremadura, as well as the Andalusian System of Permanent Teacher Training (BOJA, n° 170, 30 August 2013).] https://www.juntadeandalucia.es/boja/2013/170/1

Deieso, D., & Fraser, B. J. (2019). Learning environment, attitudes and anxiety across the transition from primary to secondary school mathematics. *Learning Environments Research*, 22(1), 133–152. doi:10.100710984-018-9261-5

Compilation of References

Del Buey, F. D. A. M., Zapico, A. F., Palacio, E. M., Pellerano, B. D., Trigo, R. M., & Urban, P. G. (2008). Cuestionario de personalidad eficaz para la formación profesional. *Psicothema, 20*(2), 224–228. PMID:18413082

Delicado Puerto, G., & Pavón Vázquez, V. (2016). Training primary student teachers for CLIL: innovation through collaboration La formación del profesorado de educación primaria para CLIL: innovación por medio de la colaboración [Primary education teacher training for CLIL: innovation through collaboration]. *Pulso: revista de educación [Pulse: Education Magazine], 39,* 35-57.

Delicado Puerto, G., & Pavón Vázquez, V. (2016). Training primary student teachers for CLIL: innovation through collaboration. *Pulso, 39,* 35-57. https://ebuah.uah.es/dspace/handle/10017/28243

Delicado Puerto, G., & Pavón Vázquez, V. (2016). Training primary student teachers for CLIL: Innovation through collaboration. *Pulso. Review of Education, 39,* 35–57.

Delicado, G. & Pavón V. (2015). La implantación de titulaciones bilingües en la Educación Superior: el caso de la formación didáctica del profesorado bilingüe de primaria en la Universidad de Extremadura, [The implementation of bilingual qualifications in Higher Education: the case of the didactic training of bilingual primary teachers at the University of Extremadura,] *Educación y futuro, 32,* 35-64.

Delicado, G., & Pavón, V. (2016). Training primary student teachers for AICLE: Innovation through collaboration, *Pulso. Review of Education, 39,* 35–57.

Delicado-Puerto, G., Alonso-Díaz, L., & Fielden-Burns, L. V. (2022). Teaching Students, Creating Teachers: Focusing on Future Language Teachers and Their Education for Bilingual Classrooms. *TESL-EJ, 25*(4), 1–31. doi:10.55593/ej.25100a10

Della Sala, S. (2009). The use and misuse of neuroscience in education. *Cortex, 45*(4), 443. doi:10.1016/j.cortex.2008.11.012 PMID:19103447

Dengel, A., Iqbal, M. Z., Grafe, S., & Mangina, E. (2022). A Review on Augmented Reality Authoring Toolkits for Education. *Frontiers Virtual Real., 3,* 798032. doi:10.3389/frvir.2022.798032

Denzin, L. (2009). The elephant in the living room: Or extending the conversation about the politics of evidence. *Qualitative Research, 9*(2), 139–160. doi:10.1177/1468794108098034

Denzin, N. K. (2017). *The research act: A theoretical introduction to sociological methods.* Routledge. doi:10.4324/9781315134543

Deumert, A. (2005). The unbearable lightness of being bilingual: English–Afrikaans language contact in South Africa. *Language Sciences, 17*(1), 113–135. doi:10.1016/j.langsci.2004.10.002

Deutsches Institut für Internationale Pädagogische Forschung [DIPF] (Ed.) (2006). *Unterricht und Kompetenzerwerb in Deutsch und Englisch. [Teaching and competence acquisition in German and English.]* Zentrale Befunde der Studie Deutsch-Englisch-Schülerleistungen-International (DESI) [Central findings of the German-English student performance study]. Frankfurt am Main.

Dewey, J. (1938). *Experience and education.* Macmillan.

Di Bitetti, M. S., & Ferreras, J. A. (2017). Publish (in English) or perish: The effect on citation rate of using languages other than English in scientific publications. *Ambio, 46*(1), 121–127. doi:10.100713280-016-0820-7 PMID:27686730

Di Martino, E., & Di Sabato, B. (2012). CLIL implementation in Italian schools: Can long-serving teachers be retrained effectively? The Italian protagonists' voice. *Latin American Journal of Content and Language Integrated Learning, 5*(2), 73–105. doi:10.5294/laclil.2012.5.2.9

Diamond, A., Kirkham, N., & Amso, D. (2002). Conditions under which young children can hold two rules in mind and inhibit a prepotent response. *Developmental Psychology, 38*(3), 352–362. doi:10.1037/0012-1649.38.3.352 PMID:12005379

Diario Oficial de Extremadura. (2011). *ORDEN de 8 de abril de 2011 por la que se regula la convocatoria de secciones bilingües, con carácter experimental, en centros sostenidos con fondos públicos que impartan enseñanzas obligatorias en Extremadura. [ORDER of 8 April 2011 by which regulates the announcement of bilingual sections, with experimental character, in centres sustained with public funds that impart compulsory educations in Extremadura.]* Junta de Extremadura, Diario Oficial de Extremadura, 77, 9711-9731.

Díaz, F., & Cuevas, M. (2013). El Practicum I del Grado de maestro de primaria como materia que contribuye a la formación integral de los futuros maestros. [The Practicum I of the Degree of primary teacher as a subject that contributes to the integral formation of future teachers] In P. C. Muñoz, M. Raposo, M. González, M. E. Martínez, M. Zabalza, & A. Pérez (Eds.), *Un Practicum para la formación integral de los estudiantes* (pp. 231–240). Andavira.

Díez, E., & Sánchez, S. (2015). Diseño universal para el aprendizaje como metodología docente para atender a la diversidad en la universidad. [Universal design for learning as a teaching methodology to address diversity in the university.]. *Aula Abierta, 43*(2), 87–93. doi:10.1016/j.aula.2014.12.002

Disability Awareness Training. (2022). *Homepage.* DA. https://disabilityawarenesstraining.com

Djurić, Lj. (2017). Minority, foreign and non-native languages in Serbia's linguistic educational policy: Destinies and intersections. *Živi jezici, 37*(1), 397–411.

Dodick, J. (2007). Understanding evolutionary change within the framework of geological time. *McGill Journal of Education, 42*(2), 245–264. https://mje.mcgill.ca/article/view/2222

Dodick, J. T., & Orion, N. (2006). Building an understanding of geological time: A cognitive synthesis of the "macro" and "micro" scales of time. *Geological Society of America. Special Paper, 413*, 77–93. doi:10.1130/2006.2413(06)

Dodick, J., & Orion, N. (2003). Cognitive Factors Affecting Student Understanding of Geologic Time. *Journal of Research in Science Teaching, 40*(4), 415–442. doi:10.1002/tea.10083

Doiz, A., Lasagabaster, D., & Pavón, V. (2019). The integration of language and content in English-medium instruction courses: Lecturers' beliefs and practices. *Ibérica (New York, N.Y.)*, 38.

Doiz, A., Lasagabaster, D., & Sierra, J. M. (2014). CLIL and motivation: The effect of individual and contextual variables. *Language Learning Journal, 42*(2), 209–224. doi:10.1080/09571736.2014.889508

Donley, D. (2022). Translanguaging as a theory, pedagogy, and qualitative research methodology. *NABE Journal of Research and Practice*, 1–16. doi:10.1080/26390043.2022.2079391

Dörneyei, Z. (2001). *Teaching and researching motivation.* Longman.

Duarte, J., & Günther-van derMeij, M. (2022). 'Just accept each other,whiletherest of the world doesn't. Teachers' reflections on multilingual education. *Language and Education, 36*(5), 451–466. doi:10.1080/09500782.2022.2098678

Durán-Martínez, R., & Beltrán-Llavador, F. (2016). A Regional Assessment of Bilingual Programmes in Primary and Secondary Schools: The Teachers' Views. *Porta Linguarum, 25*, 79–92. https://digibug.ugr.es/handle/10481/53890. doi:10.30827/Digibug.53890

Durán-Martínez, R., & Beltrán-Llavador, F. (2020). Key issues in teachers' assessment of primary education bilingual programs in Spain. *International Journal of Bilingual Education and Bilingualism, 23*(2), 170–183. doi:10.1080/13670050.2017.1345851

Compilation of References

Durán-Martínez, R., Martín Pastor, E., & Martínez Abad, F. (2020). ¿Es inclusiva la enseñanza bilingüe? Análisis de la presencia y apoyos en los alumnos con necesidades específicas de apoyo educativo. [Is bilingual education inclusive? Analysis of the presence and supports in students with specific educational support needs.] *Bordón. Revista de Pedagogía, 72*(2), 65–82.

Education First. (2020). *EF EPI. Índice del Dominio del Inglés de EF. Una clasificación de 100 países y regiones por sus habilidades de inglés [EF EPI extension. Index of the English Domain of EF. A classification of 100 countries and regions by your English skills].* EF. https://www.ef.com.mx/epi/

Ehlich, K. (2015). *Deutschlands Zukunft ist mehrsprachig. [Germany's future is multilingual.]* Unter. http://www.tagesspiegel.de/wissen/position-deutschlands-zukunft-ist-mehrsprachig/11183286.html

Ekolu, S. O., & Quainoo, H. (2019). Reliability of assessments in engineering education using Cronbach's alpha, KR, and split-half methods. *Global journal of engineering education, 21*(1), 24-29.

Ellis, R. (2003). *Task-Based Language Learning and Teaching.* Applied Linguistics. Oxford University Press.

Ellis, R., Skehan, P., Li, S., Shintani, N., & Lambert, C. (2020). *Task-based language teaching: Theory and practice.* Cambridge University Press.

Elsobeihi, M. M., & Abu Naser, S. S. (2017). Effects of Mobile Technology on Human Relationships. *International Journal of Engineering and Information Systems, 1*(5), 110–125.

Enever, J. (2004). Europeanisation or globalisation in early start EFL trends across Europe. In C. Gnutzmann & F. Intemann (Eds.), *Theglobalisation of English and the English language classroom* (pp. 177–191). Narr.

Engel, G. (2009). EVENING – Konsequenzen für die Weiterentwicklung des Englischunterrichts in der Grundschule. [EVENING – Consequences for the further development of English teaching in primary school.] In G. Engel, B. Groot-Wilken, & E. Thürmann (Eds.), *Englisch in der Primarstufe – Chancen und Herausforderungen. Evaluation und Erfahrungen aus der Praxis [English in primary school - Opportunities and challenges. Evaluation and practical experience]* (pp. 197–221). Cornelsen.

English, C. (2016). English at Work: Global analysis of language skills in the workplace. Cambridge. https://www.cambridgeenglish.org/images/335794-english-at-work-executive-summary.pdf; https://eflmagazine.com/prove-youre-a-pro-with-the-communication-skills-for-business-english-for-it-exam/

Ericsson, K. A., & Kintsch, W. (1955). Long-term working memory. *Psychological Review, 102*(2), 211–245. doi:10.1037/0033-295X.102.2.211 PMID:7740089

Escobar Urmeneta, C. (2019). An Introduction to Content and Language Integrated Learning (CLIL) for Teachers and Teacher Educators. *CLIL Journal of Innovation and Research in Plurilingual and Pluricultural Education, 2*(1), 7–19. doi:10.5565/rev/clil.21

Estrada Chichón, J. L., & Segura Caballero, N. (2022). Analysis of CLIL teaching sequences for primary education. *Revista Interuniversitaria de Formación del Profesorado, 98*(36.2), 279-299.

Estrada Chichón, J.L., & Segura Caballero, N. (2022). Análisis de secuencias didácticas AICLE para Educación Primaria. *Revista Interuniversitaria de Formación del Profesorado, 98*(36.2), 275-295. doi:10.47553/rifop.v98i36.2.91999

Estrada-Chichón, J. L., & Zayas-Martínez, F. (2022). Dual training in language didactics of foreign language/CLIL pre-service primary education teachers in Spain. *Journal of Language and Education. 8*(1), 69-83. Natsional'nyi Issledovatel'skii Universitet "Vysshaya Shkola Ekonomiki", 2022. ISSN 24117390. DOI: , R. & Castro, A. (2012). La formación permanente del profesorado basada en competencias. Estudio exploratorio de la formación del profesorado de Infantil y Primaria, in *Educatio Siglo XXI, 30*(1), 297-322. doi:10.17323/jle.2022.11520García-Ruiz

Estrada, J. L. (2021). Diagnóstico de necesidades formativas entre maestros AICLE en formación inicial. *European Journal of Child Development. Education and Psychopathology, 9*(1), 1–16. doi:10.32457/ejpad.v9i1.1402

Estrada, J. L., & Otto, A. (2019). Timing of pedagogical intervention: Oral error treatment in EFL vs. CLIL contexts in primary education in Spain. *Journal of Language and Linguistic Studies, 15*(2), 578–586. doi:10.17263/jlls.586263

Eurobarometer (2012). *Europeans and Their Languages. Special Eurobarometer 368*. European Commission.

European Centre of Modern Languages. (August 12, 2022). *Thematic areas of ECML expertise*. ECML. https://www.ecml.at/Thematicareas/Thematicareas-Overview/tabid/1763/language/en-GB/Default.aspx

European Commission, Directorate-General for Education, Youth, Sport and Culture. (2006). *Content and language integrated learning (CLIL) at school in Europe*. Publications Office.

European Commission. (2003). *Promoting Language Learning and Linguistic Diversity: An Action Plan 2004–2006*. Publications Office of the European Union. https://op.europa.eu/en/publication-detail/-/publication/b3225824-b016-42fa-83f6-43d9fd2ac96d

European Commission. (2011). *European strategic framework for education and training (ET2020). Language learning at pre-primary school level: Making it efficient and sustainable* (Commission Staff Working Paper). European Commission. https://ec.europa.eu/assets/eac/languages/policy/languagepolicy/documents/early-language-learning-handbook_en.pdf

European Higher Education Area (EHEA). (2022, February 19). *Terms of reference of working group on learning and teaching*. Working Group on Learning & Teaching. http://www.ehea.info/Upload/WG_L&T_PT_AD_TORs%20(2).pdf

Eurostat. (2021). *Foreign Language Learning Statistics*. Publications Office of the European Union. https://ec.europa.eu/eurostat/statistics-explained/index.php?title=Foreign_language_learning_statistics

Eurydice (2017). *Key data on teaching languages at school in Europe: 2017 edition*. Publications Office. https://data.europa.eu/doi/10.2797/456818

Eurydice. (2017). *Eurydice Report: Key data on teaching languages at school in Europe*. Publications Office of the European Union.

Evnitskaya, N., & Jakonen, T. (2017). Multimodal conversation analysis and CLIL classroom practices. In A. Llinares & T. Morton (Eds.), Applied linguistics perspectives on CLIL (pp. 201-220). John Benjamins Publishing Company. doi:10.1075/lllt.47.12evn

Fábregat, S. (2016). El proyecto lingüístico de centro: Aprender más y comunicar mejor. [The language project of the center: learn more and communicate better.]. *Aula de Secundaria, 19*, 25–30.

Faltis, C. (2019). Arts-based pedagogy for teaching English learners. In L. C. Oliveira (Ed.), *The handbook of TESOL in K-12* (pp. 323–337). Wiley., doi:10.1002/9781119421702.ch21

Fang, H., & Li, M. (2018). A Study on the Training Model of the Bilingual Teachers in Local Universities and Colleges. *Studies in Literature and Language, 17*(2), 62–65. doi:10.3968/10668

Compilation of References

Fan, M., Antle, A. N., & Warren, J. L. (2020). Augmented Reality for Early Language Learning: A Systematic Review of Augmented Reality Application Design, Instructional Strategies, and Evaluation Outcomes. *Journal of Educational Computing Research*, *58*(6), 1059–1100. doi:10.1177/0735633120927489

Farshid, M., Paschen, J., Eriksson, T., & Kietzmann, J. (2018). Go boldly! Explore augmented reality (AR), virtual reality (VR), and mixed reality (MR) for business. *Business Horizons*, *61*(5), 657–663. doi:10.1016/j.bushor.2018.05.009

Ferguson, H. J., Brunsdon, V. E. A., & Bradford, E. E. F. (2021). The developmental trajectories of executive function from adolescence to old age. *Nature*, *11*, 1382–1399. PMID:33446798

Ferguson, J., & Wilson, J. C. (2011). The co-teaching professorship: Power ad expertise in the co-taught higher education classroom. *Scholar-Practitioner Quarterly*, *5*(1), 52–68.

Ferjan, N., & Kuhl, P. K. (2017). The brain science of bilingualism. *Young Children*, *72*(2), 38–44.

Fernández-Fontecha, A., O'Halloran, K. L., Wignell, P., & Tan, S. (2020). Scaffolding CLIL in the science classroom via visual thinking: A systemic functional multimodal approach. *Linguistics and Education*, *55*, 100788. doi:10.1016/j.linged.2019.100788

Festman, J., & Schwieter, J. W. (2019). Self-Concepts in Reading and Spelling among Mono- and Multilingual Children: Extending the Bilingual Advantage. *Behavioral Sciences (Basel, Switzerland)*, *9*(4), 39. doi:10.3390/bs9040039 PMID:31013920

Filipović, J. (2015). *Transdisciplinary approach to language study: The complexity theory perspective*. Palgrave Macmillan. doi:10.1057/9781137538468

Filipović, J. (2018). *Moć reči: ogledi iz kritičke sociolingvistike* [*The power of words: Essays in critical sociolinguistics.*]. Zadužbina Andrejević.

Filipović, J., & Djurić, Lj. (2021). Early childhood foreign language learning and teaching in Serbia: A critical overview of language education policy and planning in varying historical contexts. In S. Zein & M. R. Coady (Eds.), *Early language learning policy in the 21st century: An international perspective* (pp. 61–84). Springer. doi:10.1007/978-3-030-76251-3_3

Filipović, J., Vučo, J., & Djurić, Lj. (2007). Critical review of language education policies in compulsory primary and secondary education in Serbia. *Current Issues in Language Planning*, *8*(2), 222–242. doi:10.2167/cilp103.0

Fischer, B., Kongeter, A., & Hartnegg, K. (2008). Effects of daily practice on subitizing, visual counting and basic arithmetic skills. *Optometry and Vision Development*, *39*, 30–34.

Flores, N., & Rosa, J. (2015). Undoing appropriateness: Raciolinguistic ideologies and language diversity in education. *Harvard Educational Review*, *85*(2), 149–171. doi:10.17763/0017-8055.85.2.149

Forey, G., & Polias, J. (2017). Multi-semiotic resources providing maximal input in teaching science through English. In A. Llinares & T. Morton (Eds.), Applied linguistics perspectives on CLIL (pp. 145-164). John Benjamins Publishing Company. doi:10.1075/lllt.47.09for

Fortune, T. (2012). What the research says about immersion. In *Chinese Language Learning in the Early Grades: A handbook of resources and best practices for Mandarin immersion* (pp. 9–13). Asian Society., https://ilabs.uw.edu/sites/default/files/2017_FerjanRamirez_Kuhl_NAEYC.pdf

Franceschini, R. (2008). Früher Spracherwerb und frühes Lernen: Wie nutzen wir die Chancen? [Early language acquisition and early learning: How do we take advantage of the opportunities?] In Ministerium für Bildung, Familie, Frauen und Kultur des Saarlandes (Ed.). Mehrsprachiges Aufwachsen in der frühen Kindheit. Band 1. Weimar: Verlag das Netz [Saarland Ministry for Education, Family, Women and Culture (ed.). Multilingual growing up in early childhood. Volume 1 Weimar: Publisher the network], 13-20.

Franceschini, R. (2016). Multilingualism and multicompetence. In V. Cook & L. Wei (Eds.), *The Cambridge Handbook of Linguistic Multi-Competence* (pp. 97–124). Cambridge University Press. doi:10.1017/CBO9781107425965.005

Friedman, V. J. (2001). Action science: Creating communities of inquiry in communities of practice. In P. Reason & H. Bradbury (Eds.), *Handbook of action research: Participative inquiry and practice* (pp. 159–170). Sage Publications Ltd.

Friend, M. (2008). Co-teaching: A simple solution that isn't that simple after all. *Journal of Curriculum and Instruction,* 2(2), 9-19.https:// doi:10.3776/joci.2008.v2n2p9-19

Fueyo-Gutiérrez, E. F., Palacio, M. E. M., & Pellerano, B. D. (2010). Personalidad eficaz y rendimiento académico: Una aproximación integrada. [Effective personality and academic performance: an integrated approach.]. *Revista de Orientación Educacional, 24*(46), 57–70.

García-Campos, M. D., Canabal, C., & Alba-Pastor, C. (2018). Executive functions on universal design for learning_ moving towards inclusive education. *International Journal of Inclusive Education.* Advance online publication. doi:10 .1080/13603116.2018.1474955

García-González, F., Ruiz Rodríguez, L., Jiménez de Tejada, M.P., Romero López, M.C., Rams Sánchez, S., Fernández Oliveras, A., Vázquez Vílchez, M., Pla Pueyo, S., Barón López, S. D. (2021). *Didáctica de las Ciencias Experimentales II: Prácticas de Laboratorio* (3ª edición). [*Didactics of Experimental Sciences II: Laboratory Practices* (3rd edition).] Ediciones Pirámide (Grupo Anaya, S.A.).

García, O. (2009). *Bilingual education in the 21st century: A global perspective.* Wiley-Blackwell.

García, O. (2011). Theorising Translanguaging for Educators. In C. Celic & K. Seltzer (Eds.), *Translanguaging: A CUNY-NYSIEB Guide for Educators* (pp. 1–7). The City University of New York.

García, O., & Flores, N. (2012). Multilingual pedagogies. In M. Martin-Jones, A. Blackledge, & A. Creese (Eds.), *The Routledge handbook of multilingualism* (pp. 232–246). Routledge.

García, O., & Kleifgen, J. A. (2019). Translanguaging and literacies. *Reading Research Quarterly, 55*(4), 553–571. doi:10.1002/rrq.286

García, O., & Wei, L. (2014). *Translanguaging: Language, Bilingualism and Education.* Palgrave Macmillan. doi:10.1057/9781137385765

Gargrish, S., Mantri, A., & Kaur, D. P. (2020). Augmented Reality-Based Learning Environment to Enhance Teaching-Learning Experience in Geometry Education. *Procedia Computer Science, 172,* 1039–1046. doi:10.1016/j.procs.2020.05.152

Garton, S., & Copland, F. (2019). *The Routledge Handbook to Teaching English to Young Learners.* Taylor & Francis group.

Gately, S., & Hammer, C. (2005). An exploratory case study of the preparation of secondary teachers to meet special education needs in the general classroom. *Teacher Educator, 40*(4), 238–256. doi:10.1080/08878730509555364

General de Participación, D., Educativa, I., de Educación, C., & de Andalucía, J. (2011). *AICLE Secuencias didácticas. Educación Primaria y Secundaria.* https://www.juntadeandalucia.es/educacion/descargas/recursos /aicle/html/inicio.html

Compilation of References

Genesee, F. (1987). *Learning Through Two Languages: Studies of Immersion and Bilingual Education.* Newbury House.

Genesee, F. (2015), Myths about early childhood bilingualism. *Canadian Psychology, 56*(1), 6–15. doi:10.1037/a0038599

Giménez-Dasí, M., Quintanilla, L., & Fernández-Sánchez, M. (2021). Longitudinal Effects of the Pandemic and Confinement on the Anxiety Levels of a Sample of Spanish Children in Primary Education. *International Journal of Environmental Research and Public Health, 18*(24), 13063. doi:10.3390/ijerph182413063 PMID:34948673

Giroux, H. A. (1988). *Teachers as intellectuals: Toward a critical pedagogy of learning.* Greenwood Publishing Group.

Gkaintartzi, A., Vitsou, M., & Kostoulas, A. (2021). The design, implementation and evaluation of a teachers' training programme for English in the Kindergarten towards multilingual education. Paper presented at *ENRICH 2021, 1st International Conference on ELF Aware Practices for MultilingualClassrooms.* Enrich.

Gkaintartzi, A., Mouti, A., Skourtou, E., & Tsokalidou, R. (2019). Language teachers' perceptions of multilingualism and language teaching: The case of the postgraduate programme "LRM". *Language Learning in Higher Education. Journal of the European Confederation of Language Centres in Higher Education (Cercles), 9*(1), 33–54. doi:10.1515/cercles-2019-0002

Gkaintartzi, A., & Tsokalidou, R. (2018). Is translanguaging a possibility in a language class?: Theoretical issues and applications in an EFL class. In V. Kourtis-Kazoullis, T. Aravossitas, E. Skourtou, & P. P. Trifonas (Eds.), *Interdisciplinary research approaches to multilingual education* (pp. 179–196). Routledge. doi:10.4324/9781351170086-15

Gogolin, I. (1997). The "monolingual habitus" as the common feature in teaching in the language of the majority in different countries. *Per Linguam, 13*(2), 38–49.

Gómez, R. (2012). *Evaluación de la personalidad eficaz en población universitaria.* [*Evaluation of the effective personality in university population.*] [Doctoral Thesis, Universidad de Huelva].

Gómez, A. (2013). El aprendizaje integrado de la lengua española y los contenidos de áreas no lingüísticas en los proyectos lingüísticos de centro. [The integrated learning of the Spanish language and the contents of non-linguistic areas in the linguistic projects of the center.]. *Porta Linguarum, 20*, 103–115.

Gómez-Loarces, R., Ferrer G. F. & González-García F. (2019) Evolución de los modelos mentales sobre fosilización tras el proceso de enseñanza-aprendizaje [Evolution of mental models about fossilisation after the teaching-learning process]. *Revista Eureka sobre Enseñanza y Divulgación de las Ciencias [Eureka Magazine on Teaching and Dissemination of Sciences], 6*(2), 1-14. doi:10.25267/Rev_Eureka_ensen_divulg_cienc.2019.v16.i2.2102

Gómez-Parra, M. E., Huertas-Abril, C. A., & Espejo-Mohedano, R. (2021). Factores clave para la evaluación del impacto de los programas bilingües: Empleabilidad, movilidad y conciencia cultural. *Porta Linguarum. Revista Interuniversitaria De Didáctica De Las Lenguas Extranjeras, 35*, 93–104. doi:10.30827/portalin.v0i35.15453

Gonzales, G. C. (2019). Review of *Art as a way of talking for emergent bilingual youth: Afoundation for literacy in PreK-12 schools* by Berriz, B.R., Wager, A.C., and Poey, V.M. *Bilingual Research Journal, 42*(4), 513–516. doi:10.1080/15235882.2019.1686442

González, Mª T. & Cutanda, T. (2017). La formación continua del profesorado de enseñanza obligatoria: incidencia en la práctica docente y el aprendizaje de los estudiantes. [Continuing teacher training in compulsory education: impact on teaching practice and student learning.] *Profesorado. Revista de currículum y formación del profesorado, 21*(2), 103-122.

Gortázar, L., & Taberner, P. A. (2020). La incidencia del programa bilingüe en la segregación escolar por origen socio-económico en la Comunidad Autónoma de Madrid: Evidencia a partir de PISA. [The incidence of the bilingual program in school segregation by socioeconomic origin in the Autonomous Community of Madrid: Evidence from PISA.] *REICE. Revista Electrónica Iberoamericana sobre Calidad, Eficacia y Cambio en Educación, 18*(4), 219–239. doi:10.15366/reice2020.18.4.009

Gort, M., & Pontier, R. W. (2013). Exploring bilingual pedagogies in dual language preschool classrooms. *Language and Education, 27*(3), 223–245. doi:10.1080/09500782.2012.697468

Graddol, D. (2006). *English next. Why global English may mean the end of 'English as a foreign language.* British Council.

Grandinetti, M., Langellotti, M., & Ting, Y. L. T. (2013). How CLIL can provide a pragmatic means to renovate science education – even in a sub-optimally bilingual context. *International Journal of Bilingual Education and Bilingualism, 16*(3), 354–374. doi:10.1080/13670050.2013.777390

Graziano, K. J., & Navarrete, L. A. (2012). Co-teaching in a teacher education classroom: Collaboration, compromise, and creativity. *Issues in Teacher Education, 21*(1), 109–126.

Griful-Freixenet, J., Struyven, K., & Vantieghem, W. (2020). Toward more inclusive education: An empirical test of the universal design for learning conceptual model among preservice teachers. *Journal of Teacher Education.* doi:10.1177/0022487120965525

Griggs, T. (2001). Teaching as acting: considering acting as epistemology and its use in teaching and teacher preparation. *Teacher Education Quarterly*, 23-37.

Griva, E., & Sivropoulou, R. (2009). Implementation and evaluation of an early foreign language learning project in lindergarten. *Early Childhood Education Journal, 37*(1), 79–87. doi:10.100710643-009-0314-3

Guadamillas, V. & Alcaraz, G. (2017). Legislación en enseñanza bilingüe: análisis en el marco de Educación Primaria en España. [Legislation in bilingual education: analysis in the framework of Primary Education in Spain.] *Multiárea. Revista de didáctica, 9,* 82-103. doi:10.18239/mard.v0i9.1528

Guadamillas, V. (2017). Trainee primary-school teachers' perceptions on CLIL instruction and assessment in universities: A case study. *Acta Scientiarum. Education. Maringá, 39*(1), 41-53. https://dialnet.unirioja.es/servlet/articulo?codigo=5827650

Gürel, E., & Tat, M. (2017). SWOT analysis: A theoretical review. *The Journal of International Social Research, 10*(51), 994–1006. doi:10.17719/jisr.2017.1832

Gutierez, S. B. (2021). Collaborative lesson planning as a positive 'dissonance' to the teachers' individual planning practices: Characterizing the features through reflections-on-action. *Teacher Development, 25*(1), 37–52. doi:10.1080/13664530.2020.1856177

Gutiérrez Gamboa, M., & Custodio Espinar, M. (2021). CLIL teacher's initial education: a study of undergraduate and postgraduate student teachers. *Encuentro, 29,* 104-119. https://ebuah.uah.es/dspace/handle/10017/47069

Gutiérrez Gamboa, M., & Custodio Espinar, M. (2021). CLIL teacher's initial education: A study of undergraduate and postgraduate student teachers. *Encuentro, 29,* 104–119. doi:10.37536/ej.2021.29.1927

Guzmán, D. B. (2019). Technology Integration for the Professional Development of English Teachers. *Tecné, Episteme y Didaxis: TED, 46,* 157-168. http://www.scielo.org.co/scielo.php?script=sci_arttext&pid=S0121-38142019000200157

Guzmán-Alcón, I. (2019). Investigating the application of communicative language teaching principles in primary education: A comparison of CLIL and FL classrooms. *English Language Teaching, 12*(2), 88–99. doi:10.5539/elt.v12n2p88

Compilation of References

Ha Bui, T. (2022). English teachers' integration of digital technologies in the classroom. *International Journal of Educational Research Open, 3*, 100204.

Hamid, M. O., & Nguyen, H. T. M. (2016). Globalization, English language policy, and teacher agency: Focus on Asia. *The International Education Journal: Comparative Perspectives, 15(1)*, 26-44. http://openjournals.library.usyd.edu.au/index.php/IEJ/index

Hamodi, C., López Pastor, V. M., & López Pastor, A. T. (2015). Medios, técnicas e instrumentos de evaluación formativa y compartida del aprendizaje en educación superior. [Means, techniques and instruments of formative and shared assessment of learning in higher education.]. *Perfiles Educativos, 37*(147), 146–161. doi:10.22201/iisue.24486167e.2015.147.47271

Harme, B. K., Pianta, R. C., Downer, J. T., DeCoster, J., Mashburn, A. J., Jones, S. M., Brown, J. L., Cappella, E., Atkins, M., Rivers, S. E., Brackett, M. A., & Hamagami, A. (2013). Teaching through interactions: Testing a developmental framework of teacher effectiveness in over 4,000 classrooms. *The Elementary School Journal, 113*(4), 461–487. doi:10.1086/669616 PMID:34497425

Harslett, M., Harrison, B., Godfrey, J., Partington, G., & Richer, K. (2000). Teacher Perceptions of the Characteristics of Effective Teachers of Aboriginal Middle School Students. *The Australian Journal of Teacher Education, 25*(2). doi:10.14221/ajte.2000v25n2.4

Hernandez de Menendez, M., Escobar Díaz, C., & Morales-Menendez, R. (2020). Technologies for the future of learning: State of the art. *International Journal on Interactive Design and Manufacturing, 14*(2), 683–695. doi:10.100712008-019-00640-0

Hersi, A., Horan, D., & Lewis, M. (2016). Redefining 'community' through collaboration and co-teaching: A case study of an ESOL specialist, a literacy specialist, and a fifth-grade teacher. *Teachers and Teaching, 22*(8), 927–946. doi:10.1080/13540602.2016.1200543

Hill, F., Mammarella, I. C., Devine, A., Caviola, S., Passolunghi, M. C., & Szűcs, D. (2016). Maths anxiety in primary and secondary school students: Gender differences, developmental changes and anxiety specificity. *Learning and Individual Differences, 48*, 45–53. doi:10.1016/j.lindif.2016.02.006

Hillyard, S. (2011). First steps in CLIL: Training the teachers. *Latin American Journal of Content & Language Integrated Learning, 4*(2), 1–12. doi:10.5294/laclil.2011.4.2.1

Hiver, P., Whiteside, Z., Sánchez Solarte, A., & Kim, C. J. (2021). Language teacher metacognition: Beyond the mirror. *Innovation in Language Learning and Teaching, 15*(1), 52–65. doi:10.1080/17501229.2019.1675666

Hobson, A. J., Ashby, P., Malderez, A., & Tomlinson, P. D. (2009). Mentoring beginning teachers: What we know and what we don't. *Teaching and Teacher Education, 25*(1), 207–216. doi:10.1016/j.tate.2008.09.001

Honigsfeld, A., & Dove, M. G. (2016). Co-teaching ELLs: Riding a tandem bike. *Educational Leadership, 73*(4), 56–60.

Honkamaa, P., Jäppinen, J., & Woodward, C. (2007). A Lightweight Approach for Augmented Reality on Camera Phones using 2D Images to Simulate in 3D. *MUM '07: Proceedings of the 6th international conference on Mobile and ubiquitous multimedia*, (pp. 155-159). ACM. 10.1145/1329469.1329490

Horning, A. (1979). Teaching as performance. *The Journal of General Education, 31*(3), 185–194.

Hu, Y. C. (2019). Constructing a Bilingual-Education Internship Management Platform to Explore Factors Influencing College Students' Internship Outcome. *Saudi Journal of Humanities and Social Sciences, 4*(1), 21-28. ISSN 2415-6248. Doi:10.21276/sjhss.2019.4.1.3

Huang, R., Spector, J. M., & Yang, J. (2019). *Educational Technology a Primer for the 21st Century*. Springer Nature. doi:10.1007/978-981-13-6643-7

Hugill, P. J. (2016). The Power of Knowledge: How Information and Technology Made the Modern World. *Journal of Historical Geography, 52*, 123–124. doi:10.1016/j.jhg.2015.06.007

Hu, J., & Gao, X. (2021). Understanding subject teachers' language-related pedagogical practices in content and language integrated learning classrooms. *Language Awareness, 30*(1), 42–61. doi:10.1080/09658416.2020.1768265

Hultgren, A. K., & Lasagabaster, D. (2019). Plenary speeches English medium instruction: Global views and countries in focus. *Language Teaching, 52*(02), 231–248. doi:10.1017/S0261444816000380

Ibrahim, N. (2020). The multilingual picturebook in English language teaching: Linguistic and cultural identity. *Children's Literature in English Language Education, 8*(2), 12–38.

Imbernón, F. & Colén, M. T. (2015). Los vaivenes de la formación inicial del profesorado. Una reforma siempre inacabada. [The ups and downs of initial teacher training. A reform always unfinished.] *Tendencias pedagógicas, 25*, 57-76.

Imbernón, F. (2007). *Diez ideas clave. La formación permanente del profesorado. Nuevas ideas para formar en la innovación y el cambio [Ten key ideas. Ongoing teacher training. New ideas to train in innovation and change.*]. Graó.

Institut zur Qualitätsentwicklung im Bildungswesen [Institute for quality development in education] [IQB]. (2019). *VERA VER gleichs Arbeiten in der 3. und 8 [VERA comparative work in the 3rd and 8th grades]*. IQB

Ioannou Georgiou, S. (2011). Guidelines for CLIL Implementation in Primary and Preprimary Education. Unter. http://www.academia.edu/15067157/Guidelines_for_CLIL_Implementation_in_Primary_and_Preprimary_Education

Ioannou-Georgiou, S., & Pavlou, P. (2011). *Guidelines for CLIL implementation in primary and pre-primary education*. PROCLIL, European Comission.

Ioannou-Georgiou, S., & Ramírez Verdugo, M. D. (2011). Stories as a tool for teaching and learning in CLIL. In S. Ioannou-Georgiou & P. Pavlou (Eds.), *Guidelines for CLIL implementation in primary and pre-primary education* (pp. 137–155). European Commission.

Iqbal, M. Z., Mangina, E., & Campbell, A. G. (2019). Exploring the use of Augmented Reality in a Kinesthetic Learning Application Integrated with an Intelligent Virtual Embodied Agent. *2019 IEEE International Symposium on Mixed and Augmented Reality Adjunct (ISMAR-Adjunct)*, (pp. 12-16). IEEE. 10.1109/ISMAR-Adjunct.2019.00018

Irie, K., Ryan, S., & Mercer, S. (2018). Using Q methodology to investigate pre-service EFL teachers' mindsets about teaching competences. *Studies in Second Language Learning and Teaching, 8*(3), 575–598. doi:10.14746sllt.2018.8.3.3

Isaeva, A., Semenova, G., Nesterova, Y., & Gudkova, O. (2021). Augmented reality technology in the foreign language classroom in a non-linguistic university. *XIV International Scientific and Practical Conference State and Prospects for the Development of Agribusiness-INTERAGROMASH 2021, (Vol. 273*, Article 12119). 10.1051/e3sconf/202127312119

Jackson, O. (2022). *Task-Based Language Teaching*. Cambridge University Press. doi:10.1017/9781009067973

Jalongo, M. R., Rieg, S. A., & Helterbran, V. R. (2007). *Planning for learning: Collaborative approaches to lesson design and review*. Teachers College Press, Columbia University.

Jansen, B. R. J., Hofman, A. D., Straatemeier, M., van Bers, B. M. C. W., Raijmakers, M. E. J., & van der Maas, H. L. J. (2014). The role of pattern recognition in children's exact enumeration of small numbers. *British Journal of Developmental Psychology, 32*(2), 178–194. doi:10.1111/bjdp.12032 PMID:24862903

Compilation of References

Jegede, O. (2011). Code Switching and Its Implications for Teaching Mathematics in Primary Schools in Ile-Ife, Nigeria. *Journal of Education and Practice, 2*(10), 41–54. https://www.iiste.org/Journals/index.php/JEP/article/view/78 1

Jenkins, J. (2015). Repositioning English and multilingualism in English as a lingua franca. *English in Practice, 2,* 49-85. doi:10.1515/eip-2015-0003

Jensen, E. (1998). *Teaching with the brain in mind.* Association for Supervision and Curriculum Development.

Jeřábek, T., Rambousek, V., & Wildová, R. (2014). Specifics of Visual Perception of The Augmented Reality in The Context of Education. *Procedia: Social and Behavioral Sciences, 159,* 598–604. doi:10.1016/j.sbspro.2014.12.432

Jewitt, C., & Kress, G. R. (2008). *Multimodal literacy.* Peter Lang.

Jiménez-Catalán, R. M. (2016). Vocabulary profiles in English as a foreign language at the end of Spanish primary and secondary education. *RLA. Revista de Lingüística Teórica y Aplicada, 54*(1), 37–50. doi:10.4067/S0718-48832016000100003

Johnson, D. W., & Johnson, R. T. (2018). Cooperative learning: The foundation for active learning. In *Active Learning-Beyond the Future.* IntechOpen.

Jordan, N. C., Kaplan, D., Locuniak, M. N., & Ramineni, C. (2007). Predicting first-grade math achievement from developmental number sense trajectories. *Learning Disabilities Research & Practice, 22*(1), 36–46. doi:10.1111/j.1540-5826.2007.00229.x

Jovanović, A., & Mastilo, M. (2022). Formación de profesores de ELE para la enseñanza formal de los niños de la edad temprana: el caso de Serbia [Training of ELE teachers for formal teaching of early age children: the case of Serbia.]. *Anali Filološkog fakulteta [Annals of the Faculty of Philology], 34*(2), forthcoming.

Jovanović, A. (2016). *Waking up from the university dream. Intersection of educational ideologies and professional identity construction.* Lambert Academic Publishing.

Jovanović, A., & Filipović, J. (2013). Spanish teacher education programs and community engagement. *Hispania, 96*(2), 283–294. doi:10.1353/hpn.2013.0056

Jover, G., Fleta, T., & González, R. (2016). La Formación inicial de los Maestros de Educación Primaria en el contexto de la enseñanza bilingüe en lengua extranjera. *Bordón. Revista de Pedagogía, 68*(2), 121–135. doi:10.13042/Bordon.2016.68208

Jubran, S. M., & Arabiat, R. M. (2021). Using Translation in the Framework of Learning a Foreign Language from Learners' Perspectives. *Multicultural Education, 7*(8). doi:10.5281/zenodo.5167622

Julius, S. M. & Madrid, D. (2017). Diversity of Students in Bilingual University Programs: A Case Study, *The International Journal of Diversity in Education. 17*(2), 17-28. ISSN (print): 2327-0020, (online): 2327-2163.

Junta de Andalucia. (2011). *Boletín Oficial de la Junta de Andalucía, 135,* de 12 de Julio de 2011, 6-19. https://www.juntadeandalucia.es/boja/2011/135/boletin.135.pdf

Junta de Andalucia. (2015). *Boletín Oficial de la Junta de Andalucía, 60,* de 23 de Marzo de 2015, 9-696. https://www.juntadeandalucia.es/boja/2015/60/BOJA15-060-00831.pdf

Kalantzis, M., & Cope, B. (2012). *Literacies.* Cambridge University Press. doi:10.1017/CBO9781139196581

Kamwangamalu, N. M., & Virasamy, C. (1999). Zulu peer-tutoring in a multiethnic English-only classroom. *Tydskrif vir Taalonderrig, 33*(1), 60–71.

Kao, Y. T. (2022). Understanding and addressing the challenges of teaching an online CLIL course: A teacher education study. *International Journal of Bilingual Education and Bilingualism, 25*(2), 656–675. doi:10.1080/13670050.2020.1713723

Karagozlu, D. (2021). Creating a Sustainable Education Environment with Augmented Reality Technology. *Sustainability, 13*(11), 5851. doi:10.3390u13115851

Kasule, D., & Mapolelo, D. (2005). Teachers' strategies of teaching primary school mathematics in a second language: A case of Botswana. *International Journal of Educational Development, 25*(6), 602–617. doi:10.1016/j.ijedudev.2004.11.021

Kaufman, E. L., Lord, M. W., Reese, T. W., & Volkmann, J. (1949). The discrimination of visual number. *The American Journal of Psychology, 62*(4), 498–525. doi:10.2307/1418556 PMID:15392567

Kayapinar, U. (2021). *Teacher Education. New Perspectives*. IntechOpen Book Series. doi:10.5772/intechopen.94952

Kelly, M., Grenfell, M., Allan, R., Kriza, C., & McEvoy, W. (2004). *European profile for language teacher education: A frame of reference*. European Commission Brussels.

Kenney, S. (2005). Nursery Rhymes: Foundation for Learning (pp. 28-31). *General Music Today, 19*, 28–31. doi:10.1177/10483713050190010108

Kenyon, V. (2016). How can we improve mathematical vocabulary comprehension that will allow students develop higher-order levels of learning? *The STeP Journal, 3*(2), 47–61. http://insight.cumbria.ac.uk/id/eprint/2460/

Keong, Y. C., Sardar, S. S., Mahdi, A. A. A., & Husham, I. M. (2016). English-Kurdish Code Switching of Teachers in Iraqi Primary Schools. *Arab World English Journal, 7*(2), 468–480. doi:10.24093/awej/vol7no2.32

Kerr, P. (2016). Questioning 'English-only' classrooms: Own-language use in ELT. In G. Hall (Ed.), *The Routledge handbook of English language teaching* (pp. 513–526). Routledge. doi:10.4324/9781315676203-43

Kersten, K. (2010). DOs and DONT's bei der Einrichtung immersiver Schulprogramme. [DOs and DONT's in setting up immersive school programs.] In Bongartz, C.M.; Rymarczyk, J. (Eds.). Languages Across the Curriculum, 71-92. Peter Lang.

Kersten, K. (Ed.). (2010). *ELIAS – Early Language and Intercultural Acquisition Studies: Final Report*. Magdeburg University: ELIAS.

Kersten, K. (2005). Bilinguale Kindergärten und Grundschulen: Wissenschaft und Praxis im Kieler Immersionsprojekt. [Bilingual kindergartens and primary schools: Science and practice in the Kiel immersion project.] In P. Baron (Ed.), *Bilingualität im Kindergarten und in der Primarstufe. Zukunftschancen für unsere Kinder [Bilingualism in kindergarten and primary school. future prospects for our children]* (pp. 22–33). Niemieckie Towarzystwo Oswiatowe.

Kessler, G. (2018). Technology and the future of language teaching. *Foreign Language Annals, 51*(1), 205–218. doi:10.1111/flan.12318

Khan, T., Johnston, K., & Ophoff, J. (2019). The Impact of an Augmented Reality Application on Learning Motivation of Students. *Advances in Human-Computer Interaction, 2019*, Article 7208494. doi:10.1155/2019/7208494

Kihara, S., Jess, M., McMillan, P., Osedo, K., Kubo, K., & Nakanishi, H. (2021). The potential of Lesson Study in primary physical education: Messages from a longitudinal study in Japan. *European Physical Education Review, 27*(2), 223–239. doi:10.1177/1356336X20932950

Kim, S. (2021). 'Butter balla here!': The functions of humor in primary English classrooms in Korea. *English Teaching, 76*(3), 115–137. doi:10.15858/engtea.76.3.202109.115

Compilation of References

Kirsch, C., Aleksić, G., Mortini, S., & Andersen, K. (2020). Developing multilingual practices in early childhood education through professional development in Luxembourg. *International Multilingual Research Journal, 14*(4), 319–337. doi:10.1080/19313152.2020.1730023

Klein, E. J., Taylor, M., Onore, C., Strom, K., & Abrams, L. (2013). Finding a third space in teacher education: Creating an urban teacher residency. *Teaching Education, 24*(1), 27–57. doi:10.1080/10476210.2012.711305

Knezek, G., & Christensen, R. (2002). Impact of New Information Technologies on Teachers and Students. *Education and Information Technologies, 7*(4), 369–376. doi:10.1023/A:1020921807131

Koshiro, U. (1990). 'The Ordinary and the Extraordinary: Language and the Puppet Theatre. In L. R. Komniz & M. Levinson (Eds.), *The Language of the Puppet, Komninz.* The Pacific Puppetry Center Press.

Kossybayeva, U., Shaldykova, B., Akhmanova, D., & Kulanina, S. (2022). Improving teaching in different disciplines of natural science and mathematics with innovative technologies. *Education and Information Technologies, 27*(6), 1–23. doi:10.100710639-022-10955-3 PMID:35233175

Kostoulas, A. (2018). *A language school as a complex system: Complex systems theory in English language teaching.* PeterLang. doi:10.3726/b11892

Kostoulas, A. (2019). Repositioning language education theory. In A. Kostoulas (Ed.), *Challenging boundaries in language education* (pp. 33–50). Springer. doi:10.1007/978-3-030-17057-8_3

Kostoulas, A., & Stelma, J. (2017). Understanding curriculum change in an ELT school in Greece. *ELT Journal, 71*(3), 354–363. doi:10.1093/elt/ccw087

Kotsopoulos, D. (2007). Mathematics discourse: "It's like hearing a foreign language. *Mathematics Teacher, 101*(4), 301–305. doi:10.5951/MT.101.4.0301

Krashen, S. (1981). *Second language acquisition and second language learning.* Pergamon Press.

Krashen, S. (1998). Comprehensible output. *System, 26*(2), 175–182. doi:10.1016/S0346-251X(98)00002-5

Krashen, S. D. (2015). Remarks on language acquisition and literacy: Language acquisition and teaching, free reading, and its consequences, the use of the first language, writing, and the great native speaker teacher debate. *Indonesian JELT, 10*(1), 1–17.

Krause, L. S., & Prinsloo, M. (2016). Translanguaging in a township primary school: Policy and practice. *Southern African Linguistics and Applied Language Studies, 34*(4), 347–357. doi:10.2989/16073614.2016.1261039

Kroesbergen, E. H., van Luit, J. E. H., van Lieshout, E. C. D. M., van Loosbroek, E., & van de Rijt, B. A. M. (2009). Individual differences in early numeracy: The role of executive functions and subitizing. *Journal of Psychoeducational Assessment, 27*(3), 226–236. doi:10.1177/0734282908330586

Kruchten, P., Nord, R., & Ozkaya, I. (2019). *Managing Technical Debt-Reducing Friction in Software Development.* Addison-Wesley Professional.

Kuhn, D. (1999). A developmental model of critical thinking. *Educational Researcher, 28*(2), 16–26. doi:10.3102/0013189X028002016

Kultusministerkonferenz [KMK]. (2006). *Konzepte für den bilingualen Unterricht – Erfahrungsbericht und Vorschläge zur Weiterentwicklung [Concepts for bilingual teaching - field report and suggestions for further development].* KMK. https://www.kmk.org/fileadmin/Dateien/veroeffentlichungen_beschluesse/2006/2006_04_10-Konzepte-bilingualer-Unterricht.pdf

Kurniawan, Y., & Luhukay, D. (2014). ERP Conceptual Model for School Using 4+1 View Model of Architecture. *International Journal of Information and Electronics Engineering, 4*(3), 201–208. doi:10.7763/IJIEE.2014.V4.435

Kuschmierz, P., Meneganzin, A., Pinxten, R., Pievani, T., Cvetković, D., Mavrikaki, E., Gra, D., & Beniermann, A. (2020). Towards common ground in measuring acceptance of evolution and knowledge about evolution across Europe: A systematic review of the state of research. *Evolution (New York), 13*(18), 1–24. doi:10.118612052-020-00132-w

Kusumoto, Y. (2018). Enhancing critical thinking through active learning. *Language Learning in Higher Education, 8*(1), 45–63. doi:10.1515/cercles-2018-0003

Kvale, S. (2007). *InterViews: An introduction to qualitative research interviewing.* SAGE.

Lacar, J. B. (2021). Inclusive Education at the Heart of Mainstream Language Pedagogu: Perspectives and Challenges. *International Journal of Linguistics. Literature and Translation, 4*(1), 124–131. doi:10.32996/ijillt

Ladilova, A., & Schroder, U. (2022). Humor in intercultural interaction: A source for misunderstanding or a common ground builder? A multimodal analysis. *Intercultural Pragmatics, 19*(1), 71–101. doi:10.1515/ip-2022-0003

Lahuerta, A. (2020). Analysis of accuracy in the writing of EFL students enrolled on CLIL and non-CLIL programmes: The impact of grade and gender. *Language Learning Journal, 48*(2), 121–132. doi:10.1080/09571736.2017.1303745

Lai, J. Y., & Chang, L. T. (2021). Impacts of Augmented Reality Apps on First Graders' Motivation and Performance in English Vocabulary Learning. *SAGE Open, 11*(4), 1–13. doi:10.1177/21582440211047549

Lao, C., & Krashen, S. (2014). Language acquisition without speaking and without study. *Journal of Bilingual Education Research and Instruction, 16*(1), 215–221.

Lasagabaster, D. (2011). English achievement and student motivation in CLIL and EFL settings. *Innovation in Language Learning and Teaching, 5*(1), 3–18. doi:10.1080/17501229.2010.519030

Lasagabaster, D. (2022). *English-Medium Instruction in Higher Education (Elements in Language Teaching).* Cambridge University Press., doi:10.1017/9781108903493

Lasagabaster, D., & Doiz, A. (2017). A longitudinal study on the impact of CLIL on affective factors. *Applied Linguistics, 38*(5), 688–712.

Lasagabaster, D., & Doiz, A. (Eds.). (2016). *CLIL experiences in secondary and tertiary education. In search of good practices.* Peter Lang. doi:10.3726/978-3-0351-0929-0

Lasagabaster, D., & Ruiz de Zarobe, Y. (2010). *AICLE in Spain: Implementation, Results and Teacher Training.* Cambridge Scholars.

Lasagabaster, D., & Ruiz de Zarobe, Y. (Eds.). (2010). *CLIL in Spain: Implementation, Results and Teacher Training.* Cambridge Scholars Publishing.

Laverick, E. K. (2018). *Project-based learning.* ELT Development Series. TESOL Press.

Lazăr, A. (2016). Suggestions on Introducing CLIL in Primary Schools. *2016 8th International Conference on Electronics, Computers and Artificial Intelligence.* 10.1109/ECAI.2016.7861134

Leach, R. J. (2016). *Introduction to Software Engineering* (2nd ed.). Taylor & Francis Group.

Lee, C. D., & Daiute, C. (2019). Introduction to Developmental Digital Technologies in Human History, Culture, and Well-Being. *Human Development, 62*(1-2), 5–13. doi:10.1159/000496072

Compilation of References

Lee, J., Joswick, C., & Pole, K. (2022). Classroom play and activities to support computational thinking development in early childhood. *Early Childhood Education Journal*. doi:10.100710643-022-01319-0

Leontjev, D., & DeBoer, M. (Eds.). (2020). *Assessment and Learning in Content and Language Integrated Learning (CLIL) Classrooms: Approaches and Conceptualisations*. Springer Nature.

Levine, G. S. (2011). *Code Choice in the Language Classroom*. Multilingual Matters. doi:10.21832/9781847693341

Lewin, K., & Grabbe, P. (1945). Conduct, knowledge, and acceptance of new values. *The Journal of Social Issues*, *1*(3), 53–64. doi:10.1111/j.1540-4560.1945.tb02694.x

Lewis, C., Perry, R., & Hurd, J. (2004). A deeper look at lesson study. *Educational Leadership*, *61*(5), 18–22.

Lewis, C., & Tsuchida, I. (1998). The basics in Japan: The 3 C's. *Educational Leadership*, *55*(6), 32–37.

Ley 4/2011 de 7 de marzo, de Educación de Extremadura (BOE n° 70, de 23 de marzo). Mérida, Consejería de Educación y Empleo, Junta de Extremadura.

Libarkin, J. C., Anderson, S. W., Beilfuss, M., & Boone, W. (2005). Qualitative Analysis of College Students' Ideas about the Earth: Interviews and Open-Ended Questionnaires. *Journal of Geoscience Education*, *53*(1), 17–26. doi:10.5408/1089-9995-53.1.17

Libarkin, J. C., Kurdziel, J. P., & Anderson, S. W. (2007). College student conceptions of geological time and the disconnect between ordering and scale. *Journal of Geoscience Education*, *55*(5), 413–422. doi:10.5408/1089-9995-55.5.413

Liebel, G., Burden, H., & Heldal, R. (2017). For free: Continuity and change by team teaching. *Teaching in Higher Education*, *22*(1), 62–77. doi:10.1080/13562517.2016.1221811

Lillo, J. (1995). Ideas de los alumnos y obstáculos epistemológicos en la construcción de los conceptos fósil y fosilización. [Students' ideas and epistemological obstacles in the construction of fossil concepts and fossilization.] *Enseñanza de las Ciencias de la Tierra 3*(3), 149-153. https://raco.cat/index.php/ECT/article/view/88245

Lin, A. (1996). Bilingualism or Linguistic Segregation? Symbolic Domination, Resistance and Code-Switching in Hong Kong Schools. *Linguistics and Education*, *8*(1), 49–84. doi:10.1016/S0898-5898(96)90006-6

Lin, A. (2013). Classroom Code-Switching: Three Decades of Research. *Applied Linguistics Review*, *4*(1), 195–218. doi:10.1515/applirev-2013-0009

Lin, A. M., & He, P. (2017). Translanguaging as dynamic activity flows in CLIL classrooms. *Journal of Language, Identity, and Education*, *16*(4), 228–244. doi:10.1080/15348458.2017.1328283

Liou, H. H. (2017). The Influences of the 2D Image-Based Augmented Reality and Virtual Reality on Student Learning. *Journal of Educational Technology & Society*, *20*(3), 110–121. https://www.jstor.org/stable/26196123

Little, D., & Kirwan, D. (2019). *Engaging with linguistic diversity: A study of educational inclusion in an Irish primary school*. Bloomsbury Academic. doi:10.5040/9781350072053

Liu, Y. (2020). Translanguaging and trans-semiotizing as planned systematic scaffolding: Examining feeling-meaning in CLIL classrooms. *English Teaching & Learning*, *44*(2), 149–173. doi:10.100742321-020-00057-z

Llevot-Calvet, N. (2018). *Advanced Learning and Teaching Environments. Innovation, Contents and Methods*. Intech Open Book Series. doi:10.5772/intechopen.68354

Llinares, A., & Lyster, R. (2014). The influence of context on patterns of corrective feedback and learner uptake: A comparison of CLIL and immersion classrooms. *Language Learning Journal*, *42*(2), 181–194. doi:10.1080/09571736.2014.889509

Llinares, A., Morton, T., & Whittaker, R. (2012). *The roles of language in CLIL*. Cambridge University Press.

Llinares, A., Morton, T., & Whittaker, R. (2012). *The Roles of Language in CLIL*. Cambridge University Press.

Longhurst, G. J., Stone, D. M., Dulohery, K., Scully, D., Campbell, T., & Smith, C. F. (2020). Strength, Weakness, Opportunity, Threat (SWOT) Analysis of the Adaptations to Anatomical Education in the United Kingdom and Republic of Ireland in Response to the Covid-19 Pandemic. *Anatomical Sciences Education*, *13*(3), 301–311. doi:10.1002/ase.1967 PMID:32306550

López-Hernández, A. (2021). Initial teacher education of primary English and CLIL teachers: An analysis of the training curricula in the universities of the Madrid Autonomous Community (Spain). *International Journal of Learning. Teaching and Educational Research*, *20*(3), 132–150. doi:10.26803/ijlter.20.3.9

López-Pastor, V. M. (2011). Best practices in academic assessment in higher education: A Case in formative and shared assessment. *Journal of Technology and Science Education*, *1*(2), 25–39.

Lorenzo, F. (2008). Instructional discourse in bilingual settings: An empirical study of linguistic adjustments in content and language integrated learning. *Language Learning Journal*, *36*(1), 21–33. doi:10.1080/09571730801988470

Lorenzo, F. (2016). Competencia en comunicación lingüística: Claves para el avance de la comprensión lectora en las pruebas PISA. [Competence in linguistic communication: keys to the advancement of reading comprehension in the PISA tests.]. *Review of Education*, *374*, 142–158.

Lova, Mª., Bolarín, Mª. J., & Porto, M. (2013). Programas bilingües en Educación Primaria: Valoraciones de docentes. [Bilingual programs in Primary Education: teacher assessments.]. *Porta Linguarum*, *20*, 253–268.

Lovorn, M., & Holaway, C. (2015). Teachers' perceptions of humour as a classroom teaching, interaction, and management tool. *The European Journal of Humour Research*, *3*(4), 24–35. doi:10.7592/EJHR2015.3.4.lovorn

Lo, Y. (2020). *Professional Development of CLIL Teachers*. Springer. doi:10.1007/978-981-15-2425-7

Lu, Y. H. (2020). A Case Study of EMI Teachers' Professional Development: The Impact of Interdisciplinary Teacher Collaboration. *RELC Journal*, *0033688220950888*. doi:10.1177/0033688220950888

Lv, Z., Lloret, J., & Song, H. (2021). Real-time image processing for augmented reality on mobile devices. *Journal of Real-Time Image Processing*, *18*(2), 245–248. doi:10.100711554-021-01097-9

Lyster, R. (2007). *Learning and teaching languages through content. A counterbalanced approach*. Benjamins. doi:10.1075/lllt.18

Lyster, R., & Ranta, L. (1997). Corrective feedback and learner uptake: Negotiation of form in communicative classrooms. *Studies in Second Language Acquisition*, *19*(1), 37–66. doi:10.1017/S0272263197001034

Macaro, E., & Lee, J. H. (2013). Teacher Language Background, Codeswitching, and English-only Instruction: Does Age Make a Difference to Learners' Attitudes? *TESOL Quarterly: A Journal for Teachers of English to Speakers of other Languages and of Standard English as a Second Dialect*, *47*(4), 717–742. . doi:10.1002/tesq.74

Macaro, E. (2018). *English Medium Instruction: Content and Language in Policy and Practice*. Oxford University Press. doi:10.30687/978-88-6969-227-7/001

Compilation of References

Madden, G. J., Petry, N. M., Badger, G. J., & Bickel, W. K. (1997). Impulsive and self-control choices in opioid-dependent patients and non-drug- using control participants: Drug and monetary rewards. *Experimental and Clinical Psychopharmacology*, *5*(3), 256–262. doi:10.1037/1064-1297.5.3.256 PMID:9260073

Madrid, D., & Trujillo, F. (2001). Reflexiones en torno a la formación del profesorado especialista en lenguas extranjeras. [Reflections on the training of teachers specializing in foreign languages.] in Francisco Javier Perales Palacios, Antonio Luis García Ruiz y Luis Rico (eds.) Las didácticas de las áreas curriculares en el siglo XXI. Granada: Grupo Editorial Universitario, 1771-1778.

Madrid, D., & Pérez-Cañado, M. L. (2018). Innovations and challenges in attending to diversity through CLIL. *Theory into Practice*, *57*(3), 241–249. doi:10.1080/00405841.2018.1492237

Madrid, M., & Madrid, D. (2014). *La formación inicial del profesorado para la educación bilingüe [Initial teacher training for bilingual education.]*. Editorial Universidad de Granada.

Mages, W. (2020). Educational drama and theatre pedagogy: An integral part of training English-as-a-foreign-language teachers. *Scenario*, *1*(1), 12–24. doi:10.33178cenario.14.1.2

Magnusson, P., & Godhe, A. L. (2019). Multimodality in Language Education—Implications for Teaching. *Designs for Learning*, *11*(1), 127–137. doi:10.16993/dfl.127

Mahan, K. R. (2022). The comprehending teacher: Scaffolding in content and language integrated learning (CLIL). *Language Learning Journal*, *50*(1), 74–88. doi:10.1080/09571736.2019.1705879

Maharani, S. (2016). The use of puppet: Shifting speaking skill from the perspective of students' self-esteem. *Register Journal*, *9*(2), 101–126. doi:10.18326/rgt.v9i2.170-186

Majid, S. N. A., & Salam, A. R. (2021). A Systematic Review of Augmented Reality Applications in Language Learning. *International Journal of Emerging Technologies in Learning*, *16*(10), 18–34. doi:10.3991/ijet.v16i10.17273

Maluleke, M. (2019). Using code-switching as an empowerment strategy in teaching mathematics to learners with limited proficiency in English in South African schools. *South African Journal of Education*, *39*(3), 1–9. doi:10.15700aje.v39n3a1528

Mangen, A., & Velay, J.-L. (2010). Digitizing literacy: reflections on the haptics of writing. *Advances in Haptics*. https://www.intechopen.com/articles/show/title/digitizing-literacy-reflections-on-the-haptics-of-writing

Mañoso-Pacheco, L., & Sánchez-Cabrero, R. (2022). Perspectives on the Effectiveness of Madrid's Regional Bilingual Programme: Exploring the Correlation between English Proficiency Level and Pre-Service Teachers' Beliefs. *Education Sciences*, *12*(8), 522. doi:10.3390/educsci12080522

Mariño Avila, C. M. (2014). Towards implementing CLIL at CBS (Tunja, Colombia). *Colombian Applied Linguistics Journal*, *16*(2), 151–160. doi:10.14483/udistrital.jour.calj.2014.2.a02

Marlina, R. (2013). Globalization, internationalization, and language education: An academic program for global citizens. *Multilingual Education*, *3*(1), 5. doi:10.1186/2191-5059-3-5

Marqués Ibáñez, A. (2017). Kamishibai: An intangible cultural heritage of Japanese culture and its application in Infant Education. *Képzésésgyakorlat: Training and practice*, *15*(1-2), 25-44.

Marrahí-Gómez, M., & Belda-Medina, J. (2020). The Application of Augmented Reality (AR) to Language Learning and its Impact on Student Motivation. *International Journal of Linguistics Studies*, *2*(2), 7–14. doi:10.32996/ijls.2022.2.2.2

Marsh, D. (2002). CLIL/EMILE. The European dimension: actions, trends and foresight potential. Jyväskylä: UniCOM.

Marsh, D. (2002). *Integrating language with non-language content, in a dual-focused learning environment*. CLIL/EMILE-The European Dimension: Actions, Trends and Foresight Potential.

Marsh, D. (2012). *Content and language integrated (CLIL) A development trajectory*. Servicio de publicaciones de la Universidad de Córdoba.

Marsh, D. (2017). Preface. In D. Lee Fields, 101 Scaffolding techniques for language teaching and learning: EMI, ELT, ESL, CLIL, EFL (pp. 9-10). Octaedro S.L.

Marsh, D. (Ed.). (2002). *CLIL/EMILE. The European dimension. Actions, trends, and foresight potential*. University of Jyväskylä. http://urn.fi/URN:NBN:fi:jyu-201511093614

Marsh, D. (2013). *Content and Language Integrated Learning (CLIL). A development trajectory*. Servicio de Publicaciones de la Universidad de Córdoba.

Marsh, D. (Ed.). (2002). *CLIL/EMILE—The European Dimension: Actions, Trends and Foresight Potential*. European Commission.

Marsh, D., & Langé, G. (Eds.). (1999). *Implementing Content and Language Integrated Learning: A Research-Driven Foundation Reader*. University of Jyväskylä.

Marsh, D., Mehisto, P., Wolff, D., & Frigols, M. J. (2010). *European framework for CLIL teacher education: A framework for the professional development of CLIL Teachers*. European Centre for Modern Languages.

Martín del Buey, F., Granados, P.; Martín, Mª E., Juárez, A., García, A. & Álvarez, M. (2000). *Desarrollo de la Personalidad Eficaz en Contextos Educativos. [Effective Personality Development in Educational Contexts.]* Marco Conceptual. FMB.

Martín Pastor, M. E., & Durán Martínez, R. (2019). La inclusión educativa en los programas bilingües de educación primaria: un análisis documental. [Educational inclusion in bilingual primary education programs: a documentary analysis.] Revista complutense de educación.

Martínez-Agudo, J. D. D., & Fielden-Burns, L. V. (2021). What key stakeholders think about CLIL programmes: Commonalities and differences of perspective. *Porta Linguarum: revista internacional de didáctica de las lenguas extranjeras*, (35), 221-237. doi:10.30827/portalin.v0i35.15320

Massler, U., & Burmeister, P. (2010). *CLIL und Immersion. Fremdsprachlicher Sachfachunterricht in der Grundschule [Concepts for bilingual teaching - field report and suggestions for further development]*. Westermann.

Mattheoudakis, M., Alexiou, T., & Laskaridou, C. (2014). To CLIL or Not to CLIL? The Case of the 3rd Experimental Primary School in Evosmos. In N. Lavidas, A. Alexiou, & A. Sougari (Eds.), *Major Trends in Theoretical and Applied Linguistics* (Vol. 3, pp. 215–234). De Gruyter Open Poland. doi:10.2478/9788376560915.p13

Mawela, A. S., & Mahlambi, S. B. (2021). Exploring teachers' views on code-switching as a communicative technique to enhance the teaching of mathematics in grade 4. *International Journal of Educational Methodology*, 7(4), 637–648. doi:10.12973/ijem.7.4.637

Maybin, J., Mercer, N., & Stierer, B. (1992). Scaffolding: learning in the classroom. In K. Norman (Ed.), Thinking Voices. The Work of the National Oracy Project (pp. 186–195). Hodder & Stoughton.

Mayilyan, H. (2019). Implementation of Augmented Reality Globe in Teaching-Learning Environment. *2019 IEEE Conference on Multimedia Information Processing and Retrieval (MIPR)*, (pp. 389-390). IEEE. 10.1109/MIPR.2019.00078

Compilation of References

May, L., & Abdul, A. (2020). Teachers' use of code-switching in ESL classrooms at a Chinese vernacular primary school. *International Journal of English Language and Literature Studies, 9*(1), 41–55. doi:10.18488/journal.23.2020.91.41.55

May, S. (2014). *The multilingual turn: Implications for SLA, TESOL and bilingual education.* Routledge.

McDougald, J., & Pissarello, D. (2020). Content and language integrated learning: In-service teachers' knowledge and perceptions before and after a professional development program. *Íkala. Revista de Lenguaje y Cultura, 25*(2), 353–372. doi:10.17533/udea.ikala.v25n02a03

McLeod, S. (2017). Kolb's learning styles and experiential learning cycle. *Simply psychology, 5.*

McMillan, P., & Jess, M. (2021). Embracing complex adaptive practice: The potential of lesson study. *Professional Development in Education, 47*(2-3), 273–288. doi:10.1080/19415257.2021.1884588

Medina, J. L. & Pérez, M. J. (2017). La construcción del conocimiento en el proceso de aprender a ser profesor: la visión de los protagonistas. [The construction of knowledge in the process of learning to be a teacher: the vision of the protagonists.] *Profesorado. Revista de currículum y formación del profesorado, 21*(2), 17-38.

Mehisto, P., Marsh, D., & Frigols, M. J. (2008). *Uncovering CLIL content and language integrated learning in bilingual and multilingual education.* Macmillan.

Mehisto, P., Marsh, D., & Frigols, M. J. (2008). *Uncovering CLIL, Content and Language Integrated learning in Bilingual and Multilingual Education.* Macmillan.

Mehisto, P., Marsh, D., & Frigols, M. J. (2008). *Uncovering CLIL: Content and language integrated learning in bilingual and multilingual education.* Macmillan Education.

Mehisto, P., Marsh, D., & Frigols, M. J. (2008). *Uncovering CLIL: Content and language integrated learning in bilingual education and multilingual education.* MacMillan.

Melara Gutiérrez, F. J., & González López, I. (2016). Sketching the figure of a bilingual teacher: Designing a profile of competencies. *Revista Española de Pedagogía, 74*(264), 357–380.

Melara Gutiérrez, F. J., & González López, I. (2016). Trazos para el diseño del perfil competencial de la figura del maestro bilingüe. *Revista Española de Pedagogía, 264,* 357–380. https://revistadepedagogia.org/lxxiv/no-264/trazos-para-el-d iseno-del-perfil-competencial-de-la-figura-del-maestro-bilin gue/101400001955/

Mellado, V., Blanco, L., & Ruiz, C. (1998). A framework for learning to teach science in initial primary teacher education. *Journal of Science Teacher Education, 9*(3), 195–219. https://www.jstor.org/stable/43156195. doi:10.1023/A:1009449922079

Melo-Pfeifer, S. (2015). Multilingual awareness and heritage language education: Children's multimodal representations of their multilingualism. *Language Awareness, 24*(3), 197–215. doi:10.1080/09658416.2015.1072208

Mendoza, N. B., Cheng, E. C., & Yan, Z. (2022). Assessing teachers' collaborative lesson planning practices: Instrument development and validation using the SECI knowledge-creation model. *Studies in Educational Evaluation, 73,* 101–139. doi:10.1016/j.stueduc.2022.101139

Mercer, N., Wegerif, R., & Major, L. (Eds.). (2020). *The Routledge international handbook of research on dialogic education.* Routledge.

Merrett, F., & Tang, W. M. (1994). The attitudes of British primary school pupils to praise, rewards, punishments and reprimands. *The British Journal of Educational Psychology, 64*(1), 91–103. doi:10.1111/j.2044-8279.1994.tb01087.x

Meyer, O. (2010). Introducing the CLIL-pyramid: Key strategies and principles for quality CLIL planning and teaching. *Basic issues in EFL-teaching and learning*, 11-29.

Meyer, O., Halbach, A., & Coyle, D. (2015). A pluriliteracies approach to teaching for learning. *ECML-Council of Europe*. https://pluriliteracies. ecml.at/Portals/54/publications/plu riliteracies-Putting-apluriliteracies-approach-into-practice
. pdf

Meyer, A., Rose, D. H., & Gordon, D. (2016). *Universal design for learning: Theory and practice*. CAST Professional Publishing.

Meyer, O. (2010). *Towards quality-CLIL: successful planning and teaching strategies*. Pulso.

Meyer, O. (2012). Introducing the CLIL pyramid: Key strategies and principles for quality CLIL planning and teaching. In M. Eisenmann & T. Summer (Eds.), *Basic issues in EFL teaching and learning* (pp. 265–283). Universitätsverlag WINTER.

Meyer, O. (2013). Introducing the CLIL-Pyramid: Key Strategies and Principles for CLIL Planning and Teaching. In M. Eisenmann & T. Summer (Eds.), *Basic Issues in EFL Teaching* (pp. 295–313). Universitätverlag Winter.

Meyer, O., & Coyle, D. (2017). Pluriliteracies Teaching for Learning: Conceptualizing progression for deeper learning in literacies development. *European Journal of Applied Linguistics*, 5(2), 199–222. doi:10.1515/eujal-2017-0006

Mihaljević Djigunović, J. (2012). Attitudes and motivations in early foreign language learning. *CEPS Journal*, 2(3), 55–74. doi:10.26529/cepsj.347

Milla Lara, M. D., & Casas Pedrosa, A. V. (2018). Teacher Perspectives on CLIL Implementation: A Within-Group Comparison of Key Variables. *Porta Linguarum*, 29, 159–180. https://www.ugr.es/~portalin/articulos/PL_numero29/8_MARIA%2 0DOLORES%20MILLA.pdf. doi:10.30827/Digibug.54032

Milla, R., & García Mayo, M. P. (2021). Teachers' and learners' beliefs about corrective feedback compared with classroom behaviour in CLIL and EFL. In K. Talbot, S. Mercer, M.-T. Gruber, & R. Nishida (Eds.), *The psychological experience of integrating language and content* (pp. 112–133). Multilingual Matters. doi:10.21832/9781788924306-012

Milla, R., & García Mayo, M. P. (in press). Feedback in CLIL: Teachers' oral and written choices and learners' response. In *D. Benegas & S. Zappa-Hollman, The Routledge Handbook of Content and Language Integrated Learning*. Routledge.

Miller, G. A. (1956). The magical number seven, plus or minus two: Some limits on our capacity for processing information. *Psychological Review*, 63(2), 81–97. doi:10.1037/h0043158 PMID:13310704

Miller, R. M., Chan, C. D., & Farmer, L. B. (2018). Interpretative phenomenological analysis: A contemporary qualitative approach. *Counselor Education and Supervision*, 57(4), 240–254. doi:10.1002/ceas.12114

Ministerio de Educación y Formación Profesional (2022). *Boletín Oficial del Estado, 52*, 24386-24504. https://www. boe.es/eli/es/rd/2022/03/01/157

Miranda, E., Vergara, O. O., Cruz, V. G., García-Alcaraz, J. L., & Favela, J. (2016). Study on Mobile Augmented Reality Adoption for Mayo Language Learning. *Mobile Information Systems*, 2016, 1069581. doi:10.1155/2016/1069581

Miras Páez, E., & Sancho Pascual, M. (2017). La enseñanza de ELE a niños, adolescentes e inmigrantes. [The teaching of ELE to children, adolescents and immigrants.] In A. M. Cestero & I. Penadés (Eds.), *Manual del profesor de ELE [ELE Professor's Manual]* (pp. 865–912). Servicio de Publicaciones de la Universidad de Alcalá.

Compilation of References

Mischel, W., Shoda, Y., & Rodriguez, M. L. (1989). Delay of gratification in children. *Science*, *244*(4907), 933–938. doi:10.1126cience.2658056 PMID:2658056

Mishina, L., & Wallace, A. (2004). *Relations between the use of puppetry in the classroom, student attention and student involvement*. Brooklyn College.

Mitchell, J., & Marland, P. (1989). Research on teacher thinking: The next phase. *Teaching and Teacher Education*, *5*(2), 115–128. doi:10.1016/0742-051X(89)90010-3

Modupeola, O. R. (2013). Code-switching as a Teaching Strategy: Implications for English Language Teaching and Learning in a Multilingual Society. *Journal of the Humanities and Social Sciences*, *14*(3), 92–94. doi:10.9790/1959-1439294

Montilva, J., Barrios, J., Besembel, I., & Montilva, W. (2014). A Business Process Model for IT Management Based on Enterprise Architecture. *CLEI Electronic Journal*, *17*(2), 3. doi:10.19153/cleiej.17.2.3

Moore, P., & Lorenzo, F. (2015). Task-based learning and content and language integrated learning materials design: Process and product. *Language Learning Journal*, *43*(3), 334–357. doi:10.1080/09571736.2015.1053282

Morán, C., Molina, S., & Sales, G. (2012). Aportaciones científicas a las formas de agrupación del alumnado. [Scientific contributions to the forms of grouping of students.]. *Revista de Organización y Gestión Educativa*, *2*, 13–18.

Morton, T. (2010). Using a Genre-Based Approach to Integrating Content and Language in CLIL. In C. Dalton-Puffer, T. Nikula, & U. Smit (Eds.), *Language Use and Language Learning in CLIL Classrooms* (pp. 81–104). John Benjamins., doi:10.1075/aals.7.05mor

Msimanga, A. (2015). Code-switching in the Teaching and Learning of Science. In R. Gunstone (Ed.), *Encyclopedia of Science Education* (pp. 160–161). Springer. doi:10.1007/978-94-007-2150-0_408

Muhammad, A., Khan, K., Lee, N., Imran, M. Y., & Sajjad, A. S. (2021). School of the Future: A Comprehensive Study on the Effectiveness of Augmented Reality as a Tool for Primary School Children's Education. *Applied Sciences (Basel, Switzerland)*, *11*(11), 5277. Advance online publication. doi:10.3390/app11115277

München, S. (2004). *Staatsinstitut für Schulqualität und Bildungsforschung München 2004: Lehrplan Sozialkunde [State Institute for School Quality and Educational Research Munich 2004: Social studies curriculum.]*. ISB. http://www. isb-gym8-lehrplan. de/contentserv/3.1. neu/g8. de/index. php

MUR. (Ministero Università della Ricerca (Italian Ministry of Education). (2012). Indicazioni Nazionalie Nuovi Scenari [National Indicators and New Scanarios]. MUR. Https://Www.Miur.Gov.It/Documents/20182/0/Indicazioni+Naziona li+E+Nuovi+Scenari/

Murillo, J., Almazán, A., & Martínez Garrido, C. (2021). La elección de centro educativo en un sistema de cuasi-mercado escolar mediado por el programa de bilingüismo. [The choice of educational center in a quasi-school market system mediated by the bilingualism program.] *Revista Complutense de Educación, 32(*1), 89-97. doi:10.5209/rced.68068

Murphy, V. (2014). *Second language learning in the early school years trends and contexts*. Oxford University Press.

Muszyńska, A., Urpí, C., & Gałązka, A. (2017). Teacher education through drama. CLIL practice in the Spanish context. Formación del profesorado a través de la dramatización: Práctica en el Aprendizaje Integrado de Lengua y Contenido en el contexto español [Teacher training through dramatization: Practice in Content and Language Integrated Learning in the Spanish context]. *Estudios Sobre Educación*, *32*, 179–195.

Naharro, M. (2019). Moving towards a revolutionary change in multilingual education: Does CLIL live up to the Hype? *Journal of e-Learning and Knowledge Society, 15*(1). Italian e-Learning Association. https://www.learntechlib.org/p/207524/

Nash, H., & Snowling, M. (2006). Teaching new words to children with poor existing vocabulary knowledge: A controlled evaluation of the definition and context methods. *International Journal of Language & Communication Disorders*, *41*(3), 335–354. doi:10.1080/13682820600602295 PMID:16702097

National Academies of Sciences, Engineering, and Medicine (2017). Promoting the Educational Success of Children and Youth Learning English: Promising Futures. *The National Academies Press*. doi:10.17226/24677

Navarro-Pablo, M., & Jiménez, E.G. (2018). Are CLIL Students More Motivated?: An Analysis of Affective Factors and their Relation to Language Attainment. *Porta Linguarum: revista internacional de didáctica de las lenguas extranjeras*, *29*, 71–90. . doi:10.30827/Digibug.54023

Nel, N., & Müller, H. (2010). The impact of teachers' limited English proficiency on English second language learners in South African schools. *South African Journal of Education*, *30*(4), 635–650. doi:10.15700aje.v30n4a393

Nezhyva, L. L. (2020). Perspectives on the use of augmented reality within the linguistic and literary field of primary education. *CEUR Workshop Proceedings*, *2731*, 297–311. https://ceur-ws.org/Vol-2731/paper17.pdf

Nguyen, T. T. (2018). *Interactional corrective feedback: a comparison between primary CLIL in Spain and primary CLIL in Vietnam* [Unpublished doctoral dissertation, Universidad Autónoma de Madrid, Spain].

Nguyen, M. H., & Dang, T. K. A. (2020). Exploring teachers' relational agency in content–language teacher collaboration in secondary science education in Australia. *Australian Educational Researcher*, *48*(4), 1–18. doi:10.100713384-020-00413-9

Nicholson, H. (2005). *Applied drama: The gift of theatre*. Palgrave Macmillan. doi:10.1007/978-0-230-20469-0

Nicolás, S. (2015). Introduction. In S. Nicolás Román & J. J. Torres Núñez (Eds.), *Drama and CLIL. A new challenge for the teaching approaches in Bilingual Education* (pp. 21–23). Peter Lang. doi:10.3726/978-3-0351-0832-3/11

Nieto Moreno de Diezmas, E., & Custodio Espinar, M. (2022). *Multilingual education under scrutiny: A critical analysis on CLIL implementation and research on a global scale*. Peter Lang., doi:10.3726/b20079

Nikolaidis, A. (2022). What is Significant in Modern Augmented Reality: A Systematic Analysis of Existing Reviews. *Journal of Imaging*, *8*(5), 145. doi:10.3390/jimaging8050145 PMID:35621909

Nikolov, M., & Mihaljević Djigunović, J. (2011). All shades of every color: An overview of early teaching and learning of foreign languages. *Annual Review of Applied Linguistics*, *31*, 95–119. doi:10.1017/S0267190511000183

Nikula, T. (2016). CLIL: A European Approach to Bilingual Education. In N. V. Deusen-Scholl & S. May (Eds.), *Second and Foreign Language Education* (pp. 1–14). Springer International Publishing., doi:10.1007/978-3-319-02323-6_10-1

Nikula, T., Dafouz, E., Moore, P., & Smit, U. (2016). *Conceptualizing integration in CLIL and multilingual education*. Multilingual Matters. doi:10.21832/9781783096145

Nikula, T., & Moore, P. (2019). Exploring translanguaging in CLIL. *International Journal of Bilingual Education and Bilingualism*, *22*(2), 237–249. doi:10.1080/13670050.2016.1254151

Nilsson, M. (2019). Foreign language anxiety: The case of young learners of English in Swedish primary classrooms. *Apples. Journal of Applied Language Studies*, *13*(2), 1–21. doi:10.17011/apples/urn.201902191584

Nishanthi, R. (2018). The importance of Learning English in Today World. *The International Journal of Trend in Scientific Research and Development*, *3*(1), 871–874. doi:10.31142/ijtsrd19061

Compilation of References

Nitsch, C. (2007). Mehrsprachigkeit: eine neurowissenschaftliche Perspektive. [Multilingualism: a neuroscientific perspective.] In T. Anstatt (Ed.), *Mehrsprachigkeit bei Kindern und Erwachsenen. Erwerb, Formen, Förderung [Multilingualism among children and adults. Acquisition, forms, promotion]* (pp. 47–68). Attempto.

Nonaka, L., & Takeuchi, H. (1995). *The knowledge creating company: How Japanese companies create the dynamics of innovation.* Oxford University Press.

Ntelioglou, B. Y. (2011). 'But why do I have to take this class?' The mandatory drama-ESL class and multiliteracies pedagogy. *Research in Drama Education, 16*(4), 595–615. doi:10.1080/13569783.2011.617108

Nukuto, H. (2017). Code Choice Between L1 and the Target Language in English Learning and Teaching: A Case Study of Japanese EFL Classrooms. *Acta Linguistica Hafniensia, 49*(1), 85–103. doi:10.1080/03740463.2017.1316631

Nunan, D. (2004). *Task-based Language Teaching.* Cambridge University Press. doi:10.1017/CBO9780511667336

Nurutdinova, A. & Bolotnikov, A. (2018). Study of Foreign Experience in Bilingual Education: Case Study: System of Higher (Professional) Education. *Current Issues of Linguistics and Didactics: The Interdisciplinary Approach in Humanities and Social Sciences* (CILDIAH-2018), 50. doi:10.1051/shsconf/20185001211

Nyati-Ramahobo, L., & Orr, J. R. (1993). Primary education and language teaching in Botswana. In K. D. Samway & D. McKeon (Eds.), *Common Threads of Practice: Teaching English to Children Around the World* (pp. 99–109). TESOL.

Object Management Group. (2022). *Web site.* OMG. https://www.omg.org

OECD. (2018). The Future of Education and Skills. *Education, 2030.* https://www.oecd.org/education/2030-project/contact/E2030%20Position%20Paper%20(05.04.2018).pdf

OECD. (2020). *How language learning opens doors.* OECD. https://www.oecd.org/pisa/foreign-language/opens-doors.pdf

Ortega, J. L. (2015). La realidad de la enseñanza bilingüe. [The reality of bilingual education.] In *Cuadernos de Pedagogía, 458,* 61-68.

Otheguy, R., García, O., & Reid, W. (2019). A translanguaging view of the linguistic system of bilinguals. *Applied Linguistics Review, 10*(4), 625–651. doi:10.1515/applirev-2018-0020

Otto, A., & Estrada Chichón, J. L. (2021). Analysing EMI assessment in higher education. *Revista Tempos E Espaços Em Educação, 14*(33), e15475. doi:10.20952/revtee.v14i33.15475

Otto, A., & Cortina-Pérez, B. (2022). *Content and Language Integrated Learning in Pre-primary Education: Moving Towards Developmentally Appropriate Practices.* Springer International.

Otwinowska, A., & Foryś, M. (2017). They learn the CLIL way, but do they like it? Affectivity and cognition in upper-primary CLIL classes. *International Journal of Bilingual Education and Bilingualism, 20*(5), 457–480. doi:10.1080/13670050.2015.1051944

Oxford Academic. (2013) *Call for Papers.* English Language Teaching Journal. (https://academic.oup.com/eltj/article-abstract/67/2/NP/532236

Özmen, K. S., & Balçıkanlı, C. (2015). Theatre acting in second language teacher education. In S. Nicolás Román & J. J. Torres Núñez (Eds.), *Drama and CLIL. A new challenge for the teaching approaches in Bilingual Education* (pp. 77–106). Peter Lang.

Paavola, S., Lipponen, L., & Hakkarainen, K. (2004). Models of innovative knowledge communities and three metaphors of learning. *Review of Educational Research*, *74*(4), 557–576. doi:10.3102/00346543074004557

Palacios, F. J., Gómez, M. E., & Huertas, C. (2018). Formación inicial del docente de AICLE en España: Retos y claves. [Initial CLIL teacher training in Spain: Challenges and keys.] *Estudios Franco-Alemanes 10*, 141-161. https://dialnet.unirioja.es/servlet/articulo?codigo=8019873

Palamar, S. P. (2021). *Formation of readiness of future teachers to use augmented reality in the educational process of preschool and primary education*. AREdu 2021: 4th International Workshop on Augmented Reality in Education, Kryvyi Rih, Ukraine. https://ceur-ws.org/Vol-2898/paper18.pdf

Palviainen, Å., Protassova, E., Mård-Miettinen, K., & Schwartz, M. (2016). Two languages in the air: A cross-cultural comparison of preschool teachers' reflections on their flexible bilingual practices. *International Journal of Bilingual Education and Bilingualism*, *19*(6), 614–630. doi:10.1080/13670050.2016.1184615

Pappa, S., Moate, J., Ruohotie-Lyhty, M., & Eteläpelto, A. (2019). Teacher agency within the Finnish CLIL context: Tensions and resources. *International Journal of Bilingual Education and Bilingualism*, *22*(5), 593–613. doi:10.1080/13670050.2017.1286292

Paramita, P. P., Anderson, A., & Sharma, U. (2020). Effective Teacher Professional Learning on Classroom Behaviour Management: A Review of Literature. *The Australian Journal of Teacher Education*, *45*(1), 61–81. doi:10.14221/ajte.2020v45n1.5

Paran, A. (2013). Content and language integrated learning: Panacea or policy borrowing myth? *Applied Linguistics Review*, *4*(2), 317–342. doi:10.1515/applirev-2013-0014

Paris, S., & Wingrad, P. (1990). How metacognition can promote academic learning and instruction. In B. F. Jones & L. Idoles (Eds.), *Dimensions of thinking and cognitive instruction* (pp. 15–51). Lawrence Erlbaum Associates.

Park, J.-E. (2014). English co-teaching and teacher collaboration: A microinteractional perspective. *System*, *44*, 34–44. doi:10.1016/j.system.2014.02.003

Patton, M. Q. (2002). Two decades of developments in qualitative inquiry: A personal, experiential perspective. *Qualitative Social Work: Research and Practice*, *1*(3), 261–283. doi:10.1177/1473325002001003636

Pavlenko, A., & Dewaele, J.-M. (2004). Language and emotions: A crosslinguistic perspective. *Journal of Multilingual and Multicultural Development*, *25*(2-3), 2–3.

Pavón Vázquez, V. (2014). Enhancing the quality of CLIL: Making the best of the collaboration between language teachers and content teachers. *Encuentro*, *23*, 115–127.

Pavón Vázquez, V., Ávila López, J., Gallego Segador, A., & Espejo Mohedano, R. (2015). Strategic and organisational considerations in planning content and language integrated learning: A study on the coordination between content and language teachers. *International Journal of Bilingual Education and Bilingualism*, *18*(4), 409–425. doi:10.1080/13670050.2014.909774

Pavón Vázquez, V., & Ellison, M. (2013). Examining teacher roles and competences in Content and Language Integrated Learning (CLIL). *Linguarum Arena*, *4*, 65–78.

Pavón Vázquez, V., & Gaustad, M. (2013). Designing bilingual programmes for higher education in Spain: Organizational, curricular and methodological decisions. *International CLIL Research Journal*, *1*(5), 82–94.

Compilation of References

Pavón Vázquez, V., Lancaster, N., & Bretones Callejas, C. (2020). Keys issues in developing teachers' competences for CLIL in Andalusia: Training, mobility and coordination. *Language Learning Journal, 48*(1), 81–98. doi:10.1080/095 71736.2019.1642940

Pavón, V. (2014). Perfil y competencia metodológica del profesorado para el Aprendizaje Integrado de Contenidos y Lenguas Extranjeras. [Profile and methodological competence of teachers for Content and Foreign Language Integrated Learning.] *Enclave docente, 5*, 8-13.

Pavón, V., & Ellison, M. (2013). Examining teacher roles and competences in content and language integrated learning (CLIL). *Linguarum Arena*, 4, 65-78. https://ojs.letras.up.pt/index.php/LinguarumArena/issue/view /293

Pavón, V., & Pérez, A. (2017). Enhancing disciplinary literacies: Languages of schooling and whole-school language projects in Spain. *European Journal of Applied Lingüistics*, 5, 153–175.

Pavón, V., & Rubio, F. D. (2010). Teachers concerns and uncertainties about the introduction of CLIL programmes. *Porta Linguarum, 14*, 45–58.

Pedrinaci, E. (1996). Sobre la persistencia o no de las ideas del alumnado en geología. [On the persistence or not of the ideas of the students in geology.] *Alambique*, 7, 27-36. http://hdl.handle.net/11162/25350

Pedrinaci, E., & Berjillos, P. (1994) Concepto de tiempo geológico: orientaciones para su tratamiento en la educación secundaria. [Concept of geological time: orientations for its treatment in secondary education.] *Enseñanza de las Ciencias de la Tierra, 2* (1), 240-251. https://raco.cat/index.php/ECT/article/view/88138

Pellicer García, M. P. (2017). *Analysis of corrective feedback in a multilingual classroom context from a CLIL perspective.* [Unpublished doctoral dissertation, Universitat de València, Spain].

Pena Díaz, C., & Porto Requejo, M. D. (2008). Teacher beliefs in a CLIL education Project. *Porta Linguarum, 10*, 151–161. doi:10.30827/Digibug.31786

Pennycook, A. (2007). The myth of English as an international language. In P. S. Makoni & A. Pennycook (Eds.), *Disinventing and reconstituting languages* (pp. 90–115). Channel View Publications.

Pennycook, A. (2017). *The Cultural Politics of English as an International Language.* Routledge. doi:10.4324/9781315225593

Pérez Cañado, M. L. (2015). Evaluating CLIL programs: Instrument design and validation. *Pulso. Review of Education, 39*, 79–112.

Pérez Cañado, M. L. (2015). Training Teachers for plurilingual education: a Spanish case study. In D. Marsh, M. L. Pérez Cañado, & J. Ráez Padilla (Eds.), *CLIL in Action: Voices from the Classroom* (pp. 165–187). Cambridge Scholars Publishing.

Pérez Cañado, M. L. (2016). Stopping the "pendulum effect" in CLIL research: Finding the balance between Pollyanna and Scrooge. *Applied Linguistics Review, 8*(1), 79–99. doi:10.1515/applirev-2016-2001

Pérez Cañado, M. L. (2016). Teacher training needs for bilingual education: In-service teacher perceptions. *International Journal of Bilingual Education and Bilingualism, 19*(3), 266–295. doi:10.1080/13670050.2014.980778

Pérez Cañado, M. L. (2017). CLIL teacher education: Where do we stand and where do we need to go? In M. E. Gómez Parra & R. Johnstone (Eds.), *Educación Bilingüe: tendencias educativas y conceptos claves* (pp. 129–144). Ministerio de Educación Cultura y Deporte.

Pérez Cañado, M. L., & Lancaster, N. K. (2017). The effects of CLIL on oral comprehension and production: A longitudinal case study. *Language, Culture and Curriculum, 30*(3), 300–316. doi:10.1080/07908318.2017.1338717

Pérez Murillo, M. D., & Steele, A. J. (2017). Initial Teacher Education for CLIL at Primary Education Level in Madrid: Key Issues and Challenges. In M. E. Gómez Parra & R. Johnstone (Eds.), *Educación Bilingüe: Tendencias Educativas y Conceptos Clave. Bilingual Education: Educational Trends and Key Concepts* (pp. 221-233). Ministerio de Educación. https://sede.educacion.gob.es/publiventa/educacion-bilinge-t endencias-educativas-y-conceptos-claves--bilingual-education al-trends-and-key-concepts/educacion-investigacion-educativa -lenguas/22107

Pérez, A. (2012). *Evaluación de programas bilingües: Análisis de resultados de las secciones experimentales de francés en el marco del Plan de Fomento del Plurilingüismo en Andalucía [Evaluation of bilingual programs: Analysis of results of the experimental sections of French within the framework of the Plan for the Promotion of Multilingualism in Andalusia.]*. Servicio de Publicaciones.

Pérez, A., Lorenzo, F., & Pavón, V. (2016). European bilingual models beyond linguafranca: Key findings from AICLE french programs. *Language Policy, 15*, 485–504. https://doi.org/10.1007/s10993-015-9386-7

Pérez-Cañado, M. L. (2021). Inclusion and diversity in bilingual education: A European comparative study. *International Journal of Bilingual Education and Bilingualism.* doi:10.1080/13670050.2021.2013770

Pérez-Cañado, M. L. (2018). Innovations and challenges in CLIL teacher training. *Theory into Practice, 57*(3), 1–10. doi:10.1080/00405841.2018.1492238

Pérez-Cañado, M. L. (2020). CLIL and elitism: Myth or reality? *Language Learning Journal, 48*(1), 4–17. doi:10.108 0/09571736.2019.1645872

Pérez-Cañado, M. L. (2020). Common CLIL (Mis)conceptions: Setting the Record Straight. In M. T. Calderón-Quindós, N. Barranco-Izquierdo, & T. Eisenrich (Eds.), *The Manifold Nature of Bilingual Education* (pp. 1–30). Cambridge Scholars Publishing.

Pérez-López, D., & Contero, M. (2013). Delivering educational multimedia contents through an augmented reality application: A case study on its impact on knowledge acquisition and retention. *The Turkish Online Journal of Educational Technology, 12*(4), 19–28. http://www.tojet.net

Perez-Vidal, C., & Roquet, H. (2015). The linguistic impact of a CLIL Science programme: An analysis measuring relative gains. *System, 54*, 80–90. doi:10.1016/j.system.2015.05.004

Petrov, P. D., & Atanasova, T. V. (2020). The Effect of Augmented Reality on Students' Learning Performance in Stem Education. *Information (Basel), 11*(4), 209. doi:10.3390/info11040209

Petrovych, O. B. (2021). The usage of augmented reality technologies in professional training of future teachers of Ukrainian language and literature. Proceedings of the 4th International Workshop on Augmented Reality in Education (AREdu 2021). Kryvyi Rih, Ukraine. May 11, 2021. *CEUR Workshop Proceedings, 2898*, 315–333. https://ceur-ws. org/Vol-2898/paper17.pdf

Peyton, J. (2002). The use of puppet. *English Education Journal* (EEJ), 216-228. http://erepository.unsyiah.ac.id/EEJ

Pfenninger, S. (2016). All good things come in threes: Early English learning, CLIL and motivation in Switzerland. *Cahiers de l'ILSL, 48*(48), 119–147. doi:10.26034/la.cdclsl.2016.429

Compilation of References

Pfenninger, S. E., & Singleton, D. (2017). *Beyond age effects in instructional L2 learning: Revisiting the age factor.* Multilingual Matters.

Phillipson, R. (1992). *Linguistic imperialism.* Oxford University Press.

Phillipson, R. (2009). *Linguistic imperialism continued.* Routledge.

Pica, T., Kanagy, R., & Falodun, J. (1993). Choosing and using communication tasks for second language instruction and research. In S. Crookes & S. M. Gass (Eds.), *Tasks and Language Learning: Integrating Theory and Practice* (pp. 9–34). Multilingual Matters.

Pierce, L. J., Klein, D., Chen, J. K., Delcenserie, A., & Genesee, F. (2014). Mapping the unconscious maintenance of a lost first language. *Proceedings of the National Academy of Sciences of the United States of America, 111*(48), 17314–17319. doi:10.1073/pnas.1409411111 PMID:25404336

Pimm, D. (1991). Communicating mathematically. In K. Durkin & B. Shire (Eds.), *Language in Mathematical Education* (pp. 17–23). Open University Press.

Pizarro Ruiz, J. P., Raya, J. J., Castellanos, S., & Ordóñez, N. (2014). La personalidad eficaz como factor protector frente al Burnout. [Effective personality as a protective factor against Burnout.] *Revista Iberoamericana de educación, 66,* 143-158.

Pižorn, K. (2009). *Dodatni tuji jeziki v otroštvu (Pregledna evalvacijska študija) [Additional foreign languages in childhood(A critical review)].* Ljubljana.

Plano-Clark, V. L. (2019). Meaningful integration within mixed methods studies: Identifying why, what, when, and how. *Contemporary Educational Psychology, 57,* 106–111. doi:10.1016/j.cedpsych.2019.01.007

Pla-Pueyo, S., González-García, F., & Ramos-García, A. M. (2021). Los fósiles y el profesorado en formación de Educación Primaria en la Universidad de Granada [Fossils and Primary Education pre-service teachers at the University of Granada]. *Lucas Mallada, Revista de Ciencias, 23,* 125-126. https://dialnet.unirioja.es/servlet/articulo?codigo=8166799

Pla-Pueyo, S., González-García, F., & Ramos-García, A.M. (in preparation). ¿Cómo tratan los libros de Educación Primaria los contenidos sobre tiempo geológico, fósiles y evolución? [How do primary school books deal with content on geological time, fossils and evolution?] *Enseñanza de las Ciencias. Revista de investigación y experiencias didácticas [Science Teaching. Magazine of investigation and didactic experiences].*

Pla-Pueyo, S., González-García, F., Ramos-García, A. M., & Ramón-Ballesta, A. (2022a). *Educación geológica formal y no formal de los estudiantes del Grado en Educación Primaria en la Universidad de Granada (España) [Formal and non-formal geological education of the students of Primary Education Teacher Training at the University of Granada (Spain)].* Paper presented at the XXI Simposio sobre Enseñanza de la Geología, Guadix, Granada.

Pla-Pueyo, S., González-García, F., Ramos-García, A. M., & Ramón-Ballesta, A. (2022b). *Gymkhana paleontológica por la Facultad de Ciencias de la Educación (Universidad de Granada, España) [Palaeontological gymkhana at the Faculty of Educational Sciences (University of Granada, Spain)].* Paper presented at the XXI Simposio sobre Enseñanza de la Geología, Guadix, Granada.

Pla-Pueyo, S., Ramos-García, A. M., & González-García, F. (2022). *Are future Primary Education teachers ready for bilingual education?* Paper presented at the meeting CIEB VIII 2022, Jaén, Spain.

Pliatsikas, C. (2020). Understanding structural plasticity in the bilingual brain: The Dynamic Restructuring Model. *Bilingualism: Language and Cognition, 23*(2), 459–471. doi:10.1017/S1366728919000130

Pliatsikas, C., Johnstone, T., & Marinis, T. (2014). Grey matter volume in the cerebellum is related to the processing of grammatical rules in a second language: A structural voxel-based morphometry study. *Cerebellum (London, England)*, *13*(1), 55–63. doi:10.100712311-013-0515-6 PMID:23990323

Poarch, G.J., & Bialystok, E. (2015). Bilingualism as a Model for Multitasking. *Developmental review*, *35*, 113–124.

Pokrivčáková, S. (2015). CLIL in Slovakia: projects, research, and teacher training (2005-2015). In S. Pokrivčáková, et al. (Eds.), CLIL in foreign language education: e-textbook for foreign language teachers. Nitra, Eslovakia: Constantine the Philosopher University.

Porcedda, M. E., & González-Martínez, J. (2020). CLIL Teacher Training: Lacks and Suggestions from a Systematic Literature Review. *Enseñanza & Teaching: Revista Interuniversitaria de Didáctica*, *38*(1), 49–68. doi:10.14201/et20203814968

Poulin-Dubois, D., Blaye, A., Coutya, J., & Bialystok, E. (2011). The effects of bilingualism on toddlers' executive functioning. *Journal of Experimental Child Psychology*, *108*(3), 567–579. doi:10.1016/j.jecp.2010.10.009 PMID:21122877

Prabhu, N. S. (1987). *Second language pedagogy* (Vol. 20). Oxford University Press.

Pressman, R. (2010). *Software Engineering, A practitioner's approach*. McGraw-Hill Companies, Inc.

Pulinx, R., & Van Avermaet, P. (2014). Linguistic diversity and education: dynamic interactions between language education policies and teachers' beliefs : a qualitative study in secondary schools in Flanders (Belgium). *Revue Francaisede LinguistiqueAppliquee, 19*(2), 9-27. doi:10.3917/rfla.192.0009

Qian, X., Tian, G., & Wang, Q. (2009). Codeswitching in the primary EFL classroom in China – Two case studies. *System, 37*(4), 719–730. doi:10.1016/j.system.2009.09.015

Ramos de Robles, S. L., & Espinet, M. (2013). Una propuesta fundamentada para analizar la interacción de contextos AICLE en la formación inicial del profesorado de ciencias. [A well-founded proposal to analyze the interaction of CLIL contexts in the initial training of science teachers.]. *Enseñanza de las Ciencias, 31*(3), 27–48. https://ensciencias.uab.cat/article/view/v31-n3-ramos-espinet. doi:10.5565/rev/ec/v31n3.777

Ramos, F., Delicado, G., & Alonso, L. (2021, July 25th). Student teaching in Spain in the time of COVID. *Language magazine. Improving Literacy and Communication*. https://www.languagemagazine.com/2021/07/25/student-teaching-in-spain-in-the-time-of-covid/

Ramos-García, A. M., & Fernández-Viciana, A. (2022). La formación en AICLE de los futuros docentes de Educación Primaria. [CLIL training for future primary school teachers.] In J. R. Guijarro Ojeda & R. Ruiz Cecilia (Eds.), *Investigación e innovación en lengua extranjera: una perspectiva global. Research and innovation in foreign language teaching: A global perspective* (pp. 477–493). Tirant lo Blanch.

Rao, Z., & Yu, P. (2019). Teaching English as a foreign language to primary school students in East Asia: Challenges and future prospects. *English Today, 35*(3), 16–21. doi:10.1017/S0266078418000378

Rea-Dickins, P. (2000). Classroom assessment. *Teaching and learning in the language classroom*, 375-401.

Redondo, B., Cózar-Gutiérrez, R., González-Calero, J. A., & Sánchez Ruiz, R. (2020). Integration of Augmented Reality in the Teaching of English as a Foreign Language in Early Childhood Education. *Early Childhood Education Journal*, *48*(2), 147–155. doi:10.100710643-019-00999-5

Reiser, B., & Tabak, I. (2014). Scaffolding. In R. Sawyer (Ed.), *The Cambridge Handbook of the Learning Sciences* (pp. 44–62). Cambridge University Press. doi:10.1017/CBO9781139519526.005

Compilation of References

Remer, R., &Tzuriel, D. (2015). "I Teach Better with the Puppet" –Use of Puppet as a Mediating Tool in Kindergarten Education– an Evaluation. *American Journal of Educational Research, 3(*3), 356-365. doi:10.12691/education-3-3-15

Report, R. R. (2021). Multilab direct replication of Flavell, Beach and Chinsky (1966): Spontaneous verbal rehearsal in a memory task as a function of age. *Advances in Methods and Practices in Psychological Science, 4*, 1–20.

Resnawati, A., Kristiawan, M., & Puspita Sari, A. (2020). Swot Analysis of Teacher's Professional Competency. *International Journal of Progressive Sciences and Technologies, 20*(1), 17–25. https://ijpsat.org/index.php/ijpsat/article/view/1704/924

Resnick, L. B. (1989). Developing mathematical knowledge. *The American Psychologist, 44*(2), 162–169. doi:10.1037/0003-066X.44.2.162

Reyes, R. G., & ... . (2016). Private Label Sales through Catalogs with Augmented Reality. In *Handbook of Research on Strategic Retailing of Private Label Products in a Recovering Economy (Coord. Mónica Gómez-Suárez y María Pilar Martínez-Ruiz)* (pp. 275–305). Business Science Reference (An imprint of IGI Global).

Richards, J. C. (2005). *Communicative language teaching today*. SEAMEO Regional Language Centre.

Richards, J. C., & Rodgers, T. S. (2014). *Approaches and Methods in Language Teaching* (3rd ed.). Cambridge University Press. doi:10.1017/9781009024532

Richards, J., Platt, J., & Weber, H. (1986). *Longman Dictionary of Applied Linguistics*. Longman. doi:10.1177/003368828601700208

Richland, L. E., Morrison, R. G., & Holyoak, K. J. (2006). Children's development of analogical reasoning: Insights from scene analogy problems. *Journal of Experimental Child Psychology, 94*(3), 249–273. doi:10.1016/j.jecp.2006.02.002 PMID:16620867

Rischawy, N. (2016). *Bilinguale Züge an Realschulen in Bayern. Vergleichsstudien zum Zuwachs englischsprachiger Fertigkeiten und Kompetenzen im Rahmen des Modellversuchs. [Bilingual traits at secondary schools in Bavaria. Comparative studies on the increase in English-language skills and competences within the framework of the pilot project.]* [Dissertation, Katholische Universität Eichstätt-Ingolstadt].

Ritter, R., Wehner, A., Lohaus, G., & Krämer, P. (2020). Effect of same discipline compared to different-discipline collaboration on teacher trainees 'attitudes towards inclusive education and their collaboration skills. *Teaching and Teacher Education, 87*, 102955. doi:10.1016/j.tate.2019.102955

Roberts, T. A., Vadas, P. F., & Sanders, E. A. (2018). Preschoolers' alphabet learning: Letter name and sound instruction, cognitive processes, and English proficiency. *Early Childhood Research Quarterly, 44*, 257–274. doi:10.1016/j.ecresq.2018.04.011

Robinson, P. (1997). State-of-the-art: SLA research and language teaching. *The Language Teacher Online, 2*(7), 7–16.

Rohrbach, N., Hermsdörfer, J., Huber, L. M., Thierfelder, A., & Buckingham, G. (2021). Fooling the size-weight illusion-Using augmented reality to eliminate the effect of size on perceptions of heaviness and sensorimotor prediction. *Virtual Reality (Waltham Cross), 25*(4), 1061–1070. doi:10.100710055-021-00508-3

Romano, M., Díaz, P., & Aedo, I. (2020). Empowering teachers to create augmented reality experiences: The effects on the educational experience. *Interactive Learning Environments*, 1–18. doi:10.1080/10494820.2020.1851727

Romero Alfaro, E., & Zayas Martínez, F. (2017). Challenges and opportunities of training teachers for plurilingual education. In J. Valcke & R. Wilkinson. Integrating content and language in higher education. Perspectives on professional practice, (pp. 205-225). Frankfurt am Main, Peter Lang.

Romero-Alfaro, E., & Zayas-Martínez, F. (2017). Challenges and opportunities of training teachers for plurilingual education. Integrating Content and Language in Higher Education. Perspectives on Professional Practice, 205 - 226. Peter Lang GmbH, 2017. ISBN 978-3-631-68126-8. doi:10.3726/978-3-653-07263-1

Romero, M. F. & Jiménez. (2014). El practicum del MAES y la formación inicial en la enseñanza de lenguas: Entre la realidad y el deseo. [The practicum of the MAES and initial training in language teaching: between reality and desire.]. *Lenguaje y Textos, 39*, 49–58.

Romero, M. F. (2014). *(Coord.). La escritura académica: diagnóstico y propuesta de actuación. Una visión desde los Grados de Magisterio* [*Academic writing: diagnosis and proposal for action. A vision from the Degrees of Teaching.*]. Octaedro.

Romero, M. F., & Trigo, E. (2015). Herramientas para el éxito. [Tools for success.]. *Cuadernos de Pedagogía, 458*, 16–21.

Romeu, M. C., Cerezo, E., & Llamas, E. (2020). Thinking skills in Primary Education: An Analysis of CLIL Textbooks in Spain. *Porta Linguarum: revista internacional de didáctica de las lenguas extranjeras [International Journal of foreign language diadetcs]*, (33), 183-200.

Roopa, D., Prabha, R., & Senthil, G. A. (2021). Revolutionizing education system with interactive augmented reality for quality education. *Materials Today: Proceedings, 46*(9), 3860–3863. doi:10.1016/j.matpr.2021.02.294

Rose, D. & Meyer, A. (2002). Teaching Every Student in the Digital age: Universal Design for Learning. Harvard Education Press.

Rose, D. (2001). Universal Design for Learning. *Journal of Special Education Technology, 16*(4), 64–67. doi:10.1177/016264340101600411

Roski, M., Walkowiak, M., & Nehring, A. (2021). Universal Design for Learning: The More, the Better? *Education Sciences, 11*(4), 164. doi:10.3390/educsci11040164

Ross, J. A. (2006). The reliability, validity, and utility of self-assessment. *Practical Assessment, Research & Evaluation, 11*(1), 10. doi:10.7275/9wph-vv65

Roussel, S., Joulia, D., Tricot, A., & Sweller, J. (2017). Learning subject content through a foreign language should not ignore human cognitive architecture: A cognitive load theory approach. *Learning and Instruction, 52*, 69–79. doi:10.1016/j.learninstruc.2017.04.007

Rowe, M. L. (2012, September). A longitudinal invetigation of the role of quantity and quality of child-directed speech in vocabulary developent. *Child Development, 83*(5), 1762–1774. doi:10.1111/j.1467-8624.2012.01805.x PMID:22716950

Ruiz de Zarobe, J. M., Sierra, & F. Gallardo del Puerto (2011). *Content and Foreign Language Integrated Learning. Contributions to multilingualism in European contexts*. Peter Lang.

Ruiz de Zarobe, Y. (2011). Which language competencies benefit from CLIL? An insight into applied linguistics research. In Y. Ruiz de Zarobe, J. M. Sierra, & F. Gallardo del Puerto (Eds.), *Content and Foreign Language Learning. Contributions to Multilingualism in European Contexts* (pp. 129–153). Peter Lang. doi:10.3726/978-3-0351-0171-3

Ruiz Pérez, M. C. (2019). The Practice of Bilingualism in Andalusia, Spain. *International Journal for Infonomics, 12*(4), 1916–1919. doi:10.20533/iji.1742.4712.2019.0197

Ryan, K. (1986). *The induction of new teachers*. Phi Delta Kappa Educational Foundations.

Compilation of References

Saadeh, H., Al Fayez, R. Q., Al Refaei, A., Shewaikani, N., Khawaldah, H., Abu-Shanab, S., & Al-Hussaini, M. (2021). Smartphone Use Among University Students During COVID-19 Quarantine: An Ethical Trigger. *Frontiers in Public Health*, *9*, 600134. doi:10.3389/fpubh.2021.600134 PMID:34381747

Sailer, M., Murböck, J., & Fischer, F. (2021). Digital learning in schools: What does it take beyond digital technology? *Teaching and Teacher Education*, *103*, 103346. doi:10.1016/j.tate.2021.103346

Salomé, F., Casalis, S., & Commissaire, E. (2022). Bilingual advantage in L3 vocabulary acquisition: Evidence of a generalized learning benefit among classroom-immersion children. *Bilingualism: Language and Cognition*, *25*(2), 242–255. doi:10.1017/S1366728921000687

Salvador-Garcia, C., & Chiva-Bartoll, Ò. (2017). CLIL in teaching physical education: Views of the teachers in the Spanish context. *Journal of Physical Education and Sport*, *17*(3), 1130–1138.

San Isidro, X. (2017). *CLIL in a multilingual setting: a longitudinal study on students, families and teachers*. University of the Basque Country.

San Isidro, X., & Lasagabaster, D. (2019). Monitoring of Teachers' Views on Both CLIL and the Development of Pluri-literacies: A Longitudinal Qualitative Study. *English Language Teaching*, *12*(2), 1–16. https://files.eric.ed.gov/fulltext/EJ1202200.pdf. doi:10.5539/elt.v12n2p1

Sanahuja, A., Moliner García, M., & Moliner Miravet, O. (2020). Organización del aula inclusiva: ¿Cómo diferenciar las estructuras para lograr prácticas educativas más efectivas? [Organization of the inclusive classroom: How to differentiate the structures to achieve more effective educational practices?]. *Revista Complutense de Educación*, *31*(4), 497–506. doi:10.5209/rced.65774

Sánchez, S., & Díez, E. (2013). La educación inclusiva desde el currículum: el Diseño Universal para el Aprendizaje. [Inclusive education from the curriculum: Universal Design for Learning.] En H. Rodríguez Navarro & L. Torrego Egido, (Coords.), Educación inclusiva, equidad y derecho a la diferencia: transformando la escuela (pp. 107-119). [Inclusive education, equity and the right to difference: transforming the school (pp. 107-119).] Wolters Kluwer.

Sánchez-Cabrero, R., Estrada-Chichón, J. L., Abad-Mancheño, A., & Mañoso-Pacheco, L. (2021). Models on Teaching Effectiveness in Current Scientific Literature. *Education Sciences*, *11*(8), 409. doi:10.3390/educsci11080409

Santagata, R., & Guarino, J. (2012). Preparing future teachers to collaborate. *Issues in Teacher Education*, *21*(1), 59–69.

Sasson, I., Yehuda, I., & Miedijensky, S. (2021). *Innovative learning spaces: class management and universal design for learning*. Learning Enviroments Research. doi:10.100710984-021-09393-8

Saville-Troike, M., & Barto, K. (2016). *Introducing second language acquisition*. Cambridge University Press. doi:10.1017/9781316569832

Scheffler, P., &Domioska, A. (2018). Own-language use in teaching English to preschool children. *ELT Journal, 72*(4), 374-83. doi:10.1093/elt/ccy013

Schleifer, P., & Landerl, K. (2011). Subitizing and counting in typical and atypical development. *Developmental Science*, *14*(2), 280–291. doi:10.1111/j.1467-7687.2010.00976.x PMID:22213901

Schroeder, S., & Chen, P. (2021). Bilingualism and COVID-19: Using a second language during a health crisis. *Journal of Communication in Healthcare*, *14*(1), 20–30. doi:10.1080/17538068.2020.1864611

Schröter, T., &MolanderDanielsson, K. (2016). English for young learners in Sweden: Activities, materials and language use in the classroom. *Litteraturochspråk, 11*, 47–73.

Schumm, J., Vaughn, S., & Leavell, A. (1994). Planning Pyramid: A framework for planning for diverse students' needs during content instruction. *The Reading Teacher, 47*, 608–615.

Schwarz, M., & Gorgatt, N. (2018). "Fortunately, I found a home here that allows me personal expression": Co-teaching in the bilingual Hebrew-Arabic-speaking preschool in Israel. *Teaching and Teacher Education, 71*, 46–56. doi:10.1016/j.tate.2017.12.006

Seidlhofer, B. (2007). Common property: English as a lingua franca in Europe. In J. Cummins & C. Davison (Eds.), *International Handbook of English Language Teaching* (pp. 137–149). Springer. doi:10.1007/978-0-387-46301-8_11

Setati, M., & Adler, J. (2000). Between languages and discourses: Language practices in primary multilingual mathematics classrooms in South Africa. *Educational Studies in Mathematics, 43*(3), 243–269. doi:10.1023/A:1011996002062

Setiawan, J. E. (2013). *Teacher's Belief and Student's Perception Regarding Content and Language Integrated Learning: A Case Study at SMA YPVDP Bontang* [Unpublished doctoral dissertation, Samarinda, Indonesia: Mulawarman University].

Shaban, M. S., Wahed, A., & Ismail, A. (2013). Exploring the nature of cooperation between teachers usingEnglish and those using Arabic as the medium of instruction in teaching ofclasses in United Arab Emirates. *American International Journal of Contemporary Research, 3*(8), 25–37. doi:10.30845/aijcr

Sharipova, I. (2021). Factors effecting friendly atmosphere in application educational technologies in ESP English language classes. *International Journal of Word Art*, 170–176. doi:. doi:10.26739/2181-9297-2021-2-27

Sharma, B., & Mantri, A. (2020). Assimilating Disruptive Technology: A New Approach of Learning Science in Engineering Education. *Procedia Computer Science, 172*, 915–921. doi:10.1016/j.procs.2020.05.132

Shavard, G. (2022). Teacher agency in collaborative lesson planning: Stabilising or transforming professional practice? *Teachers and Teaching, 28*(5), 1–13. doi:10.1080/13540602.2022.2062745

Shinga, S., & Pillay, A. (2021). Why do teachers code-switch when teaching English as a second language? *South African Journal of Education, 41*(1, Supplement 1), 1934. Advance online publication. doi:10.15700aje.v41ns1a1934

Sigrist, R., Rauter, G., Riener, R., & Wolf, P. (2013). Augmented visual, auditory, haptic, and multimodal feedback in motor learning: A review. *Psychonomic Bulletin & Review, 20*(1), 21–53. doi:10.375813423-012-0333-8 PMID:23132605

Simonova, O., & Kolesnichenko, A. (2022). The effectiveness of the augmented reality application in foreign language teaching in higher school. *SHS Web of Conferences, 137*, 01025. 10.1051hsconf/202213701025

Siqueira, D. S. P., Landau, J., & Paraná, R. A. (2018). Innovations and challenges in CLIL implementation in South America. *Theory into Practice, 57*(3), 196–203. doi:10.1080/00405841.2018.1484033

Skolnick Weisberg, D. (2008). The seductive allure of neuroscience explanation. *Journal of Cognitive Neuroscience, 20*(3), 470–477. doi:10.1162/jocn.2008.20040 PMID:18004955

Skutnabb-Kangas, T. (2012). Linguistic human rights. In P. M. Tiersma & L. M. Solan (Eds.), *The Oxford handbook of language and law* (pp. 235–247). Oxford University Press. doi:10.1093/oxfordhb/9780199572120.013.0017

Smith, F. (1976). *Comprehension and Learning: A conceptual Framework for Teachers*. Richard C. Owen Publishers.

Smith, J. A., & Eatough, V. (2011). Interpretative phenomenological analysis. In E. Lyons & A. Coyle (Eds.), *Analyzing qualitative data in psychology* (pp. 35–50). SAGE.

Smith, J. A., Flowers, P., & Larkin, M. (2009). *Interpretative phenomenological analysis. Theory, method and research.* SAGE.

Compilation of References

Smit, U., & Dafouz-Milne, E. (2012). Integrating content and language in higher education: An introduction to English-medium policies, conceptual issues and research practices across Europe. *AILA Review, 25*(1), 1–12. doi:10.1075/aila.25.01smi

Soares, C. T., Duarte, J., & Günther-van der Meij, M. (2020). 'Red is the colour of the heart': Making young children's multilingualism visible through language portraits. *Language and Education, 35*(1), 22–41. doi:10.1080/09500782.2020.1833911

Soboleva, A. V. (2019). A cognitive-style inclusive approach as a means of learner-centered EFL teaching mode implementation. In C. Denman & A. Al-Mahrooqi (Eds.), *Handbook of research on curriculum reform initiatives in English education* (pp. 122–135). IGI Global. doi:10.4018/978-1-5225-5846-0.ch008

Sommerville, I. (2016). *Software Engineering* (10th ed.). Pearson Education Limited.

Sörenson, R. (2008). *Seeing dark things.* Oxford University Press. doi:10.1093/acprof:oso/9780195326574.001.0001

Spain. (2007). Order ECI/3857/2007. *Boletín Oficial del Estado [Official State Bulletin],* No. 312. https://www.boe.es/eli/es/o/2007/12/27/eci3857

Srinivas Rao, P. (2019). The Role of English as a Global Language. *Research Journal of English, 4*(1), 65–79.

Stecker, G. C. (2019). Using Virtual Reality to Assess Auditory Performance. *The Hearing Journal, 72*(6), 20–23. doi:10.1097/01.HJ.0000558464.75151.52 PMID:34113058

Steelandt, S., Thierry, B., Boihanne, M. H., & Dufour, V. (2012). The ability of children to delay gratification in an exchange task. *Cognition, 122*(3), 416–425. doi:10.1016/j.cognition.2011.11.009 PMID:22153324

Stoller, F. (2006). Establishing a Theoretical Foundation for Project-Based Learning in Second and Foreign Language Contexts. In G. H. Beckett & P. C. Miller (Eds.), *Project-Based Second and Foreign Language Education: Past, Present, and Future* (pp. 19–40). Information Age.

Strom, K. J. (2015). Teaching as assemblage: Negotiating learning and practice in the first year of teaching. *Journal of Teacher Education, 66*(4), 321–333. doi:10.1177/0022487115589990

Strom, K. J., & Martin, A. D. (2017). *Becoming-teacher: a rhizomatic look at first-year teaching.* Springer. doi:10.1007/978-94-6300-872-3

Strom, K. J., & Viesca, K. M. (2021). Towards a complex framework of teacher learning-practice. *Professional Development in Education, 47*(2-3), 209–224. doi:10.1080/19415257.2020.1827449

Sun, J. (2013). Globalization and language teaching and learning in China. *International Journal on Integrating Technology in Education, 2*(4), 35–42. doi:10.5121/ijite.2013.2404

Swan, M. (2005). *Legislation by Hypothesis: The Case of Task-Based Instruction.* Applied Linguistics. Oxford University Press.

Sweller, J. (1998). Cognitive load during problem solving: Effects on learning. *Cognitive Science, 12*(2), 257–285. doi:10.120715516709cog1202_4

Tagnin, L., & Ríordáin, M. N. (2021). Building science through questions in Content and Language Integrated Learning (CLIL) classrooms. *International Journal of STEM Education, 8*(1), 1–14. doi:10.118640594-021-00293-0

Tardieu, C., & Dolitsky, M. (2012). *Integrating the task-based approach to CLIL teaching.* Cambridge Scholars Publishing.

Teed, R., & Slattery, W. (2011). Changes in Geologic Time Understanding in a Class for Preservice Teachers. *Journal of Geoscience Education*, *59*(3), 151–162. doi:10.5408/1.3604829

Thagard, P. (2000). *Coherence in thought and action*. MIT. doi:10.7551/mitpress/1900.001.0001

Thagard, P. (2006). *Hot thought: Mechanisms and application of emotional cognition*. MIT Press. doi:10.7551/mitpress/3566.001.0001

The Curriculum Development Council. (2017). *English Language Education. Key Learning Area Curriculum Guide (Primary 1-Secondary 6)*. Curriculum Development Council. https://www.edb.gov.hk/en/index.html

The Economic Times. (2018). Meet the new Google translator: An AI app that converts sign language into text, speech. *The Economic Times*. https://economictimes.indiatimes.com/magazines/panache/meet-the-new-google-translator-an-ai-app-that-converts-sign-language-into-text-speech/articleshow/66379450.cms?from=mdr

Then, D. C. O., & Ting, S. H. (2011). Code-switching in English and science classrooms: More than translation. *International Journal of Multilingualism*, *8*(4), 299–323. doi:10.1080/14790718.2011.577777

Thomas, M. H., & Dieter, J. N. (1987). The positive effects of writing practice on integration of foreign words in memory. *Journal of Educational Psychology*, *79*(3), 249–253. doi:10.1037/0022-0663.79.3.249

Ting, Y. L. T. (2010). CLIL appeals to how the brain likes its information: examples from CLIL-(Neuro) Science. *International CLIL Research Journal*, *1*, 1–18. http://www.icrj.eu/13/article1.html

Ting, Y. L. T. (2013). CLIL-Biology Towards IGCSE: Content and Language Integrated Learning Towards International Science Standards. *ELTons 2013 Award for Innovative Writing*. https://www.britishcouncil.org/contact/press/eltons-2013-winners

Ting, Y. L. T., Stillo, L., & Barci, G. (2022). Helping Mother Nature Compost Faster: Using Chemistry to Transform Trash into Treasure. *ELTons 2022 Award for Innovative in Learner Resource*s. https://www.teachingenglish.org.uk/article/eltons-innovation-awards-2022-finalists

Ting, Y. L. T. (2010). Pineapple please! *English Teaching Professional*, *71*, 24–26.

Ting, Y. L. T. (2022). Tertiary-level STEM and EMI: Where EFL and content meet to potentiate each other. *English Language Teaching Journal*, *76*(2), 194–207. doi:10.1093/elt/ccab093

Ting, Y. L. T. (n.d.). Preparing teachers for CLIL. In M. L. Pérez Cañado & P. Romanowski (Eds.), *The Cambridge Handbook of Multilingual Education*. Cambridge University Press.

Tomlinson, C. A. (2014). *The differentiated classroom: Responding to the needs of all learners* (2nd ed.). ASCD.

Topping, K. J. (2009). Peer assessment. *Theory into Practice*, *48*(1), 20–27. doi:10.1080/00405840802577569

Travé, G. (2013). Un estudio sobre las representaciones del profesorado de Educación Primaria acerca de la enseñanza bilingüe. [A study on the representations of primary education teachers about bilingual education.]. *Review of Education*, *361*, 1–14. doi:10.4438/1988-592X-RE-2011-361-149

Trend, R. D. (1998). An investigation into understanding of geological time among 10- and 11-year-old children. *International Journal of Science Education*, *20*(8), 973–988. doi:10.1080/0950069980200805

Trend, R. D. (2000). Conceptions of geological time among primary teacher trainees, with reference to their engagement with geosciences, history and science. *International Journal of Science Education*, *22*(5), 539–555. doi:10.1080/095006900289778

Compilation of References

Trujillo, F. (2010). La competencia lingüística como proyecto de centro: Retos, posibilidades y ejemplificaciones. [Language competence as a school project: challenges, possibilities and exemplifications.]. *Lenguaje y Textos, 32,* 35–40.

Tsybulsky, D. (2019). The team teaching experiences of pre-service science teachers implementing PBL in elementary school. *Journal of Education for Teaching, 45*(3), 244–261. doi:10.1080/09589236.2019.1599505

Tucci, C. (2019). Inglese, dopo 13 anni di scuola solo uno studente su tre capisce ciò che ascolta. *Sole 24 Ore* [English, after 13 years of school only one in three students understand what they hear. *Only 24 Hours.*].

Tzima, S., Styliaras, G., & Bassounas, A. (2019). Augmented Reality Applications in Education: Teachers Point of View. *Education Sciences, 9*(2), 99. doi:10.3390/educsci9020099

Ulrich, M., Keller, J., Hoenig, K., Waller, C., & Grön, G. (2014). Neural correlates of experimentally induced flow experiences. *NeuroImage, 86,* 194–202. doi:10.1016/j.neuroimage.2013.08.019 PMID:23959200

UML. (2022). *Web site to Unified Modeling Language.* UML. http://www.uml.org/what-is-uml.htm

UNESCO. (2014). Global Citizenship Education: Preparing learners for the challenges of the 21st century. UNESCO.

UNESCO. (2017). *La educación transforma vidas.* [*Education transforms lives.*] Organización de las Naciones Unidas para la Educación, la Ciencia y la Cultura [United Nations Education, Scientific, and Cultural Center]. https://unesdoc.unesco.org/ark:/48223/pf0000247234_spa

Üstünel, E., & Seedhouse, P. (2005). Why that, in that language, right now? Code-switching and pedagogical focus. *International Journal of Applied Linguistics, 15*(3), 302–325. doi:10.1111/j.1473-4192.2005.00093.x

Valverde-Berrocoso, J., Fernández-Sánchez, M. R., Revuelta Dominguez, F. I., & Sosa-Díaz, M. J. (2021). The educational integration of digital technologies preCovid-19: Lessons for teacher education. *PLoS One, 16*(8), e0256283. doi:10.1371/journal.pone.0256283 PMID:34411161

Van de Craen, P., Lochtman, K., Ceuleers, E., Mondt, K., & Allain, L. (2007). An interdisciplinary approach to CLIL learning in primary schools in Brussels. In C. Dalton-Puffer & U. Smit (Eds.), *Empirical Perspectives on CLIL Classroom Discourse* (pp. 253–274). Peter Lang.

van den Berg, M., Slot, R., van Steenbergen, M., Faasse, P., & van Vliet, H. (2019). How enterprise architecture improves the quality of IT investment decisions. *Journal of Systems and Software, 152,* 134–150. doi:10.1016/j.jss.2019.02.053

Vázquez-Ben, L., & Bugallo-Rodríguez, A. (2020). Teaching to teach the model of evolution in Primary Education: an experience with preservice teachers. In B. Puig, P. Blanco Anaya, M. J. Gil Quílez, & M. Grace (Eds.), *Biology Education Research. Contemporary topics and directions* (pp. 323–334). Servicio de Publicaciones de la Universidad de Zaragoza. https://zaguan.unizar.es/record/89959/files/BOOK-2020-124.pdf#page=323

Verdello Primary School. (2016). Verdello Primary School Curriculum. Verdello Primary School. https://www.icverdello.edu.it/wp-content/uploads/2016/10/INGLESE-1.pdf

Vilkancienė, L., & Rozgienė, I. (2017). CLIL teacher competences and attitudes. *Sustainable Multilingualism, 11*(1), 196–218. doi:10.1515m-2017-0019

Villa, A., & Poblete, M. (2004). Practicum y evaluación de competencias. [Practicum and evaluation of competences.] Profesorado. Revista de currículum y formación del profesorado, 8(2), 1-19.

Villabona, N., & Cenoz, J. (2022). The integration of content and language in CLIL: A challenge for content-driven and language-driven teachers. *Language, Culture and Curriculum, 35*(1), 36–50. doi:10.1080/07908318.2021.1910703

Villaescusa, M. I. (Coord). (2021). *Diseño Universal y Aprendizaje Accesible. Modelo DUA-A.* [*Universal Design and Accessible Learning. Model DUA-A.*] Generalitat Valenciana.

Vitsou, M., Papadopoulou, M., & Gana, E. (2020). Getting them back to class: A project to engage refugee children in school using drama pedagogy. *Scenario, 2*(2), 42–59. doi:10.33178cenario.14.2.3

Vygotsky, L. S. (1978). *Mind in society: The development of higher psychological processes.* Harvard University Press.

Walqui, A. (2006). Scaffolding instruction for English language learners: A conceptual framework. *International Journal of Bilingual Education and Bilingualism, 9*(2), 159–180. doi:10.1080/13670050608668639

Wattendorf, E., Westermann, B., Zappatore, D., Franceschini, R., Lüdi, G., Radü, E. W., & Nitsch, C. (2001). Different languages activate different subfields in Broca area. *NeuroImage, 6*(13), 624. doi:10.1016/S1053-8119(01)91967-6

Wernicke, M., Hammer, S., Hansen, A., & Schroedler, T. (Eds.). (2021). *Preparing teachers to work with multilingual learners.* Multilingual Matters.

Westphal, L. E. (2013). *Differentiating Instruction with Menus for the Inclusive Classroom. Science.* Routledge., doi:10.4324/9781003234296

Widdowson, H. G. (1994). The ownership of English. *TESOL Quarterly, 28*(2), 377–389. doi:10.2307/3587438

Widdowson, H. G. (2003). *Defining issues in English language teaching.* Oxford University Press. Stelma, J. & Kostoulas, A. (2021). *The intentional dynamics of TESOL.* De Gruyter. Stelma, J., & Fay, R. (2019). An ecological perspective for critical action in applied linguistics. In A. Kostoulas (Ed.), *Challenging boundaries in language education* (pp. 51–69). Springer.

Williams, L., Parthasarathy, P., & Molnar, M. (2021). Measures of Bilingual Cognition-From Infancy to Adolescence. *Journal of Cognition, 4*(1), 45. doi:10.5334/joc.184 PMID:34514316

Willis, D., & Willis, J. (2007). *Doing Task-Based Teaching.* Oxford University Press.

Wilson, G. L., & Blednick, J. (2011). *Teaching in tandem: Effective co-teaching in the inclusive classroom.* ASCD.

Wilson, M. (2002). Six views of embodied cognition. *Psychonomic Bulletin & Review, 9*(4), 625–636. doi:10.3758/BF03196322 PMID:12613670

Wode, H., Burmeister, P., Daniel, A., & Rhode, A. (1996). Die Erprobung von deutsch-englisch bilingualem Unterricht in Schleswig-Holstein: Ein erster Zwischenbericht. [The testing of german-English bilingual teaching in Schleswig-Holstein: A first interim report.]. *Zeitschrift für Fremdsprachenforschung, 7*(1), 15–42.

Wolff, D. (2012). The European framework for CLIL teacher education. *Synergies Italie,* (8), 105–116.

Word Book (Universal). (2022). *Web site.* Apple. https://apps.apple.com/us/app/wordbook-universal/id364030280

Word Lens. (2022). *Web site.* WL. https://universoabierto.org/2016/06/24/word-lens-traductor-de-realidad-aumentada/

Yildiz, E. P. (2021). Augmented Reality Research and Applications in Education. In D. Cvetković (Ed.), *Augmented Reality and Its Application.* Intech Open., doi:10.5772/intechopen.99356

Yin, R. (2003). *Case study research.* Sage Publications.

Zabala, A., & Arnau, L. (2007). *11 ideas clave: Cómo aprender y enseñar competencias* [*11 key ideas: How to learn and teach competencies.*]. Graó.

Compilation of References

Zabalza, M. A. (2011). El practicum en la formación universitaria: Estado de la cuestión. [The practicum in university education: state of the art.]. *Review of Education, 354,* 21–43.

Zayas-Martínez, F., & Estrada-Chichón, J. L. (2020). Instructed Foreign Language Acquisition (IFLA) at a Faculty of Education: German for Primary Schoolteachers under a CLIL Model. In Innovación Docente e Investigación en Educación. Avanzando en el proceso de enseñanza-aprendizaje, (pp. 1103 – 1113). Dykinson.

Zeichner, K. M. (2010). Nuevas epistemologías en formación del profesorado. Repensando las conexiones entre las asignaturas del campus y las experiencias de prácticas en la formación del profesorado en la universidad. [New epistemologies in teacher training. Rethinking the connections between campus subjects and internship experiences in teacher training at the university.] *Revista Interuniversitaria de Formación del Profesorado,* (68), 123-149.

Zein, S., & Coady, M. R. (Eds.). (2021). *Early language learning policy in the 21ˢᵗ century: An international perspective.* Springer. doi:10.1007/978-3-030-76251-3

Zhu, X., & Vanek, N. (2017). Facilitative Effects of Learner-directed Codeswitching: Evidence from Chinese Learners of English. *International Journal of Bilingual Education and Bilingualism, 20*(7), 773–787. doi:10.1080/13670050.2 015.1087962

Zuljevic, V. (2007). Puppetry *and language development in a first-grade library reading program: a case study.* [Doctoral dissertation, Washington State University]. ProQuest Dissertations and Thesis database. (UMI No. 3268779).

Zydatiß, W. (2000). Bilingualer Unterricht in der Grundschule. [Bilingual education in primary school.] Ismaning: Hueber.

Zydatiß, W. (2004). Sachfachlicher Kompetenzerwerb im bilingualen Sachfachunterricht. [Subject-related competence acquisition in bilingual subject teaching.] In A. Bonnet (Ed.), *Didaktiken im Dialog. Konzepte des Lehrens und Wege des Lernens im bilingualen Sachfachunterricht [Didactics in dialogue. Concepts of teaching and ways of learning in bilingual subject teaching]* (pp. 89–90). Lang.

About the Contributors

José Luis Estrada Chichón studied at the University of Oviedo, Spain, and at the University of Ulster, Northern Ireland. In 2017, he received his Ph.D. in language teaching from the University of Cádiz, Spain. He is currently working at the University of Cádiz as a lecturer of foreign languages didactics, bilingual education, and the CLIL approach. He worked before at Nebrija University, Spain, in the double bachelor's degrees in Modern Languages and Translation –of which he was also the director–, and Infant and Primary Education, as well as in the master's degree in bilingual education. His main research interests focus on language teaching-learning, foreign/second language acquisition in the classroom, bilingual education and teacher training, having published several articles in these academic fields.

Francisco Zayas Martínez studied in Cádiz, while spending long periods of time in England and Germany, and started his career as a university teacher in 1994. He was awarded his Ph.D. degree in 2002 for his thesis "La literature en la enseñanza del alemán como segunda lengua". Currently, he is full professor of German and Foreign Language Didactics at the University of Cádiz and member of the research group Estudios Multidisciplinares de la Enseñanza de Lenguas Extranjeras (Multidisciplinar Studies on Foreign Language Teaching). Professor Zayas Martínez has published several books and articles about 'German as a Foreign Language' and 'Foreign Language Acquisition and Learning', and has designed didactic materials for German, English, or Spanish. Between 2003 and 2011 he developed and directed the University School of Foreign Languages (CSLM - Centro Superior de Lenguas Modernas) at the University of Cádiz. In the last years, he has been working in the field of 'CLIL teaching in Higher Education'.

***

Amaia Aguirregoitia is an assistant professor at the Department of Didactics of Language and Literature at the University of the Basque Country (UPV/EHU). She has been working for the EHU/UPV since 2003. Her research interests span both educational computer science and teaching English as a foreign language. Some of her work has been on applying computer science and augmented reality (AR) to learn English as a foreign language. In the CLIL area, she has explored the use of technology to analyse the difficulty of texts as well as the integration of music, video, and AR to learn content through English.

Laura Alonso-Díaz is an associate professor in the Educational Sciences Department of the University of Extremadura in Caceres, at the Teacher Training College. She is Director of Employment and Apprenticeship Programs of the University of Extremadura. Her research topics include e-learning,

About the Contributors

teachers and social educators' training, bilingualism. She was awarded for teaching excellence in Social Sciences in 2014. From 2013 to 2016, she was the former Vice-Dean of Internship & Teaching Practice. She participated in a Marie Curie European Project related to ICT and intercultural affairs.

Heiner Böttger is a full professor of English Didactics and EFL at the Catholic University of Eichstaett-Ingolstadt, Germany. Chairman of the Early Language Learning Advisory Board, founded in Munich. Present research focuses on the preconditions for language learning within the language acquisition process. Explores how children develop communicative competences, which language strategies they use and when, the brain processes underlying language development, and the jigsaw pieces for acquiring three or more languages. Has published over 230 papers on English didactics and language research.

Francesca Costa is Associate Professor in English Language and Linguistics at the Università Cattolica del Sacro Cuore of Milan. She has also been a lecturer-trainer on EMI since 2016 and a teacher-trainer on CLIL since 2001. She taught English Linguistics at Università Cattolica del Sacro Cuore in Milan from 2002 to 2017, Scientific English at Università degli Studi di Pavia from 2006 to 2014 and English for Primary Education at Università degli Studi di Bergamo from 2017 to 2019. Her area of research focuses on applied linguistics, the teaching and learning of the English language at all levels of education (from primary to university) with a particular focus on codeswitching and translanguaging, Bilingual Education, CLIL (Content and Language Integrated Learning), ICLHE (Integrating Content and Language in Higher Education), EMI (English-medium Instruction) and scientific English. She graduated in Modern Languages from the Università degli Studi of Milan and holds a Bachelor degree in Science and a Doctorate in Education, Department of Languages (UK).

Magdalena Custodio Espinar was born in Granada, Spain in 1971. She received her PhD in Education in 2018 from Complutense University of Madrid. In 2019 she received the Extraordinary Doctorate Award. She graduated with honors from the same university and has Master's Degrees in Management and Leadership of Schools from UNIR (The International University of La Rioja) Logroño, La Rioja, Spain, and Teaching Spanish as a Second Language from Camilo José Cela University, Madrid, Spain. She was Technical Advisory Teacher for the Regional Ministry of Education, Madrid, Spain. She is currently teaching and researching in the Faculty of Human and Social Sciences at Comillas Pontifical University. Research interests include teacher training, didactic programming, CLIL, FLT, ELT, EMI, and co-teaching. She is Honorary Member of the Japan CLIL Pedagogy Association (J-CLIL).

Gemma Delicado-Puerto is an Associate Professor in the English Department of the University of Extremadura. She is Director of Mobility Strategy at University of Extremadura. She studied at Kalamazoo College, EEUU. She completed her Master of Arts at Western Michigan University, EE.UU. She holds a PhD in Humanities from the University of Chicago, EE.UU. Her research topics include languages in ICTs, bilingualism and internationalisation. She was awarded for teaching excellence in Humanities in 2017. She is being engaged in several European projects, including a Marie Curie. She is a former Associate Dean for International Affairs.

Ramiro Durán-Martínez is an associate professor in the English Studies Department at the University of Salamanca. He started his career as an Official School of Languages teacher and since 1997 he has dedicated his time to training ESOL teachers in the Primary and Secondary education sector. He

445

About the Contributors

has collaborated in international teaching placement schemes and participated in postgraduate courses in the areas of English Language Teaching and Bilingual Education. He has published several books and papers in these fields and he is currently engaged in research projects in the area of bilingual education and attention to diversity.

Valerio Ferrero is a PhD student at the University of Turin. He works on equity in education, democratic schooling, Philosophy for Children and language education. He is the author of several essays on these topics.

Isabel María Garcia Conesa has a degree in English Studies from the University of Alicante and a PhD from the National University of Distance Education (UNED). She is currently working as an associate professor at the Centro Universitario de la Defensa in San Javier (Spain). She has been awarded a scholarship by the Franklin Institute (University of Alcala de Henares, Spain) and the Radcliffe Institute for Advanced Study (Harvard University, USA), where she conducted a pre-doctoral research stay in the year 2012. Among her main lines of research, we can highlight the role of different women in literature and culture of the United States in contrast to Francophone writers. She also focuses on the study of the history of the teaching of English and gender studies.

Anastasia Gkaintartzi holds a PhD from the Department of Early Childhood Education, Aristotle University of Thessaloniki, specializing in bi/multilingualism and education in the field of Sociolinguistics. She is a member of the teaching staff at the Department of Language and Intercultural Studies, University of Thessaly, Greece. She is also a tutor at the Hellenic Open University in long-distance learning MA Programmes. She has participated in various research projects on multilingualism and plurilingual, inclusive education and is also an associate member of the ECML programme PALINGUI. She has widely published in international journals on bi/multilingualism and language teaching, migration (identities, llanguage ideology, translanguaging, inclusion) and plurilingual education.

Francisco González-García is a senior lecturer since 1995, Ph. D. in Biological Sciences, BA in Sociology and Political Sciences. Former Head of the Department of Experimental Sciences Education for 8 years, some other managerial positions for over ten years at the University of Granada. Scientific divulgator and columnist in local newspapers from Granada.

Ana Jovanović is an associate professor at the Department of Iberian Studies, Faculty of Philology, University of Belgrade. She graduated from the Department of Iberian Studies at the University of Belgrade and completed her master's and doctoral studies at Purdue University (USA). Her primary research interests reflect her transdisciplinary approach to topics related to second language acquisition, curriculum development, critical pedagogy, and intercultural education. She published two monographs and over 30 peer-reviewed articles in edited volumes and journals. She is currently the vice-president of the Association for Foreign Languages and Literatures of Serbia.

Antonio D. Juan has a degree in English Studies from the University of Murcia and a PhD from the National University of Distance Education (UNED) with the positive accreditation by the ANECA body, being given the Extraordinary Doctorate Award. He is currently working as a professor at the International University of La Rioja. He has been awarded a scholarship by University College (Cork,

About the Contributors

Ireland), the Franklin Institute (University of Alcala de Henares, Spain) and the Radcliffe Institute for Advanced Study (Harvard University, USA), where he conducted a pre-doctoral research visit in the year 2012. He is currently a member of the scientific committee of several national and international journals as well as a member of the editorial board of several international journals. He also belongs to the organizing and scientific committee of several conferences organized by the Athens Institute for Education and Research (Greece). Among his main lines of research we can emphasize the following aspects: cultural studies in the United States; gender issues associated with the role of women in the Anglo-American literature; or the teaching practice and process of English.

Achilleas Kostoulas is an applied linguist at the Department of Primary Education at the University of Thessaly. He holds a PhD and an MA in Teaching English to Speakers of Other Languages from the University of Manchester (UK), and an BA in English Language and Literature from the University of Athens (Greece). He has published extensively on issues of second/foreign language education and the psychological aspects of language teaching and learning.

Noelia Ruiz-Madrid is a Senior Lecturer at Universitat Jaume I, Spain, where she lectures Academic English, English language learning and teaching and digital genres at graduate and postgraduate level. Her research interests are MDA (Multimodal Discourse Analysis), academic and professional genres, and digital genres as well as ICLHE (Integrated Content and Language in Higher Education) and EMI. Her publications have appeared in Iberica, Discourse Studies, International Journal of English Studies, Language and Communication and Journal of English for Academic Purposes.

Cristina Manchado Nieto is an acting official adjunct professor in the Social Sciences, Languages and Literature Didactics Department of the University of Extremadura. She is also a Ph.D. student on bilingual education in the Innovation in Teacher Training Programme of the University of Extremadura. She studied Translation and Interpreting at the University Pablo de Olavide (Seville, Spain) and she holds three master's degrees (trade and marketing, teacher training, and Social Sciences research), and she has participated in several congresses, in the coordination and organisation of events and projects. Her research line focuses on bilingual education and didactics of foreign languages.

Lidia Mañoso-Pacheco has a PhD in English Linguistics, and is an Assistant Professor at the Faculty of Teaching Training and Education, Universidad Autónoma de Madrid. She works as a teacher trainer at the Department of Philology and its Didactics. Her research interests mainly focus on applied linguistics to English teaching and critical discourse analysis of media texts.

Elena Martín Pastor is an associate professor in the Didactics, Organization and Research Methods Department of the University of Salamanca. She teaches at the Faculty of Education and the Faculty of Psychology. She is a member of the research project titled "La atención a la diversidad en los programas bilingües de educación primaria: análisis del grado de inclusión del alumnado con necesidad específica de apoyo educativo", funded by the Spanish Ministry of Science and Innovation. She has published in the areas of inclusive education, teacher training and inmigrant students.

Ruth Milla is an assistant professor at the Faculty of Education of Bilbao (University of the Basque Country, UPV/EHU), where she teaches undergraduate courses on FL teaching. Dr Milla is a member of

447

About the Contributors

the Language and Speech research group (() and her research interests include EFL and CLIL contexts, teacher training, teachers' and learners' beliefs, and FL teaching techniques such as corrective feedback and collaborative writing.

Tanja Müller has been a research assistant at the Chair of English Didactics at the Catholic University of Eichstaett-Ingolstadt since 2011 and at the University Computer Centre at KUEI since 2020. Since 2021, she has also been a research assistant in the DFG project BLUME at the University of Wuerzburg/Bavaria

Sila Pla-Pueyo is a university lecturer and a writer. She currently works at the University of Granada with Early Childhood and Primary Education pre-service teachers. As a geologist and as a former English instructor, her research interests focus on the bilingual and non-bilingual teaching of contents related to geological time, palaeontology and evolution.

Ana María Ramos-García is a full-time lecturer at UGR since 2006. She holds a BA in Modern Languages, a MA in Bilingual Education and Ph. D. in English Linguistics. She has over five years' experience in teaching EFL at school and high-school level and over fifteen years' experience in teacher-training. Concerning research, she is particularly interested in ELT/EFLT, translation and bilingual education.

Gerardo Reyes Ruiz is an Actuary by training from the Faculty of Sciences-UNAM; He studied a Specialty in Econometrics in the Postgraduate Studies Division of the Faculty of Economics-UNAM. He obtained a Master's and Doctorate (with a scholarship from CONACYT and the Carolina Foundation) in Business Studies (actuarial profile) from the Faculty of Economics and Business of the University of Barcelona, Spain. In the Doctorate, he graduated with the highest honors awarded to a thesis of this nature; that is, obtainment of the qualification of Excellent Cum Laude. Later he did a postdoctoral stay at the Center for Economic, Administrative, and Social Studies (CIECAS) of the National Polytechnic Institute (IPN). His work experience has been in public education institutions (UNAM, UAEM, IPN, Centro de Estudios Superiores Navales-CESNAV) where he has had the opportunity to teach classes in Bachelor's, Specialty, Master's, and Doctorate.

Celina Salvador-Garcia is an Assistant Professor at Universitat Jaume I. Her academic research agenda focuses on methodological innovation and educational research. Hitherto, her research has mainly examined Content and Language Integrated Learning and Service Learning. She has published several articles that are stored in the main international databases focused on educational innovation. She is a member of the Endavant research group. She has participated in some research and innovation projects financed with public funds. In addition, she has carried out national and international research stays.

Y.-L. Teresa Ting is a tenured full-time Researcher at the Department of Chemistry & Chemical Technologies at the University of Calabria, Italy. She obtained her PhD in Neurobiology (Kent State, USA), studying learning and memory processes in rat-brain models, in vivo and in vitro, and taught Functional Human Neuroanatomy to medical students. After moving to Italy, she started teaching English to Italian students, for which she obtained an MA-ED in TEFL (East Anglia, UK). She researches how to apply cognitive neuroscience understandings regarding how the brain learns (or not) towards the design of STEM-instruction materials, using some in classroom research (ELTJ, IJBEB, etc.). A set

About the Contributors

of her upper-secondary CLIL-science materials received the 2013 ELTons Award for 'Innovative Writing'; in 2022 another set of STEM-materials for lower-secondary placed alongside BBC and National Geographic; she has written learning-materials for CUP. Teresa is also involved with teacher professional development for CLIL, EFL and Subject-instruction in Europe.

Laura Torres Zúñiga is a Lecturer at the Department of Philologies and Didactics of the Universidad Autónoma de Madrid, where she teaches English Language, Syllabus Design and Children's Literature in English to pre-service teachers of all educational stages. Her research interests center on contemporary short narrative forms, English language teaching and active learning methodologies.

Teresa Valverde-Esteve is an associate professor at the Department of Didactics of Physical Education, Arts and Music, at Universitat de València (Spain). She lectures Didactics of Physical Education and Body Expression at graduate and postgraduate students. Her research interests are focused on the benefits of the practice of Physical Education for Health, Social Justice, as well as the Pedagogical Models that Physical Education can be taught through, such as the CLIL, Non-linear Pedagogy or Service Learning, among others.

Magda Vitsou holds a PhD in Drama in Education from the Department of Theatre Studies, University of Peloponnese, Greece. She is a member of the Laboratory Teaching Staff in the Department of Early Childhood Education, University of Thessaly. She has majored in "Puppetry in education and art therapy", in London School of Puppetry and she has been certified in the development of levels of certification of the knowledge of Greek language as foreign / second. Her scientific interests and publications focus on issues of Drama in Education, puppetry, bilingualism and social life of minority groups. She has contributed to several research projects related to drama in education and school inclusion of students from minority background.

Index

A

Action Science 186-187, 189, 192, 201-204, 207
Action Theory 207
Active Education 64
Affective Filter 31-32, 40
Age-Appropriate Academic Language 273
Age-Appropriate Disciplinary and Academic Thinking Skills and Literacies 290
Andalusia 93, 106, 172, 352, 372, 377-378, 382, 391
Anxiety 30-31, 34-36, 40, 61, 137, 196-197, 288, 305
Art-Based Learning 70, 75, 77, 89
Assessment 18, 43, 45, 52-54, 57-59, 61, 63, 70, 78, 84, 94, 103, 114-115, 119, 122-124, 143, 145, 159, 167, 169, 203, 243, 255-257, 285-287, 290, 304, 317, 319, 343, 372-374, 381
Attention 3, 13, 30, 48-49, 52, 63, 68, 70, 80-81, 87, 90, 94, 113, 131, 140, 145, 148, 152, 155-156, 168, 186, 189, 193-197, 200, 202, 259, 261-262, 264, 267, 279, 282, 285, 295, 304, 326, 392
Augmented Reality 141-142, 321-322, 328-329, 342-349

B

Basque Autonomous Community 134
Bilingual education (BE) 1-4, 6, 8, 10-11, 13, 15, 18, 22-33, 40-48, 50-56, 58-59, 68, 70-71, 73, 77-82, 89-103, 105, 110-114, 118-120, 131-138, 140-142, 146-147, 149-151, 153-154, 156, 158-161, 163-171, 176, 178-180, 183, 186-190, 192-202, 208-209, 211-218, 221, 223, 226-231, 237-242, 245, 247-254, 260-263, 265-270, 272-276, 278-280, 282-285, 290-299, 301-314, 316, 320, 322-331, 333-336, 339-342, 352-355, 357-359, 362, 364, 368-371, 378-379, 381-392
Bilingual Programs 30-31, 90-91, 100-103, 106, 108, 155-156, 159, 161, 164, 174, 230, 373
Bilingual Science Teaching 351-352, 371, 378

Bilingual Track Internship 107
Bilingualism 13, 19-20, 22-23, 34-37, 39-40, 59-60, 64, 71, 83, 85, 87, 95, 103, 143, 145, 172, 174-176, 206, 210, 212-214, 230, 233-234, 256, 287, 317, 343, 347, 373, 376-377, 391
Bridge-Language 67, 70, 73, 89

C

Classroom Practice 41, 46, 51-52, 65, 197, 382
CLIL 1-4, 6, 8-11, 13, 15, 18-24, 27-29, 31-35, 37-56, 58-64, 81, 90-91, 99, 102-105, 107, 109-125, 129-145, 147-159, 161, 163-164, 166, 171-174, 204-206, 210-213, 232-235, 237-242, 245-246, 248-250, 252-257, 259-261, 264, 273-275, 283-290, 292-295, 298-302, 304-318, 351-360, 366-379, 381-383, 390-391
CLIL Lesson Planning 110, 112-114, 125, 131, 143
CLIL Tasks Design 292
CLIL Training 45, 59, 90, 125, 138-139, 141, 353, 377, 382-383
Code-Switching 22, 24-25, 27-30, 32-34, 37-38, 40, 56, 283
Cognitive Flexibility 23, 40, 327
Collaboration 10-11, 18, 20, 30, 46-48, 51, 54, 56, 69-70, 77-79, 81, 83, 86-87, 90, 93, 95, 97-99, 104, 111-112, 114, 119-120, 124, 143, 148, 152, 175, 187, 189, 196, 198-199, 201, 204, 208, 316, 373, 390
Collaborative Competence 109-110, 112-113, 116-120, 122, 125, 204, 382
Collaborative Teaching 1, 3, 10, 21, 89, 113, 203
Communicative Task 145
Competence 13, 23-24, 28, 42-43, 45, 48, 52-54, 57-58, 68-71, 73, 78, 89, 91-92, 103, 105-106, 109-113, 116-120, 122, 125, 130-132, 138, 143, 156, 158-159, 167, 176, 188, 190, 194, 199, 204, 207-210, 214, 216-219, 221, 225, 227-229, 232, 235, 252, 260, 273, 275, 285-286, 352-355, 367, 369, 371,

Index

373, 382, 385

Competency 29, 43, 58, 110-111, 120, 125, 209, 218, 377

Computer System 349

Content and Language Integrated Learning (CLIL) 1-4, 6, 8-11, 13, 15, 18-24, 27-29, 31-35, 37-56, 58-64, 81, 90-91, 99, 102-105, 107, 109-125, 129-145, 147-159, 161, 163-164, 166, 171-174, 204-206, 210-213, 232-235, 237-242, 245-246, 248-250, 252-257, 259-261, 264, 273-275, 283-290, 292-295, 298-302, 304-318, 351-360, 366-379, 381-383, 390-391

Cooperative Learning 1, 3, 15, 19, 21, 50, 52

Co-Teaching 69-70, 77-78, 83, 85-90, 107, 109, 113, 122, 189, 195-196, 198, 200-201, 204-207

Critical Thinking 1, 3, 13, 19, 21, 55, 205, 207, 372

Curriculum Integration 292, 309

D

Didactics 23, 44, 52, 59, 104-105, 211, 232, 235, 237-238, 241-242, 253, 351-352, 354-355, 357, 359, 367, 372, 374

Diversity 24, 35, 44, 50, 64, 70, 76-77, 79-80, 82, 85-87, 89, 93, 105, 113, 155, 157-158, 161, 163, 169, 171, 173-176, 181, 190

Drama 70, 73, 76-77, 83-84, 87-89, 379, 381-385, 389-392

E

Early Language Education 70, 186, 190, 194

Effective Personality 237-238, 245-247, 249, 251-257

Elementary School 35, 43-44, 55, 58-59, 157, 206, 208-210, 212-214, 216, 218-219, 223-226, 229-232, 235, 271, 287

Elicitation 131, 145, 193, 219

EMI 20, 23, 109-110, 113, 119, 122-124, 260, 289, 352, 367, 378

English 19-20, 23, 27-29, 32, 34-40, 43, 45, 50, 56, 63, 67-71, 73-89, 91, 99, 108, 110-113, 118, 120, 122-123, 129, 134, 136-140, 142-143, 145, 147, 149-151, 153-154, 164, 172-173, 176, 190, 208-209, 211-219, 221, 223, 225-233, 235, 237, 239, 245-246, 248-252, 259-262, 264, 266-268, 270-276, 279-289, 293, 313, 319, 321, 324-327, 329, 331-344, 346-349, 351-357, 368, 370-372, 377-379, 381-385, 389-390

English Medium Instruction 23, 110, 129, 260, 287

F

Foreign Language 20, 22-24, 27, 31, 33, 35-41, 44-45, 59-61, 93, 102, 104, 106-107, 109-111, 113-114, 118, 129-131, 136, 138-139, 145, 156, 158, 167, 172-173, 175, 187, 190, 193, 204-205, 208-214, 216-217, 219, 230-233, 235-236, 240, 250, 260-261, 265, 271, 273, 275, 279-280, 282-285, 287-290, 294, 323, 325, 342-343, 345, 347-348, 352-354, 356, 374, 377, 390

Foreign Language Anxiety 31, 40, 61, 288

Foreign Language Teaching 44, 129, 231-232, 348, 354, 377

Foreign Languages 23, 41, 44, 76, 89-90, 92, 99, 105, 120, 150, 154, 156-157, 190, 206, 210, 212-214, 231-232, 255, 268, 292

Functional-Language 291

G

Global Teacher 107

Global Teachers 90, 94

Greece 67-69, 75, 82, 86

Groupings 155, 161, 163, 168, 171-172, 178, 265, 311, 314, 352

H

Haptics 259, 261, 282, 284-285, 288

Hardware 327, 330, 332-333, 349

Higher Education 19, 61, 64, 85, 103-106, 109-110, 123-124, 189, 204-205, 238, 243, 246, 251, 254-256, 342, 377, 382

Higher Order Thinking 145, 237, 240-241, 294, 302

Higher Order Thinking Skills (HOTS) 131, 145-146, 302, 304, 312, 317

I

Immersion 24, 28, 35, 46, 64, 92, 99, 142, 144, 208, 210-213, 216, 232-236, 333

Implicit Learning and Teaching 208, 236

Incidental learning 382, 392

Inclusion 51, 74, 79, 86, 138, 146, 155, 159, 174-176, 191, 213, 310

Inclusive Education 155, 157, 172-175, 189

Information system (IS) 327-328, 349

Initial CLIL education 125

Input 6, 19, 23, 28, 47-48, 50, 52, 54, 62, 70-71, 78-79, 81-83, 131, 163, 216-218, 227, 236, 240, 257, 262-263, 265-266, 270, 279-280, 283-285, 291,

451

295, 297, 300, 303-304, 306, 308, 316

Instructional Materials for Student-Centered Classroom Dynamics 291

Internship 46, 55, 59, 90, 93, 95, 97-98, 104, 107, 120-121

Interpretative Phenomenology 186, 207

Intrinsic Motivation 31, 33, 40, 194

Italian Primary School 41, 43, 65

Italy 41-46, 51, 58-64, 245, 259, 261-262, 379, 381-384, 390, 392

L

L1 24, 28-31, 33, 39-41, 44-46, 48, 50-51, 131-132, 134, 136, 138, 140, 148-149, 152-153, 265-266, 268, 273, 279, 281, 283-285

Language Acquisition 22-23, 27, 31, 37, 47, 62, 107, 144, 212-214, 216, 230, 232-233, 236, 240, 292-293, 317-318, 343

Language Development 69, 80, 88, 208, 213, 215, 226-227, 236

Language Teacher Education 111, 123, 143, 186-188, 343, 391

Learning in Two Languages 61, 208-210, 213-217, 219, 225, 229-231, 236

Learning Menu 176, 180-182

learning-Practice Approach 237-239, 241-242, 245, 252-253

Lesson Study 241, 253, 256-257

Lexis 273, 379, 382, 385

Linguistic 1, 15, 19, 22, 24, 27, 29-30, 33, 35, 37, 39, 41-42, 44-55, 59, 62, 65, 67-71, 73-74, 76-77, 79-83, 86-89, 91-92, 94, 97, 99, 104-105, 108, 111-112, 119, 130, 132, 141-142, 144, 156, 158-159, 163, 165, 190, 204, 208, 213-217, 233, 252, 255, 286, 288, 294-295, 297-299, 301-302, 304, 308, 312-317, 347, 352-355, 357, 359, 368, 371, 382-383, 389

Literacy-Focused Instruction 260, 291

Literacy-Focused Language-Instruction 291

Lower Order Thinking Skills (LOTS) 131, 146, 302, 312, 316-317

M

Mainstream Education 109, 155

Materials Design 124, 259, 270, 353

Mathematics 22, 25, 27-29, 31-38, 40, 209, 211, 214, 219, 221, 223, 225, 230, 235, 256, 286, 290

Metacognition 51, 171, 185, 192, 201, 204, 206-207

Metalinguistic Competencies 41, 65

Methodological Training 18, 24, 94, 99, 255, 351, 353, 378

Mixed Methods 237, 251, 253-255, 257

Motivation 22-23, 31, 33-34, 37, 39-40, 51, 53, 61, 97, 134, 136-140, 142, 148, 150, 152, 154-156, 158, 160-162, 171, 173, 187, 194, 196, 202, 246, 248, 251-253, 285-286, 297, 300, 305, 314, 325, 342, 345-346, 371

Multilingua Franca 73, 89

Multilingual Education 19-20, 59, 62-63, 67-69, 83-85, 97, 124, 141, 144, 157, 186-187, 190, 201, 203, 205-206, 289, 346, 375

Multilingual, Inclusive Teaching Approach 89

Multilingualism 39-40, 46, 51, 63, 67-69, 71-72, 77, 79, 82-88, 92-93, 95, 106, 110, 125, 129, 141, 155, 186, 209, 230, 233-236, 238, 289, 319

Multimodal Communication 1, 3, 21, 190

Multimodal Learning 176

Multimodality 1, 3-4, 18, 20, 155, 159, 161, 163, 166, 171

N

New Languages 321, 325, 339

New Technologies 91, 322, 325-326, 328-329, 340-341, 349

NLA 351, 355, 378

Numeracy Development 259

O

Oral Communication 1, 3, 6, 21

Output 23, 47-48, 64, 67-68, 78, 81-82, 86, 131, 240, 257, 265-266, 285, 301, 306, 390

P

PBL 114, 120, 125, 163, 206

Pedagogical Affordance 18, 21

Pedagogical Translanguaging 1, 3, 8-9, 21, 67, 73, 76, 84, 140, 146

Pedagogy 1-3, 19, 34-35, 52, 60, 65, 68, 70, 84-85, 87-88, 110, 112, 143, 187, 203, 207, 298, 318, 340, 356, 373, 391

Peer Assessment 257

Play 8, 31, 41, 43, 48-49, 53, 76, 93, 119, 193, 196-197, 264, 287, 290, 314-315, 379, 381-382, 384-386, 389, 392

Plot 384-385, 392

Plurilingual Approaches 71, 89

Plurilingual Competence 71, 89, 188, 190, 207, 373

Index

Practicum 82, 97-100, 103-104, 106-107, 187, 191

Primary Education 1, 3, 19-20, 22, 25-26, 28, 32, 36, 39, 44, 61, 64, 68, 94-95, 97-100, 104, 108-114, 116, 120, 129-130, 133-134, 139-141, 143, 150, 154-155, 157, 161, 164, 166-167, 174-175, 190, 238, 245, 255, 292, 308, 347, 352, 354-357, 366-369, 371-374, 376-379, 381, 383, 390

Primary School 22-23, 25, 27-29, 31, 34, 36-38, 41, 43-45, 65, 79, 86, 95, 121, 132, 135, 140, 155-156, 190-191, 193, 209, 218, 230-233, 235, 239, 273, 286, 289, 321, 331, 346-347, 374, 376-377, 381, 383-385, 389-390, 392

Primary School in Italy 43, 45, 392

Programming 155, 161, 165, 168, 238, 297, 304, 307, 316-317, 329-330, 334-336, 341

R

Recast 146

S

Scaffold 8, 22, 28-29, 141, 161, 190-191, 278-279

Scaffolding 4, 19-20, 52, 102, 107, 123, 130-131, 134, 136, 140-142, 144, 146, 148, 152, 161-163, 171, 174-176, 215-216, 229, 240, 253, 294, 301, 303-304, 306, 308, 316-317, 357, 389

Science 19-22, 25, 27, 31, 33-35, 38, 40, 43, 55-57, 64-65, 140, 150, 154, 156, 161, 164, 167, 176, 186-187, 189, 192, 201-204, 206-207, 209, 211, 230, 233, 256, 261, 274, 287-289, 308, 319, 323, 343-344, 348, 351-352, 354-356, 370-371, 373, 375-379, 381-385, 389-390, 392

Science Play 379, 381, 384, 392

Self-Efficacy 161, 238, 245-246, 248, 251-253, 257, 261

Self-Esteem 30, 87, 238, 245-246, 249-250, 252-253, 257

Self-Realization 238, 245-247, 250-253, 257

Service-Learning 186-187, 189-196, 198-202, 207, 251, 254-255

Sketch 68, 392

Social Self-Realization 238, 245-246, 250-253, 257

Software 135, 324, 327-335, 345-350

Spanish as a Foreign Language 193

Student-Centered Approaches 161, 163

Subject Literacy 290

SWOT 100-101, 107, 352, 369-370, 372, 374-375, 377

T

Tandem Teaching 186-187, 189, 192-193, 195-196, 198-199, 201, 207

Task-Based Learning and Teaching (TBLT) 295

TBL 114, 125

Teacher Collaboration 20, 87

Teacher Competences 125, 188, 203, 255, 373

Teacher Education 2, 13, 34, 36, 39, 41, 43-46, 48-49, 54, 59, 63-65, 67-69, 88, 110-112, 118, 122-125, 132, 143, 173, 175, 186-191, 195, 203-205, 237-238, 245, 251, 254-257, 319, 343, 345, 348-349, 353, 373, 375-376, 391

Teacher Training 2, 6, 11, 13, 15, 18, 20, 41-42, 44-45, 47, 49, 53, 55, 58-59, 67, 92-94, 98-99, 103-105, 107-108, 124, 129-130, 132-133, 135, 140, 142-143, 145, 155, 164, 209, 215, 229-230, 237-238, 253, 256, 352-356, 370-373, 375-379, 381-382, 390-391

Teacher Training College 94, 99, 108

Teacher Training Programme 67

Teaching 1, 3-4, 10, 15, 18-21, 23-25, 27-45, 47-53, 58-64, 68-70, 73, 78-79, 81, 83-86, 88-89, 91-93, 97-99, 102-107, 109-114, 116, 118, 120, 122-124, 126, 129-130, 132-133, 136-141, 143, 145, 148-154, 156-165, 168, 171-176, 186-213, 215-217, 219, 229-242, 248, 250-257, 259, 261-262, 265, 272, 286-298, 301-302, 317-319, 321-322, 324-330, 340-348, 351-355, 358, 368-374, 376-378, 381, 383, 390-391

Teaching-Learning 21, 24, 30, 33, 138, 156, 159, 162, 164-165, 168-169, 238, 243, 252, 321-327, 329, 341, 344, 346, 351-352, 354-355, 357-358, 374

Techniques 6, 13, 47-49, 52, 56, 60, 69-70, 73, 76-77, 79, 89, 123, 130-134, 136-138, 140-141, 146, 148, 150, 152, 194, 243, 255, 293, 303, 316, 326, 379, 381-382, 384, 390

Training 2, 6, 9, 11, 13, 15, 18, 20, 24, 29, 33, 41-42, 44-47, 49, 53, 55, 58-59, 61, 63, 65, 67, 78, 85, 87, 90-100, 102-109, 112, 120, 123-125, 129-130, 132-145, 147-148, 151-152, 155, 157, 161, 164, 201, 205, 209, 213, 215, 229-230, 237-238, 253-256, 261-262, 264, 272, 321, 323-325, 327, 329, 331-332, 334-335, 339-340, 342, 344, 347, 351-356, 370-379, 381-383, 390-391

Translanguaging 1, 3, 8-9, 18-21, 24, 36-37, 39-40, 60, 67, 69-70, 73-74, 76, 79, 81, 83-85, 89, 130-131, 140-142, 145-146, 203

U

UDL 155-157, 159-161, 163-164, 166, 171

UML diagrams (Unified Modeling Language) 350

University of Extremadura 90, 94-95, 97, 99-100,

104, 108
University of Granada 255, 292, 351-352, 356-357, 369-371, 373, 376-378

V

Virtual reality 339, 341-344, 346, 348, 350
Virtual Teacher-Training Workshop 260, 291
Vocabulary 27, 29, 36, 39, 48, 50, 52, 54, 56, 58, 76, 81, 131, 134, 137, 140, 148-150, 152-153, 167, 183, 196-197, 213, 215-216, 227, 229, 240, 253, 259, 264-267, 270, 273-274, 284-285, 288, 312-314, 321, 323-324, 335, 342, 346, 357, 368, 389-390

W

Whole Language 259, 282, 284
Working Memory 261, 263-265, 267, 269-270, 274-275, 280, 284-286, 290

Y

Young Learners 67, 76, 80-81, 83, 88-89, 186-187, 190-193, 201-202, 218, 259-260, 262, 264-266, 273, 284-285, 288, 319, 343-344

Recommended Reference Books

IGI Global's reference books are available in three unique pricing formats:
Print Only, E-Book Only, or Print + E-Book.

Shipping fees may apply.

www.igi-global.com

Participatory Pedagogy

ISBN: 9781522589648
EISBN: 9781522589655
© 2021; 156 pp.
List Price: US$ 155

Transformative Pedagogical Perspectives on Home Language Use in Classrooms

ISBN: 9781799840756
EISBN: 9781799840763
© 2021; 282 pp.
List Price: US$ 185

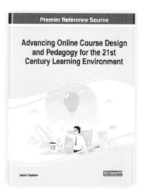

Advancing Online Course Design and Pedagogy for the 21st Century Learning Environment

ISBN: 9781799855989
EISBN: 9781799856009
© 2021; 382 pp.
List Price: US$ 195

Deep Fakes, Fake News, and Misinformation in Online Teaching and Learning Technologies

ISBN: 9781799864745
EISBN: 9781799864752
© 2021; 271 pp.
List Price: US$ 195

Enhancing Higher Education Accessibility Through Open Education and Prior Learning

ISBN: 9781799875710
EISBN: 9781799875734
© 2021; 252 pp.
List Price: US$ 195

Connecting Disciplinary Literacy and Digital Storytelling in K-12 Education

ISBN: 9781799857709
EISBN: 9781799857716
© 2021; 378 pp.
List Price: US$ 195

Do you want to stay current on the latest research trends, product announcements, news, and special offers?
Join IGI Global's mailing list to receive customized recommendations, exclusive discounts, and more.
Sign up at: **www.igi-global.com/newsletters.**

Publisher of Timely, Peer-Reviewed Inclusive Research Since 1988

www.igi-global.com   Sign up at www.igi-global.com/newsletters   facebook.com/igiglobal   twitter.com/igiglobal   linkedin.com/igiglobal

Ensure Quality Research is Introduced to the Academic Community

Become an Evaluator for IGI Global Authored Book Projects

 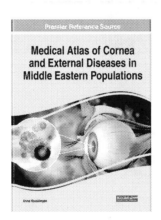 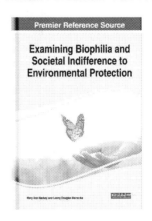 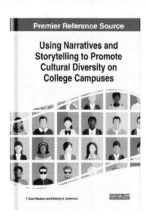

The overall success of an authored book project is dependent on quality and timely manuscript evaluations.

Applications and Inquiries may be sent to:
development@igi-global.com

Applicants must have a doctorate (or equivalent degree) as well as publishing, research, and reviewing experience. Authored Book Evaluators are appointed for one-year terms and are expected to complete at least three evaluations per term. Upon successful completion of this term, evaluators can be considered for an additional term.

If you have a colleague that may be interested in this opportunity, we encourage you to share this information with them.

Easily Identify, Acquire, and Utilize Published
Peer-Reviewed Findings in Support of Your Current Research

IGI Global OnDemand

Purchase Individual IGI Global OnDemand Book Chapters and Journal Articles

For More Information:
www.igi-global.com/e-resources/ondemand/

Browse through 150,000+ Articles and Chapters!

Find specific research related to your current studies and projects that have been contributed by international researchers from prestigious institutions, including:

- Accurate and Advanced Search
- Affordably Acquire Research
- Instantly Access Your Content
- Benefit from the InfoSci Platform Features

"It really provides an excellent entry into the research literature of the field. It presents a manageable number of highly relevant sources on topics of interest to a wide range of researchers. The sources are scholarly, but also accessible to 'practitioners'."

- Ms. Lisa Stimatz, MLS, University of North Carolina at Chapel Hill, USA

Interested in Additional Savings?

Subscribe to
IGI Global OnDemand *Plus*

Learn More

Acquire content from over 128,000+ research-focused book chapters and 33,000+ scholarly journal articles for as low as US$ 5 per article/chapter (original retail price for an article/chapter: US$ 37.50).

6,600+ E-BOOKS.
ADVANCED RESEARCH.
INCLUSIVE & ACCESSIBLE.

IGI Global e-Book Collection

- Flexible Purchasing Options (Perpetual, Subscription, EBA, etc.)
- Multi-Year Agreements with **No Price Increases** Guaranteed
- **No Additional Charge** for Multi-User Licensing
- No Maintenance, Hosting, or Archiving Fees
- Transformative **Open Access Options** Available

Request More Information, or Recommend the IGI Global e-Book Collection to Your Institution's Librarian

Among Titles Included in the IGI Global e-Book Collection

Research Anthology on Racial Equity, Identity, and Privilege (3 Vols.)
EISBN: 9781668445082
Price: US$ 895

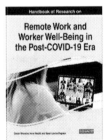

Handbook of Research on Remote Work and Worker Well-Being in the Post-COVID-19 Era
EISBN: 9781799867562
Price: US$ 265

Research Anthology on Big Data Analytics, Architectures, and Applications (4 Vols.)
EISBN: 9781668436639
Price: US$ 1,950

Handbook of Research on Challenging Deficit Thinking for Exceptional Education Improvement
EISBN: 9781799888628
Price: US$ 265

Acquire & Open

When your library acquires an IGI Global e-Book and/or e-Journal Collection, your faculty's published work will be considered for immediate conversion to Open Access *(CC BY License)*, at no additional cost to the library or its faculty *(cost only applies to the e-Collection content being acquired)*, through our popular **Transformative Open Access (Read & Publish) Initiative**.

For More Information or to Request a Free Trial, Contact IGI Global's e-Collections Team: <u>eresources@igi-global.com</u> | 1-866-342-6657 ext. 100 | 717-533-8845 ext. 100

Have Your Work Published and Freely Accessible
Open Access Publishing

With the industry shifting from the more traditional publication models to an open access (OA) publication model, publishers are finding that OA publishing has many benefits that are awarded to authors and editors of published work.

Freely Share Your Research | Higher Discoverability & Citation Impact | Rigorous & Expedited Publishing Process | Increased Advancement & Collaboration

Acquire & Open

 When your library acquires an IGI Global e-Book and/or e-Journal Collection, your faculty's published work will be considered for immediate conversion to Open Access *(CC BY License)*, at no additional cost to the library or its faculty *(cost only applies to the e-Collection content being acquired)*, through our popular **Transformative Open Access (Read & Publish) Initiative**.

Provide Up To **100%** OA APC or CPC Funding

Funding to Convert or Start a Journal to **Platinum OA**

Support for Funding an **OA Reference Book**

IGI Global publications are found in a number of prestigious indices, including Web of Science™, Scopus®, Compendex, and PsycINFO®. The selection criteria is very strict and to ensure that journals and books are accepted into the major indexes, IGI Global closely monitors publications against the criteria that the indexes provide to publishers.

WEB OF SCIENCE™   Compendex   Scopus

PsycINFO®    **IET Inspec**

Learn More Here: For Questions, Contact IGI Global's Open Access Team at openaccessadmin@igi-global.com